KU-246-091

3D MODEL RECOGNITION FROM STEREOSCOPIC CUES

3D MODEL RECOGNITION FROM STEREOSCOPIC CUES

A stereogram of the members of the consortium arranged for free-fusion by crossing the eyes.

AIVRU	John Mayhew (5) John Frisby (14) John Porrill (17) Jonathan Bowen (18) Tony Pridmore (19) Stephen Pollard (20) Chris Brown (not shown) Chris Dunford (Comp Sci, not shown)
Edin CSci	Andrew Blake (7) Andrew Zisserman (15) Gavin Brelstaff (3)
Edin AI	Bob Fisher (4) Pat Ambler (13) Jonathan Aylett (10) Mark Orr (9)
GEC	Bernard Buxton (11) Iain Graydon (16) Brendan Ruff (not shown)
IBM	Rodger Hake (1) John Knapman (12) Mike Gray (8) Rodney Cuff (not shown)
ICIS	Christopher Longuet-Higgins (2)
RAL/SERC	Tony Lucas (6)

3D MODEL RECOGNITION FROM STEREOSCOPIC CUES

Edited by

John E. W. Mayhew and John P. Frisby

The MIT Press
Cambridge, Massachusetts
London, England

This book was printed and bound in the United States of America.

Library of Congress Cataloging-in-Publication Data

3D model recognition from stereoscopic cues / edited by John E.W. Mayhew and John P. Frisby.
p. cm. — (Artificial intelligence)
Includes bibliographical references.
ISBN 0-262-13243-5
1. Robot vision. I. Mayhew, John E. W. II. Frisby, John P. III. Series: Artificial intelligence (Cambridge, Mass.)
TJ211.3.A14 1991
621.36'7—dc20 90-19241
CIP

CONTENTS

Series Foreword

Artificial intelligence is the study of intelligence using the ideas and methods of computation. Unfortunately, a definition of intelligence seems impossible at the moment because intelligence appears to be an amalgam of so many information-processing and information-representation abilities.

Of course psychology, philosophy, linguistics, and related disciplines offer various perspectives and methodologies for studying intelligence. For the most part, however, the theories proposed in these fields are too incomplete and too vaguely stated to be realized in computational terms. Something more is needed, even though valuable ideas, relationships, and constraints can be gleaned from traditional studies of what are, after all, impressive existence proofs that intelligence is in fact possible. Artificial intelligence offers a new perspective and a new methodology. Its central goal is to make computers intelligent, both to make them more useful and to understand the principles that make intelligence possible. That intelligent computers will be extremely useful is obvious. The more profound point is that artificial intelligence aims to understand intelligence using the ideas and methods of computation, thus offering a radically new and different basis for theory formation. Most of the people doing work in artificial intelligence believe that these theories will apply to any intelligent information processor, whether biological or solid state.

There are side effects that deserve attention, too. Any program that will successfully model even a small part of intelligence will be inherently massive and complex. Consequently, artificial intelligence continually confronts the limits of computer-science technology. The problems encountered have been hard enough and interesting enough to seduce artificial intelligence people into working on them with enthusiasm. It is natural, then, that there has been a steady flow of ideas from artificial intelligence to computer science, and the flow shows no sign of abating.

The purpose of The MIT Press Series in Artificial Intelligence is to provide people in many areas, both professionals and students, with timely, detailed information about what is happening on the frontiers in research centers all over the world.

Patrick Henry Winston
J. Michael Brady
Daniel Bobrow

3D MODEL RECOGNITION FROM STEREOSCOPIC CUES

I THE GRANT PROPOSAL

Introduction by the Editors

1 ORGANISATION OF THE BOOK

The research reported in this book is the outcome of a large multi-site industry/academe consortium funded (c.£1.2m) by the U.K.'s Alvey Programme in advanced information technology. The research papers are grouped under the three projects that formed the organisational structure of the consortium. The section on each project has an editorial introduction based mainly on excerpts from the original research proposal. These excerpts have been left largely verbatim to preserve the flavour of the thinking that guided the consortium's efforts.

The editors have attached to their introductory sections reviews entitled ***What Really Happened?*** These allow the reader some insight into the strengths and weaknesses of pursuing fundamental computer vision research within a large multi-site consortium. The editors draw their own conclusions about how things went as a whole in a final ***Summing Up*** at the end of this section.

In this opening section to the book we provide a brief background to the origins of the consortium. We then give an overview of the research grant proposal, and finally we thank the many people who helped the consortium get underway.

2 BACKGROUND

The research proposal for the consortium was entitled *3D Surface Representations and 3D Model Invocation from Stereoscopic Cues*. The proposal arose directly from the 3D IKBS-VISION PROJECT written by Mayhew as part of the *IKBS Architecture Study* (1983) commissioned by the Science & Engineering Research Council (SERC) and the Department of Industry.

Mayhew's 3D IKBS-VISION PROJECT document evolved from lengthy discussions over a period of a year or so between many interested parties, industrial and academic. A meeting held on 30 September 1983 of 34 scientists and engineers from 16 institutions endorsed its main outlines and discussed how a detailed research proposal should be developed. The outcome was *An Overview of the 3D IKBS-VISION PROJECT* written by Frisby. This served as a scene-setting appendix to the final research grant proposal of the consortium submitted to the Alvey IKBS Committee for its approval. An abridged version of this *Overview* is given in the next section by way of introducing the consortium as a whole. It is reproduced largely verbatim, thereby ensuring an authentic introduction to the background leading to the papers contained in this book, and its 1983 date should be borne in mind.

Most sites in the consortium began their work on 1st October 1984, with funding lasting for 3 years.

3 OVERVIEW OF THE RESEARCH GRANT PROPOSAL (Written 1983)

3.1 Research Goals and Target Applications

The proposed research is concerned with solving problems in the design of a general purpose machine vision system capable of delivering useful 3D visual competences to an automated mobile robot system and/or an assembly task work station. Lack of a good visual 'front end' capable of extracting useful 3D information about a robot's immediate environment has been one of the major factors preventing the automation of many industrial tasks, including vehicle guidance and pick-and-place manipulations. The potential value of equipping robots with this competence is widely recognised internationally and various industrial competitors overseas are working on the problems involved. It is important that the UK establishes its ability to compete in this field.

The field of 3D machine vision is a large one, with many different approaches being explored. The guiding strategy adopted in the 3D IKBS-VISION PROJECT has been to select an approach which exploits the existing research strengths of certain UK academics while meeting the expressed interests of the industrial collaborators. The resulting proposals are not therefore presented as an exhaustive account of all that 'could or should' be done in the UK in this major field. Rather, they are offered as a focussed attack on some central problems in image understanding using an approach that this group of academics and their industrial collaborators believes will lead to useful applications in the medium term (3-5 years). The programme will be scientifically rewarding by furthering basic knowledge about some classical issues in AI-oriented image understanding.

3.2 Status as an Alvey IKBS Research Theme

SERC's *IKBS Architecture Study* classified the 3D IKBS-VISION Project as a 'Research Theme'. We are content with that designation because it suits its character, namely a club[1] of cooperating scientists and engineers engaged in basic research who intend to deliver results applicable to a variety of possible products by tackling various fundamental problems in building a general purpose 3D vision system. The view of the club is that it is best to address and solve these general questions prior to launching a demonstrator project.

Many Alvey planning papers have advised that basic research must be recognised as an essential part of the Alvey endeavour. For example, the *IKBS Architecture Study* recommended that "high quality, speculative research, both

[1] The 'club' referred to here is not the Alvey Vision Club. The latter was founded later and had a much larger membership, joining together participants in Alvey's IKBS and Man-Machine Interface computer vision programmes.

also include useful global metrical information such as an estimate of an object's size.

4 SEGMENTATION AND DESCRIPTION OF COMPLEX SMOOTH SURFACE REGIONS

If a complete depth map of a surface region has been recovered from the stereo range data, then it may be desirable to recover a description of the surface shape within the region boundaries. In the proposed representation a surface region is defined as a region of the depth map enclosed by surface orientation or depth discontinuities, or occlusion or extremal boundaries. A surface region is thus C1 continuous and may be either simple or complex. We describe as simple a surface region in which the magnitudes of the principal curvatures may vary over the surface but in which the signs of the principal curvatures do not. Thus a simple surface contains no inflexions of curvature and in these terms the quadratic surfaces are simple. It is proposed that complex surfaces can be segmented into regions along the lines of curvature corresponding to the extreme and/or the inflexions of the principal curvatures (Brady, 1982; Hoffman, 1983). If the result of 'interpolation' over the segmentation is itself a complex surface, then a further stage of segmentation can be applied and so on until a simple surface is obtained. This successive segmentation and 'interpolation' over an increasingly coarser (but not spatially blurred) sample of the surface data points can be used to recover a description of the surface over its natural scales. The quotes around interpolation are to suggest that the qualitative description of the surface recovered from the straight line polygonal hull of the segmentation control points may be sufficient and so avoid the cost of repeated full interpolations.

5 SURFACE INTERPOLATION

Reference was made above to the desirability of developing methods for interpolating surfaces between the sparse depth map delivered by PMF. This topic is explored here in more depth and the work that Blake plans in this area is described.

The interpolation process will be considered in close conjunction with the objective of labelling depth discontinuities and other surface properties. Also, the interpolated surface must be consistent with the original intensity data, in the sense that where the intensity distribution can be wholly or partly predicted from 3D surface structure (and in particular from surface discontinuities) such predictions should agree with the original intensity data.

5.1 Surface Interpolation and Labelling Discontinuities

It is well known that interpolation of sparsely distributed values in an array, to form a smooth 2D function, can be achieved in a highly parallel manner. For example, stretching an elastic membrane over a fixed wire frame is just such an interpolation and if the form z(x,y) is made at discrete points over a regular x,y grid, then at each point the height value is successively replaced by the average of the heights of its near neighbours. On the wire frame itself, height values remain fixed. This replacement continues until height values at all points have converged. The algorithm is local in that the average computed at each point involves only the point's near neighbours and parallel because averages can be computed simultaneously at all grid points. Given a suitable parallel machine, such an algorithm can be executed rapidly; this is important in a vision system for which real-time performance is required. This algorithm is a simple example of what are generally called 'relaxation algorithms'. The simple interpolation algorithm just described can be regarded as performing an optimisation over an x,y grid to minimise the energy (elastic potential energy) of the membrane. A different choice of energy function results in a different sort of interpolation and in many cases it is still possible to minimise the energy by relaxation (Ullman, 1979). For instance Terzopoulos (1982) uses a more complex energy function - for interpolating stereo disparity data - that represents the energy of a thin plate rather than a membrane. Such a plate resists flexion and torsion and therefore its surface remains free of fractures and creases (it is continuously differentiable). In general the visible surface is not continuous and the interpolation procedure has no ability to locate discontinuities in the surface and its gradient. Rather it requires the location of discontinuities to be determined in advance so that the interpolation process can be inhibited across them. Thus interpolation proceeds only within the boundaries defined by the discontinuities, resulting in a piecewise continuous surface.

However, discontinuities are a very important part of the surface description and it is important to locate them reliably. It is attractive to try and incorporate discontinuity detection into the interpolation process. Intuitively this is plausible if one thinks of trying to fit a smooth surface everywhere, but allowing discontinuities to form where the 'strain' on the surface becomes too great. Blake (1983a, 1983b) describes how this can be done for the somewhat restricted case of discontinuities in a piecewise constant surface map. It is achieved by imposing 'weak continuity constraints' (Hinton, 1977, introduced weak constraints in a rather different context) to express the expectation that the surface 'varies smoothly almost everywhere' (Marr, 1982). Such constraints are only broken where the data to which the surface is being fitted (eg raw disparity data) forces a discontinuity. The ease with which constraints may be broken is controlled by a constant (the 'penalty constant'). A high penalty results in few discontinuities and a low one produces many - giving greater detail - so that the scale of the segmentation of the surface into continuous pieces is controlled by the penalty constant. The scheme described in Blake (1983a,b) has no ability to detect gradient discontinuities, or to cope with extensive smooth surfaces at large angles of tilt or large curvature, and is therefore unable to construct visible surface maps for general scenes. However it works well within its limitations - it has been tested finding discontinuities in image intensity data (which is not sparse) - and promises to be susceptible to the necessary generalisation by incorporating an energy function like that of Terzopoulos and modifying the algorithm to work with sparse data.

5.2 Consistency of the Surface Map with Intensity Data

Information from left and right images is combined in stereopsis to produce the disparity map, but there may be still further information in the intensity images that is relevant to the construction of the surface map. It is clear that the distribution of intensity constrains the surface map (via the image irradiance equation) and Ikeuchi and Horn (1981) show how the shape of a continuous surface patch can be recovered (by a relaxation algorithm) from intensity data. In practice, of course, this is likely to be complicated by lack of precise knowledge of the ambient illumination. Intensity data also contain powerful clues about the location and type of surface and illumination discontinuities (Barrow and Tenenbaum, 1978; Witkin, 1982). Stereopsis can make partial use of such information, eg in the figural continuity constraint (Mayhew and Frisby, 1981). Further use of the information could be made by specifically enabling discontinuity formation, during construction of the surface map, where there are discontinuities in intensity of the appropriate type. For example, this would apply where the tangency condition (Barrow and Tenenbaum, 1978) is satisfied, indicating the presence of an occluding edge, but not along surface markings.

5.3 Summary of Work Proposed on Surface Interpolation

It is proposed, starting from the Pollard, Mayhew and Frisby stereo algorithm (PMF), to design and implement an algorithm for surface reconstruction. This will draw on work already done on interpolation by relaxation (Terzopoulos, 1982) and on labelling discontinuities by the use of weak constraints (Blake, 1983b) combined and extended to maintain consistency of the surface map with intensity data. The work will include investigating the potential for fast multilevel processing (processing at a variety of coarse and fine resolutions, as in Terzopoulos, 1982, and Glaser, 1983) and the applicability of parallel, statistical methods for solving optimisation problems (Metropolis et al, 1953; Hinton and Sejnowski, 1983). As the work develops consideration will be given to suitable parallel architectures for efficient implementation of the surface reconstruction algorithms.

B WHAT REALLY HAPPENED?

The 2.5D Sketch Project was soon redefined and renamed as the REV Graph Project (***R****egions*, ***E****dges*, ***V****ertices*), and enlarged to include explicitly the Wire Frame Completion project (WFC), whose goal was to recover the 3D wireframe scene description from edge-based stereo.

The REV Graph proposal (Blake and Mayhew, 1987) was a design for a low level image processing architecture owing much to the blackboard metaphor (Hayes-Roth, 1985), the notion of intrinsic images (Barrow and Tenenbaum, 1978), and visual routines (Ullman, 1982). Some of the component modules or 'knowledge sources' were eventually developed and are described in the papers that follow. One particular KS was to identify specularities. Specularities may on the one hand be regarded as a source of noise, but if correctly identified may also provide a source of information concerning the curvature of the surface. Brelstaff, a graduate student of Blake worked on the problems both of identifying [17] and exploiting [18] specular reflections. The result was an augmented version of Sheffield's PMF that excised specular features to avoid matching errors arising from their violation of epipolar constraints.

Stereoscopic disparities of specularities were actually used to determine the curvature of the underlying surface by Zisserman , Giblin and Blake (1989). It has recently been shown that curvature perception in human stereoscopic vision is similarly influenced by specularities (Blake and Bulthoff 1990).

Another knowledge source specified in Blake and Mayhew (1987) was a stereo module specialised for dealing with highly textured surfaces. This culminated in the PhD work of McLauchlan in AIVRU on the Needles stereo algorithm which is described in paper [20].

The REV Graph architecture was explored only in prototype form in the context of the WFC Project. The ANIT system (Mayhew, 1989; Booth and Mayhew, 1989), which has explored some of the good ideas from Brooks' (1986) subsumption architecture, has its antecedents in this work, and is currently being transferred to a transputer environment.

The WFC Project was originally implemented in Lisp by Bowen and metamorphosed into the Consistency Maintenance System (CMS) reported in [19]. This built on the ideas of Herman and Kanade (1986) for wire frame model acquisition and those of De Kleer (1986) for consistency maintenance. The system was never fully integrated into AIVRU's TINA vision processing environment for tedious technical reasons related to the evolution of increasing incompatibility between Sun graphics, Lisp, C and Unix with each generation of the operating system as the project continued.

The WFC Project reached its zenith in the development of Geomstat by Porrill [12], a geometrical reasoning module. Exploiting Gauss-Markov optimal estimation techniques, Geomstat is a system for the integration of edge and curve descriptions (and their associated error models) to recover 2D and 3D geometric descriptions of surfaces and their intersections. Recent attempts to integrate Geomstat with a usable Lisp-based intelligent front-end have again struggled against the continuing inadequacy of the Lisp-C-graphics interface on Sun workstations.

The work on qualitative meta-feature descriptions was begun with Ian Graydon of GEC in a project using the Hough transform to find rows of blobs. The project then metamorphosed into a method for recognising planar objects using methods derived from the work of Bolles and Fischler (1981) which used focus features to devise a strategy to minimise the computational overhead of the maximal clique algorithm. This work was reported to the 1986 Alvey Vision Conference (for which no formal proceedings were published - hence no report is included here; Graydon left the project before a formal paper could be prepared for journal publication).

B (contd) Notes Provided by Blake

The remaining major component of the 2.5D sketch project concerned the recovery of surface discontinuities and descriptions. At the beginning of the project, Blake showed that the continuous surface reconstruction scheme of Grimson (1982), elaborated by Terzopoulos (1983), was flawed. It was unsuitable for what is now sometimes called *Active Vision* because it lacked viewpoint invariance [13] . The resulting instability of reconstructed surfaces was most pronounced when stereoscopic features were sparse, precisely the conditions under which reconstruction was supposed to be most useful! At the same time the emphasis of the problem shifted. What was the purpose of extrapolating surfaces through large tracts of empty space? Instead, the primary role of surface reconstruction in vision seemed to be the recovery of surface discontinuities on textured surfaces, where they would not have been visible monocularly.

Blake and Zisserman decided to concentrate on the reconstruction of surfaces complete with their discontinuities.

In the absence of established methods in the spline literature, it was natural to combine the idea of 'weak continuity' constraints with viewpoint invariance [14]. The earlier *Graduated Non-Convexity* (GNC) algorithm (Blake 1983a,b) was extended to deal with the 'weak membrane'. It turned out to be very effective experimentally, efficient compared with stochastic techniques [15], and provably correct for a significant class of signals. This led to the investigation of a whole family of reconstruction problems involving discontinuities, subsequently published in a book (Blake and Zisserman 1987). Variational analysis established some remarkable properties, in particular the stability of the weak membrane in noise and in scale-space. Unlike the Gaussian case (Witkin 1983), the new scale-space proved to be 'uniform' so that discontinuities at different scales were in perfect registration [16]. Around the same time, Mumford and Shah (1985) made major contributions to the variational analysis which were combined with Blake and Zisserman's own results in the book. At that time, analysis was completed only for the case of one-dimensional signals and hence, of course, for two dimensional signals with translational symmetry. Mathematicians are, even now, struggling with the full two-dimensional problem.

REFERENCES

Barrow, H.G. & Tenenbaum, J.M. (1978) Recovering intrinsic scene characteristics from images. In *Computer Vision Systems*, A.R. Hanson & Riseman, E.M. (eds.), Academic Press: New York. Pp. 3-26.

Baumgart, B.G. (1972) Winged edge polyhedral representation. STAN-CS-320, AIM-179, Stanford AI Lab.

Binford, T. O. (1982) Survey of model-based image understanding systems. *Internat. J. Robotics Res.* **1** 18-62.

Blake, A. (1983a) The least-disturbance principle and weak constraints. *Pattern Recognition Letters* **1** 393-399.

Blake, A. (1983b) *Parallel computation in low-level vision.* PhD Thesis, University of Edinburgh.

Blake, A., and Mayhew, J. E. W. (1987) Alvey 2.5D sketch project: Proposed structure for a development system. *AI Vision Research Unit Memo No 9*, University of Sheffield.

Blake, A. and Zisserman, A. (1987) *Visual reconstruction.* MIT Press: Cambridge, Mass.

Blake, A. and Bulthoff, H. H. (1990) Does the brain know the physics of specular reflection? *Nature* **343** 165-168.

Bolles R. C. and Fischler M. A. (1981) A RANSAC-based approach to model fitting and its applications to finding cylinders in range data. *Proc. Int. Joint Conf. AI 1981.* 637-643. Vancouver, B. C., Canada.

Booth, C. and Mayhew, J.E.W. (1989). Implementing a behavioural decomposition. Poster at *Intelligent Autonomous Systems Two*, Amsterdam, December 1989.

Brady, M. (1982) Criteria for representations of shape. *MIT AI Laboratory Memo.*

Brooks, R. A. (1986) A robust layered control system for a mobile robot. IEEE *Journal of Robotics and Automation* **2** 14-23.

De Kleer, J. (1986) An assumption based TMS. *Artificial Intelligence* **28** 127.

Draper, S. W. (1981) *Reasoning about depth in line-drawing interpretation.* PhD Thesis, University of Sussex.

Glaser, F. (1983) Multilevel relaxation in low-level computer vision. In *Multiresolution image processing and analysis*, A. Rosenfeld (ed.), Springer-Verlag.

Grimson, W. E. L. (1982) *From images to surfaces.* MIT Press: Cambridge, USA.

Hayes-Roth, B. (1985) A blackboard architecture for control. *Artificial Intelligence* **26** 251.

Herman, M. and Kanade, T. (1986) Incremental reconstruction of 3D scenes from multiple, complex images. *Artificial Intelligence* **30** 289.

Hinton, G. H. (1977) *Relaxation and its role in vision.* PhD Thesis, University of Edinburgh.

Hinton, G. E. and Sejnowski, T. J. (1983) Analysing cooperative computation. *Proc. 5th Conf. Cognitive science*, Rochester, New York.

Hoffman, D.D. (1983) *Representing shape for visual recognition.* PhD Thesis, Dept. of Psychology, MIT, Cambridge, Mass.

Ikeuchi, K. and Horn, B. K. P. (1981) Numerical shape from shading and occluding boundaries. *Artificial Intelligence* **17** 141-184.

Kanade, T. (1981) Recovery of the three dimensional shape of an object from a single view. *Artificial Intelligence* **17** 409-460.

Marr, D. (1982) *Vision.* San Francisco: W H Freeman & Co.

Mayhew, J.E.W. & J.P. Frisby (1981) Towards a computational and psychophysical theory of stereopsis. *Artificial Intelligence* **17** 349-385.

Mayhew, J. E. W. (1989) The ANIT system: Architecture for *N*avigation and *I*ntelligent *T*racking. *AI Vision Research Unit Memo Memo No 48*, University of Sheffield.

Metropolis, N., Rosenbluth, A. W., Rosenbluth, M. N., Teller, A. H. and Teller, E. (1953) Equation of state calculations by fast computing machines. *Journal of Chemical Physics* **6** 1087.

Mumford, D. and Shah, J. (1985) Boundary detection by minimising functionals. *Proc. IEEE CVPR Conf.* **22.**

Terzopoulos, D. (1982) Multilevel reconstruction of visual surfaces. *MIT AI Lab Memo 671*, Cambridge, Mass.

Terzopoulos, D. (1983) The role of constraints and discontinuities in visible-surface reconstruction. *Proc Int. Joint Conf. AI 1983* 1073-1077.

Ullman, S. (1979) Relaxation and constrained optimization by local processes. *Computer Graphics and Image Processing* **10** 115-125.

Ullman, S. (1984) Visual routines. *Cognition.* **18** 97-160.

Witkin, A.P. (1982) Intensity based edge classification. *Proc. AAAI Conference* 36-41.

Witkin, A. P. (1983) Scale-space filtering. *Proc. Int. Joint Conf. AI 1983* 1019-1022.

Zisserman, A., Giblin, P. and Blake, A. (1989) The available information to a moving observer from specularities. *Image and Vision Computing* **7** 38-42.

geometry in an image pre-processing stage prior to potential matches being established in order to exploit the simplicity of horizontal epipolars.

For any particular industrial application of the work proposed here, it will either be assumed that the camera geometry is known and fixed, or for applications where it is necessary to have a stereo camera system able to change its convergence, it will be assumed that the development of special purpose techniques suitable for the particular application will be the most economical way of proceeding. Future developments may cast doubt on these assumptions but, for the present at least, the PMF Project does not ask for resources to build a general-purpose stereo camera control system capable of keeping track of its own dynamic geometry by measuring its camera positions and/or by estimating these from analyses of the images themselves.

4 Project A: OPTIMISATION OF PMF

PMF treats the stereo correspondence problem as one of optimising the number of matches subject to the constraint that no pair of matches violates the chosen DG limit. It would in principle be possible to search serially for solutions consistent with this requirement; indeed, one possible way of implementing PMF would be to start at one corner of an image and set up an exhaustive search tree while proceeding through the entire image searching for branches that break the constraint, which would then be eliminated. However, in order to achieve the speed required in a practical application, it is desirable to utilise a parallel algorithm that computes the membership of the optimal set of matches using only local operations.

Considerable investigation of the merits of a DG limit treated as a local constraint has resulted in the adoption of the iterative update scheme set out in [2]. Nevertheless, the updating support equation used in that scheme is not intended to offer a formally satisfactory solution to the global optimisation problem but is simply a way of finding matches that are well supported locally, without violation of a DG limit, and which at the same time can be demonstrated empirically to produce a satisfactory global solution. The support equation used in [2], plus others currently under development that utilise local DG support to select matches, now stands in need of detailed mathematical examination within the framework of constrained optimisation). The objective here is to prove either that this equation (or similar) guarantees a solution of the global DG optimisation problem; or to devise suitable changes that do guarantee this result; or of course to arrive at some principled analysis of inherent limitations in using local DG support if no global optimisation is possible (the latter seems unlikely given the successful demonstrations of PMF to date).

The aim of Project A is to explore this question formally. Dr S A Lloyd, of GEC and who has the requisite mathematical skills and relevant experience in relaxation algorithms, will lead this project under the overall supervision of Dr M McCabe, also of GEC. Lloyd will work in collaboration with Pollard, Mayhew and Frisby of AIVRU.

5 Project B: FAST HARDWARE FOR PMF

It is impossible to give any useful estimates of the potential speed of PMF from the current implementation. The greatest proportion of the code/time involves reading in masses of data from files and the construction of large structures to represent primitives and their possible matches. But as has already been mentioned, using a DG limit does appear to be open to fast parallel processing techniques, and certainly PMF's iterative update scheme has been designed with this in mind. The fact that less than six iterations are needed to achieve a high measure of consistency for all the examples shown in [1] indicates that a fast implementation of PMF should be attainable and this is the goal of Project A.

This project will be conducted at GEC which is already engaged on various projects for parallel processor architectures and special purpose hardware for signal processing. Specifically, these include the design of a VLSI parallel processor architecture (GRID) and the development of a corresponding parallel programming environment. These facilities and the associated expertise will be exploited in Project A, with PMF's irregular as well as sparse data array posing interesting and fundamental questions with considerable potential relevance to other areas.

Dr J Wiejak of GEC will be responsible for ensuring the progress of this work, working in collaboration with Pollard, Mayhew and Frisby on questions relating to PMF's design and performance. Wiejak has already been involved with Dr B Buxton (GEC) and Dr H Buxton (Queen Mary College, University of London) in the design of efficient parallel algorithms for the convolutions required by stereo and optical flow computations (implemented on the DAP at Queen Mary College). Close liaison with their work will be maintained.

II WHAT REALLY HAPPENED?

1 Project A: OPTIMISATION OF PMF

This work culminated in the paper by Sheelagh Lloyd [4] which showed that a DG limit could be cast successfully within an optimisation framework.

2 Project B: FAST HARDWARE FOR PMF

This project did not develop as planned although the eventual outcome was highly satisfactory.

Immediate changes in project goals were dictated by two main factors. First, Jan Wiejak left GEC before completing much work. Secondly, GEC management reviewed their priorities and decided to redeploy resources away from PMF and towards building a pipelined architecture for the Canny edge detector. The reasoning behind this decision was as follows: (a) work on fast hardware for PMF was deemed premature until progress was made on Project A; and (b) as all foreseeable industrial applications of computer vision by GEC would depend on a fast edge detector, effort should first be concentrated in that area. Accordingly, Brendan Ruff was assigned by GEC to develop special purpose hardware for the Canny edge detector and the successful outcome of that work is described in [8]. The upshot of these changes was that developing a version of PMF suitable for the GRID parallel processor did not take place (the GRID project was transferred to other parts of GEC and eventually emerged as a product, MARADE - Marconi Array Demonstrator).

Meanwhile, a collaboration in Sheffield University between its newly appointed Chair of Computer Science, Professor

Doug Lewin[2], Gordon Manson of that Department, and Chris R Brown in AIVRU, led to a GEC-funded 1-year pilot research project aimed at devising a transputer-based architecture capable in principle of running PMF in under <1 sec. This work produced sufficiently encouraging results (see paper [9] by Brown and Chris Dunford, the latter being an assistant employed by Lewin and Manson) for it to be continued by GEC after the end of the Alvey grant. This continuation took the form of an SERC/ACME-funded GEC/AIVRU collaboration to build MARVIN[3], a transputer-based fast vision engine for running AIVRU's suite of computer vision programs (called TINATOOL[4]). That device, due in no small measure to Brown's new assistant Mike Rygol who joined AIVRU from INMOS, finally achieved the original Alvey grant objective of PMF in <1 sec, albeit about 2 years after the initial target date. In view of this, a short report on the MARVIN machine is included here as [10], despite that work not being funded under the Alvey grant.

3 ADDITIONAL RESEARCH ON THE DISPARITY GRADIENT LIMIT

The optimisation work by Lloyd prompted additional research at GEC into the mathematical properties of the DG limit. Harit Trivedi, a colleague of Lloyd and Margaret McCabe, proved with Lloyd that imposing a DG limit of less than 2 implies that matches preserve the topology of images in the sense of ensuring view-to-view continuity [5].

This result led John Porrill (a postdoctoral research assistant employed on the Alvey grant in AIVRU) to find a simplified proof of the Trivedi-Lloyd theorem and, more importantly, to show that an isotropic DG limit is only one member of a whole family of measures of continuity which impose scene-to-view and view-to-view Lipschitz continuity [2].

4 ADDITIONAL RESEARCH AT GEC

Papers [6] and [7] by Trivedi are enclosed which describe methods of estimating stereo and motion parameters. Although not envisaged in the original grant proposal, this work has proved influential and [6] forms the basis for one of AIVRU's current schemes for achieving camera calibration (Thacker and Mayhew, 1990). Trivedi's paper's are included here both for that reason and to illustrate the fact that members of the consortium were able, indeed encouraged, to pursue research topics well beyond those originally conceived in the Alvey grant proposal.

5 DEVELOPING THE PMF ALGORITHM

Many developments and evaluations of the PMF algorithm have been conducted by Stephen Pollard in AIVRU over the past 6 years ([1], [2], [3]; see also his PhD thesis: Pollard, 1985).

For example, more thorough empirical investigations of PMF on artificial images [2] confirmed the early claim that enforcing a DG limit well below the theoretical limit for opaque objects of 2 imposes negligible restrictions on the worlds that can be dealt with while at the same time serving admirably to exclude ghost matches, most of which generate DGs above 1.0.

Also, more extended evaluations of PMF have been run on natural images (using Canny edge points as matching primitives instead of the Marr-Hildreth zero crossings used previously). This work continued to demonstrate the power and convenience of using a local neighbourhood support scheme incorporating a DG limit. However, it also demonstrated the desirability of building into PMF more global constraints [3]. Hence procedures exist in the current version of the algorithm which explicitly exploit: (a) figural continuity along strings of edge points (cf. the STEREOEDGE algorithm of Mayhew and Frisby, 1978); and (b) the ordering constraint along epipolars.

Further refinements of the PMF algorithm include: speeded-up processing by restricting initial matching to 'seed points'; allowing matches between primitives of opposite contrast sign when all else fails; and better ways of dealing with the special problems posed by horizontal edges.

Much of this development work on PMF work has been done after the end of the Alvey grant but [3] is included to bring the present account of PMF up to date.

6 CONCLUDING REMARKS

The PMF Project played a crucial role in facilitating development and evaluation of the PMF algorithm, itself the backbone of much of the low level image processing work done in AIVRU. The next section of the book (on the 2.5D Sketch Project) describes how the matches generated by PMF were used in the recovery of useful 3D scene geometry for supporting the pick-and-place demonstration that was the culmination of AIVRU's Alvey-supported research (see paper [29]). That demonstration was far from real-time: it took about one hour from capturing a single 256x256 stereo image pair to the robot picking up the object! More recent developments, relying on the MARVIN architecture running much improved code, have brought the self-same demonstration down to 5-10 secs [10].

GEC have benefited from the PMF Project in various ways. The first tangible outcome was their receipt (along with all other participating sites) of a copy of AIVRU's computer vision suite (TINATOOL) at the end of the Alvey project (1987). More recently, continuation via a SERC/ACME grant of the good collaborative relationship built up under Alvey led Bernard Buxton to commission from AIVRU a clone of the MARVIN fast vision engine. That device was delivered to GEC in May 1990, together with a great deal of code for running many component modules of TINATOOL. It is now being used to mount a number of vision based vehicle guidance demonstrators in a collaborative ESPRIT project (VOILA: P2502).

All GEC staff directly working on the PMF Project as it was originally conceived have now left the company. We would particularly like to express our gratitude to Drs McCabe, Lloyd and Trivedi for their assistance in bringing the project to a successful conclusion, albeit not quite the one envisaged at the outset.

---

[2] We note with regret that Professor Lewin died before this project was brought to completion.

[3] MARVIN: ***M****ultiple* ***AR****chitecture for* ***VI****sio****N***

[4] See the introductory overview of the 3D Model-Based Vision Project in Section III for an explanation of this acronym.

how it implies a further cone restricting the nature of surfaces in the viewed world that can satisfy the disparity gradient limit. Because the gradient of the world cone is approximately that of the disparity cone scaled by the ratio of the viewing distance, z, to the interocular separation, I (Appendix 1), the world cone does not impose a very severe constraint on the nature of surfaces that can satisfy it.

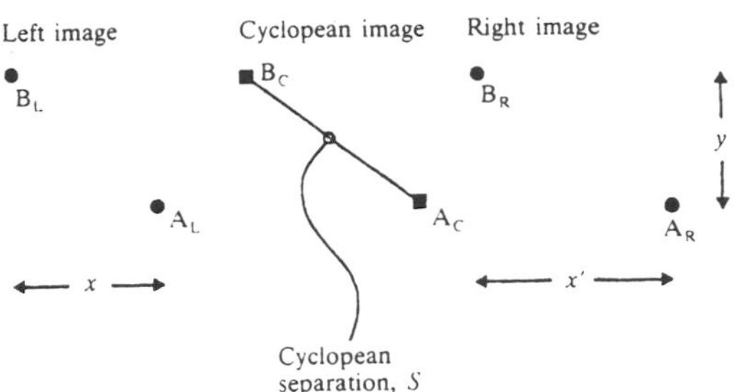

Figure 1 Definition of disparity gradient. Consider a stereogram comprising the left and right halves shown in the figure. When A_L is matched to A_R, and similarly for B, the disparity gradient between them, as defined by Burt and Julesz (1980), is the difference in the disparity divided by their cyclopean separation, S. The latter is give by the distance between the midpoints of the two pairs of dots (located at A_C and B_C respectively). Hence:

$$S = \{[{}^1/_2(x + x')]^2 + y^2\}^{1/2}.$$

As the changes in disparity between the two matches is x' - x, the cyclopean disparity gradient, Γ_D, between A_C and B_C is given by:

$$\Gamma_D = |x' - x|[{}^1/_4(x + x')^2 + y^2]^{1/2}.$$

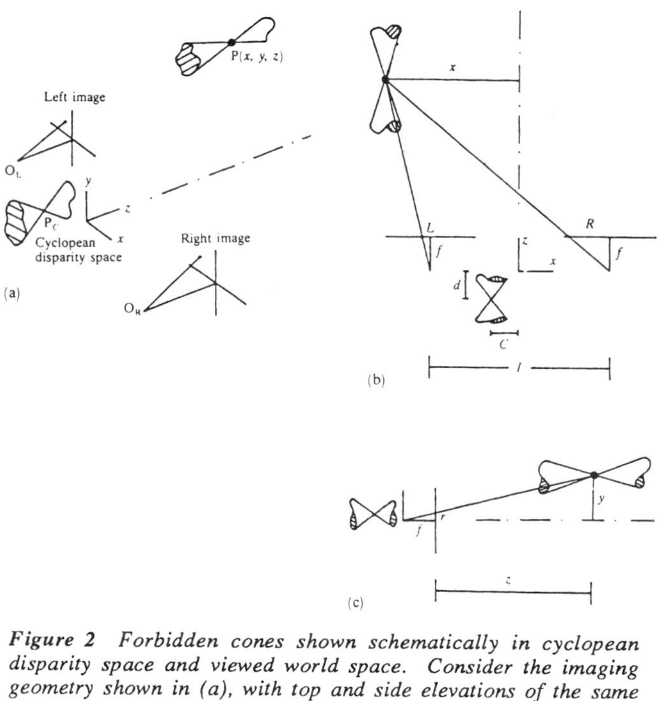

Figure 2 Forbidden cones shown schematically in cyclopean disparity space and viewed world space. Consider the imaging geometry shown in (a), with top and side elevations of the same shown in (b) and (c) to aid the presentation. The principle axes of the left and right imaging devices are parallel and have a interocular separation I . The left and right image planes are shown in front of the respective optical centres O_L and O_R for the pictorial simplicity. A world viewed space is defined with respect to a coordinate frame located midway between O_L and O_R with axes arranged as in the figure. The location of point P with respect to this frame is given by (x, y, z). The projections of P into the left and right image planes are given by (L, r) and (R, r) respectively. A cyclopean disparity space has also been constructed with its origin coincident with that of the world viewed space. In this space the point P_C corresponding to P in the viewed world space is located at (C, r, d), where C is the mean horizontal component of the projection into the left and right images given by ${}^1/_2(L+R)$, and d is the disparity defined as d = R - L.

From the definition of disparity gradient given in figure 1 it follows that the illustrated cone-shaped 'forbidden zone' will exist within the cyclopean disparity space around the point P_C. Other points that lie between the forbidden cone will violate the disparity gradient limit with respect to P_C. A second cone is shown in the viewed world space to illustrate that the forbidden cone in disparity space imposes an approximately similarly-shaped restriction on the allowable depth relationship between points lying on the surfaces that constitute the visual world. It is shown in Appendix 1 that the gradient of this second cone is approximately related to that of the first by z/I. Hence at any reasonable viewing distance the constraint imposed upon the structure of the world by a disparity gradient limit of 1 is not very severe. Note that the geometry in figure 2 is only schematic. Moreover, the described approximate relationship between world and disparity gradients holds only if z is large with respect to x, y, and I (see Appendix 1).

For example, planar surfaces with maximal slopes of up to 74° will be tolerated at a viewing distance of 6 interocular units, rising to 84° for 10 interocular units. Hence, at any reasonable viewing distance only a small proportion of planar slopes will have disparity gradients upon them that violate the limit of 1.

Turning to nonplanar surfaces, the disparity gradient limit will in general be satisfied on many types of surfaces provided they do not recede too rapidly from the viewer. Furthermore, surfaces satisfying the requirements need not be C1 smooth (ie they need not be everywhere differentiable with continuous derivative): mathematically, the disparity and world cones can be described as determining Lipschitz functions of order 1 with $K = 1$ and $K = z/I$ respectively (Appendix 2).

Intuitively, one can say that $K = 1$ in disparity space will permit world surfaces to be 'jagged but not too jagged'. The amount of allowable 'jaggedness' will depend upon the relationship of interocular distance to viewing distance. As will be illustrated later, such a rule provides considerable disambiguating power in terms of solving the stereo correspondence problem while not being overly restrictive about allowable scene surfaces. Furthermore, it is not necessary to assume that the disparity gradient limit need be satisfied between all correct matches in order that disambiguation can be achieved. Hence the Lipschitz condition provides only a conservative estimate of the class of surfaces that satisfy our constraint.

So far it has been demonstrated that the correct matches derived from the elements arising from most planar and many jagged surfaces will lie within a disparity gradient limit of 1.0 (given always small interocular separation with respect to viewing distance). But, as implied above, disambiguation needs also to rely upon there being a low probability that this limit will be satisfied by incorrect matches by chance. The convergent-to-divergent disparity range allowed between a pair of matches in order that they satisfy a disparity gradient limit of 1.0 is exactly twice their cyclopean separation. From this it follows that the probability that two points from one image can find incorrect matches that satisfy the disparity gradient limit by chance is almost directly proportional to their cyclopean image proximity [Appendix 3]. Hence at close proximities it is very unlikely that a pair of matches will 'accidentally' satisfy the disparity gradient limit. Thus a distinguishing feature that allows the identification of correct matches from the pool of 'possibles' is that the disparity gradients between the former almost always lie within a limit of 1.0, whereas between the latter this is not the case, especially at close image proximities.

Burt and Julesz (1980) pointed out that one way of viewing a disparity gradient is as a measure of figural disparity between a pair of matches because its size reflects both figural dimensions on which such a 'dipole' can differ - orientation and length. Similarly, it is possible to characterise the degree of satisfaction of the disparity gradient limit between matches in a fused binocular structure as a measure of the figural similarity of the projections of that structure into the two stereo halves. Hence an alternative description of stereo projections that will satisfy the disparity gradient limit is that they conform to a 'constraint of figural similarity', and simple observation of stereograms of most natural scenes shows that they satisfy this requirement almost everywhere. Hence it is possible to summarise this section by saying that, for a wide range of surface structures, because of the similarity of the vantage points of the two eyes the projected figural structures that constitute the left and right images will in general be sufficiently similar to allow corresponding points to be identified by using the strategy of finding the best figural matches available.

3 ADDITIONAL CONSTRAINTS UTILISED BY PMF

As well as the disparity gradient constraint discussed in the last section, PMF also exploits two other constraints: (i) the *epipolar constraint*, a limitation on the possible locations of matching points; and (ii) the *uniqueness* constraint, a limitation on the number of matches allowed for a single image entity. Both these constraints are used in a variety of other stereo algorithms.

3.1 The epipolar constraint

For the class of stereo imaging geometries with which we are concerned, ie those in which the optical axes of the two imaging devices lie in the same plane, all matching primitives appear on left/right pairs of (straight) epipolar lines (Baker 1982; see figure 3). Thus points along one member of the epipolar pair can only match with points situated along the other member, and vice versa. In the special case where the principal axes are in fact parallel, all epipolar pairs will be horizontal and matching points will be found on corresponding rasters.

As with many other algorithms PMF uses this constraint to restrict the search for possible matches to one dimension. In current versions of PMF it is assumed that the camera geometry is in fact parallel or at least approximately so. In the natural scene stereograms considered below the inter-camera separation was at least one tenth the distance to the fixation point. Given that our images are 128 x 128 pixels square and cover a visual angle of at most 10 deg, a vertical disparity of no more than a half a pixel will exist at the very corners of the image. Hence for the work reported here seeking matches along corresponding rasters is an adequate approximation to the correct epipolar geometry.

In PMF all potential matches within the (large) disparity range of +/- 30 pixels (corresponding to a Panum's fusional area of up to 5 deg) that satisfy a matching criterion for left/right

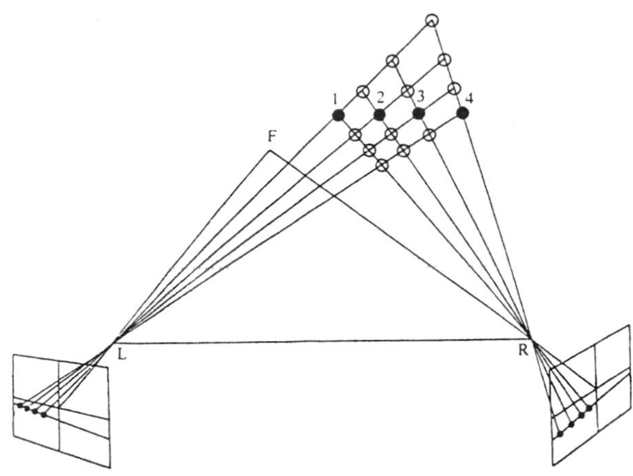

Figure 3 *Epipolar Geometry and the stereo correspondence problem. In the imaging geometries with which we are concerned the optical axes of the left and right imaging devices (LF and RF respectively) lie in a single plane and thus intersect at the fixation point F (possibly at infinity). Consider the plane, 1LR, formed by a single point in that space, labelled 1, and the optical centres of the two imaging devices, L and R. The plane 1LR is then said to intersect the two image plates along a pair of epipolar lines. Furthermore, as a result of the fact that all points along 1L and all the points along 1R are (by definition) limited to lie in the plane 1LR, all possible ghost matches associated with the point 1 must also lie in that plane and therefore project to the same pair of epipolar lines. The same is also true for all and only all the other points that lie in that same plane, for example points 2, 3, and 4 in the figure. In short, matching points can only be found along a corresponding pair of epipolar lines. The possible ghost matches that exist in this case are shown in the figure as open circles, with closed circles portraying the physically existing points that gave rise to them.*

image primitives are selected for subsequent disambiguation. The choice of matching criterion depends upon the nature of the adopted primitives, a decision which is in turn domain-dependent. PMF makes no specific requirements about what the nature of these should be, except that they should reflect scene entities. For artificial stereograms we simply use the points defined when the stimuli are being created (see figures 4-6, 9 and 10). For natural images we have found it convenient to use edge-like primitives given by zero crossings identified after the application of a single high-frequency Marr-Hildreth operator (Marr and Hildreth 1980; see figures 7 and 8). For the latter, potential matches have been restricted to those that can be formed between zero crossings of the same contrast sign and roughly similar orientation. In some domains it may also be possible to determine a measure of the 'goodness' of a match (eg degree of figural similarity of its constituent primitives) that can be made use of in the disambiguation procedure by weighting the relative importance of potential matches.

3.2 The uniqueness constraint

Owing to the fact that only rarely will a feature project into one member of a stereo pair such that it neatly masks an identical feature farther away which nevertheless remains visible in the other stereo half, it follows that matches of image primitives extracted from the two images should be unique, ie each image primitive will participate in just one match. Only in the unlikely case just mentioned, which violates the general position assumption with regard to viewpoint, would it be legitimate for a single primitive from one image to be matched with two primitives in the other.

Notice that the uniqueness constraint is itself implied by a disparity gradient limit of 1 (Burt and Julesz 1980). If a single point identified in one image is allowed to match with a pair of points identified in the other (cf Panum's limiting case), then the disparity gradient between the two matches is 2.

4 THE PMF ALGORITHM

We have developed a stereo correspondence algorithm called PMF based on the foregoing considerations. It has two distinct stages of processing.

First, the matching strength of each potential match is computed from the sum of contributions received from all potential matches in its neighbourhood that satisfy the disparity gradient of 1 with respect to it. We find a neighbourhood defined by a circle of radius 7 pixels satisfactory for all textures so far considered. Because the probability of a neighbouring match falling within the limit by chance increases (almost linearly) with its distance away from the match under consideration (section 2 and Appendix 3), the contribution of a match is weighted inversely by its distance away. Uniqueness is exploited at this stage by requiring that at most one match associated with a single primitive in one or other image makes a contribution to the matching strength.

Second, on the completion of this procedure, correct matches are chosen on the basis of matching-strength scores by using a form of discrete relaxation (Rosenfeld et al 1976). At the first iteration any matches which have the highest matching strength for both of the two image primitives that formed them are immediately chosen as 'correct', ie matches are selected whose primitives have no higher matching-strength scores with any other matches they can form. Then, in accordance with the uniqueness constraint, all other matches associated with the two primitives that formed each chosen match are eliminated from further consideration. This allows further matches, that were not previously either accepted or eliminated, to be selected as correct because they now have the highest strengths for both constituent primitives. Usually only four or five iterations are needed to propagate the uniqueness constraint in this way to the point at which the disambiguation process of PMF is complete and satisfactory (see section 6).

It is important to emphasise the fact that PMF is only interested in the quantity of within-disparity-gradient-limit support that exists for a particular match. Hence the extent to which the disparity gradient limit is offended in the neighbourhood of a candidate match does not directly affect the selection procedure of PMF. This design feature is perfectly in line with the justification given in section 2 for seeking within-disparity-gradient-limit support as the disparity gradient limit need not necessarily be satisfied everywhere.

We have also thought it sensible not to weight contributions by the actual magnitude of their disparity gradients, but instead to treat all within-disparity-gradient-limit contributions homogeneously. This makes sense for the stereo correspondence problem, as there seems to be no reason to penalise any perturbations that lie within the range that is to be expected in the stereo projections of interest. However, many other functions using disparity gradients could be employed. In one interesting example suggested by Prazdny (1985), the strength of the support that flows between a pair of matches is scaled in a gaussian fashion with respect to the size of the disparity gradient between them.

A further point to notice in this implementation of PMF is that within-disparity-gradient-limit support is sought independently from all possible matches in the neighbourhood of the match under consideration. This means that it is possible that two or more matches that give within-disparity-gradient-limit support might not themselves share a within-limit disparity gradient. This design feature has been dictated by considerations of computational efficiency. Further research is in hand with the object of examining the desirability of insisting on within-neighbourhood support consistency.

Although the use of a disparity gradient limit in PMF was stimulated by observations of the human visual system, various details of its design were shaped by more practical constraints introduced by the need to achieve reasonable efficiency and robustness on [near]-state-of-the-art computer machinery. The speed criterion is met by the intrinsically parallel nature of the structure of PMF: each matching strength could, on appropriate computer architecture, be computed independently. Extensive examination of its performance on various artificial and natural stereo images bears out satisfaction of the robustness requirement. These two factors suggest that PMF might prove valuable for industrial application in the short term.

5 HORIZONTAL SECTIONS

Our current implementation does not address fully the special difficulties posed by horizontal edge segments, a characteristic shared with all other stereo algorithms we know, many of which simply ignore horizontal sections altogether. Such segments have the dual problems of being difficult to locate (their locations can easily migrate onto an adjacent raster/epipolar line) and of being intrinsically ambiguous (points along a horizontal edge segment in one image can potentially match all points along the corresponding edge segment in the other image). The first of these problems will be met in future implementations of PMF by the inclusion of a small two-dimensional search window for near-horizontal sections. As for the second, it is clear that for long segments it will be difficult or impossible to identify matches correctly using only information based upon disparity gradients and hence some later stage of interpolation seems mandatory. Note, however, that horizontal segments can still provide figural similarity information for other matches if not always for themselves, which means that they should not be excluded from consideration by the early stages of PMF.

6 PERFORMANCE EXAMPLES

No common basis exists in the literature for assessing the performance of stereo algorithms in terms of either the images/scenes to be used or measures of performance for them. This deficiency represents a severe problem in evaluating different algorithms. Here we report some examples of the quantitative performance of PMF on a series of artificial stereograms and we show some qualitative results for a variety of natural scene stereograms which are not amenable to quantitative assessment at the present time.

For the artificial images, where the points to be matched can be specified accurately, we report the percentages of points (i) matched correctly, (ii) matched incorrectly, and (iii) left unmatched. We provide these measures for a range of surfaces chosen to sample the hardest problems typically found in many natural scenes, such as steep slopes, shears, and transparencies.

In the case of natural images, there are difficulties in providing quantitative measures because there is no simple definition of what constitutes a point to be matched. In most tests of stereo algorithms on natural scenes the points used are the outputs of an edge operator of some kind, which poses problems about whether it is the operator or the stereo algorithm which is deficient. In common with most other papers in the field, therefore, we simply present illustrations of PMF's treatment of natural images without attempting any quantitative assessment, using for this purpose primitives provided by a high-spatial-frequency Marr-Hildreth edge operator.

For the representative cross-section of performance examples presented in this section (both natural and artificial), PMF was run with the set of parameter values for allowable matching range, neighbourhood support zone, etc., described earlier. Alterations in any or all of these produced little appreciable change in the performance of PMF as long as extremes were avoided. Furthermore, the performance of PMF was largely unaffected by the addition of even quite large quantities of noise (eg the addition of more than 30% extra unmatched points to either or both halves of the artificial stereograms).

6.1 Artificial stereograms

The primitives of the pair of images that formed the artificial stereograms (figures 4-6) were positioned at the intersections of a 128 x 128 pixels square grid. Each grid point had the same probability (0.1) of carrying an image primitive, subject to the same number of points occurring on each line ($n = 13$). The ambiguity problem posed by these stereograms (as measured by the density of possible matches) was generally greater than that observed in the natural images (figures 7 and 8). This was partly because the densities of the primitives themselves were greater, and partly because the primitives were all identical so that it was not possible to restrict the set of initial matches by requiring left/right primitives for a match to be similar in contrast and orientation. For the various examples of artificial images shown below, each primitive had on average six possible matches in the other image.

6.1.1 Sloping surfaces As shown in section 2, stereo images of sloping surfaces will satisfy a disparity gradient limit of 1.0 provided the slope they depict is not too great (and assuming camera geometry typical of human stereo vision). Furthermore, even if the slope in one direction violates the disparity gradient limit it need not necessarily be violated in all other directions, and hence it is still possible that PMF may be successful. This needs to be borne in mind when considering the fact that PMF often does better than the limit would seem on the face of it to allow.

The performance of PMF for slopes was examined on surfaces of the kind shown in figure 4a, which depicts a surface whose vertical cross-section is a triangular wave. In this case the stereogram has a peak-to-trough separation of 20 pixels and a peak-to-trough disparity difference of 10 pixels; hence the disparity gradient in the vertical direction is approximately 0.5 and in the horizontal direction zero. Measures of the performance of PMF for such surfaces were obtained for peak-to-trough disparities ranging from 4 pixels to 36 pixels with 2-pixel intervals (corresponding to a range in vertical component of disparity gradient of 0.2 to 1.8). The result of running PMF on 4a is given in 4b with intensity used to code disparity (with crossed-eye viewing darker points are closer). Over 99% of the disparity values recovered from this stereogram are correct with the few errors being almost equally divided between incorrectly matched and unmatched points. The percentage of points matched correctly is plotted in figure 4c against the size of the vertical component of the disparity gradient present over the whole range of such images.

As can be seen from the graph, the performance of PMF is excellent for disparity gradients up to about 1.0, always being able to identify an excess of 98% of the true matches. Beyond this imposed limit, performance tends to fall off with only about 50% of correct matches being obtained for a disparity gradient of 1.8. As explained above, the fact that PMF copes at all with disparity gradients larger than the limit of 1 is a result of the fact that the disparity gradients are not as large in other directions.

6.1.2 Depth discontinuities and lacy surfaces

The depth profile of the stereogram in figure 5a consists of a vertical square wave. Hence the surface it depicts includes a number of depth discontinuities. Figures 5b and 5c show that PMF copes quite well at the corresponding disparity shears, although it can be seen that it fails to match a small number of the points correctly. Similar results were also obtained for vertically oriented square waves, with the exception that some points close to the disparity shears are obscured in one or other image and thus remain correctly unmatched.

The good level of performance achieved for depth discontinuities illustrates the fact that PMF is able to make use of the within-disparity-gradient-limit structure that lies to either side of the shear and at the same time ignore the fact that the limit is exceeded across it. The desirability of this characteristic is clear-cut (see earlier remarks in section 4 regarding the objective of not penalising perturbations lying within the range to be expected in the stereo projections of interest). The underlying reason why PMF achieves this goal is that it takes advantage of such within-disparity-gradient-limit support as exists; it does not impose a cost if neighbouring primitives fall outside the limit (cf Prazdny 1985).

The same property is apparent in the way in which PMF is able to deal with the lace surface portrayed in figure 6. Here the within-limit neighbourhoods that facilitate disambiguation are actually superimposed on top of each other. Whilst it is clear that the performance of PMF is considerably worse for this lace surface, in that only two thirds of the points in each depth plane are matched correctly, the results are qualitatively in keeping with human performance (comparable quantitative data not being available for human vision)[2].

6.2 Natural images

Figures 7 and 8 portray the stages of stereo processing for two very different natural image pairs, each of which is 128 x 128 pixels square. Zero crossings serving as edge-like primitives were extracted from each image with the use of a single high-frequency (w = 4 pixels) Marr-Hildreth operator (Marr and Hildreth 1980). In the figures the resulting edge primitives are portrayed with a grey level proportional to their contrast strengths (darker primitives have a greater absolute contrast value). The orientation and the contrast polarity associated with a primitive were used to restrict the initial set of matches.

---

2 This issue is considered in more detail in Pollard and Frisby (1990) Transparency and the Uniqueness Constraint in Human and Computer Stereo Vision, *Nature* (in press).

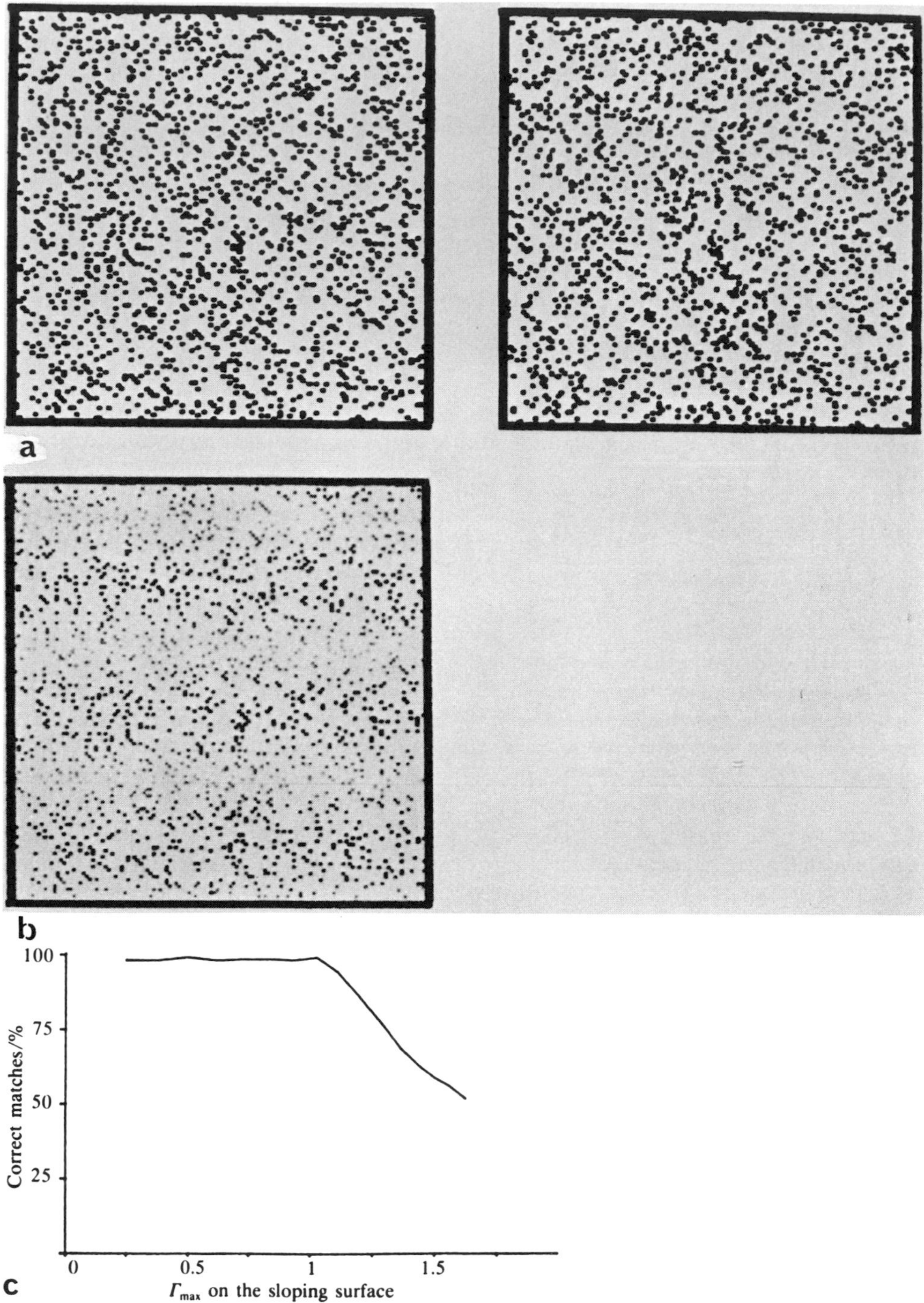

Figure 4 *Random-dot stereograms used to test the capacity of PMF to deal with sloping faces. (a) An example of a stereogram portraying a triangular waveform oriented horizontally, with peak-to-trough disparity amplitude equal to 10 pixels (each stereo half comprised of 128 x 128 pixels, of which about 10% are shown as black dots) and with maximum disparity gradient,* Γ_{max}, *on each sloping face equal to 0.5. (b) The result of applying PMF to (a), 99% of correct matches were found by PMF and these are shown with their disparities coded by intensity [darker points shown as the closest when (a) is viewed with cross-eye fusion]. (c) The correctly located matches recovered by PMF for triangular waveforms with varying* Γ_{max}. *See text for further details.*

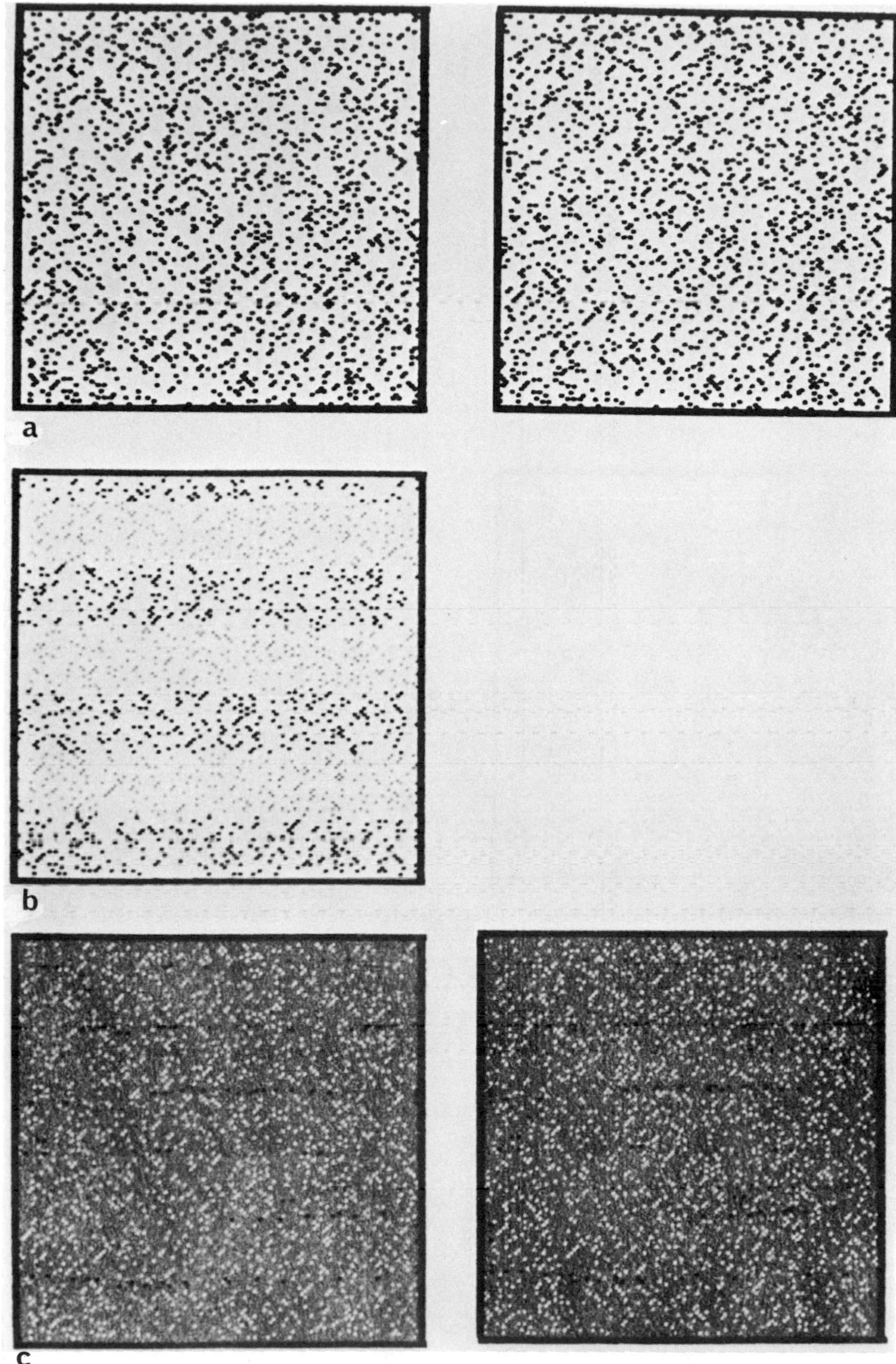

Figure 5 *Random dot stereogram used to test the capacity of PMF to deal with depth shears. (a) Stereogram portraying a square wave orientated horizontally and with peak-to-trough amplitude of 5 pixels. (b) Over 95% of points are matched correctly, with 4.5 matched incorrectly and a further 0.5% being left incorrectly unmatched. (c) A reconstruction of the stereogram displayed in (a) after processing with PMF. Dots matched correctly are shown white (hence the mid-grey back-ground), and the remainder are shown black. It can be seen that the performance of PMF is in general good with a few incorrect or missing matches confined to some parts of the borders of the shears. See text for further details.*

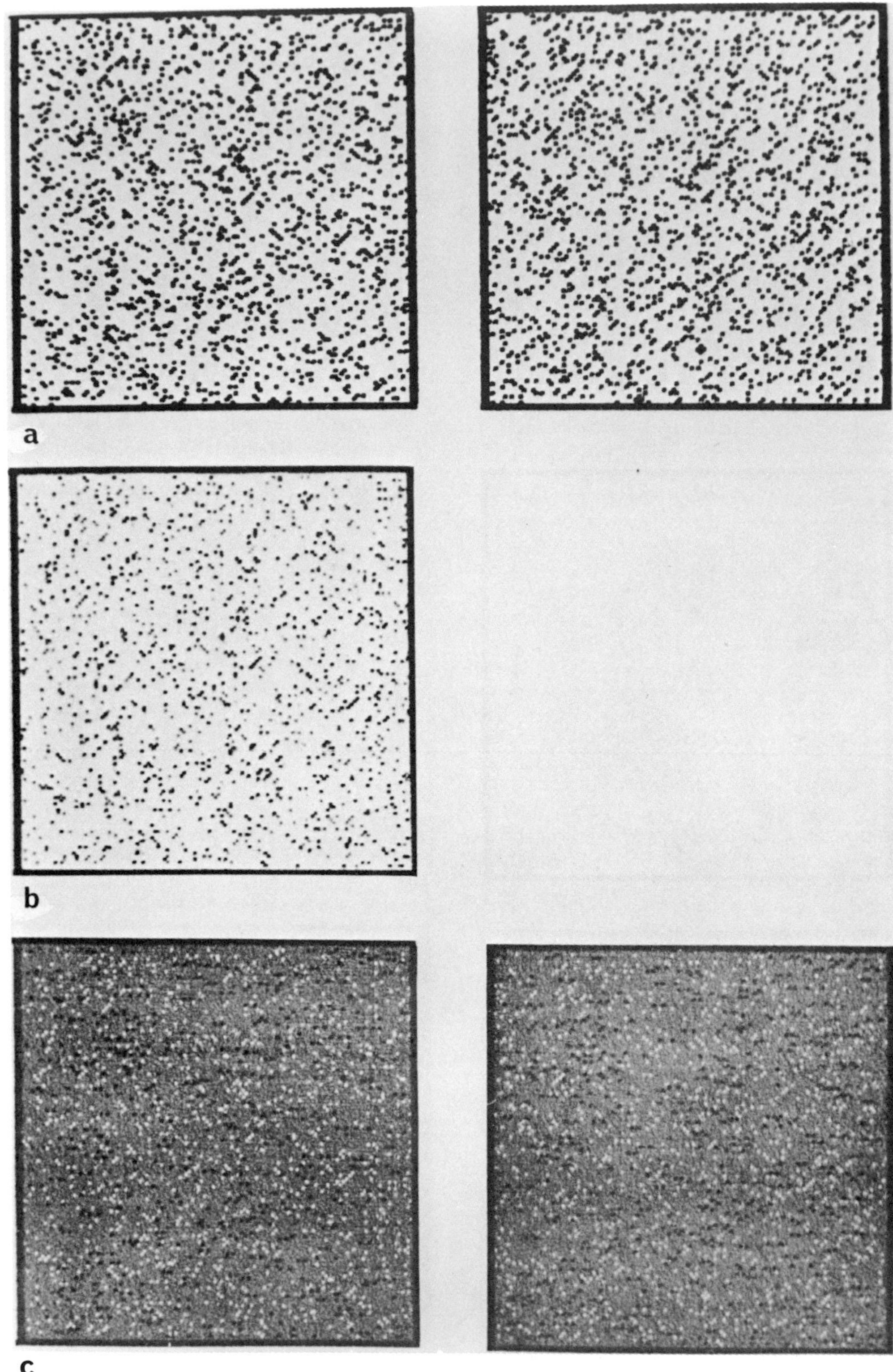

Figure 6 Random-dot stereogram used to test the capacity of PMF to deal with superimposed transparent surfaces. (a) Stereogram portraying two superimposed planar surfaces with a disparity difference of 5 pixels. (b) The correct matches (64%) located by PMF for this stereogram. Of the remainder, 35.5% were matched incorrectly and 0.5% were left incorrectly unmatched. (c) A reconstruction of the stereogram displayed in (a) after processing with PMF. Dots matched correctly are shown white and the remainder are shown black. See text for further details.

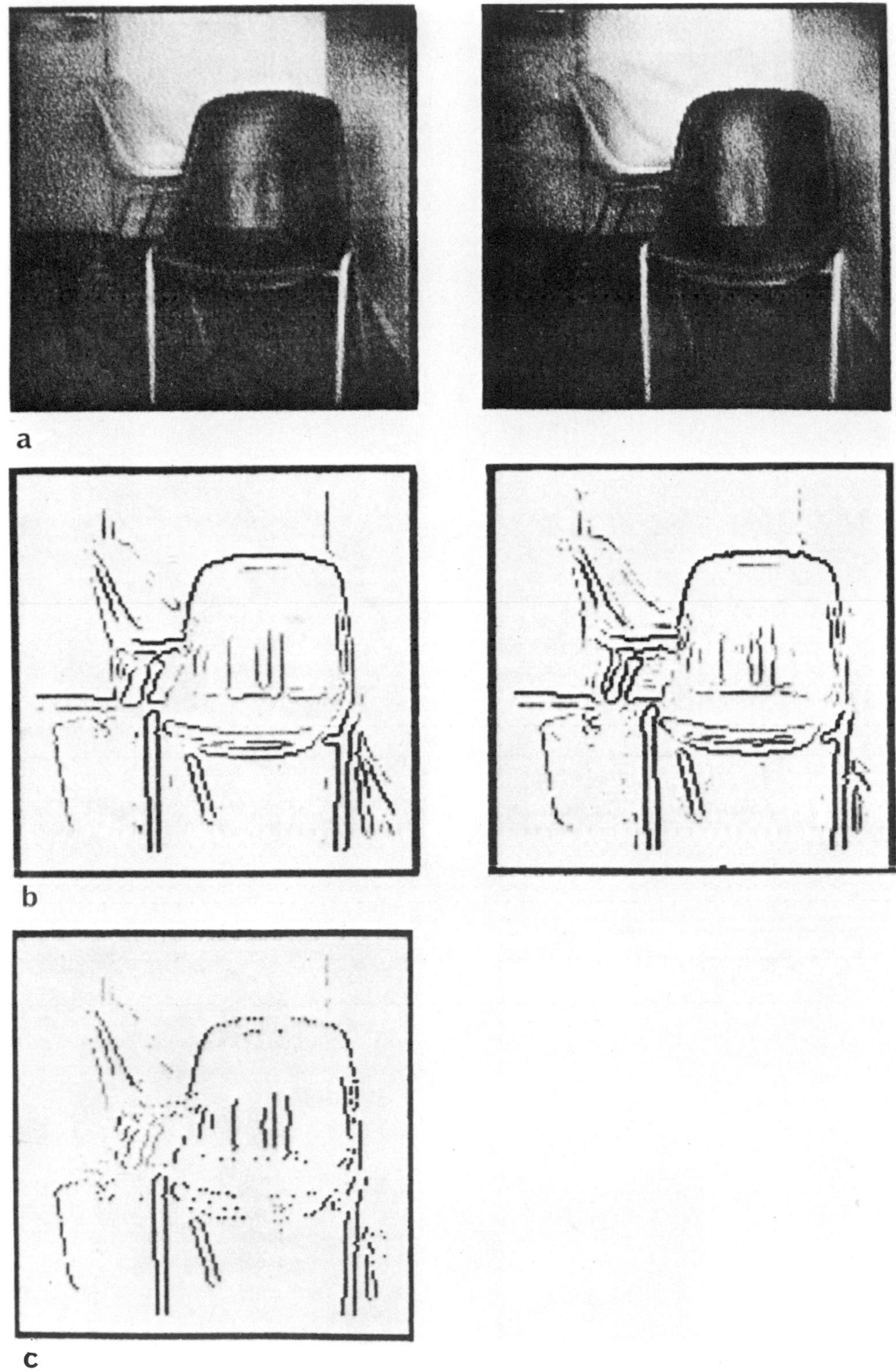

Figure 7 The performance of PMF on a stereo pair comprised of natural images of an office scene. (a) Stereo pair arranged suitably for cross-eyed fusion. (b) Edge-like primitives extracted with the use of a Marr-Hildreth operator. (c) Matches found by PMF, with intensity used to code relative disparities (dark = near, faint = far). See text for details.

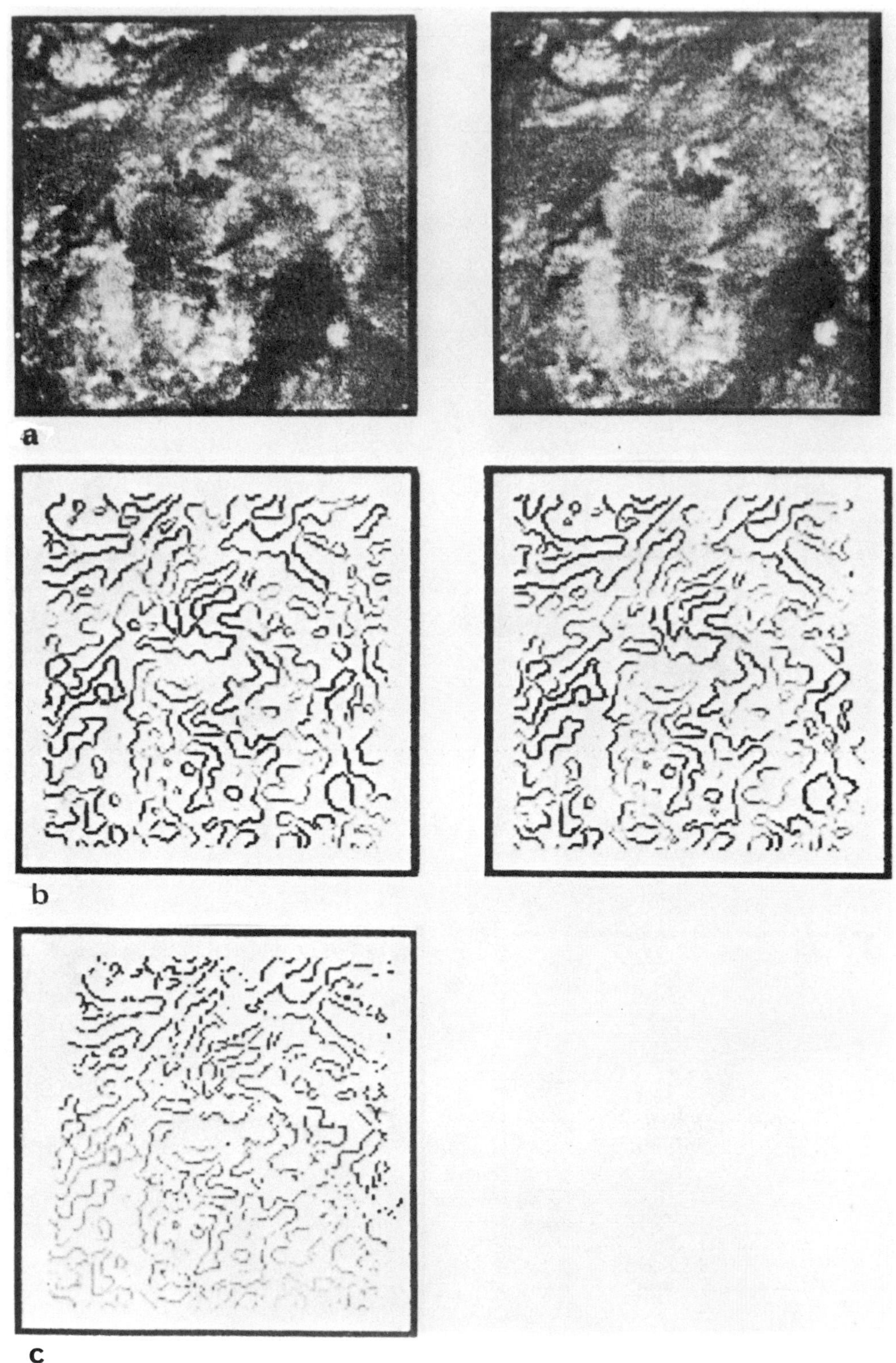

Figure 8 A further example of the performance of PMF on natural images, this time a rocky terrain viewed from above. Details as for figure 7.

The disparity gradient limit was again used to determine the allowable differences in orientation: a matched edge segment was not allowed between left and right zero crossings whose orientations were so different as to imply that the disparity gradient existing along a binocular line formed from those orientations would exceed the disparity gradient limit.

The 'goodness' of each match was given by the contrast strength of the weakest of its two constituent edges rather than as a function of the similarity of their orientation and contrast values. A goodness measure of the latter kind was thought to be inappropriate, given that changes in orientation and contrast do occur between the stereo projections with which we are concerned. Using a simple contrast measure has the advantage that it gives preference to the more reliable data, given that strength of an edge (its absolute contrast value) is directly related to its reliability (whether or not it is likely to be noise).

The disparity information (approximating for present purposes to relative depth) recovered from the matches identified as correct by PMF is displayed in the form of a cyclopean edge image in which disparity is encoded by edge intensity (darker points are closer to the imaging device). These points that remained unmatched by PMF are not displayed in these images.

Figure 7 is of a simple office scene, the edges recovered from which are quite sparse in comparison to those encountered in the artificial stereograms above. Nevertheless, despite the fairly small neighbourhood window exploited in PMF, it is able to cope quite easily with this scene. Figure 8 involves a natural scene that is more like those encountered in the artificial stereograms as it has a dense distribution of image primitives. It portrays a rocky terrain viewed from above, presenting therefore a similar task to that solved by human operators in the field of photogrammetry from aerial photographs. For both of these stereograms it can be seen that for the most part the resulting disparity output is at least qualitatively correct, the main exception being the horizontal sections located in the office scene (see remarks in section 5).

The accuracy to which depths can be measured in natural scenes is directly dependent upon the accuracy to which edges can be located in their images. In the example above, edges are only located to the nearest pixel, but it would be easy to locate the majority of strong edges to a tenth or even a hundredth of a pixel. The use of more accurately located image primitives would not interfere with the robustness of PMF.

7 HOW PMF RELATES TO OTHER THEORIES OF STEREOPSIS

As we have already stated, the theoretical justification for PMF is the fact that, for the stereo projections for which it is designed, the majority of disparity gradients that exist between correct matches will be less than 1. In this section we discuss how this constraint relates to others that have been considered in the literature on stereo algorithms. We do not, however, give a full review of the field as the theoretical aspects of many stereo algorithms have little in common with PMF.

7.1 The constraint of surface continuity

As outlined in the introduction, Marr and Poggio (1976) chose to base their theory of stereo disambiguation upon the observation that "matter is cohesive, it is separated into [reasonably large] objects", from which they derived their constraint of local surface smoothness. Whatever they might want to imply in detail by the notion of 'surface smoothness', it is clear that the way a disparity gradient limit is imposed in PMF explicitly allows many jagged (ie 'non-smooth') surfaces. An illustration of the 'degree of jaggedness' allowed by a disparity gradient limit of 1 is given by the random-dot stereogram portrayed in figure 9. At no point do any disparity gradients in this stereogram exceed 1 and yet the perceived surface is not obviously well described as smooth. This surface satisfies the Lipschitz condition discussed above and, as can be seen from the figure, the performance of PMF on it is extremely good. An example of the performance of PMF on a stereogram which depicts a surface that does not satisfy the Lipschitz condition is given in figure 10. The performance for this stereogram is rather better than may be expected for a surface that is so far from smooth, providing a further illustration that the Lipschitz condition is a rather conservative estimate of the class of surfaces suitable for PMF.

This suggestion that the use of a disparity gradient by PMF is not usefully characterised as imposing a surface smoothness constraint is further supported by the observation that there exist perfectly smooth surfaces that violate the disparity gradient limit of PMF. Even a planar surface can provide many violations of this limit if it recedes sufficiently rapidly. This is therefore another reason for distinguishing between Marr and Poggio's surface smoothness constraint and that developed here in terms of surfaces needing (conservatively) to meet a Lipschitz criterion.

7.2 The ordering constraint

It has been pointed out that stereo projection almost always preserves the order of primitives extracted from the two images along matching epipolar lines (Baker 1982; Mayhew 1983). The underlying reason for this is that it is geometrically impossible for points arising from the same opaque surface to be differently ordered in the two images (different orderings can come about only for scenes comprised of surfaces of small extent such as isolated small blobs or thin wires). Hence order has been exploited explicitly to constrain the selection of matches in a number of stereo algorithms (eg Baker and Binford 1981; Arnold 1982; Ohta and Kanade 1983).

It has been frequently noted that order reversals correspond to disparity gradients of magnitude greater than 2 (eg Burt and Julesz 1980; Mayhew 1983). Hence a limit of 1 will prevent matches that violate the ordering constraint from mutually supporting each other and to that extent a limit of 1 can be said to be a conservative implementation of the ordering constraint. However, we think there are some difficulties with that notion, particularly if it is used to justify the design of PMF.

First, the ordering constraint and its associated disparity gradient limit of 2 are concerned only with events along epipolar lines. The disparity gradient limit between epipolars can be in principle infinite even for opaque surfaces. PMF uses its limit isotropically, and justification for this cannot logically be sought just in terms of the physical limits that are possible along epipolars.

Second, we have found that a limit of 2 is not sufficiently restrictive for disambiguating purposes. Hence some other justification for a lower limit is required, even if attention is directed only to disparity gradients between points on the epipolars themselves. It may be helpful to point out in this context that a limit of 1 prevents the separation of a pair of points along an epipolar line in one image from being greater than three times the separation of a corresponding pair in the

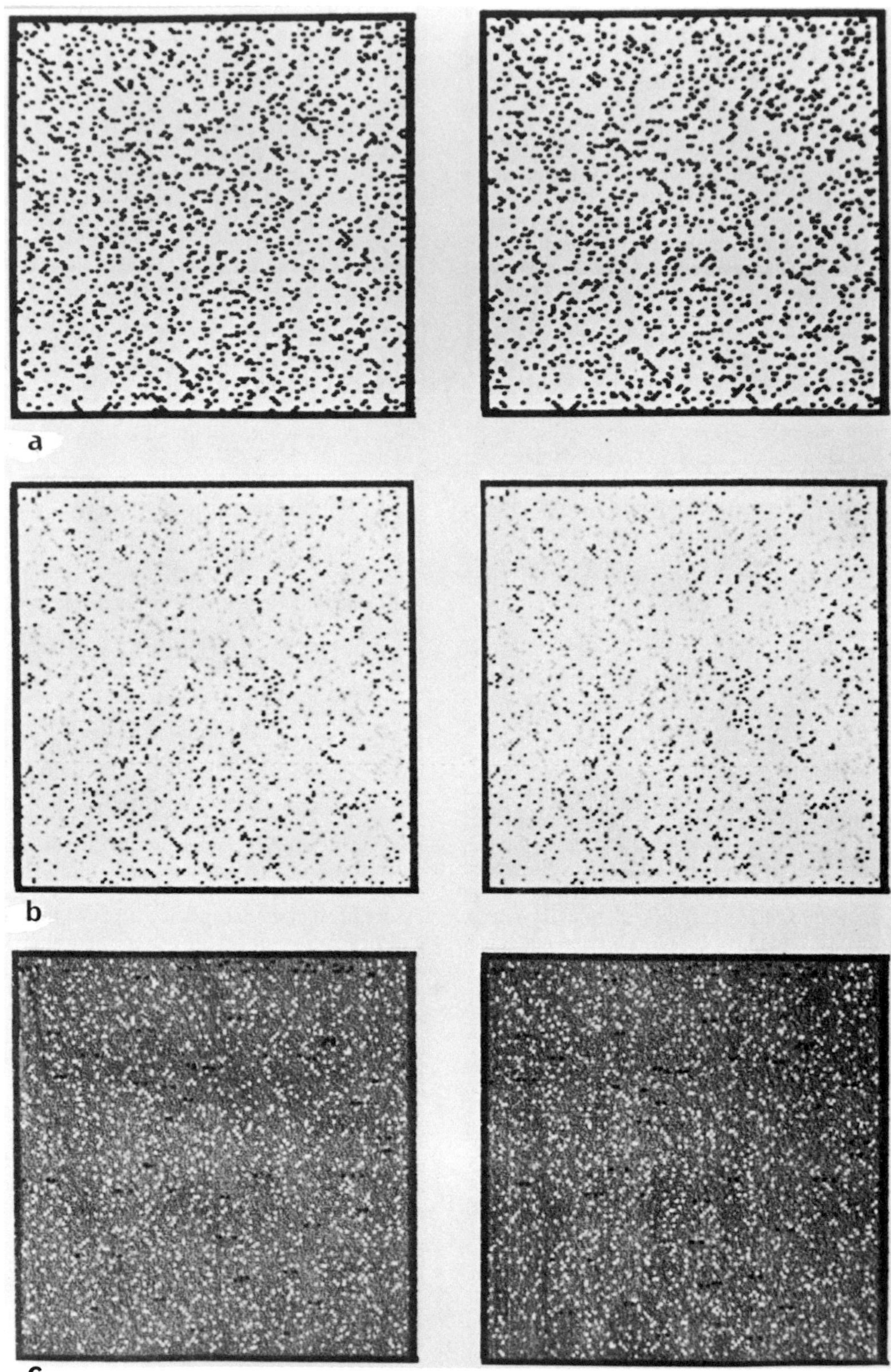

Figure 9 Random-dot stereogram used to test the capacity of PMF to deal with jagged surfaces. (a) A stereogram in which the disparities were randomly selected from a range of 6 pixels except that they everywhere had to satisfy a disparity gradient limit of 1. (b) Dots matched by PMF are shown on the right-hand side with intensity used to code relative disparity (again, dark = near, faint = far, for the cross-eyed fusion of the original stereogram). For comparison the correct relative disparities are shown on the left-hand side with the same intensity code being used. The similarity between these figures brings out the fact that PMF found the vast majority of correct matches (93%). To help further in this regard, the positions of the dots in these two images have been adjusted such that when the two are fused as though there were a stereo pair, the correct matches are seen to lie in a plane, with the very few incorrect matches seen as dots lying outside the plane occupied by the majority. (c) A reconstruction of the stereogram displayed in (a) after its processing by PMF. Dots matched correctly are shown white and the remainder are shown black. See text for further details.

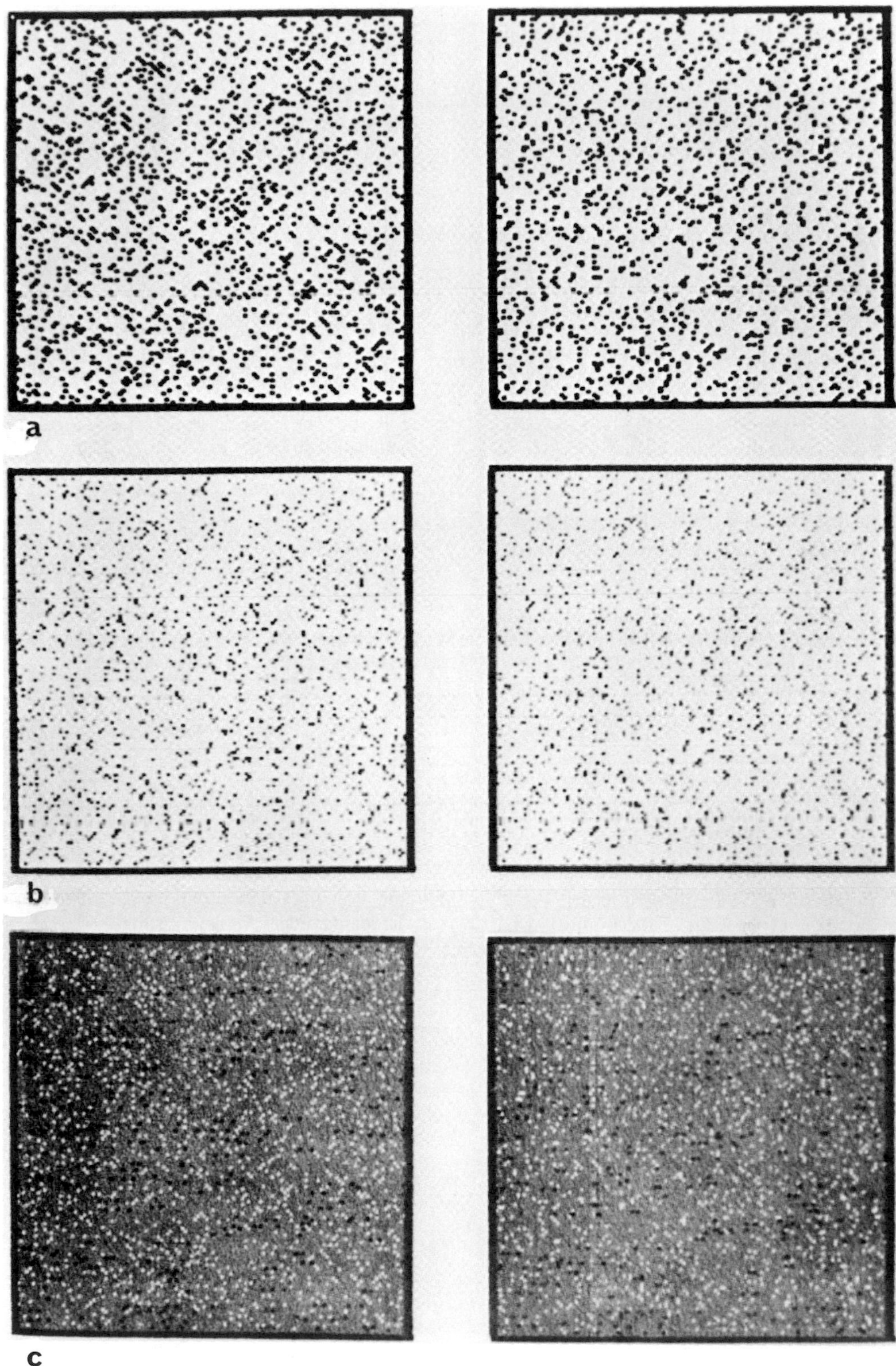

Figure 10 A second random-dot stereogram used to test the capacity of PMF to deal with jagged surfaces. (a) A stereogram made by selecting disparities at random from a gaussian distribution of zero mean disparity and standard deviation 2 pixels with no limit on allowable disparity gradients. Hence there are many severe local variations in disparity. Despite this, PMF manages to match correctly over 79% of dots; (b) and (c) display this competence on using the method of figures 9b and 9c. The text gives further details.

other; a gradient limit of 2 on the other hand allows the separation in one image to be infinitely larger than that in the other.

7.3 The constraint of figural continuity

Our previous stereo algorithm (STEREOEDGE: Mayhew and Frisby 1980, 1981) was based on taking advantage of the figural continuity that existed between the two images. Edge-like primitives were matched on the basis of their continuity and the similarity of their geometrical structure. That algorithm was justified in terms of the surface continuity constraint, and we continue to believe that that justification was appropriate for that algorithm. When surfaces do happen to be locally spatially continuous, then their edges and extended surface markings must be spatially continuous also: hence the rationale for the stereo combination rule of STEREOEDGE of preferring disparity matches which preserve figural continuity (see also Grimson 1984).

As we have already discussed in section 2, it is clear that a disparity gradient limit also provides a limit upon the allowable geometrical deformation that exists locally between the two images. For instance, if the disparity gradient limit were in fact zero, then the two images would have to be locally figurally identical. Imposing a limit of 1 allows some dissimilarity in the figural structures that constitute the two images. Hence, PMF can be viewed as effecting a correlation between stereo halves in which the figural distortions that characterise the differences between left and right stereo projections are not allowed to lower the correlation score. This way of considering PMF shows that it is a natural development of the STEREOEDGE algorithm. However, PMF has the advantage that its matching primitives are not restricted to extended edge segments.

8 SUMMARY

We have demonstrated the considerable disambiguating power that results from imposing a limit on the magnitude of allowable disparity gradients in order that matches are allowed to support one another. Imposing such a limit does not greatly limit the class of allowable surfaces. We have developed a simple stereo algorithm that utilises disparity gradients in a cooperative manner (Fender and Julesz 1967; Julesz 1971) to solve the stereo disambiguation problem and have illustrated its performance on a variety of natural and artificial stereograms. The rationale underlying the use of the disparity gradient limit has been contrasted with other computational treatments of the stereo correspondence problem.

Note added in proof Since the submission of this paper further results have been obtained regarding the mathematical details of the imposition of a disparity gradient limit (see Trivedi and Lloyd 1985; Pollard et al 1985).

Acknowledgements We would like to thank John Porrill and Tony Pridmore for their valuable advice and Chris Brown for his technical assistance. PMF was first invented on SERC Research Grant GR/B.43265 and was the subject of further development by S B Pollard supported on a SERC CASE studentship jointly supervised by Dr M M McCabe of GEC/Hirst Laboratories and Dr S A Lloyd. JEWM is supported by Alvey/SERC contract GR/D/1679.6.

REFERENCES

Arnold R D, (1982) *Automated Stereo Perception* PhD thesis, Stanford University, Stanford, CA, USA

Baker H H, (1982) *Depth from edge and intensity based stereo*, AI Memo 347, Stanford University, Stanford, CA, USA

Baker H H, Binford T O, (1981) Depth from edge and intensity based stereo in *Proceedings of 7th IJCA* (Los Altos, CA: William Kaufmann) 631-636

Burt P, Julesz B, (1980) Modifications of the classical notion of Panum's fusional area *Perception* **9** 671-682

Fender D, Julesz B, (1967) Extensions of Panum's fusional area in binocularly stabilised vision *Journal of the Optical Society of America* **57** 819-830

Grimson W E L, (1984) Computational experiments with a feature based stereo algorithm, AI Memo 762, MIT, Cambridge, MA, USA

Julesz B, (1971) *Foundations of Cyclopean Perception* (Chicago: University of Chicago Press)

Marr D, (1982) *Vision* (San Francisco: W H Freeman)

Marr D, Hildreth E, (1980) Theory of edge detection *Proceedings of the Royal Society of London, Series B*, **207** 187-217

Marr D, Poggio T, (1976) A cooperative computation of stereo-disparity *Science* **194** 283-287

Marr D, Poggio T, (1979) A theory of human stereo vision *Proceedings of the Royal Society of London, Series B*, **204** 301-328

Mayhew J E W, (1983) Stereopsis in *Physical and Biological Processing Images* eds O J Braddick, A C Sleigh (New York: Springer) 204-216

Mayhew J E W, Frisby J P, (1980) The computation of binocular edges *Perception* **9** 69-86

Mayhew J E W, Frisby J P, (1981) Psychophysical and computational studies towards a theory of human stereopsis *Artificial Intelligence* **17** 349-386

Ohta Y, Kanade T, (1983) Stereo by intra- and inter-scanline search using dynamic programming Technical Report CMU-CS-83-162, Carnegie Mellon University, Pittsburgh, PA, USA

Pollard S B, Porrill J, Mayhew J E W, Frisby J P, (1985) Disparity gradient, Lipschitz continuity and computing binocular correspondences in *Proceedings of the Third International Symposium of Robotics Research, Gouviex, France* (Cambridge, MA: MIT Press) in press

Prazdny K, (1985) Detection of binocular disparities *Biological Cybernetics* (in press)

Rosenfeld A, Hummel R, Zucker S W, (1976) Scene labelling by relaxation operations *IEEE Transactions on Systems, Man, and Cybernetics* **6** 420-433

Trivedi H P, Lloyd S A, (1985) The role of disparity gradient in stereo vision *Perception* in press

Tyler C W, (1973) Stereoscopic vision: cortical limitations and a disparity scaling effect *Science* **181** 276-278

[2] Disparity Gradient, Lipschitz Continuity, and Computing Binocular Correspondences

Stephen B Pollard, John Porrill, John E W Mayhew and John P Frisby

AI Vision Research Unit
University of Sheffield, Sheffield S10 2TN, UK

Reprinted, with permission of MIT Press, from Faugeras, O D and Giralt, G (Eds) *Robotics Research: The Third International Symposium*, 1986, 19-26.

Abstract

A theoretical formulation of the stereo correspondence problem and an algorithm for its solution are described. One way of characterising the stereo matching problem is to find a one-to-one locally continuous mapping between the two eyes' subject to the epipolar geometry. This abstract formulation unfortunately provides no algorithmic *mechanism* with which to obtain the solution. This has long been recognised and researchers in the field have been concerned to identify and exploit heuristic continuity and smoothness constraints to resolve the stereo ambiguity problem (for a review see Mayhew 1983). One such constraint, motivated by psychophysical observation (Burt and Julsez 1980), is the disparity gradient constraint which was first exploited heuristically in the PMF stereo algorithm (Pollard et al 1985). The disparity gradient constraint enforces Lipschitz continuity on the mappings between the eyes' views, on the surfaces in the scene and on the depth map. The Lipschitz constant (corresponding to the limiting disparity gradient) provides a free parameter that can be exploited algorithmically. Accordingly we also examine how varying the value of the disparity gradient limit effects both the disambiguating power of the PMF algorithm, and restricts the range of surface orientations that can be fused (full details can be found in Pollard *et al* 1985; Pollard 1985).

1. Introduction

Suppose we have a stereo pair of views of n points in space. The only purely geometrical constraint on matching between the two views is that matches should lie on corresponding epipolar lines. In principle this would be enough. For generic views of generic point sets no two points will lie on the same epipolar and so every point has a unique match. In practice we do not deal with generic point sets; quantisation error also forces points into the same epipolar *raster*. Further matching constraints are thus required for uniqueness.

Objects in the world are usually bounded by continuous opaque surfaces. If we assume that the observed feature points lie on such a surface so as to be simultaneously visible to both eye's we arrive at the *ordering constraint* (see: Baker and Binford 1981; Burt and Julesz 1981; Baker 1982; Mayhew 1983; Yuille and Poggio 1984; Ohta and Kanade 1985): points on the same epipolar line are in the same order in both eyes' views. Once again the matching problem is solved in principle. Points are matched in left-to-right order along epipolars, starting with the leftmost in each view. Again this is not sufficient in practice; the two eyes' views will not cover the same area, so the leftmost points will not both be available; also extra unmatchable noise points will be present. A further constraint is required. One possibility is to propagate information between rasters exploiting figural continuity (Mayhew and Frisby 1980, 1981) since continuous edges in the scene will project to continuous curves in the image (see also: Baker 1982; Grimson 1983, Ohta and Kanade 1985). Once we have matched one point on such a curve, we can follow it continuously across rasters (note that a practical definition of continuity would be required here).

Another between-rasters constraint that has proved useful is based on the concept of *disparity gradient limit* (derived from psychophysical observations: Burt and Julesz 1980a, 1980b; Tyler 1973, 1974, 1975). It is the basis of a successful feature based stereo matching algorithm (the PMF algorithm: Pollard *et. al.* 1984, 1985; Pollard 1985). Disparity gradient can be thought of as a simple measure of continuity, and the disparity gradient limit encapsulates previous stereo constraints in a strong form. For example, enforcing a disparity gradient limit of $DG<2$ requires that the observed surface be Lipschitz continuous (this is defined in the Appendix) and not self-occluding; a recent result by Trivedi & Lloyd (1985) shows that it also imposes continuity on the mapping between the two eyes' views. This can be considered as an algorithmic description of the continuous and opaque nature of most surfaces in the world. Some simple transparent self-occluding surfaces (*e.g.* a pair of transparent planes at different depths), though not satisfying the disparity gradient limit globally, can be built up from surfaces patches which do satisfy this limit locally (this is similar to the concept of a *cohesiveness* discussed by Prazdny 1985). The set of such surfaces forms a wider domain in which disparity gradient limit is still a useful tool for disambiguation, and in fact the PMF algorithm can cope with such *lace curtain* stereograms (see Pollard *et al* 1985).

2. Disparity Gradients and Lipschitz Continuity

In this section we will show that an isotropic disparity gradient limit is only one member of a whole family of measures of continuity which impose scene-to-view and view-to-view Lipschitz continuity. In the process we obtain a simplified proof of the result of Trivedi & Lloyd (1985) on view-to-view continuity. In §3 the PMF stereo algorithm (Pollard *et al* 1985) which exploits the disparity gradient constraint will be briefly described.

2.1. Properties of the Disparity Gradient Limit Constraint

Let L and R be the left and right views of a given scene (they could be regions in the image planes, or finite sets of feature points). If points $p \in L$ and $p' \in R$ have been than one match for a single primitive that satisfies the gradient limit, only the stronger contributes to the matching strength.

3.2. Resolving ambiguity

Uniqueness is enforced via a simple discrete iterative winner take all procedure. At each iteration those matches having the highest matching strength for both of the two image primitives forming them are immediately chosen as *correct*, ie matches that are maximal with respect to both lines of sight are selected. Subsequently, alternative matches associated with the two primitives that form each selected match can be eliminated from further consideration. This allows further matches, not previously either accepted or eliminated, to be selected as correct provided that they now have the highest strengths for both constituent primitives. In practice convergence of this procedure usually occurs after only 4 or 5 iterations, with the overwhelming majority of matches being identified at the first iteration.

3.3. Support

It is important to emphasise the fact that PMF is only interested in the quantity of within-disparity gradient limit support that exists for a particular match. The extent to which the disparity gradient limit is violated in the neighbourhood of a candidate match does not directly effect PMF's selection procedure. Alternatively, it would be possible to reduce the strength of a match in accordance with the number of points over the neighbourhood that did not possess matches that satisfied the gradient limit. However it cannot be assumed that a moderate disparity gradient limit will be satisfied everywhere. The disparity gradients that exist across depth shears, for example, will generally be large. Fortunately the satisfaction of the gradient limit that exists to either side of the discontinuity is generally sufficient to resolve ambiguity in their vicinity.

3.4. Consistency

A further point to note is that within-disparity gradient support is sought independently from all possible matches in the neighbourhood of the match under consideration. Hence it is possible that two or more matches that give within-disparity gradient limit support might not themselves share a within-limit disparity gradient. An alternative approach would be to require that all matches that give support be mutually consistent, that is the disparity gradient limit must be satisfied amongst them. However the computational overheads involved in recovering the best such score are prohibitive even for quite small neighbourhoods. Hence this requirement is relaxed in the design of PMF for reasons of computational efficiency. The effect of this simplification is illustrated below.

4. Statistics of Projection

In practice the selection of a suitable limiting disparity gradient in PMF is doubly constrained. On the one hand the chosen limit should provide sufficient generality, ie it should admit as wide a range of surfaces as possible. And on the other it should provide sufficient disambiguating power to resolve any ambiguity that may be present. In this section we shall examine the statistics of stereo projection in order to show that the restriction on the set of possible surfaces resulting from the imposition of a moderate disparity gradient limit is not severe.

Proposition 3 relates gradients in the scene to disparity gradients in the image. Expressing the world gradient as tan s and rearranging gives

$$DG = \frac{I}{d} \cdot \tan s$$

Notice how the magnitude of the disparity gradient is scaled with respect to the viewing parameters I and d. Generally, for viewing systems approximating that of the human visual system, d is large in comparison to I and the vast majority of disparity gradients in the image will be small. Following Arnold and Binford (1980), also reported by Kass (1984), it is possible to derive a probability density function for disparity gradient based upon the assumption that surface orientation is uniformly distributed over the gaussian sphere (details in Pollard 1985). That is

$$Pdf(DG) = \frac{\cos(\tan^{-1}(\frac{DG}{a}))a}{a^2 + DG^2}$$

where

$$a = \frac{I}{d}$$

for DG in the range 0 to infinity.

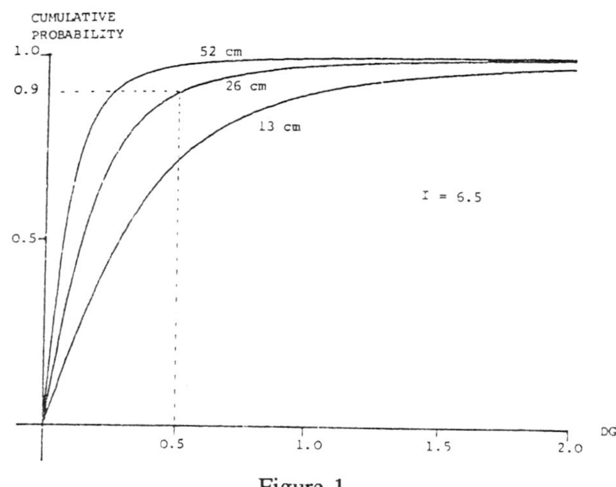

Figure 1

In figure 1 the cumulative density function is plotted for a range of d values representative of the distances for which binocular stereo is considered to be an important depth cue in human vision. The inter-ocular separation I is assumed to be 6.5cm. Inspection of figure 1 clearly shows that at any reasonable viewing distance the majority of disparity gradients will be small. For example, less than 10% of world surfaces viewed at more than 26cm will present with disparity gradient in excess of 0.5. Hence one can argue that to enforce a disparity gradient well below the *theoretical* limit (of 2) imposes negligible restrictions on the *worlds* that can be fused by the stereo algorithm.

5. Disambiguation

So far it has been demonstrated that the binocular projections of most planar and many jagged surfaces will present small disparity gradients almost everywhere (given always that interocular separation is small with respect to viewing distance). Consequently, assuming some cohesiveness of the world, the disparity gradients that exist between the correct matches of the image features that describe the structure of the viewed surfaces will almost always be within a moderate limit. But, as implied above, disambiguation also needs to rely upon there being a low probability for this limit to be satisfied between incorrect matches (also called ghosts for convenience) of the same image features.

This section presents the results of a simple computational experiment designed to illustrate the effect on disambiguating power of varying the magnitude of the limiting disparity gradient. For this purpose it is convenient to consider the matching problem associated with patterns of random point features (dots generated to 32 bit floating point resolution) of a uniform density. Whilst this restriction is not entirely satisfactory, the ambiguity problem associated with dot patterns makes them typical of some of the most problematic textures that exist in natural imagery.

5.1. Strength Ratios

For our purposes disambiguating power is defined as the extent to which it is possible to distinguish those matches that are correct from their associated ghosts. The ratio of incorrect to correct match strength provides a useful metric in this regard. If this ratio is generally small the resulting disambiguation power will be sufficient to resolve the vast majority of correct matches even in the presence of large quantities of noise and/or close to disparity discontinuities. Experimental results are presented in the form of a frequency distribution compiled as a result of a large number of independent trials. At each trial:

(i) a single dot is chosen from a random dot pattern

(ii) the strength of its correct match is computed by matching the dot with the same dot in an identical dot pattern

(iii) the strength of an incorrect match is computed by matching the dot with a dot in an independent dot pattern

(iv) their ratio is computed

(v) this single contribution is added to the distribution

The magnitude of the strength of a correct match, given by (ii), is equivalent for all situations in which the gradient limit is satisfied amongst the correct matches, ie where the word projects as a suitable Lipschitz disparity surface. This follows from the fact that in such situations the matching strength of PMF is only dependent upon the projection into the left image. For noiseless data, the matching strength for a correct match (CS) will receive a single contribution from each dot in the neighbourhood.

$$CS = \sum_{i \in N} \frac{1}{S(i)}$$

where N is the set of dots in the neighbourhood and $S(i)$ is the physical separation of dot i.

For an incorrect match only those dots in the neighbourhood that have matches that satisfy the gradient limit by chance are allowed to contribute to the matching score.

$$IS = \sum_{i \in N} \frac{INDG(i)}{S(i)}$$

where $INDG(i)$ is a boolean that is satisfied only if there exists a match for dot i that satisfies the disparity gradient limit with respect to the match under consideration.

Figure 2 presents the normalised frequency distribution of strength ratios (IS/CS) (obtained over 1000 independent trials) for several values of limiting disparity gradient. The random dot patterns used were of uniform density with 0.1 dots per unit area [pixel] and the neighbourhood size was of 7 units radius. A vertical matching range of one unit was allowed for matching each dot in the neighbourhood. In the absence of noise the maximum possible ratio magnitude is 1. Hence good disambiguating power is characterised by a distribution of strength ratios clustered about some value much less than 1. This is the case where the disparity gradient is of moderate size, ie in the range between 0.5 and 1 (even within this range considerably better disambiguation power is achieved with the lower limit). Beyond such values the degree of deformation allowed between the two images (without affecting the matching strength) increases rapidly, and thus the disambiguation power provided falls off equally rapidly. A disparity gradient limit of 2 (approximated by a limit of 1.99), the *physical* limit along epipolar lines, provides almost no disambiguating power when used in this way; almost all incorrect matches obtain the same quantity of within-gradient support as their associated correct matches.

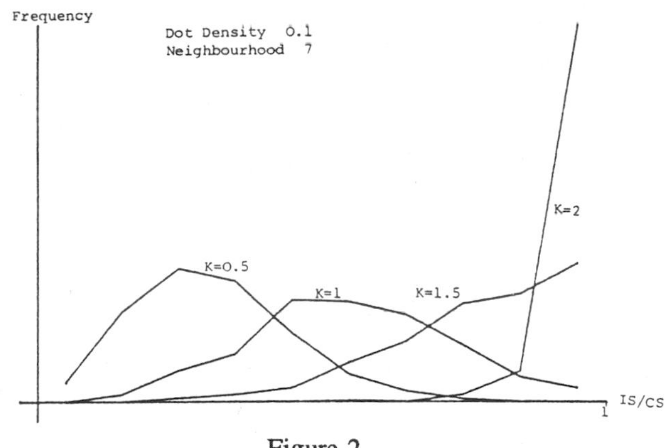

Figure 2

5.2. Mutual Consistency

It is also possible to examine the effect on the matching strength computation of PMF of the decision to relax the mutual consistency constraint. Matching strengths for correct matches remain the same as by definition correct matches defined here will all mutually satisfy the gradient limit over the extent of the neighbourhood. For incorrect matches, however, it is necessary to search the set of possible matches for each dot in the neighbourhood for the mutually consistent subset that maximises the matching strength, the initial set being limited to those matches, of each dot, that satisfy the gradient limit with respect to the match in question. Frequency distributions for mutually consistent matches are displayed in figure 3 for gradient limits 0.5, 1 and 1.5 (1.99 being too expensive to compute).

Some improvement, for each chosen value of the disparity gradient limit, is observed. However the overall trend of disambiguating power decreasing with the magnitude of the gradient limit still occurs. In practical terms the actual improvement in disambiguation power that is gained for a small disparity gradient limit, such as 0.5, is not appreciable when compared with the computational simplicity of computing matching strengths without insisting upon consistency. Enforcing mutual consistency in this way is combinatorially explosive, being closely related to the max clique problem (which is known to be NP complete; see Aho, Hopcroft and Ullman 1974).

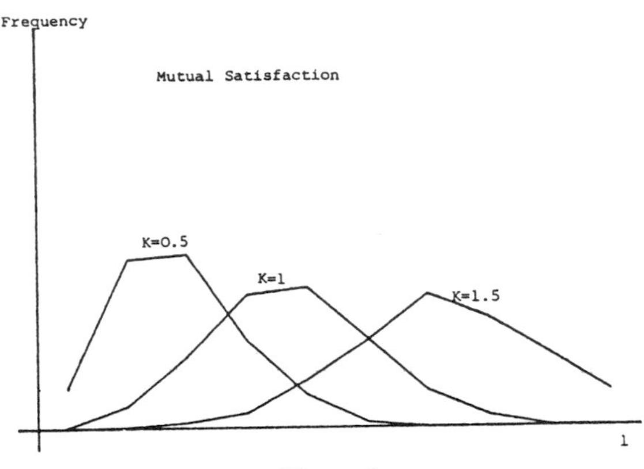

Figure 3

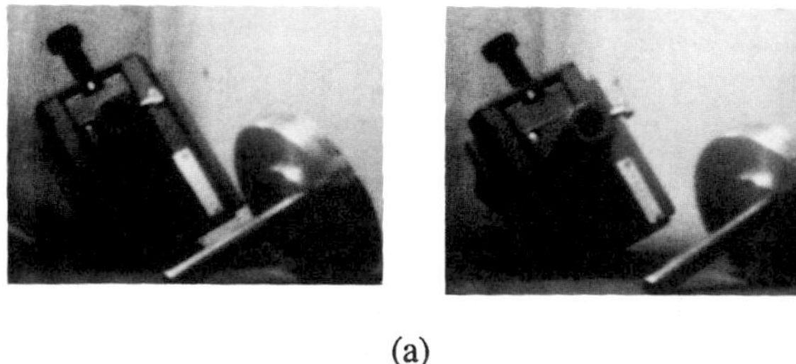

(a)

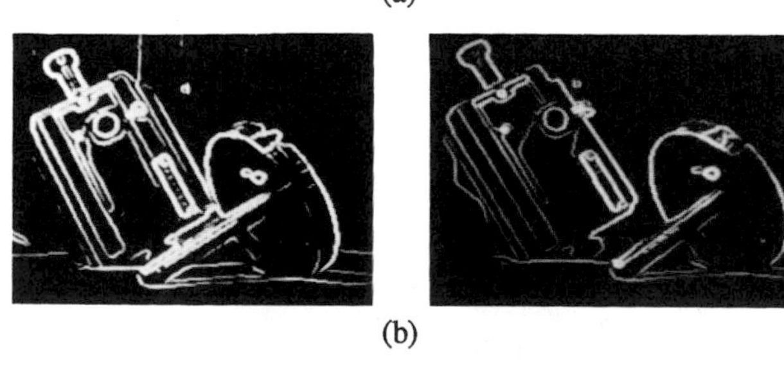

(b)

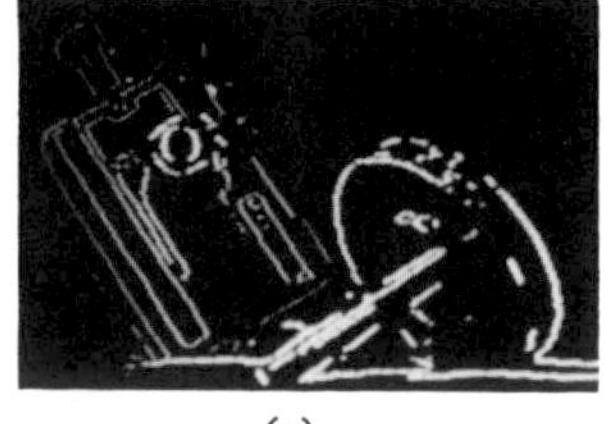

(c)

Figure 4

6. Examples of Performance

Two examples of the performance of the PMF algorithm on natural scenes are given here. The adopted disparity gradient limit is that reported by Burt and Julesz (1980a,1980b) for the human visual system, ie DG=1. Note that in terms of generality and disambiguating power this provides a fairly liberal constraint.

The stereogram given in figure 4(a) is representative of a simple industrial scene. Each image is 256 pixels square. Edge-like primitives, identified with a single scale (σ=2) Canny edge detector (Canny 1983) are displayed in (b), with intensity used to code edge contrast. As edge primitives are represented as pixels the constraint provided by epipolar geometry is implemented by limiting search to corresponding rasters in the two images (vertical disparities between the two images are always less than half a pixel). Potential matches are limited to a disparity range of $\pm$30 pixels and are required to be of the same contrast polarity and of a similar orientation. The actual limit on reorientation is given by the magnitude of the disparity gradient limit. Hence near vertical edge segments are allowed to reorient more so than horizontal ones. Disparity data recovered from matches selected by PMF (with a neighbourhood of radius 10 pixels) is displayed in (c) as a cyclopean image with intensity used to approximate relative depth (brighter points are closer to the imaging device). Unmatched points are not displayed.

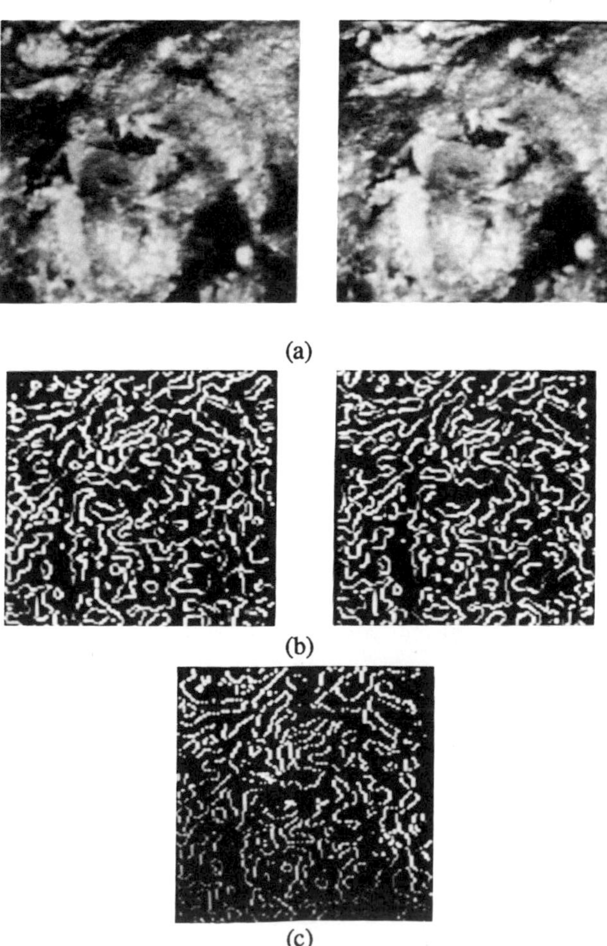

(a)

(b)

(c)

Figure 5

A very different scene is the subject of the stereogram in figure 5(a). It portrays a rocky terrain viewed from above, presenting therefore a similar task to that solved by human operators in the field of photogrammetry from aerial photographs. The images are just 128 pixels square. All other parameters are the same as those used to process figure 4. The edge-like primitives in (b) are provided by a single high frequency (ω=5) Marr-Hildreth operator (Marr and Hildreth 1980). Disparity data is presented in (c) with intensity coding depth.

7. Concluding Comments

This paper has explored the theoretical and practical justifications for the use of the disparity gradient constraint in stereo matching. It has been shown that provided the gradient limit is less than 2 Lipschitz continuity is enforced between the stereo images and furthermore both the world and the cyclopean disparity map will be Lipschitz (with respect to a cyclopean coordinate frame). The selection of a suitable gradient limit is subject to pragmatic constraints. It has been shown that a moderate gradient limit (between 0.5 and 1) captures the statistics of small baseline stereo projection and provides considerable disambiguating power. The PMF stereo algorithm exploits the local satisfaction of the gradient limit in a simple and computationally attractive fashion. The strength of each match could, on a suitable computer architecture, be computed entirely in parallel and because of the considerable disambiguating power provided by the gradient limit in a single pass over the images.

References

Aho A. V., J. E. Hopcroft and J. D. Ullman (1974) *The design and analysis of computer algorithms,* Addison Wesley.

Arnold R. D. and T. O. Binford (1980) Geometric constraints in stereo vision, *Soc. Photo-Optical Instr. Engineers,* 238, 281-292.

Baker H. H. (1982) Depth from edge and intensity based stereo, *PhD Thesis,* University of Illinois.

Baker H. H. and T. O. Binford (1981) Depth from edge and intensity based stereo, *IJCAI 7,* Vancouver, B. C., 631-636.

Burt P. and B. Julesz (1980a) A disparity gradient limit for binocular fusion, *Science* 208, 615-617.

Burt P. and B. Julesz (1980b) Modifications of the classical notion of Panum's fusional area, *Perception* 9, 671-682.

Canny J. F. (1983) Finding edges and lines in images, *MIT AI Lab. Memo* 720.

Grimson W. E. L. (1983) Computational experiments with a feature base stereo algorithm. *MIT AI Lab. Memo* 762.

Kass M. H. (1984) Computing stereo correspondence, *MSc Thesis,* Dept. of Elect. Eng. and Computer Sci., MIT, Cambridge, Mass.

Marr D. and E. Hildreth, (1980) Theory of edge detection, *Proc. R. Soc. London B* 207 187-217.

Marr D. and T. Poggio (1976) The cooperative computation of stereo disparity, *Science* 194 283-287.

Marr D. and T. Poggio (1979) A theory of human stereo vision, *Proc. R. Soc. London B* 204 301-328.

Mayhew J. E. W. (1983) *Stereopsis, in Physiological and Biological Processing of Images,* O. J. Braddick and A. C. Sleigh (Eds), Springer Verlag, Berlin, 204-216.

Mayhew J. E. W. and J. P. Frisby (1980) The computation of binocular edges, *Perception* 9, 69-86.

Mayhew J. E. W. and J. P. Frisby (1981) Psychophysical and computational studies toward a theory of human stereopsis, *Artificial Intelligence* 17, 349-386.

Ohta and Kanade (1985) Stereo by two-level dynamic programming, *IJCAI* 9, Los Angeles, 1120-1126.

Pollard S. B. (1985) Identifying correspondences in binocular stereo, *PhD Thesis,* Department of Psychology, University of Sheffield.

Pollard S. B., Mayhew J. E. W. and Frisby J. P. (1984) PMF: A stereo correspondence algorithm using a disparity gradient limit, *paper presented at ECVP* 7, *Perception* 13 *(abstract only).*

Pollard S. B., Mayhew J. E. W. and Frisby J. P. (1985) PMF: A stereo correspondence algorithm using a disparity gradient limit, *Perception (in press).*

Prazdny (1985) Detection of binocular disparities, *Biol. Cyb. (in press).*

Trivedi H. P. and S. A. Lloyd (1985) The role of disparity gradient in stereo vision, *Comp. Sys. Memo* 165, GEC Hirst Research Centre, Wembley, England.

Tyler C. W. (1973) Stereoscopic vision: cortical limitations and a disparity scaling effect, *Science* 181, 276-278.

Tyler C. W. (1974) Depth perception in disparity gratings, *Nature* 251, 140-142.

Tyler C. W (1975) Spatial organization of binocular disparity sensitivity, *Vision Research* 15, 583-590.

Yuille A. L. and T. Poggio (1984) A generalised ordering constraint for stereo correspondence, *MIT AI Memo* 777.

Appendix: Norms, Lipschitz conditions, and Continuity

A norm $\|\cdot\|$ on a vector space V is a map

$$V \to \mathbf{R} : a \to \|a\|$$

with the three properties

$$\|a\| \geq 0$$

$$\|\lambda a\| = |\lambda| \, \|a\|$$

$$\|a + b\| \leq \|a\| + \|b\|$$

for all $a,b \in V$ and $\lambda \in \mathbf{R}$. A function $f: V \to W$ is Lipschitz order α, ($0<\alpha<1$) constant K if

$$\|f(y) - f(x)\|_W \leq K \, \|y - x\|_V^{\alpha}$$

for all $x,y \in V$. Such a Lipschitz function is always continuous since for any $\varepsilon>0$ by putting $\delta=(\varepsilon/K)^{1/\alpha}$ we have

$$\|f(y) - f(x)\|_W \leq \varepsilon$$

whenever

$$\|y - x\|_V \leq \delta$$

A function is a homeomorphism if it is one-to-one and it and its inverse are continuous, and hence if it and its inverse are Lipschitz.

If f is Lipschitz order 1 constant K then if it is also differentiable its gradient has magnitude bounded by K. This Lipschitz condition can thus be regarded as a measure of jaggedness intermediate between continuity and bounded differentiability.

In practical situations we are working with functions defined only at a finite set of points. For such functions the notions of continuity and differentiability are meaningless. We can however calculate the Lipschitz constant K and this will give us a simple measure of *continuity*. In practice continuity always means a particular choice of bound on K. For example we may have a set of image points on adjacent screen rasters. We will say that they form a continuous curve if the change in position between rasters is less than, say, 2 pixels. This is a Lipschitz condition order 1 constant 2. The mathematical definition of continuity is not useful here since any finite set of points lies on some continuous curve.

[3] Implementation Details of the PMF Stereo Algorithm

Stephen B Pollard, John E W Mayhew and John P Frisby

AI Vision Research Unit,
University of Sheffield, Sheffield S10 2TN, UK

INTRODUCTION

This paper describes the current version of the PMF stereo algorithm. The two preceding papers (Pollard, Mayhew and Frisby, 1985 [1]; Pollard, Porrill, Mayhew and Frisby, 1985 [2]) were largely concerned with the theoretical considerations that have underpinned the general design philosophy of PMF. Within that general framework a great deal of scope exists for particular implementation details. The ones described here attend to the twin requirements of robustness and efficiency on state of the art computer machinery. Also, this implementation incorporates some features from other stereo algorithms aimed at exploiting more global constraints than those embedded in the original PMF.

CONTROL STRUCTURE

Figure 1 provides an overview of the control structure. Processing stages are represented as rectangular boxes, and decisions as diamonds. The algorithm makes three iterations through a fixed sequence of processing stages. Once selected, matches remain fixed for any remaining iterations. For selection, matches must satisfy a number of matching criteria based upon gradient support, figural continuity, and the satisfaction of the ordering constraint.

POTENTIAL MATCH SELECTION

The physical locations of potential matches satisfy the epipolar constraint. In particular, it is assumed that the edges to be matched have arisen from a simplified parallel camera geometry in which the imaging planes of each camera are coplanar, the inter-ocular axis parallel to it, and the images arrays similarly oriented. Under such conditions the epipolar constraint becomes a same-raster constraint, thereby simplifying the process of match selection. Whilst this restriction may seem severe, it is in practice straightforward to rectify edge locations to give the appearance that they arose from a parallel camera geometry provided that the true camera geometry is known to reasonable accuracy. Thus rectification assumes either a priori knowledge or some form of calibration process to determine the physical camera geometry. In the examples of the performance of PMF shown below we have used the method of calibration from Tsai (1986) to recover a suitable approximation to the physical camera geometry.

Initial ranges of allowable image disparity can be either (1) preset arbitrarily: for later performance examples they were fixed to +/- half the size of the images; or (2) selected using disparity histogramming (based upon Shirai and Nishimoto, 1986) to set initial disparity ranges for each region of the image (16 by 16).

Matches between edges are restricted to have differences in left and right image orientations that could have arisen from a disparity gradient (DG) of 1.0. Hence edges that have orientations close to vertical are allowed to reorient to a greater extent than those close to horizontal. The sign and physical contrast of a pair of edges can also be used to determine both their matchability and matching strength. In the initial stages of the algorithm the contrast of a pair of matching edges must agree to a factor of 3. The strength of a match is the product of the individual contrast values, thus giving greater weight to matches between more robust edges.

SELECT SEED POINTS

A strategy aimed at fast yet reliable matching is to begin by seeking a set of strong seed point matches which can be used to guide selection of subsequent matches. This is done by trying to match at first only a subset of all the edge points available. So, only every nth point on an edge string is considered (currently n=4) as a seed point, and only every mth point along a string can give support (currently m=2). Figure 2 illustrates these concepts.

COMPUTE WITHIN-DG-LIMIT SUPPORT

In figure 3 the small circles p, p', p'', i, and j' represent edge point primitives (the edge strings of which they form a part are not shown). Matching is initiated from left image primitives and two potential matches for p are illustrated with the lines labelled pp' and pp''. Support for each of these matches is sought from the potential matches of other left image primitives lying within the neighbourhood support circle (of radius r not drawn to scale) shown around p. Just one supporting match ij' is illustrated for the match pp': note that ij' lies within the disparity gradient limit with respect to pp'.

The local neighbourhood support scheme is run with the DG limit set to 0.5, a value which provides better disambiguating power than 1.0 (Pollard, 1985). The size of the support neighbourhood is set to be a function of the image size (currently a default radius of 20 pixels for 256x256 images, a radius of 40 pixels for 512x512 images). The underlying concern here is to ensure that the support neighbourhood is large enough to provide good disambiguation while not being so large that processing time is spent needlessly.

ENFORCE WITHIN-DG-LIMIT SELECTION

From the list of potential matches for a given left image seed point candidate, choose the strongest match *unless* there exists in the neighbourhood a point with a stronger match that exceeds DG=1.5 with respect to the match under consideration. If a selection is made, eliminate from further consideration at this stage (they may get reconsidered later): (i) all other matches for the given left image edge primitive, and (ii) those that violate the gradient limit with respect to the selected match.

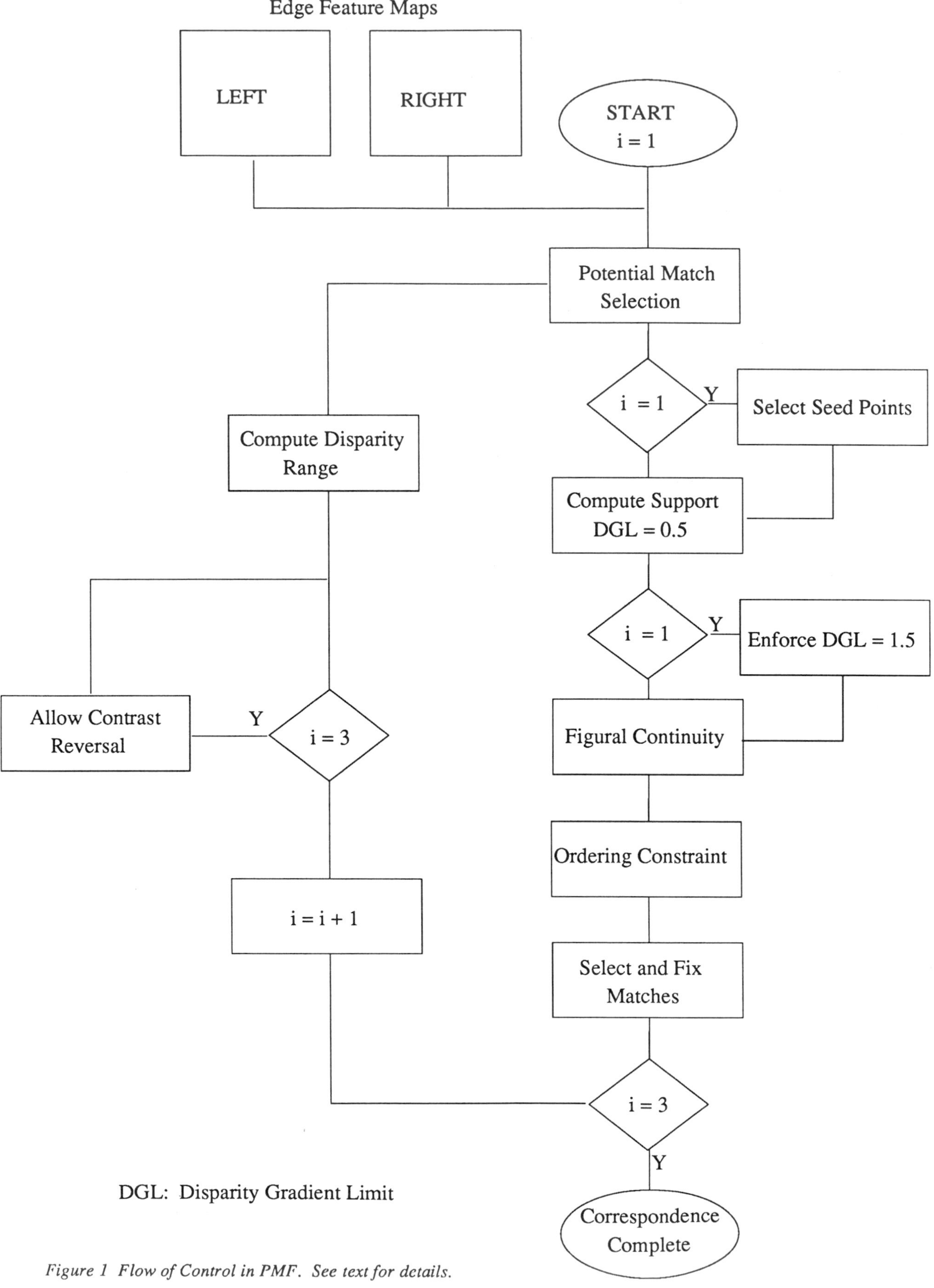

Figure 1 Flow of Control in PMF. See text for details.

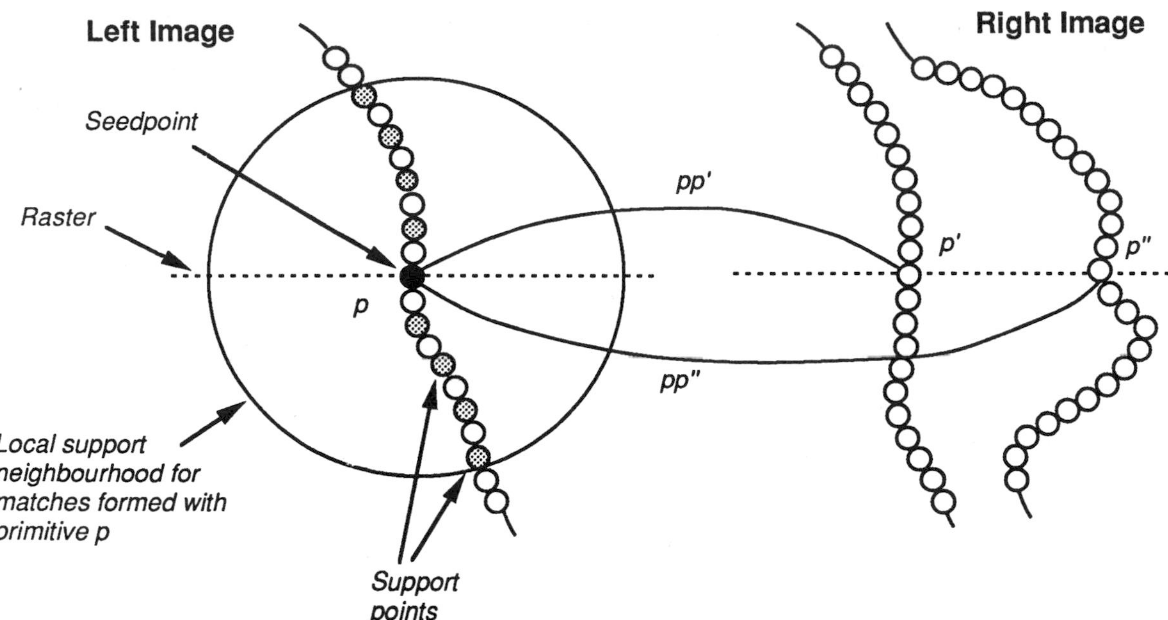

Figure 2 Selection of Seed Point Matches. The small circles represent edge point primitives comprising edge strings. Matching is initiated from left image strings and at first only every nth point comprising a left hand string is considered for matching. Such points are termed 'seed points'. Two potential matches for the seed point primitive p are shown, pp' and pp". Support for each of these matches is sought within the neighbourhood support circle shown around p (radius not drawn to scale), with every mth primitive along the string evaluated for the support it offers (the dotted circles illustrate m=2).

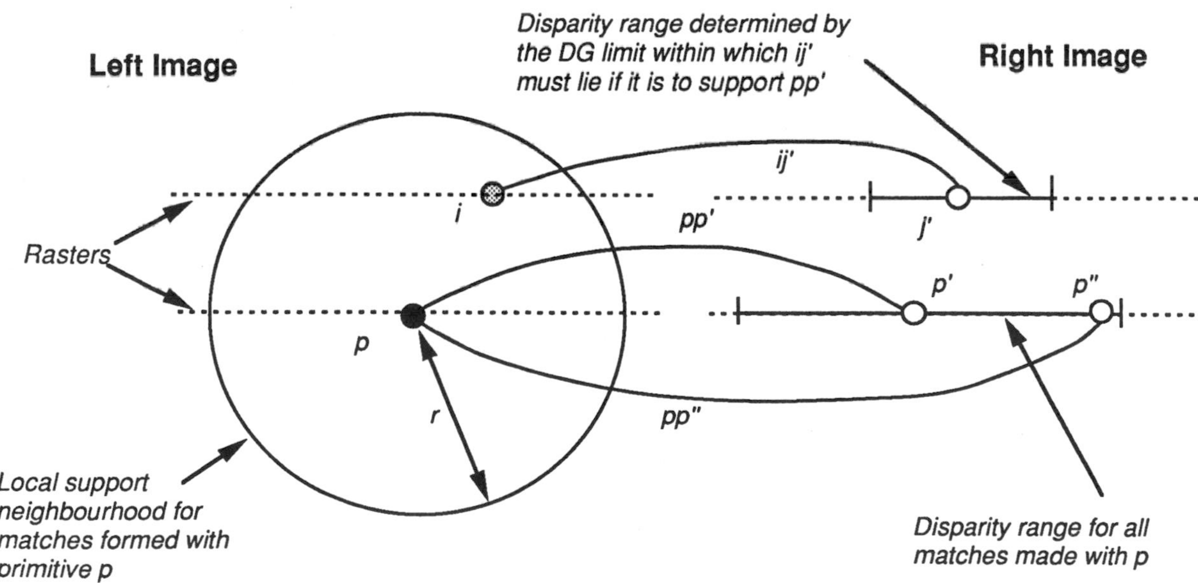

Figure 3 Neighbourhood Support. See text for details.

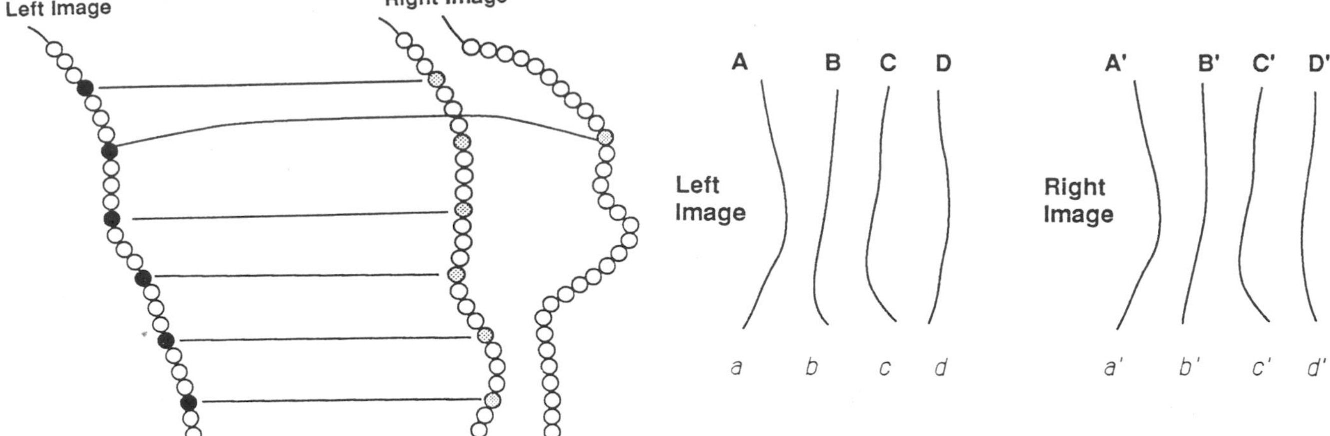

Figure 4 Exploiting the Figural Continuity Constraint by Matching Strings of Edge Points as a Whole. Lines connecting left and right image strings depict matches between initial seed points. The second line from the top shows a match whose right image primitive lies within a different edge string from those of all other matches. This fact is discovered and the discrepant match killed off.

Figure 5 Imposing the Ordering Constraint Explicitly. Suppose strings of points existed in the two images as shown, each with associated strengths a, b, ... c', d'. Suppose also that the correct matches were AA', BB', CC' and DD'. If matches AA', BD', CC' and DB' were initially chosen then the violation of the ordering constraint by matches BD' and DB' would be noted. The weakest strings whose elimination from matching would remove the violation are then discovered, and their primitives freed for reconsideration by later stages of matching.

The rationale for the *unless* proviso is that if there exists a stronger match in the neighbourhood that offends a quite steep disparity gradient limit then this is evidence that the match under consideration might well be false. It should not therefore be selected as a seed point on which to base other selections.

The selection rule is applied iteratively. If a stronger match exists then no selection is made on that iteration. If the stronger match gets killed off (by not getting selected as a seed point itself) then any selection held over may be allowed to proceed on the next iteration.

The above selection procedure implements the uniqueness constraint by allowing only one match per primitive but it does so only with respect to the left image points. Uniqueness is not imposed with respect to right image points as well (as happened in early versions of PMF) except later on via a greater use of the ordering constraint

FIGURAL CONTINUITY

The figural continuity constraint is exploited by counting the seed points along each string of edge points, and selecting that string which contains the majority of seed point matches. This operation marks a shift from the fairly local operations embedded in the neighbourhood support stage to much more global operations that can in principle span quite large regions of the image (in fact the whole image if an edge happens to traverse right across it). Seed point matches to the 'wrong' edge string get killed off at this stage (figure 4).

This stage copes with mild 'wallpaper illusion' problems caused by similar but not identical edge strings. Of course, there is no way to solve the ambiguity problem posed by repeating identical surface texture elements (the *real* wallpaper illusion problem) unless some disambiguating information can be propagated from the 'edges of the wallpaper'.

Finding matches between seed points is also done by a species of figural grouping. The procedure employed simply extrapolates from seed points along edge strings except that it can 'jump over gaps' caused by unmatchable edge points. The latter typically arise when left and right image edge points fall outside the allowable orientation limit required for matching (justified by the compatibility constraint and guided by the disparity gradient limit, as in PMF). This tends to happen when the edge string meanders due to local image noise, or closely neighbouring edges cause interference in the locations of Canny edge point locations. When small gaps of this kind are crossed, left image edge points lacking a match due to the gap in the right image do not have a disparity value attached to them.

ORDERING CONSTRAINT

It sometimes happens, particularly in image regions with few edges, that whole strings of edges points are incorrectly matched using the figural continuity procedures outlined above. A check is imposed to discover and remedy such problems using the ordering constraint explicitly and qualitatively. For example, suppose there exist strings *A*, *B*, *C*, *D* in the left image, each with a strength that is the sum of the strengths of the matches along them (not just length of string). Then if the matches for these strings in the right image violate the ordering constraint (figure 5), then the rule is to kill the weakest strings that result in the ordering constraint being satisfied. The primitives thereby 'released' from matching are considered (along with others also remaining unmatched) in subsequent stages.

Figure 6 Performance on a rock stereogram. (a) Grey level stereo images arranged for cross-eyed fusion. (b) Matched Canny edge points from the left image coded for relative depths with far=light and near=dark. (c) Smooth depth profile obtained from matches in b with the viewpoint from the top left hand side with respect to the other images.

a

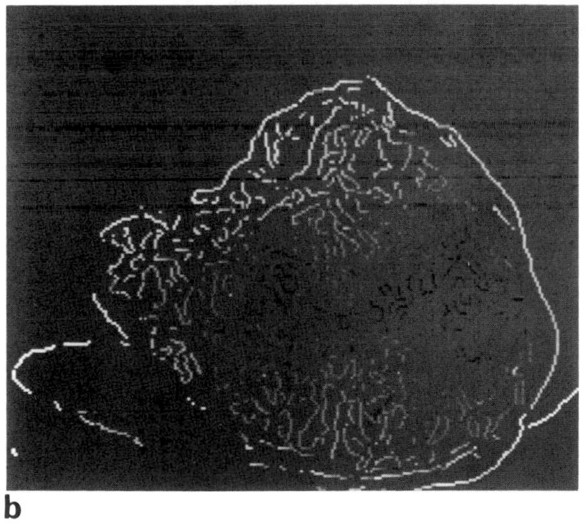

b

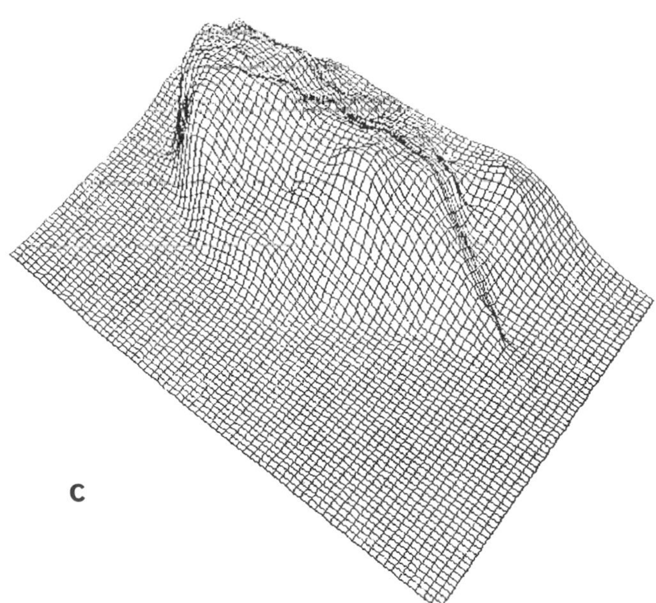

c

[4] Binocular Stereo Algorithm Based on the Disparity-Gradient Limit and Using Optimization Theory

S A Lloyd[1]

GEC Research Limited
Hirst Research Centre, Wembley, HA9 7PP, UK

Reprinted, with permission of Butterworth Scientific Ltd, from *Image and Vision Computing*, 1985, **3**, 177-181.

ABSTRACT

A new algorithm for stereo matching is presented, based on the idea of imposing a limit on disparity gradients allowed in the matched image. The matching problem will be expressed as one of maximizing a certain function, subject to constraints. Standard methods from optimization theory may then be used to find a solution.

Keywords: stereo matching, disparity gradient, optimization

Binocular stereo vision is the process by which three-dimensional structure is recovered from a pair of images of a scene taken from slightly different viewpoints. The difference in positions causes relative displacements or disparities of corresponding items in the images, and these disparities enable the depth to be calculated by triangulation.

There are three main stages in any binocular stereo algorithm: detecting and locating features to be matched, matching features, and calculating depths. When the camera geometry is known, the last of these stages is trivial. The method used for the first stage has been described elsewhere[1], so this paper will be concerned with the second stage. It will assume that a set of edge points, together with their orientations, has been extracted from each image.

The algorithm to be presented is based on the idea of imposing a limit on disparity gradients allowed in the matched image[2,3]. The disparity gradient between a pair of matched points is given by the ratio of the change in their disparity to the distance between their locations in the monocular image (Figure 1).

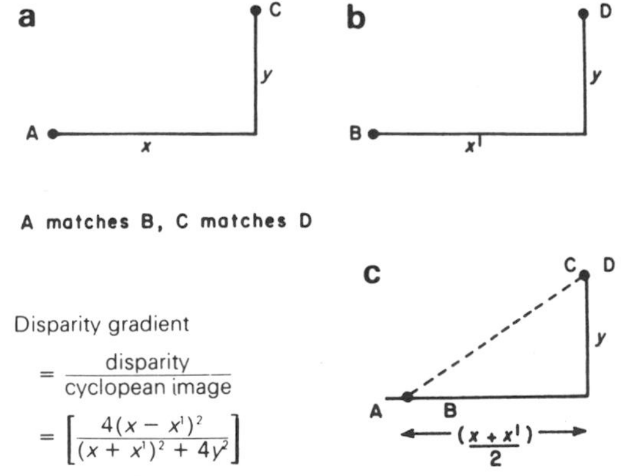

Figure 1. Definition of disparity gradient: a, left image; b, right image; c, cyclopean image

[1] Now with Hewlett Packard Laboratories
Filton Road, Stoke Gifford, Bristol, BS12 6QZ, UK.

It is related to the degree to which the surface on which the two points lie recedes from the observer; or, if the points lie on different surfaces, to the depth between those surfaces. The idea of using a disparity gradient limit is that matches of neighbouring primitives, when considered as a pair, should have a small disparity gradient. Pollard *et al*[2] have developed several algorithms, both iterative and noniterative, which implement this idea, and they have demonstrated their efficiency on a range of natural and synthetic images. These algorithms, however, have little mathematical basis, and the iterative versions have not been proved to converge. The aim of this work was, therefore, to produce an implementation of the idea of disparity-gradient limit based on optimization theory.

CONSTRUCTING A POOL OF POSSIBLE MATCHES

It will be assumed that the cameras are set up so that corresponding edges are constrained to lie in corresponding rows. Edges are then allowed to match provided they have the same contrast sign and similar orientations. The precise definition of similar orientations is that the angles are either within 30° of each other or lie within an 'orientation similarity' limit derived from the disparity gradient limit

$$\frac{4(\tan\theta - \tan\varphi)^2}{(\tan\theta + \tan\varphi)^2 + 4(\tan\theta - \tan\varphi)^2} < L_{dg}^2$$

Where L_{dg} is the disparity gradient limit. This condition is dependent on the edge orientation, the closer an edge is to vertical in one image, the greater the range of potential orientations that can arise in the other image.

OPTIMIZATION APPROACH

To use optimization theory, it is necessary to find a function to be maximized. In other words, a score must be defined for each way of matching the images, so it is possible to say when a match is a good one. Suppose that the images have been matched. For edge i in the left image and edge j in the right image, the decision variable x_{ij} is defined by

$$x_{ij} = \begin{cases} 1 & \text{if } i \text{ matches } j \\ 0 & \text{otherwise} \end{cases}$$

For edges i and k in the left image and edges j and l in the right image, a compatibility factor $q(i,j,k,l)$ can be defined in some way to represent the compatibility of matching i to j and k to l. For example q could be defined as

$$q(i,j,k,l) = \begin{cases} 1 & \text{if disparity gradient limit is satisfied} \\ 0 & \text{otherwise} \end{cases}$$

Then a global measure of the goodness of the match is

$$F(\mathrm{x}) = \sum_{i,j,k,l} q(i,j,k,l) x_{ij} x_{kl}$$

where $\mathbf{x} = (x_{11}, ..., x_{MN})$, ie the number of pairs of matches, each weighted by its compatibility factor. This is the function that will be maximized.

To apply optimization theory, the definition of the decision variables x_{ij} will be extended to be the probability that edge i matches edge j. Then the uniqueness constraint can be written

$$\sum_j x_{ij} \leq 1 \text{ for all } i$$

$$\sum_i x_{ij} \leq 1 \text{ for all } j$$

The following conditions must also hold

$$x_{ij} \geq 0 \text{ for all } i,j$$

$$x_{ij} = 0 \text{ if } i \text{ is not allowed to match } j$$

The region in MN-dimensional space fefined by the above conditions is called the feasible region. The problem is now to find the point in the feasible region with the largest value of F. If F were convex, this maximum would occur at a vertex of the feasible region. It can be shown[4] that any vertex of this region has the property that $x_{ij} = 0$ or 1 for all i,j, so a decision would be made. Unfortunately, it is not clear whether F is convex or not. In practice, however, this has not been a problem.

GRADIENT METHODS

The idea of a gradient method of solution is to begin with an initial feasible solution and, at each iteration, to determine a direction **r** in which to move so that by moving in this direction the value of F is increased, while remaining within the feasible region.

For the feasible region described above, the direction **r** must satisfy

$$\sum_j r_{ij} \leq 0 \text{ for all } i \text{ such that } \sum_j x_{ij} = 1$$

$$\sum_j r_{ij} \leq 0 \text{ for all } j \text{ such that } \sum_i x_{ij} = 1$$

$$r_{ij} \geq 0 \text{ for all } i,j, \text{ such that } x_{ij} = 0$$

$$r_{ij} = 0 \text{ if } i \text{ is not allowed to match } j.$$

The 'best' direction is that which maximizes $\nabla F.\mathbf{r}$ subject to $\mathbf{r.r} = 1$ and the conditions above. This is the direction in which the surface slopes most steeply, but this does not necessarily mean that moving in this direction will yield the greatest increase in F, nor that moving in this direction at each iteration will be the best strategy. It is, however, certainly a good direction in which to move. Unfortunately, finding the best direction is difficult because of the nonlinear constraint $\mathbf{r.r} = 1$. An aproximation to the best direction can be found by replacing this constraint by $\sum|r_{ij}| = 1$, and this (almost) linear programming problem can be solved by the restricted basis entry simplex method[5].

DESCRIPTION OF ALGORITHM

For ease of notation, several sets will be defined. Let

$$R = \{i \mid \textstyle\sum_j x_{ij} = 1\}$$
$$S = \{j \mid \textstyle\sum_i x_{ij} = 1\}$$
$$Z = \{(i,j) \mid x_{ij} = 0\}$$
$$I = \{(i,j) \mid i \text{ is not allowed to match } j\}.$$

To find **r**, the direction in which to move, the following optimization problem must be solved at each iteraton: maximize $\nabla F.\mathbf{r}$ subject to

$$\sum_j r_{ij} \leq 0 (i \in R)$$

$$\sum_i r_{ij} \leq 0 \; (j \in S)$$

$$r_{ij} \geq 0((i,j) \in Z)$$

$$r_{ij} = 0((i,j) \in I)$$

$$\sum_{i,j} |r_{ij}| = 1$$

It will be assumed that the compatibility factors q are symmetric, that is$q(i,j.k.l) = q(k,l,i,j)$. Then

$$\nabla F = (Q_{11}, ..., Q_{MN})$$

where

$$Q_{ij} = 2\sum_{k,l} q(i,j,k,l)\, x_{kl}$$

If either $R \neq \{l, \ldots, M\}$ or $S \neq \{l, \ldots, N\}$, then the solution to the problem can be found as follows

Let k,l be such that $k \in R$, $l \in S$ and

$$Q_{kl} = \max_{\substack{i \in R \\ j \in S}} Q_{ij}$$

Let r,t,u be such that $(r,u) \in Z$, $t \in S$ and

$$D_{rtu} = Q_{rt} - Q_{ru} = \max_{\substack{(i,k) \in Z \\ j \in S}} (Q_{ij} - Q_{ik})$$

Let s,v,w be such that $(w,s) \in Z$, $v \in R$ and

$$E_{svw} = Q_{vs} - Q_{ws} \max_{\substack{(k,j) \in Z \\ i \in R}} (Q_{ij} - Q_{kj})$$

Note that, depending on R and S, some of these quantities may not exist. Provided that $R \neq \{1, ..., M\}$ or $S \neq \{1,...,N\}$, however, at least one of these will exist. Then there are three cases.

(i) If $Q_{kl} \geq {}^1/_2 D_{rtu}$, ${}^1/_2 E_{svw}$, then
$r_{kl} = 1, r_{ij} = 0$ for all $(i,j) \neq (k,l)$

(ii) If ${}^1/_2 D_{rtu} > Q_{kl}$, ${}^1/_2 E_{svw}$, then
$r_{it} = 1, r_{ru} = -1, r_{ij} = 0$ otherwise

(iii) If ${}^1/_2 E_{svw} > Q_{kl}$, ${}^1/_2 D_{rtu}$, then
$r_{vs} = 1, r_{ws} = -1, r_{ij} = 0$ otherwise

If $R = \{1, ..., M\}$ and $S = \{1, ..., N\}$, then the problem is harder. In this case, a possible direction can be found as follows. Let r,t,u,v be such that (r,u), $(r,t) \in Z$ and

$$G_{rtuv} = Q_{rt} - Q_{vt} - Q_{ru} + Q_{vu} = \max_{\substack{(i,l) \in Z \\ (k,j) \in Z}} (Q_{ij} - Q_{il} - Q_{kj} + Q_{kl})$$

Let w,x,y be such that (w,y), $(z,x) \in Z$, $(z,y) \in I$ and

$$H_{wxyz} = Q_{wx} - Q_{wy} - Q_{zx} = \max_{\substack{(i,l) \in Z \\ (k,j) \in Z}} (Q_{ij} - Q_{il} - Q_{ki})$$

There are then two cases

(iv) If ${}^1/_4 G_{rtuv} \geq {}^1/_3 H_{wxyz}$, then
$r_{rt} = r_{vu} = 1$, $r_{ru} = r_{vt} = -1$, $r_{ij} = 0$ otherwise

(v) If ${}^1/_3 H_{wxyz} > {}^1/_4 G_{rtuv}$, then
$r_{wx} = 1$, $r_{wy} = r_{zx} = -1$, $r_{ij} = 0$ otherwise

Having chosen a direction $\mathbf{r}$ in which to move, it is now necessary to find a distance λ such that $(\mathbf{x} + \lambda\mathbf{r})$ belongs to the feasible region and $F(\mathbf{x} + \lambda\mathbf{r})$ is as large as possible. In other words, λ must satisfy

$$\sum_j \left(x_{ij} + \lambda r_{ij}\right) \leq 1 \quad \text{for all } i$$

$$\sum_i \left(x_{ij} + \lambda r_{ij}\right) \leq 1 \quad \text{for all } j$$

$$\left(x_{ij} + \lambda r_{ij}\right) \geq 0 \text{ for all } i,j$$

and must maximize

$$F(x + \lambda r) - F(x) = \lambda^2 \sum r_{ij} r_{kl} q(i,j,k,l) + 2\lambda \sum x_{ij} r_{kl} q(i,j,k,l).$$

In the cases given, simple calculation yields the following values for λ.

(i) $\left(1 - \sum_j x_{kj},\ 1 - \sum_i x_{il}\right)$

(ii) $\left(x_{ru},\ 1 - \sum_i x_{it}\right)$

(iii) $\left(x_{ws},\ 1 - \sum_j x_{vj}\right)$

(iv) $\left(x_{ru},\ x_{vt}\right)$

(v) $\left(x_{wy},\ x_{zx}\right)$

This method, although yielding an approximation to the best direction, is clearly slow and highly nonparallel, since at each iteration no more than four x_{ij} are changed. It is possible, however, to use the same ideas but increase the speed and parallelism by doing the computation given above for each row at the same time. This is possible because the images are assumed to be such that corresponding edges lie in corresponding rows.

CHOOSING AN INITIAL FEASIBLE SOLUTION

Since the function being maximized may be highly nonconvex and have many local maxima, the starting point is important. If the probabilities are set as equal as possible, the initial value of the function should be small, and so the algorithm should have a better chance of finding the global maximum. If the starting point were near a local maximum a gradient algorithm would be more likely to find that local maximum instead of the global one. Initially, the probabilities were all set to $1/N$ where

$$N = \max\left(\max_i \#\{j \mid (i,j) \in I\},\ \max_j \#\{i \mid (i,j) \in I\}\right)$$

Then certainly $\sum_j x_{ij} \leq 1$ for all i and $\sum_i x_{ij} \leq 1$ for all j.

This choice, however, meant that the algorithm spent a long time increasing all the x_{ij} so that the sums were nearer to one, so the starting point now used is

$$x_{ij} = \frac{1}{\max\left(N_i, M_j\right)} \quad \text{where } N_i = \#\{j \mid (i,j) \in I\} \text{ and } M_j = \#\{i \mid (i,j) \in I\}$$

Then, again the inequalities are satisfied. This strategy seems to be successful.

COMPATIBILITY FACTORS

The value of $q(i,j,k,l)$ should fall off as i and k (or j and l) move further apart. It is computationally convenient to define a neighbourhood $N(i)$ round each point i, and define q to be zero if j does not lie in $N(i)$. The general form for q was taken to be

$$q(i,j,k,l) = \begin{cases} \dfrac{p(i,j,k,l)}{1 + d(i,j,k,l)} & k \in N(i), k \neq i \\ & l \in N(j), l \neq j \\ 0 & \text{otherwise} \end{cases}$$

where $N(i)$ is the $(2n + 1) \times (2n + 1)$ window centred on i, and $d(i,j,k,l)$ is the square of the average of the distance between i and k and the distance between j and l. Several different definitions for $p(i,j,k,l)$ were investigated.

$$p(i,j,k,l) = \begin{cases} 1 & \text{if } G_d < L_{dg} \\ 0 & \text{otherwise} \end{cases}$$

or

$$p(i,j,k,l) = \begin{cases} 1 - G_d^2/L_{dg} & \text{if } G_d < L_{dg} \\ 0 & \text{otherwise} \end{cases}$$

where G_d is the disparity gradient.

RESULTS

The algorithm was implemented in C on a VAX 11/750 running under Unix, and tested on a number of images both real and synthesized. The first two pairs of images presented here are random-dot stereograms, which enable quantitative evaluation of the algorithm's performance. Each pair depicts three planes: the bottom plane extends over the whole image, while the top two planes occupy a square in the centre of the image. The top plane is transparent, but the middle plane is opaque. The images are presented for crosseyed viewing in Figures 2 and 3 respectively. The disparities of the three

Figure 2. Random-dot stereogram 1: a, right image; b, left image

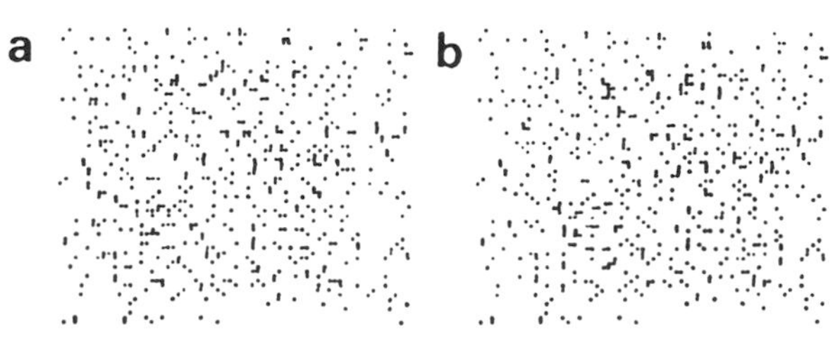

Figure 3. Random-dot stereogram 2: a, right image; b, left image

planes are 0,1 and 2 in figure 2, and 0,1 and 3 in Figure 3. Thus, in the second case the disparity gradient limit of 0.7 is violated by neighbouring points lying on different planes. The results are summarized in Table 1.

Table 1. Results of algorithm on random-dot stereograms

Stereogram number	Total number of points	Number matched wrongly	Number left unmatched	% correctly matched
1	618	9	38	92
2	603	56	34	85

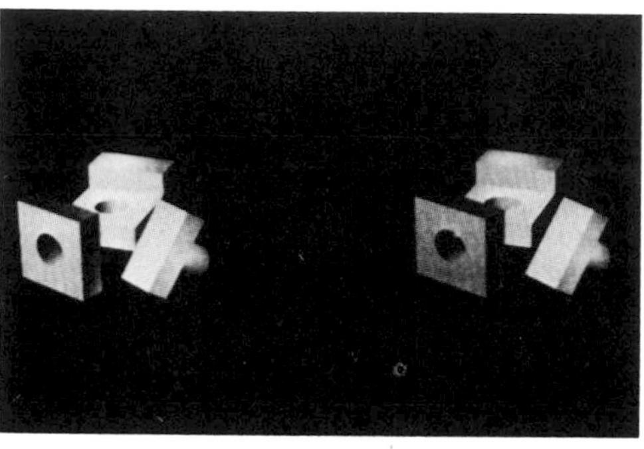

Figure 4. Synthesized pair of images: right image (left); and left image (right)

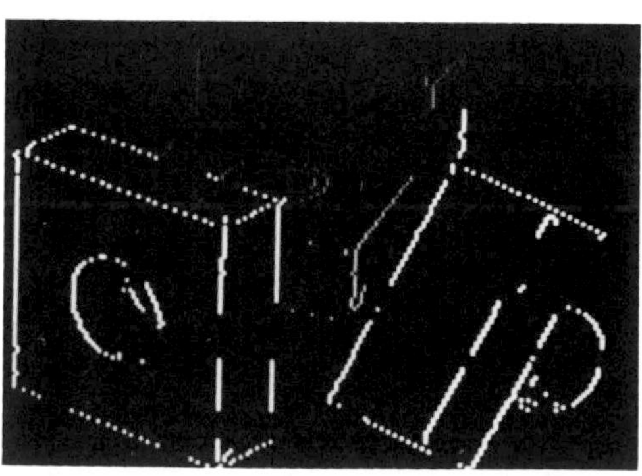

Figure 5. Intensity-coded depth from Figure 4

A synthesised pair of images is shown in Figure 4. The result of the algorithm on this pair is displayed intensity coded (bright is near) in Figure 5 and is displayed as a perspective projection from a different angle in Figure 6. Finally, a pair of real images of a piece of rock is shown in Figure 7, and the result, intensity coded, displayed in Figure 8.

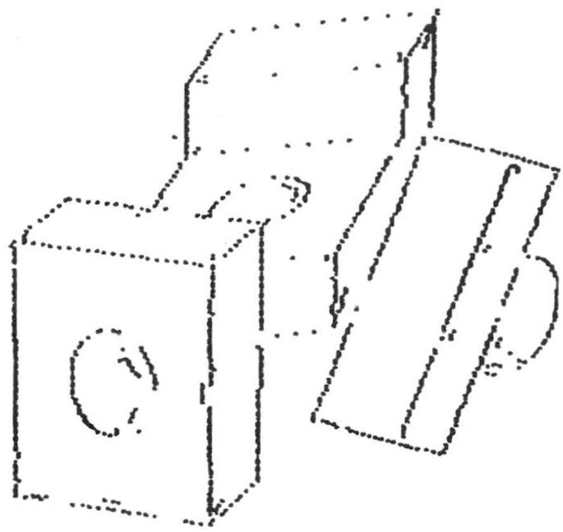

Figure 6. Perspective view of objects in Figure 4

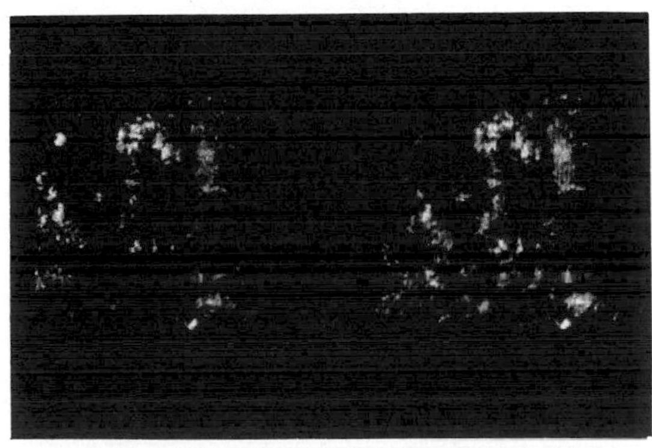

Figure 7. Pair of images of rock: right image (left), left image (right)

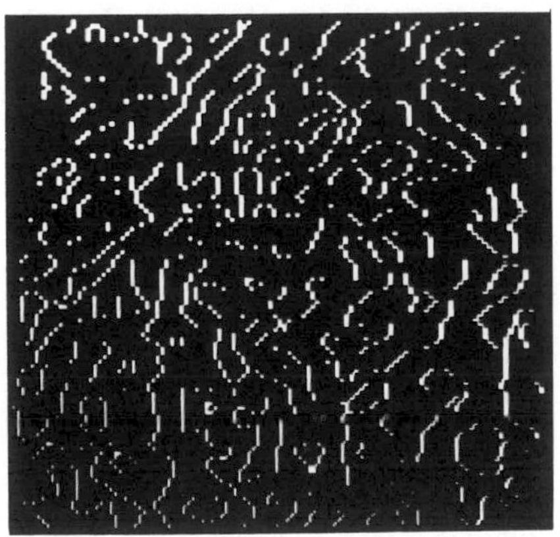

Figure 8. Intensity-coded depth from Figure 7

CONCLUSIONS

The algorithm has been seen to perform well on a range of real and synthesized images, even when the disparity-gradient limit is exceeded.

REFERENCES

1 Lloyd, S.A., (1985) Dynamic programming algorithm for binocular stereo vision. *GEC J. Res.* **3**(1), 18-24.

2 Pollard, S.B., Mayhew, J.E.W. and Frisby, J.P. (1985). PMF: a stereo correspondence algorithm using a disparity gradient limit. *Perception* **14**, 449-470.

3 Trivedi, H.P. and Lloyd, S.A. (1985). The role of disparity gradient in stereo vision. *Perception* **14** 685-690.

4 Garfinkel, R. and Neuhauser, G. (1972) *Integer programming*, Wiley, New York.

5 Hadley, G. (1964) *Nonlinear and dynamic programming*, Addison Wesley, Wokingham UK.

[5] # The Role of Disparity Gradient in Stereo Vision

Harit P Trivedi[1] and Sheelagh A Lloyd[2]

GEC Research Laboratories
Hirst Research Centre, Wembley, HA9 7PP, UK

Reprinted, with permission of Pion Ltd, from *Perception*, 1985, **14**, 685-690.

Abstract

Burt and Julesz experimentally demonstrated that, in addition to Panum's fusional area, a quantity defined by them and named disparity gradient also plays a crucial part in deciding whether the human visual system would be able to fuse the images seen by the left and right eyes. The physical meaning of this quantity remains obscure despite attempts to interpret it in terms of depth gradient. Nevertheless, it has been found to be an effective selector of matches in stereo correspondence algorithms. A proof is provided that a disparity gradient limit of less than 2 implies that the matches between the two images preserve the topology of the images. The result, which is invariant under rotations and under relative as well as overall magnifications, holds for pairs of points separated in *any* direction, not just along epipolar lines. This in turn can be shown to prevent correspondences being established between points which would have to be located in three dimensions on a surface invisible to one eye, assuming opaque surfaces.

1 Introduction

Binocular stereo vision entails reconstructing depth information from two images of a three-dimensional (3-D) scene taken from slightly different viewpoints. This involves establishing correspondences between points (solving the 'correspondence problem') and computing the depth by triangulation. In computer vision, provided that the camera geometry is known, this last step is trivial, and so solving the correspondence problem guarantees stereopsis.

In the case of human vision, there is also the concept of binocular fusion, which is when a stereoscopically presented image appears single, and this is not the same as stereopsis. It is well known that stereopsis can occur with fusion (eg depth perception despite diplopia), and fusion without stereopsis (eg in amblyopes). For computer vision, of course, there is no concept of fusion. Burt and Julesz (1980a, 1980b) conducted some interesting experiments to investigate the effect of nearby points on binocular fusion. They defined the disparity gradient (figure 1) between two nearby points as the difference in their disparities divided by their separation in visual angle, and demonstrated that fusion of at least one point fails when this gradient exceeds a critical value (approximately 1). Although their experiments were necessarily concerned with horizontal disparities only (since the arrangement of human eyes means that vertical disparities are usually very small), the definition of disparity gradient is

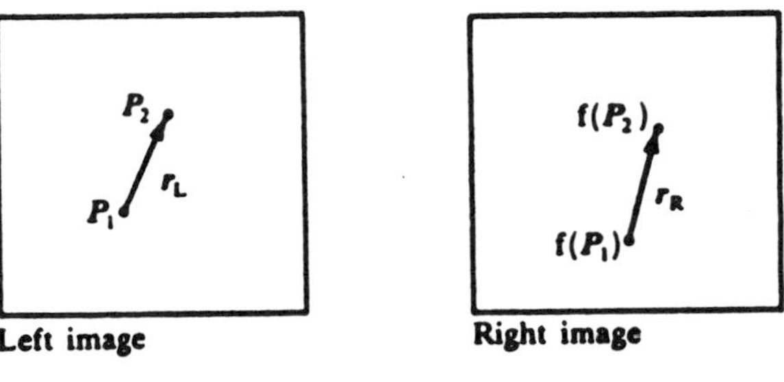

Figure 1. Vector r_L in the left image and the corresponding vector r_R in the right image. The disparity gradient is defined as $|r_L - r_R|/{}^1/_2|r_L + r_R|$.

not restricted to points with only horizontal disparities. There will be situations in computer vision (eg large vergence and/or gaze angles) where points will have both horizontal and vertical disparities, so it is useful to keep the concept of disparity general and not restrict the considerations to horizontal disparities only.

Despite the fact that this limit applies to fusion, which is meaningless in a computer vision context, the disparity gradient limit has provided a powerful disambiguator of correspondences in several stereo algorithms (Lloyd 1984; Pollard et al 1985). The success of these algorithms is perhaps surprising: why should a constraint on human fusion be a good constraint for computer stereopsis? Equally, why should the disparity gradient limit be a good constraint in human vision? There are certainly some empirical reasons: most false matches will cause the disparity gradient limit to be exceeded and so will be rejected by the algorithm, whereas most pairs of correct matches will satisfy the disparity gradient limit (Pollard et al 1985). Even on surfaces containing apirs of points exceeding the disparity gradient limited (consider, for example, a plane inclined away from the viewer so that it is close to horizontal), there will still be many pairs of points with disparity gradient less than the limit, and so the algorithm may still be able to solve the correspondence problem correctly. While not disputing in any way the success of these algorithms, we were, however, still unconvinced of the reasons for this success.

---

1 now with BP International Ltd, Sunbury Research Centre, Chertsey Road, Sunbury-on-Thames, Middlesex, TW16 7LN, UK.

2 now with Hewlett Packard Laboratories, Filton Road, Stoke Gifford, Bristol, BS12 6QZ, UK.

We therefore propose an explanation of the disparity gradient limit based on the physics of image formation. This suggests a reason why it is sensible, both for human fusion and for computer stereopsis, to impose a disparity gradient limit. We shall show that imposing a disparity gradient limit of less than 2 ensures that no matches will be made between points that would have to be located in space on a surface invisible to one eye (assuming opaque surfaces). Observe that the converse (that all pairs of points on a non-self-occluding opaque surface satisfy the disparity gradient limit) does not follow; the example mentioned earlier of a plane inclined away from the viewer would be an obvious counter example. Imposing a disparity gradient limit is a conservative policy; it prevents false matches, but also disallows some correct ones. Burt and Julesz suggest a figure of 1, although some of their experimental data might suggest a higher figure. This is still safely below 2 and in perfect accord with our theory. It is interesting to note that, when restricted to pairs of points lying on the same epipolar line, a disparity gradient limit of less than 2 reduces to the familiar 'ordering constraint' used in many stereo algorithms, which demands that points on an epipolar line lie in the same order in both images.

We shall, in fact, show that imposing a disparity gradient limit of less than 2 ensures that the correspondence between the two images preserves their topology. In other words:

(a) each point in the left image corresponds to a unique point in the right image and vice versa;

(b) if we were given one image painted on a rubber sheet, we could, without tearing the shet or glueing it to itself, deform it so that we obtained the other image.

This may seem very obscure, but if we consider how the two images arise, things may become clearer. Let us suppose that we have a continuous non-self-occluding surface as in figure 2. Now, for each eye, the projection which transforms the surface into the image preserves the topology, and so each image must have the same topology as the surface does. Hence they must have the same topology as each other. Conversely, if we have a self-occluding surface as in figure 3, the appropriate matches will not preserve the topology. This can be seen quite easily by considering the point E, where the ray from D intersects the surface again. In the left eye the image of this point will appear in the same place as the image of D, that is D_L, whereas the two will be distinct in the right image. So D_L in the left image corresponds to two points (D_R and E_R) in the right image, and this implies that the topology cannot be preserved since condition (a) above would be violated.

2 Proof

Suppose that we have two images $\mathbf{I}_L$ and $\mathbf{I}_R$ and a correspondence f between them. So, for each point P in $\mathbf{I}_L$, we know the point or points in $\mathbf{I}_R$ corresponding to P. Suppose further that f obeys the disparity gradient limit of $2k$ (where $k< 1$), that is, if P_1 and P_2 are points in $\mathbf{I}_L$, then

$$\Gamma_D = \frac{\left|(P_1 - P_2) - \left[\mathrm{f}(P_1) - \mathrm{f}(P_2)\right]\right|}{\frac{1}{2}\left|(P_1 - P_2) + \left[\mathrm{f}(P_1) - \mathrm{f}(P_2)\right]\right|} \leq 2k < 2 .$$

In order to prove that the topology is preserved, we need to show that

(i) f is one-to-one (ie each point in $\mathbf{I}_R$ corresponds to a unique point in $\mathbf{I}_L$);
(ii) f^{-1} is one-to-one (ie each point in $\mathbf{I}_L$ corresponds to a unique point in $\mathbf{I}_R$);
(iii) f is continuous (roughly, nearby points in $\mathbf{I}_R$ correspond to nearby points in $\mathbf{I}_L$);
(iv) f^{-1} is continuous (roughly, nearby points in $\mathbf{I}_L$ correspond to nearby points in $\mathbf{I}_R$).

Since the disparity gradient limit is symmetric, we need only prove (i) and (iii), and then (ii) and (iv) will follow by symmetry.

In order to prove (i), suppose that a single point P_R in $\mathbf{I}_R$ corresponds to two points in P_{1L} and P_{2L} in $\mathbf{I}_L$. Consider the disparity gradient, Γ_D, between this pair of matches:

$$\Gamma_D = \frac{2|(P_{1L} - P_{2L}) - 0|}{|(P_{1L} - P_{2L}) + 0|} = 2 .$$

But this is not allowed because we are supposing that all the disparity gradients are less than 2. So P_R must correspond to a unique point P_L in $\mathbf{I}_L$: that is, f is one-to-one.

We now need to prove that f is continuous. Suppose that P_1 and P_2 are two distinct points in $\mathbf{I}_L$ and let us write $\mathbf{r}_L = P_1 - P_2$ and $\mathbf{r}_R = \mathrm{f}(P_1) - \mathrm{f}(P_2)$. In order to prove continuity we need to show that whatever smal positive number e we are given, we can always find another positive number d so that

$|\mathbf{r}_L| < d$ implies that $|\mathbf{r}_R| < e$.

The proof which follows is straightforward but technical. We simply suppose that $|\mathbf{r}_L| < d$ and apply the fact that f obeys the disparity gradient limit of $2k$ with $k < 1$, and deduce that

$$|r_R| < d\frac{2^{1/2}(1+k)^2}{1-k^2} .$$

Turning this round, we see that, given e, we simply choose

$$d = e\frac{2^{-1/2}(1-k^2)}{(1+k)^2}$$

and we are done. It is now clear why we need to stipulate that $k < 1$.

We now give the details of the proof.

Let us write $\mathbf{r}_L = (x_L , y_L)$ and $r_R = (x_R , y_R)$. Suppose that $|\mathbf{r}_L| < d$, then $|x_L|, |y_L| < d$. Now the disparity gradient limit can be rewritten

$$(x_L - x_R)^2 + (y_L - y_R)^2 \leq k^2\left[(x_L + x_R)^2 + (y_L + y_R)^2\right]$$

or

$$x_R^2\left(k^2 - 1\right) + 2x_L x_R\left(k^2 + 1\right) + x_L^2\left(k^2 - 1\right) + k^2(y_L + y_R)^2 - (y_L - y_R)^2 \geq 0.$$

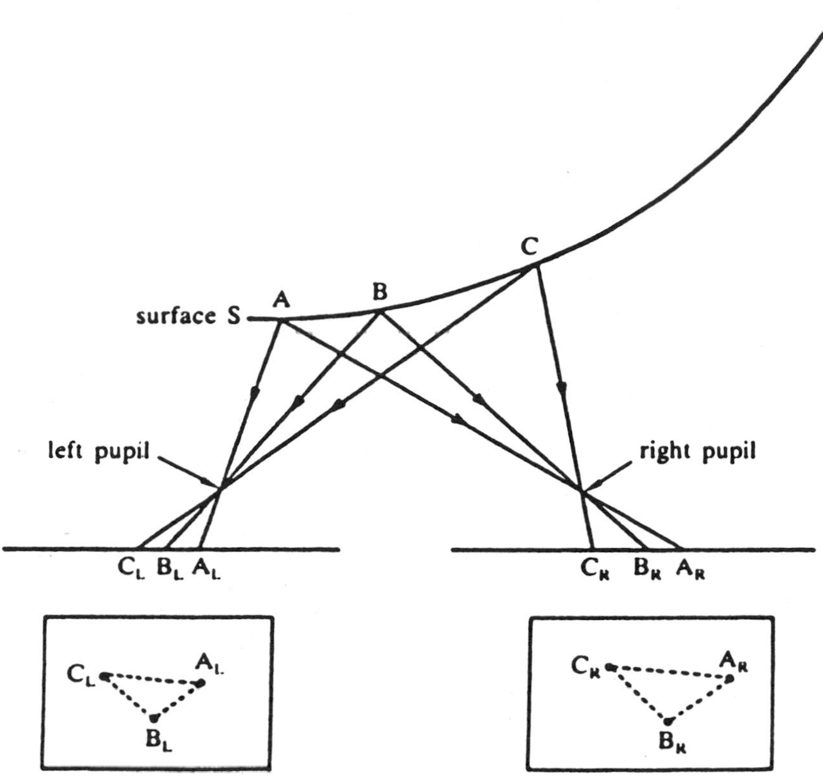

Figure 2 (Above) Points A, B, and C on a surface S (A, B, C not meant to lie on the intersection of the surface S and a plane) and their images. (Below) The two images are topologically equivalent.

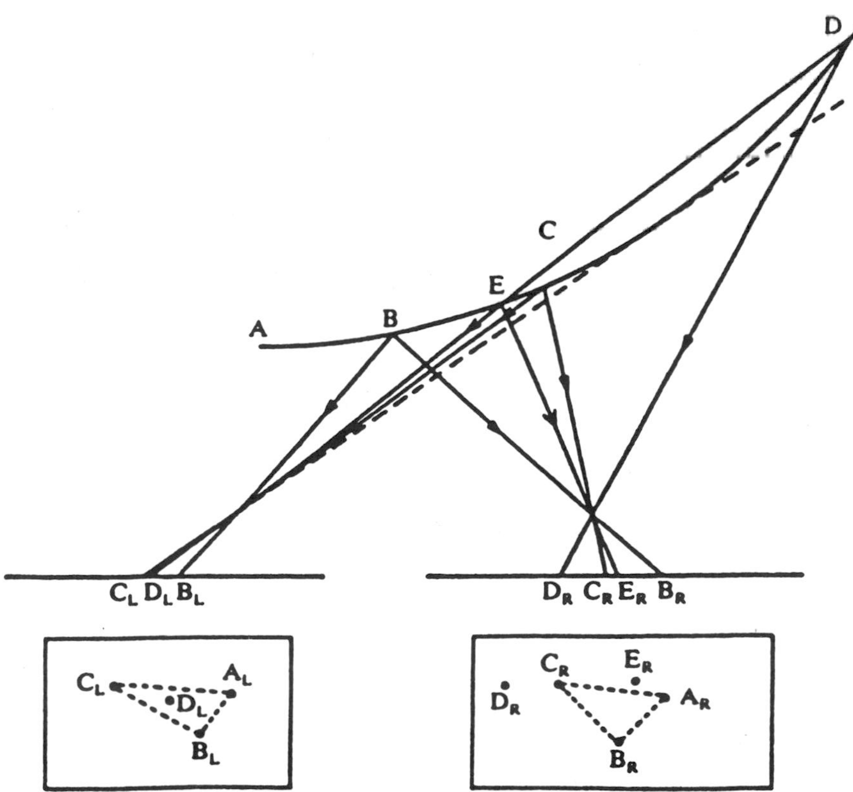

Figure 3 (Above) Surface S of figure 2. In addition, points D and E and a tangent ray passing through the left eye are also shown. (Below) The topologies of the two images are clearly not equivalent.

This is a quadratic in x_R, and the coefficient of x_R^2 is negative. The above inequality can only be satisfied when there are two real roots and x_R lies between them. The condition for the quadratic to have real roots is that

$$4x_L^2(k^2+1)^2 - 4(k^2-1)\left[x_L^2(k^2-1)+k^2(y_L+y_R)^2-(y_L-y_R)^2\right] \geq 0$$

or

$$-(1-k^2)^2 y_R^2 + 2y_L y_R (1-k^2)(1+k^2) + 4k^2x_L^2 - (1-k^2)^2 y_L^2 \geq 0.$$

Again, this is a quadratic in y_R with leading coefficient negative. It has two real roots, so the inequality is satisfied when

$$\frac{2y_L(1-k^4)-4k(1-k^2)|r_L|}{2(1-k^2)^2} \leq y_R$$

$$y_R \leq \frac{2y_L(1-k^4)+4k(1-k^2)|r_L|}{2(1-k^2)^2}$$

or

$$\frac{y_L(1+k^2)-2k|r_L|}{1-k^2} \leq y_R \leq \frac{y_L(1+k^2)+2k|r_L|}{1-k^2}$$

So certainly

$$|y_R| \leq d\frac{(1+k)^2}{1-k^2}.$$

The two roots of the quadratic in x_R are

$$\frac{-2x_L(1+k^2)\pm 2\{4k^2x_L{}^2-(k^2-1)[k^2(y_L+y_R)^2-(y_L-y_R)^2]\}^{1/2}}{2(1-k^2)}$$

Now

$$k^2(y_L+y_R)^2-(y_L-y_R)^2 \leq d\frac{4k^2y_L^2}{1-k^2}$$

(since the left-hand side is a quadratic in y_R with maximum value the expression on the right-hand side) so

$$|x_R| \leq \frac{2d(1+k^2)+2\left[4k^2x_L^2+4k^2y_L^2\right]^{1/2}}{2(1-k^2)} \leq d\frac{(1+k)^2}{1-k^2}$$

Hence

$$|r_R| < d\frac{2^{1/2}(1+k)^2}{1-k^2}$$

So, given $e > 0$, take $d = e[2^{-1/2}(1-k^2)/(1+k)^2]$, and then $|r_L| < d$ implies that $|r_R| < e$. Hence f is continuous. This is the end of the proof.

Note that the result is invariant to rotations and to relative as well as overall magnifications.

3 Discussion

In their attempt to incorporate the notion of disparity gradient limit in Panum's fusional area, Burt and Julesz (1980a) mention a "cone-shaped forbidden zone, symmetric about the line of sight" around a point object. This is readily understood in terms of our explanation if the cone is taken to be defined by the surface $k = 1$ passing through the point. (The extended lines of sight to each eye lie on this surface, for instance.) Then the matches between the left and the right images of the original point (at the tip of the cone) and other points - some inside and some outside the cone - will not, in general, preserve the topology of the images.

Our interpretation of the disparity gradient limit constraint in view of what we have said so far is that the human visual system expects to find *surfaces*, and that it expects the surfaces to be opaque. If a vision system is to solve the stereo correspondence problem *before* interpolating surfaces through the three-dimensional points so computed, the equivalent topology (or disparity gradient limit) constraint along with this interpretation would guarantee that no part of the surface will be obscured by another: a very powerful guarantee ensuring no conflict between stereo matching and surface interpolation at a subsequent stage of processing.

4 Conclusion

We have proved that a disparity gradient limit of less than 2 implies topological equivalence between left and right images. Further, we have shown that this guarantees that a group of three-dimensional points obeying the disparity gradient limit cannot lie on a surface which would have been obscured to one eye. Incorporation of the disparity gradient limit constraint in stereo matching makes it possible to proceed to surface interpolation in a bottom-up fashion.

References

Burt, P. and Julesz, B. (1980a) Modifications of the classical notion of Panum's fusional area. *Perception*, **9**, 671-682.

Burt, P. and Julesz, B. (1980b) A disparity gradient limit for binocular fusion. *Science*, **208**, 615-617.

Pollard, S.B., Mayhew, J.E.W., Frisby, J.P. (1985) PMF: A stereo correspondence algorithm using a disparity gradient limit. *Perception*, **14**, 449-470.

Lloyd, S.A. (1984) A new stereo algorithm. Memo CSRL/157, GEC Research Laboratories, Hirst Research Centre, Wembley, UK.

[6] Estimation of Stereo and Motion Parameters using a Variational Principle

Harit P Trivedi

BP Research Centre
Sunbury-on-Thames, TW16 7LN, UK

Reprinted, with permission of Butterworth Scientific Ltd, from *Image and Vision Computing*, 1987, **5**, 181-183.

The problems of extracting 3D structure from stereo or motion parameters from optic flow are now analytically tractable but numerically ill-conditioned. A variational principle is proposed which alleviates ill-conditioning and saturates rapidly with data so that even a small excess (over a minimal number) of data points yields accurate results. It involves no adjustable parameters (unlike many applications of the regularization theory) and no assumptions about measurement errors, which, in fact, it seeks to estimate and minimize. The technique is illustrated with image resolutions varying from 1024 to 128 pixels square, using between 6 and 30 data points (5 data points define a unique solution) perturbed by at most 0.2 pixels. The error in the computed direction of translation was 2.7 deg in the worst case (128 x 128 pixels, 15 data points). It was 1.2 deg with only six data points for an image 1024 square.

Keywords: stereo vision, motion, optic flow, variational principle

The low-level computer vision problems of determining camera geometry from stereo images and object motion and structure from optic flow (or a time sequence of images) are ill-conditioned. Tsai and Hyang (1984), for example, reported a staggering 54% error in the model parameters for only a 1% error in the data. Fang and Huang (1984) also observed similar symptoms of numerical instability.

Researchers have responded to this difficulty (for example, Yasumoto and Medioni, 1985) by using the regularization techinque (Tikhonov and Arsenin, 1977), following the lead of Poggio (Poggio T, 1985). This involves additional constraints, which are quite often heuristic, and each constraint entails a weighting coefficient, which, in practice at least, has to be chosen judiciously if not with some degree of foreknowledge.

In this paper, a variational principle is formulated which involves no additional constraints, has no adjustable parameters (such as weighting coefficients), 'corrects' each data point, and yields errors entirely in terms of the image measurables. As one usually knows something about the accuracy of the device, the precision of edge-location, etc, one can judge the quality of the computed solution from the estimated measurement error.

VARIATIONAL PRINCIPLE

Let the model equation be $f(\mathbf{x}, \mathbf{a}) = 0$, where $\mathbf{x}$ denotes a data point and $\mathbf{a}$ denotes the model parameters. Allowing for error in the data measurements, a correction $\delta\mathbf{x}(i)$ is sought to satisfy exactly

$$f[\mathbf{x}(i) + \delta\mathbf{x}(i), \mathbf{a}] = 0 \qquad \text{for } i = 1, 2, \ldots, N \qquad (1)$$

This will not determine $\delta\mathbf{x}(i)$ uniquely, of course, and so we impose a subsidiary condition and select that $\delta\mathbf{x}(i)$ in each instance i for which the size of the correction

$$|\delta\mathbf{x}(i)|^2 = [\delta x_1(i)]^2 + \ldots + [\delta x_m(i)]^2 \qquad (2)$$

is the smallest. That is,

$$f[\mathbf{x}(i) + \delta\mathbf{x}(i),\mathbf{a}] = 0 \qquad |\delta\mathbf{x}(i)|^2 \text{ minimum } \forall\, i \qquad (3)$$

By defining the size of the correction by Equation (2), all the components of a data measurement have been put on an equal footing. It is also implied that the absolute correction is the most meaningful. While this is so in our application domain (the measured data are the coordinates of image points), these assumptions are not necessarily universal, and, in general, the size of the correction must be defined in a way appropriate to the problem at hand. If the $\delta\mathbf{x}$ values are required to obey constraints, the equation above must be solved subject to those constraints.

Let the kth component of the formal solution of Equation (3) be written as

$$\delta\mathbf{x}_k(i) = g_k[\mathbf{x}(i), \mathbf{a}] \qquad k === 1, \ldots, m \qquad (4)$$

Neglecting second- and higher-order terms in the Taylor series of expansion of f in Equation (3) above, it can be determined that

$$\mathbf{g}(\mathbf{x},\mathbf{a}) = -f\nabla f/|\nabla f|^2 \qquad (5)$$

Then

$$E(i) = |\delta x(i)|^2 = \sum_{k=1}^{m} g_k\left[x(i), a\right]^2 \qquad (6)$$

is the minimum correction to $\mathbf{x}(i)$ given $\mathbf{a}$, and

$$e = \sum_{i=1}^{N} E(i) \qquad (7)$$

is the minimum total correction to the sampled data, given $\mathbf{a}$. This, then, is the varational quantity to be minimized with respect to the latter, the model parameters. It generates that solution which, for the smallest correction to the sampled data, enables the model equation to be satisfied exactly at each (corrected) data point.

Application of variational principle to sample problem

No of data points	Image resolution	1 - ê.ê'	$\left[\sum_i (\hat{e}_i - \hat{e}_i')^2\right]^{\frac{1}{2}}$	cos^{-1}(ê.ê') (deg)	1 - **T**.**T**'	$\left[\sum_i (T_i - T_i')^2\right]^{\frac{1}{2}}$	cos^{-1}(**T**.**T**') (deg)
6	1024^2	2.4×10^{-7}	6.9×10^{-4}	0.040	2.3×10^{-4}	5.0×10^{-3}	1.2
7	1024^2	2.7×10^{-7}	7.3×10^{-4}	0.042	2.3×10^{-4}	5.0×10^{-3}	1.2
8	1024^2	3.3×10^{-7}	8.1×10^{-4}	0.047	1.1×10^{-4}	3.4×10^{-3}	0.85
9	1024^2	2.5×10^{-7}	7.1×10^{-4}	0.040	4.9×10^{-5}	2.2×10^{-3}	0.57
10	1024^2	1.7×10^{-7}	5.9×10^{-4}	0.034	1.6×10^{-6}	1.0×10^{-5}	0.10
15	1024^2	1.3×10^{-7}	5.0×10^{-4}	0.029	2.1×10^{-5}	1.4×10^{-3}	0.37
30	1024^2	1.7×10^{-9}	5.9×10^{-5}	0.0034	6.5×10^{-7}	2.4×10^{-4}	0.066
15	512^2	6.3×10^{-7}	1.1×10^{-3}	0.064	1.9×10^{-5}	1.4×10^{-3}	0.36
15	256^2	3.4×10^{-6}	2.6×10^{-3}	0.15	1.2×10^{-4}	3.0×10^{-3}	0.9
15	128^2	9.2×10^{-6}	4.3×10^{-3}	0.25	1.1×10^{-3}	9.3×10^{-3}	2.7

Computed solution (ê',T') and true solution (ê,T): [ê.ê = ê'.ê' = 1, **T**.**T** = **TT'** = 1]
An image is a unit square, unit distance from the optic centre. The error is a uniformly distributed random value bounded by $|\Delta x| < 0.2$ pixels, $|\Delta y| < 0.2$ pixels. As a result, the absolute of the error doubles as the image resolution halves (from 1024 value to 512 etc). The results correspond to $T_1{:}T_2{:}T_3 = 1{:}0.1{:}0.2$ and the rotation $R = R_z(0.03)R_y(0.2)R_z(0.05)$, the angles being in radians. The depth varied between 5 and 100 interocular units.

EXAMPLE

Image coordinates **x** and **x'** in the left and right images of a stereo pair corresponding to every scene point obey the relation[1,6,7]

$$\sum_{i,j=1}^{3} x_i' Q_{ij} x_j = 0 \tag{8}$$

where x'_3, $x_3 = 1$. The primed coordinates refer to the right image and the unprimed to the left. The matrix **Q** = **RS** is defined in terms of the rotation matrix **R** and the antisymmetric matrix **S** related to the translation vector **T** = (T_1, T_2, T_3) by

$$S = \begin{bmatrix} 0 & T_3 & -T_2 \\ -T_3 & 0 & T_1 \\ T_2 & -T_1 & 0 \end{bmatrix} \tag{9}$$

perspective projection being assumed.

The aim is to determine the matrices **R** and **S** of the stereo geometry, given N data points. This is found to be an ill-conditioned problem. That is, errors in the data are amplified when the model parameters are determined from the (imperfect) data. We have used g of Equation (5) to apply our method to this problem. Each point was perturbed by a random amount (both horizontally and vertically) bounded by ± 0.2 pixel. The distribution of pertubation over the points was uniform. The results are summarized in Table 1. The rotation matrix was parametrized using Euler parameters[8], which are real unlike the Cayley-Klein parameters) and are distinct from Euler angles. For completeness,

$$R = \begin{bmatrix} e_0^2 + e_1^2 - e_2^2 - e_3^2 & 2(e_1 e_2 + e_0 e_3) & 2(e_1 e_3 - e_0 e_2) \\ 2(e_1 e_2 - e_0 e_3) & e_0^2 - e_1^2 + e_2^2 - e_3^2 & 2(e_2 e_3 + e_0 e_1) \\ 2(e_1 e_3 + e_0 e_2) & 2(e_2 e_3 - e_0 e_1) & e_0^2 - e_1^2 - e_2^2 + e_3^2 \end{bmatrix} \tag{10}$$

where $e_0^2 + e_1^2 + e_2^2 + e_3^2 = 1$. Since Equation 8 clearly leaves the overall scale of **T** undetermined, it was fixed by setting **T**.**T** = 1.

RESULTS AND CONCLUSIONS

A variational principle, the minimum correction principle, has been constructed to deal with ill-conditioned problems. A minimum correction to the sampled data is sought, such that the corrected data obeys exactly the model equation in each instance (or, to be precise, through the first order in the corrections, at least).

Unlike some applications of the regularization theory, the minimum correction principle involves no adjustable parameters. In fact, it seeks to estimate data errors by minimizing them with respect to the model parameters and requires no assumptions to be made about them. The principle has been illustrated with various image resolutions, from 1024 to 128 pixels square, using between six and 30 data points perturbed by at most 0.2 pixels. The error in the computed direction of translation was 2.7 deg in the worst case (image resolution 128 x 128 with 15 data points. It was 1.2 deg with only six data points for an image 1024 square. (It should be recalled that five data points are needed to even define a solution.) The accuracy of the rotational parameters is much greater, as observed by Tsai and Huang (1984). (There is an explanation for this behaviour, although it is not directly

Table 2. Comparison of least squares method (singular value decomposition based) and minimum correction principle for different field of view angles.

Resolution	No of matches	tan θ = 0.5		tan θ = 0.25	
		Least sq	Min corr	Least sq	Min corr
1024	6	-	1.2	-	1.8
1024	7	-	1.2	-	1.7
1024	8	-	0.9	-	1.2
1024	9	64	0.6	69	1.0
1024	10	1.7	0.1	7.7	1.1
1024	15	0.3	0.4	2.7	1.2
1024	30	0.5	0.07	0.4	0.05
512	15	0.3	0.4	1.0	1.1
256	15	10.0	0.9	74	1.1
128	15	64	2.7	141	1.0

[tan θ = (1/2) image width (or height)/focal length]. Camera geometry and data errors are as in Table 1.

connected with this work. The variation with respect to **T**, subject to a normalization constraint, can be performed analytically in both methods. The result is that **T** has to be an eigenvector of a matrix depending on the data measurements and **R**; hence the observed behaviour.) The four Euler parameters are characterized by a direction in a 4D Euclidean space. The error in the computed direction (of rotation) was found to be minuscule (0.25 deg at most). No compelling theoretical grounds have yet been found that might explain why this method works so well. To this extent, it remains an empirical method.

The method is numerically stable and saturates rapidly, so that a single extra data point usually suffices. It is insensitive to the addition or removal of data points (stability). The numerical value of the functional E is the estimated total error in the sampled data. For 'true' model parameters, the correction to each component of data is just the negative of the error in its measured value. Knowing the precision of the data measurements *a priori* (from factors like resolution, quantization, device accuracy, etc), one can judge the solution quality by comparing these two quantities. For example, a higher than expencted value of $E(i)$ can expose a rogue data point.

When the exact solution of the model Equation (5) with corrected data is impracticable, a linear approximation (keeping only constants and linear terms in δx) can be made. The stereo and motion results above were obtained using this approximation.

Our error measures are independent of the laboratory coordinate frame. To compare the performance of the varational principle with other methods, a conventional least-squares calculation (using singular value decomposition) was performed for two different field-of-view angles. The results are compared in Table 2. While the variational method produces smaller errors, the more striking finding is that the results of the least-squares method look far bettwer than one might have expected, given the notoriety of this particular problem. The importance of choosing appropriate (ie coordinate frame invariant) error measures to evaluate and compare methods cannot be overemphasized.

Although this method entails more work, it seems to handle adequately the ill-conditioned problem of determining stereo geometry even with a single extra data point. Certain 'degenerate' configurations of data points, as pointed out by Longuet-Higgins (1984) and Tsai and Huang (1984), cause the '8-point algorithm' [1,7] for solving for the eight ratios of **Q** in Equation (8) to break down. The method described here does not suffer from this problem as the variation is performed directly with respect to the parameters of rotation and translation.

ACKNOWLEDGEMENTS

It is a pleasure to thank Bernard Buxton for the many useful discussions during the course of this work.

REFERENCES

Tsai, R. Y. and Huang, T. S. (1984). Uniqueness and estimation of three-dimensional motion parameters of rigid objects with curved surfaces. *IEEE Trans. Pattern Anal. & Mach. Intell.* **6**, 13-26.

Fang, J-Q. and Huang, T.S. (1984). Some experiments on estimating 3D motion parameters of a rigid body from two consecutive image frames. *IEEE Trans. Pattern Anal. & Mach. Intell.* **6**, 545-554.

Yasumoto, Y. and Medioni, G. (1985). Experiments in estimation of 3D motion parameters from a sequence of image frames. *Proc. I.E.E.E. Conference on Computer Vision & Pattern Recognition*, San Francisco, CA, U.S.A., 89-94.

Tikhonov, A.N. and Arsenin, V.Y. (1977) *Solutions of ill-posed problems.* V.H. Winston, Washington, DC. U.S.A.

Poggio, T. (1985) Early vision: from computational structure to algorithms and parallel hardware. *Computer Vision, Graphics Image Proc.*, **31**, 139-155.

Thompson, E.H. (1959) A rational algebraic formulation of the problem of relative orientation *Photogramm. Record*, **3**, 152-159 (especialy Note 2).

Longuet-Higgins, H.C. (1981) A computer algorithm for reconstructing a scene from two projections. *Nature* **293**, 133-135.

Goldstein, H. (1980) *Classical mechanics (2nd edn)* Addison-Wesley, Reading, MA, U.S.A., p.153 and appendix B.

Longuet-Higgins, H.C. (1984) The reconstruction of a scene from two projections - configurations that defeat the 8-point algorithm. *Proc. 1st Conf. Appl. of AI*, Denver, CO, U.S.A. 395-397.

[7] On the Reconstruction of a Scene from Two Unregistered Images

Harit P Trivedi

GEC Research Limited
Hirst Research Centre, Wembley, HA9 7PP, UK

ABSTRACT

It is sometimes desirable to compute depth from unregistered pairs of images. I show that it is possible to calculate the two 'epicentres' and the relation governing pairs of epipolar lines, given 8 corresponding points in the two images in any coordinate system. This reduces the matching problem to one dimensional searches along pairs of epipolar lines and can be readily automated using any stereo algorithm. Depth, however, does not seem to be derivable without extra information. I show how to compute depth in two such instances, each involving two 'pieces' of information.

1. INTRODUCTION

One often encounters unregistered pairs of stereo images (e.g. in microscopy) from which three dimensional information is nevertheless desired. This provided the motivation for the work reported here. Longuet-Higgins (1981) has shown that the camera geometry is fixed (assuming perspective projection) by the coordinates of 8 corresponding points in a certain coordinate frame. The latter entails knowledge of the 'natural origins' (defined as the point where the respective optic axis meets the image plane) and the orientations of both the image coordinate systems - in other words, the registration information. He also gave an algorithm to compute depth given this information. When images are unregistered, however, neither the natural origins nor the relative image orientation may be known. To what extent can one then succeed in recovering structure (depth)?

I show that it is possible in the absence of any registration information whatever (i.e., given just the 8 corresponding points in *arbitrary* image coordinate systems) to work out the location of the 'epicentres' - where the interoccular axis intersects the image planes and through which all epipolar lines pass - and the relation governing pairs of epipolar lines (defined in section 4), one in each image. This reduces the rest of the matching problem to one dimensional searches along pairs of epipolar lines - which can be automated using any stereo algorithm. Although it seems that structure cannot be inferred from the image data alone in the absence of any registration information whatever, full registration information is also not necessary. For example, given either (a) the direction of displacement (two direction cosines) of one camera with respect to the optic axis of the other, or, (b) the orientation of the optic axis (two angles) of one camera with respect to that of the other, I show how structure can be recovered.

2. BACKGROUND

I keep to the notation used by Longuet-Higgins (1981). Let a point in the scene have 3D coordinates (X_1, X_2, X_3) and (X'_1, X'_2, X'_3) with respect to the left and the right optic centres. Then its left and right image coordinates (measured from the natural origins) are $(x_1, x_2) = (X_1/X_3, X_2/X_3)$, and $(x'_1, x'_2) = (X'_1/X'_3, X'_2/X'_3)$, in the units of their respective focal lengths. Thus image coordinates $x_3 = 1 = x'_3$, so that $x_i = X_i/X_3$ and $x'_i = X'_i/X'_3$ (i,j = 1,2,3).

Let the right camera position and orientation be obtained by displacing the left camera by a vector **t** and then rotating it so that its new orientation can be obtained from the old by applying the the rotation matrix **R**. Then the two sets of 3D coordinates are related by $X'_j = R_{jk}(X_k - t_k)$, implicit summation convention implied hereinafter. Now from the cartesian components of **t**, construct an antisymmetric matrix

$$\mathbf{S} = \begin{bmatrix} 0 & t_3 & -t_2 \\ -t_3 & 0 & t_1 \\ t_2 & -t_1 & 0 \end{bmatrix}.$$

Longuet-Higgins shows that the matrix **Q** = **RS** satisfies the relations

* Now with BP Research, Sunbury, Middlesex

$$X'_i Q_{ij} X_j = 0, \qquad (i,j=1,2,3) \tag{1}$$

and hence

$$x'_i Q_{ij} x_j = 0 \qquad (i,j=1,2,3) \tag{2}$$

for any point. Notice that (1) and (2) continue to hold under image magnification and length-scale changes to the displacement **t**. For convenience, one chooses $|\mathbf{t}| = 1$. Given eight independent pairs of corresponding points - barring special cases (see Longuet-Higgins (1984)) -, it is straightforward to compute the 8 independent ratios of the elements of **Q** as solutions to an 8 by 8 linear simultaneous system of equations. In the same paper, Longuet-Higgins also shows how to extract **R** and **t** (from **Q**), and hence structure.

3. TRANSFORMATION UNDER ROTATION AND TRANSLATION

Now consider a rotation of the right image (described by the rotation matrix $\mathbf{R}_{z'}(g)$) about its optic axis - the z' axis - by some angle 'g' as introducing registration error in the orientation. By writing (2) as a matrix equation

$$\mathbf{x}'^T \mathbf{Q}\ \mathbf{x} = 0; \tag{3}$$

i.e.,

$$(\mathbf{R}_{z'}(g)\mathbf{x}')^T(\mathbf{R}_{z'}(g)\mathbf{Q})\mathbf{x}=0, \tag{4}$$

we immediately see that the image pair still satisfies an equation of the form (2) but with

$$\mathbf{Q} \rightarrow \mathbf{Q}' = \mathbf{R}_{z'}(g)\mathbf{Q}. \tag{5}$$

All that needs to be done to get things right is to absorb the extra rotation in **R**, i.e.,

$$\mathbf{R} \rightarrow [\mathbf{R}_{z'}(g)\mathbf{R}]. \tag{6}$$

Next we consider the effect of displacing the image origins by (u_1,u_2) and (u'_1,u'_2) in the left and the right images respectively. Then $x_i \rightarrow \xi_i = x_i - u_i$, and $x'_i \rightarrow \xi'_i = x'_i - u'_i$, $(i=1,2,3;\ u_3 = u'_3 = 0)$. Starting with (2) yields, by algebraic manipulation, the relation

$$\xi'_i Q''_{ij} \xi_j = 0, \ \ or,\ (\xi')^{\mathrm{T}}\mathbf{Q}''\xi = 0; \tag{7}$$

where

$$u_3 = 0 = u'_3, \tag{7a}$$

$$Q''_{ij} = Q_{ij}, \quad (i,j=1,2) \tag{7b}$$

$$Q''_{13} = Q_{13} + r, \tag{7c}$$

$$Q''_{23} = Q_{23} + s, \tag{7d}$$

$$Q''_{31} = Q_{31} + r', \tag{7e}$$

$$Q''_{32} = Q_{32} + s', \tag{7f}$$

$$Q''_{33} = Q_{33} + t_0 + t'_0 + v; \tag{7g}$$

i.e.,

$$\mathbf{Q} \rightarrow \mathbf{Q}'' = \begin{bmatrix} Q_{11} & Q_{12} & Q_{13}+r \\ Q_{21} & Q_{22} & Q_{23}+s \\ Q_{31}+r' & Q_{32}+s' & Q_{33}+t_0+t'_0+v \end{bmatrix}. \tag{8}$$

Here

$$\begin{bmatrix} r \\ s \end{bmatrix} = \begin{bmatrix} Q_{11} & Q_{12} \\ Q_{21} & Q_{22} \end{bmatrix} \begin{bmatrix} u_1 \\ u_2 \end{bmatrix}, \tag{9a}$$

$$\begin{bmatrix} r' & s' \end{bmatrix} = \begin{bmatrix} u'_1 & u'_2 \end{bmatrix} \begin{bmatrix} Q_{11} & Q_{12} \\ Q_{21} & Q_{22} \end{bmatrix}, \tag{9b}$$

$$t_0 = Q_{31}\,u_1 + Q_{32}\,u_2, \tag{9c}$$

$$t'_0 = u'_1 Q_{13} + u'_2 Q_{23}, \tag{9d}$$

and

$$v = r'u_1 + s'u_2 = u'_1 r + u'_2 s. \tag{9e}$$

Combined rotations and translations of the image coordinate systems can be readily described by replacing **Q** in (7)-(9) with **Q**$'$ of (5). The image coordinates, therefore, always obey a relation of the form (2), or equivalently, (3), whatever the coordinate system. Using this observation, I show how to work out the locations of the epicentres and the relation governing pairs of epipolar lines.

4. EPICENTRES AND EPIPOLAR LINES

Where the interoccular axis intersects the image planes are the two epicentres. Now imagine a family of planes passing through the interoccular axis. Each such plane intersects each image plane in a straight line (which naturally passes through the respective epicentre), giving rise to pairs of epipolar lines. Let the left and the right epicentres be located at (π_1,π_2) and (π'_1,π'_2). The equation of a straight line of slope m passing through (π_1,π_2) is $(\xi_2 - \pi_2) = m(\xi_1 - \pi_1)$. Similarly, denoting by m' the slope of the corresponding epipolar line, the equation of the latter is $(\xi'_2 - \pi'_2) = m'\ (\xi'_1 - \pi'_1)$. [The geometric motivation presented here is not essential. One can simply postulate the existence of epicentres and epipolar lines and the arguments go through.] Now any point on a certain epipolar line in one image can match any point on the corresponding epipolar line in the other image. Given that all matched points obey (7), one obtains by inserting for ξ'_2 and ξ_2 from the linear equations above into the matrix representation of (7), that

$$\begin{bmatrix} \xi'_1, & m'(\xi'_1 - \pi'_1)+\pi'_2, & 1 \end{bmatrix} \mathbf{Q}'' \begin{bmatrix} \xi_1 \\ m(\xi_1-\pi_1)+\pi_2 \\ 1 \end{bmatrix} = 0 \tag{10}$$

for all values of ξ_1 and ξ'_1. The left hand side is a second order inhomogeneous polynomial in ξ_1 and ξ'_1 and can vanish identically if and only if the coefficient of each term vanishes. This yields four equations. The first of them, arising from the vanishing coefficient of the $(\xi_1\xi'_1)$ term, immediately gives the relation

$$m = -(Q''_{11} + m'Q''_{21})/(Q''_{12} + m'Q''_{22}) \qquad (11)$$

governing the slopes of a pair of epipolar lines. Note that it is independent of the normalisation of $\mathbf{Q}''$. The solution to the rest of the matching problem can be mechanised by the use of any stereo algorithm.

The condition that the coefficient of the term in ξ'_1 must vanish yields, after substituting (11) for m, a polynomial in m' which must vanish. Equating the coefficient of each power of m' to zero gives two linear inhomogeneous equations in the two unknowns π_1 and π_2:

$$\begin{bmatrix} Q''_{11} & Q''_{12} \\ Q''_{21} & Q''_{22} \end{bmatrix} \begin{bmatrix} \pi_1 \\ \pi_2 \end{bmatrix} = - \begin{bmatrix} Q''_{13} \\ Q''_{23} \end{bmatrix}. \qquad (12)$$

Similarly, the condition that the coefficient of the term in ξ_1 vanish yields

$$\begin{bmatrix} \pi'_1 & \pi'_2 \end{bmatrix} \begin{bmatrix} Q''_{11} & Q''_{12} \\ Q''_{21} & Q''_{22} \end{bmatrix} = - \begin{bmatrix} Q''_{31} & Q''_{32} \end{bmatrix}. \qquad (13)$$

That the constant term also vanishes can be verified by inserting the coordinates of the two epicentres in (7) and using (12) and (13). In the process, one obtains two interesting equations - one for each epicentre:

$$[\pi'_1, \pi'_2, 1]\mathbf{Q}'' = 0, \qquad (14)$$

and

$$\mathbf{Q}''[\pi_1, \pi_2, 1]^T = 0; \qquad (15)$$

implying that

$$\det|\ \mathbf{Q}''\ | = 0. \qquad (16)$$

This serves as a check on the accuracy of the data and the calculations.

Alternatively, observing that the last row and column of $\mathbf{Q}''$ in (8) are linear combinations of the rows and columns of $\mathbf{Q}$, it is readily seen that $\det|\ \mathbf{Q}''\ | = 0$ if and only if $\det|\ \mathbf{Q}\ | = 0$. That $\det|\ \mathbf{Q}\ | = 0$ follows from the fact that $\det|\ \mathbf{Q}\ | = \det|\ \mathbf{R}\ |.\det|\ \mathbf{S}\ |$, and it can be verified that $\det|\ \mathbf{S}\ | = 0$.

Starting with (3) and using the equivalents of (14) and (15) in the 'natural' coordinate system, i.e.,

$$[p'_1, p'_2, 1]\mathbf{Q} = 0, \qquad (14a)$$

and

$$\mathbf{Q}[p_1, p_2, 1]^T = 0, \qquad (15a)$$

where (p_1, p_2) and (p'_1, p'_2) are the epicentres in the natural coordinate system, an alternative form of $\mathbf{Q}''$ can also be given:

$$Q''_{ij} = Q_{ij},\ (i,j = 1,2)$$
$$Q''_{i3} = Q_{i1}(u_1 - p_1) + Q_{i2}(u_2 - p_2),\ (i=1,2)$$
$$Q''_{3i} = (u'_1 - p'_1)Q_{1i} + (u'_2 - p'_2)Q_{2i},\ (i=1,2)$$
$$Q''_{33} = (u'_1 - p'_1)Q''_{13} + (u'_2 - p'_2)Q''_{23},$$
$$= Q''_{31}(u_1 - p_1) + Q''_{32}(u_2 - p_2). \qquad (17)$$

5. SCENE RECONSTRUCTION

Longuet-Higgins gives a method of recovering structure from $\mathbf{Q}$. He also points out three equations relating the diagonal and the off-diagonal elements of the matrix $\mathbf{Q}^T\mathbf{Q}$ (his eqn. (17)), the rotation matrix dropping out in the process. Three equations are not sufficient to determine the four unknowns u_1, u_2, u'_1 and u'_2 needed to recover $\mathbf{Q}$ from (8) or (17). Thus given $\mathbf{Q}''$ alone, it does not seem possible to recover $\mathbf{Q}$ (whence structure).

It is possible to recover structure, however, given either (a) the direction of displacement of one camera with respect to the optic axis of the other, or, (b) the orientation of the optic axis of one camera with respect to that of the other. Note that $Q_{ij} = Q''_{ij}$, $(i,j=1,2)$. From the image data, therefore, one can obtain three ratios between these four elements. Now, from $\mathbf{Q}=\mathbf{RS}$,

$$Q_{11} = t_2R_{13} - t_3R_{12}, \quad Q_{12} = t_3R_{11} - t_1R_{13},$$
$$Q_{21} = t_2R_{23} - t_3R_{22}, \quad Q_{22} = t_3R_{21} - t_1R_{23}. \qquad (18)$$

Given $\mathbf{R}$, and using $\mathbf{R}_i \times \mathbf{R}_j = \mathbf{R}_k$, ($i,j,k$ cyclic permutations of 1,2,3), where $\mathbf{R}_m$ refers to the mth row of $\mathbf{R}$ regarded as a vector, (18) yields

$$t_1 = (R_{11}Q_{22} - R_{21}Q_{12})/R_{32},$$
$$t_2 = (R_{12}Q_{21} - R_{22}Q_{11})/R_{31},$$
$$t_3 = (R_{13}Q_{21} - R_{23}Q_{11})/R_{31},$$
$$= (R_{13}Q_{22} - R_{23}Q_{12})/R_{32}. \qquad (19)$$

The two expressions for t_3 in (19) provide an accuracy check. More importantly, it can happen that the right image (say) was rotated about its original position. This corresponds to an unknown rotation about the z' axis - represented by $\mathbf{R}_{z'}(g)$, g being the angle. The two expressions for t_3 then force a constraint on $tan(g)$. To see this, write the final rotation matrix as

$$\mathbf{R} \rightarrow [\mathbf{R}_{z'}(g)\mathbf{R}],$$

where R is known (for example, (Arfken 1970)). That is,

$$\mathbf{R} \rightarrow \begin{bmatrix} cos(g) & sin(g) & 0 \\ -sin(g) & cos(g) & 0 \\ 0 & 0 & 1 \end{bmatrix} \begin{bmatrix} R_{11} & R_{12} & R_{13} \\ R_{21} & R_{22} & R_{23} \\ R_{31} & R_{32} & R_{33} \end{bmatrix}. \quad (20)$$

Equating the two expressions for t_3 in (19) and substituting for the new **R** from (20), one obtains

$$tan(g) = -a/b, \quad (21)$$

$$a = (R_{13}Q_{21} - R_{23}Q_{11})/R_{31} - (R_{13}Q_{22} - R_{23}Q_{12})/R_{32},$$

$$b = (R_{23}Q_{21} + R_{13}Q_{11})/R_{31} - (R_{23}Q_{22} + R_{13}Q_{12})/R_{32}.$$

There are two possible solutions for g, given $tan(g)$. If the two images are coarsely aligned (by eye, say) then the small angle solution is the desired solution.

Next consider known displacement (t_1, t_2, t_3). Denoting the ratio Q_{11}/Q_{12} by a_x (computed from data measurement), and setting $R_{11}/R_{12} = a_1$ and $R_{13}/R_{11} = a_2$, it can be readily shown that

$$a_2 = t_3(a_1 + a_x)/(t_2 + a_x t_1) = f_1(a_1) \quad (22)$$

is a linear function of a_1. Similarly, denoting the ratio Q_{22}/Q_{21} by a_y (measured), and setting $R_{21}/R_{22} = b_1$ and $R_{23}/R_{22} = b_2$, it can be verified that

$$b_2 = t_3(b_1 + a_y)/(t_1 + a_y t_2) = f_2(b_1) \quad (23)$$

is a linear function of b_1. Then

$$R_{11}^2 + R_{12}^2 + R_{13}^2 = 1, \quad \text{and} \quad R_{21}^2 + R_{22}^2 + R_{23}^2 = 1$$

imply

$$R_{11}^2 = (1 + a_1^2 + f_1^2(a_1))^{-1} \quad (24)$$

and

$$R_{22}^2 = (1 + b_1^2 + f_2^2(b_1))^{-1}. \quad (25)$$

The rotation matrix **R** is characterised by the four unknowns R_{11}, R_{22}, a_1 and b_1, and has the form

$$\mathbf{R} = \begin{bmatrix} R_{11} & a_1 R_{11} & f_1(a_1)R_{11} \\ b_1 R_{22} & R_{22} & f_2(b_1)R_{22} \\ R_{31} & R_{32} & R_{33} \end{bmatrix}, \quad (26)$$

where

$$R_{31} = R_{11}R_{22}[a_1 f_2(b_1) - f_1(a_1)], \quad (26a)$$

$$R_{32} = R_{11}R_{22}[b_1 f_1(a_1) - f_2(b_1)], \quad (26b)$$

and

$$R_{33} = R_{11}R_{22}(1 - a_1 b_1). \quad (26c)$$

Every relationship following from the equation $\mathbf{R}_i \times \mathbf{R}_j = \mathbf{R}_k$, $(i, j, k$ cyclic permutations of 1,2,3) gives

$$a_1 + b_1 + f_1(a_1)f_2(b_1) = 0. \quad (27)$$

Since $f_1(a_1)$ and $f_2(b_1)$ are linear functions of a_1 and b_1 respectively, (27) takes the form

$$c_1 a_1 b_1 + c_2 a_1 + c_3 b_1 = c_4,$$

or

$$b_1 = (c_4 - c_2 a_1)/(c_3 + c_1 a_1); \quad (28)$$

where

$$c_1 = t_3^2, \quad (28a)$$

$$c_2 = (t_2 + a_x t_1)(t_1 + a_y t_2) + a_y t_3^2, \quad (28b)$$

$$c_3 = (t_2 + a_x t_1)(t_1 + a_y t_2) + a_x t_3^2, \quad (28c)$$

and

$$c_4 = -a_x a_y t_3^2. \quad (28d)$$

There is now the last piece of unused information, the ratio $Q_{22}/Q_{11} = a_{yx}$ (measured). Writing this out explicitly, squaring it [to get rid of the square- roots from (24) and (25)], and using (22)-(28), one obtains a fourth degree polynomial equation in a_1 :

$$\begin{aligned} & a_1^4[a_{yx}^2 h_1 h_2 - h_3 h_4] + \\ & a_1^3[a_{yx}^2(e_1 h_2 + h_1 e_2) - (e_3 h_4 + h_3 e_4)] + \\ & a_1^2[a_{yx}^2(d_1 h_2 + e_1 e_2 + h_1 d_2) - (d_3 h_4 + e_3 e_4 + h_3 d_4)] + \\ & a_1[a_{yx}^2(d_1 e_2 + e_1 d_2) - (d_3 e_4 + e_3 d_4)] + \\ & [a_{yx}^2(d_1 d_2) - d_3 d_4] = 0 \; ; \end{aligned} \quad (29)$$

where

$$n_1 = a_x n_2, \quad n_2 = t_3/(t_2 + a_x t_1),$$

$$n_3 = a_y n_4, \quad n_4 = t_3/(t_1 + a_y t_2); \quad (29a)$$

$$d_1 = (t_3 - t_1 n_1)^2,$$

$$d_2 = (1 + n_3^2)c_3^2 + 2n_3 n_4 c_3 c_4 + (1 + n_4^2)c_4^2,$$

$$d_3 = (1 + n_1^2),$$

$$d_4 = [(t_3 - t_1 n_4)c_4 - n_3 c_3 t_1]^2; \quad (29b)$$

$$e_1 = -2t_1 n_2(t_3 - t_1 n_1),$$

$$e_2 = 2[(1+n_3^2)c_1 c_3 + n_3 n_4(c_1 c_4 - c_2 c_3) - c_2 c_4(1+n_4^2)],$$

$$e_3 = 2n_1 n_2,$$

$$e_4 = -2[(t_3 - t_1 n_4)c_4 - n_3 c_3 t_1][c_1 n_3 t_1 + c_2(t_3 - t_1 n_4)]; \quad (29c)$$

and

$$h_1 = (t_1 n_2)^2,$$

$$h_2 = (1 + n_3^2)c_1^2 - 2c_1c_2n_3n_4 + (1 + n_4^2)c_2^2,$$
$$h_3 = (1 + n_2^2),$$
$$h_4 = [c_1n_3t_1 + c_2(t_3 - t_1n_4)]^2. \quad (29d)$$

Efficient subroutines exist (e.g. NAG) for obtaining the four roots of the polynomial. Having obtained a_1, **R** can be calculated using (22)- (26) and (28). Since **R** is real, only real roots are of interest. Of the real roots, only that which yields positive depth (both X_3 and $X'_3 > 0$) for all points is acceptable. Empirically, the polynomial always appears to have two real roots. Each root has a single combination of the signs of R_{11} and R_{22} which yields positive depths for all data points. The nonveridical solution, however, produces a large origin shift (typically five times the image width) in one image, and small depths (typically a few tenths of the interoccular distance). If the positions of the natural origins are known even roughly (e.g., they may be known to lie somewhere within the pictures), the veridical solution can be chosen quite unambiguously.

Given **t** it is thus possible to compute **R**, and vice versa. Hence **Q** can also be computed. From (8) or (17), after rescaling **Q**″, the unknown coordinates (u_1, u_2) and (u'_1, u'_2) of the natural origins can also be obtained. The image coordinates can then be appropriately transformed into their natural systems, whence depth can be calculated by the method prescribed by Longuet-Higgins:

$$X_3 = [(\mathbf{R}_1 - x'_1\mathbf{R}_3)\cdot\mathbf{t}]/[(\mathbf{R}_1 - x'_1\mathbf{R}_3)\cdot\mathbf{x}], \quad (30)$$

$$X_1 = x_1X_3, \quad X_2 = x_2X_3, \quad (31)$$

and

$$X'_j = R_{jk}(X_k - t_k). \quad (j,k = 1,2,3) \quad (32)$$

Note that $\mathbf{x}, \mathbf{x}', \mathbf{X}, \mathbf{X}'$ are now in the natural image coordinate system.

6. SUMMARY

Given 8 corresponding points in two images without any registration information whatsoever, it is possible to calculate the two epicentres and the relation governing the pairs of epipolar lines. The rest of the matching problem reduces to one dimensional searches along the epipolar lines and can be automated using any stereo matching algorithm.

Although it would appear that structure cannot be inferred from the image data alone in the absence of any registration information whatever, full registration information is also not necessary. For example, given either (a) the direction of displacement (two direction cosines) of one camera with respect to the optic axis of the other, or, (b) the orientation of the optic axis (two angles) of one camera with respect to that of the other, methods were described to obtain structure.

7. ACKNOWLEDGEMENTS

It is a pleasure to thank Bernard Buxton for his critical reading of the manuscript.

8. REFERENCES

[1] Longuet-Higgins H C, "A computer algorithm for reconstructing a scene from two projections", **Nature**, 293 (1981) 133-5.

[2] Longuet-Higgins H C, "The reconstruction of a scene from two projections - configurations that defeat the 8-point algorithm", in the *Proceedings of the First International Conference on the Applications of Artificial Intelligence* , Denver, Colorado, USA (1984) 395-7.

[3] Arfken G, *Mathematical methods for physicists.* New York, USA: Academic Press. (1970) pp 178-181 (second edition).

[4] The NAG (Numerical Algorithms Group) Fortran Library, subroutine C02AEF.

[8] A Pipelined Architecture for the Canny Edge Detector

Brendan P D Ruff

GEC Research Limited
Hirst Research Centre, Wembley, HA9 7PP, UK

Abstract

Low level vision algorithms deal with information at the pixel level. Their output is more abstract, meaningful, and compact, as it deals with the structure underlying the scene. General purpose processors are well suited to dealing with abstractions that require flexible processing, more so than they are to the simple and repetitive pixel processing task, a task that does not make use of control flow sophistication. Because of this dichotomy in processing style, a fixed low level front-end processor suggests itself as a dedicated real-time data "abstractor", presenting as its output data relevant, in this case, to edge based stereo processing. The stereo system will deal with the abstracted data at the same scene rate but slower data rate on a general purpose, and possibly parallel, processor. The low-level edge detection algorithm implemented, the Canny edge detector [1] , will be partitioned into a cascade of simpler operations in the dataflow, or **pipelined** manner, to exploit the algorithm's inherent structure.

1 Introduction

The Pipelined Canny system has been designed around the requirements of the PMF stereo algorithm [2] to remove the load of low-level processing from TINA [3] , a stereo 3-D modelling system with capabilities for object manipulation. The goal of any vision system is to operate in step with its environment, reacting to stimuli with sufficiently small processing lag so that a sensible response may be made. Biological systems perform this through massive, though slow, parallelism. Machines are limited in parallelism through size, but operate with many orders of magnitude greater speed. However, general purpose processors have large control time overheads in arranging data for processing and thus cannot achieve the full processing potential of silicon technology. This is not as serious a restraint in the symbolic processing for scene understanding as it is in the early processing of the massive amounts of pixel data thrown at the vision system. A pre-processor is required with control information designed implicitly into its architecture so removing time penalties. This processor, the Canny edge detector for the stereo vision system, extracts edge information from the intensity map of the image, so reducing the data volume from the square of the image luminosity array's dimension to the order of that data volume divided by sigma squared, where sigma is the standard deviation of the Gaussian used in the blurring operation of Canny.

2 The Canny Edge Operator

The Canny edge operator is an optimal edge detector addressing the twin goals of sensitivity and localisation. The processing involves several sophisticated operations. The pipelined Canny has an architecture that divides the processing task into many small stages. These may be grouped together into the following functional units as suggested in the original thesis by J.Canny [1].

1. 2-D Gaussian convolution with the image luminoscity array
2. Gradient and orientation calculation
3. Non-Maximal gradient suppression based upon the the gradient at a pixel and its two nearest neighbours along the gradient direction.
4. Interpolation of the maximum gradient position to sub-pixel accuracy based upon qaudratic or other fitting.
5. Thresholding with hysteresis to grow back weak edges but to allow greater noise immunity by setting a high threshold.

Each unit itself will be further sub-divided until 'nuclear' units are defined for processing as will be demonstrated in later sections.

These functional units are self contained, dealing with input data from the previous unit and producing an output. The final output of the system is a set of edges with gradient strength, orientation, and a sub-pixel offset to the edge in either the X or Y direction.

3 Pipelining philosophy

The pipeline approach to algorithm design is to represent the algorithm in the data flow representation. However all parts of the network are synchronous allowing one period of the pipeline clock to perform the operation within each part of the network. Thus an algorithm that is composed as a cascade of operations is divided into simple

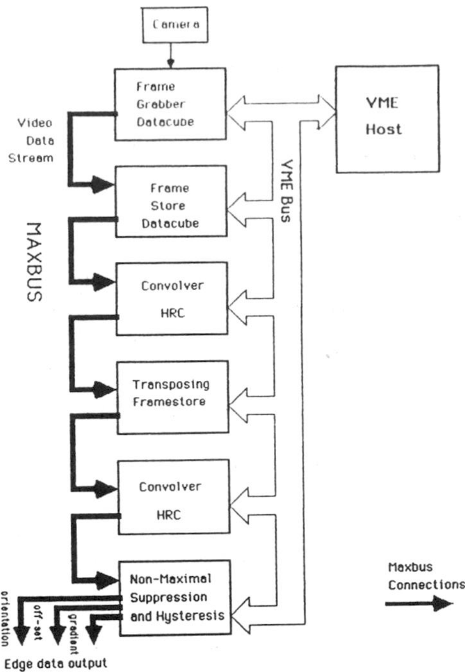

Figure 1: Front-End Edge Detector System

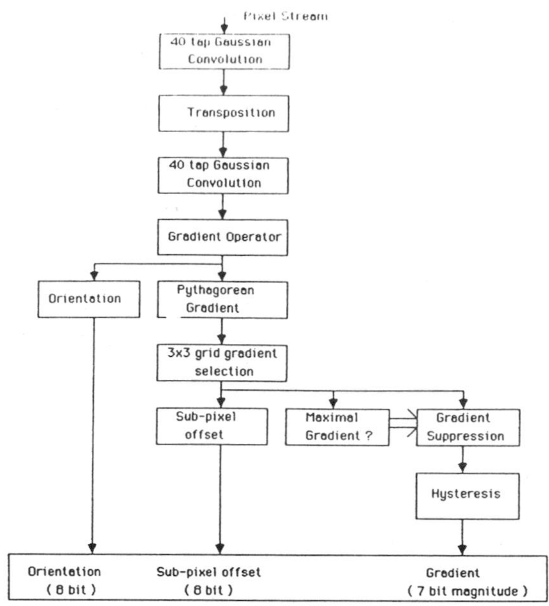

Figure 2: Pipeline of Modules within the Canny Edge Detector

operations, units, that may be performed within a single beat of the pipeline clock. The units are then cascaded so that each unit processes its input during the period between clocks in order that it presents its output to the next unit in the pipeline at the next clock period. It is the ordering of the units that allows input data to be processed in parts until emerging from the pipeline. It is then clear that each stage of the pipeline is busy during every beat of the clock, this being the strength of the pipeline processor. The penalty for such a distributed cascaded processor lies in the time latency between data entering the processor and later emerging. However one piece of processed data emmerges at every clock beat. For image analysis systems the latency induced by a pipelined processor is unlikely to affect performance as a latency of even several frames corresponds to several million stages in the pipeline but only a few milliseconds latency.

4 Pipelined Edge Detector

The edge detector is partitioned over several circuit boards in a standardised environment for its development and for interface to other processors for further analysis. Data is acquired with a frame grabber and then output in non-interlaced format over the Maxbus [4] video bus to a chain of three pipelined modules and an additional frame-store. Data is transmitted between modules on the Maxbus as is the final output of the pipeline. Figure.1 shows this system. Note that each module is additionally interfaced to the VME bus for control purposes. This environment coincides with all of Datacube's image processing modules and also with the MARVIN transputer system being developed as the processing engine upon which TINA is to execute.

The edge detector is composed of a chain of several modules. Figure.2. Each module is internally pipelined. The modules perform the following functions:

1. The first convolver performs a 40-point Gaussian convolution of the pixel stream.

2. The second transposes the output array of the convolver.

3. The third board performs a second 40-point convolution with an 8-bit result.

4. The fourth board performs the non-maximal suppression and hysteresis algorithm.

These modules define the functional parts of the Canny edge detector whose output is a data set containing zeroes for points not containing inflections, but for inflection points three pieces of data are given designed to interface with the TINA system:

1. the edge (gradient) orientation (8-bit orientation code)

2. the edge strength (8-bit sign magnitude)

3. the sub-pixel offset (8-bit sign magnitude) within the pixel to the edge position measured to an accuracy of 0.02 pixels for high contrast edges, degrading to 0.5 pixels for unit contrast edges.

This offset is measured either in the image 'vertical' or 'horizontal' direction according to which is nearest to the true gradient direction. Note that if the gradient is zero the other pieces of data should be disregarded.

It then remains to describe the architecture of each board.

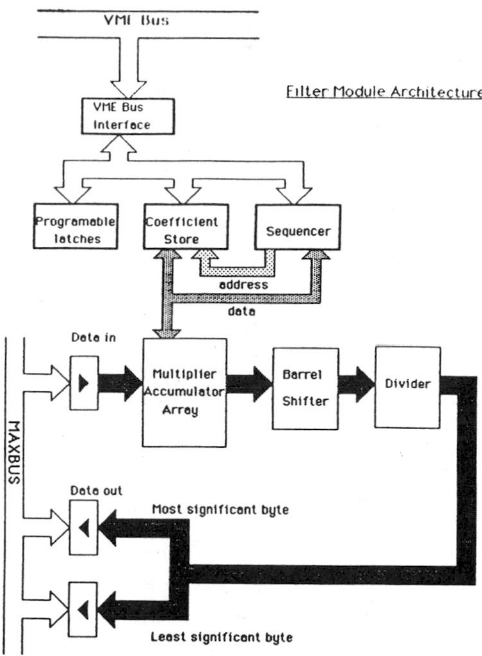

Figure 3: Convolver Architecture

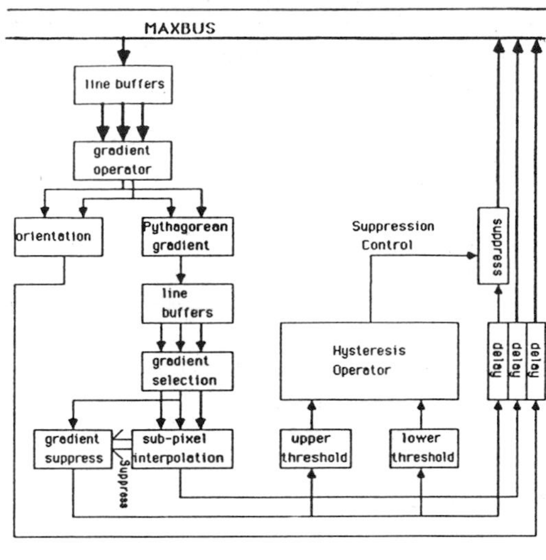

Figure 4: Non-Maximal Suppression and Hysteresis Module

5 Architecture of the boards within the edge detector

5.1 Convolver architecture

Figure.3 shows the architecture of the convolver. The convolver board receives an 8-bit data stream from the Maxbus and performs a 40-point convolution of this data with a 40-point programmable mask of 9-bit twos complement coefficients. The result is converted into sign magnitude format then arithmetically shifted left or right by up to 16 bits. This is programmable. The shifted result is divided by a 16 bit factor using a multiplicative division technique. The result is then either converted again to twos complement format or left as a magnitude only result. The 16-bit result requires two Maxbus ports for output. The shifting and dividing stage is fully programmable to allow format adjustment and normalisation.

Operations are synchronised to the data stream with timing information supplied by the Maxbus timing port, P3. Control of the board's operation is effected via the VME bus. Various programmable latches control the functions of the board. The coefficient memory is fully read/write accessible to the VME bus for mask definition. The board behaves both as a Maxbus slave and a VME slave as is required for stream processing under the Maxbus philosophy.

Standard MSI TTL integrated circuits and PALs dominate the design. VLSI parts are used in the convolution. The convolution is implemented with five single chip multiplier-accumulator arrays each of which contain eight multiplier-accumulators of 8-bit data and 9-bit coefficient precision producing a 26 bit result.

5.2 Non-maximal suppression (NMS) and hysteresis module

This module houses two cascaded pipelined processors, figure.4. The first performs the non-maximal gradient suppression, outputting gradient strength, sub-pixel offsets, and edge orientation. The second performs the hysteresis edge thresholding algorithm. This produces, on a 3 line array, two single bit maps of the upper thresholded edges and lower thresholded, weak, edges. A third map is produced which consists of the upper thresholded, strong, map with any of the lower thresholded edges adjacent to the strong edges logically ORed onto it. This map then becomes the strong edge map of the next iteration of the algorithm. The weak edge map is unchanged. A number of iterations of this pipelined algorithm reduces edge noise considerably while incurring only a very low hardware overhead.

5.3 Non-maximal suppression, NMS

Eight-bit magnitude data is input from the maxbus. A gradient operator based upon a differencing convolution with the mask (1,0,-1) in horizontal and vertical image directions produces the partial derivatives of the already blurred image. Orientation and pythagorean gradient are then calculated via fast look up tables. Based upon the gradient direction, the central gradient and its two nearest neighbours are selected and passed to a processor that calculates the sub-pixel offset to the maximum, if the central gradient is indeed a maximum. This is performed in a fast look-up table based upon the difference of the central and largest other gradient compared to the smaller, giving only a 14 bit look-up. Otherwise the gradient is suppressed by asigning it a zero value. Gradient values are passed as a 10MHz stream to the hysteresis processor while orientation and sub-pixel offset data is input to delay elements to synchronise their final emergence to the maxbus with the output of the hysteresis.

5.4 Hysteresis

This algorithm initially builds up an upper and lower thresholded edge gradient map by performing a thresholding of the gradient with programmable upper and lower thresholds. The pipelined logical processor in figure.4 generates as its output a single bit specifying an edge or non-edge decision, suppressing noise edges. The gradient is delayed to synchronise it with the emergence of the decision from the processor. The gradient is then suppressed or maintained in accordance with the outcome of the decision.

6 Hardware design philosophy

Pipelined modules are simple encapsulated processors. Each performs its function within the time period of the pipeline clock. This naturally defines a highly modular design philosophy. Specification of interfaces between each module and module function are sufficient to define the module so that detailed design may be delegated to allow highly parallel development. Design testability is simplified as custom data may be inserted at any stage in the pipeline to test the proceeding pipelined unit. Test vectors of the output of the preceding unit must be generated.

7 Example of Pipelined circuitry

This example illustrates the pipelined technique for processor design for a simple operation performed at a rate of 10MHz.

Imagine that some second order polynomial for a group of 4 adjacent pixels, in a square, is to be calculated. Figure.5 shows how this may be performed. A line buffer is a set of N registers set head to tail to allow data to be delayed by N clock cycles, where N is the length of a line. The operation performed causes a latency of N cycles for the line delay, 1 cycle for a registered buffering to allow all four pixels to be accessed simultaneously. Squaring is performed by look-up table, an operation that can take as little as about 40ns (nano-seconds) up to 150ns or more for slower memory devices. In general, a 15-bit look up table will not be faster than 70ns, but an 8-bit table could be as fast as 20ns. The output of the square look-up tables is registered to allow synchronisation to the pixel clock so that the input to the next set of arithmetic units is stable. A set of additions is performed in three tiers to allow adequate processing time for each stage. It is possible that the square law look-up table and an addition stage could have been cascaded in one registered section (100ns time slice) and that two or more of the additions could have also been performed in one registered section. The propagation delay of these devices compared to the

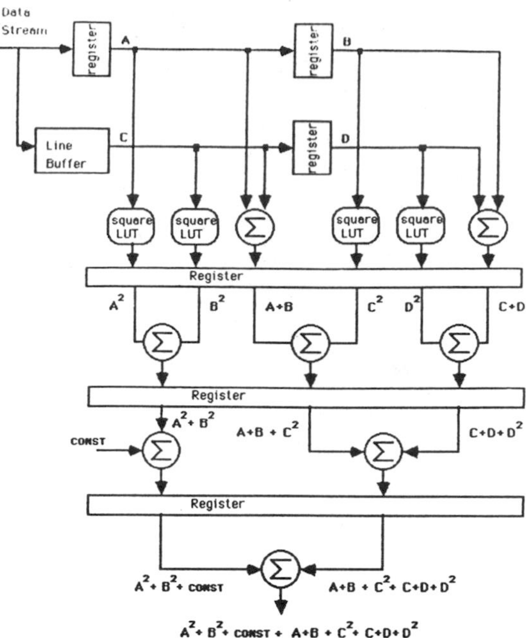

Figure 5: An Example of Pipelining

pipeline clock period will determine the number and size of operations to be performed as a cascade in one registered section of the pipeline.

8 Adapting to Industrial Applications

The pipelined or *data flow* architecture is highly suitable for design in custom VLSI circuits. The modular architecture and unidirectional flow of data in the pipeline allow for a standard-cell design approach (design using libraries of modular logic circuits) with cells linked by very regular and short interconnection. It is envisaged that an extreme compression of circuit area is possible through the custom approach. This will in turn allow very small size for the processor, more suitable to autonomous guided vehicles. Identifiable areas for size reduction through the custom silicon design approach within the Canny architecture are:

1. For smaller Gaussian convolutions a single chip solution is possible for an 8x8 array of multipliers with line buffering on-chip. This reduces the Gaussian convolution to the convolver and interface circuitry.

2. Non-maximal suppression for this architecture requires extensive use of look-up tables, already near their present limit in VLSI, but custom circuits would allow integration of line buffers and registers, multiplexers for the pixel and gradient selection network, either on separate chips or on one of the look-up table chips.

3. Hysteresis may be performed with a single chip incorporating the line buffers, logic network, and

Figure 6: A Widget Scene

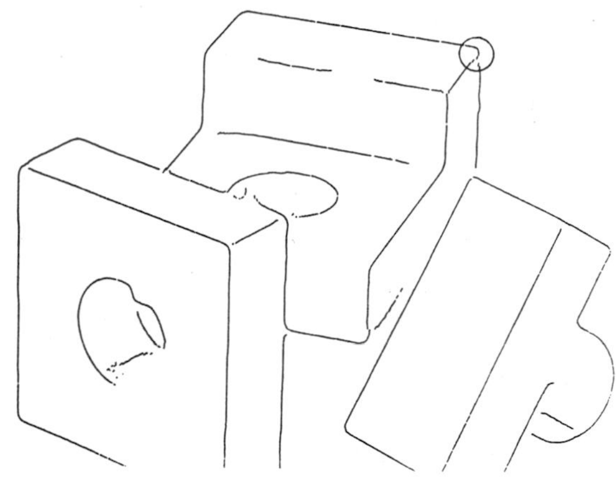

Figure 7: Canny Edge Detected Scene

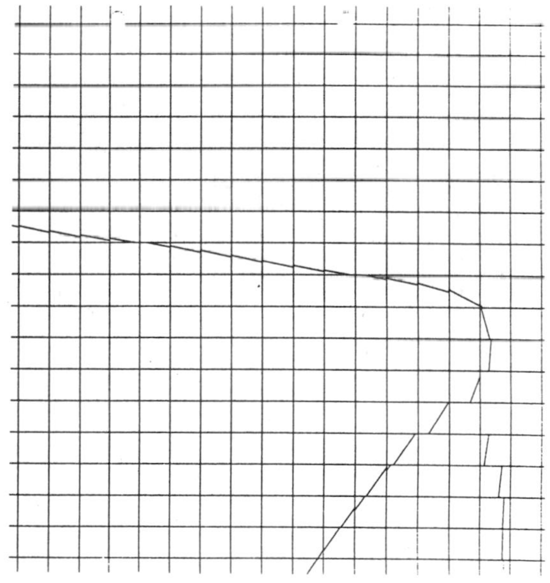

Figure 8: An expansion of the circled corner in figure 7 The graduations represent pixel boundaries

threshold selectors.

It is envisaged that the edge operator could be compressed into about seven integrated circuits for the computation, each around the 28 pin dual-in-line size. Additional cicuitry is required for interfacing to the VME bus and MAXBUS. The convolution, non-maximal suppression and hysteresis could then be performed on a single circuit board to provide a compact front-end processor for edge based stereo systems.

9 Simulations

The version of the Canny operator chosen for pipelined implementation uses integer arithmetic, restricted to 8-bits for the gradient and 8-bits for the final convolution output though the full resolution of the 9-bit coefficient and 8-bit pixel data is maintained until a final format adjustment reduces it to 8-bits. This accuracy is the minimum required sufficient to maintain to 0.02 pixel accuracy of high contrast edges using wide Gaussian convolution. Precision less than this degrades this performance. This precision is, however, quite convenient for standard 8-bit data paths.

Some simulations results are presented in figures 6,7,8. These show, respectively, a simulated widget scene generated by WINSOM [5] , a Canny edge map of the scene, and an expanded corner junction of the edge map to illustrate sub-pixel acuity (the grid represents pixel boundaries).

Theoretical edge positional accuracies are given below for the edge detector measured upon a test image of a circle of radius 60 pixels using a Gaussian of sigma 1.0, where the contrast across the circle boundary is varied between 2 to 200.

Intensity (0..255)	Mean magnitude error in edge position (pixels)
2	.48
20	.05
200	.02

Figure 9: Edge Positional Error for the Pipelined Edge Detector

10 Discussion

It has been shown how pipelining an algorithm can lead to a fast hardware architecture. It is clear that some algorithms are susceptible to the pipeline, or dataflow, architecture, in particular many of the low level vision algorithms, the algorithms typically used as the 'front end' to an image analysis system. Further, the real-time processing possible with this design philosophy allows the abstraction of higher level data to reduce data rate. This data is scene dependent, asynchronous to the input pixel stream and of a much reduced volume compared to the pixel data volume. It is hoped that the next layer on the analysis ladder of an image processing system will deal with this data in one, or several frame times, to produce higher level, yet still real-time, abstractions. For the PMF stereo algorithm implemented on a transputer network this is possible. It is hoped that a VLSI version of the system will allow a compact standard front-end processor for higher level vision engines.

References

[1] J F Canny. A computational approach to edge detection. *IEEE Trans Pattern Anaysis and Machine Intelligence*, PAMI-8(6):679–698, 1986.

[2] Stephen B Pollard, John E W Mayhew, and John P Frisby. PMF - a stereo correspondence algorithm using a disparity gradient limit. *Perception*, 14(4):449–470, 1985.

[3] J Porrill, S B Pollard, T P Pridmore, J B Bowen, J E W Mayhew, and J P Frisby. Tina: The sheffield vision system. *Proceedings of the International Joint Conference on Artificial Intelligence*, pages 1138–1144, 1987.

[4] Datacube Inc. Maxbus specification manual. Technical report, 1985.

[5] P Quarendon. Winsom user's guide, report number uksc 123. Technical report, IBM Scientific Centre, Winchester, Hants, 1984.

[9] Parallel Architectures for Fast 3D Machine Vision

Chris R Brown and Chris M Dunford

AI Vision Research Unit
University of Sheffield, Sheffield S10 2TN, UK

1. Introduction

The *TINA* software suite, developed within *AIVRU* during the period 1984 to 1987, has demonstrated an encouraging level of visual competence by delivering (from stereoscopic TV images of a relatively cluttered scene) three-dimensional edge-based geometrical scene descriptions sufficiently accurate to guide a robot arm in a pick-and-place task. Against this success must be offset the large computational effort required to pass even a single image through the *TINA* suite.

This paper describes work undertaken by *AIVRU* to develop a computing engine of realistic cost, yet powerful enough to provide three-dimensional machine vision at speeds commensurate with the real-time needs of an assembly robot, or an autonomous guided vehicle. Firstly, we make some observations about the opportunities for exploiting parallel MIMD architectures and other specialised hardware, including sequential pipelined frame-rate processors. Secondly, we discuss the results of a pilot study in which parallel implementations of the *Canny* edge detector and the PMF stereo matching algorithm were implemented on an array of eight transputers. Thirdly, we describe '*Marvin*' - a Multi-processor ARchitecure for VIsioN, currently being developed within *AIVRU*.

To give some idea of the extent of improvement in speed being sought, it is interesting to examine the CPU time required to process an image through the *TINA* suite at the time it was originally demonstrated, which for a typical scene at 256 by 256 resolution are shown in Table 1. These times were obtained on a Sun 2 with a *SKY* floating point accelerator.

Process Stage	Time (sec)
Canny (Edge detection)	428
Rectify (Convert to parallel camera geometry)	57
PMF (Stereo matching)	1118
Connect (Establish connectivity of 3-D edges)	214
GDB (Classify connected edges as lines & arcs)	1442
Model Matcher (Find 3-D match of edge model)	300
TOTAL:	**3559**

Table 1

Exactly what is implied by 'real-time' operation of the system is open to debate, but a throughput of 1 image per second is probably the minimum requirement. In addition, a move to higher resolution (say 512 by 512) images is desirable. We seek, therefore, a speed increase of order 10,000.

Much work is in progress within *AIVRU* to reduce the computational load by refinement of the algorithms; for example by restricting the areas of image which are processed to specific regions of interest, and to further reduce the amount of searching by predicting forward within a sequence of images. The work reported here however, is concerned with the provision of more raw computing power, through the use of parallel MIMD architectures.

The transputer is an ideal candidate as a processing unit in such a system, and our work centres around the use of this device. A powerful 32-bit processor in its own right, it has four high-speed serial links that enable the construction of highly parallel architectures without the system engineering problems and bus bandwidth limitations experienced by shared memory designs. The transputer's flexibility and price allow a modular system to be constructed for prototyping fast vision systems, without imposing a heavy financial burden.

2. The Exploitation of Parallelism

In this section we discuss the parallelism inherent in the *TINA* processing stages, and how this might be exploited. The discussion focusses mainly on the use of a transputer array, although some comments on the use of specialised pipelined hardware are also made. It is important to note that we seek opportunities for parallelism on quite a large scale. Schemes which allow us to exploit, say, two or three transputers are simply not worthwhile. Thus, the extent to which any given scheme can be extended to greater numbers of transputers, and the extent to which a linear increase in speed is achieved, are important issues.

Three types of parallelism can be identified within the processing stages: *spatial*, *featural*, and *temporal*. We will consider these in turn.

2.1 Spatial Parallelism

Each processor is allocated a patch of the image. This is appropriate for operators which require access to relatively small pixel neighbourhoods, such as Canny and *PMF*. Load-balancing (that is, arranging for each processor to have the same amount of work to do) can be performed by adjusting the size of the patches. Although in principle a decomposition into a 2-D array of rectangles could be used (see *Fig.* 2), in practice the use of 'slices' (rectangles extending the full width of the image) is easiest (*Fig.* 1). If 2-D decomposition is used, it is difficult to adjust the size of the patches to balance the processing load, and still have the patches tesselate the image. Also, because of the 'raster scan' order in which digital video busses operate, it is somewhat easier from an engineering standpoint to distribute data in complete rasters.

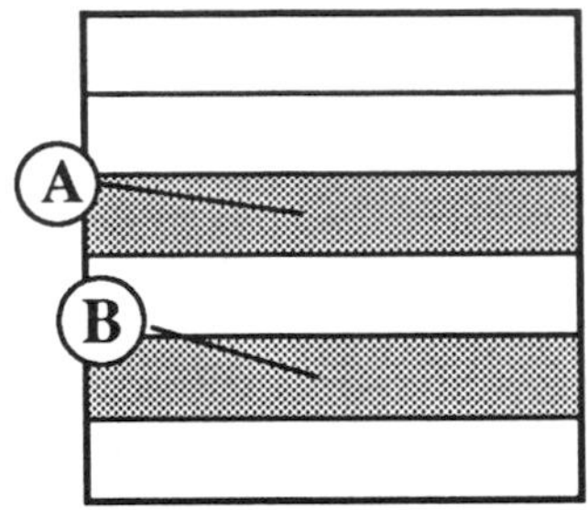

Fig 1. 1-D Spatial Partitioning

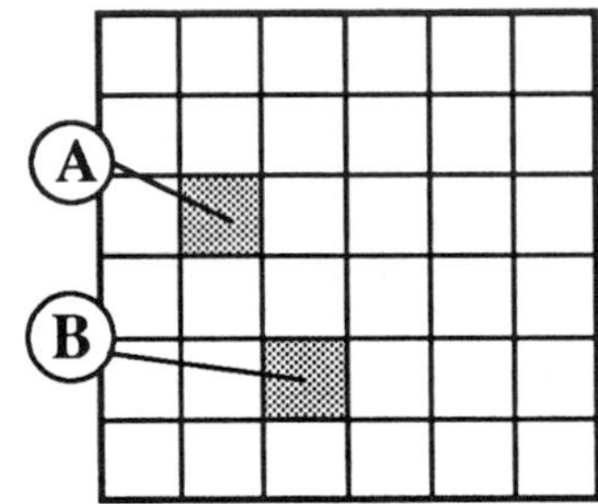

Fig 2. 2-D Spatial Partitioning

2.1.1 Data flow within spatially parallel systems

The data flow within spatially parallel systems is complicated by the fact that most algorithms require access to pixel neighbourhoods surrounding the pixels for which they are to deliver output. This can be handled in various ways:

(a) By migrating data at the slice boundaries across the transputer links. The order of processing may be important, especially in iterative algorithms such as *PMF*. For example, if all slices are processed top-to-bottom, and slice 4 needs complete or partial results from slice 3 etc., processing activity will ripple down through the slices and parallelism will be lost.

(b) By duplication of effort at the slice boundaries. That is, a slice's transputer will replicate some of the processing which its neighbour is performing on pixels near the slice boundary. The input slice will be bigger than the output slice.

These considerations lead to the following observation: if the width of the slice allocated to a processor is reduced, the processor spends a larger proportion of its time either talking to its neighbour or duplicating its neighbour's efforts. If the slice becomes narrower than the algorithm's neighbourhood size, this effect dominates and little speed increase is obtained. This yields a (very approximate) upper limit on the number of transputers which can be gainfully employed in this way of

```
image size/neighbourhood size
```

Taking *image size* = 512 and *neighbourhood size* = 8, yields an upper limit of 64 processors. At present, this value is larger than the number of transputers we have the money to buy -- though not by a large factor.

An alternative form of spatial parallelism could arise from multiple region of interest processing, in which a number of relatively small rectangular regions of the image have been identified as worthy of detailed processing. In this case the regions will not necessarily be horizontal slices, and there is no requirement for them to tesselate the image.

2.1.2 Load Balancing in Spatially Parallel Systems

Load balancing, as mentioned earlier, can be accomplished by adjusting the size of the slices. The computational load of some operations, such as *Canny*, is relatively insensitive to the actual content of the image. For others, such as *PMF*, cluttered regions take much longer. Since pictures (usually) have the important bits in the middle, a load-balanced partitioning will typically have wide slices at the top and bottom edges and narrower slices in the middle. Partitioning adjustments are ideally carried out before processing an image, if the 'cost' of processing each raster can be somehow evaluated before hand. For example, a simple count of the number of edges found by *Canny* could be used to guide a pre-partitioning of the data prior to *PMF*. Alternatively, if the system is being used to process a series of images, partition sizes can be adjusted after each image has been processed, on the assumption that each image in the sequence has a similar 'complexity distribution' to its predecessor.

2.2 Featural Parallelism

Each processor is allocated a subset of the geometrical features in the image (See *Fig.* 3). This is appropriate for

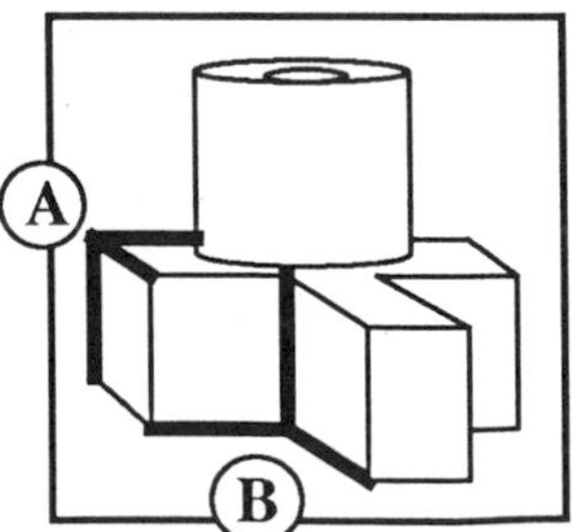

Fig 3. Featural Partitioning

operations on lines and regions which potentially could span large distances across the image. The rules by which features are allocated to processors are less obvious than for spatial parallelism, but could continue to have a spatial basis; for example, each processor is allocated a slice; features are allocated to processors on the basis of which slice their top-most point lies in. The real problems lie in the transformation of the data structures between spatial-parallel and feature-parallel stages, and in efficiently re-distributing the data around the processor array.

Load balancing in this scheme could be performed by using a 'processor farm', consisting of a master processor and a number of worker processors. The master keeps a list of busy and idle workers, and assigns 'work packets' to processors as they become idle. (A work packet might be, for example, an attempt to match a geometric feature in the image with a pre-computed object model). The fundamental characteristic of a processor farm is that the workers do not need to communicate or synchronise with one another. Processor farms are automatically load-balanced, and it is very easy to add more transputers; the master simply needs to be made aware of the increased number of workers. A desirable characteristic of a processor farm is a topology which provides short data paths between the master and all of its workers. Given that transputers have only four links, a ternary tree is perhaps sensible. The transputer is well-suited as a worker node as its design allows the passing of data from one link to another in parallel with the actual work process running on it. CPU time is required only to initiate the operation, thereafter DMA logic in the links carries out the transfer with minimal inpact on the CPU. The master task should ensure that this overlap of processing and transferring data is exploited. Further, efficient processor farms reduce the CPU overhead and maximise the communications bandwidth of the network by sending small numbers of large messages in preference to large numbers of small ones.

2.3 Temporal Parallelism

Temporal Parallelism, or *pipelining*, refers to the use of several processing elements in series, with each element responsible for one stage of the processing. Typically this provides N-fold parallelism for only small values of N, simply because there are conceptually only a few stages in the pipeline. In practice each element could be a group of transputers which themselves employed spatial or featural parallelism. For example, one might envisage 4 groups as shown in *Fig.* 4. Different numbers of transputers are placed in each group to balance the processing loads of the various stages. Effective parallelism is achieved only if a continuous flow of images are to be processed, so that, for example, processor group *D* is processing image *N*, whilst group *C* is processing image *N+1*, and so on.

Insofar as it provides opportunity to use more transputers, pipelining increases the throughput of the system, but it does not reduce the overall latency from image acquisition to delivery of the geometry. For example, suppose each processor group in the pipelined system of Fig. 4 were able to perform its task in, say, 0.5 seconds. The pipeline would thus deliver fresh 3-D geometry every 0.5 seconds, but each one would be 2.0 seconds out of date. The same number of transputers employed without pipelining would achieve a four-fold increase in the fineness of the spatial or featural parallelism, thus (assuming the load was balanced) completing each processing stage in 0.125 seconds. It would still deliver results every 0.5 seconds, moreover, each would be only 0.5 seconds out of date.

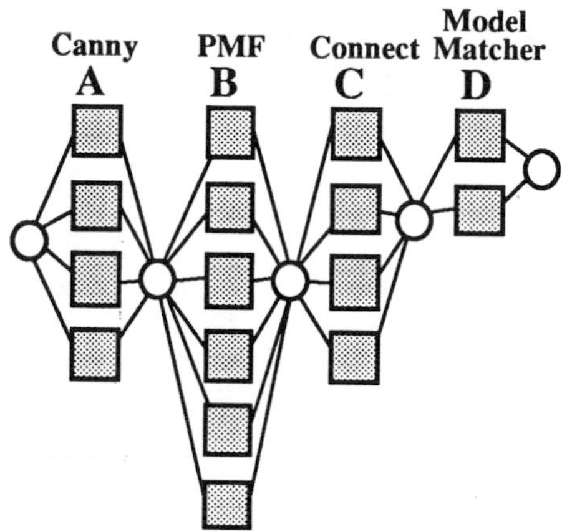

Fig. 4. Pipelining of Transputer Groups

These comments apply when general purpose processors are used at each stage in the pipeline, such that each processor is actually able to turn its hand to all processing stages. A very different picture emerges when we consider the use of specialised pipelined hardware which runs at video frame-rate. Such hardware offers extremely high performance for very specific tasks, of which convolution is a good example. Typical of this type of device is the *MaxVideo* range of modules manufactured by Datacube, Inc.

Whatever the hardware, pipelining also creates difficulties where feed-forward predictive techniques are used to reduce the computational load. It is difficult to see how results derived from image *N* could influence the processing of image *N+1*, if that image is already well through the pipeline.

3. Pilot Study

A pilot study (carried out in the Dept. of Computer Science at Sheffield University during 1986-87 with funding from GEC) implemented three of the algorithms at the front end of the *TINA* suite on a tranputer array. These are the *Canny* edge detector, the *PMF* stereo algorithm, and an edge-grouping stage. (These correspond to the 'Canny' 'PMF' and 'Connect' stages in the table of timings shown earlier). The system comprised a network of 8 T414 transputers each with 1 Mbyte of memory, with a Research Machines '*Nimbus*' PC as host. The algorithms were coded in *Occam II*, using the Inmos Transputer Development System (TDS).

3.1 Pilot Implementation of Canny

3.1.1 The *Canny* edge detector algorithm takes a 2-D intensity map as input, and identifies positions ('edgels') at which the intensity gradient is a local maximum. The algorithm has four stages: gaussian convolution, differentiation, non-maximal suppression, and thresholding with hysteresis.

3.1.2 Exploitation of parallelism within Canny

Canny is essentially a pixel based algorithm, which (apart from the thresholding stage) requires only local neighbourhood access to pixels. Therefore, a (1-D) spatial partitioning of the image was adopted. As with all algorithms which require access to pixel neighbourhoods, complications arise at the slice boundaries. In the case of the convolution and non-maximal suppression stages, these problems can be solved by supplying each transputer with input data which includes a few rasters adjacent to the slice for which the processor is responsible for generating output. That is, the input slice is bigger than the output slice.

In the case of the 'thresholding with hysteresis' stage, the problem is less easily solved. This stage is implemented by imposing two thresholds, T_l and T_h, on edge strength. Edges with strength above T_h are unconditionally accepted. Those with strength below T_l are rejected. Then for each marked edgel, a search for a neighbouring edgel with strength between T_l and T_h is made. If one is found, it is marked to be kept, and then in turn its neighbours are examined, and marked. Effectively this is a recursive line following algorithm. Finally, when all high contrast edges have been examined, (and lower contrast segments have been followed and marked), the thresholding stage terminates. All unmarked edges are then discarded. This algorithm allows isolated weak edgels to be discarded whilst allowing weak points in otherwise strong edges to survive.

Because of the slice partitioning of the image, provision must be made to allow the line follower to follow lines across slice boundaries. This is implemented by having each transputer request one raster from the transputers processing the neighbouring slices. The hysteresis procedure operates on the whole of the slice and each of these two rasters. At the end of the iteration, these two rasters (which may have been modified -- i.e. some edgels may have been marked) are returned to the appropriate transputers which compare them with the original rasters sent out. If they detect a new marked edge on this raster, they apply the line follower to it, which will mark the edgels comprising any line segment extending from it into the slice. In turn this may cause the slice edge raster to be modified again (if the line loops back towards the slice boundary), which will precipitate another iteration. These iterations continue until all transputers detect no change to the raster they previously transmitted. Typically the number of iterations will be one or two for nearly all images, unless a line wobbles across a slice boundary several times. In any event, each iteration consumes only a small amount of processing time as the line follower is being applied to only one or two points on the raster.

3.1.3 Pilot study -- Canny timings

Table 2 shows the time in seconds taken to execute Canny on a 256x256 image (similar to the one used for the timings in Table 1) using a network of 2, 4, or 8 transputers, both with and without load balancing. Due to the memory requirements of the program, no slice size adjustment was possible using two transputers, as each had sufficient memory to store only 128 rasters.

Condition	Number of Transputers		
	2	4	8
No load balancing	4.4	2.4	1.5
With load balancing	---	2.1	1.1

Table 2

3.2 Pilot Implementation of PMF

PMF is a stereo matching algorithm. Is takes as input a stereoscopic pair of edge maps, and attempts to match corresponding edgels in the two images. From the measured disparity of each matched pair, and the known camera geometry, a 3-D edge map is generated.

3.2.1 The PMF algorithm

The algorithm is not described in detail here. Essentially it consists of two distinct stages. The first establishes a matching strength for each potential match, computed from some measure of edge quality (for example, contrast strength), of every other potential match in the neighbourhood (typically about 15 pixels in diameter). Each contribution is weighted inversely by its distance away. This is the match generation phase, and is relatively fast, accounting for typically 5% of *PMF*'s total run time.

There follows the disambiguation phase which chooses the correct matches using a form of discrete relaxation. Matches which have the highest matching strength for both of the two image primitives forming them are immediately chosen as correct. To satisfy the uniqueness constraint, all other matches associated with these primitives are then discarded. Other matches that were not previously accepted or rejected are then considered again. Typically four or five iterations of this are needed to provide satisfactory disambiguation.

3.2.2 Exploitation of parallelism within PMF

PMF is essentially a local neighbourhood operation, albeit one in which communication with neighbouring pixels is frequent. The neighbourhood in the match generation phase is inherently anisotropic, as matches are sought only along corresponding horizontal rasters. These considerations again suggest the use of a 1-D spatial partitioning. Once again, problems arise at the slice boundaries.

Two methods of having the transputer acquire neighbouring rasters were investigated. These are the *slice overlap* method, and the *slice communication* method.

The simpler slice overlap approach requires each transputer to apply the match generation phase of *PMF* not only to the rasters within the slice to be processed, but also the *N* (typically 10) neighbouring rasters above and below. Thus, no transputer communication is required as all the data required for the disambiguation phase for the slice is already computed and held in memory. During the disambiguation phase, only the match strengths of edgels within the slice are altered, and matches are rejected or accepted accordingly. The match strengths of the neighbourhood rasters are not altered, nor are they rejected. This is not a true implementation of *PMF*, and it was anticipated that this could cause irregularities in the depth map at the slice boundaries. It transpired that although the disambiguation power was slightly reduced, the depth map was still of good quality, and not greatly different from the original serial implementation. Because there is no communication between the transputers, and hence no synchronisation, the time taken to process the slice varies considerably with complexity.

The slice communication method initially sends each transputer only those rasters within its slice. The match generation phase is then executed for each of the slice rasters. Before and after each iteration of the disambiguation phase, N neighbourhood rasters are copied from the neighbouring transputers. This approach ensures that matching strengths of the slice neighbour rasters are always updated and correct. This method gives a more satisfactory result than the slice overlap method. The timing variations are much less because the raster communication at the start of each iterations effectively forces the transputers to synchronise.

3.2.3 Load Balancing of PMF

A simple 1-D pre-partitioning of the data was performed by allocating roughly equal numbers of edgels to each transputer. This simple algorithm reduces the time taken by the slowest transputer by as much as 50%. A more complete algorithm to pre-partition the data would need to take into account other factors such as the distribution of edgels as well as their numbers, but no simple rule could be found which was effective. Further investigation might yield a more effective measure, but a requirement of the measure is that it is quick to compute, else more time could be lost than gained.

It would in principle be possible to re-partition the image after each iteration in the disambiguation phase. However, this re-distribution of rasters could be so substantial that large pieces of the image would need to be transmitted across several transputers. Instead, it was felt that load balancing would be best performed between images (assuming an image sequence), by controlling the initial distribution of the slices into the transputer array.

In this pilot study, only a single pair of images was available, so a re-partitioning of the *same* image was performed to simulate the effect of pre-partitioning the next image in the sequence.

3.2.4 Pilot Study -- PMF Timings

Table 3 shows timings for the same 256x256 image used in the pilot implementation of *Canny*, using 8 transputers.

It is particularly interesting to note how ineffective the pre-partitioned load balancing is (i.e. based on distributinq equal numbers of edgels to each transputer), as evidenced by the 3-15 second timing spread. The computational load of one raster of *PMF* depends not only on the number of edges but also their distribution. (A large number of edges close together take longer to disambiguate than the same number more evenly spread). This is reflected in the much wider range of slice sizes in the post-partitioned results.

3.3 Fixed versus Floating Point Arithmetic

This pilot study placed some emphasis on the avoidance of floating-point arithmetic by using scaled integer arithmetic wherever fractional accuracy was required. This was sensible in view of the fact that the T414 transputer has no floating point hardware. The T800 transputer being used in the new system can, remarkably, multiply two floating point numbers in less than one third the time taken to multiply two integers. This turns the tables -- it may be that in the future it should be integer arithmetic we should avoid!

	Pre-partitioned data		Post-partitioned data	
	Time	Slice sizes	Time	Slice sizes
Slice Overlap Method:	3-15	36,20,15,14,17,15,16,37	7-9	63,19,7,4,4,11,13,4
Slice Communication Method:	5.1-5.9	36,20,15,14,17,15,16,37	4.3-5.0	43,26,13,6,10,14,16,4

Table 3

3.4 Some comments on Occam II

The study did not find that the *occam* language is any better for program development than other languages with which the authors are familiar, such as *Pascal* and *C*, although the large number of compile time checks can reduce the number of potential runtime bugs. However, *occam* provides tighter control in a parallel processing environment and maps very efficiently onto the transputer instruction set.

Occam II has several shortcomings for the programmer used to procedural languages such as *C* and *Pascal*. Only the most basic data types are available: integers, booleans, and reals of different lengths, together with arrays of these types. Absent from occam are facilities such as pointers, record structures, and enumerated types. The transputer implementation of occam also requires static data allocation -- dynamically allocated structures such as record heaps or linked lists are not available. The lack of dynamic memory allocation further prohibits the use of recursion, requiring the programmer to resort to 'manual' simulations using loops and explicit parameter stacks.

Nonetheless, *occam* does offer considerable advantages to the parallel systems programmer. Networks of parallel processes can be set up very easily, and interconnected by 'occam channels' -- an abstraction of a serial inter-process communication channel which implements a *rendez-vous* between the two processes, and which corresponds directly to the behaviour of a transputer link. Networks of parallel processes can be implemented on a single transputer then later migrated onto an appropriate multi-processor network by the addition of a very small amount of configuration information, and without changes to the code itself.

4. MARVIN

4.1 Introduction

The work currently in progress as part of the *Fast Vision Project* in *AIVRU* centres around the construction of a hybrid computing engine containing both pipelined frame-rate hardware and an MIMD transputer array, with fast data paths between them. We call this machine *Marvin*.

4.2 Marvin Hardware Architecture

4.2.1 Hardware Components

The hardware architecture of the system is shown in *Fig.*

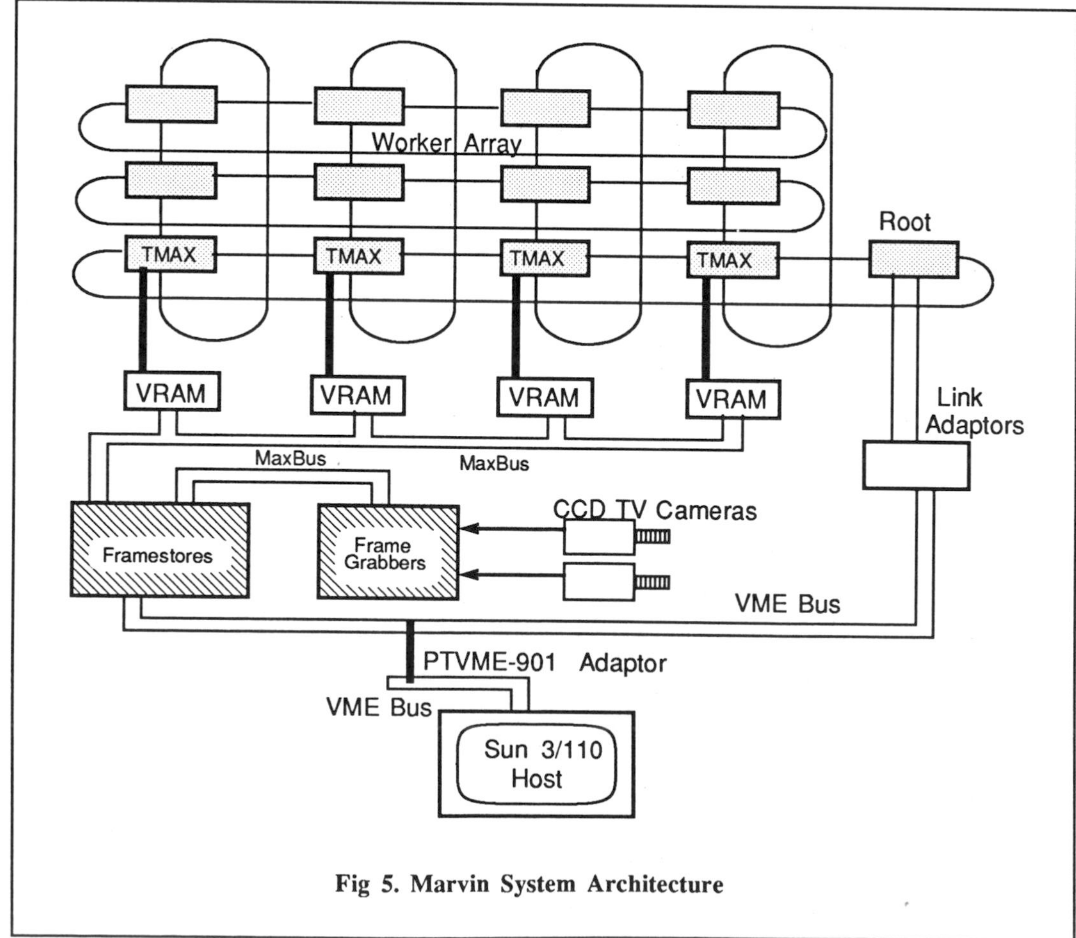

Fig 5. Marvin System Architecture

5. It consists of the following major components:

(1) A *Sun-3* workstation, referred to as the *host* machine.

(2) Datacube framestores and frame grabbers ('Digimax') providing for the acquisition, storage, and display of TV images using conventional interlaced TV timing. Two frame grabbers facilitate simultaneous acquisition of stereo images from two (synchronised) cameras.

(3) A network of transputers, referred to as *worker* processors, connected via Inmos serial links into a rectangular array. (The system will actually have an eight by three array. Only four columns are shown in the figure for simplicity). Each worker consists of a T800 floating point transputer with 2 Mbytes of memory. The workers in the bottom row of the array have an additional 1 Mbyte of video memory which is dual-ported between the transputer and the frame-rate digital video bus (MaxBus). In other respects they are functionally equivalent to the other rows. This bottom row are referred to as *TMAX* (Transputer-MAXbus) processors.

(4) One additional transputer module referred to as the *root* processor. This module is functionally equivalent to the workers and is special only as regards its strategic placement between the worker array and the host machine.

4.2.2 Datapaths

The datapaths within the system are as follows:

(1) Inmos serial links running at 20 Mbits per second provide interconnectivity within the worker array.

(2) The Datacube framestores are fully mapped into the Sun's address space via the VME (A24D16) bus. There are six 512x512 framestores, collectively providing 1.5 Mbytes of image storage.

(3) The framestores are dual ported onto a set of four *MaxBus* interconnects. Each interconnect provides an 8-bit parallel, byte-serial data stream at video frame rate. *MaxBus* is not a bus in the usual sense. It has no address lines, and no general arbitration scheme. Rather, it is a point-to-point data path. The spatial position of a pixel in the image is inferred from its temporal position in the data stream relative to frame sync, line sync, and pixel dot clock signals. The peak data rate (per *MaxBus*) is 10 Mbytes/sec; the average rate (over a 40 msec. frame) is 6.4 Mbytes/sec. The video memories on the *TMAX* processors are also dual-ported onto these *MaxBus* interconnects. Region-of-interest circuitry within this interface allows each *TMAX* to participate in *MaxBus* transfers (both in and out of the *TMAX* memories) within a software-selectable region of interest of the image. (See *Fig*. 6). This allows, for example, a pair of stereo images held in the framestores to be distributed across the row of *TMAX* processors within a single frame time. The architecture is clearly designed to exploit 1-D spatial parallelism.

(4) Two links on the root processor are connected to the Sun host via Inmos link adapters which are mapped into the Sun's VME address space. Each provides a serial byte stream between the Sun and the network of workers. The maximum data transfer rate acheivable here is limited by the rate at which the host 68020 processor can execute the loop which copies the bytes across, and is only about 120Kbyte/sec; however this is not crucial to the performance of the system as this data path is used only for initial downloading of code and for relatively short control messages.

4.2.3 Rationale

Our choice of network topology is made not as the result of any detailed study but simply because it is richly interconnected, regular, and (we believe) 'sensible'. We do not believe that there is some magic topology awaiting discovery which somehow resonates with the problem and offers supra-linear speedup. Of course, some topologies are demonstrably better than others, for specific applications. However, the adoption of a specialised topology is only appropriate if the process structure and patterns of dataflow are already well understood, and unlikely to change. Neither condition holds in our case. Indeed, the scenarios we envisage involve a variety of vision tasks, with different logical structures and operating on different time scales, executing on the

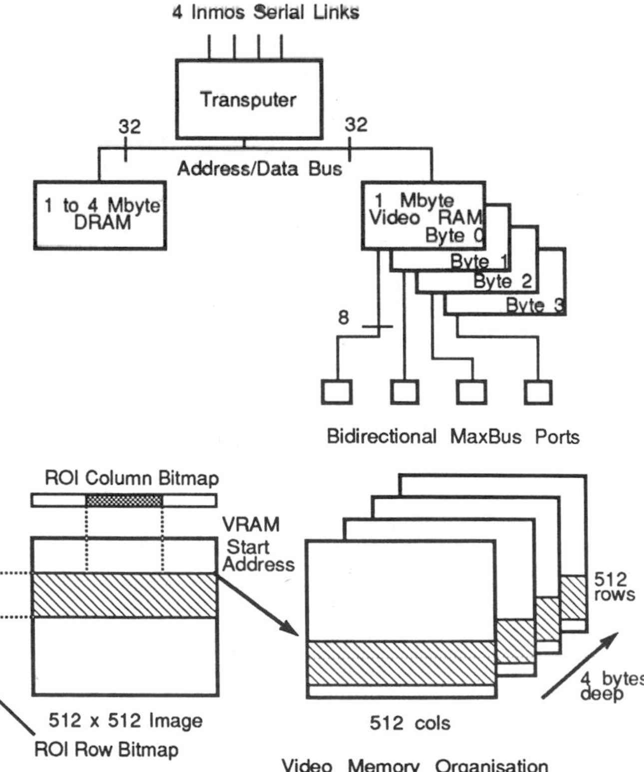

Fig 6. Architecture of TMAX Processor

a shared interrupt signal).

Resident on each TMAX is a server providing network-wide facilities. Any task on any processor may request operations from these servers. Such operations include region-of-interest acquisition, data plotting and low level control operations. Access to these operations is via a library of function calls.

The entire system is programmed in Parallel C and runs within a locally developed run-time environment [2]. The model of parallelism adopted is based upon Communicating Sequential Processes (CSP) where the system comprises a number of sequential processes executing concurrently and communicating via *channels* [3]. Our run-time environment allows all processes throughout the system to communicate with each other via *virtual* channels, allowing (addressed) messages to be exchanged between processes that have no knowledge of the hardware topology.

The root processor performs no vision processing but holds the highest levels of the *control architecture* and runs various servers to provide host facilities to the rest of the network.

Worker processors provide various repertoires of *resources* which are requested to do work by other processes in the control architecture, employing a *client-server* model. The development of this technique has greatly simplified the addition of new competences to the system.

Vision processing is broken down into a number of *tasks* each of which may itself be multi-threaded. (A "thread" is a lightweight process that may share code and data with other threads.) Numerous copies of the vision task bundles are distributed across the network. Each of these tasks receives a control message that contains all of the necessary run-time parameters for that task. This technique allows dynamic changes of operation in the system.

CONTROL ARCHITECTURE

System control is hierarchical and distributed. At any level in the hierarchy, the system comprises a small and manageable number of processes each with a well-defined interface, allowing simplified interaction within the system.

A simplified version of the control architecture is shown in figure 2 where higher levels of the hierarchy are towards the centre. The top levels of the control hierarchy are resident upon the root transputer. A control thread is created on the root processor for each sub-group of processors performing the vision processing allowing asynchronous control, if necessary. A central thread, the highest level in the hierarchy, controls the operation of the vision processes via these threads. Each vision process has no built-in knowledge of where its data comes from or where results are to be sent. The action of the machine is completely fluid, all dataflow being determined by the control architecture at run-time.

Each vision process communicates with its (superior) control thread upon completion with a small reply packet. The controller then uses this information to instruct the task performing the next processing stage. In this way the various tasks are kept independent from each other as much as possible.

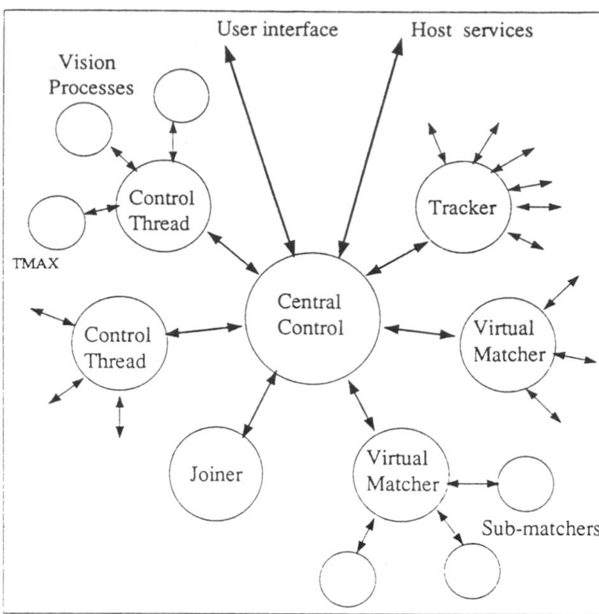

Figure 2 Control Architecture

Some of the tasks require asynchronous control operations. In this case, control information is received by a separate thread running within the task, allowing control information to be asynchronously decoupled from data flow.

The MARVIN Software Infrastructure [2] allows us to ignore the physical communication paths between tasks and the physical interconnections between processors, allowing any *logical* topology to be chosen and changed dynamically.

Figure 2 highlights the principle of the distributed control paradigm. It is easy to see that control of a parallel system is made simple and "open" using this technique as opposed to, say, a completely centralised or data driven organisation. The user may then interface with the system via the top level of control.

RECOVERY OF 3D SCENE GEOMETRY

This vision system is derived from the AIVRU TINA system [4] which employs edge based stereo triangulation as a basis for three dimensional description.

We employ spatial parallelism by dividing both left and right images into 8 horizontal slices approximately 64 rasters wide. A small overlap (2 rasters) between adjacent slices is incorporated to avoid boundary effects and simplify the processes of recombination that occur later. There is a limit to how thin the image slices can be made without adversely effecting the reliability of the stereo matching process. However, potential does exist for further subdivision of images in the horizontal direction with a small increase in the complexity of the stereo matching algorithm.

Each image slice pair is acquired simultaneously into an allotted TMAX, controlled remotely by the control task on the root processor. The pair of transputers vertically adjacent to the TMAX are used to process the left and right image slices in parallel. The size of the right image slice is adjusted to take into account the warping effect of the rectification of edge locations into a parallel camera geometry. This is determined from a copy of the calibration data resident upon each processor (this may be updated dynamically to allow for updated calibration estimates to be incorporated).

Obtaining Edges

Edges are obtained to sub-pixel acuity from grey-level images by a single scale high frequency application of the Canny edge operator [5]. The high frequency operator used here employs a gaussian mask of sigma 1.0. Convolution is computationally expensive but fortunately the two dimensional gaussian smoothing can be achieved through two 1 dimensional convolutions (i.e. first along the rows and then the columns). However, it is our preferred intention, in the longer term, to use specialised convolution boards directly on the MAXBus video stream.

Each Canny process obtains the raw image slice from a TMAX with a simple parameterised function call. The Canny task processing the left image slice packs the resultant edgemap into a data packet and sends it to a collection thread running within the right Canny task. Upon completion, the right Canny task and the collection thread rendezvous and send a reply to the control thread, on the root processor. Following detection, edge strings are formed by linking edge pixels (edgels) into chains of connected components.

Stereo Matching

We use a locally developed algorithm, PMF [4], for stereo matching. In PMF, matches between edges from the left and right images are preferred if they mutually support each other through a disparity gradient constraint and if they satisfy a number of higher level grouping constraints, most notably uniqueness, ordering (along epipolars) and figural continuity.

The PMF task runs on the processor that now holds both edgemaps (the one that held the right image slice). The edge structures are organised so as to make both spatial location and connectivity explicit. To avoid major data transfer and recomputation the PMF control packet (sent from the root) simply contains a pointer to the edge structures in the memory shared by the threads.

Geometrical Elements

As well as being matched, edge strings are processed to recover descriptions of the two dimensional geometrical elements they may represent. This process is currently limited to straight line descriptions though in previous implementations we have also recovered circular descriptions, and are currently developing methods to identify ellipses. The algorithm uses a recursive fit and segment strategy. Segmentation points are included when the underlying edge string deviates from the current line fit.

Robustness of the system (and its speed) relies upon the fact that a heuristic search strategy is used to identify those regions of strings/segmented sub-strings that are most amenable to straight line fit. The actual fit is computed by orthogonal regression.

Given descriptions of the two dimensional geometry (in a single view) and the results of the application of the stereo algorithm to the underlying edge strings, it is possible to recover three dimensional geometrical descriptions. Disparity values can be obtained along the 2D geometrical descriptors for each matched edge point. A second stage of 2D fitting (in arc length against disparity) computes the fit in disparity space. Finally, disparity data is projected into the world using transformations based upon the camera calibration. The sequence of operations taking place on each pair of processors is shown in figure 3.

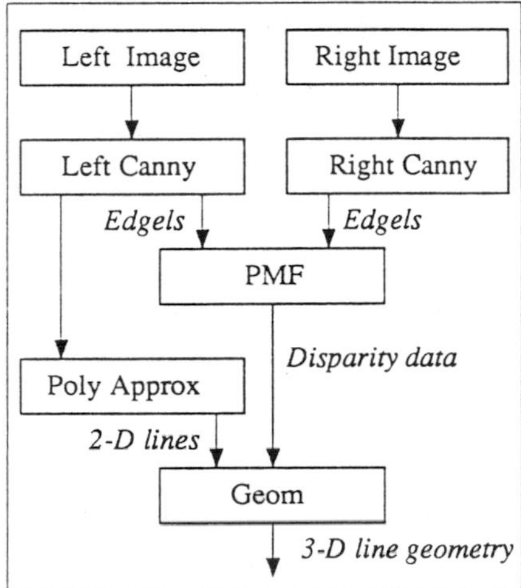

Figure 3. Data flow for recovery of scene geometry for each image pair slice

At this point in the processing, the 3D geometry from the current scene is spatially distributed across a number of processors. This data needs to be integrated into one data set as if it came from a single processor. A Joiner task (figure 5) communicates with all of the 3D geometry tasks, receiving both 2D and 3D information. These descriptions are optimally combined where valid 2D connectivity is identified between image slices. Upon completion, the Joiner returns the integrated geometry to the main control task resident on the root processor. The controller then forwards this information to a number (defined at run-time) of model matcher tasks distributed throughout the network.

Figure 4 shows an example of the 3D geometry recovered from a scene, projected over a ground plane.

One important consideration in this parallel vision system is that the computation of descriptions higher in the processing chain is dependent upon large amounts of previously computed data. For example the 3D data structure is dependent upon both 2D polygonal approximations and the matched edges. Accordingly, the use of the traditional processor farm is inappropriate as the amount of data flow required would make it unusable.

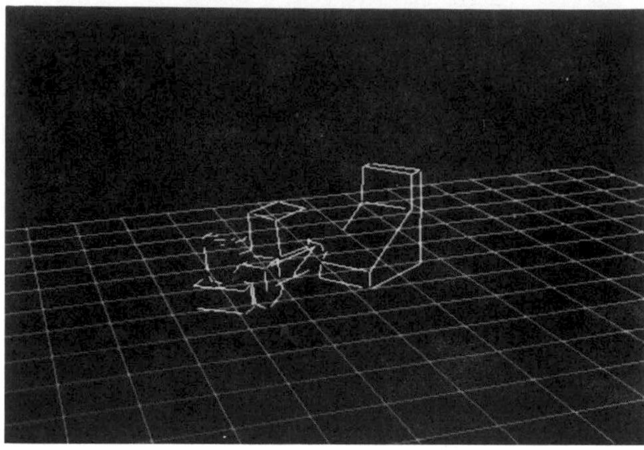

Figure 4. 3D Geometry with ground plane

MODEL MATCHING

The model matcher is able to give accurately the position and rotation of modelled objects (defined in terms of their 3D geometrical primitives) from the geometry recovered by the earlier processing stages.

The adopted strategy [6] is to base initial matching hypotheses on congruencies identified between 3D scene descriptions and a chosen subset of features from the model. Following hypotheses, potential matches are ranked on the basis of the extent to which further support exists for the three dimensional transformation they implicitly represent (between model and scene). The algorithm exploits ideas from several sources: the use of a partial pairwise geometrical relationships table to represent object model and scene description from Grimson and Lozano-Perez [7], the least squares computation of transformations by exploiting the quaternion representation for rotations from Faugeraus et al [8], and the use of focus features from Bolles et al [9].

Whilst exhaustive search for maximal cliques of consistent scene and model descriptions is avoided, the algorithm still requires a considerable amount of searching to be performed. Furthermore, the computational expense of the algorithm (which increases roughly linearly with the scene complexity) is replicated for each modelled object when implemented on a sequential machine.

The most obvious way to exploit the architecture of MARVIN in the model matching phase is to run multiple instances of the model matcher on different processors, thereby searching the same data for different models. This limits the parallelism to the number of models being searched for and is still too computationally time-consuming. A further degree of parallelism is obtained by employing a multi-level control architecture within the matching process itself. The model matching process is decomposed into separate searches for feature sets from the modelled object in the spirit of *characteristic views* [10]. A characteristic view in this scenario is deemed to consist of a set of geometrical features of the object that are consistent with a range of closely related viewpoints of the object. This, in effect, allows the distribution of the search tree over a number of processors.

To realise this in a consistent manner, a *virtual matcher* is used. The virtual matcher receives a control message describing the name of the model to become its responsibility and a list of processors available for use (allocated at run-time, typically 6) which have a resident matching task which will be instructed to search the scene geometry for a particular characteristic view of the object. The virtual matcher obtains all relevant information about the model (from files on the host machine) and the current geometry (from the Joiner) and distributes this information to its subordinates. The virtual matcher retains a precomputed grasp position, specifying a pick-up position in the coordinate frame of the model description. Each subordinate matcher attempts to locate a *subset* of the model features.

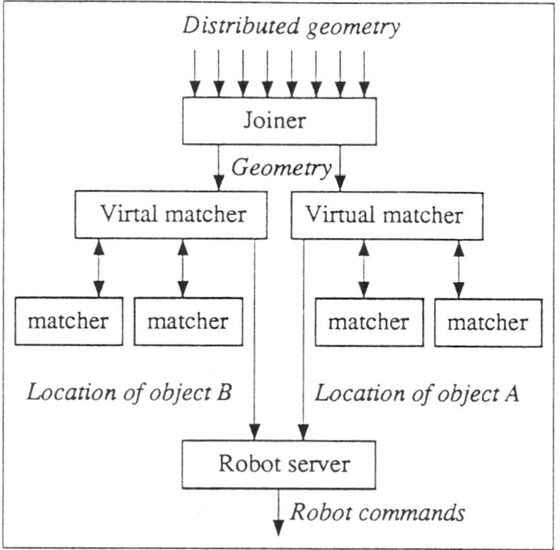

Figure 5 Geometry joining and object location for two objects (A & B) each with two subordinate matchers

Upon completion, the virtual matcher chooses the best match obtained from all of its subordinates and feeds the object location and grasp position (now transformed into the world coordinate frame) up to the next higher level of the control hierarchy. A virtual matcher is used for each model to be located in the scene with the resources of the entire network being shared between them.

This technique allows a search to be made for multiple objects (with no extra time penalty) in a consistent, flexible and highly efficient manner (figure 5). Figure 6 shows the reprojection of three matched models onto the original image along with their grasp positions.

Figure 6. Matched models

CONTROLLING THE ROBOT ARM

A UMI robot controlled by an IBM PC is used to perform the pick and place. The IBM PC is in turn connected to a SUN 3 workstation over a serial line. MARVIN may talk to any SUN in our network by means of the UNIX socket mechanism. Facilities provided by our run-time environment allow any task on any transputer to open and communicate with sockets to the outside world [2].

Each virtual model matcher returns a rotation and position of the relevant object. This information is used to transform a precomputed grasp position from the model coordinate frame to the world coordinate frame.

This information is sent over a socket to a server controlling the robot (figure 5) on a remote machine according to an agreed protocol, specifying the name of the model, where to pick it up and what to do with it. MARVIN need have no concern with solving the inverse kinematics, camera to robot transformations and path planning in order to pick the objects from the workspace, these issues are computed in different areas of the *computer* network. An example of the robot picking up a widget is shown in figure 7.

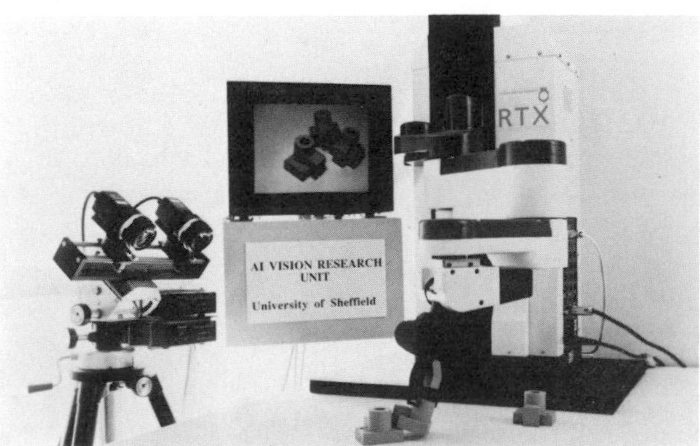

Figure 7. Robot picking up a widget

The *hand-eye* calibration (the transformation between camera space and robot space) is obtained by using TINA to locate a flag held in the gripper of the robot arm. This is repeated numerous times in various positions of the robot workspace. A least-squares method is used to obtain the best transformation.

CONCLUSIONS

A multiprocessor transputer-based vision system has been described. We have employed two different techniques to utilise the parallel hardware. The recovery of the scene geometry employs *spatial* parallelism by decomposing the image pairs into horizontal image slices. This is a natural approach as depth data is obtained by matching elements between left and right images. The requirement to transfer image data quickly into the heart of the network is overcome by means of the MAXbus and TMAX cards, making the architecture of MARVIN well suited to exploiting spatial parallelism.

The model matching process is parallelised on a *featural* basis, using a hierarchical control strategy. Our run-time environment provides a suitable framework for integrating processing modules by allowing processors to provide various resources to be utilised by any other requesting processes.

Using MARVIN we have a system that in a former incarnation took well over one hour to to locate *one* object, now runs in around 10 seconds, locating *numerous* objects, making it far more practicable to perform interactive "what-if" experiments and thus bringing this level of visual competence ever closer to the industrial domain.

A more detailed breakdown of processing timings for a typical scene is shown in table 1. The two vision processes which have benefited most from being parallelised are the Canny and model matching stages, the two most costly tasks on a sequential machine.

Over the entire sequence of operations from grabbing the image to obtaining four matched models we achieve an average performance per processor of over 80%. This figure relates the estimated time taken by one processor to the time taken by 24 processors.

Building a parallel vision system on a multi-processor architecture has usefully demonstrated the applicability of parallel techniques to machine vision. Designing the machine around a set of general purpose processors such as the transputer, rather than dedicated hardware has given us a high performance machine whilst retaining flexibility.

All knowledge gained from experiences with MARVIN will be highly relevant in the building of a next-generation machine which will utilise the forthcoming H1 transputer and further frame-rate hardware enabling us to start to approach real-time processing with a general purpose machine.

Work is in hand to implement a parallel feature tracker on MARVIN which will follow (at near real-time) features identified as being those from a modelled object. This beacon tracking is to provide some of the information required to enable our in-house vehicle to navigate through an unknown environment.

Vision Process	Time (ms)
Canny	5500
PMF	1000
2D Geometry	100
3D Geometry	200
Geometry joining	100
Model Matching	1600
System Overheads	1000
Total	~10000

Table 1. Processing times

REFERENCES

1. **Brown C. and Rygol M.** (1989), "Marvin : Multiprocessor Architecture for Vision", *Proceedings of the 10th Occam User Group Technical Meeting*

2. **Brown C. and Rygol M.** (1990), "An Environment for the Development of Large Applications in Parallel C", *Transputer Applications '90*

3. **Hoare C.A.R.** (1985), Communicating Sequential Processes, *Prentice-Hall International.*

4. **Porrill J, Pollard S B, Pridmore T P, Bowen J, Mayhew J E W, and Frisby J P** (1987) "TINA: The Sheffield AIVRU vision system", *IJCAI 9, Milan 1138-1144.*

5. **Canny J** (1986), "A computational approach to edge detection", *Trans. Patt. Anal. & Mach. Intell, 679-698, PAMI-8.*

6. **Pollard S B, Porrill J, Mayhew J E W and Frisby J P** (1986) "Matching geometrical descriptions in three space", *Image and Vision Computing, Vol 2, No 5 (1987) 73-78.*

7. **Grimson W.E.L. and T. Lozano-Perez** (1984), "Model based recognition from sparse range or tactile data", *Int. J. Robotics Res. 3(3): 3-35.*

8. **Faugeras O.D. and M. Hebert** (1985), "The representation, recognition and positioning of 3D shapes from range data", *Int. J. Robotics Res*

9. **Bolles R.C., P. Horaud and M.J. Hannah** (1983), "3DPO: A three dimensional part orientation system", *Proc. IJCAI 8, Karlshrue, West Germany, 116-120.*

10. **Freeman H. and Chakravarti I.** (1980), "The Use of Characteristic Views in the Recognition of Three-Dimensional Objects", *Pattern Recognition in Practice, pp 277-288, Gelsema and Kanal (Eds), North-Holland.*

III 2.5D SKETCH PROJECT

Introduction by the Editors

A THE GRANT PROPOSAL (Written 1983)

1 OBJECTIVES

The objective of the 2.5D Sketch Project is to develop methods for deriving from the depth map delivered by the PMF Project a representation of the 3D structure of the visible surfaces in the scene. The 2.5D Sketch is conceived here as an intermediate-level representation serving as the input representation for the 3D Model-Based Vision Project as well as being able to support in its own right various lower-level tasks such as some forms of trajectory planning, robot guidance, grasp planning etc.

It is proposed that the output representation of the 2.5D Sketch Project be a relational structure describing the vertices, edges, and faces in the scene and their adjacency and connectivity relationships. This structure is in some ways analogous to the winged edge shape representation used by Baumgart (1972) to describe polyhedral objects. That representation is basically a pointer-record structure in which the nodes/records correspond to the elements (vertices, edges, regions) and the arcs/pointers express the adjacency and connectivity relationships. Such a relational structure is extendable, and quite general; it is envisaged that the records will contain fields containing not only the geometrical coordinates of the entities, but also, as far as can be recovered, both their qualitative and quantitative 3D descriptions. It would be premature to attempt to specify further the details of the representation to be used for the 2.5D Sketch Project, and wherever the term 'winged edge' is used hereafter it is to be understood as a generic label rather than a commitment to a precise form of relational structure.

2 LOCATION AND DESCRIPTION OF SURFACE DEPTH AND SURFACE ORIENTATION DISCONTINUITIES

The basis of the proposed 2.5D scene description is the discovery and identification of the surface regions bounded by depth and surface orientation discontinuities. The labelling and classification of surface orientation and depth discontinuities is a necessary precursor to grouping the scene into regions. An important stage in the labelling and description of the regions in the scene is to identify and label the ground plane. If the stereo camera geometry is known (as it will be) the labelling of the ground contact edges of the objects in the scene will in general be relatively straightforward.

The information delivered by PMF is local, sparse and noisy. Its range data output is tied to image description entities such as zero crossing segments, and although in many cases these derive from the projection of surface orientation discontinuities, boundaries and occlusions, the sign of the edge, and the direction of the occluding-occluded relationship is not explicitly represented by PMF. There are several strategies for the recovery of this information which the 2.5D Sketch Project will evaluate.

One possibility is to use a stage of surface interpolation either directly integrated with the stereo correspondence process or else operating over its output. Ideally the interpolation process should be self-monitoring and break at surface depth and orientation discontinuities, otherwise a subsequent 'edge detection' process is required to detect and label the surface depth and orientation discontinuities. It is anticipated that surface interpolation will be a substantial part of the 2.5D Sketch Project with detailed proposals described below.

Alternatively, because the profile of the local stereo disambiguating support (particularly if augmented by some form of grey level correlation working within the constraints of edge based stereo; see the PMF Project) will often constrain the choice of the sidedness of occlusions, it should be possible to obviate the necessity of an independent stage of surface interpolation in many cases. And in others, this information could be used to help direct the interpolation.

Another possibility is to exploit the propagation of 3D information from cues in the 2D image or primal sketch features as in classical line labelling schemes (Kanade, 1981; Draper, 1981; for a review, Binford, 1982) though the resolution of the low level visual processing needed for such a scheme may be prohibitive.

A robust system will probably need the intelligent conjunction of all these and possibly other strategies to recover surface shape descriptions. It will also probably need to incorporate information about the illumination characteristics of the scene, eg for the principled treatment of specularities and shadows.

3 QUALITATIVE META-FEATURE DESCRIPTIONS

It is the intention of the proposal to develop procedures to recover 3D features and their relationships from the depth map of the scene using only image/depth map descriptive processes and without recourse to higher level semantics. The obvious basis for the relationship between features is their connectivity, eg surface regions connected across edges derived from surface orientation discontinuities, vertices connected along such edges etc. It is likely however that other 3D topological relationships will also prove useful descriptors. For example, if an object contains a row of holes within a face then the colinear grouping over the individual image features provides a gestalt that can be exploited in the model invocation and recognition process. We thus propose that if a global feature can be reliably and cheaply computed from the depth map, and if it is a potentially useful index into the 3D model catalogue capable of guiding the initial stages of the recognition process, then such gestalts should be part of the 2.5D Sketch description. Typically such meta-features would be colinearities and parallel lines but symmetries might also be included as might simple prototypical shapes. These meta-features could theoretical and practical .... is extremely important for the health of the programme overall .... it must not become the poor relation" (Main Report, 1983, Vol 1, Section 8.3.5). In the field of the present proposal, concentration on particular applications at this early stage could easily stifle progress by generating application-specific strategies. That said, however, it should also be emphasised that the proposal is *not* directed towards the design of a 'completely general purpose visual system', which would of course be a quite premature goal at the present time. Rather, the proposal is solidly based on substantial recent achievements by various members of the club in the domain of general purpose 3D vision from optic flow and stereoscopic cues, and the domain of model-based interpretation. This prior work, which has obvious potential application to vehicle guidance and robot assembly tasks in many industrial settings, augurs well for the 3D IKBS-VISION Project spawning a demonstrator project in 3-5 years time.

3.3 Relationship to Other Research Programmes

Any worthwhile club is composed of like-minded members sharing certain fundamental preconceptions about how to proceed with their cooperative endeavour. The 3D IKBS-VISION proposal is fortunate to have just that basis, while being large enough to avoid the obvious danger of becoming in-grown. In short, the proposal is supported by a coherent and manageable team, spread widely over various organisations but nevertheless able to work well together, as demonstrated by the successful initial preparation of the 3D IKBS-VISION proposal and by its recent endorsement by the members of the club (no mean achievement given their wide distribution, geographically and academically). We strongly urge that this identity be maintained and exploited by the Alvey Directorate.

3.4 The Two Consortia Comprising the IKBS Research Theme

It is proposed that the two consortia will address problems in acquiring depth information from optical flow and stereoscopic disparity cues. The advantage of using these cues is that they are general purpose in character and that internationally accredited expertise exists in the club in both fields. Each of these topics is the subject of well advanced plans for the creation of academic/industrial research consortia, whose scope includes the utilisation of depth information for 3D model invocation and verification.

A basic objective of the optical flow and stereopsis proposals is to compute a type of 3D scene description that has come to be known in the field of image understanding as the '2.5D Sketch'. This is a viewer-centred representation making explicit the disposition, orientations and distances of visible surfaces in the scene (a meaning that is not to be confused with other uses of this term). Thus the 2.5D Sketch is conceived here as an intermediate-level representation serving as the database for subsequent 3D model invocation as well as being a representation able to support in its own right various lower-level tasks such as some forms of trajectory planning, robot guidance, grasp planning etc (see later). The attempt to build a 2.5D Sketch distinguishes the present proposal from those which proceed directly and solely from 2D image descriptions to 3D models.

The desirability for a wide range of tasks (though not all of course) of an intermediate level representation expressing the depth relationships of visible surfaces is widely recognised in AI laboratories in the USA working on 3D machine vision. As the objects of interest are usually volumetric in character, it makes obvious sense in the design of guidance and manipulation systems capable of dealing with them to provide access to a database that describes scene surfaces in terms of their spatial distributions in 3D. Building such a representation using optical flow and stereoscopic cues has demonstrably paid handsome dividends in biological vision systems, greatly facilitating, for example, the identification of figure from ground. Using a 2.5D Sketch based on these cues should enable better exploitation of the strategy of 'segmentation by recognition', because of the opportunities presented for object recognition via the identification of clusters of 3D surface features characteristic of target objects (see later).

3.5 Constituent Projects of the Consortium Working from Stereoscopic Cues

This consortium [whose work is the subject of this book] proposes three projects, integrated around the theme of building a real-time (<1 sec) stereo processor capable of supporting the creation of 3D surface representations suitable for equipping a robot assembly task workstation with useful 3D visual competences, including the capacity for 3D model invocation and verification. The three projects are as follows:

The PMF Project is based on a computational theory of stereopsis developed over a number of years at Sheffield by Mayhew and Frisby, and recently extended by Stephen Pollard, one of their postgraduates holding a CASE award in collaboration with Margaret McCabe of GEC. This work has produced a simple but highly effective stereo correspondence algorithm called PMF. The underlying principles on which PMF is based are described [in Section II of this book], which also provides illustrations of its performance. The PMF Project is also directed at developing special purpose hardware for implementing PMF.

The 2.5D Sketch Project has as its overall goal the development of ways of using the pointilliste range data delivered by PMF to create descriptions about the nature of the surface boundaries and surface regions that are present in the scene (e.g. methods of labelling depth edges as concave, convex, occluding, extremal, etc. and regions as cylindrical, planar, synclastic, antisynclastic, etc.) This work is central to the objective of building a 2.5D Sketch representation.

The 3D Model-Based Vision Project will be concerned with the utilisation of the 3D scene geometry delivered by the 2.5D Sketch Project for the purposes of 3D model invocation and verification. The distinguishing characteristic of this work will be the development of methods to match 3D structures extracted from the depth map with 3D structures in an object model catalogue (not, as in almost all current object recognition schemes, to match 2D structures extracted from the image with 2D virtual image structures predicted from the object model and imaging geometry).

There will be two main groups involved on the 3D Model-Based Vision Project. The one at Sheffield will be led by Mayhew who proposes to use object models comprised of a 3D relational structure of clusters of 3D surface features that remain stable over a restricted but nevertheless reasonably broad range of viewpoints of a given 3D object. This representation should facilitate the indexing of the model catalogue and the partitioning of the matching task.

Table 1: Participants of the Consortium

GEC Hirst Research Centre
Wembley
Dr Margaret M McCabe*
Dr Harit Trevedi
Mr Ian Graydon
*Dr Bernard Buxton**
Dr Sheelagh A Lloyd*
Dr Jan Wiejak*
Mr Brendan Ruff

IBM UK Ltd Scientific Centre
Winchester
Mr Rodger Hake*
Dr Michael Gray
Dr John Knapman
Dr Rodney Cuff

AI Vision Research Unit
University of Sheffield
*Prof John E W Mayhew**
*Dr Stephen B Pollard**
*Dr Chris R Brown**
*Prof John P Frisby**
Dr John Porrill
Dr Tony Pridmore

Department of Artificial Intelligence
University of Edinburgh
Mr Robin Popplestone*
Dr Robert B Fisher
Mr Jonathan C Aylett
Mrs Pat Fothergill
Dr Mark J L Orr

Department of Computer Science
University of Edinburgh
*Dr Andrew Blake**
Dr Gavin Brelstaff
Dr Andrew Zisserman

Centre for Research in Perception & Cognition
University of Sussex
*Prof H Christopher Longuet-Higgins**

Individuals denoted with * were either cited in the research grant proposal &/or closely involved in its planning. All others were recruited once the proposal was awarded or deployed to work on it by their companies. Individuals who were on the project throughout its life are shown in italics.

Dr Buxton was closely involved in his role as coordinator of the optic flow consortium in the IKBS Image Interpretation Research Theme. Dr Brelstaff was a CASE student supported by IBM UK Scientific Centre.

The other group is at Edinburgh and will be led by Robin Popplestone[2] who is presently developing the robot language RAPT-2 under a contract from Rutherford Laboratory. One important goal of this work is to equip RAPT-2 with sufficient visual competence for 3D model invocation and verification such that visually acquired data can be used in programming a sequence of actions to cause a robot to unpack, say, a motor from a box and install it in a machined location.

3.6 Participants of the Consortium

See Table 1 above and also the frontispiece photograph.

3.7 Criteria for Evaluation

A document entitled *An Outline of a Strategy for Pattern Analysis Within the Alvey Programme* written by Julian Ullman proposed various criteria against which proposals of the present type should be evaluated. We believe that the 3D IKBS-VISION proposal successfully meets these criteria, as follows:

[*Warning Note from the Editors.* There is probably no limit to what some people will say to get their proposals funded.]

1 *ENHANCEMENT OF UK COMPETENCE & COMPETITIVENESS*? Yes.

2 *WIN PLACES FOR UK IN WORLD MARKETS?* The proposal is concerned with 'basic research' and hence is not directed at developing a market product in the short term. Nevertheless, industrial collaborators believe there should be medium-term market benefits.

3 *WELL-BALANCED PARTNERSHIP WITH OTHER WORK IN IT?* The proposers believe that the work is timely in terms of other work in Information Technology, such as that concerned with parallel processors, the development of robot object level languages etc.

4 *VIABLE TRAJECTORY TO THE MARKET PLACE?* See comments under 2 above. The key feature here is the keen involvement of large UK firms who look forward to marketing applications in the medium-term.

5 *A GENUINELY COLLABORATIVE CONSORTIUM?* The programme has a clear integrating theme. Evidence that participants really do want to work together is the series of fruitful meetings that has already taken place in drawing up the proposal. Also, certain participants are already involved in collaborative research (e.g. via CASE studentships, shared publications).

6 *EVIDENCE OF TECHNICAL COMPETENCE?* The records of the participants should be used to form an opinion on this.

---

[2] Popplestone left the project about the time that the grant was approved, whereupon Pat Ambler (later to become Pat Fothergill) and Bob Fisher took over his role. Fothergill later left the project on her move to Aberdeen.

7 *COMPLEMENTARY CONSTITUENTS OF THE CONSORTIUM?* The proposal blends together diverse competences in optic flow, stereopsis, hardware, image processing, artificial intelligence, robot objective languages, mathematics, psychophysics, and industrial machine vision applications.

8 *MANAGEMENT & ADMINISTRATION?* McCabe and Frisby have been nominated as Industrial and Academic Coordinators respectively of the consortium as a whole, with Lloyd leading the PMF Project, Blake leading the 2.5D Sketch Project, and Mayhew leading the 3D Model based Vision Project. It is envisaged that each project leader will be responsible for drawing up a detailed research plan in conjunction with the Consortium Coordinators. The latter will between them provide an overall organisational structure to ensure good integration of research at different sites, as well as serving as the interface between the Consortium and the Alvey Directorate.

3.8 Concluding Remarks

The targets of the consortium are substantial but not unrealistic. They are founded on a great deal of prior work at Sheffield, Edinburgh, Sussex, IBM and GEC, and they bring together expertise in mathematics, optimisation techniques, VLSI hardware, robot programming languages, industrial machine vision applications, and computational and psychophysical studies of human vision. A great deal of effort will be necessary to attain the targets specified but we think that effort worthwhile, both in terms of the importance of the fundamental scientific issues and in terms of the potential benefits to UK industry.

4 LINKS TO OTHER IKBS CONSORTIA

The *3D IKBS-VISION PROJECT* in fact spawned two[3] large consortia which together were entitled the *Alvey IKBS Image Interpretation Research Theme*. Its Industrial and Academic Coordinators were respectively Margaret McCabe (GEC) and Frisby.

The consortium dealt with in this book took as its starting point the recovery of useful 3D scene geometry from single pairs of stereoscopic images. Its Coordinator was Mayhew and its participating institutions were the universities of Edinburgh, Sheffield and Sussex, GEC (Hirst Research Centre, Wembley), and the IBM UK Ltd Scientific Centre (Winchester).

The Coordinator of the second consortium was Bernard Buxton (GEC). It had the same general goals but started from an analysis of optic flow. Its participating institutions were Queen Mary College (London University), GEC, BAEd and Plessey. Much of the work carried out by GEC in this consortium is presented in the recent book by Murray and Buxton (1990), also published by MIT Press.

It was intended that the two consortia should be run largely independently, but with coordinators attending the major meetings of each consortium to seize on any possibilities for integration that might arise. This is in fact what happened and there is no doubt that various contacts between the two consortia were helpful in developing the research.

[3]There was a third consortium mentioned in the original proposal, to be led by Andrew Sleigh of RSRE Malvern, but its participants soon withdrew to join with other more related work funded by Alvey's Man-Machine Interface Directorate.

5 ACKNOWLEDGEMENTS

As noted at the outset, the research reported in this book was funded by the U.K.'s Alvey Programme in advanced information technology. The latter was launched in the early 1980's as one response to the perceived threat to UK manufacturing industry of Japan's announcement of its intention to build Fifth Generation Computers. Alvey had four branches: the present consortium fell under the *Intelligent Knowledge Based Systems Directorate* led by Dr David Thomas. His enthusiastic support for the consortium, coupled with his vast expertise in finding ways through research funding bureacracies, had much to do with the research getting underway soon after the Alvey Programme received final government approval. We are very grateful for his help.

We are also grateful for the role played by Brian Oakley, Director of the Alvey Programme, who at all times was most supportive of the consortium.

The *IKBS Architecture Study* (which invited Mayhew to write his 3D IKBS-VISION PROJECT proposal) was chaired by John Taylor, co-chaired by Karen Sparck-Jones, and coordinated by Bill Sharpe and Gareth Williams. All members of the consortium have good reason to thank those individuals, and indeed the many others involved in preparation of the *Study*. The reason is that their work coincided with the early stages of the work of the Alvey Committee. This meant that when the Alvey Programme was approved, the existence of the *Study* enabled the IKBS Directorate of Alvey to get off to a flying start, the main outlines of its mission statement being already in place. This in turn led to the work reported here being started about a year or so ahead of the other computer vision projects funded by Alvey under its Man-Machine Interface Directorate.

GEC and IBM continue to be close collaborators of AIVRU. We are exceedingly appreciative of the medium to long-term perspective they have shown in supporting our research over the past 6 years. In IBM Dr Rodger Hake and Dr John Knapman have been outstanding in their backing. In GEC, we wish to note the first-rate support from Prof Dennis Scotter (Manager of GEC's Long Range Research Laboratory) and Prof Cyril Hilsum (GEC's Director of Research), but most of all the tireless support of Bernard Buxton[4].

We would also like to mention to mention the special role played by Prof Christopher Longuet-Higgins. He agreed early on to act as a consultant for the consortium. This led him to attend all major meetings, during which he injected his usual large number of constructive and insightful remarks. During this period he solved an important problem in structure-from-motion (included here as paper [30]).

Finally, this book would not have emerged without the assistance of Grace Crookes, AIVRU's secretary funded by

[4] Bernard Buxton (of GEC) was seminal figure throughout. Indeed, he and Mayhew recollect making a decision to get the whole project underway in Buxton's kitchen late one night in 1982, though doubt must be cast on the reliability of that recollection given the quantities consumed.

Alvey to assist with coordination of the consortium. We thank her for exceptional competence and patience, both during the Alvey period and subsequently. It has been said that trying to organise academics is rather like trying to herd cats. If anyone is in good position to judge the truth of that remark it is Grace.

6 SUMMING UP

An unusual feature of this book is that each of the subsequent sections starts with the original grant proposal. This is followed by scientific papers recording what emerged. This enables readers to form their own judgements on the success or otherwise of the Consortium in meeting its objectives. (Readers who are not so inclined can of course skip the introductory sections.) We will not therefore attempt an overall review of the scientific content ourselves although we do provide commentaries at the end of each section that highlight certain aspects of the work. Here we simply record some of our general reactions to the Consortium and its work.

***Amazing That It Happened At All**
Given the current European science climate, in which many large industrial/academic consortia exist funded by ESPRIT, it is easy to forget that the consortium way of financing U.K. academics is relatively novel. Certainly for us, Alvey was a 'first go' at participating in, and indeed coordinating, this sort of large-scale scientific activity. The view we have come to is that Alvey was an heroic effort to get the UK's IT effort into the 20th century before it ended, and one that was remarkably successful. The shame is that the remarkable spirit of collaboration which Alvey created, was not seized upon in a suitable follow-up programme aimed at bringing Alvey's research achievements nearer to the market place. Brian Oakley (Alvey's Director) has lamented this failure in a recent review of Alvey (Oakley and Owen, 1990) and we see no reason to disagree with him.

***Collaboration Is Possible**
Alvey introduced us to the benefits of proper travel funding for inter-site visits. It is easy to forget how difficult it was, indeed usually quite out of the question, for U.K. academics to get on the train to visit colleagues in other institutions. The travel money simply was not there (of course, this can still be a difficult problem for academics on standard non-collaborative grants). Alvey changed all that for us, and as a result we had many and vigorous discussions with consortium members, from which we benefited considerably. Amongst other things, these gave us an insight into the problems experienced by large industrial companies in mounting basic research. It is very clear to us that that endeavour cannot be left to them alone: the role of universities in tackling long-term fundamental issues is crucial. This may seem an obvious point to make but in a decade of university cutbacks and government insistence on academics finding industrial backing for their work, it perhaps needs saying very loudly and very often. Nor do we think industry disagrees; certainly our Alvey industrial sponsors (GEC and IBM) concur. In any event, we found the scientific discussions within the consortium extremely helpful and we hope this is visible in the papers in this book. For us, the inter-relationships between the work conducted at the various sites is evidence that the consortium did achieve that elusive goal of the 'whole being more than the sum of its parts'.

***Collaboration is Difficult**
It came as a bit of a surprise to us to realise in the compilation of this book that the consortium spawned not a single inter-site publication. Presumably this was because, despite the many visits and workshops, the underlying reality was still that at the end of the day individual sites knew they would be judged individually in future rounds of grant getting. Another problem was the rather frequent changes of personnel, especially, as it turned out to our surprise, within the industrial partners. Despite these factors, some code was ported between sites. For example, we benefited greatly from IBM's body modeller WINSOM (see [27]), and we circulated to everyone who wanted it a copy of TINA, AIVRU's stereo-based computer vision environment (see [29]). But it hardly needs pointing out that the character of the consortium was never intended to be that of a closely inter-twined multi-site software house bringing forth a large software product. We were not building a 'demonstrator'. Far from it: the consortium was a club of colleagues who agreed to pursue the goal of enhanced understanding of a set of inter-related research issues, their work genuinely enlarged by inter-consortium debates but in the end conducted separately.

***Medium term Pay-offs For Industry**
It has taken a further two years after the end of our Alvey grant to build a device (MARVIN - paper [10]) that can deliver useful 3D scene geometry from stereo at industrially relevant rates. That achievement fits the time frame we set for ourselves at the outset (3-5 years). On the other hand, it would be foolish to pretend that MARVIN is now an 'off-the-shelf answer'. It offers scope for immediate industrial exploitation but it is better regarded as the precursor of a new device that builds on its performance. Such work is now being planned between AIVRU and GEC. Other sites have had their own follow-up programmes.

***The Alvey Vision Conferences**
These became an annual event, beginning in September 1985. They have covered a wide range of topics but with emphasis on the 'image understanding' approach to recovering useful 3D scene descriptions, rather than on the 'pattern recognition' one with its customary attack on 2D problems. The success of these meetings has been such that they are to continue post-Alvey under the auspices of the newly-formed *British Machine Vision Association* (BMVA). This new organisation combines the Alvey vision community with members of the *British Pattern Recognition Association*. That outcome of Alvey is in itself no mean achievement.

REFERENCES

Oakley, B. and Owen, K. (1990) *Alvey: Britain's Strategic Computing Initiative*. MIT Press

[11] Segmentation and Description of Binocularly Viewed Contours

Tony T Pridmore, John Porrill and John E W Mayhew

AI Vision Research Unit
University of Sheffield, Sheffield S10 2TN, UK

Reprinted, with permission of Butterworth Scientific Ltd, from *Image and Vision Computing,* 1987, **5**, 132-138.

Abstract

Edge-based binocular correspondence produces a sparse disparity map, available information being distributed along space curves which project to matched image edges. To become useful these contours must be parsed into describable sections. We present a novel view of the segmentation/description process and describe an effective algorithm based on our model.

1. Introduction

The segmentation of arbitrary contours into meaningful sections is a longstanding problem receiving much attention. The goal of the present work is a description of the fragmented 3D contours to be found in edge-based binocular disparity data (figure 1). This representation provides a stepping stone to the construction of a complete wire frame model of the viewed scene.

Contour segmentation is typically seen as the identification either of discontinuities[1–7] or of describable subsections[8–10] operations which are usually treated as dual. As we are interested in providing primitive descriptions to higher processes we tend toward the latter view, though the algorithm reported here combines both approaches. Local segmentation operators are used to hypothesise discontinuities which are only retained if they delimit one or more describable segments. A contour is considered describable if the mean-squares residual associated with the most likely approximating primitive falls below some threshold. No attempt is made to accurately locate discontinuities, nor is a complete description required. In our view the primary goal of a bottom-up segmentation process should be to locate only those data sets which may be reliably described. This conservative approach provides an alternative to algorithms that obtain a fuller description at the cost of imposing interpretations which may not be appropriate.

Present (2D) approximation systems typically assume that a single primitive, usually a straight line, is sufficient to describe viewed curves. Most are based on computationally expensive split/merge algorithms guided by some measure of the accuracy of the approximation and terminating when an adequate description has been achieved (cf.[11]). For real scenes it is not clear that a single primitive will suffice. Furthermore, the generalisation of these techniques to multiple primitives is non-trivial and may involve optimisation theory (e.g. [12]).

Segmentation operators are more flexible; if descriptions are derived after discontinuity detection a wider set of primitives may be considered. It has, however, been argued[13] that reliable segmentation cannot be achieved without reference to the local structure of the data. A further problem is that a given discontinuity may not give rise to a unique, identifiable data item. It is quite probable, given the noise inherent in the disparity map, that the exact location of a particular discontinuity will not be covered by the data at all.

In the algorithm discussed below, simple segmentation operators provide heuristic guidance to a contour description process. This reduces the number of approximations attempted while allowing multiple primitives to be considered and relieving the segmentation operators of the responsibility of accurate discontinuity localisation.

In the following we describe segmentation and description techniques and present a recursive segmentation/description algorithm based upon the above considerations. Input to this algorithm are ordered strings of disparity measurements obtained via the Canny edge detector[14], PMF[15] and CONNECT[16].

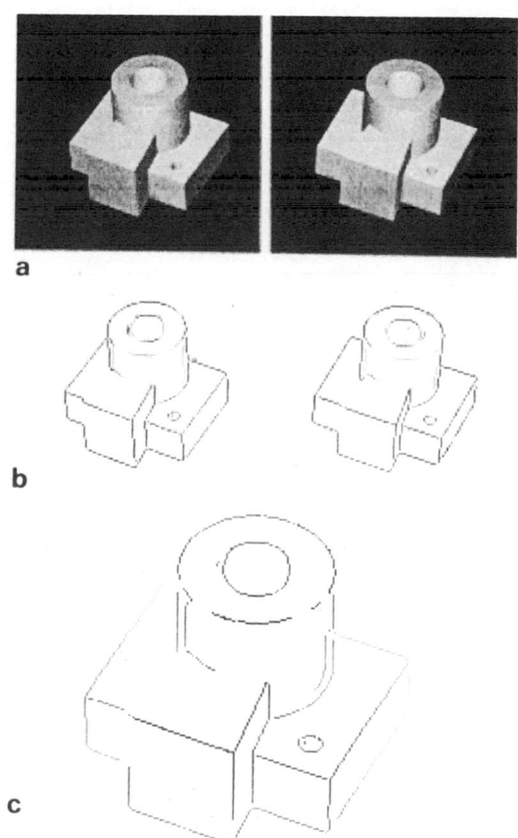

*Figure 1. Typical input data obtained from a pair of IBM Winsom images via PMF. The images (a), 256*256 pixels with 256 grey levels presented for cross-eyed fusion, give rise to edge assertions (b). The edge detector is a Canny operator with σ 1.0. Correspondence produces the sparse disparity map (c). Disparities are coded dark to light with increasing depth.*

2. Segmentation

Two operators are employed, recording curvature (κ) and its derivative ($\dot{\kappa}$) as functions of arc length. Both κ and $\dot{\kappa}$ estimates are obtained by differentiation of a locally approximating quadratic. Peaks in these measurements are assumed to mark discontinuities in orientation and curvature respectively, a supposition that is common in the literature[2–5,7].

It has long been appreciated that the performance of a given differential operator depends heavily upon the relative spatial extent, or scale, of the device and the features to which it is applied[17]. This observation has led to recent explorations of Scale Space[18,4]. Although the construction of a multiple scale representation is beyond the scope of the current project, the algorithm presented here does use smoothing to alleviate quantisation noise before computing curvature properties. The technique applied is the diffusion method of Porrill et. al.[19]. Only a small amount of smoothing is necessary; diffusion roughly equivalent to a gaussian of σ 2.5 is usually sufficient. When significantly larger σ are used peaks tend to migrate, making even approximate localisation difficult. After smoothing quadratics are fitted through triples of adjacent points.

Peaks (and troughs) in κ and $\dot{\kappa}$ are detected by thresholding absolute values. When examining $\dot{\kappa}$ it is important not to tag the side lobes of zero-crossings associated with peaks in curvature. For this reason supra-threshold $\dot{\kappa}$ estimates are only marked if no significant peaks in κ are found within a given neighbourhood. Asada and Brady[4] give the following expression for the arc length between the side lobes of a zero crossing caused by an angular discontinuity θ between contour segments with curvatures κ_1, κ_2 where σ is the standard deviation of an initial gaussian smoothing function:

$$d_{corner}=\frac{\sigma^2}{\phi}\left[\left[\kappa_1-\kappa_2\right]^2+\frac{4\phi^2}{\sigma^2}\right]^{\frac{1}{2}}$$

For a pure corner in which

$$\kappa=\kappa_1=\kappa_2$$

this simplifies to

$$d_{pure}=2\sigma$$

Assuming all angular discontinuities to be pure and the peak to lie approximately mid-way between the side lobes, we impose the condition that no significant curvature peak may lie within σ units of arc length of a marked peak in curvature difference. A curvature peak is considered significant if its absolute value is greater than the threshold that would be applied if such features were being sought. The use of diffusion means that our σ, the diffusion scale, is only an approximation to the gaussian parameter. It appears, however, to be a sufficiently close approximation for current purposes.

Note that κ and $\dot{\kappa}$ are measured in world, as opposed to disparity, coordinates. The transformation from disparity to world scales the depth component with respect to the other dimensions. Hence if curvature properties were estimated in disparity space the depth component would be compressed, playing a reduced role in segmentation. Segmenting in real coordinates allows depth information to contribute fully to all measurements. The increased error brought about by the disparity->world scaling does not appear to affect the segmentation process unduly, though the computation of mean squares residuals is greatly complicated. As quantisation error in disparity is isotropic in all three directions, the approximation techniques described below are applied to disparity values[20].

3. Description

In the current scheme, extrema in κ and $\dot{\kappa}$ serve to suggest likely areas of discontinuity; before any final decision can be made a geometrical description of the surrounding contour is required. An input string may be classified as a straight line, circular arc, planar or undescribable space curve. Mathematical details of the techniques involved are presented elsewhere[20], here we discuss the algorithm by which they are applied.

Given a set of points, orthogonal regression[20–22] supplies mean-squares residuals and metrical descriptions of the best fit plane, straight line and point. The residuals, related by the expression $res_{point}>res_{line}>res_{plane}$, are examined in decreasing order of magnitude, the first to fall below threshold[*] being taken as representative of the true description. Should all the residuals be above threshold, a default space curve tag is assigned. Short strings often match each primitive with a high degree of accuracy, in which case curves are assumed to be locally straight.

After regression, plane curves are passed to a three point circle fitting routine. If the circle residual is below threshold it is accepted, otherwise the plane descriptor becomes the primary representation. Although the choice of points may affect the residual, constraints imposed by CONNECT[16] force input strings to be at least Lipschitz continuous[23]. It is therefore unlikely that any significant discontinuities will be due to noise, making point selection less critical. As a further safeguard points are chosen from diffused data. This could introduce error if the data were heavily diffused, though it seems unlikely given the limited smoothing used here. As the extension of regression techniques to circle fitting is computationally expensive[22], the reduced cost of a three point fit easily outweighs its potential disadvantages.

Difficulties arise when describing curves containing horizontal segments. In such cases the binocular correspondence problem is effectively insoluble and any disparity values obtained must be considered unreliable. To avoid erroneous data, residual components arising from horizontal sections are computed in the image plane[20]. Geometrical descriptions, however, are always computed in 3-D, using non-horizontal data. Horizontal disparity elements are detected by thresholding the orientation of matched edge assertions. Although this method cannot solve the problem in its entirety, it does represent a first attempt to improve initial disparity measurements on the basis of later processing. If an input string is entirely horizontal its disparity values are used and the resulting segment(s) labelled.

4. An Algorithm

The segmentation/description scheme presented here admits many possible algorithms. We concern ourselves with a single example, known as GDF (Geometrical Descriptive Filter). Processing begins with a call to the description algorithm, thereafter focusing attention on strings not immediately represented by a single straight or circular segment. Planar and undescribed space curves are passed to a recursive segmentation algorithm which may be summarised thus:-

(1) $\dot{\kappa}$ estimates arising from non-horizontal data are thresholded at 90% of their maximum value, supra-threshold data being tagged as possible segmentation points. Should the string be entirely horizontal all of the data is used.

(2) Tags are removed from any points which fail the side-lobe test

(3) If no $\dot{\kappa}$ tags remain or all substrings are below the required length, extrema in κ are sought. A threshold is again set at 90% of the maximum (non-horizontal) value and (non-horizontal) supra-threshold points tagged.

(4) If all hypothesised substrings fall below the length threshold horizontal data is removed by segmenting at the ends of horizontal sections.

(5) If no acceptably long segments result the description reverts to the previous plane or space curve representation, otherwise long substrings are passed to the descriptive processes. Any classified as space or plane curves are further subdivided by recursive application of the segmentation procedure.

GDF seeks the longest acceptable primitives while segmenting at the largest κ and/or $\dot{\kappa}$ values. Peaks in $\dot{\kappa}$ are sought first. If all hypothesised segmentation points are rejected κ values are examined. Should κ fail to provide an acceptable segmentation horizontal data is removed by placing segmentation points at the ends of horizontal sections. If this also fails the representation reverts to the previous space or planar curve description. Note that the length threshold measures the number of data points available, rather than the absolute length of the curve: reliable classification of short strings is problematic. Hypothesised segments of above threshold length are then passed to the description algorithm. After classification, any remaining plane or space curves are recursively segmented. In this way strings are subdivided until either a satisfactory representation is obtained or the segments remaining fall below a length threshold. On termination, a GDB (Geometrical Descriptive Base) format[25] file is produced.

In peak detection the choice of threshold is critical, being subject to a trade-off. If thresholds are set too high, extrema will be missed and the data only partially segmented, typically leading to extra plane and/or space curve descriptions. Underestimating may, on the other hand, lead to oversegmentation, breaking long strings into arbitrarily small segments. Both effects reduce the information content of the final representation, though the former is more serious. Later processes should be able to recover from fragmented data, though the computational cost incurred may be considerable. GDF sets thresholds dynamically at 90% of the maximum absolute value of the appropriate operator. An alternative strategy[8,11] would be to segment at the maximum. This, however, would restrict the system to marking a single discontinuity on each recursion. Under the current scheme it is common for several peaks to be marked, speeding segmentation and reducing the number of approximations required. As thresholds are set just below maximum the danger of marking noise is small. On successive recursions operator maxima, and therefore the thresholds applied, become smaller. GDF is, therefore, (trivially) guaranteed to terminate.

Note that a simple threshold is applied; no suppression of non-maximal estimates is assumed. As a result, most peaks/troughs generate a pair of segmentation points, one either side of the local extremum. An interesting feature of this technique is the way in which the distance between segmentation point and local extremum increases with the spatial extent of the discontinuity. Hence GDF tends to locate fine scale discontinuities with a greater degree of accuracy. This has the secondary effect that strings having rapidly changing properties are rarely passed to the descriptive processes.

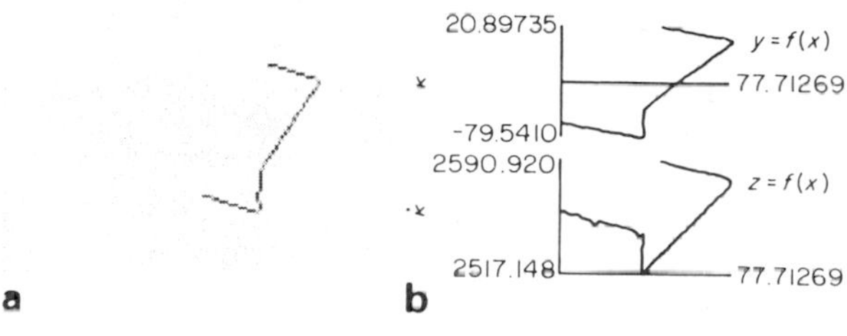

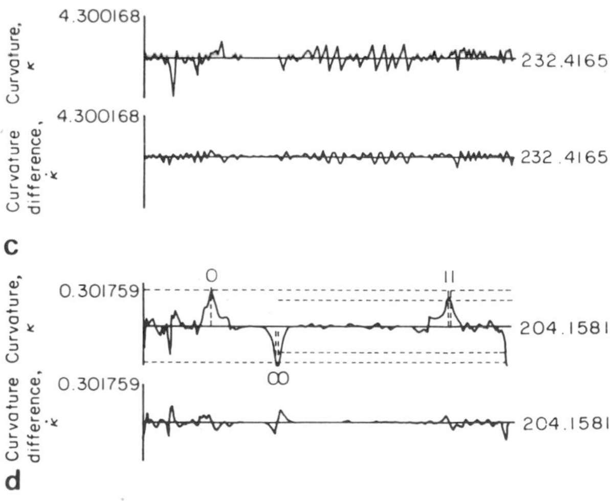

Figure 2. Recursive segmentation/description. b) data arising from the line highlighted in a). c) κ and $\dot{\kappa}$ values before diffusion. d) smoothed κ, $\dot{\kappa}$ plots (σ = 2.5). Segmentation points are marked by vertical lines tagged with recursion depths.

The approximation algorithm, where possible, extrapolates descriptions of non-horizontal edges into unreliable, horizontal data. If this is to be effective, horizontal strings must only contribute segmentation points as a last resort; the descriptive processes should first be given every chance to correct erroneous data. Threshold selection and application is, therefore, normally limited to non-horizontal depth estimates. Some strings are, however, entirely horizontal, in which case unreliable measurements must be used. Horizontal data introduces problems the techniques employed here can only begin to solve. The removal of horizontal segments when both differential operators fail to produce an acceptable segmentation is an explicit recognition of this limitation.

Figure 2 illustrates the application of GDF to the data of figure 1. The plots shown in fig. 2b display 3D position estimates, y and z coordinates as functions of x, arising from the line highlighted in figure 2a. Raw κ and $\dot{\kappa}$ values, obtained before diffusion and plotted as functions of arc length, are presented in figure 2c. Diffusion (σ=2.5) produces the smoothed plots shown in figure 2d. Note that three clearly distinguishable peaks have emerged. Dashed vertical lines represent segmentation points found by GDF, each tagged with an integer specifying the depth of recursion at which the discontinuity was identified. Threshold values, and the strings to which they were applied, are marked by horizontal dotted lines. The final representation in this case comprised three straight segments.

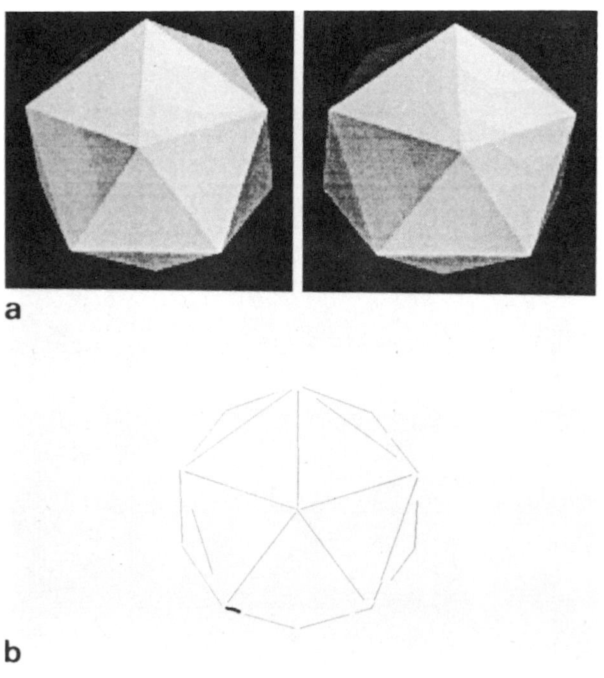

Figure 3: IBM Winsom generated test data. a) stereo images of a unit icosahedron viewed at 6 interocular distances. b) GDB representation. Circles are represented by broad lines, straight segments by fine.

Although the differential operators are said to hypothesise segmentation points, no hypotheses are ever fully rejected. All intermediate representations are recorded, building for each string a tree comprising non-terminal planar and/or space curve nodes and leaves representing straight or circular arcs. Note, however, that no attempt is made to produce a fuller description by combining segments. As Blake and Mayhew[26] point out, unrestricted computation of geometrical information is expensive and may lead to representations that are redundant given the task at hand. Even so, it is still sensible to exploit information obtained as a side effect of the normal description procedure.

5. Examples and Evaluation

The most important evaluation criterion for any 3D vision system is the extent to which it allows subsequent tasks to be performed. In the present case this clearly depends upon the geometrical accuracy of the contour descriptions supplied. As prior processing stages exert considerable influence on the final representation, any examination of GDF output incorporates some evaluation of the lower level components of the system.

Figures 3 and 4 show test data used to examine the accuracy of the GDB representation. To avoid camera calibration error, IBM Winsom generated images were employed. In these and all subsequent examples a Canny[14] edge operator (σ = 1.0), PMF[15] , CONNECT[16] and GDF (diffusion scale 2.5) were applied to the original 256*256 pixel, 256 grey level images. Figure 3 shows the images and GDB description arising from a unit icosahedron viewed at 6 interocular distances (approximately human reading distance). In figure 4 the icosahedron is intersected with a sphere, generating circular faces of known size, position and orientation.

Comparison of line equations derived from the Winsom model with straight line descriptors contained in GDF output shows a mean absolute error of 0.58 degrees in the internal angles of the icosahedron. The mean absolute error in line orientation is 0.24 degrees. Note that PMF was unable to match the horizontal edge at the bottom of the figure, this is an extreme example. Correspondence is usually achieved, though the resulting disparity data is always unreliable. Positional error was estimated by measuring the perpendicular distance from the mid-point of the GDB description to the true line, the mean error being 6.24 pixels. Winsom measures distances in image units, although no conversion to external units is possible, this is clearly a small error.

A similar examination of circle descriptions (figure 4b) shows a mean absolute error in circle radii and centre position of 0.71 and 1.20 pixels respectively. Each circle is associated with a plane descriptor. The mean absolute error in the internal angles of these planes is 2.05 degrees, while the mean absolute error in plane orientation is 2.49 degrees. Most circles give rise to some horizontal edges. Horizontal sections in the data of figure 4 are marked in figure 5a. Figure 5c shows the position estimates attributed to the arc highlighted in figure 5b. Note the flattened depth plot in the horizontal region, despite this distortion the circle description is recovered satisfactorily. In this case the error in plane orientation is 1.72 degrees, the circle radius and centre having errors of 1.38 and 2.01 pixels respectively. It will be noted that full circles apparent in the original images (figure 4a) are represented in GDF output by pairs of semi-circles. This is a result of missing data in the edge detection phase. Although image noise is limited by the use of Winsom, such problems may still occur.

It is clear from the above that useful 3D descriptions can be derived, via GDF, from edge based disparity data. An important question, however, concerns the stability of the GDB representation over changes in viewpoint. Although noise in edge detection and the number and position of horizontal edges are obviously view-dependent, some measure of stability is to be expected. Figure 6 shows natural image pairs and GDB representations of two views (separated by a rotation of approximately 180 degrees) of a wire, seen from approximately four interocular distances. Under this geometry 250 pixels is approximately equal to 1 cm. Note that the location of segmentation points and the geometry of the final representation are similar. The most noticeable error arises in the radii of the small circular arcs close to the free end of the wire. A considerable amount of data is required if circles are to be recovered accurately, examination of the longer arc parallel to the short segment of figure 6d shows a reduced error. As a further test, GDF output has been successfully exploited in the model matching work of Pollard et. al[27]. A more detailed experimental evaluation of GDF may be found in Pridmore[24].

6. Conclusion

GDF has been implemented and appears both effective and robust. Several features should be stressed:

Segmentation operators provide heuristic control to contour description processes.

Descriptions obtained from non-horizontal data are, where possible, extrapolated into horizontal regions.

No attempt is made to label the exact positions of discontinuities. Rather we report the end points and geometrical properties of the largest acceptable approximating segments.

GDF makes no strong assumptions about viewed curves, preferring instead to capture only those sections which may be closely approximated by a set of simple primitives.

The construction of a complete wire frame from GDF output is currently being investigated.

7. Discussion Note

The use of thresholding is often justifiably criticised in the image processing literature on the grounds that it reduces generality: thresholds for edge detection for example often need to be tuned to particular world domains and/or imaging conditions.

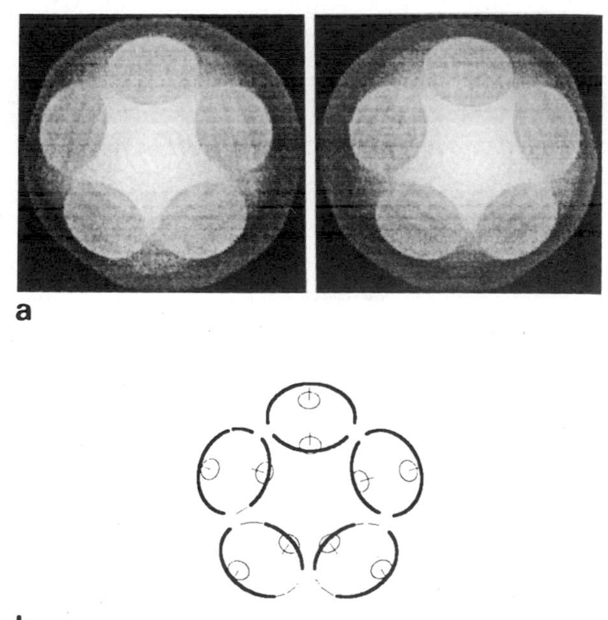

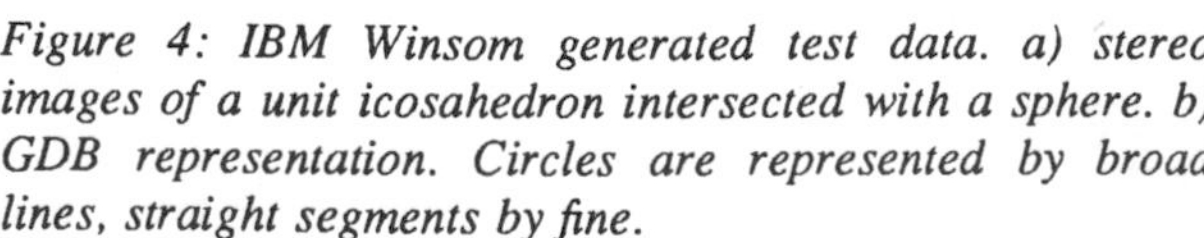

Figure 4: IBM Winsom generated test data. a) stereo images of a unit icosahedron intersected with a sphere. b) GDB representation. Circles are represented by broad lines, straight segments by fine.

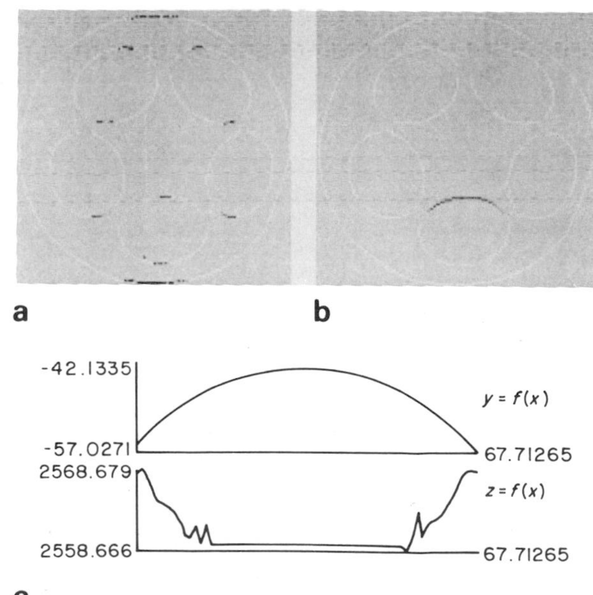

Figure 5. The effect of horizontal edges. a) disparity map obtained via PMF from the object of figure 4. Horizontal segments are drawn in black, other data in white. Position plots, y and z as functions of x, associated with the circular arc marked in black in (b) are presented in (c). Note the distorted z values arising from horizontal data.

This criticism is not applicable to our use of thresholds during curve fitting because those thresholds are to do with how any given set of edge locations can best be described geometrically. This is a different issue from how those edge tokens are obtained in the first place. Different edge operators will of course yield different edge tokens, and hence they would lead our system to produce different geometric descriptions. But that is not in itself a valid criticism of the use of thresholds within the processes we propose for obtaining geometric descriptions. We think it may be necessary to emphasise this point in view of the comments made by a referee. The residual values we threshold during orthogonal regression can be interpreted as measuring the standard deviation of error in edge location given a particular geometric fit (if errors in edge locations are assumed to be distributed normally which seems reasonable). Hence our use of thresholding is approximately equivalent to applying a χ^2 test of goodness of fit. The current threshold of 0.5 pixels amounts to the requirement that any accepted geometric description is unlikely to deviate from the data at any point by more that about one pixel.

Acknowledgements

We would like to thank Stephen Pollard and John Frisby for comments and advice and Chris Brown for his valuable technical assistance. This research was supported by SERC project grant no. GR/D 16796.

References

1 **Rosenberg, B.,** The Analysis of Convex Blobs, *Computer Graphics and Image Processing*, 1, pp 183-192, (1972).

2 **Davis, L.S.,** Understanding Shape: Angles and Sides, *IEEE Transactions on Computers*, C-26, 3, pp 236-242, (1977).

3 **Freeman H., and Davis, L.S.** A Corner Finding Algorithm for Chain Coded Curves, *IEEE Transactions on Computers*, C-26, pp 297-303, (1977).

4 **Asada, H., and Brady, J.M.,** The Curvature Primal Sketch, *MIT AI Memo*, 758, (1984).

5 **Sakai, T., Nagao, N, and Matsushima, H.,** Extraction of Invariant Picture sub-structures by Computer, *Computer Graphics and Image Processing*, 1, pp 81-96, (1972).

6 **Feng, H.Y., and Pavlidis, T.,** Finding Vertices in a Picture, *Computer Graphics and Image Processing*, 2, pp 103-117, (1973).

7 **Shirai, Y.,** Analysing Intensity Arrays Using Knowledge About Scenes, in *The Psychology of Computer Vision*, ed. P.H. Winston, McGraw-Hill, (1975).

8 **Ramer, U.,** An Iterative Procedure for the Polygonal Approximation of Plane Curves, *Computer Graphics and Image Processing*, 1, pp 244-56, (1972).

9 **Pavlidis, T.,** Waveform segmentation through Functional Approximation, *IEEE Transactions on Computers*, C-22, 7, pp 689-97, (1973).

10 **Pavlidis, T., and Horowitz, S.L.,** Segmentation of Plane Curves, *IEEE Transactions on Computers*, C-23, 8, pp 860-70, (1974).

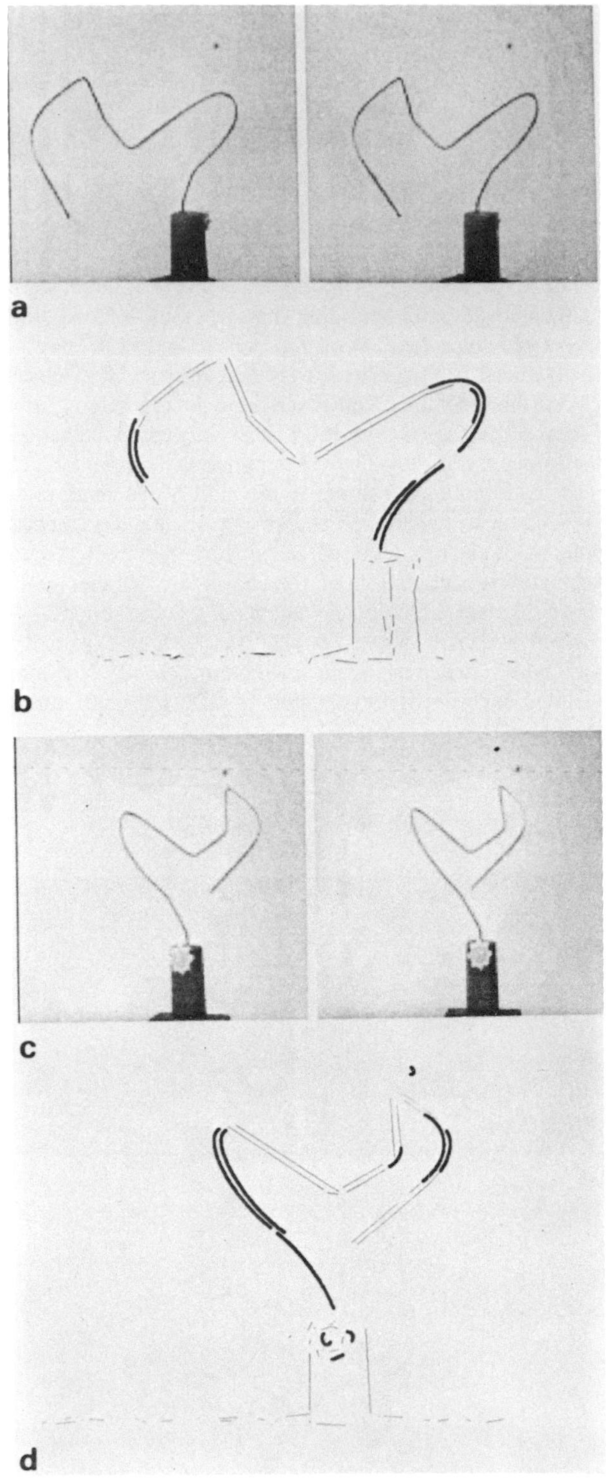

Figure 6: Stability over changes in viewpoint. a), c) natural stereo images of a bent wire taken from viewpoints separated by a rotation of approximately 180 degrees. b), d) GDB representations. The descriptions obtained are qualitatively and quantitatively similar.

11 **Ballard, D.H.,** Strip Trees: A Hierarchical Representation for Curves, *Communications of the Association for Computing Machinery*, 24, 5, pp 310-21, (1981).

12 **Plass, M., and Stone, M.,** Curve-Fitting with Piecewise Parametric Cubics, *Computer Graphics*, 17, 3, pp 229-239, (1983).

13 **Leclerc, Y., and Zucker, S.W.,** The Local Structure of Image Discontinuities in One Dimension, *McGill University Computer Vision and Robotics Laboratory Technical Report*, TR-83-19R, (1983).

14 **Canny, J.F., Finding Edges and Lines in Images,** *MIT AI memo*, 720, (1983).

15 **Pollard, S.B., Mayhew, J.E.W. and Frisby, J.P.,** PMF: A Stereo Correspondence Algorithm Using a Disparity Gradient Limit, *Perception*, 14, pp 449-470, (1985).

16 **Pridmore, T.P., Mayhew J.E.W., and Frisby, J.P., Production Rules for Grouping Edge-based Disparity Data,** Paper presented at the Alvey Image Interpretation Conference, Sussex University, and *AIVRU Memo*, 015, (1985).

17 **Marr, D., and Hildreth, E.,** Theory of Edge Detection, *Proc. Roy. Soc. Lond.*, B207, pp 187-217, (1980).

18 **Witkin, A.P., Scale Space Filtering,** *Proc. 8th IJCAI*, Karlsruhe, W. Germany, pp 1019-1023, (1983).

19 **Porrill, J., Mayhew, J.E.W., and Frisby, J.P.,** Scale Space Diffusion: Planes and space Curves, *AIVRU memo*, 018, (1986).

20 **Porrill, J., Pridmore, T.P., Mayhew, J.E.W., and Frisby, J.P.,** Fitting Planes, Lines and Circles to Stereo Disparity Data, *AIVRU memo*, 017, (1986).

21 **Pearson, K.,** On Lines and Planes of Closest Fit to Systems of Points in Space, *Phil. Mag. VI,* 2, pp 559, (1901).

22 **Ballard, D.H., and Brown, C.M.,** *Computer Vision*, Prentice Hall, (1982).

23 **Pollard, S.P., Porrill, J., Mayhew, J.E.W., and Frisby, J.P.,** Disparity Gradient, Lipschitz Continuity and Computing Binocular Correspondences, *Proc 3rd ISRR*, Gouviex, France, (1986).

24 **Pridmore, T.P.,** PhD Thesis, University of Sheffield, forthcoming.

25 **Pridmore, T.P., Bowen, J.B., and Mayhew, J.E.W.,** Geometrical Description of the CONNECT Graph #2, The Geometrical Base Description: A Specification, *AIVRU Memo*, 012, (1985).

26 **Blake, A., and Mayhew, J.E.W.,** Alvey 2&1/2-D Sketch Project: Proposed Structure For a Development System, *AIVRU Memo* , 009, (1985).

27 **Pollard, S.B., Porrill, J., Mayhew, J.E.W., and Frisby, J.P.,** Matching Geometrical Descriptions in Three Space, *Alvey Computer Vision and Image Interpretation Meeting and Image and Vision Computing (submitted)*, (1986).

[12] The Optimal Combination of Multiple Sensors Including Stereo Vision

John Porrill, Stephen B Pollard and John E W Mayhew

AI Vision Research Unit
University of Sheffield, Sheffield S10 2TN, UK

Reprinted, with permission of Butterworth Scientific Ltd, from *Image and Vision Computing*, 1987, **5**, 174-180.

Abstract

The statistical combination of information from multiple sources is considered. The particular needs of the target application, stereo vision, require that the formulation be adequate to deal with highly correlated errors and constraints, and that it deal naturally with geometrical data.

1. Introduction

Stereo viewing of an object supplies partial information that can have unacceptably large errors in depth. To build up a more accurate and complete model of the object we would like to view it from many positions and match and combine these views. In a preliminary experiment using artificially generated stereo images the views were matched[1], transformed into the same frame, and combined by a weighted least squares method. Since the data was artificial we had access to the true camera motion when performing the transformation, and the merging behaved correctly. However when the estimate of camera motion supplied by the matcher was used, the resulting model, rather than gradually firming up, gently disintegrated; the errors in the model were correlated with the error in estimated camera motion and accumulated rather than cancelled. In attempting to overcome this we found that it could fruitfully be regarded as a multiple sensor problem (one stereo sensor for each view) the object being to combine these sources of information when their relative calibration is imperfectly known. Although our main interest is stereo vision we shall try to discuss this problem in full generality, using stereo vision only as an illustration.

The combination of information from multiple sensors including vision-like sensors is of immediate practical importance in robotics where one can find many examples of ad hoc combination rules. For example the Intelligent Mobile Platform described by Crowley[2] combines maps of its surroundings obtained from an ultrasonic range sensor into a 'composite local model' by averaging.

Recent treatments have attempted to find a solution which is optimal in some sense. For example the refinement of stereo data by a stationary Kalman filter has been described by Faugeras et al.[3], and Durrant-Whyte[4] has considered the problem of statistical combination of sensors, each of which has its own reference frame, while retaining geometrical consistency between frames. The treatment given here draws largely from these two sources.

2. Statistical Combination

What are the benefits of statistical combination of information? Firstly there is a reduction in error proportional to the square root of the number of similar observations. This is welcome and in many applications is the whole aim of data combination, but in stereo vision, where we might have a typical error in an observed angle of five degrees say, the one hundred observations needed to reduce the error to a respectable half a degree are not likely to be available.

Even though stereo can be very inaccurate the errors are highly anisotropic: lateral errors are much smaller than depth errors. If two stereo views from different known positions are available we can largely eliminate this anisotropy and give much better localisation in depth. This illustrates a general point that the combination of information from sensors with complementary anisotropies can be very beneficial. We can represent the error of each sensor by a confidence ellipsoid and we require statistical combination laws to perform the book-keeping task of 'intersecting' these ellipsoids. One common way of simplifying the mathematics of statistical combination is to majorise the error covariance matrices by diagonal matrices since they are much easier to handle. This replaces error ellipsoids by their smallest enveloping spheres. Since we believe that error anisotropy can be on our side, we cannot make use of this method.

Another source of increased accuracy can be the imposition of constraints. For example if we see that three lines almost intersect we may hypothesise the existence of a trihedral vertex. A statistical model allows us to test this hypothesis and if it is accepted to optimally adjust the data to satisfy the constraint and accurately specify the vertex. The data could thus be adjusted to achieve consistency with a symbolic (region, edge, vertex graph) description of the data.

3. Gauss-Markov Estimation Theory

The simplest and best-developed theory of statistical combination of measurements deals with minimum variance estimators for linear measurement equations, these are maximum likelihood estimators when the noise is Gaussian. Though the robustness of such methods is open to question (we will discuss this later) they are mathematically very attractive. If we try to impose linear constraints (which are essentially exact measurements) the error covariance matrix becomes singular, and the classical Gauss-Markov theorem fails though a generalisation is available to deal with this case. Since this gives an essentially complete theoretical basis for the treatment of linear measurements, we will summarise the results here, based on an elegant treatment of the theory as an application of the Moore-Penrose pseudo-inverse by Albert[5]. Morrison[6] also deals with the subject of linear models and gives more statistical background.

4. Linear Measurement Equations and Linear Constraints

The state to be estimated is a vector $\mathbf{x} \in \mathbf{R}^m$, the measurement and noise are vectors $\mathbf{z}, \mathbf{u} \in \mathbf{R}^n$, and the measurement equation is assumed to be linear

$$\mathbf{z} = H\mathbf{x} + \mathbf{u}$$

where the 'plant matrix' H is $n \times m$. The noise $\mathbf{u}$ is taken to be Gaussian with zero mean and covariance matrix R. This formulation is more general than it looks since if we also have a prior estimate $\mathbf{x}_0$ with prior covariance S_0 and $\mathbf{x}$ is subject to linear constraints $C\mathbf{x} = \mathbf{c}$ we can form a composite equation of exactly the same form

$$\tilde{\mathbf{z}} = \begin{pmatrix} \mathbf{z} \\ \mathbf{x}_0 \\ \mathbf{c} \end{pmatrix} = \begin{pmatrix} H \\ 1 \\ C \end{pmatrix} \mathbf{x} + \begin{pmatrix} \mathbf{u} \\ \mathbf{v} \\ \mathbf{w} \end{pmatrix} = \tilde{H}\mathbf{x} + \tilde{\mathbf{u}}$$

where the covariance of the composite measurement error $\tilde{\mathbf{u}}$ is

$$\mathrm{Cov}[\tilde{\mathbf{u}}] = \tilde{R} = \begin{pmatrix} R & 0 & 0 \\ 0 & S_0 & 0 \\ 0 & 0 & 0 \end{pmatrix}$$

From now on we assume we are dealing with this general situation and drop the tildes. It is easy to see that the matrix R will be singular when constraints (essentially exact measurements) are present. Since R is symmetric and positive and it has a unique positive symmetric square root

$$V = R^{1/2} \qquad R = V^2.$$

To manipulate such singular matrices we will need a generalisation of the concept of the inverse M^{-1} of a matrix M to general matrices. This is given by the Moore-Penrose pseudo-inverse

$$M^+ = \lim_{\delta \to 0} (M^t M + \delta^2 1)^{-1} M^t$$

for details of its properties and many uses see Albert[5]. A discussion of the role of other generalised inverses in estimation theory can be found in Mitra[6].

We include the possibility that the measurement $\mathbf{z}$ may not be sufficient (even when exact) to determine the state $\mathbf{x}$ completely. When this is so there are still linear functionals of $\mathbf{x}$ which can be estimated from the given measurements, the estimable linear functionals.

5. Definition

The functional $\mathbf{y} = L\mathbf{x}$ is said to be *estimable* if it has an unbiased linear estimate $\hat{\mathbf{y}} = M\mathbf{z}$ (that is an estimate such that $E[\hat{\mathbf{y}}] = \mathbf{y}$) for some matrix M.

Theorem

The $\mathbf{y}$ above is estimable if and only if

$$LH^+H = L$$

that is, if and only if

$$\mathrm{Range}(L^t) \subseteq \mathrm{Range}(H^t)$$

More simply, the rows of L must be linear combinations of the rows of H.

In particular taking $L = 1$, $\mathbf{x}$ itself is estimable only if H has full row-rank.

The generalised Gauss-Markov theorem now gives us the best estimate of estimable $\mathbf{y}$'s.

Theorem

Let $\bar{V} = V(1 - HH^+)$ and $G = H^+(1 - (\bar{V}^+V)^t)$ and let $\hat{\mathbf{x}} = G\mathbf{z}$ then

a) $E[\hat{\mathbf{x}}] = H^+H\mathbf{x}$ (this is the 'estimable part' of $\mathbf{x}$).

b) If $\mathbf{y}$ as above is estimable, then its best linear unbiased estimator is $\hat{\mathbf{y}} = L\hat{\mathbf{x}}$

c) If the error covariance $R = V^2$ is non-singular

$$\hat{\mathbf{x}} = (H^t R^{-1} H)^+ H^t R^{-1} \mathbf{z}$$

This last can be recognised as the usual formula for the weighted least squares estimate of $\mathbf{x}$ with a pseudo-inversion replacing the inversion.

Suppose we now wish to find the estimate of $\mathbf{y}$ given that $\mathbf{x}$ satisfies a further set of constraints $C\mathbf{x} = \mathbf{c}$. We could extend the measurement equation further so as to include these constraints as extra measurements but we can also write down extensions to the results above which solve this problem directly.

Theorem

Let $M = H(1 - C^+C)$. Then $\mathbf{y}$ is estimable given the additional constraints if and only if $LM^+M = L$ that is, if and only if $\mathrm{Range}(L^t) \subseteq \mathrm{Range}(M^t)$

All $\mathbf{y}$'s which were estimable without the constraints are still estimable, and some more may become estimable (for example $C\mathbf{x}$ is obviously estimable as $\mathbf{c}$ whatever its status before).

Theorem

Let M be as above and let

$$\bar{V} = V(1 - MM^+)$$
$$G = (1 - C^+C)\, H^+\, (1 - (\bar{V}^+V)^t)$$

and

$$\hat{\mathbf{x}} = C^+\mathbf{c} + G(\mathbf{z} - HC^+\mathbf{c})$$

then

a) $E[\hat{\mathbf{x}}] = C^+\mathbf{c} + M^+M\mathbf{x}$

b) If $\mathbf{y}$ is estimable its best linear unbiased estimator is given by $\hat{\mathbf{y}} = L\hat{\mathbf{x}}$.

If we want to test the hypothesis that the constraint holds given the previous measurement $\mathbf{z}$ we first calculate the estimators $\hat{\mathbf{x}}$ and $\hat{\mathbf{x}}_C$ for $\mathbf{x}$ before and after imposing the constraint. Each estimate tries to minimise the weighted sum square error, but the second minimisation is constrained, so its residual will be larger. The increase in residual

$$\delta\varepsilon = (\mathbf{z} - H\hat{\mathbf{x}}_C)^t R^+ (\mathbf{z} - H\hat{\mathbf{x}}_C) - (\mathbf{z} - H\hat{\mathbf{x}})^t R^+ (\mathbf{z} - H\hat{\mathbf{x}})$$

measures the distortion of the data required to impose the constraint. A maximum likelihood test of the constraint can be performed by testing $\delta\varepsilon$ as a central χ^2 variable with $\mathrm{Rank}(HH^+ - MM^+)$ degrees of freedom (this is the number of independent constraints imposed). In general we will not be testing alternative hypotheses against another, if we were we would need to discuss the power of this test, details can be found in Morrison[6].

6. Recursive Least Squares

The theory as described above covers all our needs, but is very unwieldy computationally and conceptually. A great simplification is achieved by considering the recursive computation of estimators and residuals when single scalar measurements and constraints are added sequentially. Of course this has practical application since data acquisition is often serial in nature.

Suppose we have already performed some measurements and let A be the matrix which projects vectors perpendicular to the estimable subspace of the state space $\mathbf{R}^n$ (so if $\mathbf{y}$ is estimable then $A\mathbf{y} = 0$) if we have performed measurements sufficient in principle to determine $\mathbf{x}$ then $A = 0$. Let $\hat{\mathbf{x}}$ be our present estimate of the estimable part of $\mathbf{x}$ and let the covariance of this estimate be $\hat{S}$. Let the residual so far be ε.

Now suppose we make a single scalar measurement

$$z = \mathbf{h}^t\mathbf{x} + u \qquad \mathrm{var}[u] = \sigma^2$$

with measurement noise uncorrelated with the noise in our previous measurements. Then we can give update rules for A, $\hat{S}$, $\hat{\mathbf{x}}$, and ε. There are two cases: firstly if the new measurement direction $\mathbf{h}$ has already been sampled *i.e.* if $A\mathbf{h} = 0$ then:

$$A' = A$$

$$\hat{S}' = \hat{S} - \frac{(\hat{S}\mathbf{h})^t(\hat{S}\mathbf{h})}{\sigma^2 + \mathbf{h}^t\,\hat{S}\,\mathbf{h}}$$

$$\mathbf{k} = \frac{\hat{S}\mathbf{h}}{\sigma^2 + \mathbf{h}^t\,\hat{S}\,\mathbf{h}}$$

$$\varepsilon' = \varepsilon + \frac{(z - \mathbf{h}^t\,\mathbf{x})^2}{\sigma^2 + \mathbf{h}^t\,\hat{S}\,\mathbf{h}}$$

if the measurement is in a new direction

$$A' = A - \frac{(A\mathbf{h})(A\mathbf{h})^t}{\mathbf{h}^t\,A\,\mathbf{h}}$$

$$\hat{S}' = \hat{S} - \frac{(\hat{S}\mathbf{h})(A\mathbf{h})^t + (A\mathbf{h})(\hat{S}\mathbf{h})^t}{\mathbf{h}^tA\mathbf{h}} + \frac{\sigma^2 + \mathbf{h}^t\hat{S}\mathbf{h}}{(\mathbf{h}^tA\mathbf{h})^2}(A\mathbf{h})(A\mathbf{h})^t$$

$$\mathbf{k} = \frac{A\mathbf{h}}{\mathbf{h}^t\,A\,\mathbf{h}}$$

$$\varepsilon' = \varepsilon$$

in either of these cases the new estimate is given as

$$\hat{\mathbf{x}}' = \hat{\mathbf{x}} + \mathbf{k}\,(z - \mathbf{h}^t\hat{\mathbf{x}})$$

In this formulation the equations form a stationary Kalman filter for sequential scalar measurements. As an alternative to storing and updating the matrix A if one knows that certain components of $\mathbf{x}$ have not been measured one can assign them very large variances initially.

A problem with the recursive application of this update rule is that a sequence of successive measurement must be mutually independent, this is a major restriction. One case in which this is not a problem is when we need to impose a sequence of constraints, since constraints can always be treated as independent if they are not redundant or inconsistent. The imposition of a single scalar constraint (that is a measurement with $\sigma = 0$) when we have sufficient previous measurements that $\mathbf{x}$ itself is estimable (so $A = 0$) is remarkably simple, the update rule is

$$\hat{S}' = \hat{S} - \frac{(\hat{S}\mathbf{h})\,(\hat{S}\mathbf{h})^t}{\mathbf{h}^t\,\hat{S}\,\mathbf{h}}$$

$$\mathbf{k} = \frac{\hat{S}\mathbf{h}}{\mathbf{h}^t\,\hat{S}\,\mathbf{h}}$$

$$\hat{\mathbf{x}}' = \hat{\mathbf{x}} + \mathbf{k}\,(z - \mathbf{h}^t\,\mathbf{x})$$

$$\varepsilon' = \varepsilon + \frac{(z - \mathbf{h}^t\,\mathbf{x})^2}{\mathbf{h}^t\,\hat{S}\,\mathbf{h}}$$

The maximum likelihood test of the constraint treats $\varepsilon' - \varepsilon$ as χ^2 on one degree of freedom for Gaussian errors.

7. Measurement Primitives

To allow a measurement process to return only vectors in $\mathbf{R}^n$ is conceptually limiting. Often the type of process we want to consider is more naturally regarded as measuring and returning a more complex geometrical primitive. For example a simple touch sensor might 'measure' a plane by returning a point on it; an inaccurately calibrated stereo rig might attempt to measure the projective transformation between its own visual world and the real world. Of course such primitives, however complex, can always be encoded into vectors in $\mathbf{R}^n$, the point is that this should be done in a way that reflects their natural geometric structure.

Suppose we are dealing with a class of geometric primitives forming a smooth manifold M (most of the entities we are interested in satisfy this condition: points, lines, planes, circles, rotations, projective transformations ...). An error prone measurement of such a primitive can be thought of as sampling from a random process on M. How are the statistics of such processes to be specified? If we choose local coordinates 'sensibly' in a neighbourhood U of some point of M, that is, a chart

$$\phi : U \to \mathbf{R}^n$$

assigning coordinates $\phi(\pi) = \mathbf{x} = (x^1, x^2, \cdots, x^n)^t$ to points π of M we can say that a process is 'approximately normal' with mean a given primitive $\mu \in M$ if the probability distribution of $\mathbf{x}$ has the approximate form

$$p(\mathbf{x}) \propto \exp\left(-\frac{(\mathbf{x}-\mathbf{m})^t\,R^+\,(\mathbf{x}-\mathbf{m})}{2}\right)$$

where $\mathbf{m} = \phi(\mu)$, and the probability density function is non-negligible only inside U. Under changes of coordinates that are approximately affine over the support of the probability distribution (using the summation convention)

$$x^{i'} = x_0^{i'} + A_j^{i'}\,x^j + \cdots$$

(A is the Jacobian matrix of the transformation) the mean transforms like a vector and the covariance matrix $R^{ij} = E[x^ix^j]$ like a second rank tensor

$$m^{i'} = m^i + x_0^{i'} \qquad R^{i'j'} = A_k^{i'}\,A_l^{j'}\,R^{kl}$$

To discuss what is meant by a 'sensible' choice of coordinates would lead into very deep waters indeed. Stated simply, the coordinates chosen should not be too distorted with respect to the underlying symmetries of the manifold (all the manifolds in which we are interested have such symmetries) at the scale of description required. For example, if we are describing a point on the unit sphere polar coordinates are fine near the equator, and singular at the poles. We can describe a probability distribution with peak near to a pole adequately in terms of these coordinates only if it has very small variance.

A problem with local coordinates is that they are often inconvenient for the description of geometrical relationships. For example the condition that two unit vectors be perpendicular is not a pretty sight when written out in polar coordinates. However we often have an alternative global description (in this case as a vector $\mathbf{n}$ with $\mathbf{n}\cdot\mathbf{n} = 1$) in which such relationships are easily expressed. The problem with such descriptions is that they tend to involve non-linear constraints (the condition $\mathbf{n}\cdot\mathbf{n} = 1$ above, for example). This second description (which we will call the global description) will in general be an an embedding of M in a higher dimensional space $\mathbf{R}^N$.

$$\iota : M \to \mathbf{R}^N : \pi \to \xi = (\xi^1, \xi^2, \ldots, \xi^N)^t$$

(*e.g.* for the two dimensional manifold of unit vectors it is the natural embedding as the sphere in $\mathbf{R}^3$). We want to choose local coordinates in such a way that transformation between the local and global descriptions is simple, In general this will require that we deal with affine approximations to the transformation, but we this is no great loss, since our statistics can only deal with affine transformations. These will take the form

$$\xi = \xi_0 + F_x\, \mathbf{x} \qquad \mathbf{x} = f_\xi\, (\xi - \xi_0)$$

where F_x and f_ξ are $N \times n$ and $n \times N$ matrices respectively, and ξ_0 represents the origin of the local coordinate system. The local coordinates should be attached to the primitive rigidly, in the sense that a rigid motion in space preserves the form of the matrices F_x and f_ξ. The systematic use of these representations can simplify and mechanise the problem of deriving measurement equations and constraints.

8. Sensors and Constraints

For our purposes a sensor observes a measurement primitive ξ, its internal state (motion since last view, miscalibration, *etc.*) is described by another primitive σ, and it returns a third primitive ζ as measurement. If the measurement were exact the relationship between the three would typically have the form

$$\mathbf{h}(\zeta, \sigma, \xi) = 0$$

Choose local coordinates about the actual measurement ζ. On the assumption of small approximately normal errors we know that the true measurement ζ is related to the actual measurement ζ_0 by

$$\zeta = \zeta_0 + F_z\, \mathbf{z} \qquad \mathbf{z} = N(0, R)$$

If we have estimates σ_0 and ξ_0 of the other two quantities and introduce local coordinates about these estimates we can linearise the equation (with obvious choice of notation) as

$$\tilde{\mathbf{z}} = -\mathbf{h}(\zeta_0, \sigma_0, \xi_0) = \left[\frac{\partial \mathbf{h}}{\partial \sigma}\cdot F_s\,,\ \frac{\partial \mathbf{h}}{\partial \xi}\cdot F_x\right]\begin{pmatrix}\mathbf{s}\\ \mathbf{x}\end{pmatrix} + \frac{\partial \mathbf{h}}{\partial \zeta}\cdot F_z\, \mathbf{z} = \tilde{H}\tilde{\mathbf{x}} + \tilde{\mathbf{u}}$$

This is a linear measurement equation for the perturbations $\mathbf{x}$, $\mathbf{s}$ where the measurement error has covariance

$$\tilde{R} = \mathrm{cov}[\tilde{\mathbf{u}}] = \frac{\partial \mathbf{h}}{\partial \zeta}\, F_z\, R\, F_z^t\, \frac{\partial \mathbf{h}}{\partial \zeta}^t$$

This equation can now be treated by Gauss-Markov theory. However if we wish to perform each component $\tilde{z}_i$ of the measurement sequentially they must be independent, that is, the matrix $\tilde{R}$ must be diagonal. This is unlikely to be the case. As stated previously we do not wish to majorise $\tilde{R}$ by a diagonal matrix, since this loses information. One solution is to find the eigenvectors $\mathbf{e}_i$ of $\tilde{R}$ and apply the the scalar measurements

$$\mathbf{e}_i^t\, \tilde{\mathbf{z}} = \mathbf{e}_i^t\, \tilde{H}\tilde{\mathbf{x}} + \mathbf{e}_i^t\, \tilde{\mathbf{u}}$$

sequentially since these are independent.

A second approach is to extend our state space to include the measurement $\mathbf{z}$ and to regard the equation above as a set of constraints on the augmented state vector. If we ensure that the set of constraints is not redundant then they can be applied sequentially.

In order to justify the above linearisations we must be able to obtain good initial estimates of the state and calibration. In particular the total sensor information available must be sufficient in the absence of error to determine all the unknowns which have non-linear descriptions or measurement equations; the purpose of the statistical method is to optimise this estimate.

9. Sensor Combination

The above analysis allows us to outline a framework for sensor combination that is conceptually very attractive. We have a world containing a list of primitives with estimated positions $(\xi_1, \xi_2, \cdots)$ and a set of independent sensors whose calibrations with respect to the world frame are estimated as $(\sigma_1, \sigma_2, \cdots)$. The world frame can be chosen for convenience, as the frame of our most important sensor for example. The state vector is the list $(\mathbf{s}_1, \mathbf{s}_2, \cdots, \mathbf{x}_1, \mathbf{x}_2, \cdots)$ of corrections which must be made to the calibrations and world primitives. Each of these corrections is referred to an intrinsic frame attached to the primitive, initially each will be zero.

If a measurement of the form of the last section is made, the error in the measurement is adjoined to the state space and the covariance matrix of the measurement adjoined to the state covariance. The measurement equation is then applied as a series of constraints. If the measurement itself is a primitive of interest it can be kept in the state vector, otherwise it is dropped. At any stage we can apply the corrections specified in the state vector to the primitives, this does not require any change in the state covariance, since such changes would be second order small quantities. If we want to change our world frame, we need only change our global representations of the primitives, the corrections and the state covariance being attached to the intrinsic frame of the primitives.

We will now describe the above process in some detail in a case study of the multiple stereoview problem.

10. The Stereo Sensor

Our immediate application of the above analysis is to stereo data. This is provided by a 'sensor' which is a combination of error prone processing stages: acquisition of a pair of images, edge detection to sub-pixel acuity by a Canny operator[8], stereo edge matching by the PMF algorithm[9], and finally plane, line and circle fitting to produce the geometrical descriptive base (GDB)[10].

11. Description of Stereo Primitives

The most reliable part of the GDB is a list of straight edges found in the scene (this is the basic input to our matcher). The endpoints of these edges are not very informative due to unpredictability in segmentation, so the measurement primitive which we output is essentially a straight line in three space. We need a convenient global description of these primitives; the most convenient is as a pair of vectors $(\mathbf{p}_0, \mathbf{v}_0)$ where $\mathbf{p}_0$ is the position of a point on the line and $\mathbf{v}_0$ is its direction vector. We now choose vectors $\mathbf{v}_1$, $\mathbf{v}_2$ such that the $\mathbf{v}_i$ form a basis, and add these to our description of the line in the GDB, this then forms an intrinsic reference frame which will be carried with the line throughout its history.

Any nearby line can be described by a position vector and a direction vector

$$\mathbf{p} = \mathbf{p}_0 + p_1\mathbf{v}_1 + p_2\mathbf{v}_2$$

$$\mathbf{v} = \mathbf{v}_0 + v_1\mathbf{v}_1 + v_2\mathbf{v}_2$$

(note that $\mathbf{v}$ is unit to first order) and we use (p_1, p_2, v_1, v_2) as local coordinates on the line manifold. The transformations between local and global descriptions are thus

$$\begin{bmatrix}\mathbf{p}\\ \mathbf{v}\end{bmatrix} = \begin{bmatrix}\mathbf{p}_0\\ \mathbf{v}_0\end{bmatrix} + \begin{bmatrix}\mathbf{v}_1 & \mathbf{v}_2 & 0 & 0\\ 0 & 0 & \mathbf{v}_1 & \mathbf{v}_2\end{bmatrix}\begin{bmatrix}p_1\\ p_2\\ v_1\\ v_2\end{bmatrix}$$

$$\begin{bmatrix}p_1\\ p_2\\ v_1\\ v_2\end{bmatrix} = \begin{bmatrix}\mathbf{v}_1^t & 0\\ \mathbf{v}_2^t & 0\\ 0 & \mathbf{v}_1^t\\ 0 & \mathbf{v}_2^t\end{bmatrix}\begin{bmatrix}\mathbf{p}-\mathbf{p}_0\\ \mathbf{v}-\mathbf{v}_0\end{bmatrix}$$

12. Error Estimation

We must now estimate the error with which our system localises a line. For such a complex sensor a complete description of the error process is impossible. We will describe two ways to approximate it.

First we will consider an idealised situation where we are observing not lines, but sets of n collinear points. These are matched without error between left and right images.

The imaging process is assumed to produce equal uncorrelated errors of variance σ^2 in their left and right image X-coordinates and the left image Y coordinate, so that fitting a line by orthogonal regression in (X_L, X_R, Y_L)-space (disparity space) is optimal[10]. This then produces a centroid position error of variance σ^2/n and an angular error of variance $12\sigma^2/nl^2$ where l is the length of the line in disparity space.

In terms of local line coordinates in disparity space the error covariance is thus (1_2 is the 2×2 unit matrix)

$$S_{\text{disp}} = \frac{\sigma^2}{n}\begin{bmatrix}1_2 & 0\\ 0 & \frac{12}{l^2}1_2\end{bmatrix}$$

We must transform this result to world coordinates. If the Jacobian matrix of the map from disparity space to the world is J Then

$$\begin{bmatrix}\mathbf{p}-\mathbf{p}_0\\ (\mathbf{v}-\mathbf{v}_0)|J\mathbf{v}_0|\end{bmatrix} = \begin{bmatrix}J & 0\\ 0 & J\end{bmatrix}\begin{bmatrix}\mathbf{p}-\mathbf{p}_0\\ \mathbf{v}-\mathbf{v}_0\end{bmatrix}_{\text{disp}}$$

Using the transformation above the error covariance of the description in the world is thus

$$S = \begin{bmatrix}\Sigma & 0\\ 0 & \frac{12}{l^2|J\mathbf{v}_0|^2}\Sigma\end{bmatrix}$$

where

$$\Sigma_{ij} = \frac{\sigma^2}{n}\mathbf{v}_i^t\, JJ^t\, \mathbf{v}_j \qquad i, j = 1, 2$$

if $\mathbf{p}_0$ is taken as the projection of the disparity space centroid into the world.

The above idealisation is very unrealistic for two main reasons. Firstly the stereo matching of continuous lines mixes the horizontal errors with the vertical errors; for lines with making angles θ with the horizontal which are close to zero depth values are highly inaccurate (when $\theta = 0$ matching is impossible). A crude way of compensating for this is to multiply J by a matrix producing an expansion factor of $1/\sin\theta$ in depth before using the above formulae. Secondly the points detected on continuous lines are not randomly scattered about the line, but wander slowly from one side of the line to the other. This can be compensated for by replacing n by a smaller effective number of points on the line which counts these wanderings. Though crude, this model then captures most of the essential information about stereo errors.

As an alternative to the calculation of an *a priori* covariance we can try to estimate the covariance from our data. Fit a line $(\mathbf{p}_0, \mathbf{v}_0)$ to the data, the true line being The true line is $(\mathbf{p}, \mathbf{v})$ with local coordinates as above. Suppose one of the data points (x, y, z) projects to $(X, Y) = (x/z, y/z)$ in the left image. Let $\mathbf{a} = (X, Y, 1)^t$. The condition that this image point lies on the projection of the true line into the image is $\mathbf{p}\cdot(\mathbf{a}\times\mathbf{v}) = 0$ which linearises to

$$\mathbf{p}_0\cdot(\mathbf{a}\times\mathbf{v}_0) + p_1\, \mathbf{v}_1\cdot(\mathbf{a}\times\mathbf{v}_0) + p_2\, \mathbf{v}_2\cdot(\mathbf{a}\times\mathbf{v}_0) + v_1\, \mathbf{p}_0\cdot(\mathbf{a}\times\mathbf{v}_1)$$

If we assume no prior knowledge, then by walking down the string of points imposing this constraint in each image, we can simultaneously correct our initial line and build up its covariance matrix.

13. Geometrical Constraints

We would like a module embodying the theory above to be available to a geometrical reasoning system as a knowledge source aiding in the interpretation of a single stereo view. As the geometrical reasoning system hypotheses geometrical relationships (orthogonality, coincidence of lines etc.) the module is able to assign likelihoods to these hypotheses, and if they are accepted, to correct the data to be consistent with the current under-

[13] Viewpoint-Invariant Reconstruction of Visible Surfaces

Andrew Blake

Department of Computer Science
University of Edinburgh, Edinburgh EH9 3JZ, Scotland,UK

An earlier and shorter version of this paper was published in the *Proceedings of the National Conference on Artificial Intelligence*, 1984, 23-26, published by William Kaufman.

Abstract

Stereoscopic vision delivers a sparse map of the range to various "matched" points or contours, in the field of view. This paper addresses the problem of explicitly reconstructing a smooth surface that interpolates those points and contours. It is argued that any scheme for surface reconstruction should be viewpoint-invariant; otherwise the reconstructed surface would "wobble" as the viewpoint changes.

Progress has been made towards obtaining viewpoint-invariant reconstruction. A scheme has been implemented in 2-D and found to be relatively invariant to changes of viewpoint. Some remaining theoretical problems are outlined.

1 Introduction

In this paper we consider aspects of the task of generating geometrical information from stereo vision, extending the conclusions of a previous paper [4]. The aim is to derive as rich a geometric description as possible of the visible surfaces of the scene - a "viewer-centred representation of the visible surfaces" [12]. Principally this is to consist of information about surface discontinuities and surface orientation and curvature. Ideally it would be desirable to label discontinuities, and generate smooth surfaces between them, all in a single process. Some preliminary work has been done towards achieving this [3] but here we restrict discussion to reconstruction of smooth surfaces.

Grimson [9] discusses the task of interpolating smooth surfaces inside a known contour (obtained from stereo e.g. [13], [11], [9], [2]). He shows how surface interpolation can be done by minimising a suitably defined surface energy, the "quadratic variation". The interpolating surface that results is *biharmonic* and under most conditions is defined uniquely. Terzopoulos [18] derives, via finite elements, a method of computing a discrete representation of the surface; the computation uses relaxation which is widely favoured for minimisation problems in computer vision [22], largely because of its inherent parallelism. Both Grimson and Terzopoulos suggest that the surface computed represents the configuration of a thin plate under constraint or load.

In this paper we first point out that the faithfulness of the computation to the physical thin plate holds only under stringent assumptions - assumptions that do not apply for the intended use in representing visible surfaces. It is argued that physical thin plates do not anyway have the right properties for surface interpolation - it is not desirable to try and model one. Secondly, the effect of biharmonic interpolation is investigated in its own right. We show that it lacks 3-D viewpoint-invariance and demonstrate, with 2-D examples, that this results in an appreciable "wobble" of the reconstructed surface as the viewpoint is varied.

An alternative method of surface reconstruction is proposed, minimising a surface energy that is invariant to changes of viewpoint. However there is a problem of non-uniqueness: there may be more than one minimising surface - a surface that *locally* minimises the surface energy. As viewpoint changes, the surface delivered by an optimisation process could "flip" from one local minimum to another, resulting in loss of viewpoint-invariance. The best compromise seems to be the mixed membrane/plate. The membrane on its own is stable and viewpoint-invariant, with unique minimum energy solutions, but the reconstructed surface is not smooth. The plate, on the other hand, is smooth but not viewpoint-invariant. A mixture of the two energies gives a controlled trade-off between smoothness and viewpoint-invariance.

2 The thin plate

Accurate mathematical modelling of a thin plate is fraught with difficulties and, in general, generates a somewhat intractable, non-linear problem. Under certain assumptions however the energy density on the plate can be approximated by a quadratic expression; minimising the total energy in that case is equivalent to solving a linear partial differential equation with linear boundary conditions. The partial differential equation determines the displacement $u(x, y)$ of the plate, in the z-direction

*Current address: Dept. Engineering Science, Parks Rd., Oxford OX1 3PJ.

(the viewer direction), that interpolates a set of matched points. These matched points are assumed to be available as the output of stereopsis. With an approximate representation of the plate in a discrete (sampled) space, using finite differences or finite elements, the linear differential equation becomes a set of simultaneous linear equations. These can be solved by relaxation. The assumptions necessary to approximate the surface energy by quadratic variation are analysed by Landau and Lifshitz [10] and we enumerate them:

1. The plate is thin compared with its extent.

2. The displacements of the plate from its equilibrium position $z = 0$ are substantially in the z-direction; transverse displacement is negligible.

3. The normal to the plate is everywhere approximately in the z-direction.

4. The deflection of the plate is everywhere small compared with its extent.

5. The deflection of the plate is everywhere small compared with its thickness

Assumption 1 is acceptable - indeed intuitively it is preferable to use a thin plate that yields willingly to the pull of the stereo-matched points. Assumption 2 may also be acceptable if the pull on the plate from each matched point is normal to the plate. The remaining assumptions 3-5 are the ones which prove to be stumbling blocks for reconstruction of visible surfaces.

Assumption 3 is clearly unacceptable: any scene (for example, a room with walls, floor, table-tops etc.) is liable to contain surfaces at many widely differing orientations. By no means will they all be in or near the frontal plane (i.e. normal to the z-direction), though it seems that human vision may have a certain preference for surfaces in the frontal plane (Marr, 1982). In particular, surfaces to which the z-axis is almost tangential are of considerable interest: it is important to be able to distinguish, in a region of large disparity gradient, between such a slanted surface and a discontinuity of range (caused by occlusion).

Assumption 4 and the even stronger assumption 5 are again unacceptably restrictive. In fact assumption 5 can be removed at the cost of introducing non-linearity that makes the problem considerably harder; the non-linear formulation takes into account the stretching energy of the plate as well as it bending energy. It is this energy that represents the unwillingness of a flat plate to conform to the surface of a sphere rather than to, say, a cylindrical or other developable surface. Even without assumption 5, assumption 4 on its own is still too strong because it requires the scene to be relatively flat - to have an overall variation in depth that is small compared with its extent in the xy plane. This is clearly inapplicable in general.

One conclusion from the foregoing review of assumptions is that that faithfulness of visible surface reconstruction to a physical thin plate model is undesirable. This is because of the stretching energy discriminating against spherical surfaces, which is not generally appropriate in surface reconstruction. In fact, happily enough, we saw that quadratic variation is *not* an accurate description of the surface energy of a thin plate precisely because it omits stretching energy, so biharmonic interpolation does *not* exhibit this discrimination.

We now declare ourselves free from any obligation to adhere to a physical thin plate model and will explore the geometrical properties of biharmonic interpolation.

3 Biharmonic interpolation

We now examine biharmonic interpolation in its own right. A variety of forms of such interpolation are possible and the one preferred by Grimson [9] is to construct that surface $z = f(x,y)$ that (uniquely) minimises the quadratic variation

$$F = \int A \, dx \, dy \quad \text{where} \quad A = f_{xx}^2 + f_{yy}^2, \tag{1}$$

subject to the constraints that $f(x,y)$ passes through the stereo-matched points[1]. Landau and Lifshitz show [10] that the solution to this minimisation satisfies the biharmonic equation

$$\nabla^2 \nabla^2 f = 0, \tag{2}$$

under certain boundary conditions. For instance when the edges of the surface are fixed (constrained, for example, by stereo-matched points) the condition is that

$$f \text{ is fixed and } \partial^2 f / \partial n^2 = 0, \tag{3}$$

where $\partial / \partial n$ denotes differentiation along the normal to the boundary. Consider the effect on a simple shape such as a piece of the curved wall of a cylinder, assuming that the surface is fixed on the piece's boundary. It is easy to show that a cylindrical surface defined by

$$f(x,y) = \sqrt{a^2 - x^2} \tag{4}$$

does not satisfy $\nabla^2 \nabla^2 f = 0$, so we cannot expect the surface to be interpolated exactly. Grimson [9] demonstrates this: his interpolation of such a boundary conforms to the cylindrical surface near the boundary ends but sags somewhat in the middle.

To return to the definition in (1), a serious objection to using quadratic variation to define surface energy is that it is not invariant under change of 3D coordinate frame. As (Brady and Horn, 1983) point out, it is isotropic in

[1] An alternative formulation attaches the surface $f(x,y)$ to matched points by springs, allowing some deviation of the surface from the points.

2D - invariant under rotation of axes in the xy plane. However, under a change of coordinate frame in which the z-axis also moves, the quadratic variation proves not to be invariant.

Is it altogether obvious that 3D invariance is required? Certainly the situation is not entirely isotropic in that the visible surface is single valued in z - any line perpendicular to the image plane intersects the visible surface only once - the z-direction is special. On the other hand it is also desirable that the interpolated surface should be capable of remaining the same over a wide range of viewpoints. Specifically, given a scene and a set of viewpoints over which occlusion relationships in the scene do not alter, so that the points matched by stereo do not change, the reconstructed surface should remain the same over all those positions. Such a situation is by no means a special case and is easy to generate: imagine, for example, looking down the axis of a "beehive" (fig 1). There is

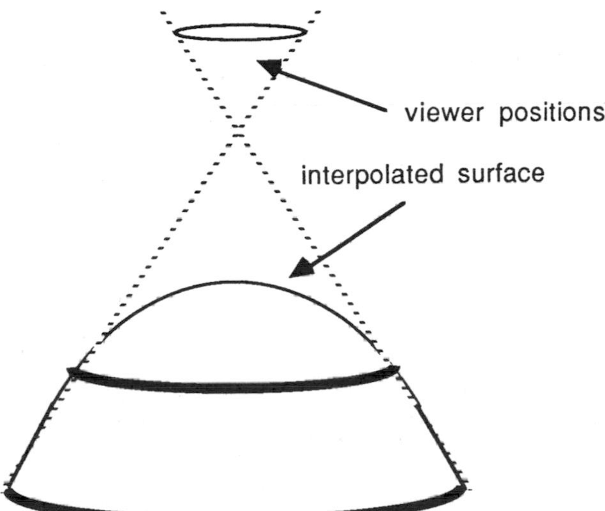

Figure 1: **Viewpoint-invariant surface reconstruction.** *The two solid rings can be interpolated by a "beehive"-shaped surface. Within the cone of viewer directions shown, the lower ring is not obscured by the upper one. It is argued that, for viewer directions lying in that cone, the interpolated surface should remain static (invariant) in 3-D.*

no change of occlusion over a range of viewer directions that lie inside a certain cone. The reconstructed surfaces of both beehive and table should remain static in 3D as viewpoint varies within that cone. The point is that, over such a set of viewpoints, the available information about the surface does not change; neither then should there be any change in the estimate of its shape[2]. Without invariance, a moving viewer would perceive a wobbling surface.

[2]Since the short version of this paper [4] appeared there has been some logomachy in the literature over the term "viewpoint-invariance". It has apparently been misunderstood by some as referring to invariance over *all* viewpoints, who proposed instead a cacology that was allegedly more accurate. What our term refers to, of course, is invariance over *some set* of viewpoints.

To demonstrate the wobble effect, surface interpolation using quadratic variation has been simulated in 2-D (fig 2) over a range of viewpoints. In the 2-D case, biharmonic interpolation simply fits a piecewise cubic polynomial to set of points. There is continuity of second derivative at those points and the second derivative is zero at the end-points. In other words, interpolation in 2-D reduces simply to fitting cubic splines [6]. As expected, the wobble effect is strong when boundary conditions are such that the reconstructed surface is forced to be far from planar.

4 A viewpoint-invariant surface energy

4.1 Deriving the energy expression

In order to obtain the desired invariance to viewpoint while still constraining the surface to be single valued along the direction of projection, the interpolation problem can be reformulated as follows: first surface energy is defined for an arbitrary 3D surface, defined by

$$g(x, y, z) = 0 \tag{5}$$

then the single value constraint is applied, that g must have the form

$$g(x, y, z) = f(x, y) - z \tag{6}$$

In this way we can generate a new energy expression to replace (1) that does have 3D invariance, because it is defined in terms of surface properties. The energy is:

$$F = \int E dS \text{ where } E = \kappa_1^2 + \kappa_2^2. \tag{7}$$

and where κ_1, κ_2 are principal curvatures and dS is the area of an infinitessimal surface element. This can be expressed quite straightforwardly, as a non-linear function of the derivatives [7]. It is not the *only* possible invariant energy but is consistent with the old expression (1) when $f_x = f_y = 0$ - the normal to the surface lies everywhere along the viewer direction. It is approximately consistent if the surface normal is everywhere close to the viewing direction. This is simply assumption 3, for the thin plate approximation, appearing again. Indeed, this consistency property leads to a proof that (1) is not in general an invariant expression: for a given surface element dS, we know that

- EdS is invariant with respect to change of coordinate frame
- $Adxdy = EdS$ in one coordinate frame but not in certain others

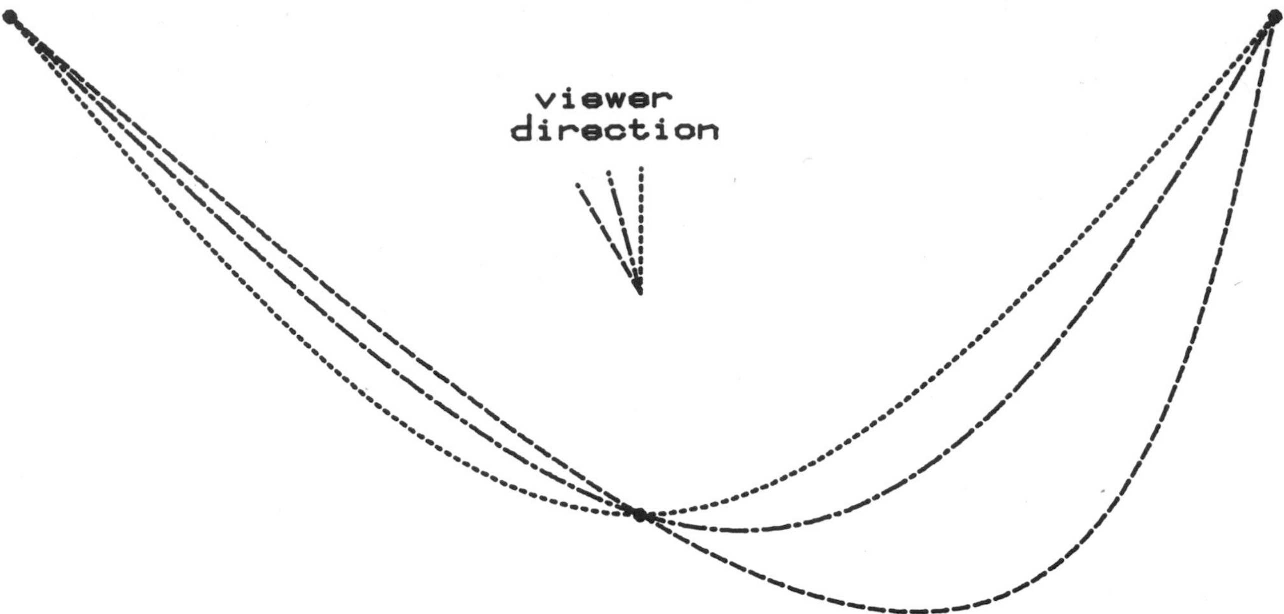

Figure 2: **Biharmonic interpolation scheme.** *Here is an example of the interpolation scheme operating in 2-D rather than 3-D. The curve interpolates 3 points (marked by circles). As the viewer direction varies from 0 to 30 degrees there is marked movement of the interpolating curve. Clearly the scheme is far from invariant to change of viewpoint.*

therefore $A dx dy$ cannot be invariant under change of coordinate frame.

The original energy (1) has a unique minimum [9] but for the new energy the situation is more complicated. To understand this we will consider, for simplicity, a 2-D form of the new energy:

$$F = \int_{x=x_1}^{x=x_2} E(f_x, f_{xx})\, \mathrm{d}s \tag{8}$$

where

$$E(t,u) = u^2(1+t^2)^{-3}$$

and the arc length $\mathrm{d}s = w(f_x)\,\mathrm{d}x$ with

$$w(t) = \sqrt{1+t^2}.$$

A standard result from the calculus of variations [1] states a certain sufficient set of conditions for a minimum of F to exist, one of which, in the case of (8), is that:

$$\exists a > 0, p > 1, \text{ s.t. } \forall t, u, E(t,u)w(t) \geq a|u|^p + b. \tag{9}$$

This condition is not satisfied as $E(t,u)$ becomes arbitrarily small for large enough t. This problem can be circumvented by restricting f to a family of functions whose normal is nowhere perpendicular to the line of sight - say at most 85° away. Now the term in u is bounded below. However, the boundary of this set of functions (defined by a condition $|u| < U$ for some U) is coordinate-frame dependent. So a local minimum f of F is guaranteed to be invariant (to small changes of viewpoint) if it lies in the interior of this set. If it lies on the boundary it may be viewpoint-dependent.

Note that, by the Morse-lemma [14], an f which locally minimises F in one coordinate frame (u,l) also minimises F in another frame (u',l'), provided that the change of frame is a "diffeomorphism". This property is needed for viewpoint-invariance of f. The change of frame is not diffeomorphic if, somewhere on the surface, the gradient becomes unbounded in the new frame. This is as expected: the surface acquires an extremal contour in the new frame and some of the previously reconstructed surface is lost to view. Clearly there is no viewpoint-invariance in this situation.

There remains a more serious problem: that of uniqueness. The integrand of (8) fails to satisfy a certain sufficient condition for uniqueness [21] because it is not convex. It can easily be shown that its Hessian matrix with respect to u, l is not positive definite. Therefore the integrand $E(u,l)w(u)$ is not convex in u, l. In the absence of convexity there may be more than one extremal function (non-uniqueness). Practical methods of finding local minima (such as the descent method used in the discrete computation in the next section) are coordinate frame dependent. Both the initial state (initial estimate of f) and the path taken from that state depend on the coordinate frame. This would not matter if there were a unique minimum; in each coordinate frame the descent method would reach that minimum, albeit via different paths. However if there are several local minima, the final state may flip from one to another as the coordinate frame is varied. This would cause viewpoint-invariance to be lost.

A certain modification of the energy in (8) can be shown to make it's integrand convex, at least asymptotically. The modified energy is

$$F = \int (E + K) w dx \tag{10}$$

where K is a positive constant. The additional term Kw adds a component of energy that is simply proportional to the length of the curve $f(x)$ between endpoints. In three dimensions this is simply the energy of an elastic membrane — energy is proportional to surface area. If K is very large, so that the membrane term dominates the energy F, the effect, in 2D, is simply to link the interpolated points by straight lines. Moreover the integrand is convex in the limit of large K. That is, the term $Kw(u)$ in (10) is convex in u because its second derivative

$$K w_{uu} = K \left(1 + u^2\right)^{-3/2} \tag{11}$$

is positive everywhere. The convexity result for the membrane holds also in 3D.

The membrane limit may be inappropriate to visible surface reconstruction because gradient discontinuities are introduced at interpolated points. (A drawn bow-string has a V-shaped kink at the archer's finger). An *intermediate* value of K produces a compromise between invariant interpolation and avoiding high curvature at interpolated points. Examples are shown in the next section. Note that the mixed membrane/plate is only approximately invariant. To make it fully invariant, it would be necessary to find a *convex, viewpoint-invariant set in u, l space over which the integrand is a convex function*. This is shown, in the appendix, to be impossible.

The modified energy (10) can easily be extended to the full 3-D case simply by adding a positive constant K to the integrand, as before. In 3-D, for large K, the surface behaves as a membrane having minimal area (and creases). An intermediate K achieves a compromise, as in 2-D.

5 Discrete computation in 2-D

Interpolation in 2-D, using the mixed membrane/plate of the previous section, has been implemented on a computer, using a parallel, iterative method. First the energy is expressed in a discrete form, by a finite element approximation [17]. Trial functions are represented as quadratic piecewise polynomials. A quadratic spline basis [6] allows the piecewise polynomials to be represented as vectors, each of whose components affects the energy function only locally. Hence when one of these components is adjusted only a local computation is necessary to update the total energy. This situation is typical of optimisation by parallel relaxation [22]. Computation is further simplified by approximating the energy (8) within each polynomial piece. The gradient u, in a polynomial piece, is approximated by its average value over that piece. A simple application of the patch test [17] shows that this is allowable.

The discrete scheme has been applied to the problem of fig 2, for which interpolation with quadratic variation was shown to be viewpoint-dependent. In practice, for an appropriate choice of K, the interpolated curve is very nearly static over viewpoints in the range $\pm 30^o$ (fig 3), without excessively high curvatures.

6 Conclusion

We have shown that:

1. Biharmonic interpolation does not accurately model a thin plate and, in any case, a thin plate model would be inappropriate for use in surface interpolation.

2. Biharmonic interpolation of the visible surface is not viewpoint-invariant and that, in specific 2-D cases, this lack of invariance certainly causes significant surface wobble.

3. A proposed alternative reconstruction scheme uses an energy that is a function of surface curvature and area — the mixed membrane/plate. In 2-D simulation the scheme appears to be relatively invariant to change of viewpoint. However the theoretical basis for invariance is still incomplete, because of problems demonstrating uniqueness. A possible line of investigation to try and resolve this would examine the Euler equation of the energy integrand. This would define the extrema. It might reveal, for instance, that for large values of the parameter K, any extremal surface must approximate to the surface of minimal area. In that case, reconstruction is, at least approximately, invariant to change of viewpoint.

4. If the visual task does not require smoothly interpolated surfaces then a computational membrane can be used which *is* viewpoint-invariant.

5. Before attempting to proceed to a full 3-D implementation, it is worth questioning whether it is anyway appropriate to perform full, explicit reconstruction of a surface as a range-map. An alternative would be to represent the surface in terms of prototype (e.g. quadric) surface patches [8], [15]. Such a representation could be computed from a range map; but a more direct route would be to perform surface reconstruction using the surface patches themselves, thus eliminating the need for the range map as an intermediate representation. This direct route might be

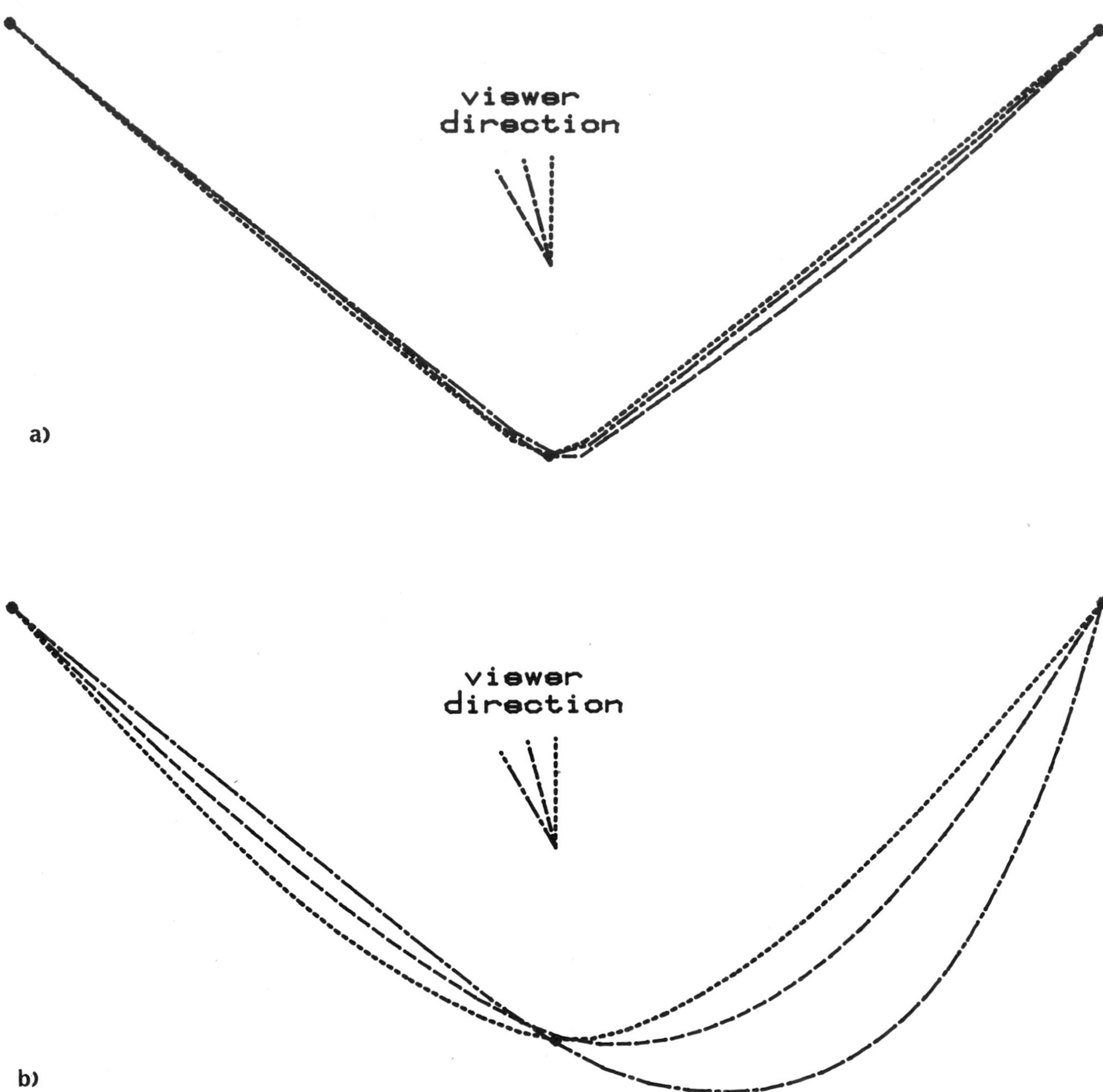

Figure 3: **Implementation of the proposed scheme.** *Compare results here with those for quadratic variation, in fig 2. The new scheme (a) is, for a modest value of the parameter K, fairly independent of viewpoint. As the parameter K is decreased there is more viewpoint dependence (b).*

attained by restricting the admissible family of functions in the finite element method to assemblies of prototype patches, and finding the member of that family with lowest energy.

6. The problem of detecting discontinuities has not been dealt with in this paper. Terzopoulos [19] suggests labelling zero-crossings of the reconstructed surface $f(x,y)$ as discontinuities. However, this method is not viewpoint-invariant (fig 5). Further work is needed here: one possibility is to incorporate a penalty for surface discontinuities into the surface energy function, an extension[3] of the method in [3].

7. The principle of 3-D invariance appears to be important in 2-1/2D sketch processes. Another potential area of application is shape-from-shading. The inferred shape of a beehive (fig 1) with a lambertian surface should be viewpoint-invariant, as with shape-from-stereo.

Acknowledgement

The author is grateful to Professor J. Ball and to Dr J. Mayhew and Professor J. Frisby for valuable discussion, to John Canny for pointing out an error in a previous version of this paper and to Andrew Zisserman for valuable comments.

References

1. Akhiezer,N.I. (1962). *The calculus of variations.* Blaisdell, New York.
2. Baker,H.H. (1981). Depth from edge and intensity based stereo. *IJCAI conf. 1981*, 583-588.
3. Blake,A. (1983). *Parallel computation in low-level vision.* Ph.D. Thesis, University of Edinburgh, Scotland.
4. Blake,A. (1984). Reconstructing a visible surface. *Proc AAAI conf. 1984*, 23-26.
5. Brady,M. and Horn,B.K.P. (1983). Rotationally symmetric operators for surface interpolation. *Comp. Vis. Graph. Image Proc.*, 22, 70-94.
6. de Boor,C. (1978). *A practical guide to splines.* Springer-Verlag, New York.
7. do Carmo,M.P. (1976). *Differential geometry of curves and surfaces.* Prentice-Hall, Englewood Cliffs, USA.
8. Faugeras,O.D. and Hebert,M. (1983). A 3-D recognition and positioning algorithm using geometrical matching between primitive surfaces. *IJCAI 83*, 996-1002.

[3] see the paper by Blake and Zisserman, in this volume.

9. Grimson,W.E.L. (1982). *From images to surfaces.* MIT Press, Cambridge, USA.
10. Landau,L.D. and Lifschitz,E.M. (1959). *Theory of elasticity.* Pergamon.
11. Marr,D. and Poggio,T. (1979). A computational theory of human stereo vision. *Proc. R. Soc Lond. B*, 204, 301-328.
12. Marr,D. (1982). *Vision.* Freeman, San Francisco.
13. Mayhew,J.E.W and Frisby,J.P. (1981). Towards a computational and psychophysical theory of stereopsis. *AI Journal*, 17, 349-385.
14. Poston,T. and Stewart,I. (1978). *Catastrophe theory and its applications.* Pitman, London.
15. Potmesil,M. (1983). Generating models of solid objects by matching 3D surface segments. *IJCAI 83*, 1089-1093.
16. Roberts,A.W. and Varberg,D.E. (1976). *Convex functions.* Academic Press, New York.
17. G. Strang and G.J. Fix, *An analysis of the finite element method.* Prentice-Hall, Englewood Cliffs, USA, 1973.
18. Terzopoulos,D. (1983). The role of constraints and discontinuities in visible-surface reconstruction. *IJCAI 83*, 1073-1077.
19. Terzopoulos,D. (1984). *Multiresolution computation of visible-surface representations.* Ph.D. Thesis, M.I.T., Cambridge, USA.
20. Thorpe,J.A. (1979). *Elementary topics in differential geometry.* Springer-Verlag, New York.
21. Troutman,J.L. (1983). *Variational calculus with elementary convexity.* Springer-Verlag, New York.
22. Ullman,S. (1979). Relaxed and constrained optimisation by local processes. *Computer graphics and image processing*, 10, 115-125.

A. Convexity in the 2-D case

"Adding in" the convex component in (10) can make the entire integrand convex, but only over a subset of values of u, l. To see this we examine the Hessian of the integrand in (10) with respect to u, l. If the Hessian is strictly positive definite in some domain then the integrand is strongly convex there [16].

$$T(u,l) = (E(u,l) + K)w(u) \tag{12}$$

where $E = l^2 w(u)^{-6}$ and $w(u) = \sqrt{1+u^2}$. Examining the hessian of T w.r.t u, l, a necessary and sufficient condition for convexity is that the hessian be positive definite [16]. Moreover a sufficient condition for strict convexity is that the hessian be strictly positive definite. Differentiating T twice, we obtain:

$$\begin{aligned} T_{ll} &= 2w^{-5}, \\ T_{uu} &= 5(6u^2 - 10w^{-9} + Kw^{-3}), \\ T_{ul} &= -10ulw^{-7}. \end{aligned} \tag{13}$$

The eigenvalues of the Hessian are

$$\frac{1}{2}\left((T_{ll} + T_{uu}) \pm \sqrt{(T_{ll} + T_{uu})^2 - 4(T_{uu}T_{ll} - T_{ul}^2)}\right) \tag{14}$$

and, since T_{ll}, T_{uu} are positive, the smallest eigenvalue is positive iff

$$T_{ll}T_{uu} \geq T_{ul}^2. \tag{15}$$

Substituting (14) into this condition and simplifying yields the condition

$$K \geq 5\kappa^2(1 + 4u^2). \tag{16}$$

Making this inequality strict yields a condition for strict convexity.

If a viewpoint-invariant sufficient condition for convexity could be found, which also formed a convex set in u, l space, in all coordinate frames, then constrained optimisation within that set would be viewpoint-invariant. No such condition exists however. The *only* viewpoint-invariant function of u, l is κ and, from (16), κ-intervals are not convex sets in the u, l space of any viewer coordinate-frame.

[14] Invariant Surface Reconstruction using Weak Continuity Constraints

Andrew Blake and Andrew Zisserman

Department of Computer Science
University of Edinburgh, Edinburgh EH9 3JZ, Scotland

Abstract

We consider surface reconstruction schemes in which the discontinuities are included explicitly by means of weak continuity constraints. It is essential that such a scheme be viewpoint invariant. We explain how this can be achieved. Two schemes are described: an invariant membrane and an invariant plate, where the regularising terms are respectively surface area and surface curvature. Results are presented of detection of discontinuities in range data, both simulated and from a laser range finder.

1 Introduction

Much work has been carried out on the problem of reconstructing surfaces from three dimensional data. Grimson[11] discusses the interpolation of smooth surfaces. He shows how surface interpolation can be done by minimising a suitably defined energy functional. The interpolating surface that results is biharmonic and under most conditions is defined uniquely. Terzopoulos[12] extended this work by using finite elements and generalising the interpolating surface to be a mixture of "membrane" and "thin plate". The computation involved relaxation which is widely used for minimisation problems in computer vision[14], largely because of its inherent parallelism.

However, there are two fundamental problems with these optimisation approaches. Firstly, the schemes do not label discontinuities *explicitly*. They can only be located by examining the gradient, after the surface has been fitted. Discontinuities can be included explicitly if the optimisation formulation uses *weak continuity constraints*. A weak constraint is one that is usually obeyed but may be broken on occasion - when there are pressing reasons to do so. This is discussed more fully in[2,6].

The second problem is that such schemes are not *invariant*. The reconstructed scheme will "wobble" as the viewpoint varies[4]. This is because instead of using the invariant quantities of surface area and surface curvature[1], the schemes use approximations to these quantities which are not invariant to change of viewpoint. Consequently the energy of the minimum energy surface changes with viewpoint. The advantage of using approximations is that energy can be minimised by solving locally coupled linear equations, and that there is a unique minimum in each frame.

In this paper we discuss two reconstruction schemes for surface approximation which incorporate weak continuity constraints. For a weak constraint a penalty is charged each time a constraint is broken. The penalty is weighed against certain "other costs". If breaking a constraint leads (somehow) to a total saving in "other costs" that exceeds the penalty, then breaking that constraint is deemed worthwhile. The energy of the "other costs" must be invariant otherwise the existence and position of discontinuities will depend on viewpoint.

Invariant schemes incorporating weak continuity constraints are harder to minimise than the earlier schemes because

- The cost function is non - convex so that naive descent tends to stick at local minima.
- They do not give rise to linear equations.

The first scheme we consider is an invariant membrane with weak (C^0) continuity constraints. Here the "other costs" mentioned above consist of a "closeness of fit" term and a term involving surface area. Minimising the energy is a trade off between fitting the data closely, reducing the surface area, and including discontinuities.

In the second scheme the "other costs" are a measure of closeness of fit and a term involving surface curvature. There are two types of discontinuity - a discontinuity in surface depth and a discontinuity in surface orientation.

Apart from reconstructing the surface an important use of the schemes is in localising discontinuities. Local edge detection operators (such as the Canny[9]) can have poor localisation in noisy data (where a large support must be used to improve the signal to noise ratio) . The problem is accentuated if the underlying step in the data is not symmetrical (for example a step with a finite gradient on one side). However, the localisation of discontinuities using weak continuity constraints is very good even under these circumstances[5].

In our numerical implementation we have used the Graduated Non-Convexity (GNC) Algorithm[3,6] as an approximate method for obtaining the global minimum. This allows the discretised energy to be minimised by local iterative methods. The GNC algorithm has been applied to dense range data obtained from a CSG body modeller and also from a laser range finder.

2 Invariant Membrane

The non-invariant schemes are

In 1D - a weak string:

$$E = \int \{(u-d)^2 + \lambda^2 (u')^2\}\, dx + P \qquad (1)$$

In 2D - a membrane:

$$E = \int \{(u-d)^2 + \lambda^2 (\nabla u)^2\}\, dx\, dy + P \qquad (2)$$

In each case there are three terms

1. A measure of faithfulness to data (the spring term).
2. A regularising term which depends on the gradient of the function.
3. A penalty term. In 1D this adds a penalty of α for each step discontinuity. In 2D the penalty is α multiplied by the length of the discontinuity.

The manner in which the parameters λ and α influence the behaviour is found by comparing the minimum energy solutions both with and without discontinuities for certain simple data[6]. The weak membrane will adopt the lowest energy configuration. The main conclusions are that

- The parameter λ is a characteristic length.
- The ratio $h_0 = \sqrt{2\alpha/\lambda}$ is a contrast threshold, determining the minimum contrast for detection of an isolated step edge.
- The ratio $g_l = h_0/2\lambda$ is a limit on gradient, above which spurious discontinuities may be marked. If the gradient exceeds g_l one or more discontinuities may appear in the fitted function.

In the first place we consider the modifications needed to make the weak string invariant, and describe how this affects the contrast threshold and gradient limit. This is then generalised to the (2D) invariant weak membrane.

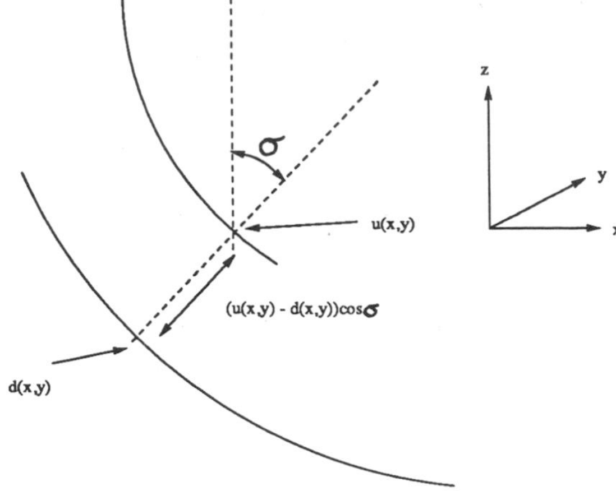

Figure 1: Invariant distance measurement: under the assumption that the surfaces u, d are roughly parallel, a fair estimate of perpendicular distance between them at (x, y) is $|u-d|\cos\sigma$.

2.1 Invariant weak string

The invariant version of (1) is

$$E = \int \{(u-d)^2 \cos^2\sigma + \lambda^2\}\, ds + P \qquad (3)$$

where

$$ds = \sqrt{1+(u')^2}dx = \sec\sigma\, dx. \qquad (4)$$

There are two changes from (1)

1. The spring term is multiplied by $\cos^2\sigma$ (where $\tan\sigma = u'$).
2. The *arc length* is used instead of $(u')^2$ in the regularising term.

Ideally instead of $(u-d)$, which is tied to a particular reference frame, the perpendicular distance between $u(x)$ and $d(x)$ (which is invariant) should be used. The $\cos^2\sigma\, ds$ term in (3) is an imperfect attempt to do this. (this is illustrated in figure 1). The inclusion of the $\cos^2\sigma\, ds$ term reduces the contribution of the spring term especially when $\cos\sigma$ is small. This occurs when the data has high gradient. Consequently the reconstructed function will be further away from the data in high gradient regions, especially if the data is noisy.

Such a correction is appropriate under the assumption that "noise" in the system derives from the surface, from surface texture for example. However this is inappropriate if the noise derives from the sensor itself, because the noise then "lives" in the viewer (sensor) frame. Instead,

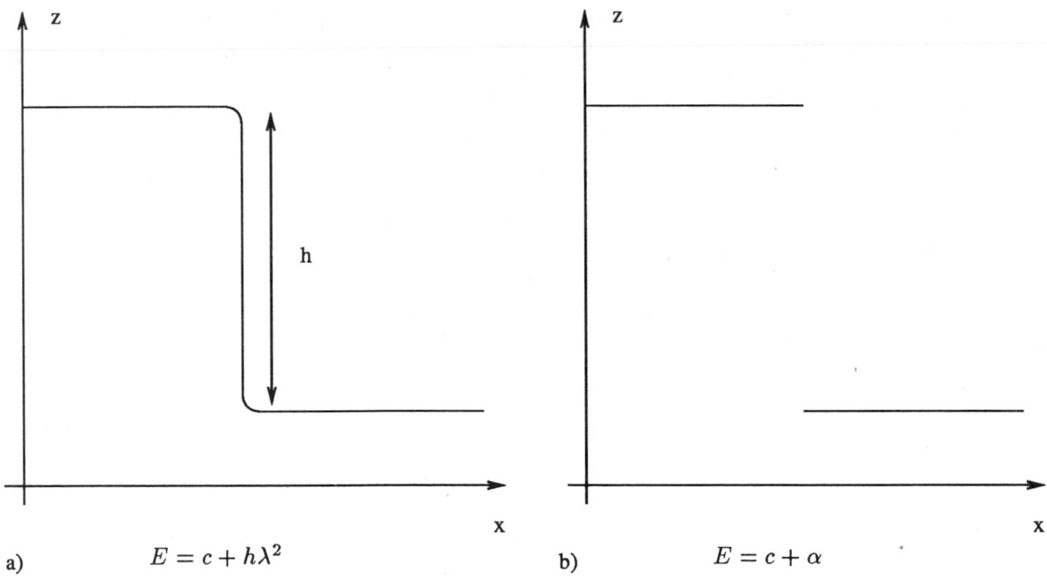

Figure 2: An isolated step (a) of height h. There are are two possible minima for the invariant weak string - a continuous function where $u(x)$ is close to $d(x)$ as in (a); or a step discontinuity (b).

the energy in that case is

$$E = \int \left\{ (u-d)^2 + \lambda^2 \sqrt{1 + (u')^2} \right\} dx + P \qquad (5)$$

The regularising term in (1) is the most obviously non-invariant part of the energy since it depends on gradient, which is clearly viewpoint dependent. The gradient can be small in one frame and (in theory) unbounded in another (for example at extremal boundaries - see later). Using the length as a regulariser, as in (3) and (5), entirely removes these problems.

Just as in the non-invariant case, there is a contrast threshold for the system. Its value is found by comparing the two possible minimum energies for data consisting of an isolated step of height h (see figure 2). If there is no discontinuity then to a first approximation (assuming $\lambda \ll h$) the energy is due solely to the length of the data

$$E = \lambda^2 (C + h) \qquad (6)$$

where h is the length of the vertical part of the step and C is the length of the horizontal part. If there is a discontinuity at the step then the minimum energy is

$$E = \lambda^2 C + \alpha \qquad (7)$$

Comparing the energies (6) and (7), the lowest energy solution will have a discontinuity if $h > \alpha / \lambda^2$.

Note there is some remission of the gradient limit g_l. This is simply because, when the surface gradient $g = u' \gg 1$, the length integrand above $\propto |g|$, rather than g^2 as for the non-invariant string. This is of most benefit near extremal boundaries where g becomes very large. This can be seen by considering a cylinder of radius r. From any viewpoint there will be an extremal boundary, and the gradient there will be extremely high (in theory unbounded). In the non-invariant string the gradient limit will certainly be exceeded and spurious discontinuities will be marked. However, in the invariant case the regularising term will be bounded by $\lambda^2 \pi r$ and so the problem is avoided. This point is clearly illustrated in the results of the range data segmentation (figure 4).

2.2 2D a weak membrane

In 2D the invariant energy is

$$E = \int \{ (u-d)^2 \cos^2 \sigma + \lambda^2 \} \, dS \; + P \qquad (8)$$

where

$$dS = \sec \sigma \, dx \, dy = \sqrt{1 + u_x^2 + u_y^2} \, dx \, dy$$

and

$$P = \alpha \times (\text{actual length of discontinuities}),$$

Each of the terms has been made invariant

1. The spring term has been corrected as in the 1D case. σ is the the surface slant.
2. The regularising term depends on the surface area.
3. The penalty involves the actual length of the discontinuity - not simply the projected length.

Note that as for the non-invariant membrane the energy is invariant to rotations in the xy plane[7].

Again it is the regularising term which has the most severe effect if it is not invariant. The arguments in 1D concerning the contrast threshold and remission from the gradient limit are equally applicable here.

The penalty term could be made invariant by incorporating slant and tilt dependent compensation as was done by Brady and Yuille[8], for perimeter measurement under back projection. However in many circumstances the change in length of a discontinuity will be small when the viewpoint varies (Consider, for example, the projection of a circle changing to an ellipse under rotation).

3 Invariant plate

In this section the invariant forms of the plate (and, in 1D, the rod) are described. For the rod the non-invariant energy is given by

$$E = \int \{(u-d)^2 + \mu^4 (u'')^2\} dx + P \tag{9}$$

This differs from the energy of a weak elastic string (1) in including the *second* derivative of u rather than the first. The energy E is "second order". Furthermore, P incorporates a penalty β for each crease (discontinuity in du/dx) and a penalty α for each step (discontinuity in u).

The 2D version comes in two varieties[11]

Quadratic variation:

$$E = \int \{(u-d)^2 + \mu^4 (u_{xx}^2 + 2u_{xy}^2 + u_{yy}^2)\}\, dx\, dy \ + P \tag{10}$$

Square laplacian:

$$E = \int \{(u-d)^2 + \mu^4 (u_{xx} + u_{yy})^2\}\, dx\, dy \ + P. \tag{11}$$

In fact any linear combination of these two is a feasible plate energy.

The invariant version for the rod is

$$E = \int \{(u-d)^2 \cos^2\sigma + \mu^4 (\kappa)^2\}\, ds \ + P \tag{12}$$

where κ is the curvature

$$\kappa = \frac{u''}{(1+(u')^2)^{3/2}} \tag{13}$$

The invariant equivalent of the square laplacian (11) is

$$E = \int \{(u-d)^2 \cos^2\sigma + \mu^4 (\kappa_1 + \kappa_2)^2\}\, dS \ + P \tag{14}$$

where κ_1, κ_2 are principal curvatures. The squared sum of curvatures

$$(\kappa_1 + \kappa_2)^2 = \frac{(Au_{xx} - 2Bu_{xy} + Cu_{yy})^2}{D^3}, \tag{15}$$

where

$$A = 1 + u_y^2 \ B = u_x u_y \ C = 1 + u_x^2 \text{ and } D = \sec^2\sigma,$$

from[10]. Note that A, B, C, D are all functions of 1st derivatives of u only. If sum of squared curvatures is to be used (the invariant form of quadratic variation) then

$$\kappa_1^2 + \kappa_2^2 = (\kappa_1 + \kappa_2)^2 - 2\kappa_1\kappa_2, \tag{16}$$

where, from[10] the gaussian curvature

$$\kappa_1\kappa_2 = \frac{u_{xx}u_{yy} - u_{xy}^2}{D^2}.$$

The effect of the D in the denominator is to reduce the influence of the regularising term. This has most effect when the surface gradients are large (for example noisy regions). In such regions the degree of smoothing in the viewer frame will be considerably reduced.

It can be shown[4] that, expressing the energy E as

$$E = \int \overline{E}(u_x, u_y, u_{xx}, u_{xy}, u_{yy})\, dx\, dy \ + P$$

$\overline{E}$ is a non-convex function of $u_x, \ldots$. So even with a fixed set of discontinuities, it is not known whether there is an optimal u to be found[13].

To overcome this problem we suggest the following approximate method. First, estimates for $u_x(x,y), u_y(x,y)$ are obtained by fitting an invariant weak membrane (8) to the rangefinder data. This yields estimates of u_x, u_y which can be inserted as constants into $\overline{E}$ which is then convex with respect to u_{xx}, u_{xy}, u_{yy}.

Another possibility is to use gradient information directly in an invariant scheme for detecting creases. There are then two passes for detecting both crease and step discontinuities. For example in 1D the invariant weak string with a small λ (3) is used to detect steps and provide some noise rejection. The gradient estimates $u'(x)$ have been regularised and thus are well behaved (bounded). These are used for the data in a scheme with energy

$$E = \int \left\{ (u' - d')^2 \cos^2\sigma + \mu^2 \left[\frac{u''}{(1+(d')^2)^{3/2}} \right]^2 \right\} ds + P \tag{17}$$

This has the additional benefit numerically that both schemes are first order (rather than second) so that the convergence of the iteration schemes is typically improved by at least an order of magnitude[6].

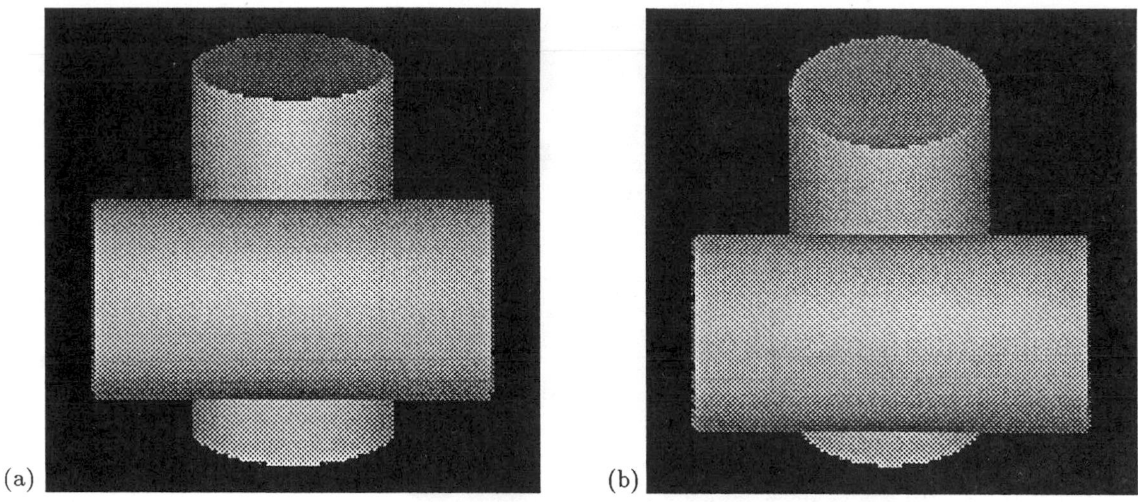

Figure 3: CSG image of two cylinders - (b) is (a) rotated by 15 degrees.

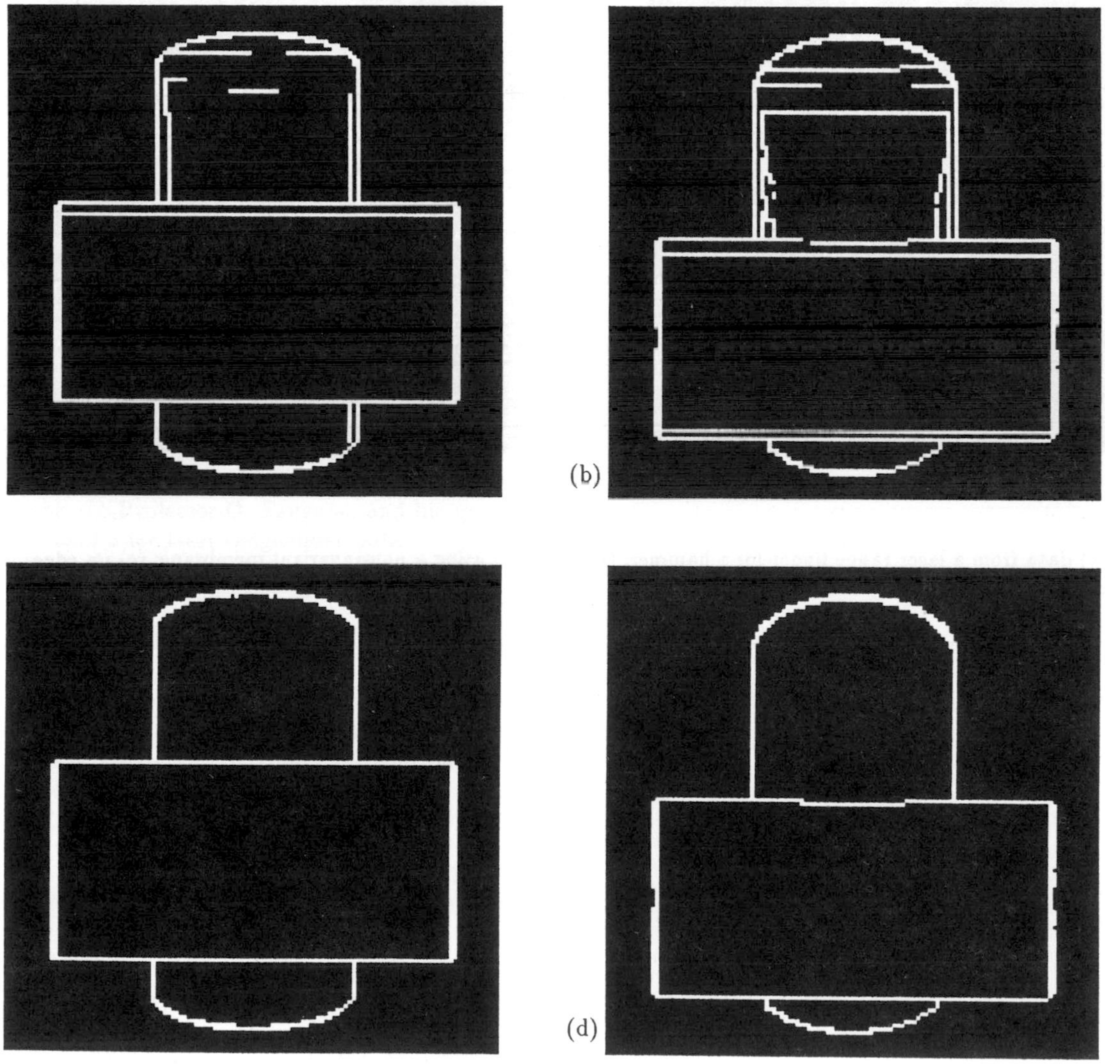

(a) (b)

(c) (d)

Figure 4: Edges detected in the depth data for the CSG cylinders (figure 3) . (a) and (b) are from a non-invariant membrane the double edges are where the gradient threshold is exceeded at the extremal boundaries. (c) and (d) are the edges detected using an invariant membrane.

[15] Comparison of the Efficiency of Deterministic and Stochastic Algorithms for Visual Reconstruction

Andrew Blake

Department of Computer Science
University of Edinburgh, Edinburgh EH9 3JZ, Scotland, UK

Abstract

Piecewise continuous reconstruction of real-valued data can be formulated in terms of non-convex optimisation problems. Both stochastic and deterministic algorithms have been devised to solve them. The simplest such reconstruction process is the "weak string". Exact solutions can be obtained for it, and are used to determine the success or failure of the algorithms under precisely controlled conditions. It is concluded that the deterministic algorithm (Graduated Non-Convexity) outstrips stochastic (Simulated Annealing) algorithms both in computational efficiency and in problem-solving power. Piecewise continuous reconstruction of real-valued data can be formulated in terms of non-convex optimisation problems. Both stochastic and deterministic algorithms have been devised to solve them. The simplest such reconstruction process is the "weak string". Exact solutions can be obtained for it, and are used to determine the success or failure of the algorithms under precisely controlled conditions. It is concluded that the deterministic algorithm (Graduated Non-Convexity) outstrips stochastic (Simulated Annealing) algorithms both in computational efficiency and in problem-solving power.

1 Introduction

Visual Reconstruction is the reduction of noisy visual data to stable descriptions. An early stage in this process involves approximating data by continuous or piecewise continuous functions. In particular this paper is concerned with optimisation formulations for such tasks. Work in this area has included analysis of shading [29, 15, 13, 4], stereo [11, 27] and optic flow [14, 24]. More recently such methods have been extended to deal with discontinuities [3, 10, 22, 5, 6, 28, 23, 2, 8, 9, 18].

Both deterministic (relaxation) algorithms and stochastic ones (simulated annealing) have been used for visual reconstruction with discontinuities. Intuitively it might seem that stochastic algorithms, using random perturbations, should be less efficient than deterministic ones. We will show in carefully controlled comparisons that this is indeed the case.

The problem chosen for study is the "weak string" which is a 1D reconstruction process susceptible both to deterministic and stochastic algorithms. It is a means of approximating a noisy function $d(x)$ by a piecewise continuous function $u(x)$. It admits of an exact solution - an important property for benchmarking purposes. Note that $u(x)$ is real-valued, not restricted to a few levels or colours. This is an important point, as in many visual applications real-valued quantities are involved and must be estimated by a reconstruction process. Moreover the deterministic algorithm to be tested (GNC [3, 8]) does not lend itself to discrete valued problems.

Evaluation of Simulated Annealing in one particular problem [12] showed that it succeeds only if the characteristic "scale" or "smoothing parameter" of reconstruction is not too great. Another study [16] shows that the deterministic GNC algorithm requires about the same computational effort to solve the real-valued "weak membrane" problem as does Simulated Annealing to perform a similar but boolean-valued reconstruction. However the state-space for a real-valued problem is so much larger (i.e. uncountable) that it is reasonable to expect that more computational effort might be required than in the boolean case. This also accords with experience of deterministic algorithms [27, 8] in which increasing precision of reconstruction results in increased computational load. Those studies also reveal other important factors in the computational load. Computation time is strongly dependent both on scale of reconstruction and on the noise content of the data. Both factors will be examined in this paper.

Benchmarks used in the paper are for 1D reconstruction, using the weak string. Although results are for 1D data, there is some justification for the conjecture that they will apply to 2D - for example to the weak membrane whose computational structure is a direct 2D analogue of the weak string. Of course there exist phenomena in certain interaction models (e.g. phase transitions in Ising models) that occur only in 2D, not in 1D. However, relevant properties for piecewise continuous reconstruction (scale and sensitivity properties, resistance to noise, "gradient

*Current address: Dept. Engineering Science, Parks Rd., Oxford.

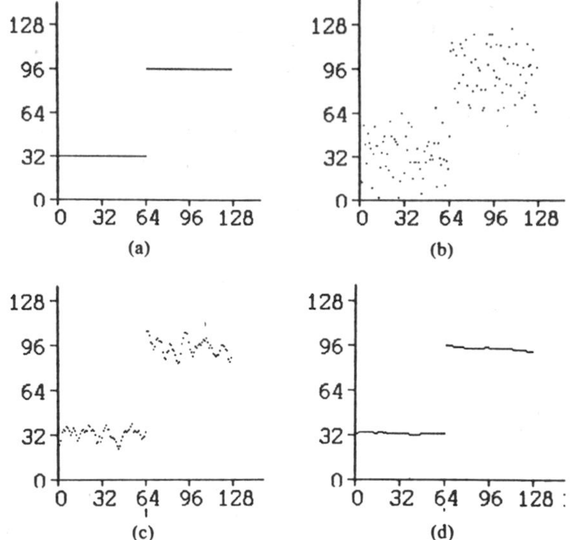

Figure 1: An isolated antisymmetric step (a) in random, uncorrelated gaussian noise of standard deviation 16 units (b) reconstructed by a weak string at small scale (c) and large scale (d).

limit") are common both to 1D and to 2D [8]. Moreover, performance of classical optimisation (i.e. with fixed rather than variable discontinuities) is known to be qualitatively similar in 1D and in 2D. And in the non-classical case, convergence of the GNC algorithm has been observed to be qualitatively similar both in 1D and in 2D.

The organisation of the paper is as follows. Section 2. defines the weak string problem and the algorithms to solve it, both deterministic and stochastic. Section 3. describes a new, exact dynamic programming solution for the weak string, to be used as an "assay" for benchmarks. Section 4. sets out results, using the benchmarks, of measurements of computational effort for deterministic and stochastic algorithms.

2 The weak string: problem and algorithms

In this section the weak string reconstruction problem is briefly described; a more detailed description is given in [8]. It is also more or less the simplest form of reconstruction for 1D signals that is capable of detecting and localising discontinuities. It is sufficiently simple that exact solutions can be computed (see next section) but sufficiently complex to be genuinely representative of a family of 1D and 2D reconstruction problems. An example of reconstruction by the weak string is given in figure 1.

2.1 The weak string

As with continuous reconstruction [11, 27] the weak string is defined in terms of functions and functionals. Given data $d(x)$ a reconstruction $u(x)$ is obtained by minimising an energy $E(u, d)$. This can be converted by means of "finite elements" [26, 30] to a discrete problem. A reconstruction

$$\mathbf{u} = \{u_i \; i = 1,..,N\}, \;\; \mathbf{l} = \{l_i \; i = 1,..,N-1\}$$

is obtained from data $\mathbf{d} = \{d_i, \; i = 1,..,N\}$ by minimising the energy E:

$$\min_{u_i, l_i} E, \text{ where } E = D + S + P \tag{1}$$

and

$$\begin{aligned} D &= \sum_1^N (u_i - d_i)^2, \\ S &= \lambda^2 \sum_1^{N-1} (u_i - u_{i+1})^2 (1 - l_i), \\ P &= \alpha \sum_1^{N-1} l_i. \end{aligned} \tag{2}$$

The constant λ, the elasticity of the string, controls the scale of reconstruction. Constant α is a penalty levied for the inclusion of a breakpoint (discontinuity) and controls resistance to noise. Sensitivity is determined by the ratio $\sqrt{\alpha/\lambda}$. As it stands, the optimisation problem is "mixed" involving both boolean (l_i) and real (u_i) variables. It has been shown [8] that the mixed optimisation can be reduced to the following problem involving only real variables:

$$\min_{u_i} F \tag{3}$$

where

$$F = D + \sum_1^{N-1} g(u_i - u_{i+1}) \tag{4}$$

and

$$g(t) = \begin{cases} \lambda^2 t^2 & \text{if } |t| < \sqrt{\alpha}/\lambda \\ \alpha & \text{otherwise.} \end{cases} \tag{5}$$

Optimal values of l_i can be obtained explicitly from the optimal u_i as follows:

$$l_i = \begin{cases} 0 & \text{if } |u_i - u_{i+1}| < \sqrt{\alpha}/\lambda \\ 1 & \text{otherwise.} \end{cases} \tag{6}$$

The system can be understood by a mechanical analogy, in terms of coupled springs as in figure 2. It can also be understood in probabilistic terms as a "Markov Random Field" (MRF) whose prior probability density for a given state is simply $\exp(-(S+P)/T_0)$, where T_0 is a constant. A sample from the MRF is observed with additive gaussian noise whose probability density is $\exp(-D/T_0)$. The joint posterior probability of a particular set $\mathbf{d}$ of observed data is therefore proportional to

$$\exp(-(S+P)/T_0)\exp(-D/T_0) = \exp(-E/T_0). \tag{7}$$

Minimising the energy E is therefore equivalent to maximising this posterior probability.

The energy $E(\mathbf{u}, \mathbf{l})$ is convex with respect to variables u_i, for fixed l_i, so that if line-variables l_i are fixed, classical optimisation procedures can be used to determine optimal u_i as in [11, 27]. But it is non-convex with respect to the variables l_i, so that when line-variables are treated as alterable classical optimisation is no longer adequate. (This is because non-convex functions may have many local minima; classical optimisation may lead to any one of them, which will not necessarily be a global minimimum.) Similarly, in the alternative form of the problem, $F(\mathbf{u})$ is non-convex with respect to the u_i - classical optimisation is no use there either. The purpose of this paper is to quantify the performance of algorithms which *are* capable of minimising some non-convex energies, including various stochastic algorithms and the deterministic "GNC" algorithm.

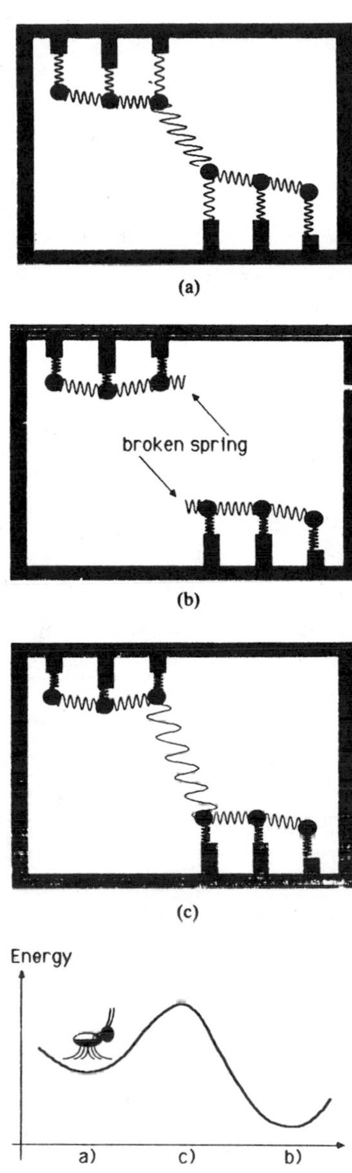

Figure 2: The weak string is like a system of conventional vertical springs with "breakable" lateral springs as shown. The states (a) and (b) are both stable, but the intermediate state (c) has higher energy than either (a) or (b). Suppose the lowest state is (b). A myopic fly with vertigo, crawling along the energy transition diagram (d), thinks state (a) is best. He has no way of seeing that, over the hump, he could get to a lower state (b). This is the "non-convexity" problem.

2.2 Stochastic optimisation

Stochastic algorithms for optimising non-convex energies have been described by various authors [25, 17, 10]. They use simulated annealing techniques in which the magnitude of successively applied random disturbances is controlled by a temperature parameter. Temperature (T) is lowered gradually according to a fixed "schedule". At high temperatures the system is able to jump out of local minima in the energy function and, as it cools, should settle into the system's ground state - its global energy minimum. The ground state can be achieved, in theory, [10] if a schedule is followed in which $T \propto 1/\log(n)$ (at the nth iteration or time-step of the system). Such a schedule takes an entirely unrealistic length of time. In practice a truncated logarithmic schedule is usually used but of course it can no longer be guaranteed that the ground state will be reached.

In this paper three variants of the simulated annealing algorithm for mixed variable problems are considered.

- The "Heatbath" (as described by Geman and Geman [10]) in which the thermal system is maintained in equilibrium as temperature decreases.
- What we will call the "Metropolis-Heatbath" algorithm in which the u_i are updated in the same way as in the Heatbath but the l_i are modified according to the Metropolis procedure [21].
- "Mixed annealing" [20] in which the u_i are updated according to a deterministic formula, but the l_i follow the Metropolis rule.

The first and last of these are included because they have been studied by other authors, and the Metropolis-Heatbath algorithm is interesting because it turns out to be the most efficient of the three, at least for the weak string problem. The three algorithms will now be described briefly.

Heatbath

Each iteration consists of N visits made to randomly picked sites i, to update u_i and then l_i. Successive new values of u_i, l_i are generated by a "Gibbs Sampler" [10] - the values are chosen randomly from their conditional distibutions. Updating l_i is done by setting $l_i = l$ where l is picked randomly from the distribution

$$P_{l_i}(l) = \\ P(l_i = l | u_j,\ j = 1,..,N;\ l_j,\ j = 1,..,N-1,\ j \neq i),$$

for $l \in \{0,1\}$. For the weak string, this distribution is easily shown from (1), (2) and (7) to be

$$P_{l_i}(l) \propto \exp\left(-\frac{\alpha l + (1-l)(u_i - u_{i+1})^2\lambda^2}{T}\right). \quad (8)$$

Similarly u_i is updated to a value u chosen randomly from the distribution

$$P_{u_i}(u) = \\ P(u_i = u | u_j,\ j = 1,..,N,\ j \neq i;\ l_j,\ j = 1,..,N-1).$$

For the weak string this is

$$P_{u_i}(u) \propto \exp\left(-\frac{(u-\mu_i)^2}{\sigma_i^2 T}\right) \quad (9)$$

where

$$\mu_i = \sigma_i^2 \left(d_i + \lambda^2((1-l_{i-1})u_{i-1} + (1-l_i)u_{i+1})\right) \quad (10)$$

and

$$\sigma_i^2 = \left((2 - l_{i-1} - l_i)\lambda^2 + 1\right)^{-1} \quad (11)$$

These formulae are of course modified for sites near the ends $i = 1, N$. Temperature T is lowered according to a truncated logarithmic schedule

$$T = T_0 \frac{\log(2)}{\log(2+n)}, \quad n \geq 0. \quad (12)$$

Metropolis-Heatbath

This algorithm works as the Heatbath except that line-variables l_i are updated according to the Metropolis procedure as follows. First calculate the energy change

$$\begin{aligned} \Delta E = &\ E(u_1,..,u_N;\ l_1,..,l_{i-1}, 1-l_i, l_{i+1},..,l_{N-1}) \\ - &\ E(u_1,..,u_N;\ l_1,..,l_{i-1}, l_i, l_{i+1},..,l_{N-1}) \end{aligned}$$

which, for the weak string,

$$= (\alpha - (u_i - u_{i+1})^2\lambda^2)(1 - 2l_i). \quad (13)$$

Then do the following:

if	$\Delta E < 0$	**then**	$l_i \rightarrow 1 - l_i$
but if	$\Delta E \geq 0$	**then**	$l_i \rightarrow 1 - l_i$ with probability $\exp(-\Delta E/T)$.

That is, if energy would be decreased the change is invariably accepted. Otherwise the decision whether to make the change is made according to the toss of a (biassed) coin.

Mixed annealing

Line variables l_i are updated as in the Metropolis-Heatbath, but the u_i are updated deterministically as follows:

$$u_i \rightarrow (1-w)u_i + w\mu_i, \quad (14)$$

where μ_i is as defined previously. Marroquin [20] uses $w = 1$ with sequential site visitation. Random site visitation with "optimal" w (a value dependent on λ and in the interval $(1,2)$ - see below under discussion of the GNC algorithm) will also be tried.

2.3 The GNC algorithm

The Graduated Non-convexity (GNC) algorithm is a deterministic procedure for optimising certain non-convex energies associated with piecewise continuous reconstruction problems [3, 5, 8]. It is based on a convex approximation $F^{(1)}$ to the energy F in (4). A family of functions $F^{(p)}$, $p \in [0,1]$ is defined such that $F^{(1)}$ is convex, $F^{(0)} \equiv F$, and $F^{(p)}$ varies continuously, in a particular prescribed manner, as p decreases from 1 to 0. For $0 \leq p < 1$ the $F^{(p)}$ are non-convex - of the whole family, only $F^{(1)}$ is convex. The $F^{(p)}$ are obtained quite simply by replacing the local interaction energy terms $g(..)$ in (4) by new energy terms $g^{(p)}(..)$ (figure 3). The GNC algorithm for the weak string is given in table 1. Detailed explanation of the algorithm will be found in [8], including such issues as how successive values of p should be chosen and norms for measurement of convergence. The GNC algorithm is distinguished in that it has been proved, for the weak string problem, to converge to the global minimum energy for a significant class of inputs $\mathbf{d}$ [8]. The proof applies more or less for the practical computer implementation of the algorithm. This is in sharp contradistinction with stochastic algorithms for which only asymptotic results have been obtained [19, 10]. The algorithm used in this paper applies to 1D dense data only. However the algorithm extends very naturally for 2D data, and also (but not quite so naturally) for sparse data.

Because the GNC algorithm is deterministic one might

Choose λ, h_0 (scale and sensitivity).
Set $\alpha = h_0^2\lambda/2$.
SOR parameter: $w = 2/(1+1/\lambda)$.
Function sequence: $p \in \{1, 0.5, 0.25, ..., 1/\lambda\}$.
Nodes: $i \in \{1, ..., N\}$.

Iterate $n = 1, 2, ...$

For $i = 2, ..., N-1$:

$$u_i^{(n+1)} = u_i^{(n)} - \omega\left\{2\left(u_i^{(n)} - d_i\right) + g^{(p)\prime}\left(u_i^{(n)} - u_{i-1}^{(n+1)}\right) + g^{(p)\prime}\left(u_i^{(n)} - u_{i+1}^{(n)}\right)\right\} / \left(2 + 4\lambda^2\right)$$

where

$$g^{(p)\prime}(t) = \begin{cases} 2\lambda^2 t, & \text{if } |t| < q \\ -\frac{1}{2p}(|t| - r)\text{sign}(t), & \text{if } q \leq |t| < r \\ 0, & \text{if } |t| \geq r \end{cases}$$

and

$$r^2 = \alpha\left(4p + \frac{1}{\lambda^2}\right), q = \frac{\alpha}{\lambda^2 r}.$$

Initially $p = 1$. Switch to successive p after convergence at current p. Appropriate modification is necessary at boundaries:

$$u_1^{(n+1)} = u_1^{(n)} - \omega\left\{2\left(u_1^{(n)} - d_1\right) + g^{(p)\prime}\left(u_1^{(n)} - u_2^{(n)}\right)\right\} / \left(2 + 2\lambda^2\right)$$

and similarly at $i = N$.

Table 1: **The GNC algorithm for the weak string (SOR version).**

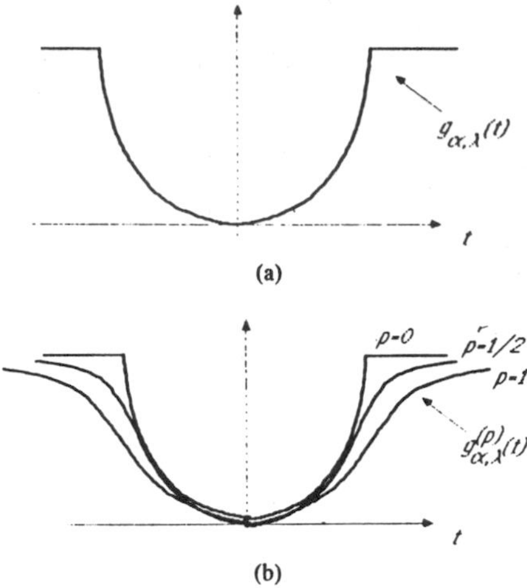

Figure 3: The energy of interaction between neighbouring sites in the weak string computation is governed by the function shown (a). The central part of the function represents a Hooke's law spring, and the outer part a spring pulled past its breaking point. The GNC algorithm replaces this function with a sequence of functions (b).

expect that it should be more efficient than algorithms employing random perturbations. This is precisely what, by controlled experiment, this paper sets out to demonstrate. Now in order to demonstrate the success or failure of an algorithm in reconstruction from a particular set of data **d** it is necessary to have some access to the correct solution **u**, **l**. For the weak string problem, the solution can be obtained from a dynamic programming algorithm described in the next section.

3 An assay for weak string benchmarks

In this section a new dynamic programming algorithm is presented that delivers an exact solution to the problem of minimising $E(\mathbf{u},\mathbf{l})$. The time-complexity of the algorithm is at worst $O(N^3)$ and can be as little as $O(N^2)$. This compares unfavourably however with GNC whose time-complexity is $O(N\lambda)$ [8]. However, because it is exact the dynamic programming algorithm can be used as an "assay" to verify that a particular reconstruction $(\mathbf{u},\mathbf{l})$ of data **d** is indeed optimal (i.e. that it globally minimises $E(\mathbf{u},\mathbf{l})$). Readers wishing to take the assay on trust and look at the results of algorithm evaluation should skip the remainder of this section.

It has already been pointed out [7] that the problem of minimising $F(\mathbf{u})$ can be solved by dynamic programming, provided the real-valued u_i are first quantised into M discrete levels. The time complexity of the resulting algorithm is then $O(NM^2)$ so M must not be too large. However the effect of coarseness of quantisation on accuracy of the solution cannot easily be analysed. Therefore the method is unusable as an assay. Mumford and Shah [22] describe an algorithm for the weak string (or at least for a closely related problem) for which u_i are not required to be quantised. But it relies on an assumption that breakpoints (values of i for which $l_i = 1$) are spaced by a distance that is large compared with the characteristic scale λ. Hence it is not usable in general. As neither of these existing algorithms is suitable for our purpose, a new one is required.

An exact dynamic programming algorithm will be described which requires no quantisation of the u_i. In many cases, moreover, its time-complexity is better than for the earlier dynamic programmming algorithm. The new algorithm will be described in outline here; some further details are given in appendix A.

Given data d_i, $i = 1, .., N$ and choices of parameters α, λ, our problem is to find a global minimum of $E(\mathbf{u},\mathbf{l})$. The first step will be to re-express energy E in terms of the set of breakpoints $\mathbf{L} = \{L_k,\ k = 0, .., K+1\}$ which take values (their positions)

$$L_k \in \{0, .., N-1\},\ 1 \leq k \leq K, \quad \text{with } L_0 = 0,\ L_{K+1} = N.$$

The constant K is to be chosen in a manner to be described later. Without loss of generality it can be assumed that $L_k \leq L_{k+1}$. Given breakpoints, line-variables l_i are

$$l_i = \begin{cases} 1 & \text{if } \exists k \text{ s.t. } L_k = i \\ 0 & \text{otherwise.} \end{cases}$$

The optimal u_i for a given set of break-points could then be obtained simply by minimising $E(\mathbf{u},\mathbf{l})$ which (remember earlier) is convex with respect to $\mathbf{u}$. Hence $\mathbf{u}$ is obtainable from any classical descent algorithm, or else by a recurrence relation with time complexity $O(N)$. In fact we will not be interested in $\mathbf{u}$ - only $\mathbf{l}$ will be required explicitly.

Once energy has been obtained in terms of breakpoints as $E(\mathbf{L})$, it will remain to observe that $E(\mathbf{L})$ is decomposable into a sum of functions each involving only two adjacent breakpoints. Therefore dynamic programming, can be applied in a standard manner, to find the optimal breakpoint set $\mathbf{L}$.

3.1 Expressing energy E in terms of breakpoints

Given a set $\mathbf{L}$ of breakpoints, energy E can be expressed as

$$E(\mathbf{L}) = \sum_{k=0}^{K} \mathcal{E}(L_k, L_{k+1}) + \sum_{k=1}^{K} Z(L_k) \tag{15}$$

where

$$Z(L_k) = \begin{cases} \alpha & \text{if } 0 < L_k < N \\ 0 & \text{otherwise (i.e. when } L_k = 0) \end{cases} \tag{16}$$

- the penalty for allowing a discontinuity - and $\mathcal{E}(L_k, L_{k+1})$ is the energy of the continuous length of reconstructed string between breakpoints L_k, L_{k+1} which, from the elastic string model, is:

$$\mathcal{E}(i,j) = \qquad (17)$$

$$\min_{u_{i+1},\ldots,u_j} \left\{ \sum_{m=i+1}^{j} (u_m - d_m)^2 + \lambda^2 \sum_{m=i+1}^{j-1} (u_m - u_{m+1})^2 \right\}$$

for $j \geq i+2$

and

$$\mathcal{E}(i,i) = \mathcal{E}(i,i+1) = 0. \qquad (18)$$

Note that when $L_k = 0$, $Z(L_k) = 0$ so that node $i = 0$ acts as a "garage" for unrequired breakpoint variables L_k, where they can rest without incurring any breakpoint penalty α. By this means the energy $E(\mathbf{L})$ can represent the energy of any weak string reconstruction with *up to* K breakpoints.

It remains actually to construct $\mathcal{E}(i,j)$ which is a triangular array since it is defined only for $j \geq i$. It is a function of $\mathbf{d}, \lambda, \alpha$ and can be constructed by means of recurrence relations. First the quantity $\mathcal{E}^\dagger(i,j,u_{j+1})$ is defined:

$$\mathcal{E}^\dagger(i,j,u_{j+1}) = \qquad (19)$$

$$\min_{u_{i+1},\ldots,u_j} \left\{ \sum_{m=i+1}^{j+1} (u_m - d_m)^2 + \lambda^2 \sum_{m=i+1}^{j} (u_m - u_{m+1})^2 \right\}$$

for $j > i$

and

$$\mathcal{E}^\dagger(i,i,u_{i+1}) = (u_{i+1} - d_{i+1})^2. \qquad (20)$$

Now from this definition it follows that the following recursive property holds, for $j > i$:

$$\mathcal{E}^\dagger(i,j,u_{j+1}) = \qquad (21)$$

$$\min_{u_j} \left\{ \mathcal{E}^\dagger(i,j-1,u_j) + \lambda^2 (u_j - u_{j+1})^2 + (u_{j+1} - d_{j+1})^2 \right\}.$$

It can now be deduced from (21) and (20), by induction on j, that $\mathcal{E}(i,j,u_{j+1})$ is a quadratic expression in u_{j+1}. From (17), (19) and (20) the quadratic expression is:

$$\mathcal{E}^\dagger(i,j,u_{j+1}) = (u_{j+1} - \overline{u}_{i,j+1})^2 \mathcal{F}_{j+1-i} + \mathcal{E}(i,j+1), \quad (22)$$

where $\mathcal{F}_m$ and $\overline{u}_{i,j}$ are constant coefficients that must be computed and, of course, $\mathcal{E}(i,j)$ is the desired triangular array whose evaluation is the goal of the entire construction above. Substitution of (22) into (21) yields mutual recurrence relations for $\mathcal{F}_m$, $\overline{u}_{i,j}$, $\mathcal{E}(i,j)$ (appendix A.) which enable $\mathcal{E}(i,j)$ to be computed.

Having obtained the triangular array $\mathcal{E}$ we are now in a position to determine K the maximum number of breakpoints. The global minimum energy $E(\mathbf{L})$ is clearly less than the energy in the absence of breakpoints, that is:

$$E(\mathbf{L}) \leq \mathcal{E}(0,N)$$

but if there are K' active breakpoints (breakpoints $L_k \neq 0$ which incur a penalty α) then

$$E(\mathbf{L}) \geq \sum_{k=1}^{K} Z(L_k) = K'\alpha.$$

Hence

$$K' \leq \frac{\mathcal{E}(0,N)}{\alpha}$$

so it is safe to choose

$$K = \left\lfloor \frac{\mathcal{E}(0,N)}{\alpha} \right\rfloor \qquad (23)$$

where $\lfloor .. \rfloor$ denotes the integer part of a real-valued quantity.

3.2 Dynamic programming

Now that energy $E(\mathbf{L})$ is in the form of a sum of local functions (15), dynamic programming [1] can be applied. Partial energy functions ϕ_k and policy functions p_k are defined:

$$\phi_0(L_1) = \mathcal{E}(0, L_1), \qquad (24)$$

$$\phi_k(L_{k+1}) = \min_{L_k \leq L_{k+1}} \phi_{k-1}(L_k) + \mathcal{E}(L_k, L_{k+1}),\ 1 \leq k \leq K \qquad (25)$$

and $p_k(L_{k+1})$ is the value of L_k that minimises (25) above. Construction of all these policy functions (as a set of K N-element tables) has time-complexity $O(KN^2)$. Then the solution for the optimal breakpoints is given by

$$L_{K+1} = N \text{ and } L_k = p_k(L_{k+1}) \text{ for } 1 \leq k \leq K. \quad (26)$$

4 Measurements of performance

The previous section described an exact algorithm usable as an assay for weak string benchmarks. In this paper, the bench used for most performance measurements will be an antisymmetric step with $N = 128$ data points:

$$d_i = \begin{cases} 32 & \text{for } 1 \leq i \leq 64 \\ 96 & \text{for } 65 \leq i \leq 128 \end{cases} \qquad (27)$$

of height $h = 64$. Varying amounts of uncorrelated, gaussian noise are added as in figure 1. The added noise has standard deviation σ and a relative measure of noise s will frequently be used

$$s = \frac{\sigma}{\sqrt{\alpha}}. \qquad (28)$$

It can be shown that, in theory [8], as s falls below $1/\sqrt{2}$, there is a very low probability of "spurious" breakpoints (i.e. other than the "real" one at $i = 64$) occurring in the weak string reconstruction. Moreover, if

$$\alpha < \frac{1}{2}h^2\lambda$$

the real breakpoint *does* appear in the reconstruction (with high probability). Provided $\sigma < 2h$, it is also located precisely correctly (i.e. at $i = 64$). These theoretical predictions have been corroborated by the assay for the data above with added noise of relative amplitude $s = 0.1, 0.2, 0.4$, with $\alpha = 1600$ and a variety of trial values of $\lambda \in [2, 16]$. Numerical details are given in appendix B. Moreover, when $s = 0.8$, the exact, weak string reconstruction contains many spurious breakpoints, also in line with theoretical expectations.

4.1 Measuring rates of convergence

The GNC algorithm, being deterministic, presents little difficulty in measurement of convergence rate. It is simply a matter of running the algorithm repeatedly at gradually increasing precision[1] (and consequently requiring more and more iterations) until breakpoints in the output agree with those in the true reconstruction. Note that only breakpoints, as represented by line-variables $\mathbf{l}$, are required to agree - $\mathbf{u}$ is not tested. This policy is justified by the following observations.

- Determination of breakpoints is the difficult part of the reconstruction problem. Once correct breakpoints are obtained, $\mathbf{u}$ can be calculated by classical relaxation procedures. This is true both of dense data as considered here, and of sparse data [27].
- The u_i are real-valued so they could never be exactly correct, only correct to within some tolerance. Choice of tolerance would be unsatisfactorily arbitrary.

The measure of computation time for the GNC algorithm is then the minimum number of iterations required for a correct output.

Comparisons between algorithms will be in terms of numbers of iterations, ignoring differences in the amount of computation involved in a single iteration which, in any case, are not appreciable.

In the case of stochastic algorithms, convergence rate is much harder to measure because of the random nature of the process. Convergence profiles vary randomly between successive runs of an algorithm. For a given run, a profile is obtained by checking, after each iteration, to see whether $\mathbf{l}$ is in the correct state. Error rate - the proportion of time for which $\mathbf{l}$ is in a state other than the correct one (computed using a time window of 100 iterations) - is plotted as a function of iteration number. Typical examples are shown in figure 4a,b. They are noisy but show a clear trend towards the correct state as the algorithm progresses. The profile in figure 4b was generated from data with 4 times as much noise as in figure 4a. Increased noise in the data has clearly led to a noisier convergence profile. In some cases the profile has been observed eventually to decay to zero error rate, although this is not the case in figure 4a,b.

An error rate threshold of 50% is a natural choice for the following reason. If it is known that the vector $\mathbf{l}^{(n)}$ (the line process at the nth iteration) is in the correct state for more than half of the iterations $n \in \{n_1, .., n_2\}$ then it is sufficient to estimate $\mathbf{l}$ to be:

$$l_i = \begin{cases} 1 & \text{if } \sum_{n=n_1}^{n_2} l_i^{(n)} > n_3 \\ 0 & \text{otherwise} \end{cases} \tag{29}$$

where n_3 is defined by

$$n_2 = n_1 + 2n_3 - 1.$$

In other words the estimated l_i is simply the value adopted by $l_i^{(n)}$ in the majority of iterations. (This is similar to the 'majority vote" criterion used in defining the class "BPP" of stochastic algorithms.) Convergence could be defined to occur at the largest n for which error rate (measured in a suitable time-window) exceeds 50%. We will adopt a practical lower bound n_L on this value by recording the smallest n for which the error rate falls below 50%. In this respect estimates of convergence rate for stochastic algorithms will be *optimistic*[2]. In the examples of figure 4a,b lower bound n_L is smaller than convergence time as defined above by a factor of 3 or so.

To allow for randomness an average rate $\overline{n}_L$ will be estimated by running the algorithm under test 10 times and computing the average of n_L for those cases in which the algorithm succeeds. (Stochastic algorithms can and do fail by locking out of the correct state - this shows up as a persistent 100% error rate.)

Cooling schedule

An analysis of optimal cooling schedules is outside the scope of this paper, but it is worth noting that a linear schedule is in some ways preferable. Logarithmic and linear schedules for the same data are compared in figure 4b,c. Convergence in the linear case occurs later but

[1] Precision is measured in terms of "absolute norm" [8] which is, in turn, computed from "dynamic norm" - a measure of the change in $\mathbf{u}$ in successive iterations.

[2] Lundy and Mees [19] suggest recording the *first* iteration at which the correct state is hit. This is a still more optimistic measure. But in the first place this is not really applicable to problems like ours that involve real variables. In the second place, even treating $\mathbf{l}$ as the state vector (i.e. ignoring $\mathbf{u}$) so that their measure *can* be applied, results turn out to be qualitatively similar to those obtained by our proposed measure.

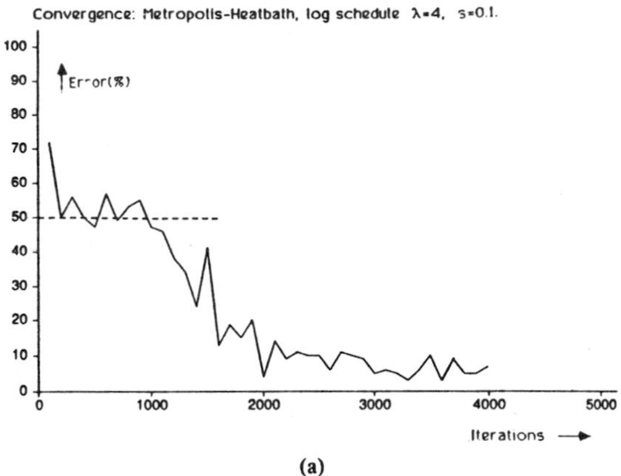

(a)

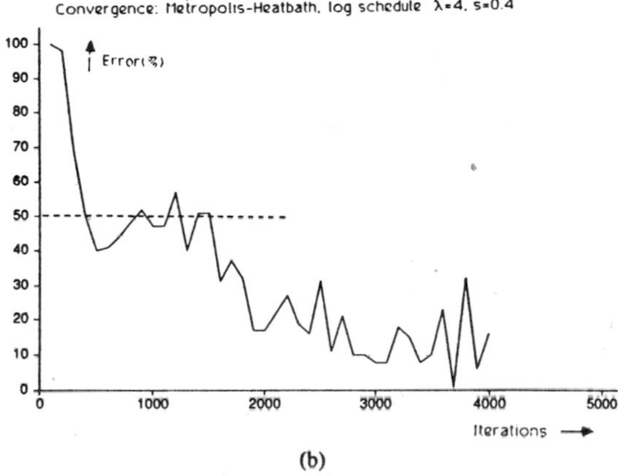

(b)

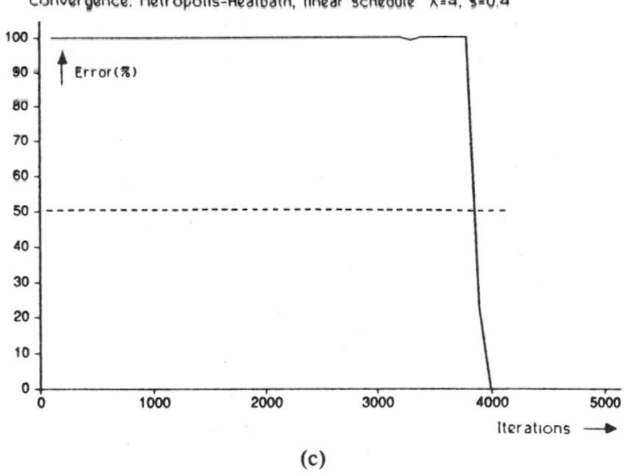

(c)

Figure 4: Convergence profiles for individual runs of the Metropolis-Heatbath algorithm. (a) Logarithmic schedule - low noise. (b) Logarithmic schedule - higher noise. (c) Linear schedule - higher noise. Error percentages are averages over 100 successive iterations.

approximately at the same temperature, roughly 10% of the starting temperature. In the logarithmic case, final temperature is strongly determined by initial temperature. Even after 10^6 iterations the final temperature is still about 5% of the initial temperature - see equation (12). In the linear case the final temperature is zero, regardless of starting temperature. Hence performance should be less critically dependent on starting temperature and the following table of results bears this out.

Percentage of successful runs

Starting temp.	Linear	Logarithmic
$T_0 = 2\alpha$	60%	0%
$T_0 = \alpha$	90%	100%
$T_0 = 0.5\alpha$	90%	20%

(Metropolis-Heatbath with $\lambda = 4$, $s = 0.4$, out of 10 runs)

Note also that, in the logarithmic case, it appears that the starting temperature must not be much less than α if the algorithm is to succeed.

In this study a logarithmic schedule with starting temperature $T_0 = \alpha$ will be used throughout.

4.2 Relative performance of stochastic algorithms

A measurement procedure for determination of success and convergence rate of stochastic algorithms has been set up. This makes it possible, first of all, to compare performance of the three stochastic algorithms described in section 2.

Performance is somewhat dependent on the relative noise level s of the data. At low noise (figure 5a) all three algorithms are successful at scales up to $\lambda = 8$. For $\lambda > 8$ the mixed annealing algorithm fails. At a higher noise level (fig 5b) the mixed annealing algorithm fails at all scales. (This continues to be true even when site visitation is random and when the optimal relaxation parameter w is used.) Mixed annealing therefore appears to be much less powerful than the other two. Of those two, Heatbath and Metropolis-Heatbath, it seems from figure 5 that each is of similar power in that they fail (figure 5b) at the same value of λ. But Metropolis-Heatbath is a little more efficient. Therefore Metropolis-Heatbath will be used in comparisons with the GNC algorithm.

4.3 Relative performance of deterministic and stochastic algorithms

At last the main purpose of the paper can be accomplished - comparison of the power of the GNC algorithm

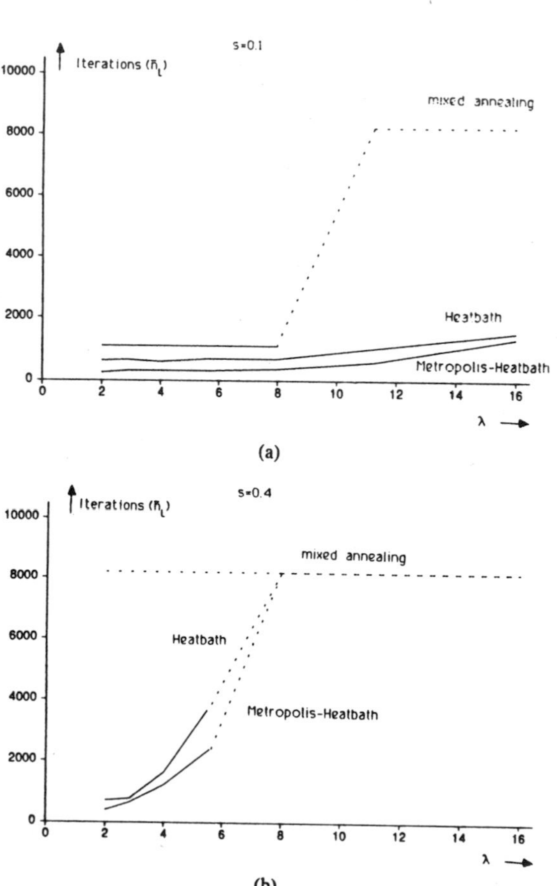

Figure 5: Comparison of stochastic algorithms. (a) Low noise. (b) Higher noise. Dotted lines indicate that algorithm failed on at least some runs.

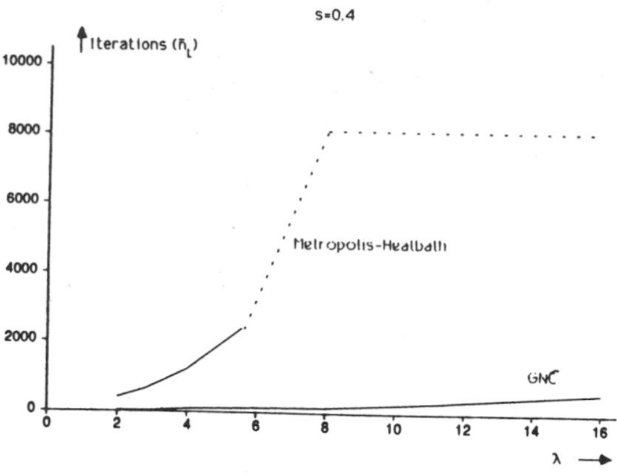

Figure 6: Comparison of stochastic and deterministic algorithms, as a function of varying scale. Dotted lines as figure 5.

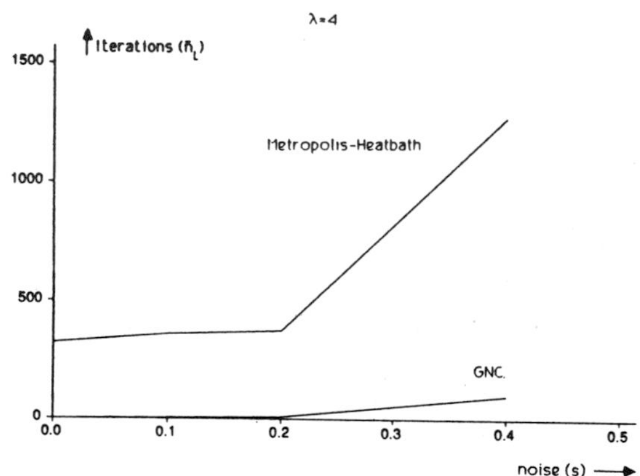

Figure 7: Comparison of stochastic and deterministic algorithms, as a function of varying scale. Dotted lines as figure 5.

with that of the chosen stochastic algorithm. Comparative results are obtained as a function both of scale λ and noise level s. Variation with scale, at moderately high noise level, shows that up to a certain critical scale Metropolis-Heatbath requires between 10 and 20 times more iterations than GNC does (figure 6). Increasing levels of noise (figure 7) and increasing scale (figure 6) cause both algorithms to do more work, though GNC remains comparatively much more efficient. Beyond the critical scale Metropolis-Heatbath fails altogether to find a solution (within 8000 iterations). This justifies the claim, made at the beginning of the paper, that GNC is both more powerful and more efficient. Figure 8 shows that these conclusions hold also for parallel (chequerboard) implementations of the algorithms.

Finally a more complex signal is shown in figure 9. Uncorrelated gaussian noise is added to give a signal-to-noise ratio of about 1:2. The result of the GNC algorithm is shown in figure 9c. Not only is the signal retrieved from

Errata for

3D Model Recognition from Stereoscopic Cues
Edited by John E. W. Mayhew and John P. Frisby

To reinforce the point that collaboration is difficult, even between editors and publisher, the pages on that subject have been transposed. In this text pages 2, 3, 4, and 5 can be found on pages 82, 83, 84, and 85 and pages 82, 83, 84, and 85 can be found on pages 2, 3, 4, and 5.

Please accept our apologies for this misprint.

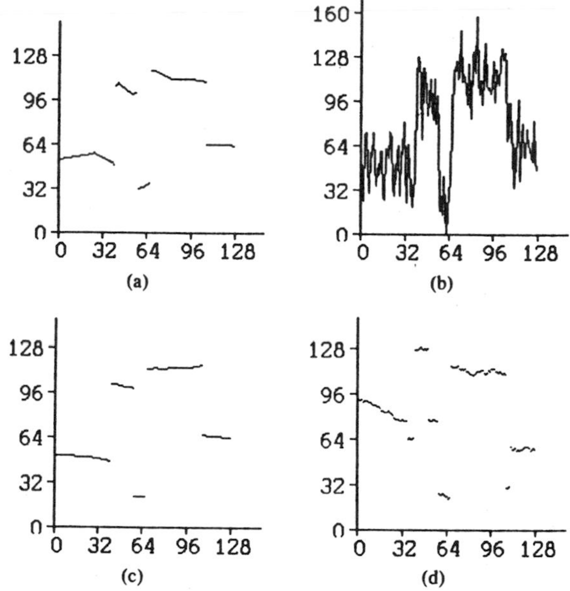

Figure 9: A more complex signal (a) with added noise (b) - signal-to-noise is roughly 1:2. Deterministic GNC algorithm produces a correct reconstruction (c) with parameters $\lambda = 16, \alpha = 5000$. Stochastic algorithm fails (d).

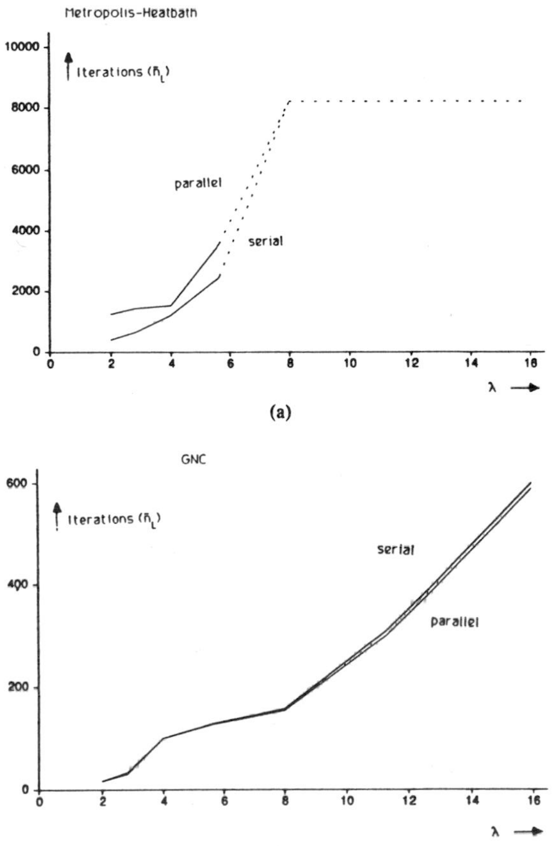

Figure 8: Comparative performance of serial and parallel algorithms at various scales. (a) Stochastic Metropolis-Heatbath. (b) Deterministic GNC.

the noise, but the reconstruction is verified by the assay. A reasonably large scale λ must be used to retrieve the signal because of the high noise level (s=0.23). (This is because high resistance to noise (large α), with reasonable sensitivity (small $\sqrt{\alpha/\lambda}$), demands large scale λ.) The stochastic algorithm can be expected to fail. This is just what it does in 100% of 10 runs. In a typical run it never visits the correct state[3]. An example state (after 8000 iterations) contains extra, spurious breakpoints (figure 9d) in addition to some correct ones.

5 Conclusions

First of all, a "test-bed" for a piecewise continuous reconstruction problem has been established, by means of the assay described in section 3. The dynamic programming algorithm is relatively straightforward to implement[4]. Reconstructions for data used in this paper have been verified by the assay for certain values of α, λ, s (appendix B.).

Comparison of the deterministic GNC algorithm with three stochastic algorithms has shown the latter to be considerably less efficient. Furthermore they are less powerful in that they cannot practically deliver correct solutions for problems involving moderately high levels of noise (and which therefore demand large scale in recon-

[3] It therefore fails even under the Lundy and Mees [19] criterion
[4] Code in POP11 is available from the author on request.

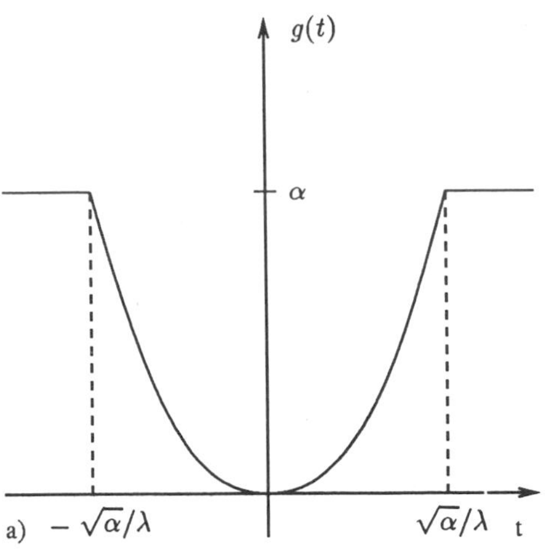

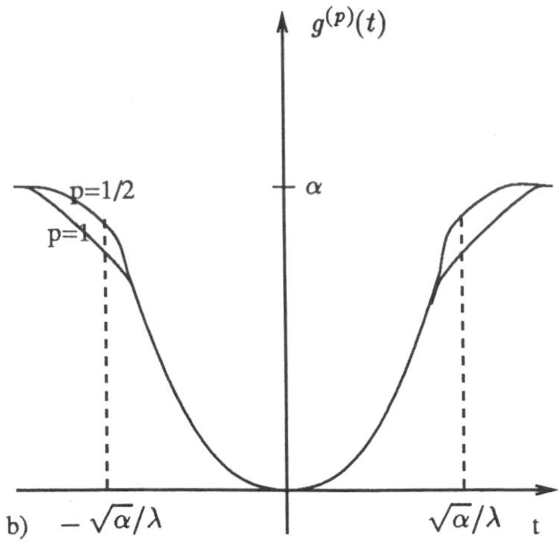

Fig 3. Neighbourhood interaction functions: (a) g for the cost function F; (b) $g^{(p)}$ for the sequence of functions $F^{(p)}$ that approximate F.

constraints to 2D data, as in edge detection or surface reconstruction. Although a dynamic programming algorithm for the 2D problem could be defined, in theory, it would involve the use of tables with up to M^N entries! For similar reasons, it is not practicable to use dynamic programming for higher order energies P, involving 2nd or higher derivatives of u. Tables of size $O(M^2)$ would be required (for P involving u''). GNC is quite usable, however, both for 2D data and for 2nd order P.

Following normal dynamic programming practice, the algorithm consists largely of constructing a pair of tables (the return function f_i and the policy function p_i) for each i, each of length M. Total storage required is therefore $O(NM)$ units. The value of $f_i(u_{i+1})$ is the minimal partial cost for $u_0..u_i$ for a given value of u_{i+1}, and $p_i(u_{i+1})$ is the value of u_i at that minimum. Having constructed the tables, there remains the task (requiring relatively insignificant computation time) of tracing back through the tables, from f_N down to f_0, to recover the optimal u_i. The complexity of the algorithm is $O(NM^2)$ - so extra precision in angle quantisation (large M) is expensive. The expense can be mitigated to some degree by "table reduction" (Papoulias 85), which works as follows. For the cost function F for the weak elastic string, it transpires that each table f_i contains a non-constant interval flanked by entries all of the same constant value. Those constant entries can be treated for computational purposes as one entry. This effectively reduces the value of M. The effective M appears, in practice, to be proportional to $\sqrt{\alpha}$ (independent of λ); so the reduction may be effective even at large λ when GNC is least efficient. In practice, reduction by a factor of up to 4 was obtained, reducing execution time by a factor of up to 16. More recently, an exact dynamic programming algorithm has been constructed, that requires no quantisation at all (Blake 89).

Comparison of GNC and dynamic programming

It has been mentioned that GNC is an approximate method, whereas dynamic programming is exact. In practice, no qualitative difference between solutions obtained from the two methods is observed (see also Blake 89); this is, in itself, a confirmation that solutions from GNC are good approximations. As for efficiency, each method has its advantages. For large values of λ GNC is slow, but (for a given α) dynamic programming continues to work well. Finally, GNC requires high precision arithmetic, unlike quantised dynamic programming. In practice (for modest values of λ) it seems that GNC is faster on a Motorola 68000, for example, if it has adequate hardware floating-point support. For smaller values of λ, GNC runs in about 1 second (SUN 2, SKY floating point, vector length N=50, λ=2). This could be expected to improve by an order of magnitude with the new 68000 floating point co-processor.

3 Scale-space properties

This section discusses the properties of scale-space descriptions of curves, under weak continuity constraints. An example was displayed in fig 1. Several notable properties are illustrated: the most striking is the uniformity of the scale-space - the locus of each discontinuity in scale space is plumb vertical. Moreover, in this scale-space, unlike gaussian scale space (Witkin, 83) in which the fingerprint theorem holds (Yuille and Poggio 84), structure is *not* preserved - discontinuities *may* be created as scale increases. We argue here that this *lack* of structure preservation is a desirable property. Four other issues are considered: how to achieve an invariant parametrisation of the curve, detection of curvature discontinuities and how to treat the "curvature limit" described in section 1, and boundary conditions for open-ended curves. Finally it is worth noting that the new scale-space has an extra parameter in addition to scale, namely angular sensitivity (Φ_0 in section 1). Plots of scale-space shown here are at fixed values of Φ_0(e.g. 45° in fig 1.).

Uniformity

It is apparent in fig 1 that the locus in scale-space of an individual feature (corner) is uniformly vertical, unlike gaussian scale spaces. This is a consequence of the theoretically predicted, spatial stability with respect to scale, that is inherent in optimal function fitting under weak continuity constraints (Blake and Zisserman 87). It arises because the extra cost in F, if a corner were slightly misplaced, is very large - far greater than the relatively modest extra costs introduced by spatially incoherent noise, or by extended but gentle curves (figure 4). Hence corners do not get misplaced.

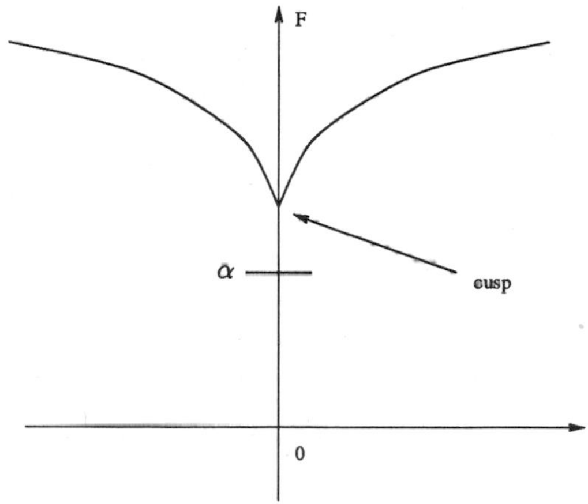

Fig.4 The uniformity property is a consequence of the sharp, cusp-like minimum in the energy F, plotted as a function of edge position. For a displacement ϵ in edge position it can be shown (Blake and Zisserman, 87) that the corresponding F is as plotted above. Hence there is a strong attraction towards $\epsilon = 0$, the true edge position.

Alternatively, in the terms of Canny's (83) performance measurers, the *localisation* is very good - as good, in fact, as a difference of boxes operator. (But it doesn't have that operator's multiple response problem!) A consequence of uniformity is that any one connected contour in scale-space must belong to only *one* physical feature on the curve. This is untrue of gaussian scale-space, as fig 5. shows.

Preservation of structure

Under weak continuity constraints, structure is not preserved as scale increases. There is an example of this in figure 1, in which a rounded corner is represented in scale space by a line that is present at large scale, but absent at small scale ($\lambda \epsilon [0,5]$). This is absolutely as it should be. The rounded corner appears smooth at small scale. It seems that the ability to represent this fact is important. Whereas structure preservation is a must with gaussian filters because it guarantees a successful tracking algorithm - tracking from fine to coarse scale picks up all zero-crossings - it is redundant under weak continuity constraints. Tracking is trivial, due to uniformity.

Invariant parametrisation

A problem with any scheme that uses arclength s to parametrise curves is that the parametrisation is defined with respect to the data rather than the *interpreted* curve $u(s)$. At small scale, this could mean extreme sensitivity to sensor and quantisation noise; in a practical vision system, this would result in curve descriptions that were unstable over time. A simple solution to this is adopted by Asada and Brady (84): they obtain their data from images, by means of an edge detector that inherently supresses noise. However there remains the lesser problem, that intermediate structure could generate distortions of scale (fig 6). An elegant solution to this problem, in the context of gaussian scale space filtering, proposed by Porril (85), subjects the curve to a simulated diffusion process. Under weak continuity constraints, an invariant scheme could conceivably be attainable by fitting a curve to data supplied as a sequence of coordinate vectors X_i, minimising curvature. Further work may be needed here.

Curvature limit and detection of discontinuities

It was explained in section 1 that $\kappa_0 = \Phi_0/2\lambda$ is a curvature limit, such that curves of curvature $\kappa > \kappa_0$ are segmented, even if there is no curvature maximum (fig 7).

Moreover the actual point of segmentation need not be particularly spatially stable. This seems to be a limitation of the scheme, for which two partial remedies are proposed. One is to note that such segmentation points exist only at large scale - but of course there may be "genuine" structure too that exists only at large scale. A better remedy is to use a higher order scheme, in which $P = \int u''^2$. This allows both *tangent* and *curvature* discontinuities to be detected, rather than tangent only. It also pushes the "spurious" segmentation problem to higher order (i.e. spurious curvature discontinuities) - but at some extra computational expense.

Boundary conditions

A very attractive property of the proposed scheme is that boundary conditions on open-ended contours are dealt with naturally. Naive gaussian filtering generates spurious discontinuities near ends of contours, which may mask genuine features near ends. Cures are of course possible, such as using modified convolution masks near ends (thus

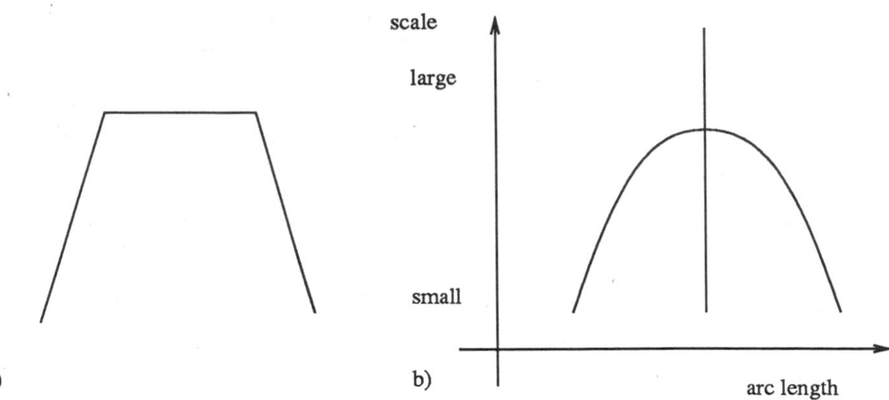

Fig 5. The gaussian scale-space generated by a polygonal contour (a), contains a bifurcation (b) which is unstable (non-transverse). It is therefore uncertain to which fine scale zero-crossing the single coarse scale zero-crossing belongs.

losing the gaussian's time-saving factorisability) or a diffusion process as above. Fig 1 illustrates the correct handling of boundary conditions: the small feature near the end is treated much like the one in the middle.

Acknowledgements

The authors thank the University of Edinburgh for provision of facilities, and the SERC for funding. A Blake is grateful for the support of the IBM Research Fellowship from the Royal Society.

References

1. Asada,H. and Brady,J.M. (1986). The Curvature Primal Sketch. *IEEE PAMI,* 8, 1, 2-14.

2. Bellman, R. and Dreyfus, S. (1962) *Applied Dynamic Programming.* Princeton University Press, Princeton, USA.

3. Blake,A. (1983a). The least disturbance principle and weak constraints. *Pattern Recognition Letters, 1, 393-399.*

4. Blake,A. (1983b). *Parallel computation in low-level vision.* Ph.D. Thesis, University of Edinburgh.

5. Blake,A. and Zisserman,A. (1985). Using weak continuity constraints. Report CSR-186-85, Dept. Computer Science, Edinburgh University, Edinburgh, Scotland. Also *Pattern Recognition Letters 6, 51-60, 1987.*

6. Blake A. and Zisserman A. *Visual Reconstruction.* MIT Press, 1987.

7. Blake A. Comparison of the efficiency of stochastic and deterministic algorithms for visual reconstruction. *PAMI 11, 1, 2-12.* Also reprinted in this volume.

8. Canny,J.F. (1983). *Finding edges and lines in images.* S.M. thesis, MIT, Cambridge, USA.

9. de Boor,C. (1978). *A practical guide to splines.* Springer-Verlag, New York.

10. Geman,S. and Geman,D. (1984). Stochastic Relaxation, Gibbs distribution, and Bayesian restoration of images. *IEEE PAMI, Nov 1984.*

11. Marroquin,J. (1984). Surface reconstruction preserving discontinuities. Memo 792, AI Laboratory, MIT, Cambridge, USA.

12. Metropolis,N., Rosenbluth,A.W., Rosenbluth,M.N., Teller,A.H. and Teller,E. (1953). Equation of state calculations by fast computing machines. *Journal of Chemical Physics,* 6, 1087.

13. Papoulias,A. (1985). *Curve segmentation using weak continuity constraints.* M.Sc. thesis, Dept. Computer Science, University of Edinburgh.

14. Perkins,W.A. (1978). A model-based system for industrial parts. *IEEE Trans. Comp.,* 27, 2, 126 - 143.

15. Porril, J., Mayhew, J.E.W. and Frisby, J.P. (1986). Scale space diffusion: plane and space curves. Research Memo 018, AIVRU, Sheffield University.

16. Terzopoulos,D. (1983). Multilevel computational processes for visual surface reconstruction, *Computer Vision Graphics and Image Processing,* 24, 52-96.

17. Witkin,A.P. (1983). Scale-space filtering. *Proc. IJCAI 1983,* 1019-1022.

18. Yuille,A.L. and Poggio,T. (1984). Fingerprints theorems. *Proc. AAAI 1984,* 362-365.

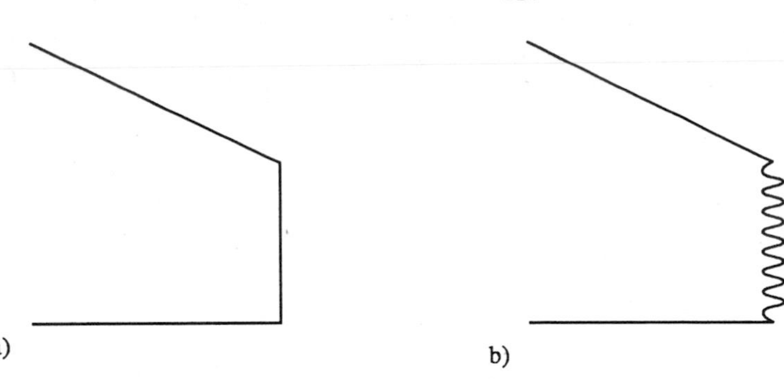

Fig 6 Non-invariance in s-parametrisation of curves. Curve (a) has two corners. Curve (b) very similar "at large scale", but has some detail between the two corners. As a result it acquires a great deal of extra arc-length between those corners, which distorts its scale-space diagram.

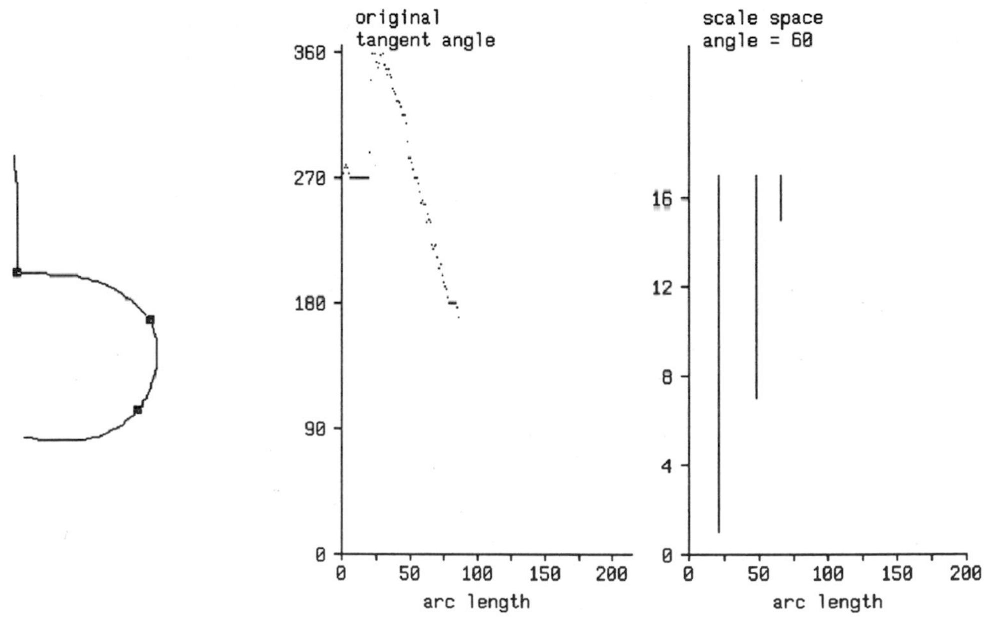

Fig 7 The gradient limit: arcs above a certain threshold curvature $\kappa_0 = \Phi_0/2\lambda$ may be segmented spuriously at larger scales.

[17] Detecting Specular Reflections Using Lambertian Constraints

Gavin Brelstaff and Andrew Blake

Department of Computer Science
University of Edinburgh, Edinburgh EH9 3JZ, Scotland, UK

Abstract

Specularities—bright image regions formed by specular reflection—are likely to be mistaken for genuine surface markings by processes that perform photometric analysis, derive motion fields from optical flow or estimate depth from binocular stereo. In addition they can be used to infer surface geometry. This paper describes a scheme for detecting specularities based on a characterisation of Lambertian surfaces. Real surfaces are not simple composites of Lambertian and specular surfaces but evidence suggests that away from specularities they do not deviate from the Lambertian model by more than a factor of 3 or so. This proves adequate to serve as a constraint for specularity detection. Two independent tests identify image regions where the constraint is violated. The detector is shown to performs well on a variety of real images. Applications: improving binocular stereo and inferring surface geometry are described using specularities produced by the detector.

1 Introduction and other work

Specular reflection occurs whenever a glossy surface reflects light incident upon it in a mirror-like fashion. Specularities—bright image regions formed by specular reflection—are useful features for any practical vision system to identify. Once identified they need no longer be mistaken for genuine surface markings by processes that match models to objects [8], derive motion fields from optical flow (see [40]) or estimate depth from binocular stereo [34,35]. They can also be used to infer surface geometry [21,37,2,13,28,5,6]. Here a scheme is described for detecting specularities based on a characterisation of Lambertian (non-specular) surfaces. Although real surfaces are not simple composites of Lambertian and specular surfaces, experimental evidence suggests that they maintain a roughly Lambertian character in regions away from specularities. Constraints derived for Lambertian surfaces are applied to real images and specularities detected in regions where the constraints are found to be violated.

*Current addresses: A. Blake, Dept. Engineering Science, Parks Rd., Oxford. G. Brelstaff, IBM UKSC, Athelstan Ho., St Clement St., Winchester.

Contemporary work on detecting specularities takes an alternative, chromatic approach [18,27]. Colour differences in the specular and non-specular components of the light reflected by certain materials are exploited. A chromatic approach can complement the achromatic (grey-level) approach described here, but only where colour differences exist—i.e. not for most metals nor for white light incident on a grey surface.

Previous work on detecting specularities in achromatic images is provided by Forbus [16]. He applied Ullman's 'S' operator [39] to images containing specularities. However his method fails for specularities that have smooth shading profiles—as produced by curved surfaces [7]. However, the second directional derivative used by the 'S' operator clearly is capable of distinguishing some specularities The "cylinder test" proposed later also makes use of it. The cylinder test provides a practical method to distinguish between smooth Lambertian and smooth specular shading variations. It is one of two independent tests developed to detect specularities. Both tests use the assumption (justified by experimental results) that surfaces maintain a roughly Lambertian character away from specularities. The tests identify regions where constraints that hold for Lambertian surfaces, are clearly violated. These regions are candidate specularities. Each test exploits a different Lambertian characteristic—as summarised below:

Name of test	Operating principle of test
Retinex-based test	Region 'too bright' to be Lambertian
Cylinder test	Peak 'too sharp' to be Lambertian

The detection scheme combines and propagates the evidence from each test to create a map of the specularities in the image. The results show that the scheme successfully detects prominent specularities in a variety of real images. No explicit model of specularities is involved. This is a great advantage because the models of composite specular and matte surface reflection that do exist require a great deal of a priori knowledge of the scene surfaces and lighting before they can be exploited. In fact the reflective properties of many common materials are poorly understood and no useful models exist for them. Before describing the details of both tests, the basis for their underlying assumptions is discussed.

2 Lambertian characteristics of real surfaces

The physical processes involved when real surfaces reflect light are very complicated, even for common materials. Some of the light incident upon a surface is directly reflected at the air-surface interface, while the rest penetrates into the sub-surface layer and may be scattered by particles contained within it. Total reflected light flux combines contributions from both direct reflection and sub-surface scattering. The directional distribution of the light reflected by the two contributing processes can be quite different. A narrow beam of incident light is scattered by the sub-surface over a wide range of directions, while direct reflection directs light back into a narrow beam aligned along the direction of mirror reflection. Direct reflection of a light source creates a specularity when formed into an image. In order to detect specularities the flux due to direct reflection must, in some sense, be separated from that due to sub-surface scattering. So, is it possible to tell apart the flux produced by the two processes and thus detect specularities? As mentioned earlier, colour differences in the flux can sometimes be exploited. This paper considers what can be done with "white" (achromatic) light. One possibility would be to use the available theories of the physical processes to model the amount and directional distribution of the light reflected by a surface and then attempt to fit the model to images. Specularities would be detected where the fitted model requires a significant proportion of direct reflection. However three facts make this approach impractical:

1. For many materials no adequate theory exists. Good models of *direct reflection* exist only for surface of certain roughness [38,3,36,15]. The Lambertian model provides a rough approximation of *sub-surface scattering*— more realistic models applying only in some circumstances [25,11,12,31].

2. Even if a material is adequately modelled a prohibitively large number of fitting parameters are involved. For example the simplest models [25] of sub-surface reflection involve at least five parameters—even more when direct reflection is included.

3. In order to interpret an image in terms of a surface model the precise directional distribution of the illumination is required.

In the absence of theory, the reflective properties of individual materials have been measured. Photometric surface properties are defined in terms of radiance, irradiance and BRDF [32,24]. For a glossy mirror-like surface the BRDF, f_r is small for all pairs of directions except those of mirror-like alignment. For a Lambertian surface it is constant: $f_r = \rho/\pi$ where ρ, known as albedo, is the ratio of the flux reflected to that which is incident. As surfaces absorb some percentage of the incident light without reflecting it ρ has a legal range $(0, 1)$. The simplicity of the Lambertian BRDF makes it a useful standard against which to compare the BRDF's of real surfaces. Naturally, matte surfaces—for which sub-surface scattering is the dominant reflection process, deviate less from this standard than glossy surfaces—which produce large variations in f_r, between mirror-like and other orientations. The specularity detector described in this paper is based on the **assumptions** that:

1. real sub-surface scattering is approximately Lambertian, producing deviations from a constant f_r of at most a factor of 3, except at geometrical conditions for specular reflection.

2. real surfaces are also roughly Lambertian for all directions of incidence and reflection, except at geometrical conditions for specular reflection.

The validity of each assumption is discussed below with reference to data taken from the theoretical and experimental literature. Each graph corresponds to a particular material—plotting the variation in the relative value of the BRDF with angle of reflection θ_r, for a fixed value of the angle of incidence θ_i. For all of the graphs the directions of incidence and reflection lie in the plane containing the local surface normal. If any measurements have been made for a material it is usually in this plane. In any case, when direct reflection acts to divert the BRDF from Lambertian the deviation is most marked in this plane.

Although isotropic sub-surface scattering [25] does not, as one might expect, result in isotropic (Lambertian) reflection, it does to within the approximation provided above—except at glancing angles. The theoretically de-

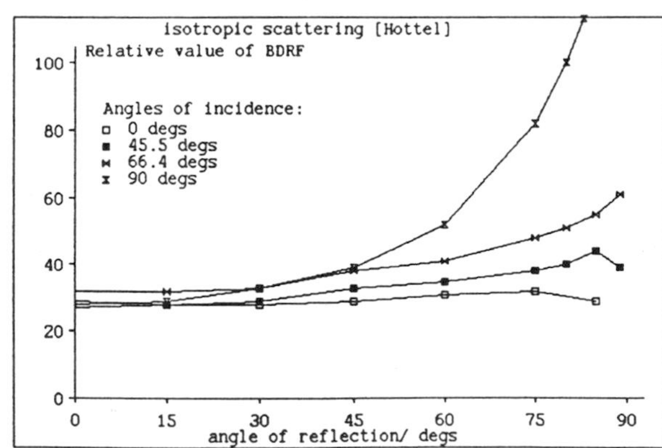

Figure 1: Theoretical prediction of BRDF for an isotropic scatter. A Lambertian surface would produce a horizontal line.

rived graphs in fig 1 show this—only at glancing angles ($\theta_i \geq 70^o$ and $\theta_r \geq 70^o$, $\theta_i \approx \theta_r$) does the BRDF grow larger—resulting in a considerable deviation from the a constant f_r. However this occurs only at or close to the geometrical conditions for specular reflection and so does not refute assumption 1. The available measurements of real, near isotropic scatters, e.g: fig 2, confirm the theoretical predictions of fig 1. Sub-surface scattering need

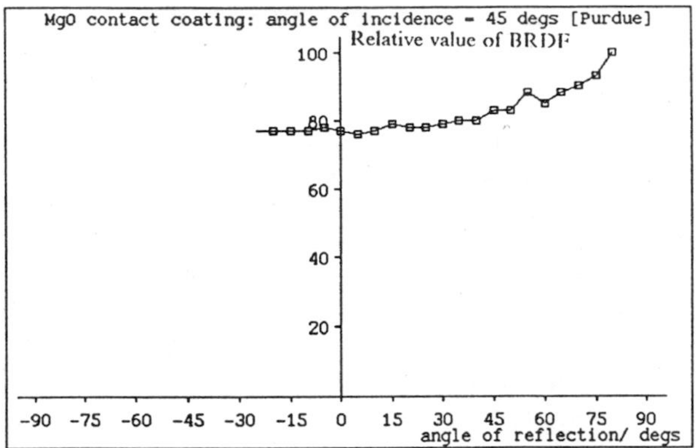

Figure 2: MgO contact coating: $\theta_i = 45°$ [36].

not be isotropic. For the example shown in fig 3 the deviation from constant f_r is by less than a factor of three. If this data is typical then assumption 1 above will be good. In order to address assumption 2 materials that

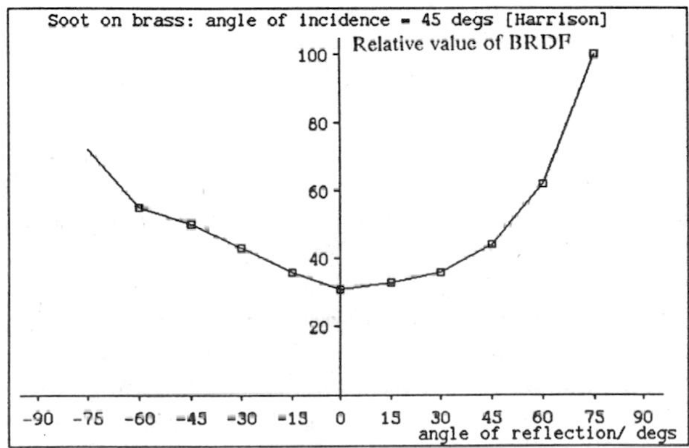

Figure 3: Soot on brass: $\theta_i = 45°$ [20].

reflect light directly must be considered. These materials are of two types:

- Metals which reflect (by electric dipole interaction) almost all incident light directly so that sub-surface scattering is negligible.
- Dielectrics which reflect (by atomic or ionic dipole interaction) some incident light directly—the rest penetrates the surface—so that sub-surface scattering can occur.

For metals with smooth surfaces $f_r \sim 0$ except for specular geometry. For dielectrics an additional component due to sub-surface scattering must be considered. Fig 4 illustrates a typical example: porcelain enamel. Here f_r is roughly constant except for the pulse-like peak at the mirror-like orientation. So for both metals and dielectrics with smooth surfaces assumption 2 looks good. The di-

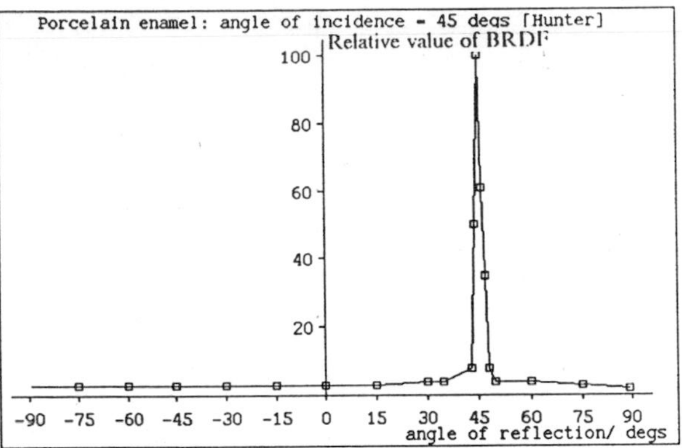

Figure 4: Porcelain enamel: $\theta_i = 45°$ [26].

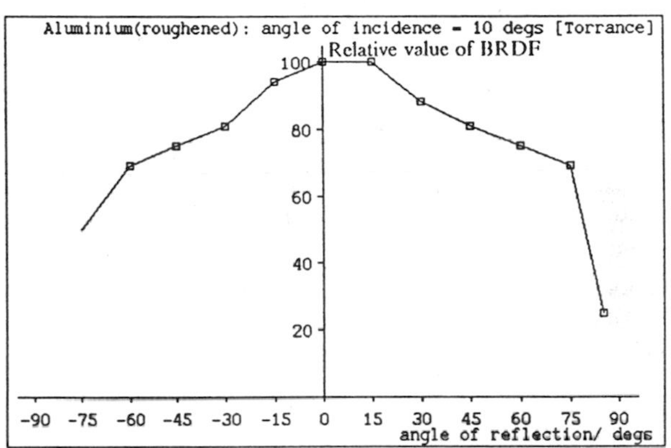

Figure 5: Aluminium (roughened): $\theta_i = 10°$ [38].

rectional distribution of directly reflected light, which is a narrow peak (fig 4) for a smooth surface, becomes a broader peak for a rough surface. The data for roughened aluminium—fig 5—illustrates just how wide the spread can be. The shape of this particular graph is explained by modeling the surface roughness as many micro-facets oriented in many different directions [38]. Although entirely due to direct reflection, the graph in fig 5 has a range that deviates from the Lambertian standard by no more than that of sub-surface scatterers (e.g. as in fig 3). So no prominent specularities should be formed. However, the graph is typical only of small angles of incidence θ_i. As θ_i increases the graph becomes more pulse-like—see fig 6. When θ_i is large the range of the graph deviates significantly from the Lambertian standard and prominent specularities are produced. The discussion above is of a rough metal surface—dielectric surfaces of similar roughness behave similarly [38]. So, the survey above—encompassing metals and dielectrics, both rough and smooth—suggests that assumptions 1 and 2 above, are good.

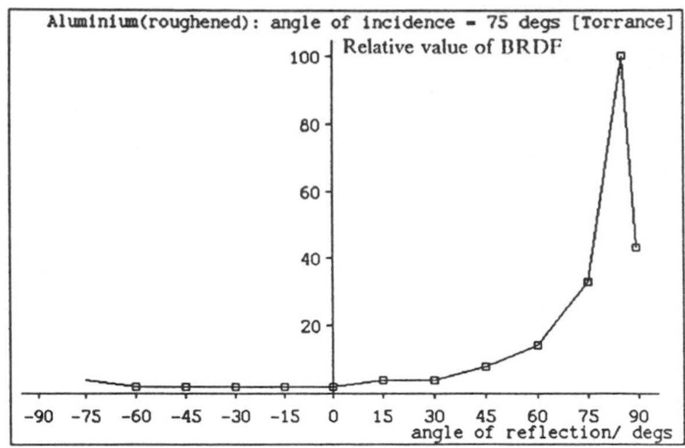

Figure 6: Aluminium (roughened): $\theta_i = 75^o$ [38].

3 Lambertian constraint on irradiance

The general specification of a material's reflective properties provided by the BRDF is independent of any considerations of the illumination. The image irradiance registered by a camera depends on the illumination as well as on the BRDF of the surface. Illumination varies across a scene. The general relationship between image irradiance, E, and the BRDF, f_r, for a given imaged point is [24]:

$$E = \int_{\omega_i} f_r L_i \cos\theta_i d\omega_i, \tag{1}$$

where the illumination at the point is fully specified by L_i: the directional distribution function of the incident radiance. The integral is over all directions encompassed by the solid angle of the incident beam ω_i. For extended or multiple illuminants it is often necessary to integrate over the entire hemisphere above the surface. The variations in E due to L_i and f_r are not, in general, separable—so that the image irradiance equation (1) is very difficult to exploit. However, for Lambertian surfaces $f_r = \rho/\pi$, so equation (1) simplifies:

$$E = \rho I; \quad I = (1/\pi) \int_{\omega_i} L_i \cos\theta_i d\omega_i, \tag{2}$$

so image irradiance can be separated into the product of albedo ρ and I: a term that quantifies the net illumination falling at the surface point. I and ρ both vary with location $\mathbf{x}$ of the point in the image. I also depends on the local surface orientation (conveniently specified by the direction of the surface normal $\hat{\mathbf{n}}$). Equation (2) can be written:

$$E(\mathbf{x}) = R_L(\hat{\mathbf{n}}(\mathbf{x}), \mathbf{x}) = \rho(\mathbf{x}) I(\hat{\mathbf{n}}(\mathbf{x}), (\mathbf{x})), \tag{3}$$

where R_L is an extension of the concept of the reflectance map familiar to computer vision. In this form the image irradiance equation is amenable to analysis in terms of the three component variations: $\rho(\mathbf{x})$, I with respect to $\hat{\mathbf{n}}$ and I with respect to $\mathbf{x}$. Any R_L that corresponds to realistic natural matte surface reflection is constrained. An upper bound on the dynamic range of R_L is established below by considering realistic limits on natural variations in $\rho(\mathbf{x})$ and $I(\hat{\mathbf{n}}, \mathbf{x})$.

3.1 Realistic dynamic range of I with respect to $\hat{\mathbf{n}}$ for natural illumination

Perfectly collimated illumination does not prevail in natural everyday circumstances. It can only be achieved in a dark-room. Light may seem to be collimated in some natural circumstances, e.g. spot-light illumination, but the collimation is not perfect. The inter-reflection of light between the surfaces of the scene adds a small non-zero component to the illumination incident along every direction. In terms of the L_i function: it is no longer non-zero only for the direction of collimation—it is non-zero everywhere. The non-zero component is often referred to as the ambient light and it accounts, very roughly for 1/3rd of the net illumination [33]. In computer graphics images with a remarkably natural appearance have been simulated using a simple illumination model incorporating a constant ambient component [14]. The "collimated plus ambient" illumination model is:

$$I(\hat{\mathbf{n}}, \mathbf{x}) = I_0(\mathbf{x}) \left(1/3 + (2/3).\max(0, \hat{\mathbf{n}} \cdot \hat{\mathbf{L}})\right), \tag{4}$$

where $\hat{\mathbf{L}}$ is the direction of collimation and I_0 is the net illumination along $\hat{\mathbf{L}}$. In this case $I(\hat{\mathbf{n}}, \mathbf{x})$ has a dynamic range of 3 over all surface orientations at a given $\mathbf{x}$. This collimated model is a worst case—for multiple sources or an extended source (e.g. a large window or the sky) the dynamic range is the same if not less. Both multiple and extended sources serve to distribute the net incident illumination over a wider range of directions. Informal experiments with a spot photometer, indoors under various lighting conditions confirm that **3** is a reasonable value.

3.2 Realistic dynamic range of $\rho(\mathbf{x})$ for natural materials

The legal range of albedo is $\rho \in (0, 1)$. Real surfaces away from specular geometries exhibit an effective albedo. In practice real dielectrics are neither perfect reflectors nor perfect absorbers and their effective albedo lies in a restricted range $\rho \in (\rho_{min}, \rho_{max})$. In operating circumstances the dynamic range of effective albedo in a scene ρ_{max}/ρ_{min} is found to have an upper bound of roughly 10. Table 1 summarises the available data. Normal-hemispherical reflectance $\rho(0; 2\pi)$ provides a useful estimate of effective albedo [7]. By simply taking the maximum and minimum values of $\rho(0; 2\pi)$ in the table a very large dynamic range: $98\%/0.3\% \sim 3000$ is obtained. When some of the materials: chemical powders, carbon black and black velvet are discounted—upon the basis that they are very rarely encountered—a much lower value prevails: $90\%/5\% \sim 18$. In fact it seems safe to use a still lower value, **10** for commonly encountered materials.

Material	$\rho(0; 2\pi)$	References
Pure powders (e.g. MgCO3)	98–80%	[17]
Sugar, Flour, Talc., Starch	90–80%	[17,22]
White paint, papers, cloth	80–60%	[17,22,36,19]
Coloured pigments:	80–8%	[17]
..Chrome yellow	80%	
..Ultramarine	8%	
Building Materials:	90–9%	[17,22]
..Clays	90–11%	
..Concrete	35–9%	
..Slates	20–10%	
..Roofing Materials	78–11%	
..Bricks	64–11%	
..Pine Wood	40%	
Peach, Pear (ripe or green)	40–20%	[22]
Coloured porcelain-enamel	70–20%	[22]
Black papers	6–5%	[22]
Black velvet	0.4%	[22]
Carbon black in oil	0.3%	[22]

Table 1: Measured values of $\rho(0; 2\pi)$ for various dielectrics.

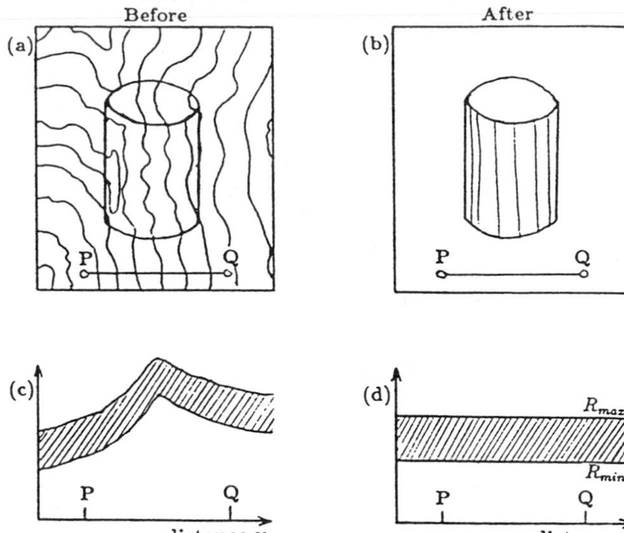

Figure 7: (a) Before retinex pre-processing, spatial variations in net illumination are present in the image irradiance signal. (b) After processing any gradual variations have been eliminated. (c) Before processing, the 30:1 dynamic range constraint does not apply. (d) After processing, it does.

4 The retinex-based test

The retinex-based test is developed to detect those specularities that are 'too bright' to be matte. This test involves *more* than identifying specularities that exceed a certain fixed brightness threshold because the appropriate threshold value varies with the spatial variations of illumination. By considering relative rather than absolute brightness the test copes with the scene-to-scene variations. Variations within a single image are removed by applying a retinex process (fig 7). After removal of spatial variations in illumination $I(\hat{\mathbf{n}}, \mathbf{x})$ the dynamic range of image irradiance, for Lambertian-like regions has an upper bound of about **30**, the product of the bounds on $\rho(\mathbf{x})$ and $I(\hat{\mathbf{n}}, \mathbf{x})$ (i.e. 10 × 3). Bright regions in an image with a dynamic range exceeding 30 are candidate specularities.

A variety of computational schemes of the retinex are available [29,23]. The implementation used here [9] is correct in its treatment of the image perimeter. Although the retinex is designed to work in a (Mondrian) world without the shading gradients introduced by surface curvature, Land [30] shows that it usefully eliminates illumination variations present in images of real curved surfaces. However, as the retinex cannot distinguish the smaller shading gradients from those due to gradual changes in the illumination level, it is apt to remove them too. This somewhat reduces the power of the test. Removal of gradual changes is done by gaussian filtering [7].

5 The cylinder test

Specularities can often be distinguished from Lambertian shading by the sharpness of their irradiance peaks. The cylinder test quantifies just how sharp a peak must be before the Lambertian interpretation can be discounted. It does this by placing an upper bound U, on the 2nd derivative of irradiance, $D(x_P)$ at the peak location, x_P along the direction of any 1-D profile through an elongated bright region (blob). Where ever $D(x_P) > U$ a specularity is detected. Very narrow profiles are excluded—they might simply be due to thin white matte lines on a dark background. A method akin to that of Asada and Brady [1] is used to extract suitable profiles [7]. The appropriate value of threshold U is computed for a given profile using its dimensions. By a worst case analysis [7], the value can be shown to be

$$U = E(x_P)/(r_1 r_2), \tag{5}$$

where $E(x_P)$ is peak irradiance and r_1 and r_2 are the image distances from the flanking edges of the profile. Establishing this expression requires two assumptions: that albedo is uniform between flanking edges[23] and the surface is locally approximately cylindrical. The second assumption is not as arbitrary as it might seem: an elongated blob is, in itself, a strong indication of a local cylindrical surface. And since the test requires only a bound on, rather than an accurate estimate of $D(x_P)$, it is robust to modest curvature along the spine of the blob. This bound holds *for all* viewer-source geometries, cylinder radii, levels of ambient illumination and portions of a cylinder.

6 Results and applications

Fig 9 show how the specularity detector performs on a set of real images. Each (256x256; 8-bit grey-level) image was acquired from a Link-Electronics 109 vidicon camera. Grey-level was approximately proportional to image irradiance. The signal's (~6 bit) dynamic range was just enough to apply the retinex-based test. Edge maps—used to initiate the profile extraction paths—were obtained using a Canny operator (width $\sigma = 1$ pixel) followed by hysteresis thresholding [10].

Both the retinex-based and cylinder tests provide strong evidence for specularities, but only mark local maxima in image irradiance. To obtain descriptions of the entire specular blob surrounding any maximum the evidence is propagated outwards. A simple but effective method of achieving this is to apply the following process at each maximum where evidence exists:

- Mark the location of the maximum inside the specular blob.
- Recursively apply the same process at any adjacent pixels which are not on the blobs edge contour (as marked in the edge map) and at which the image irradiance exceeds 2/3rds the peak value.

Although fairly arbitrary, this method produces adequate specularity maps corresponding to the maxima at which evidence was found (see fig 9). A more principled approach might fit quadratic patches to the irradiance surface of each specular blob in order to determine the extent of each blob.

The results show that both tests can and do detect genuine specularities. Neither test detects all the genuine specularities in any of the images but importantly neither test marks any false positives. On most occasions the evidence is satisfactorily propagated from the local maxima into the surrounding blobs. Occasionally it is propagated too far: Barring this minor problem, the scheme successfully combines the evidence provided by the tests to create a specularity map. However, at least one genuine specularity is missed in each test image so there is room for improvement. The specularities that are missed are often both too dim for the retinex-based test and too narrow for the cylinder test—e.g. on the left spoke in fig 9 (a). At a higher resolution they might well be detected. Once detected, both the monocular shape and the stereoscopic disparity of a specularity can be used to infer local surface shape as described in the accompanying paper [6]. Specularities should not be used as features for estimating surface depth—their apparent depths are not on the surface. Binocular stereo is improved if specularities are excised before matching and estimating the depth of surface features. Fig 8 shows how excising the detected specularity improves the depth estimated by the PMF stereo algorithm [35]. The fragmentation of the smooth surface is eliminated.

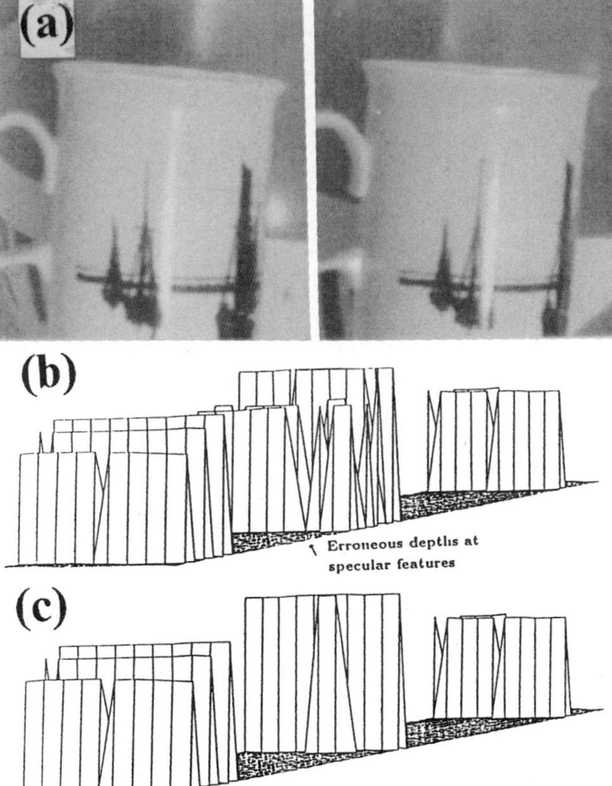

Figure 8: (a) A stereo pair of images (aligned for cross-eyed fusion). Surface plots of part of the sparse depth map from the previous figure, (b) before and (c) after excising the detected specular features.

Acknowledgements

This work was supported by SERC grant GR/D 1439.6, by the University of Edinburgh, by the Royal Society of London's IBM Research Fellowship (for AB) and by the IBM/SERC CASE Studentship (for GB). Thanks to Stephen Pollard at AIVRU, Sheffield for images. We are very grateful to Andrew Zisserman and Constantinos Marinos for helpful discussions.

References

[1] Asada H. and Brady J.M., The Curvature Primal Sketch, *IEEE Trans. PAMI*, 8, 1, (1986), 2-14.

[2] Babu M.D.R., Lee C-H. and Rosenfeld A., Determining Plane Orientation From Specular Reflectance, *Pattern Recognition*, 18, 1, (1985), 53-62.

Figure 9: (a)–(d): Series of four real images. (e)–(h): The corresponding series of detected specularities—marked in white (edges in black).

[3] Beckmann P. and Spizzichino A., *The Scattering of Electromagnetic Waves from Rough Surfaces*, MacMillan, New York, (1963).

[4] Billmeyer F.W., Lewis D.L. and Davidson J.G., Goniophotometry of Pressed Barium Sulphate, *Color Engineering, May/June*, (1971) 31-36.

[5] Blake A., Specular Stereo, *Proc. IJCAI-85*, 2, (1985), 973-976.

[6] Blake A. and Brelstaff G.J., Geometry from Specularity, *Proc. 2nd ICCV*, Florida, (1988).

[7] Brelstaff G.J., *Inferring Surface Shape from Specular Reflections*, Ph.d. Thesis, Dept. Comp. Sci., University of Edinburgh (1988).

[8] Bolle R.M. and Cooper D.B., Baysian Recognition of Local 3-D shape by Approximating Image Intensity Functions with Quadric Polynomials, *IEEE Trans. PAMI*, 6, 4, (1984), 418-429.

[9] Brelstaff G.J. and Blake A., Computing Lightness, *Pattern Recognition Letters*, 5, 129-138, (1987).

[10] Canny J.F., *Finding Edges and Lines in Images*, Masters Thesis, AI-TR 720, (1983), A.I. Lab., M.I.T.

[11] Chylek P., Light Scattering by small particles in an absorbing medium, *J. Opt. Soc. Am.* 67, 4, (1977), 561-563.

[12] Chylek P. and Wiscombe W.J., Mie Scattering between any two angles, *J. Opt. Soc. Am.* 67, 4, (1977), 572-573.

[13] Coleman E.N.Jr. and Jain R., Obtaining 3-Dimensional Shape of Textured and Specular Surfaces Using Four-Source Photometry, *CGIP*, 18, (1982), 309-328.

[14] Cook R.L. and Torrance K.E., A Reflectance Model for Computer Graphics, *ACM Trans. on Graphics*, 1, 1, (1982), 7-24.

[15] Elson J.M and Bennet J.M., Relation between the angular dependences of scattering and the statistical properties of optical surfaces, *J. Opt. Soc. Am.*, 69, 1, (1979), 31-47.

[16] Forbus K., *Light Source Effects* A.I. Memo 422, (1977), A.I. Lab., M.I.T.

[17] Forsythe W.E., *Smithsonian Physical Tables*, 9th ed., (1954), 549-559.

[18] Gershon R., Jepson A.D. and Tsotsos J.K., The Use of Color in Highlight Identification, *Proc. 1st ICCV*, London, (1987), 161-170.

[19] Gubareff G.G., Janssen J.E. and Torbourg R.H., *Thermal Radiation Properties Survey: A Review of the Literature*, Honeywell Research Center, Minneapolis, USA, (1960).

[20] Harrison V.G.W., *Definition and Measurement of Gloss*, Monograph, The Printing and Allied Trades Research Assoc. (1945).

[21] Healey G., and Binford T.O., Local shape from specularity, *CVGIP*, 42, (1988), 62-86.

[22] Hodgman C.D., *Handbook of Chemistry of Physics*, 32nd Ed, (1950-51), 2443-2445.

[23] Horn B.K.P., Determining Lightness from an Image, *CGIP*, 3 (1974) 277-299.

[24] Horn B.K.P. and Sjoberg R.W., Calculating the reflectance map, *Applied Optics*, 18, 11, (1979), 1770-1779.

[25] Hottel H.C. and Sarofim A.F., *Radiative Transfer*, McGraw-Hill, 1967.

[26] Hunter R.S., Methods of determining gloss, *J. Res. Nat. Bur. Std.*, 18, (1937) 19-39.

[27] Klinker G.J., Shafer S,A., and Kanade T., Using a color reflection model to separate highlights from object color, *Proc. 1st ICCV*, London, (1987) 145-150.

[28] Koenderink J.J. and van Doorn A,J., Photometric invariants related to solid shape, *Optica Acta*, 27, 7, (1980), 981-996.

[29] Land E.H. and McCann J.J., Lightness and Retinex Theory, *J. Opt. Soc. Am.*, 61, 1, (1971), 1-11.

[30] Land E.H., Recent advances in retinex theory and some implications for cortical computation: Color vision and natural images., *Proc. Natl. Acad. Sci. U.S.A.*, 80, (1983), 5163-5169.

[31] Mudgett P.S. and Richards L.W., Multiple Scattering Calculations for Technology, *Applied Optics*, 10, 7, (1971), 1485-1502.

[32] Nicodemus F.E., Richmond J.C., Ginsberg I.W., Hsia J.J. and Limperist T., *Geometrical Considerations and Nomenclature for Reflectance* Monograph 160, NBS, Washington D.C., (1977).

[33] Nishita T. and Nakamae E., Continuous Tone Representation of Three-Dimensional Objects Taking Account of Shadows and Interreflection, *SIGGRAPH*, 19, 3, (1985), 23-30.

[34] Ohta Y. and Kanade T., Stereo by Intra- and Inter Scanline Search Using Dynamic Programming, *IEEE PAMI*, 7, 2, (1985), 139-154.

[35] Pollard S., Mayhew J.E.W. and Frisby J.P., PMF: a stereo correspondence algorithm using the disparity gradient limit, *Perception*, 14, (1985), 449-470.

[36] Purdue University, *Thermophysical Properties of Matter*, Vols 7, 8 and 9, Plenum, New York, (1970).

[37] Thrift P. and Lee C-H., Using Highlights to Constrain Object Size and Location, *IEEE Trans. Sys, Man and Cyber.*, 13, 3, (1983), 426-431.

[38] Torrance K.E. and Sparrow E.M., Theory of Off-Specular Reflection From Roughened Surfaces, *J. Opt. Soc. Am.*, 57, 9, (1967), 1105-1114.

[39] Ullman S., On Visual Detection of Light Sources, *Biol. Cybernetics*, 21, (1976), 205-212.

[40] Verri A. and Poggio T., Against Quantitative Optical Flow, *Proc, 1st ICCV*, London, June, (1987), 201-208.

[18] Geometry from Specularities

Andrew Blake and Gavin Brelstaff

Department of Computer Science
University of Edinburgh, Edinburgh EH9 3JZ, Scotland, UK

Abstract

Relatively recently the problems for vision presented by specular reflections have begun to receive attention. In particular it has been noted that the monocular and stereoscopic appearance of specular reflections, and their dynamic behaviour, contain local shape information. Work reported here contributes to the understanding of specularity in several ways.

A new algorithm is described for accurate computation of horizontal and vertical stereoscopic disparities of specular points, relative to nearby surface points. Knowledge of such disparities is shown to restrict principal curvatures (with known light-source position) to lie on a hyperbolic constraint-curve. Monocular appearance of specularities is known also to constrain surface shape. We show that, at best, there remains a fourfold ambiguity of local surface curvature. In the case of a light source that is of unknown shape but known to be compact (in a precise sense), elongated specularities have geometrical significance. The "axis" of such a specularity, back-projected onto the surface tangent plane, approximates to a line of curvature. The approximation improves as the specularity becomes more elongated and the source more compact.

These ideas have been incorporated into an existing stereo vision system, and shown to work well with real and simulated images.

1 Introduction

Specular reflection represents both a problem and an opportunity in vision. It is a problem in that it disrupts processes such as edge-detection and stereoscopic matching, but an opportunity in that highlights or specularities are cues for surface geometry.

Clearly, to make any progress, it must be possible to detect specularities. Various processes have been proposed and tested. Some involve chromatic analysis [9,17] others achromatic analysis of intensity [25,8]. This paper addresses problems of geometric inference rather than of specularity detection but for the purposes of demonstrating a working system an achromatic specularity detector has been used. It builds on the ideas of Ullman's S-operator [25] and on the retinex process of Land and others [16,13,3], and will be the subject of a future paper.

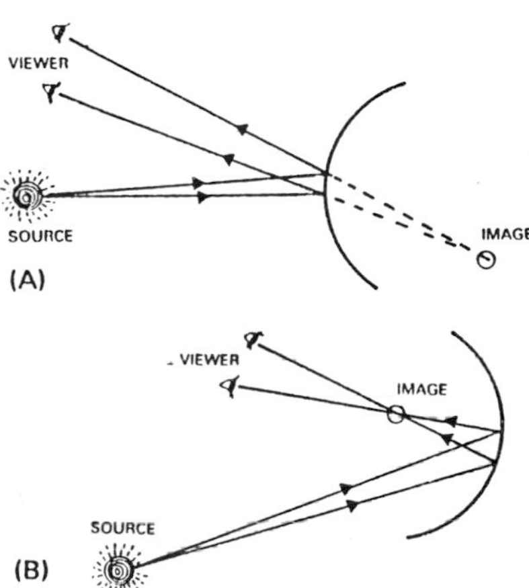

Figure 1: Specular stereo - the basic principle: specularities appear behind a convex mirror but in front of a concave one.

A discussion of the inference of shape from specularity is given by Koenderinck and van Doorn [15]. They elegantly expound the qualitative behaviour of specularities under viewer motion. Specularities travel freely in elliptic or hyperbolic regions, speeding up near parabolic lines, annihilating and being created, in pairs, on the parabolic lines. They travel most slowly in regions of high curvature and hence, for a given static viewer position, specularities are most likely to be found where curvature is high. More recently a number of quantitative analyses of specularity have emerged. Several involve active vision systems extending photometric stereo [26] to deal with and profit from specular reflection [7,14,20]. Other approaches are based on mathematical models of specular reflection, including specification of reflectance map, fixing various free parameters of the model by measure-

*Current addresses: A. Blake, Dept. Engineering Science, Parks Rd., Oxford. G. Brelstaff, IBM UKSC, Athelstan Ho., St Clement St., Winchester.

Figure 2: An example of a specularity whose "motion" relative to surface features is oblique - vertical relative disparity is not zero.

ments from individual specularities [1, 11,12]. In view of the difficulty of achieving adequate photometric models for specularity and of fixing their parameters from image data [11] it seems reasonable to try to restrict modelling to simple ray optics and the law of reflection. Koenderinck and van Doorn's work is in this vein, and other more quantitative models have been investigated [21,24,2]. In this paper we extend that theme and illustrate it by incorporating analysis of specularity in a stereoscopic vision system.

2 Stereoscopic analysis of specular reflection

The basic principle of "specular stereo" is illustrated in figure 1. According to the simple physics of curved mirrors, a specularity will appear behind a glossy, convex surface but (generally) in front of a concave one. Here this simple idea is expanded. For example, how does a specularity appear in a hyperbolic surface? Whether it appears behind or in front depends on the orientation of the surface. Even on elliptic, non-umbilic surfaces, astigmatic effects produce apparent depth variations as orientation is changed. In fact the notion of apparent depth is ill-defined here - what we actually observe are horizontal and vertical relative disparities (relative to disparities of surface features). Specularities, unlike physical surface features, need not satisfy the "epipolar" constraint [18] so vertical disparity may be non-zero. This is illustrated by the example of figure 2, in which relative displacement of the specularity in the right image (relative to the left) is oblique. Both horizontal and vertical disparities vary as the orientation of the stereo baseline changes relative to lines of curvature on the surface.

Analysis of the stereoscopic viewing geometry will establish the relationship between surface shape and measured disparities. It is helpful to consider two different kinds of analysis. The first is approximate, a linear system "driven" by the interocular separation, with disparities as its output. The characteristics of the linear system depend on surface geometry (curvature and orientation). This analysis appeared in earlier work [2] and is useful for characterising degeneracies - special alignments at which geometric inference will fail. An exact analysis is more convenient for computation as well as being more accurate and a method has been developed for accurate computation of relative disparities, together with error bounds.

2.1 Viewing geometry

The geometry for stereoscopic viewing of a specularity is shown in figure 3. Vectors $\mathbf{d}$, the stereo baseline, is assumed known, as is $\mathbf{S}$, the position of the light source [1]. The directions $\hat{\mathbf{V}}, \hat{\mathbf{W}}$ of vectors $\mathbf{V}, \mathbf{W}$ are given by the measured positions of the specularities in the left and right images. The projection of displacement vector $\mathbf{r}$ onto the left (say) image plane forms the observed relative disparity vector.

A few equations suffice to describe this geometrical arrangement. First, there are three cycles amongst the vectors:

$$\mathbf{V} + \mathbf{d} - \mathbf{r} - \mathbf{W} = 0, \tag{1}$$

[1] The assumption of known light source position is of course a strong one. However it can be computed from just one stereoscopic observation of a highlight on an object of known shape.

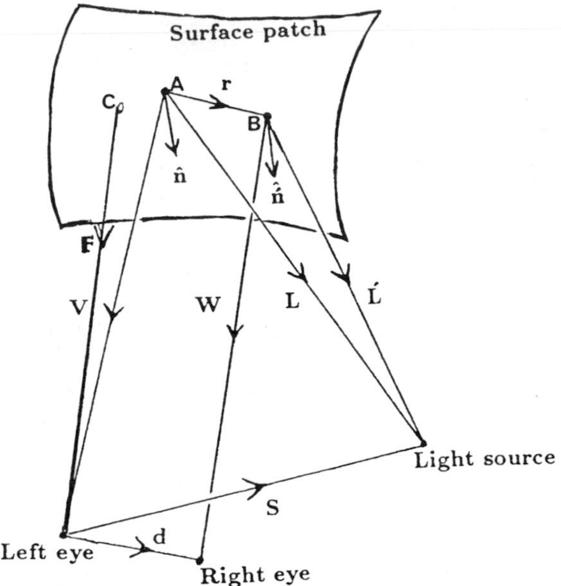

Figure 3: A smooth patch of surface is illuminated by a point source along vector $\mathbf{L}$. Light striking point A is specularly reflected along vector $\mathbf{V}$ into the left eye. Similarly, light incident at B traverses $\mathbf{W}$ into the right eye. Surface normals at A and B are $\hat{\mathbf{n}}$ and $\hat{\mathbf{n}}$ respectively. Vector $\mathbf{r}$ separates A and B. The stereo base-line lies along vector $\mathbf{d}$. A surface marking lies nearby A at C.

$$\mathbf{V} - \mathbf{L} - \mathbf{S} = 0 \tag{2}$$

and

$$\mathbf{L} - \mathbf{L}' - \mathbf{r} = 0. \tag{3}$$

The physical law of reflection is expressed in the following equations:

$$\hat{\mathbf{n}} = \frac{\hat{\mathbf{V}} + \hat{\mathbf{L}}}{|\hat{\mathbf{V}} + \hat{\mathbf{L}}|}. \tag{4}$$

$$\hat{\mathbf{n}}' = \frac{\hat{\mathbf{W}} + \hat{\mathbf{L}}'}{|\hat{\mathbf{W}} + \hat{\mathbf{L}}'|}. \tag{5}$$

Finally, the vector $\mathbf{F}$ is computed from conventional stereoscopic viewing of the surface reference mark C, and it is assumed to lie in the tangent plane to the surface at A, so that

$$(\mathbf{F} - \mathbf{V}).\mathbf{n} = 0. \tag{6}$$

Of course C does not lie *exactly* in the tangent plane, but the error is small provided the surface reference C is not too far away from the ray intersection point A (figure 4).

2.2 Computation of surface depth

We need to know surface depth $V = |\mathbf{V}|$ but, so far, know only the depth of a nearby non-specular "reference point" on the surface. In fact V can be computed from equation

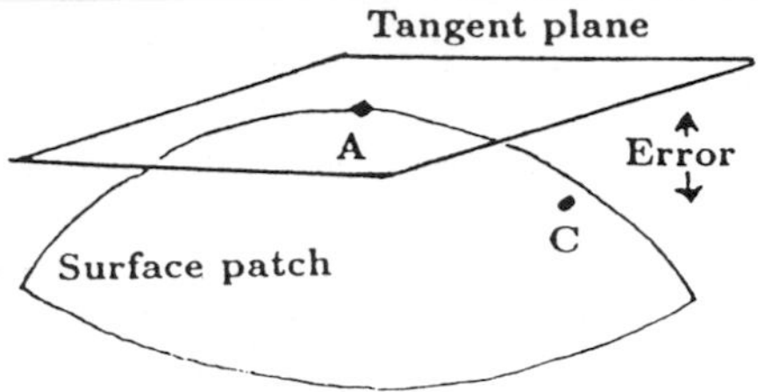

Figure 4: Point C lies on the surface at a little distance from A. Along this distance the surface curves gently out of the tangent plane. So the "tangent plane assumption" is only an approximation.

(6), given that $\hat{\mathbf{V}} = \mathbf{V}/V$ is known from the position of the specularity in the left image, by the iterative algorithm given in figure 5. This algorithm has not been

$i=0$, $|\mathbf{V}|^{(i)} = |\mathbf{F}|$.
repeat

$$\begin{aligned} i &= i+1, \\ \mathbf{V}^{(i)} &= |\mathbf{V}|^{(i)}\hat{\mathbf{V}}, \\ \mathbf{L}^{(i)} &= \mathbf{V}^{(i)} + \mathbf{S}, \\ \hat{\mathbf{n}}^{(i)} &= \left(\hat{\mathbf{V}} + \hat{\mathbf{L}}^{(i)}\right) / |\hat{\mathbf{V}} + \hat{\mathbf{L}}^{(i)}|, \\ |\mathbf{V}|^{(i)} &= \left(\hat{\mathbf{n}}^{(i)} . \mathbf{F}\right) / \left(\hat{\mathbf{n}}^{(i)} . \hat{\mathbf{V}}\right). \end{aligned}$$

while $\left||\mathbf{V}|^{(i)} - |\mathbf{V}|^{(i-1)}\right| > 0.01|\mathbf{F}|$.
$\mathbf{V} = \mathbf{V}^{(i)}$, $\hat{\mathbf{n}} = \hat{\mathbf{n}}^{(i)}$, $\mathbf{L} = \mathbf{L}^{(i)}$.

Figure 5: Iterative algorithm for computing $\mathbf{V}$, the position at which the reflected ray strikes the specular surface.

proved to converge, but seems well-behaved in practice.

2.3 Local surface shape

It is clear that, having computed $\mathbf{V}$ as above, $\mathbf{n}$ can be obtained from (4) and (2). In other words, knowing the light source position, and observing a nearby surface reference point C suffices to compute surface orientation at the specular point A.

So much for surface orientation - but what about local surface curvature? Curvature is expressed in terms of the Hessian matrix H. Choosing coordinates such that $\mathbf{x} = (x, y)$ is the restriction of $\mathbf{r} = (x, y, z)$ to the tangent plane at A:

$$z = \frac{1}{2}\mathbf{x}.(H\mathbf{x}) + O(|\mathbf{x}|^3). \tag{7}$$

(The choice of coordinates allows an arbitrary rotation in the tangent plane, which is conveniently fixed by choosing the (0,1,0) direction to be orthogonal to vector $\mathbf{V} - \mathbf{L}$.)

Differentiating (7), one can obtain

$$\delta\mathbf{n} = -H\mathbf{x} + O(|\mathbf{x}|^2). \quad (8)$$

where $\delta\mathbf{n}$ is the component of $\hat{\mathbf{n}}' - \hat{\mathbf{n}}$ lying in the tangent plane. Now $\hat{\mathbf{n}}$ is known already, so to compute $\delta\mathbf{n}$ we need $\hat{\mathbf{n}}'$ - which can be calculated from (5) if $\mathbf{W}$ is known. Observing that $\mathbf{r}.\mathbf{n} = 0$ and substituting this into (1) yields the following formula, in terms of measured quantities, for $|\mathbf{W}|$:

$$|\mathbf{W}| \approx \frac{(\mathbf{V}+\mathbf{d})\cdot\hat{\mathbf{n}}}{\widehat{\mathbf{W}}\cdot\hat{\mathbf{n}}}. \quad (9)$$

2.4 Graphical representation of geometric constraints

Measurement of $\delta\mathbf{n} = (\delta n_1, \delta n_2)$ imposes 2 independent constraints, via equation (8), on the components of the hessian H. But H is a symmetric matrix:

$$H = \begin{pmatrix} H_{xx} & H_{xy} \\ H_{xy} & H_{yy} \end{pmatrix}, \quad (10)$$

so it has 3 independent components. Clearly, further information is required to fix all 3. This can be obtained either by moving the stereo baseline or by monocular observation of the shape of the specularity. Both possibilities will be discussed in due course. In the meantime, it is natural to ask whether the 2 constraints already obtained represent *intrinsic* information about the surface - that is, do they constrain principal curvatures of the surface?

Brelstaff [4] has shown that there is indeed an intrinsic constraint. The principal curvatures κ_1, κ_2 are constrained to lie on a hyperbola. Equivalently, the corresponding principal radii of curvature r_1, r_2 lie on a hyperbola:

$$-B^2 = (r_1 - A)(r_2 - A) \quad (11)$$

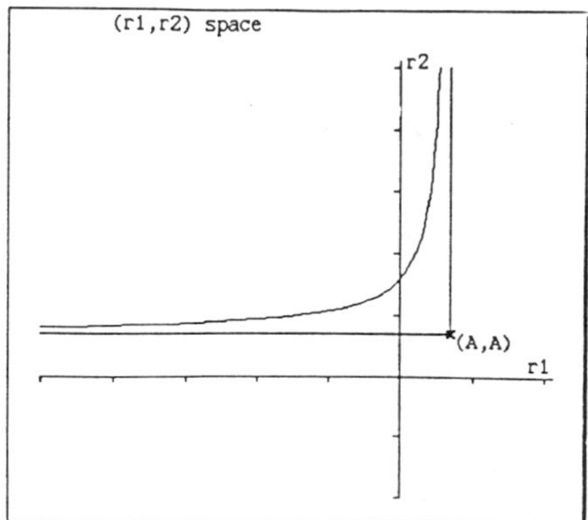

Figure 6: Stereo analysis constrains the principal radii of curvature $r_i = 1/\kappa_i$, $i = 1,2$ to lie on the upper curve of a hyperbola.

where

$$A = \frac{\delta\mathbf{n}.\mathbf{x}}{|\delta\mathbf{n}|^2} \text{ and } B = \sqrt{\frac{|\mathbf{x}|^2}{|\delta\mathbf{n}|^2} - A^2}, \quad (12)$$

as shown in figure 6. Without loss of generality, we can require $r_1 \le r_2$, so that the constraint set includes only one curve of the hyperbola. For example, the family of surfaces allowed by the constraint in figure 6 is illustrated in figure 7.

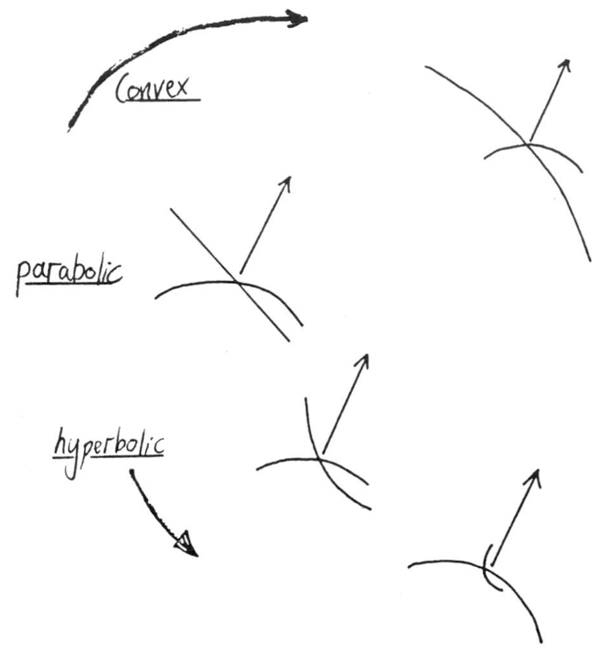

Figure 7: Specular stereo - constraints on local shape. A typical constraint, illustrated algebraically in figure 6, admits a one-parameter family of interpretations. Generally either concave or convex interpretations are excluded - in this case concave ones.

Note that a concave interpretation is excluded - the surface must be either convex or hyperbolic in this case. Generally a concave or convex interpretation is excluded according as the sign of A is positive or negative respectively - that is, according to the sign of $\delta\mathbf{n}.\mathbf{x}$. Recently a similar condition has been obtained by Zisserman et al. [27] but with the additional advantage of being independent of light source position. In that case, the discriminant is simply the scalar product of the projections onto the image plane of $\mathbf{x}$ (i.e. the relative disparity vector) and the baseline $\mathbf{d}$.

2.5 Test for umbilic points

Spheres are an interesting special case for specular stereo. Since $H = \kappa I$ on the surface of a sphere, we can see from equation (8) that $\delta\mathbf{n}$ and $\mathbf{x}$ are parallel vectors or, in practice:

$$|\delta\mathbf{n} \times \mathbf{x}| \ll |\delta\mathbf{n}||\mathbf{x}|. \tag{13}$$

If the parallelism test is passed the point *may* be umbilic - but of course this is not guaranteed. For instance it could be on any surface patch specially oriented so that one line of curvature lies (locally) in the plane of the incident and reflected rays. So the test can be used to eliminate umbilic interpretations.

3 Specular stereo as a linear system

The previous section explained how constraints on geometry can be inferred from stereoscopic observation of a specularity and a nearby non-specular "reference" point. Further analysis can be applied, linearising the relationship between displacement vector $\mathbf{x}$ and baseline vector $\mathbf{d}$. Whilst this offers no particular improvements in convenience of computation of shape constraints, it affords insights into geometric degeneracies, and clarifies the relationship with conventional stereoscopic disparity.

Simplifying previous analysis [2], the linear system can expressed as

$$2V(MH - \kappa_{VL}I)\mathbf{x} = \mathbf{w}, \tag{14}$$

where

$$\mathbf{w} = (-d_1 + d_3 \tan\sigma, -d_2)^T, \tag{15}$$

$$M = \begin{pmatrix} \sec\sigma & 0 \\ 0 & \cos\sigma \end{pmatrix}, \tag{16}$$

σ is surface slant at A, and

$$\kappa_{VL} = \frac{1}{2}\left(\frac{1}{V} + \frac{1}{L}\right) \tag{17}$$

- a term familiar from the elementary ray-optics of lenses. It can be thought of as an "apparent curvature" induced on a viewed plane, owing to the finite distances from the plane to source and viewer. This linear approximation is valid whenever the baseline is relatively short, that is, when

$$|\mathbf{d}| \ll |\mathbf{V}|\cos\sigma, \tag{18}$$

and provided the surface does not focus incoming rays to a point or line close to the centre of projection (see discussion of degeneracy below).

3.1 Horizontal and vertical disparity

One insight that equation (14) affords is that the specular stereo constraints on H depend solely on imaging geometry ($\kappa_{VL}, V, M, \mathbf{w}$) and on the displacement vector $\mathbf{x}$. So the only *measured* quantity involved is $\mathbf{x}$, which is intimately related to the relative stereoscopic disparity $\boldsymbol{\delta}$, as follows:

$$\mathbf{x} = VP\boldsymbol{\delta} \tag{19}$$

where

$$P = \begin{pmatrix} \sec\sigma & 0 \\ 0 & 1 \end{pmatrix}. \tag{20}$$

The two-component vector $\boldsymbol{\delta}$ represents the horizontal and vertical disparities of the specularity, *relative* to the disparities of the nearby surface reference point. The conventional view of stereoscopic vision is that useful depth information is encoded entirely in horizontal disparities. Vertical disparity is fixed by epipolar geometry, so its possible influence is limited to calibration of view geometry and, in human vision, an associated illusory distortion, the induced effect [19].

For specularities, this is not the case. Vertical disparity plays a strong role, in two ways. First, vertical disparities that violate epipolar geometry are *evidence* that specular reflection is occurring. Second, as we just saw, measured vertical disparity imposes an independent constraint on curvature, in addition to the one imposed by measurement of horizontal disparity. Both of these computational "truths" call for psychophysical investigation. Is either theory exploited in human vision?

3.2 Degeneracy

Inspection of the linearised imaging equation (14) reveals degeneracy when

$$\det(MH - \kappa_{VL}I) = 0.$$

What exactly is observed physically? First of all, this can happen only on non-convex surfaces (MH is negative definite on a convex surface) and even then only for special alignments - when the viewer collides with one or both "focal surfaces" [27][2]. A convex surface lies *in front* of its focal surfaces; the viewer cannot collide with a focal surface because the convex surface is in the way. When degeneracy does occur, stereoscopic analysis fails for the very simple reason that the specularity is visible only in one eye. Moreover, the focusing effect ensures that when it is visible, it is likely to be very bright.

3.3 Combining information from two baselines

A final result from the linearised view is that when two independent baselines are used, for instance when a stereo observer is in motion, the baselines should not be nearly parallel. If they are not, $\mathbf{H}$ can be recovered completely; if they are, computation of $\mathbf{H}$ is ill-conditioned. Details of the argument are given in [2].

[2]The specularity is focussed onto a line or onto a blob, according as the rank of $MH - \kappa_{VL}I$ is 1 or 0 respectively.

4 Monocular analysis of specular reflection

A simple theory of monocular analysis of specularity [2] is summarised here, and possible ambiguity of interpretation is explored. In the case of a circular source, assuming that the diameter of the source is known, there is a possible fourfold ambiguity of interpretation, corresponding roughly to independent inversion of each principal curvature, but generally accompanied by some rotation (about the surface normal) of the lines of curvature.

The geometrical arrangement for monocular viewing, with a distributed source, is shown in figure 8. It mirrors the earlier stereo geometry but with the baseline between stereo views replaced by virtual baselines between pairs of points on the source. This duality can be tapped mathematically to derive a linear mapping relating the position

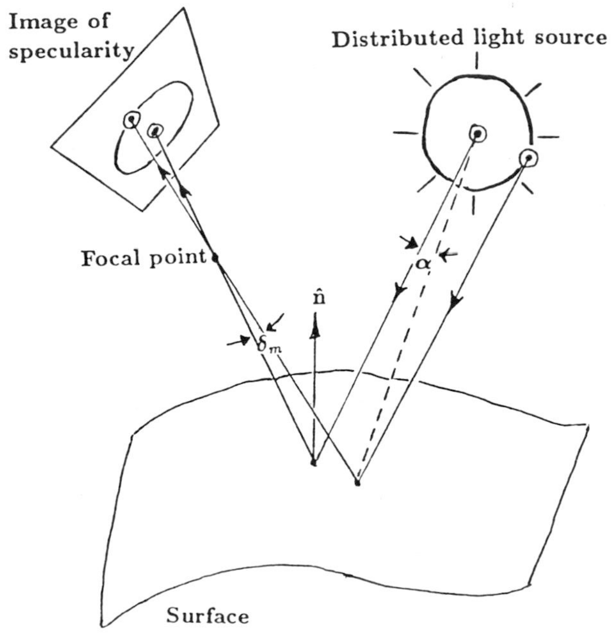

Figure 8: Monocular analysis: A distributed light source of known shape is reflected by a curved surface as a specular image region. Surface curvature information may be inferred by measuring the shape in the image. A point on the source, transforms to a point on the specularity. The angular positions of two such points are specified by α and δ_m, for source and specularity respectively.

δ_m of a specular point (in polar projection) to the angular position α on the source from which the illuminating ray came.

$$T\delta_m = \alpha \tag{21}$$

where

$$T = 2VP^{-1}MH^*P, \tag{22}$$

where

$$H^* = H - \kappa_{VL}M^{-1}, \tag{23}$$

and P, H, M, κ_{VL} are defined as previously. Since T is symmetric, the mapping is a linear scaling in two orthogonal directions.

Consider the case of a circular source, so that points on the outline of the source satisfy

$$\alpha^T\alpha = \rho^2. \tag{24}$$

The shape of the ellipse (on the polar projection) is obtained using the transformation (21) to give (using the fact that T is symmetric):

$$\delta_m^T T^2 \delta_m = \rho^2. \tag{25}$$

If we assumed the source radius ρ were known, then observation of the elliptical shape of a highlight determines T^2, via equation (25). Hence T is known up to a fourfold ambiguity (the signs of the two eigenvalues of T are unknown). Then H can be computed directly from (21), so again there are four possibilities (figure 9). These four in-

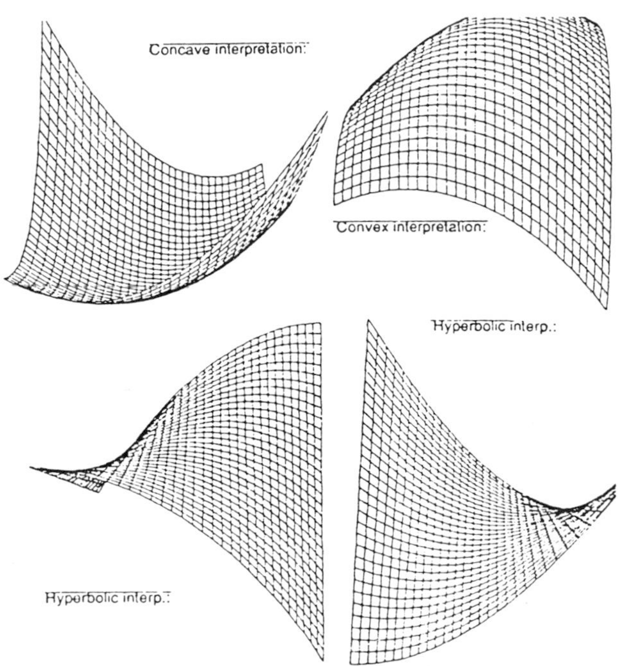

Figure 9: Observation of an elliptical specularity, with a circular source of known radius, determines local curvature up to a fourfold ambiguity, as illustrated.

terpretations generally do *not* share common lines of curvature; but the discrepancy is small if the slant is modest. Moreover, provided principal curvatures are neither small nor nearly equal in magnitude -

$$||\kappa_1| - |\kappa_2|| \gg 2\kappa_{VL}\sec\sigma,$$

the four possibilities for directions of lines of curvature collapse down to just two possibilities - this is the case in the example of figure 9.

Usually, real cameras do not form an image by polar projection, but by perspective projection. However the difference is more or less cosmetic. At a given point on the image, perspective projection is related to polar projection by a linear transformation $\delta_m = Q\mathbf{X}$, where $\mathbf{X}$ is a position vector on the projection plane, and Q is a matrix. The elliptical specularity that appears on the image plane is given by

$$\mathbf{X}^T Q^T T^2 Q \mathbf{X} = \rho^2. \quad (26)$$

Measurements made within the image plane can provide $(Q^T T^2 Q)$, from which T^2 can be computed.

4.1 Assuming a circular source

The analysis above assumed that the angular diameter (subtended at the surface) of the source was known. Often a more reasonable assumption is that the source is circular, but of *unknown* radius. There are now two possible cases.

1. The surface is locally almost flat - the magnitudes of the principal curvatures are of the order of κ_{VL} or smaller.

2. At least one principal curvature κ_1 is large - that is, it satisfies

$$\kappa_1 \gg \kappa_{VL} \sec \sigma.$$

   This is much the more likely state of affairs since specularities tend to cling to highly curved patches - hence the likelihood of observing a specularity on such a patch is relatively great. In this case, since the $2V\kappa_{VL}I$ term in (22) is negligible, and since T^2 is known up to an arbitrary multiplicative constant, H can be computed from (22) up to fourfold ambiguity *and* an arbitrary multiplicative constant. However, computed curvatures are accurate only to within $\kappa_{VL} \sec \sigma$.

So even when absolute source size is unknown, monocular observation of a specularity still allows some inference about surface shape. This is what might be expected intuitively; an elongated specularity, for example, seems to suggest very unequal principal curvatures - a locally cylindrical surface in the extreme case. In fact this particular example might be expected to hold good even when the source is not known to be circular, but merely to be "compact". That expectation is justified below.

4.2 Assuming a compact source

First we must define what is meant by a compact source. A source of compactness $K > 1$ is defined as one that is bounded by concentric circles, with radii in the ratio K : 1, as in figure 10. The most compact source is therefore a circle ($K = 1$). The absolute size of the source is assumed to be unknown.

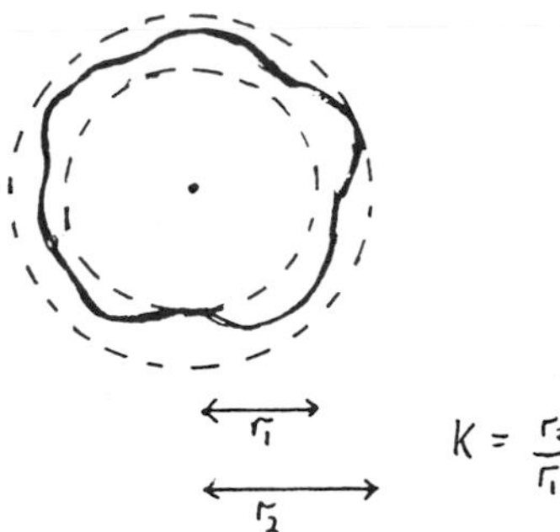

Figure 10: Definition of compact source, in terms of bounding circles.

The task now is to use the monocular specularity equations (21, 22, 23) to make some inference about surface curvature, even though the shape of the source is unknown, merely constrained. It is proposed to estimate the direction of least curvature on the surface as follows. Take the direction in which the diameter of the specular blob is greatest (figure 11), and back-project it onto the surface tangent plane. If this estimate proves reliable it provides a third constraint, in addition to the two already provided by stereoscopic analysis. Then surface curvature, represented by the three parameters of H, can be computed [2].

However, there are three problems to be addressed:

1. The direction in which the diameter of the specular blob is greatest does not correspond exactly to an eigenvector direction of T.

2. If $\mathbf{u}$ is an eigenvector of T, then in the limit that its eigenvalue $\lambda \rightarrow 0$, it can be seen from (22) that $P\mathbf{u}$ is an eigenvector of H^* (with eigenvalue 0). However, when $\lambda \neq 0$ $\mathbf{u}$ only approximates to an eigenvector of H^*.

3. Even if the eigenvectors of H^* are successfully estimated, they correspond only approximately (23) to eigenvectors of H.

What does all this amount to? Our procedure for estimating directions of lines of curvature works, but is only approximate. The approximation improves as

- the blob becomes more elongated
- the source becomes more compact
- the surface slant decreases
- the surface becomes more curved (either cylindrically or elliptically).

the problem of false matches negligible for specular features since they are usually sparse. A simple matcher, employing rough comparison of blob features, has proved sufficient in our experiments.

Geometric inference Stereoscopic and monocular inference of geometry proceed separately, as detailed in previous sections, and finally inferences are pooled. In some cases local curvature is completely determined, in others merely constrained. Results are displayed by means of appropriate graphics, together with error bounds. They are also accessible at program-level for use in model-matching, geometric reasoning or other applications.

Error treatment Each measured quantity in the stereo analysis has uncertainty associated with it; this can be represented crudely by propagation of error bounds. By combining the errors it is possible to quantify the uncertainty of the quantities in the constraint equation (14). This can be done by summing square errors [22] at each step in the analysis. This method of combination strictly only applies to independent sources of uncertainty. As the uncertainties involved here are unlikely to be completely independent, room exists for refinement.

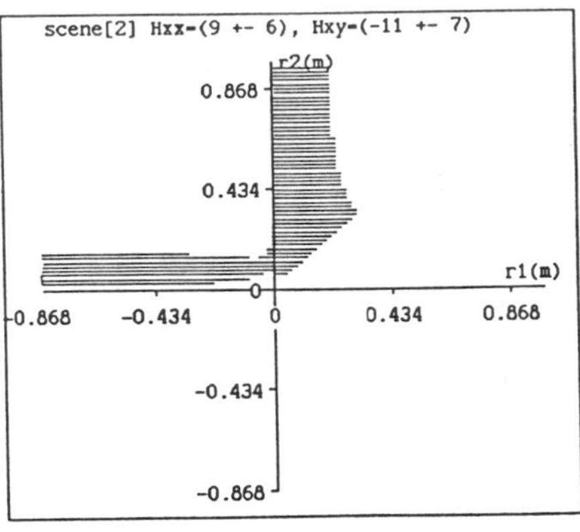

Figure 13: Constraints from stereoscopic analysis of specularity number 2, in figure 12.

An example of the system in operation is shown in figure 12. Subwindows allow user intervention at various levels, from selection of images to tracing the inference steps. Line drawings at the bottom show detected, matched specularities, labelled 1 and 2. Results of geometric inference are summarised in the display at the lower left. The ellipse and needle indicate surface orientation. Numerical slant and tilt values are also shown. The line indicates the direction of the line of least curvature - note that this appears to coincide with the axis of the cylindrical cup on which the specularity (number 2) lies. In fact the cup is not quite cylindrical, and the system has inferred (see COMBINED EVIDENCE window) that the surface is hyperbolic. Further detail can be obtained by selecting "graph" to illustrate stereoscopic and monocular inferences, and their combination. The graph for stereoscopic inference is shown in figure 13. In an ideal, error-free world it would be simply a hyperbola as in figure 6. The effect of allowing for error in the components of the Hessian H is that the hyperbola is "thickened". So on the basis of stereoscopic information, the principal curvatures may take any values in the shaded set. Note that the *directions* of the lines of curvature are not fixed, but differ for different points in the set.

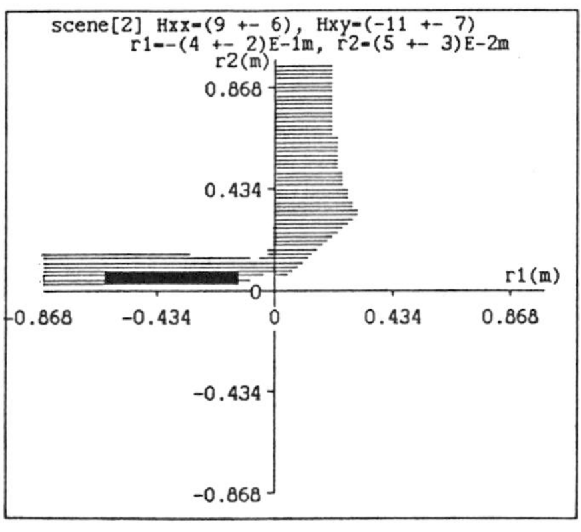

Figure 14: Combined stereoscopic and monocular constraints restrict the set of possible solutions for surface curvature to the black region.

Now when monocular information is taken into account, only a small portion of the shaded set remains feasible - shown in black on figure 14. The combination of information works very simply: the specularity is observed to be very elongated, and this more or less fixes the directions of the lines of curvature (see earlier discussion). The black region consists of those solutions from the shaded set which correspond approximately to those computed directions.

Stereoscopic analysis for the other specularity (number 1 in figure 12) is shown in figure 15. In this case the

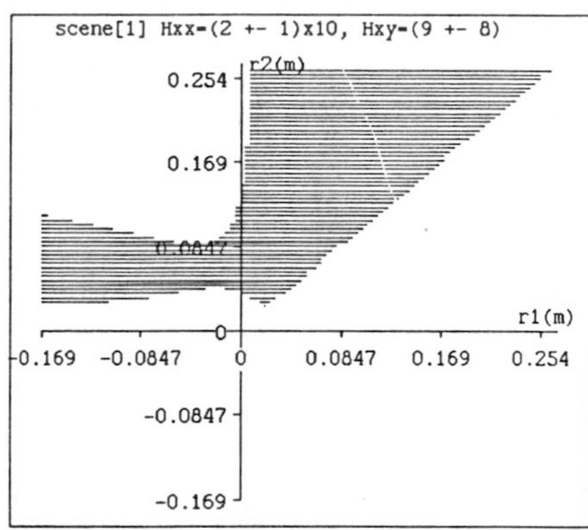

Figure 15: Stereoscopic analysis of specularity number 1 in figure 12 restricts local surface curvatures to values within the shaded set.

specularity appears as a small blob, too small reliably to determine its shape. Hence (in the absence of information about the absolute size of the source) monocular analysis does not constrain local shape any further.

The pair of stereo images in figure 16 is computer generated, using a narrow field of view to exaggerate disparities. This makes it easy to see relative displacement of specularities, and how they relate to the shape of the underlying surface. The specularity is displaced both horizontally *and* vertically relative to surface markings. That is, there are both horizontal and vertical relative disparities - a vivid illustration of the earlier assertion that specularities may break epipolar constraints. (The specularity tends to cling to the line of greatest curvature, hence the relative motion is oblique.) Indeed, the non-zero relative vertical disparity is *evidence*, in principle, that the bright blob is indeed specular. The horizontal disparity is positive, leading correctly to a prediction that the surface is convex [27]. The true values of principal curvatures (denoted by the white cross) lies within the black region that indicates predicted curvatures with error bounds. Of course the data is computer generated and free of noise, but this does at least indicate that the error bound computations, which determine the extent of the feasible set (in black) in terms of image measurement errors, are correct.

Finally, a real image (figure 17) is shown below, together with the results of geometric inference from specularity analysis. Surface curvatures have measured approximately, and fall within error bounds computed by the system. There are stereoscopic constraints as shown, but no monocular constraints; this is because the specularity is so nearly circular that ellipse axes cannot be reliably computed. Nonetheless, the shaded set does contain (just!) the measured values of surface curvature. Moreover, the black window at the bottom of the graph indicates that the system has found that the surface could be locally spherical (umbilic), according to the test described earlier (13).

6 Conclusions

Analysis of specularity is of potential assistance to geometric inference in machine vision. Stereoscopic and monocular analysis are complementary, and together can entirely determine local shape. A further role for vertical disparity has been demonstrated, in addition to its role in calibration of viewing geometry. Analysis of specularity has been incorporated into a stereoscopic vision system, and shown to yield usably accurate results. Some questions remain. How can such local shape measurements be integrated? Quantitative methods involving stereoscopic reconstruction are certainly available [11, 23] - can qualitative methods, bypassing depth maps, be found? Another question concerns motion: how much surface information can be extracted from specularities under extended displacement of the viewer?

A number of questions are raised too for human vision.

- Is vertical disparity - violation of epipolar constraints - used to identify bright features as specular?
- Can perceived surface curvature be manipulated by adjusting the disparities of a specularity?
- Can predicted fourfold ambiguity of curvature be realised in monocular views of specularities?
- Do monocular and stereoscopic analysis of specularities combine to fix perceived curvature, as predicted theoretically?
- Can the direction of displacement of a specularity in right and left stereoscopic views, resolve reversal ambiguities, as is theoretically predicted?

Acknowledgements

Discussion with A.Zisserman and with J.Mayhew, J.Frisby and S.Pollard is gratefully acknowledged. The PMF stereo system from AIVRU, Sheffield University proved invaluable and for the basis for experimentation. The support of IBM UK Scientific Centre, the Royal Society of London, the SERC and the University of Edinburgh are gratefully acknowledged.

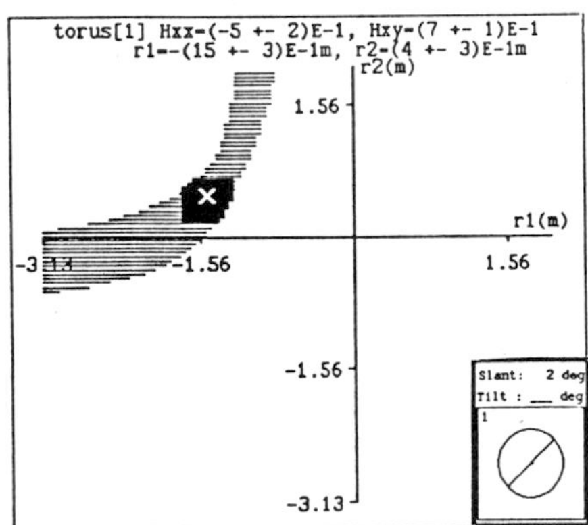

Figure 16: Inner surface of of a torus ring with surface markings (artificial images). Stereoscopic constraints, shown shaded, are restricted to the black region by monocular analysis. The correct values of curvature (used in the geometric modeller) are indicated by a white cross.

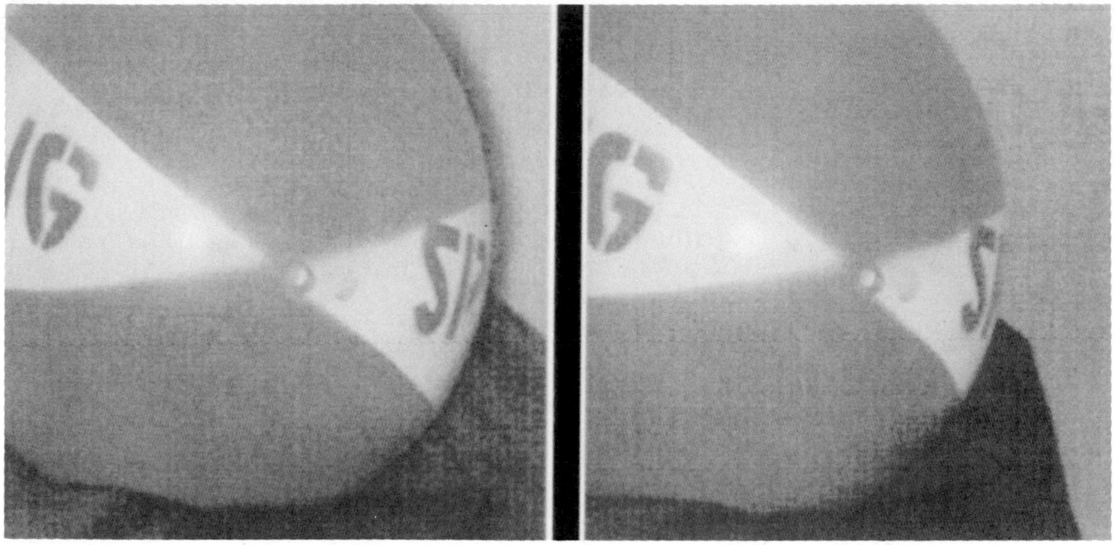

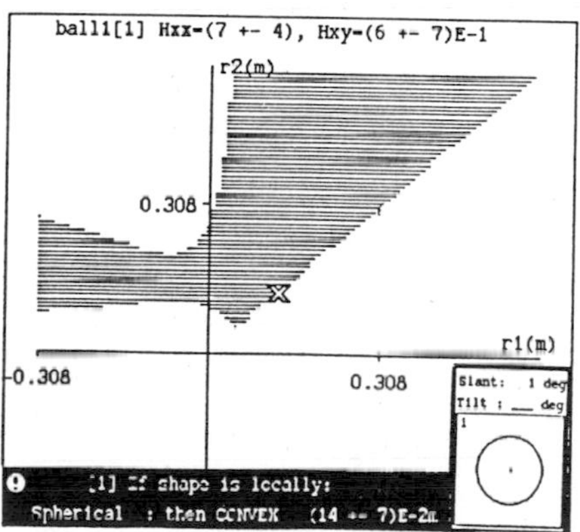

Figure 17: Beach ball of 12cm radius.

References

1. Babu, M.D.R., Lee, C-H. and Rosenfeld, A. (1985). Determining Plane Orientation From Specular Reflectance, *Pattern Recognition*, 18, 1, 53-62.

2. Blake, A. (1985). Specular Stereo. *Proc. IJCAI-85*, 2, 973-976.

3. Blake,A. (1985). Boundary conditions for lightness computation in Mondrian world. *CVGIP, 32*, 314-327.

4. Brelstaff,G.J. (1988). PhD thesis, University of Edinburgh.

5. Buchanan, C.S.B. (1987). Determining Surface Orientation from Specular Highlights, RCBV Tech. Report, RCBV-TR-87-19, University of Toronto.

6. Canny,J.F. (1983). Finding edges and lines in images. S.M. thesis, MIT, Cambridge, USA.

7. Coleman, E.N.Jr., and Jain, R. (1982) Obtaining 3-Dimensional Shape of Textured and Specular Surfaces Using Four-Source Photometry, Computer graphics and image processing, 18, 309-328.

8. Forbus, K. (1977). Light Source Effects A.I. Memo 422, A.I. Lab., M.I.T.

9. Gershon, R., Jepson, A.D. and Tsotsos, J.K. (1987). Highlight Identification Using Chromatic Information, *Proc. IJCAI87 Milan*, 752-754.

10. Grimson, W.E.L. (1981). *From Images to Surfaces* M.I.T. Press, Cambridge Mass. U.S.A..

11. Grimson, W.E.L. (1982). Binocular Shading and Visual Surface Reconstruction. M.I.T. A.I.Lab. Memo No 697.

12. Healey, G., and Binford, T.O. (1987). Local shape from specularity. Proc. First Int. Conf. on Computer Vision, London, 151-160

13. Horn, B.K.P. (1974). Determining Lightness from an Image. Computer Graphics and Image Processing, 3, 277-299.

14. Ikeuchi, K. (1981). Determining Surface Orientation of Specular Surfaces by Using the Photometric Stereo Method. IEEE Trans. PAMI, 3, 6, 661-669.

15. Koenderink, J.J. and van Doorn, A,J. (1980). Photometric invariants related to solid shape. Optica Acta, 27, 7, 981-996.

16. Land, E.H. (1983). Recent advances in retinex theory and some implications for cortical computation: Color vision and natural images. *Proc. Natl. Acad. Sci. U.S.A.* 80, (1983), 5163-5169.

17. Klinker, G.J., Shafer, S,A., and Kanade, T. (1987). Using a color reflection model to separate highlights from object color. Proc. First Int. Conf. on Computer Vision, London, 145-150.

18. Mayhew,J.E.W and Frisby,J.P. (1981). Towards a computational and psychophysical theory of stereopsis. *AI Journal*, 17, 349-385.

19. Mayhew,J.E.W. and Longuet-Higgins,H.C. (1982). A computational model of binocular depth perception. *Nature*, 297, 376-378.

20. Sanderson, A.C., Weiss, L.E. and Nayar, S.K. (1988). Structured Highlight Inspection of Specular Surfaces. *IEEE Trans. PAMI* 10, 1, 44-55.

21. Stevens,K.A. (1979). Ph.D. Thesis, MIT, Cambridge, USA.

22. Squires, G.L. (1968). *Practical Physics*, European Physics Series, McGraw-Hill, London.

23. Terzopoulos, D. (1985). Multilevel computational processes for visual surface reconstruction. *Computer Vision Graphics and Image Processing*, 24, (1985), 52-96.

24. Thrift, P. and Lee, C-H. (1983). Using Highlights to Constrain Object Size and Location. *IEEE Trans. Sys, Man and Cybernetics*, 13, 3, 426-431.

25. Ullman, S. (1976). On Visual Detection of Light Sources. *Biol. Cybernetics*, 21, (1976), 205-212.

26. Woodham, R.J. (1980). Photometric method for determining surface orientation from multiple images. Optical Engineering, 19, 1, 139-144.

27. Zisserman,A., Giblin,P.J. and Blake,A. (1988). The information available to a moving observer from specularities. *Proc. Alvey Conf. 1988.*

[19] Consistency Maintenance in the REVgraph Environment

Jonathan B Bowen and John E W Mayhew

AI Vision Research Unit
University of Sheffield, Sheffield S10 2TN, UK

Reprinted, with permission of Butterworth Scientific Ltd, from *Image and Vision Computing*, 1988, **6**, 12-15.

Introduction

The REVgraph is a data structure designed to represent a 3 dimensional model of a scene, built up from a stereo pair of 2 dimensional images. The most important levels of representation are Regions, Edges and Vertices, linked together as a graph structure, though other intermediate structures also exist.

The REVgraph is built up from our stereo processing system, TINA[1]. This system runs a Canny edge detector over both images, finds disparity values for the edge points using the PMF stereo correspondence algorithm[2] groups up the points into edge segments, and produces a geometric description of these edge segments in terms of straight lines and circular arcs[3]. The REVgraph contains representations for the outputs of all these primary stages of visual processing.

The geometric descriptions of the edge segments are typically fragmented due to noise and to the intrinsic nature of the edge detecting processes which tend to break up edges at, for example, vertices.

The use of the REVgraph is to enable reasoning processes to reconstruct a geometrically consistent description of the surfaces in the scene from the various lower levels of description. This will involve completion of broken edges, the finding of vertices and finally the identification and description of regions bounded by edges and vertices.

For the purposes of the reasoning process, any piece of data in the REVgraph may be regarded an assertion or fact. The nature of such facts will depend on the level of the data : At the edge detection level, a fact will be the presence of an intensity gradient maximum at a particular pixel. At the geometric level, it will be the direction and end points of a straight edge segment, and at higher levels the existence of a vertex or region, or ultimately the identification of a group of regions as a recognised object.

The reasoning processes required for this task utilise a set of rules that express knowledge about the task. For example, a typical rule is : "If 3 lines can be extended to meet at point Then hypothesise a vertex at that point." It is frequently a matter of considerable uncertainty as to which rules should be applied at any one time due to ambiguity in the initial data, so we require a method of exploring several alternative lines of reasoning with the ability to recover gracefully from contradictions and errors.

To this end, we have been exploring Truth Maintenance Systems (TMS) as a method for controlling the reasoning system. We have studied three particular Truth Maintenance algorithms in detail : Doyle's[4], De Kleer's[5] and McDermott's[6]. In all three we have found limitations which make them inappropriate for our domain, but all have some very attractive properties which we have tried to combine.

Truth Maintenance is concerned with taking a database of facts (or assertions) some of which may be contradictory, and, using the paths of justifications for the facts, partitioning the database into one or more self-consistent sets of facts. Such a set of self-consistent facts we will in future refer to as a solution to the truth maintenance problem. Some truth maintenance systems only follow one solution explicitly, while others follow many competing possibilities at once. Also, some only find the solution(s) when all deductive processing has been completed, while others represent explicit part-solutions at every stage through reasoning.

Existing Truth Maintenance Systems

Doyle's Truth Maintenance System was evolved for non-monotonic reasoning, where the belief of more assumptions does not necessarily lead to belief in more facts, but may result in fewer facts being believed. Thus the database of True or believed facts does not necessarily grow as further deductions are made. The system was designed to yield a single consistent set of facts as a solution. If this solution is rejected, by the discovery of a contradiction or by user intervention, the system then backtracks, at considerable expense, to find another solution.

McDermott's TMS is an attempt to reconcile Doyle's ideas with some earlier ideas of contexts. The main extension to Doyle's system is the facility for user programs to label major decision points, and for the database at that stage to be "pushed down", for easy recovery later. This would allow a certain reduction in the thrashing behaviour of TMS if such pushed down contexts were requested to be re-instated after a contradiction.

De Kleer's Assumption-Based Truth Maintenance System (ATMS) arose with the need to represent several solutions, one of which could then be chosen. Also, his algorithms are highly optimised. Part of this increase in efficiency is achieved by abandoning Doyle's non-monotonic justifications (eg If x=1 is true, then y=0 is NOT true) in favour of representing known contradictions in the database of facts explicitly. In the basic ATMS this places some restriction on the domains that the system is useful within, but in an extended version such restrictions are removed with the penalty of reduced efficiency.

Reasoning Within the REVgraph

The style of reasoning we will be using with the REV-graph is relatively straightforward. It involves a set of rules which will search for certain patterns of data in the REV-graph (antecedent data), and from this will generate new data at a different level in the graph. From here on the antecedent facts are referred to as the premises of the deduction, and the new data is referred to as the consequent of the deduction.

Due to the ambiguity in the initial data, some rules may hypothesise more than one possible consequent, and some deductions may result in geometric inconsistencies. We intend to use truth maintenance techniques to keep track of consistent solutions, and to aid decisions on which facts and deductions to disbelieve.

The following behaviours would be required of any TMS :

1) Work done towards one solution should be automatically inherited by other possible solutions wherever it is relevant.

2) Different justifications for the same fact should not become confused.

3) When a contradiction is found, the premises that gave rise to that contradiction should never be allowed to co-exist within a solution, nor should they be allowed to generate any new facts in the database.

4) A fact should not be allowed in a solution if all its paths of deduction include itself. This is known as Circular deduction and the problem is somewhat similar in nature and complexity to garbage collection of circular data structures.

5) It should be possible for the user to intervene in processing to arbitrarily add facts to or remove facts from the database.

6) It would be desirable to provide facilities for the problem solver to be able to intelligently bound the potentially very large search space. The burden of the intelligence, of course, lies with the problem solver.

There are three properties we consider to be of greatest importance for a TMS in the REVgraph :

1) At any time it must be possible to traverse a self-consistent, if incomplete, graph, as further reasoning and local inconsistency discovery can only be done by traversing the graph. This is difficult with De Kleer's scheme, as there is no notion during processing of a part solution. De Kleer states[7] "It is extremely rare for a problem solver to ask for the contents of a context." and uses this assumption to increase ATMS efficiency. We are particularly interested in cases where this assumption breaks down.

2) The initial data is ambiguous rather than wrong. Consequently the rules used for reasoning will be based largely on heuristics rather than on logical implications. Thus, in a backtracking scheme, if a fact is found to be wrong, there may be no reason to believe that its premises are wrong. It may simply be that the heuristic that generated the fact got it wrong on this occasion. None of the schemes we investigated provide what we consider to be an appropriate method for dealing with this situation.

3) Often, ambiguities may lead to radically different solutions of the graph. Rather than find one solution and then backtrack to find others, it would be more efficient to follow the development of alternative solutions in parallel, and compare final solutions to choose the "best". Doyle's TMS does not allow this, but De Kleer's ATMS was developed primarily to give this property as efficiently as possible.

The Proposed Solution : *Consistency Maintenance*

Since our reasoning system will be using heuristics rather than logically correct rules, there is less an element of solutions being True, and more of them simply being Consistent. Hence we have called our proposed system a 'Consistency Maintenance System' (CMS).

The key idea in CMS is that of the 'Context': The database of facts will be interconnected by logical dependencies, such as "Fact1 justifies Fact2, therefore Fact2 cannot exist without Fact1". Also, some of the facts may be contradictory, and therefore cannot exist in the same solution. It is possible to divide the database into subsets within which there are no contradictory facts, and no paths of justification are incomplete. Such a subset we refer to as a 'Context'.

eg Suppose :

Fact1 and Fact2 justify Fact3.
Fact4 and Fact5 justify Fact6.
Fact6 and Fact7 justify Fact8.
Fact3 and Fact6 justify Fact9.
Fact10 doesn't justify anything else.

AND Fact2 and Fact4 are known to be true,
AND Fact3 is then found to be contradictory to Fact6.

The resulting database could be broken down as in Figure 1. The proposed representation of this division of the database into contexts is :

Fact1	(1)
Fact2	(1 2)
Fact3	(1)
Fact4	(1 2)
Fact5	(2)
Fact6	(2)
Fact7	(1 2)
Fact8	(2)
Fact9	()
Fact10	(1 2)

Hence :

Context 1	Context 2
Fact1	Fact2
Fact2	Fact4
Fact3	Fact5
Fact4	Fact6
Fact7	Fact7
Fact10	Fact8
	Fact10

These contexts are consistent partitions of the global database.

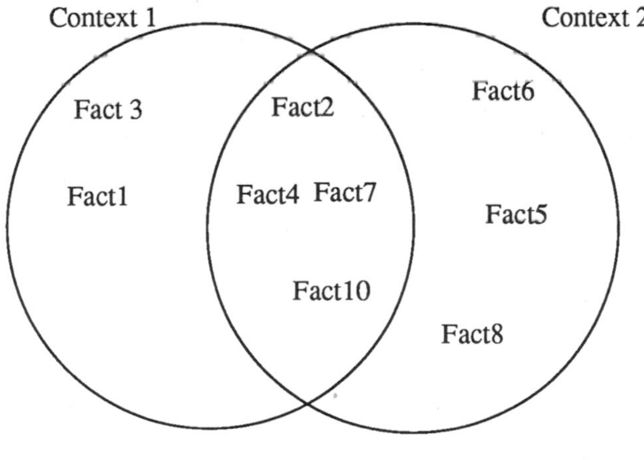

Figure 1 :- Division of Database after a contradiction

Inheritance of work between contexts

Suppose in the above example 3 more deductions were made :-

Fact1 and Fact7 justify Fact11.
Fact5 and Fact10 justify Fact12.
Fact7 and Fact10 justify Fact13.

The contexts of Fact11, Fact12 and Fact13 can be calculated from their justifications as shown in Figure 2.

Representation :

Fact1	(1)
Fact2	(1 2)
Fact3	(1)
Fact4	(1 2)
Fact5	(2)
Fact6	(2)
Fact7	(1 2)
Fact8	(2)
Fact9	()
Fact10	(1 2)
Fact11	(1)
Fact12	(2)
Fact13	(1 2)

Hence :

Context 1	Context 2
Fact1	Fact2
Fact2	Fact4
Fact3	Fact5
Fact4	Fact6
Fact7	Fact7
Fact10	Fact8
Fact11	Fact10
Fact13	Fact12
	Fact13

The rule governing inheritance is as follows :

The contexts in which a new fact is valid are the intersection of the contexts in which its premises are valid.

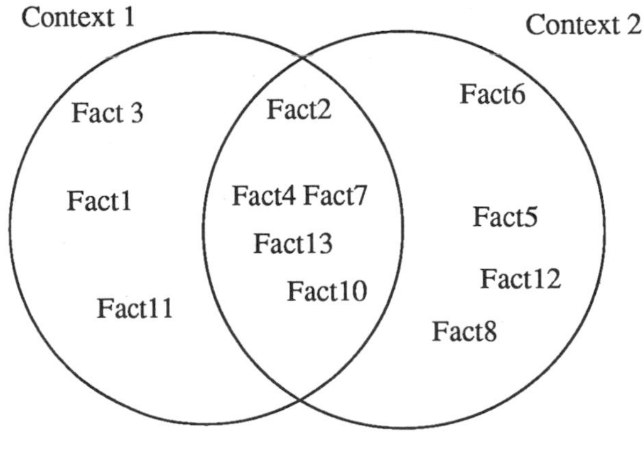

Figure 2 :- Division of Database after further deductions

Multiple Justification of Facts.

Suppose in this example that one further deduction were made :

Fact4 and Fact1 justify Fact12.

Fact12 already exists in context 2, justified by fact4 and fact10. However, the new justification makes it valid in context 1. As this does not lead to any contradictions, fact12 should now become valid in both contexts. See Figure 3.

Representation :

Fact1	(1)
Fact2	(1 2)
Fact3	(1)
Fact4	(1 2)
Fact5	(2)
Fact6	(2)
Fact7	(1 2)
Fact8	(2)
Fact9	()
Fact10	(1 2)
Fact11	(1)
Fact12	(1 2)
Fact13	(1 2)

Hence :

Context 1	Context 2
Fact1	Fact2
Fact2	Fact4
Fact3	Fact5
Fact4	Fact6
Fact7	Fact7
Fact10	Fact8
Fact11	Fact10
Fact12	Fact12
Fact13	Fact13

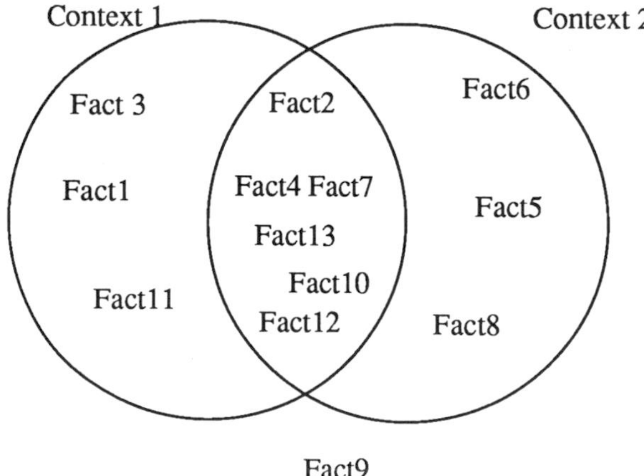

Figure 3 :- Division of Database with a multiple justification

The generalisation of the rule above is this : Each justification for a fact is valid in a set of contexts which is the intersection of the contexts in which the premises are valid. The fact itself is valid in a set of contexts which is the union of those contexts in which its justifications are valid.

The Data Dependency representation.

As processing of the REVgraph progresses, we need to record the deductions that have taken place. Following Doyle, the data structure we have decided upon is a directed graph consisting of two types of node, the 'Fact node' and the 'Data Dependency node'.

Data Dependency Node (DD-node)

The DD-node represents a single deduction by the reasoning system.

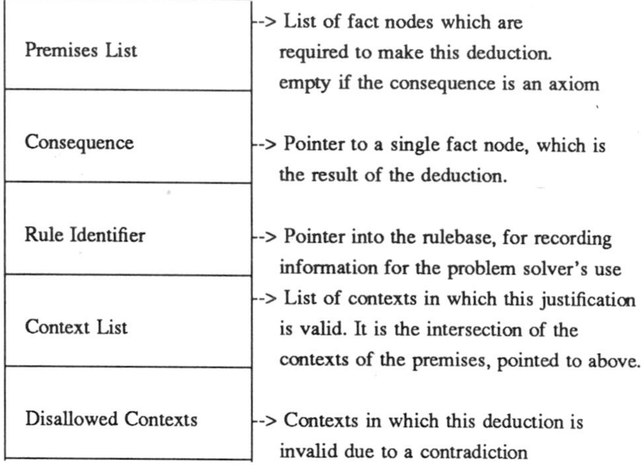

Fact Node

The fact node represents an actual item in the database.

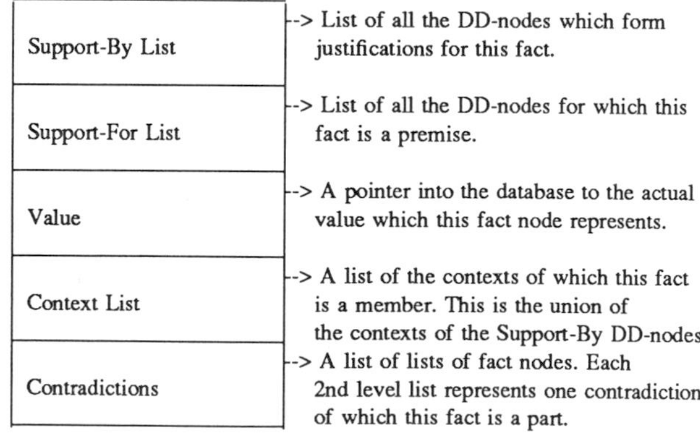

Constraints Between Facts in the Database

As we mentioned above, the development of the REVgraph will be guided by heuristics as much as by logically correct rules. The constraints between the premises and consequence of a heuristic deduction are slightly different from those between the premises and consequence of a logically correct deduction. The following descriptions apply to facts with only one justification. The generalisation to multiple justifications is given in the next section.

Suppose Fact1, Fact2 and Fact3 together are evidence for a heuristic rule to propose the existence of Fact4. Let us refer to the premise set as P, and the Consequence as C. Then, a context within which C is valid (or 'True'), must also contain the evidence for C (i.e. P must be True as well). As an example, it would be ridiculous to propose the existence of a vertex at a point if no edges terminated at that point. However, if P is True in a context, then C may or may not be True in that context, because the result of the heuristic operating on P cannot be trusted to be definitely correct. This argument can be represented in a Boolean expression :

" P heuristically justifies C " or : (P ħ C)

The Boolean table for the operator ħ is :

P	ħ	C	P heuristically justifies C
T	T	T	A context where the evidence is True and the consequence is True is valid within the CMS.
T	F	T	The evidence is True, but the consequence is not trusted, and is made False.This is valid.
F	T	F	A context where the consequence is True despite having no evidence is NOT valid within CMS.
F	F	T	A context in which neither the evidence nor the consequence is True, is valid in the CMS.

So, for this deductive step on its own, only contexts which satisfy that constraint between the evidence and consequence, may exist. The job of the CMS is to maintain those constraints properly, and never generate a context where the constraints are not satisfied, such as a context which contains C but does not contain P.

It may be noticed that for any heuristic deduction there are two possible contexts in which the premise set is true. Rather than keep track of both contexts from the outset, the CMS first follows the context that contains the consequence, but if this causes a contradiction it then falls back to the context in which the premise is true but the consequence is not. This highlights an important property of the CMS, that of maximality of the contexts represented : That is, for any context, the addition of further facts from the database to that context would necessitate a contradiction.

Logically correct, or rigorous rules : This is the kind of rule of that Truth Maintenance systems have conventionally dealt with, where if the premises are True, the consequence is undeniably True . For example, if the end-points of an edge are defined, then the direction must be the vector difference between them. Again, however, the consequence cannot exist without the evidence. Thus, if the end points of an edge are undefined, it would be silly to give a value for the direction. This can also be represented as a Boolean expression.

Defining P and C as above, let us see the effect of this statement :

"P rigorously justifies C" or : (P ŧ C)

The Boolean table for the operator ŧ is :

P	ŧ	C	P rigorously justifies C
T	T	T	A context where the evidence is True and the consequence is True is valid within the CMS.
T	F	F	A context where P is True and P rigorously justifies C, but C is False, is not valid in CMS.
F	T	F	A context where the consequence is True despite having no evidence is NOT valid within CMS.
F	F	T	A context in which neither the evidence nor the consequence is True, is valid in the CMS.

These are the constraints that the CMS must maintain between the premises and consequence of a logically correct rule. They are a little more restrictive, having fewer valid states than the heuristic implication.

Other constraints that exist within the database :

Suppose Fact1 and Fact2 and Fact3 are axioms (unjustified facts) which the user wishes to believe in, then the constraint that :

(Fact1 ∧ Fact2 ∧ Fact3) is True must hold in all contexts. i.e all contexts must contain these facts. Axioms that the user doesn't trust don't impose any constraints on contexts.

Axioms in the CMS are, in fact, represented as either heuristic or rigorous deductions. An axiom that the user trusts is represented as a rigorous deduction from "True", while untrustworthy axioms, or assumptions, are represented as heuristic deductions from "True". The treatment of heuristic deductions as explained above means that untrustworthy axioms are believed until they are found to cause a contradiction.

Also, any time a contradiction is found, an extra constraint is placed on the database : Suppose the combination of Fact1, Fact2 and Fact3 is found to be contradictory, then the constraint that ¬(Fact1 ∧ Fact2 ∧ Fact3) must hold in all contexts. i.e. no context may contain all the facts involved in a contradiction.

Generalising the operators ħ and ŧ, if a fact has several justifications of different types, the situation becomes more complicated. If P1, P2 and P3 are 3 premise sets each of which provides a rigorous justification for Fact1, and P4 and P5 are premise sets each of which provides a heuristic justification for Fact1, then the following constraint must be True :

$$((Fact1 \Rightarrow (P1 \vee P2 \vee P3 \vee P4 \vee P5)) \wedge ((P1 \vee P2 \vee P3) \Rightarrow Fact1))$$

Where each of P1 -> P5 is of the general form

(Factm ∧ Factn ∧ .... FactN).

4 and 5. Thus, the context list is now a list of special labels, rather than actual contexts.

Making sure that all the other algorithms carry over is very simple. All the operations on context lists are set operations, so in order that they carry across, it is only necessary to define set operations on context lists using the new labelling scheme.

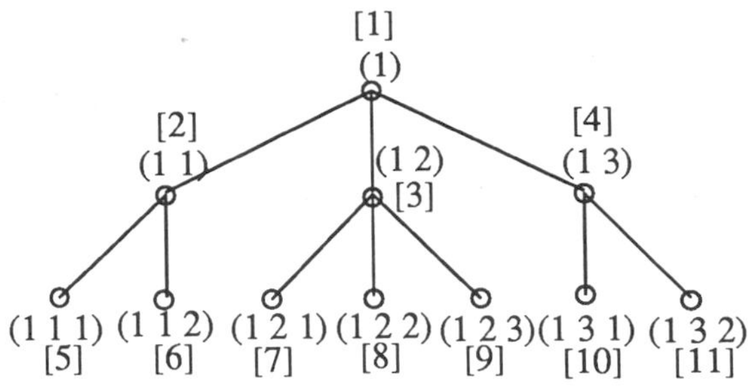

Figure 4 :- Context Tree with 2 context representations

Set Membership

To Compute Set Membership, the shorter label must be the head of the longer label :

(1 2 3) ∈ {(1 2 2)} is False

Previously :

[9] ∈ {[8]} is False

(1 2 3) ∈ {(1 2)} is True

Previously :

[9] ∈ {[7] [8] [9]} is True

Set Union

{(1 2)} ∪ {(1 3 1)} = {(1 2)(1 3 1)}

{(1 2)} ∪ {(1 2 1)} = {(1 2)}

{(1 2) (1 1 2) (1 3 1)} ∪
{(1 2 1) (1 1) (1 3 2)} =
{(1 2) (1 1) (1 3 1) (1 3 2)}

Previously :

{[7] [8] [9] [6] [10]} ∪
{[7] [5] [6] [11]} =
{[5] [6] [7] [8] [9] [10] [11]}

Set Intersection

{(1 2)} ∩ {(1 3 1)} = { ∅ }

{(1 2)} ∩ {(1 2 1)} = {(1 2 1)}

{(1 2) (1 1 2) (1 3 1)} ∩ {(1 2 1) (1 1) (1 3 2)} = {(1 2 1) (1 1 2)}

Previously :

{[7] [8] [9] [6] [10]} ∩ {[7] [5] [6] [11]} = {[7] [6]}

Set Difference

{(1 2)} – {(1 3 1)} = {(1 2)}

Previously :

{[7] [8] [9]} – {[10]} = {[7] [8] [9]}

{(1 2)} – {(1 2 1)} = {(1 2 2)
(1 2 3)}

Previously :

{[7] [8] [9]} – {[7]} = {[8] [9]}

The set difference operator requires more information than is available in the context list. To calculate the last example, reference must be made to the context tree, which is developed as contradictions occur. The set difference operator is only used at one point in the algorithms so far described, and that is when a new context is being fed forward through a heuristic DD node. The resultant contexts of the DD node is the intersection of its premises' contexts, less the contexts on its disallowed contexts list.

Comparison of CMS with Other Systems

We shall now compare the behaviour of CMS with Doyle's TMS, McDermott's TMS and De Kleer's assumption based technique. To demonstrate how they are related, we will return to the idea that the constraints discovered to exist between facts can be represented as a Boolean expression, and that valid solutions to the problem are those where the expression is True. Let us take the situation where some processing has been done, but no contradictions have been discovered.

The Boolean expression may look something like this :

```
(A ∨ B ∨ ....) ∧ (((A ∧ B) ∨ ....) ⇔ C) ∧ .... ∧ ( ..... ⇔ D)
 T   T            T   T             T                    T   T <-TMS , CMS
 T   T            T   T             F                    .   F
 T   F            T   F             T                    .   F
 T   F            T   F             F                    .   T
 F   T            F   T             T                    .   T
 F   T            F   T             F                    .   T
 F   F            F   F             T                    .   F
 F   F            F   F             F                    .   F
 T   T            T   T             T                    .   T
 .   .            .   .             .                    .   F
                  etc.
```

Up to this stage, TMS will have done no backtracking, and will be following the topmost solution. CMS will be in the same situation, whereas De Kleer will have kept track of the constraints without explicitly solving any of the truth values. Now consider what happens if a contradiction is found between A and B. This adds a new clause into the expression, $\neg(A \wedge B)$, which has this effect :

```
(A ∨ B ∨ ..) ∧ (((A ∧ B) ∨ ..) ⇔ C) ∧ .. ∧ ( .. ⇔ D) ∧ ¬(A ∧ B)
 T   T          T   T           T              T   F        F
 T   T          T   T           F              .   F        F
 T   F          T   F           T              .   T        F
 T   F          T   F           F              .   T        T <-TMS,
                                                                CMS
 F   T          F   T           T              .   T        T <-CMS
 F   T          F   T           F              .   T        T <-CMS
 F   F          F   F           T              .   T        F
 F   F          F   F           F              .   T        F
 T   T          T   T           T              .   T        T
 .   .          .   .           .              .   T        F
                etc.
```

The topmost solution has become invalid. TMS backtracks to the next highest level solution, and if, in future, this is invalidated, TMS will attempt to find the next solution down, and so on. CMS keeps track of the next several solutions, which are all the maximal contexts. De Kleer's method would set up a nogood set, but would still have the work of interpretation construction to do. Also, De Kleer's method would not be able to show alternative 'part-solutions' without doing that work, so that development of the various solutions could not be easily followed. However, the ATMS would be able to use that nogood to prevent inconsistent facts from being used together to form further deductions. McDermott's TMS will behave as Doyle's, except that in response to user requests it can also set aside other specific solutions which it can move to quickly.

The main advantages of CMS over both these systems for our problem is that it caters for both rigorous and heuristic types of rule, and it successfully keeps track of equally valid alternative solutions as processing proceeds.

There are two major disadvantages of the CMS. Although it is based on a simple idea, the machinery necessary to put it into practice is very cumbersome, and also, as the complexity of the problem increases, the performance is likely to degrade exponentially. De Kleer's methods of interpretation construction to some extent reduce this problem, but CMS is likely to grind almost to a halt as the number of contexts becomes large compared to the number of facts in the database. In our domain, the problem is well enough determined for this situation to be unlikely to occur, and we are also investigating methods of abandoning unpromising contexts during processing, thus pruning the search.

The CMS as described above has been implemented, and applied to a typical vision problem, one particular stage in the process of WireFrame Completion. A brief description of the problem, the algorithm used to solve it and the role of the CMS follows, together with results that demonstrate the existence of ambiguity to a limited extent in this particular vision problem.

Prototype WireFrame Completion (PWFC)

The 3 dimensional geometric data recovered from the low level vision suite is segmented and described in terms of straight lines and circular arcs by the segmentation algorithm. Also, individual straight lines and circles are broken up due to noise, so that much of the topology of the edges in the scene is missing at this level. The aim of the PWFC algorithm is to reconnect the geometric data to find vertices and T junctions where appropriate.

The first version of this algorithm only works on the straight lines in a scene, and was written while the mathematics for circular arc geometry was being investigated. Both these tasks are now completed and this algorithm will soon be extended to include circular arcs.

At this stage there is a certain amount of ambiguity, and it was proposed to use the CMS to aid in searching parallel possibilities. Also, all the processing up to this point has been bottom up in nature, but it should now be possible to utilise top down information where available to ease the wireframe completion task. The CMS is useful in combining bottom up information with top down directives.

When we state that an object is justified, or given a justification, what is meant is that in addition to creating that object and linking it to others in the PWFC data structures, a request is sent to the CMS giving the object, those objects which justify it and a tag relating to the point in the program that this request is made. Similarly, when we state that a contradiction is found, or that objects are contradictory, what we mean is that a request is sent to the CMS informing it that those objects in the PWFC data sturcture have been adjudged to be contradictory.

Information relating to which objects are valid which others (i.e. in the same context) is obtained by making various requests to the CMS. The CMS can basically make available information answering these two questions : "What contexts are this object valid in?", "What objects are valid in this context?". Any further information the user may require can be phrased in terms of set operations and those two questions.

Top Down Directives

(1) Focus on certain edges. The algorithm will only attempt actively to form completions (into vertices or T junctions) for a set of edges present in the interesting-wires list. Thus, if the higher level processes only demand processing of part of the scene, this can be achieved.

(2) Focus on certain pairings. The algorithm will initially attempt to form vertices between pairs of edges present on the interesting-pairs list. However, if these pairings are inconsistent, or very dubious, the use of the CMS allows the algorithm to explore other more promising routes.

(3) Restrict connections to a certain proximity. A true breadth first search algorithm will form connections between all possible combinations of edges. To restrict the search, junctions are only investigated if they occur within a user specified distance of the edge being completed.

How these top down constraints are implemented, and how the CMS is used to constrain the search using these constraints will be discussed in detail later on.

Data Structures

Wires : These represent straight lines as passed from TINA. They are introduced to the CMS as trustworthy axioms. Thus, all straight lines from TINA will exist in all solutions.

Connectors : These are straight lines that connect wires to each other, wires to vertices or wires to T junctions. These basically fill in the gaps due to noise and segmentation. How they are justified depends on the nature of the junction that is created.

Vertices : These are junctions where two wires can be extended to within a certain distance of each other in 3 dimensions at their point of intersection on the image plane. The two wires will be connected to the vertex by one connector each.

T Junctions : These are junctions where two wires meet on the image plane, but are further apart in 3 dimensions than a certain threshold. The occluded wire is connected to the T junction by one connector. The occluding wire must either directly occlude the other, or have a connector which occludes the other.

Super-vertices : where more than one vertex occur close enough to be considered the same, a super-vertex is created which groups them together. In this way, 3 or 4 directional vertices can be built up from 2 way vertices without further explicit representation.

Interesting-wires : As previously mentioned, this is a list of wires where attention is to be focussed.

Interesting-pairs : Another attention focussing list. This consists of pairs of wires, which are joined together by the completion algorithm in preference to other possibilities.

Candidate-lists : Each wire end has associated with it all the possible junctions that can be made from that wire end, within the user defined limiting radius. Initialisation of these lists is explained below.

Initialisation

Before the main algorithm can be run, various data structures must be initialised.

All the wires must be created from the GDB, and introduced to the CMS. The user must then define the limiting radius (which may be increased later), and must set the interesting-wires list.

The candidate lists must be created for the end of each wire in the interesting-wires list. This utilises the Pairwise Geometric Relations Table, which is a utility under the REVgraph. The PGRT delivers pairs of lines to the user satisfying certain user defined geometric criteria. For each such pair a number of geometric relations are calculated, which are cached in a table should that pair be requested again.

At this stage, the user may also define pairs of wires to be placed on the interesting-pairs list, but this is not necessary for the algorithm to run.

The Algorithm

The algorithm is object oriented, and arranged in a pass structure. In each pass, each of the wires in the interesting-wires list attempts to find a completion for both of its ends, in a vertex or T junction or collinearity. Between each pass, an optimal context is found, which is the basis for further completions. Also between each pass it is possible for the top down directives to be modified as the user desires.

The method we used to decide on the optimal context in this problem is very straightforward. The aim of the algorithm is to connect wires together, so the most successful context is the one in which most wire ends are connected to something. Whenever a contradiction is found, the context with the most objects is chosen for further exploration. Such contexts are often suboptimal, but this strategy gives the search a necessary breadth during each pass of the algorithm.

For each end of each interesting wire the following criteria are used to choose a new junction to create :

If the wire end is already linked to something in the current context, then no attempt is made to create a new junction. Otherwise, the candidate list of the wire end is examined as follows.

First, all those candidates which have already been used to create a junction are ignored. If there is a remaining candidate pair which is tagged as having been connected before segmentation, then that is chosen. Otherwise, any pair which appears to be parallel, close and overlapping is chosen. If there is still no successful candidate, then the interesting-pairs list is searched for the presence of any remaining candidates, and the first such candidate found will be chosen. Finally, if all else fails, the pair which would produce the junction closest to the wire end is chosen.

Junction types and constraints

When a pair is selected to be instantiated as a junction, the geometric relations provided by the PGRT are used to determine junction type. Basically, measures of collinearity, and distance between wires at their image crossing point are used to place the junction in one of these categories : Collinearity, Bar, Vertex, T junction, and Maybe-Vertex.

For a collinearity, a single connector is created, each end of which is attached to the relevant end of the two wires. The new connector is heuristically justified by the conjunction of the two wires.

For a bar, where two lines are close, parallel and overlapping, then no connector is created, but the two lines are linked directly to one another. Effectively, this provides a rigorous justification for the link, as both wires are rigorous axioms, but the link itself is not explicitly represented as an object.

For a vertex, two new connectors and a new vertex are created. The vertex is positioned in x and y according to where the wires cross on the image plane, and in depth half way between the two wires' depths at this point. The vertex is heuristically justified by the conjunction of the two wires. Each connector is rigorously justified by the vertex. If the vertex is found (by searching) to be sufficiently close to another vertex, then the new vertex is incorporated into the relevant super-vertex. The super-vertex is then heuristically justified by the new vertex.

As often happens with trihedral vertices, one wire will end up being connected to two vertices which are judged to be in the same super-vertex. Thus each vertex has one wire in common. In this case, a new connector is not created for that wire, but the existing one is re-used, and given a new justification.

For T junctions one new connector is created, and one T junction object. The connector goes between the occluded wire and the T junction. The new connector is rigorously justified by the T junction. The occluded wire may well not be occluded by the other wire directly, but rather by a connector linking that other wire to another junction of some kind. Several such connectors may exist, in different contexts, so the T junction requires a new justification for each such occluding connector that is created.

Every time a new connector is created, it is tested against all the relevant T junctions to determine if it occludes any of them. If so, the T junction is given an extra heuristic justification of the conjunction of the occluded wire and the connector.

Similarly, whenever a new T junction is created then it is tested against all the relevant connectors, and appropriate justifications are made.

If the junction type is Maybe-Vertex, then initially a T junction is created (if possible), but if a vertex is ever created close enough to this T junction, then this is taken as enough evidence for the T junction actually being a vertex, and a new vertex is created to replace the original T junction. The new vertex is then considered to be part of the same super-vertex as the vertex which was justified the upgrading of the T junction.

If a junction type is a vertex, but the extension of one wire meets the other along its length, then it is topologically convenient to represent this as a T junction. However, if such a T junction is close enough to the end of the other wire, then a vertex is created with one connector going back along the length of the wire.

The sequence of events on creating a new junction is as follows. First, all the new objects required for the junction are created, added to the lists of the relevant object type, set to point to objects they are linked to, and geometrically initialised. This thoroughly imbeds new objects into the PWFC data structure. Then, the objects must be introduced to the CMS, which involves a justification request for each new object. At this stage, any new connectors are checked against all T junctions, and any new T junctions are checked against all connectors, to see if any new justifications can be found for the relevant T junctions. The final phase is to check for contradictions, as described below. When all this has been done, a new wire end is chosen, and the process of completion starts again.

Contradiction Constraints

Any two connectors which occupy the same end of the same wire are made contradictory to each other. Any connector pair or wire and connector pair which cross on the image plane are marked as contradictory, with an exception in special circumstances. These are the two "rules" which deal with contradictions, and they are applied whenever a new connector is created.

These two rules are applied at very specific points in the program. Whenever a new connector is created, any wire it is linked to has its end checked for other links. Any other object linked to the relevant end of the wire is made contradictory to the newly created connector.

Whenever a new connector is created, it is tested against all other wires and connectors in the database to see if it crosses any of them. Every other wire and connector it crosses is made contradictory to the new connector. Such an exhaustive search for crossing objects is not totally necessary, and a little more time consuming than is desirable.

The exception to the second "rule" is when the two objects are connected to vertices which are part of the same super-vertex. The geometrical description of lines is such that the centroid of the line is known to a certain error, and the direction of the line is known to a certain error. This has the effect that the greatest positional errors are at the line ends. Consequently, when connecting up vertices of 3 or more wires, which are perfectly valid, it is often found that the component connectors in the individual 2 way vertices cross over each other, and cross over component wires. Thus the necessary exception to the connector crossing rule.

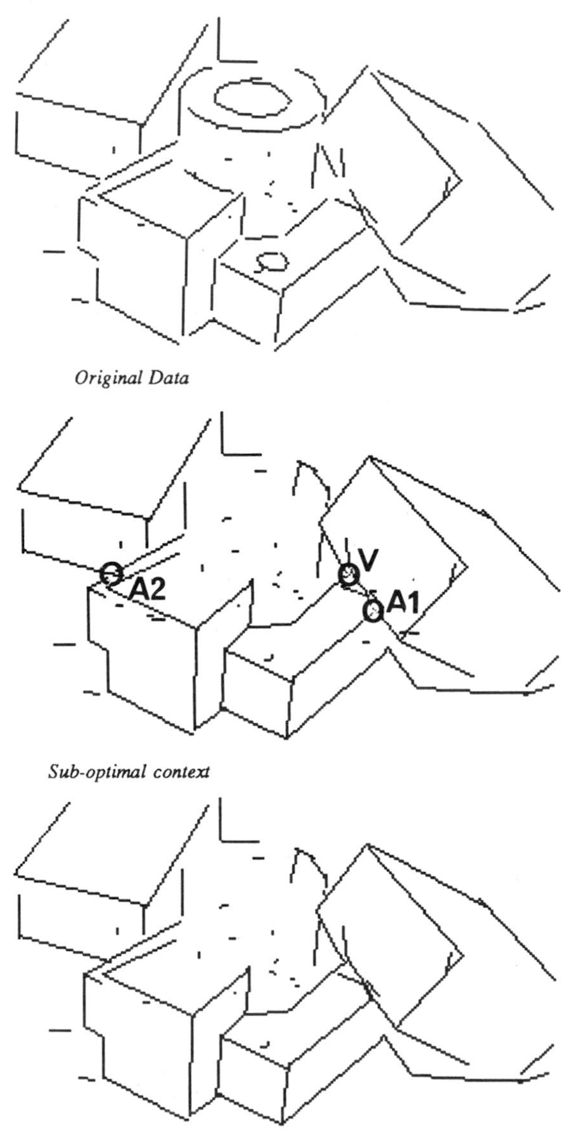

Original Data

Sub-optimal context

Optimal Context

Figure 5 :- Before and After Wireframe Completion

Results

Figure 5 shows the initial data from one image for Wireframe Completion, and 2 contexts after four passes of the algorithm. During the fifth pass, no more junctions were found, so pending further top down information processing could be said to be complete after the fourth pass. The bottom context is adjudged to be optimal, while the middle one highlights the major ambiguities.

The image contains several lines with no depth information, which account for most of the missed vertices, and some T junctions which should be vertices. The interesting wires were set to be all the wires with some depth information. The limiting radius was set to 15 image pixels, which is relatively large and likely to make the algorithm thrash a little more than is necessary. The circular arcs which should be present round the top of the central object are missing in this straight-line-only version of the algorithm. Their inclusion in the algorithm should cause several more vertices to be found.

Most of the work was done during the first pass of the algorithm, which confirms our prediction that most of the junctions are obvious, with only a few ambiguities. In total, three ambiguities were found : On the far right hand corner of the central object three T junctions are found to be alternative solutions to the local connections, though one in particular is considered optimal (labelled A1 on Figure 5). On the left hand side of the same object, three alternative solutions were eventually found, with the intuitively best solution being picked as optimal by the program. (labelled A2 on Figure 5).

The development of this latter ambiguity as the program runs is interesting, and is shown in detail in Figure 6. Initially, the worst solution is found, where the straight line on the left hand object is extended through a break in the bounding line of the central object to form a spurious T junction. (Figure 6b). This is found to be inadequate, as the bounding contour cannot be completed in such a context, so a second solution is found, which involves a T junction and vertex in close proximity, and one line segment being completely unconnected. (Figure 6c). The unconnected line segment runs close and parallel to the new connector, so close that in the display they run into each other, appearing in the figure as one thicker line rather than two distinct lines. Finally, the "correct" solution is found. (Figure 6d).

There are also some unfortunate errors in this sequence of processing. One particularly unpleasant feature is the vertex on the right hand block which involves an extension of one of the wires from the central object (labelled V on Figure 5). That wire should be occluded by the short bounding line at the rear of that object, but unfortunately there was insufficient depth information to make any completions to that line, so the spurious vertex remained.

The total number of contexts produced as a result of these ambiguities was six. The time spent by the CMS processing the various constraints was less than, though of the same order as the time spent searching for junctions and creating the necessary data structures. While we will admit that very careful thought had to be given to the structuring of the constraints, and that this particular example problem might have been more efficiently processed using a conventional breadth and bound search technique, we feel we have shown the potential value of a CMS in the vision domain, where ambiguity is comparatively infrequent, and caused by failings in heuristics rather than contradictory data. Higher level reasoning schemes which are more processor intensive, such as might attempt to start assigning surfaces to completed regions in the example would possibly benefit greatly by utilising a TMS such as this.

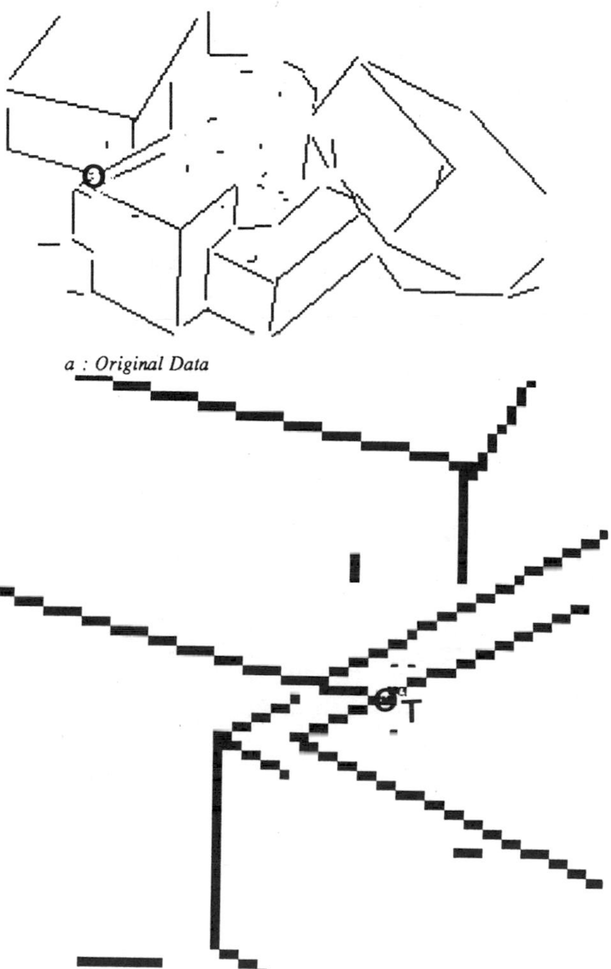

a : Original Data

b : Incorrect Solution

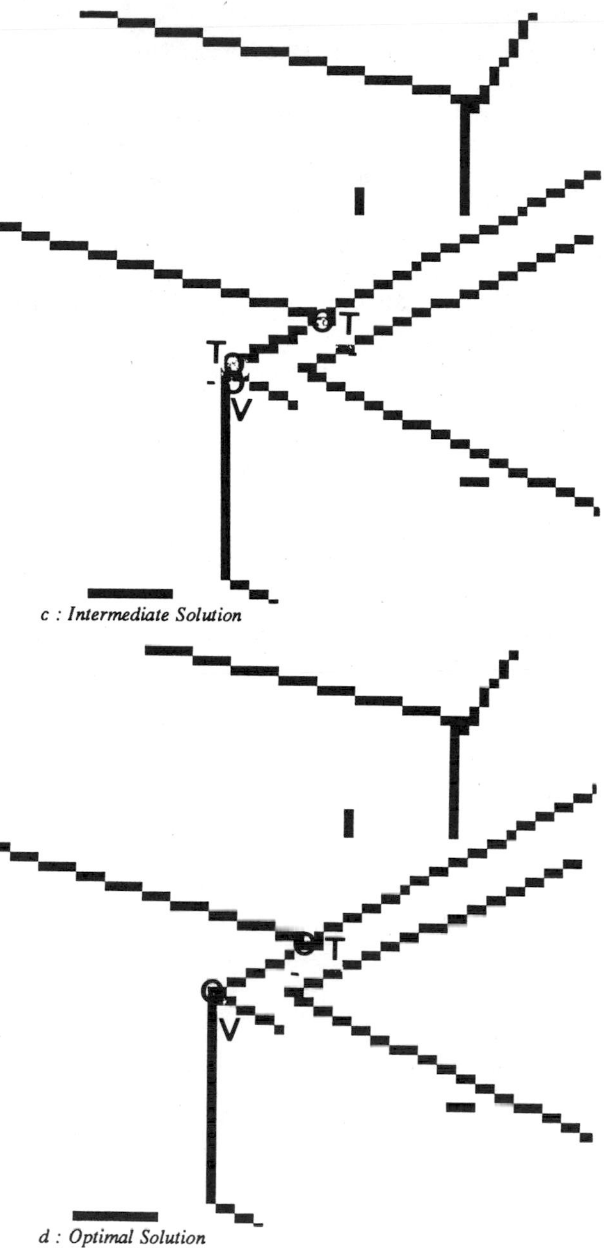

c : Intermediate Solution

d : Optimal Solution

Figure 6 : 3 Solutions to Ambiguity A2 in Figure 5

References :

1 Porrill JP, SB Pollard, TP Pridmore, JB Bowen, JEW Mayhew, JP Frisby (1987) TINA : The Sheffield AIVRU vision system, AIVRU memo 027.

2 Pollard SB, JEW Mayhew and JP Frisby (1985) PMF: A stereo correspondence algorithm using a disparity gradient limit, Perception 14, 449-470.

3 Pridmore TP, J Porrill, JEW Mayhew and JP Frisby (1985) Geometrical description of the CONNECT graph #1 : Straight lines, planes, space curves and blobs, AIVRU memo 011.

4 Doyle J (1979) A Truth Maintenance System , Artificial Intelligence 12 , 231-272.

5 De Kleer J (1984) Choices without backtracking , Proceedings National Conference on Artificial Intelligence, August 1984.

6 McDermott D (1983) Contexts and Data Dependencies : A synthesis , IEEE Pattern analysis and machine intelligence.

7 De Kleer J (1986) An Assumption-based TMS , Artificial Intelligence 28 , 127-161.

[20] Location and Description of Textured Surfaces Using Stereo Vision

Philip F McLauchlan, John E W Mayhew and John P Frisby

AI Vision Research Unit
University of Sheffield, Sheffield S10 2TN, UK

We describe a stereo algorithm, called Needles, specialised to deal with smooth textured surfaces. Constraints of local surface smoothness and global surface continuity are used to solve the correspondence problem. The algorithm is edge based. First the left image is divided into square patches, and a disparity histogram of the potential edge matches is constructed in each patch. Above-threshold peaks in the histogram are passed into a Hough transform, which fits a plane to a subset of the potential matches lying around the peak, forming local hypotheses for the range and orientation of the visual surface along with the edge matches. Next, hypotheses in adjacent, overlapping patches are connected if they share enough common matches. A region growing procedure locates large areas of mutually connected hypotheses, corresponding to continuous, possibly overlapping surfaces. When surfaces overlap, the largest one is chosen. Needles has been implemented on a Sun workstation and a Transputer network. Results are presented for two stereopairs, and compared with physical measurements.

In approaches to solving the stereo correspondence problem in computer vision to date, little explicit attention has been paid to the special problems posed by highly textured surfaces. Edge maps associated with such surfaces tend to be dense, fragmentary and noisy. These characteristics make the correspondence problem much harder to solve than normal. This paper demonstrates an algorithm, called Needles, which can overcome these difficulties for smooth surfaces by implementing a strong form of the smoothness constraint widely used in stereo algorithms.

One of the advantages of Needles is that it generates a visual surface description directly as part of the matching process. In many feature-based stereo algorithms, some species of smoothness is exploited in the form of mutual support propagated between matches that could lie on a "smooth" surface. In subsequent surface reconstruction, as proposed by Grimson [5] and Terzopoulos [15] for example, the information used in the application of the smoothness constraint at the matching stage is then discarded: a thin plate surface is fitted to all matches whether or not they supported each other. In contrast, although Needles discards most of the potential matches by application of a local smoothness constraint, final matching decisions are postponed until the stage at which a surface description is selected. Unlike algorithms that solve the correspondence problem by propagation of local constraints, such as Barnard and Thomson's [1] and PMF [10], Needles uses a combination of local and global constraints, the latter being based on continuous whole surfaces rather than local patches.

The general approach of integrating matching and surface reconstruction has been used previously, for example by Boult and Chen [2] and by Hoff and Ahuja [6]. However, Needles differs in using a global region-growing procedure to link neighbouring local patches of potential smooth-surface matches if they share a sufficient number of matches in their region of overlap. Final disambiguation is applied to the continuous surfaces formed in this way. Like [2] and [6], Needles integrates surface reconstruction and surface discontinuity detection. The global disambiguation mechanism distinguishes Needles from other algorithms that use a locally planar model of disparity, such as [6] and that of Otto and Chau [9].

1 The Needles Algorithm

The Needles algorithm is feature based, using at present edgels produced by the Canny edge detector [4]. It is assumed that at the scale at which the algorithm is applied (defined by the image patch size, see below) the variation of the visual surface from a plane is small relative to its extent. This assumption provides a very strong constraint on the possible edge matches. A brief summary of the algorithm is as follows: one image (the left) is divided into small square overlapping patches. In each patch a histogram of the disparities of the potential matches is constructed. Peaks in the histogram provide hypotheses for the disparity of the visual surface in the patch. A Hough transform then selects from the potential matches near each hypothetical disparity a set of them all of which lie near a plane. The other potential matches are rejected. Sets of matches from adjacent image patches that contain enough matches in common are labelled as connected (i.e. as part of the same surface). A region growing procedure finds large regions of mutually connected sets of matches. Where regions overlap the strongest region (in the sense defined in section 1.4 below) wins, and its matches are selected.

Needles thus uses local (within patch) matching constraints to form hypotheses for the visual surface in each patch. The incorrect hypotheses are eliminated using *global* surface connectivity information, i.e. each surface is located as a whole. Surface smoothness is used in two ways: a local smoothness constraint to generate local surface hypotheses, and a surface continuity constraint to make explicit the connectivity of the local hypotheses.

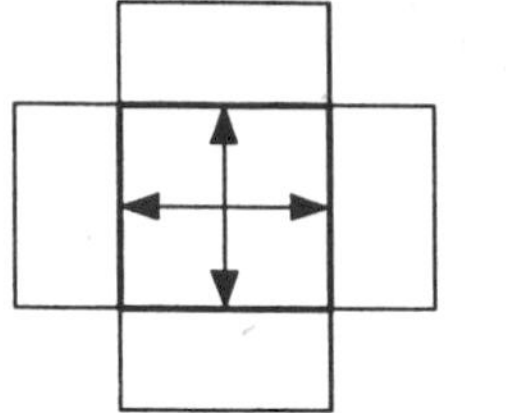

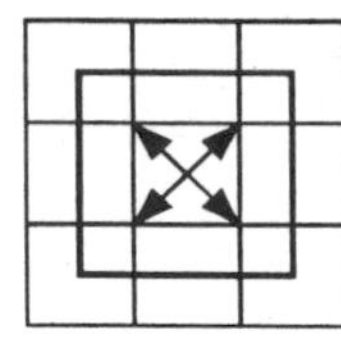

Figure 1: The four lateral (left) and four diagonal (right) neighbours of an image patch. The central patch is shown in bold. The arrows mark the differences in position of the adjacent patches with respect to the central patch.

1.1 Preprocessing

The left image of the stereopair is divided into overlapping square patches of width $H = 32$ pixels. The patches are arranged in a grid so that diagonally adjacent patches overlap by 3/4 of their length in each direction, while laterally adjacent patches overlap in half their area. Each patch thus has eight neighbours as shown in figure 1. A simple test on texture density rejects an image patch if the number of edges within it is less than a threshold[1] $2H$.

The edge positions are *rectified* to the positions they would have been in had the camera image planes been parallel[2]. This is done using camera parameters obtained from Tsai's camera calibration method [16]. Edge detection and rectification take place within AIVRU's TINATOOL stereo vision environment [12]. Corresponding edges in the two images are now assumed to lie in the same image raster. Given a pair of edges with rectified positions (x_l, y) and (x_r, y), disparity is defined as $d = x_r - x_l$.

Each edge pair lying in the same raster must satisfy five *compatibility* conditions in order to be accepted as a potential match. The conditions are:

1. The disparity of the edge pair must lie within a (large) initial range extending $0.375s$ on either side of the convergent point of the optic axes of the cameras, where s is the size of the image in pixels.
2. The contrasts of the edges are compared. If the ratio of the larger to the smaller is greater than a threshold, set at 4, the pair is excluded.
3. Neither edge can have an orientation within 5° of horizontal. Near horizontal edges give rise to large disparity measurement errors.
4. The orientation of the edges must be the same side of horizontal, i.e. an edge marking a boundary between a light region on the left and a dark region on the right can only match with another edge of the same type. This is an analogue of the contrast sign rule characterising human vision (but see [11]).
5. Edge orientations correspond to the orientations of boundaries in the images, which may be due to object boundaries, surface texture etc. For a pair of edges to be matched it must be feasible for the orientations to be projections of a boundary in the world. Since Needles imposes a disparity gradient limit on the surfaces it finds (as explained below) it is reasonable to impose a limit on the disparity gradient of the line in disparity space (x, y, d) formed by back-projecting the edge orientations. This is set to 1.

[1] Note: due to lack of space, full explanations are not given for the values of all the parameters quoted, but they are given in [8]. The quoted values have been found to give good results on all the images so far tested.

[2] This corresponds to a rotation of the cameras about their optical centres to bring the image planes into alignment.

1.2 Disparity Histogramming

A local disparity histogram [14] is constructed for each square patch. The disparity range is divided into blocks of size $0.2H$, and an accumulator assigned to each block. Each compatible edge pair contributes a vote to the corresponding disparity block. The magnitude of the vote is the *weight* assigned to the left edge of the pair. This is an integer dependent on the position of the edge within the square patch. The weighting function is a pyramid with its peak at the centre of the patch. The weights are used throughout the algorithm, and the increased weight assigned to central edges means than matches are less inclined to congregate on one side of a patch. This gives rise to more reliable connections between adjacent patches.

The histogram is smoothed by Gaussian convolution, using a mask with $\sigma = 1.5$ blocks. The peaks in the smoothed histogram are then thresholded. The threshold is set to $0.1W$, where W is the sum of the weights of the left edges in the square patch. Each peak above the threshold is localised by fitting a quadratic to the histogram accumulator values at and on either side of the peak value. The maximum of the quadratic is taken to be the disparity at the peak, which is then passed into the next stage, plane fitting.

1.3 Planar Patch Fitting by Hough Transform Method

The transformation between disparity space and world space preserves planes. The plane fitting can hence be done in disparity space. For each peak in the disparity histogram an attempt is made to fit a plane through the disparity points lying near the peak. A large number of these points will be incorrect, so direct fitting, by least squares for example, would not work. A Hough transform is used to select a large subset of the points which lie near a plane. This point set, along with the plane parameters, constitutes a local *surface hypothesis*.

For each image patch the origin of the left image coordinate system (x, y) is reset to the centre of the square. The equation of a plane in disparity space can be written as

$$d = ax + by + c \tag{1}$$

where a, b and c are constant (a and b are the disparity gradients in the x and y directions respectively). For a given point (x, y, d), eq. 1 describes a plane in parameter space (a, b, c) defining the set of values of a, b and c that give rise to a plane in disparity space passing through the point (x, y, d). Points lying on the same plane in disparity space define planes in parameter space which meet at a single point. The problem is to find that point. The standard Hough transform approach is to divide parameter space into blocks in each direction. For each point (x, y, d), and each block in parameter space that the plane in eq. 1 passes through, an accumulator assigned to the block is incremented. At the end the block whose accumulator that received the most votes is the best planar fit to the data.

The Fast Hough Transform (FHT)

The above method has two main drawbacks: large memory requirement and slowness. In order to find the plane parameters accurately, parameter space must be divided finely in all three directions, and an accumulator assigned to each block. The Fast Hough Transform (FHT) described in [7] gives considerable speed up and reduces storage requirement.

The FHT applies to those Hough transform problems in which the equation relating features to parameters is linear in the parameters. In this case each feature votes for a *hyperplane* in parameter space (a $k-1$ dimensional generalisation of a plane, where k is the dimension of parameter space). The parameters are scaled so that their initial ranges form a 'hypercube' (generalisation of a cube) in parameter space.

A coarse Hough Transform is applied to the initial 'root' hypercube in parameter space by dividing it into 2^k 'child' hypercubes formed by halving the root along each of the k dimensions and assigning an accumulator to each child. Each hyperplane passing through a child hypercube contributes a vote to its accumulator. (In fact, a hyperplane is tested for intersection with a hypercube's circumscribing 'hypersphere'. This is approximate but is faster than the exact method.) Those children receiving greater than a threshold T votes are recursively subdivided, and so on. A limit is set on the level of subdivision, which is equivalent to setting a required accuracy.

An extra speed up is possible by keeping track of which features vote for (i.e. which hyperplanes intersect) each hypercube. Only those features need be tested for intersection between hyperplane and child hypercubes, since children lie inside their parents.

Plane finding using the FHT

In the FHT plane finder, 'hyperplanes' are planes and 'hypercubes' are cubes. The initial range of the parameters are: a: is -0.6 to 0.6. b: -0.8 to 0.8. c: $d_{\text{peak}} - 0.4H$ to $d_{\text{peak}} + 0.4H$ where d_{peak} is the disparity of the peak in the disparity histogram. The vertical disparity gradient limit b is set larger than the horizontal limit a because Needles is less sensitive to the shear distortion between images caused by b than the horizontal compression/expansion caused by a, since a shear preserves the area of an image patch.

The FHT threshold T is set to $0.6W$. A lower threshold would allow a fit to a smaller number of points, but would slow the algorithm down. The value $0.6W$ has been suitable for all the stereopairs so far tested. Normalising T using W is justified since one edge can only contribute one vote to the winning hypercube (this is proved in [8]), so that the value of T used implies that at least 60% of the edges in a left image patch must be matched.

Right Image Texture Density Test

The FHT plane fitter implicitly maps the left image patch into a parallelogram-shaped patch of the right image specified by the plane parameters (a, b, c). If the two patches are indeed projections of the same surface in the world, the texture density of the two patches should be similar. This test rejects a planar fit if the right image patch contains disproportionally more edges than the left image patch (in the reverse case a good planar fit could not have been obtained in the first place). Thus the planar fit is rejected if the ratio of number of right image patch edges to left image patch edges is greater than a threshold, set to $1.5(1+a)$. $1+a$ is the ratio of areas of the patches (right/left), so the test therefore rejects the planar fit if the number of right image edges is more than 1.5 times what we would expect.

1.4 Region Formation and Hypothesis Disambiguation

The next step is to join surface hypotheses in adjacent image patches if the two surfaces agree in their area of overlap. The test is based on the number of common matches in the sets of matches selected by the FHT. If this is ≥ 5, the hypotheses are labelled as connected. When one hypothesis could be connected to several hypotheses in the same patch, the one with the best planar fit is chosen, i.e. the one reaching the highest subdivision level in the FHT, or failing that the FHT accumulator values are compared.

A region growing process now explicitly labels regions of connected hypotheses. Each hypothesis becomes part of a numbered region. Hypothesis disambiguation then eliminates all but one of the surface hypotheses in each patch, with the set of remaining hypotheses assumed to be true representations of the visual surface. Discontinuities are located implicitly at the boundaries of regions. The stages are interleaved in the following way:

1. **First region growing stage**. Regions of connected hypotheses are grown by taking those hypotheses that are connected to neighbours in all eight (lateral and diagonal) directions as 'seeds', which grow into the network of hypotheses along their connections. Such hypotheses are used in descending order of the goodness of the planar fits. A seeded region expands breadth-first along the eight connection directions.

2. **Hypothesis disambiguation**. Competition between hypotheses in an image patch is resolved according to the 'strength' S of a region, calculated by summing the FHT subdivision levels of all the hypotheses in the region. Hence region strength represents the area of the region and the strength of the hypotheses within it. In each patch, the surface hypothesis belonging to the region of highest strength is declared the winning hypothesis in the patch. Hypotheses not part of any region are rejected.

3. **Second region growing stage**. Connections to hypotheses eliminated at the previous step are removed, and all region data is nullified. The region growing step 1 is then repeated. This is necessary because step 2 may split a region into two parts, still wrongly labelled as the same region.

4. **Elimination of weak regions**. The strengths of all the regions are recalculated. Those regions whose strength S falls below a threshold (20) are removed. This is designed to eliminate only very small regions.

Each continuous textured surface in the scene should be represented as a single region. Boundaries of a region should correspond to boundaries of the surface, e.g. step discontinuities, object boundaries. Note that a region may contain a step discontinuity if a connection route exists around it.

1.5 Least Squares Plane Fitting

The final stage in the Needles algorithm is to obtain more precise estimates of the local plane surface parameters than the quantised values obtained from the FHT plane finder. For the winning hypothesis in each patch, orthogonal regression is used to fit a plane to the disparity points that contributed to the winning plane in the FHT, minimising the sum of the squared perpendicular distances of the disparity points from the plane. Mathematical details are given in [13].

2 Parallel Implementation

The most time consuming parts of Needles take place independently in each image patch. The only non-local steps are region growing and final disambiguation, which take very little time. There is therefore great scope for using parallel processing to increase efficiency. Needles has been implemented on the MARVIN Transputer architecture developed in AIVRU, which is described in [3]. Using a nine Transputer system gives approximately an eight-fold decrease in running time over a Sun 3/60. Since one processor could in theory be assigned to each image patch, this is clearly a limited parallel implementation of Needles.

3 Results

We present results for two steropairs. The first is of a human face model, shown in figure 2. The face has been fixed to a backplate, painted white and dotted using a black pen to introduce texture. The images are 512 × 512 pixels, each pixel having a grey value between 0 and 255. Figure 3 shows the orientations of the local planar patches found by the Needles algorithm, shown superimposed on the left image. Each pin is centred on the centre of an image patch. The needles (hence the name) point in the direction of the surface normal in the world. The surface of the face is shown in figure 4a, plotted in world space. This was constructed by fitting a surface to the edge disparity points. For comparison, figure 4b shows the results of running the PMF stereo algorithm [10]. This general-purpose algorithm employs a disparity gradient limit between matches that support each other, a weaker constraint than that imposed by Needles, resulting in occasional bad matches that cause glitches in the fitted surface. Since PMF is about two magnitudes faster than Needles, an obvious research direction is to try to incorporate the speed of PMF and the surface smoothness of Needles, to take advantage of both.

We have compared measurements of the face produced by Needles with height measurements of the face above the backplate made along cross-sections using a clock gauge. Both sets of measurements were relative to fixed axes marked on the backplate. The results are shown in graphs A to K of figure 5, representing the positions on the face shown in figure 4a. Solid squares mark the clock gauge data, outlined squares the Needles data. Gaps in the clock gauge data represent places where the slope was too steep for an accurate measurement to be made. Sub-millimetre accuracy has been achieved over large parts of most of the cross-sections, corresponding to sub-pixel accuracy in disparity. The large errors in graphs B, E and I seem to be caused by prominent surface features which are smoothed over by Needles, such as the eyes (E) and mouth (I).

The second stereopair, shown in figure 6, contains six more or less textured objects. The images are again 512 × 512 pixels. Figure 7 shows the planar surface normals found by Needles. Needles segmented the scene into the separate objects, in particular finding the discontinuity between the lego house and the telephone directory. The surfaces of the objects are shown in figure 8a. We also ran PMF and imposed the segmentation provided by Needles on the disparity data. The result of surface fitting is shown in figure 8b. The main difference between the results is the smoothness of the Needles surface for the telephone directory and the book. Repetitive texture, such as that on the book, is difficult for stereo algorithms to match correctly, since shifting either image by the 'wavelength' of the texture gives a match that is almost as good as the correct one. The global disambiguation mechanism employed by Needles causes the correct matches to be chosen since they will make up the largest region of connected surface patches.

4 Conclusion

We have implemented a stereo algorithm designed for smooth textured surfaces. It uses a local surface smoothness constraint and a novel global disambiguation mechanism that locates each surface as a whole. The algorithm has been implemented on a Sun and a network of Transputers. Extensions that have been made to the algorithm include crease discontinuity detection and calculation of surface curvature. These are described in [8].

5 Acknowledgements

Grateful thanks to the AIVRU vision community, especially Neil Thacker, Michael Rygol and Stephen Pollard. We also thank Nouveau Sculpture Ltd. for providing the face model, and Andrew Zisserman for the surface plotting software.

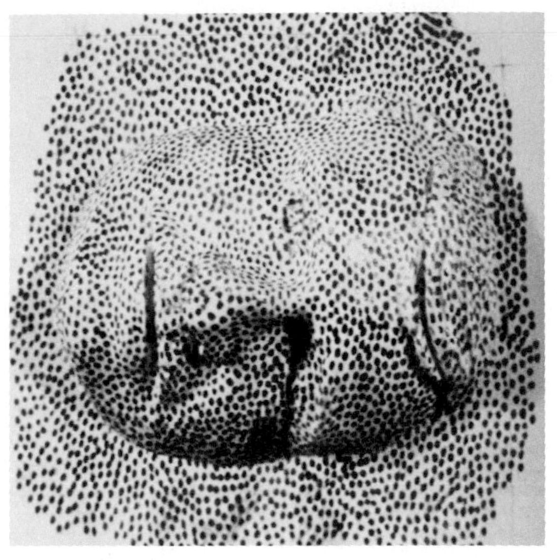

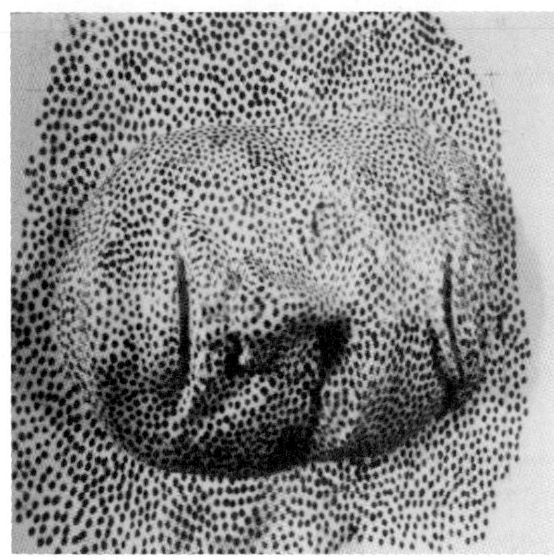

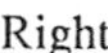

Right

Left

Figure 2: Stereopair of head model.

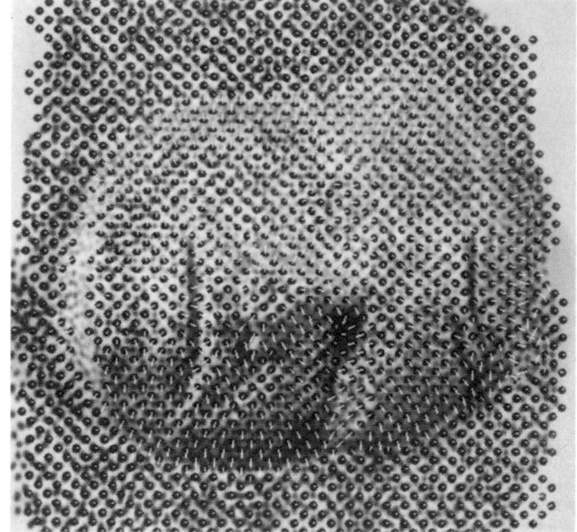

Figure 3: Local planar surface normals found by Needles algorithm.

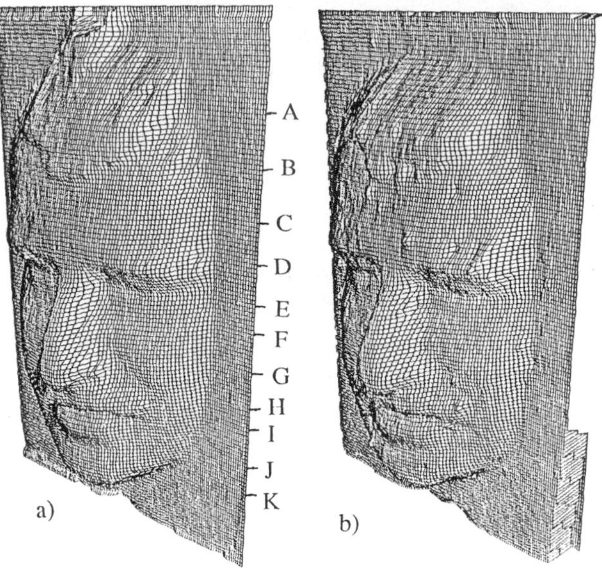

Figure 4: Surfaces of head found by a) Needles b) PMF.

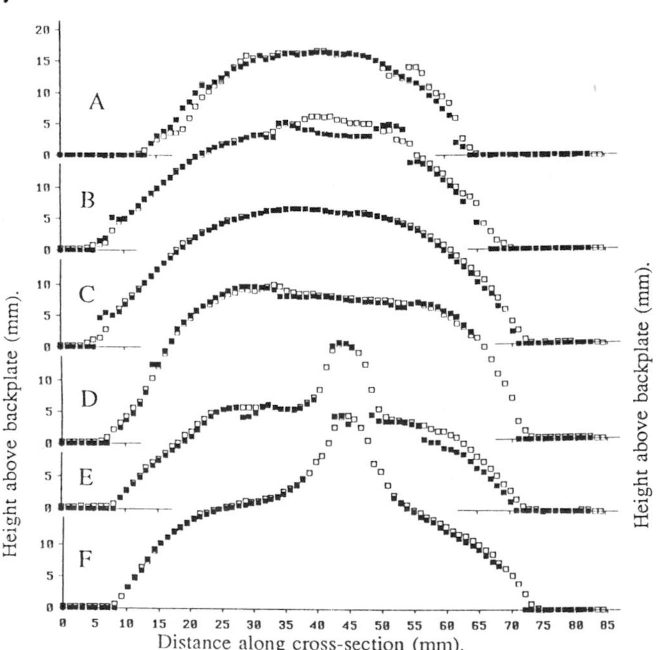

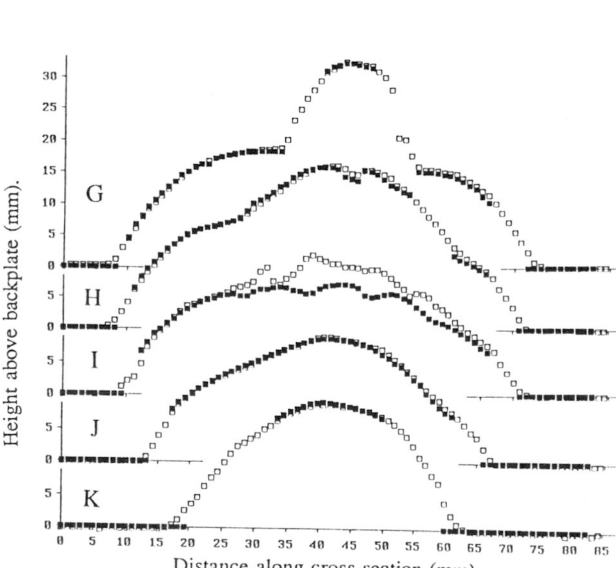

Figure 5: Cross-section graphs of head.

Right

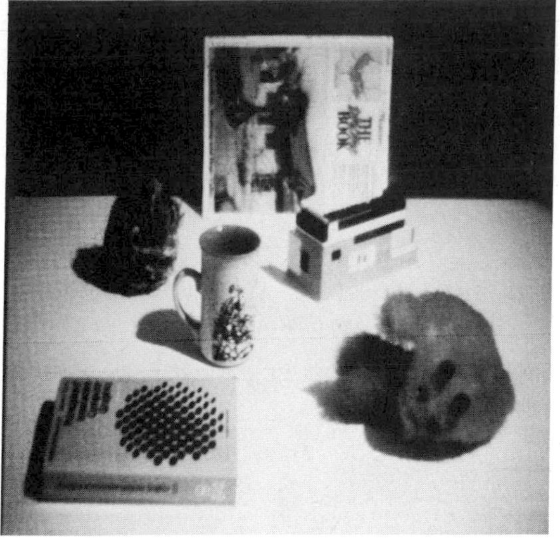

Left

Figure 6: Stereopair of six textured objects.

Figure 7: Local planar surface normals found by Needles.

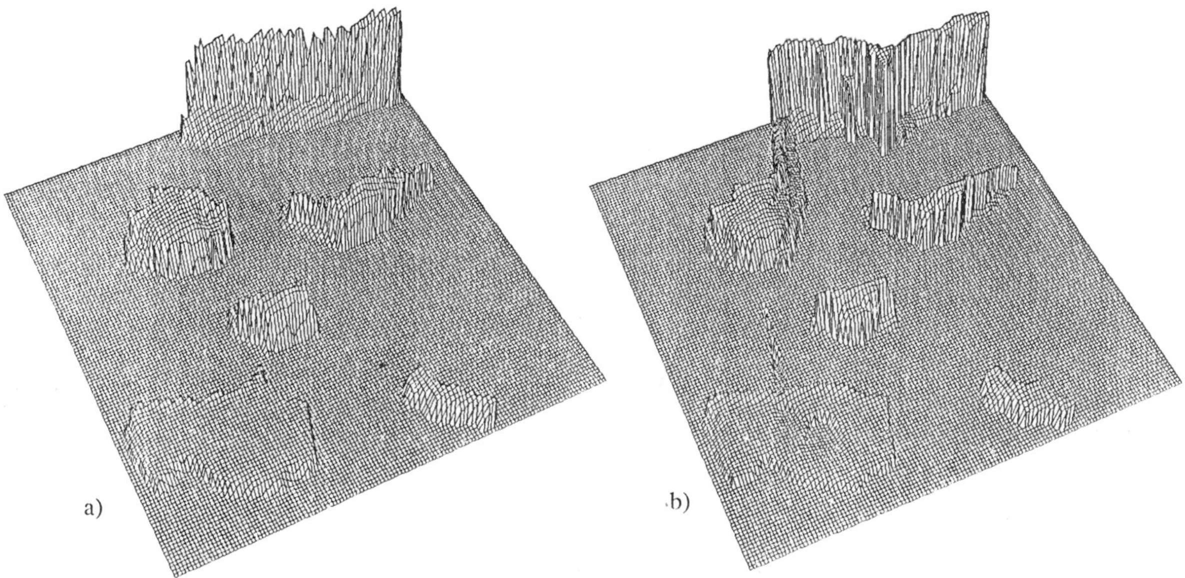

Figure 8: Surfaces of six objects, showing segmentation. a) Needles b) PMF, using segmentation provided by Needles.

References

[1] **Barnard, S.T. and W.B. Thomson** "Disparity Analysis of Images" *PAMI.* Vol. 2 No. 4 (1980) pp 333-340.

[2] **Boult, T.E. and L. Chen** "Synergistic Smooth Surface Stereo" *Proc. 2nd ICCV.* (1988) pp 118-122.

[3] **Brown, C. and M. Rygol** "An Environment for the Development of Large Applications in Parallel C" *Proc. Transputer Applications '90* (1990)

[4] **Canny, J.F.** "Finding Edges and Lines in Images" MSc thesis, MIT (1983).

[5] **Grimson, W.E.L.** *From Images to Surfaces: A Computational Study of the Human Early Visual System* MIT Press (1981).

[6] **Hoff, W. and N. Ahuja** "Surfaces from Stereo: Integrating Feature Matching, Disparity Estimation, and Contour Detection" *PAMI.* Vol. 11 No. 2 (1989) pp 121-136.

[7] **Li, H., M.A. Lavin and R.J. Le Master** "Fast Hough Transform: A Hierarchical Approach" *CVGIP.* Vol. 36 (1986) pp 139-161.

[8] **McLauchlan, P.F.** "Recovery of Textured Surfaces using Stereo Vision" PhD thesis. AIVRU, University of Sheffield (1990).

[9] **Otto, G.P.and T.K.W. Chau** "A 'Region-Growing' Algorithm for Matching of Terrain Images" *Proc. 4th AVC* (1988) pp 123-128.

[10] **Pollard, S.B., J.E.W. Mayhew and J.P. Frisby** "PMF: A Stereo Correspondence Algorithm using a Disparity Gradient Limit" *Perception.* Vol. 14 (1985) pp 449-470.

[11] **Pollard, S.B., J.E.W. Mayhew and J.P. Frisby** "Implementation Details of the PMF Stereo Algorithm" in this volume.

[12] **Porrill, J., S.B. Pollard, T.P. Pridmore, J.B. Bowen, J.E.W. Mayhew and J.P. Frisby** "TINA: The Sheffield AIVRU Vision System" *Proc. 10th IJCAI* Vol. 2 (1987) pp 1138-1144.

[13] **Porrill, J., T.P. Pridmore, J.E.W. Mayhew and J.P. Frisby** "Fitting Planes, Lines and Circles to Stereo Disparity Data" Technical Report 17. AIVRU, University of Sheffield (1986).

[14] **Shirai, Y. and Y. Nishimoto** "A Stereo Method using Disparity Histograms of Multi-Resolution Channels" *Proc. Robotics Research: 3rd Int. Symp.* (1986) pp 27-32.

[15] **Terzopoulos, D.** "Multiresolution Computation of Visible-Surface Representations" PhD thesis. MIT (1984).

[16] **Tsai, R.Y.** "An Efficient and Accurate Camera Calibration Technique for 3D Machine Vision" *Proc. CVPR '86.* (1986) pp 364-374.

IV 3D MODEL-BASED VISION PROJECT

Introduction by the Editors

A THE GRANT PROPOSAL (Written 1983)

1 OBJECTIVES

The overall objective of the 3D Model-Based Vision Project is to develop a scheme for the recognition and manipulation of 3D objects using information about the 3D structure of their visible surfaces delivered by the 2.5D Sketch Project.

Object recognition has two major components. First, there must be a collection of stored model descriptions cast within some representational scheme; and second, there must be one or more ways of associating descriptions derived from images with descriptions in the collection of models (Marr and Nishihara, 1978). The 3D Model-Based Vision Project reflects these twin requirements by having two separate, albeit closely inter-related, sub-projects. The first has as its goal the design of a representational scheme for 3D objects which is specifically tailored to address the issues and problems of describing visual objects using the kind of data structures carried by the 2.5D Sketch. This is called the YASA project. The second will be concerned with developing methods for accessing the collection of stored object models from a newly derived 2.5D Sketch. This is called the 3D Model Invocation and Verification Project.

The 3D Model-Based Vision Project will be led by Dr J E W Mayhew, working in conjunction with Dr R J Popplestone[1] in Edinburgh (Department of Artificial Intelligence) who wishes to interface 3D vision capabilities to the robot programming language RAPT-2.

2 THE YASA PROJECT

The primitives to be used in the YASA[2] recognition scheme will be 3D surface features and relationships between them. The 2.5D Sketch data structures to be used for input for YASA can be regarded as equivalent to what Brooks (1981) called the 'observation graph' but with an important difference. In the scheme proposed here both the primitives and the relationships expressed between them in the graph are three dimensional.

Brooks points out that the most important factor in predicting shape is the orientation of the object relative to the camera. The two factors which determine the 2D image are: (i) the self-occlusion relationships of the object given a specific camera geometry (ignoring other object occlusions!), and (ii) the metrical distortions produced by the projection from 3D onto 2D. In the 3D depth map the self-occlusion relationships are almost the same as for the 2D case and the representation we have chosen for the description of 3D objects (based on what Koenderink and van Doorn (1979) have called the 'visual potential' of the object) explicitly recognises and exploits self occlusion relationships. However, the depth map is not subject to the same metrical distortions as the 2D image, for whereas the 2D projection of a right angle may be acute or obtuse depending on its orientation to the imaging plane, a right angle projects into the depth map as a right angle whatever its orientation (within obvious noise and resolution limits). Thus a very important characteristic of the scheme we propose is that the matching is between 3D structures extracted from the depth map and 3D structures in the object model catalogue, and not as is the case in many current object recognition schemes, between 2D structures predicted from the object model and imaging geometry. The proposed scheme has much in common with the 3DPO project described by Bolles, Howard and Hannah (1983).

It is realised of course that image aquisition limitations may degrade the 3D data and an important concern of the YASA scheme will be the development of methods that degrade gracefully.

Binford (1982) lists several criteria for a representation of 3D shape:

a) The scope of the representation should be such that a wide range of objects can be classified and described with it.

b) The primitives of the scheme should be locally computable. They should not be simple volumetric prototypes but, rather like splines, be both general and locally generated from the imaged data.

c) The representation should make the similarity relationships between object parts and between object wholes easy to recognise and describe.

d) The appearance of the objects should be readily predicted.

e) There should be a natural coarse to fine segmentation of the object into whole/part relationships. The parts should be volumes and locally realisable, with a complex object being the 'glued' union of simpler components.

There are few differences between these and the following criteria proposed by Marr and Nishihara (1978):- primitives should be accessible (readily computed from the image data); the scope should be large and descriptions canonical (unique); and both similarities and differences between shapes should be describable.

Both Binford's and Marr and Nishihara's criteria are based on an important assumption, namely that the task domain is one of visible object recognition. The criteria that govern the design of CAD/CAM body modelling schemes are based on different requirements but nevertheless various CAD/CAM techniques have helped shape the present proposal.

---

[1] As noted previously, Robin Popplestone left Edinburgh soon after the consortium began its work, with first Pat Fothergill and then Bob Fisher taking over his role.

[2] YASA: *Y*et *A*nother *S*illy *A*cronym. Sorry - JEWM.

Recent developments in constructive solid geometry (CGS) schemes (eg PADL - see Requicha, 1980, Brown, 1982) are attempts to overcome the representational deficiencies of earlier wire frame and boundary representation CAD/CAM systems. The major problems associated with the early schemes was the difficulty in checking the 'objects' for inconsistencies, such as hanging edges or faces, and hence for automating the computations of mass properties of the object as well as its graphical display. In CSG schemes solids are represented as a tree of ordered additions and subtractions of simple volumetric primitives (eg cylinders, cubes, cones, spheres etc, the bounded intersections of quadric halfspaces) using a regularised set of Boolean operators and rigid motions. (Regularised operators prevent the construction of objects with hanging faces and edges and thus help ensure the geometrical validity of the objects). Though a considerable advance over earlier wireframe systems, in order for a designer to see what he has 'built' using CSG it is necessary for the representation to be converted to a boundary representation before it can be input to a computer graphics display.

Following discussion with C Brown at Rochester (PADL) and members of the Leeds Body Modelling Project, it is clear that notwithstanding its considerable advantages for design, CSG is not a suitable scheme for the purposes of object recognition (in terms of Binford's criteria it satisfies only criterion (a): its scope is estimated as 95% of manufactured parts; Requicha and Voelcker (1982). Moreover, if as seems likely the automation of manufacture will increasingly utilise CSG schemes then it seems that another criterion to be added to those given by Binford is that there be a valid and reliable conversation from the 3D shape representation used for body modelling and the 3D shape representation used for visual recognition and validation. The calculation of the boundary representation from the CSG representation is an example of an exact conversion between representations.

We have chosen as the primitives of representation entities which are both importantly related to the 3D geometry of the object and also readily identified or inferred from their projections into the depth map, such as the qualitative and quantitative 3D descriptions of vertices, edges and surface regions, their 3D relationships, and some simple global gestalts (see the 2.5D Sketch Project). A possible choice for the organisation of these primitives in an object model that would facilitate model invocation and verification is a data structure somewhat similar to the winged edge representation proposed by Baumgart (1972) but one which takes directly into account the viewing geometry. Here we can exploit hidden surface removal priority sorting ideas derived from computer graphics; and also what have variously been called invariant and quasi-invariant features (Attneave, 1954; Brooks, 1981), characteristic views (Hrechanyk and Ballard, 1982, and many others!), and the visual potential of the object (Koenderink and van Doorn, 1979).

The proposed representation for YASA is a hierarchical organisation of clusters of 3D features which are stable over variations in viewpoint. Consider a 3D object centred in a transparent sphere of relatively large radius compared to the depth variation in the object. Let an eye wander over the surface of the sphere, marking on it the boundaries of regions within which specific 3D surface features of the object can be seen. Repeating this operation for all the features will produce a map of the object's viewing potential containing regions of different sizes, inclusion/exclusion relationships, and degrees of overlap, with the whole defining a hierarchical organisation of clusters of 3D features, their transformations and occlusion relationships.
Another way of illustrating the proposed representation is in terms of volumes produced by the intersections of the complements of the half spaces of the boundary surfaces. Consider a planar boundary surface of an (opaque) object. It can only be seen if the viewpoint is on the non-object side of the surface. If three planes intersect to form a corner then they define a quadrant in space in which the three faces of the corner are potentially visible. That is, the junction, the edges, and the faces form a stable 3D feature cluster which is visible until the viewpoint moves out of the quadrant, the latter being an example of what will hereafter be termed a 'view solid'. The union and intersection of view solids produced by other feature clusters provides an organisation of the view potential and suggests that procedures similar to those used in the construction of the 3D solid may provide a starting point for development of methods for the computation of the object description.

There are always problems arising from occlusion, particularly those arising from the boundaries of smooth surfaces. A smooth surface can give rise to an image feature and discontinuity in the depth map as the line of sight becomes tangent to the surface. Such a feature is called an 'extremal boundary' and its status in solid body modelling boundary representations is recognised as problematic because, unlike the edges arising from the junctions of surfaces, the position of the extremal boundary is viewpoint dependent and therefore not easily represented in object centred coordinate system. For objects of revolution or rotation the extremal boundary is an important shape descriptor and the 3D space curve corresponding to the swept function is trivially part of the representation proposed here (it will be associated with a very large view solid). Another issue is occlusion discontinuities. From some viewpoints a surface will project an extremal boundary, but from others, like the nose on a face, it will not. It is envisaged that the YASA scheme will be capable of representing this sort of information, if only in qualitative and heuristic fashion.

In terms of Binford's list of criteria, the YASA representation satisfies, at least partially, all except possibly (e), i.e. that there should be a natural segmentation of the object into part/whole relationships in which the parts are locally realisable volumes. In this regard it is possible that in some cases the hierarchical nature of the YASA representation is such that a particular cutting plane would segment the object into two components, though the reason for wanting to do this may not be obvious. Possibly of greater potential application is the operation in the opposite direction, i.e. in the construction of an object out of component parts. It may be necessary to backup to the level of the CSG representation to recompute the boundary representation and from that compute the stable feature clusters that comprise the viewing potential of the new object but whether a method that merges viewing potential can be developed will need to be investigated. This issue is of particular relevance in assembly task applications that use visual verification.

3 SUMMARY OF YASA REPRESENTATION

The basis of the YASA scheme is a form of winged edge surface representation describing the 3D geometrical relations of surface features in an object centred coordinate system. It is equivalent to the boundary representation of the body model in so far as all the vertices, edges, and faces comprising the visible surface of the object are explicitly identified and described and the boundary representation could be generated for display if required (although the representation will be somewhat richer than the boundary representation as meta-feature gestalts or groupings will also be included as part of the object's description).

If there is any novelty in the YASA scheme it is by virtue of the proposal to group subsets of the 3D feature-nodes of the winged edge graph on the basis of their stability over variations in viewpoint. Thus, if the winged edge graph implicitly describes the complete viewing potential of the object the hierachical organisation of the 3D feature-node clusters is an explicit description of the viewing potential of the object that is invariant over a particular range of viewpoints but may change catastrophically outside that range. Included in this organisation of the graph will be information concerning:- any meta-feature or gestalt descriptions of the particular stable feature cluster; feature transformations (eg a edge may project as an orientation discontinuity over a certain range of viewpoints and as a depth discontinuity afterwards); and possible potential extremal boundary/occlusion relationships of smooth curved surfaces.

B WHAT REALLY HAPPENED?

The YASA Project began with Mayhew writing a series of internal AIVRU memos and a simple CSG body modeller and ray caster to explore their implications. These were written while Mike Gray of IBM Winchester wrote a boundary file evaluator for the IBM body modeller WINSOM and extended it to make explicit the external surface intersections (the surfaces, edges and vertices) organised on the basis of their visibility from viewpoints around a tesselation of the sphere surrounding the object. Gray's work was reported to an Alvey Vision Conference but regrettably he left the project after about 18 months and before producing a formal paper, which is why no report of his work is included here (Gray's paper did have some influence on the psychophysical and neurophysiological work of Perrett: see e.g. Perrett and Harries, 1988). Gray's replacement at IBM also left the project before a publishable report was attained. Thus the proposed extension of the representation to include extremal boundaries and virtual vertices (eg edges and vertices that occur only in the 2D projections of occlusion relationships between surfaces) was not completed.

Following John Knapman's assignment to leadership of the IBM effort in the consortium a change of direction in their work was made towards the Wireframe Completion Project (see Knapman's paper on cyclide patches [22]). Knapman also produced a working demonstration of a system for 3D polygonal model identification from stereo data, though not one of the envisaged YASA type [21].

As no personnel were available in AIVRU to pursue in detail the YASA-related ideas developed in Mayhew's memos, the project lapsed, though if one looks hard, traces of the kind of thinking it engendered can be found in Fisher's SMS [24].

Since the proposal was written several object recognition schemes of a very similar kind to that proposed for the YASA Project have been published. Generously interpreted, these suggest that the fundamental ideas on which it was based (which can be traced to those of Koenderink) were well-founded. An extension of Koenderink's work has been published by Joachim Rieger of GEC (Rieger, 1987, 1990).

The transfer of the TINA vision system model matcher [28,29] to the fast parallel vision system MARVIN [10] exploited ideas central to the YASA project. The combinatorial complexity of the search problem was much reduced by restructuring the object model into its characteristic views each with its own particular set of focus features. Furthermore, since the MARVIN system is able to conduct the simplified model matching task for each characteristic view in parallel, a considerable speed up is obtained.

One spin-off of the YASA project was a psychophysical study of human object recognition conducted in AIVRU by Langdon (a postgraduate student of Mayhew and Frisby). A report of that work, which as it developed became as much a pursuit of mechanisms of mental rotation as it did of canonical view-based object representations, is included here [27] as a fitting tombstone for the YASA project.

The work in the 3D Model-based Vision Project culminated in two systems integrating research within but not between sites. This reflects the nature of the collaboration enjoyed by the consortium: a loose club of communicating but autonomous modules (the platoon or Vietcong model; contrast with the nexus of interdependencies or pack of cards model).

Sheffield chose to demonstrate the results of the research in the three sub-projects (PMF, 2.5D and 3D Model-based Vision) by using stereo vision to solve the 'pick and place task' cliche [24, 25]. The system of component modules was called TINA for reasons which can no longer be remembered but *T*hat *I*s *N*o *A*nswer and *T*his *I*s *N*o *A*cronym seem to capture some of the flavour of the thinking at the time. Given the present predilection of so many industrial automation engineers to design vision out of their production lines, we might with hindsight suggest that *T*here *I*s *N*o *A*pplication might be a more appropriate interpretation. However, if flexibility is to be the touchstone of the future factory, then the best interpretation might be *T*here *I*s *N*o *A*lternative.

TINA has now been completely rewritten (almost entirely by Pollard) and provides the basis of TINATOOL, a very extensive integrated vision research environment. TINATOOL has been ported to several research sites. This experience taught us first-hand the oft-repeated warning that porting large bodies of software can be an extremely time-consuming and frustrating task as the attendant responsibilities become manifest. It should not be undertaken lightly, particularly in a consortium devoted primarily to basic research.

B (contd) Notes Added by Fisher

The work at Edinburgh started with two tracks. The first track investigated methods for applying model-based vision methods in situations where most object identities and positions are known, such as in a typical robot workcell, containing the known robot, gantry, feeders, jigs and workpiece. The remaining objects to be visually analysed may be a dropped part, or a part with an unknown orientation. A CSG model of a known scene is used by

ROBMOD (Cameron, 1984) to deduce a wire-frame model of the visible 3D edges, in an off-line process. To do this, we extended the ROBMOD body modeler to deduce boundary representations from the Constructive Solid Geometry object. ROBMOD was also extended to produce an annotated visible edge description, by analysing the object visibility from a given viewer position. This produced a list of the visible portions of the 3D object edges, including extremal boundaries.

The wire-frame edges are then matched to 3D data edges, such as those obtained from a stereo camera system. We used a set of simple position constraints to verify the matches close location, close orientation, data edge within predicted model edge, etc.). Because the 3D positions of the model and data edges should be identical, fast matching is possible, and we achieved a 1 second verification time [25].

The other track investigated model-based object recognition and location, based on surface patch evidence, such as would be represented in the REV graph. During the early part of the project, work was spent investigating the IMAGINE I system (developed for Fisher's PhD thesis, now reported as a monograph - Fisher, 1989a). This work pointed out particular problems in the areas of model representation and geometric reasoning.

As a result of the evaluations, the SMS object representation scheme (Fisher, 1987a) was designed and implemented [24]. This was a surface-based modeler to allow connecting curved surfaces, surfaces with holes, degrees of freedom and a greater variety of surface types. As any model feature could be described using expressions involving variables, models could have deformable parametric shapes (but not variable structure). A generalisation hierarchy was also included, to allow scale dependent representations. Because the volumetric features did not represent well the significant features of the object, such as might be used to suggest or confirm identity, second-order volumetric primitives were added to the models (Fisher, 1987b,c).

Since a considerable portion of model matching time was spent in appearance prediction (to derive feature visibility and self-occlusion relationships) the SMS models were designed to include a visibility submodel, listing the features visible from salient viewpoints and new viewpoint dependent features, such as extremal boundaries. This idea linked closely with the proposed YASA representation.

Another observation from the IMAGINE I system was that the geometric reasoning system was insufficiently powerful for complex problems. By examining previous 3D vision systems, Orr and Fisher (1987) identified the key geometric reasoning functions, needed for vision applications, and used these to guide the development of a new interval arithmetic geometric reasoner based on propagating bounds on quantities through a parallel network (Fisher, 1988; [23]). The network approach allowed handling of data errors, model variations including degrees of freedom, incremental position constraints, and a priori scene constraints. We observed that the forms of the algebraic position constraints tended to be few and repeated often, and hence standard subnetwork modules could be developed, with instances allocated when new position constraints were identified.

Though research on the use of these networks is continuing (e.g. Fisher, 1989b; Fisher and Orr, in press) problems overcome by the new technique included the weak bounding of transformed parameter estimates and partially constrained variables, and the representation and use of constraints not aligned with the parameter coordinate axes. The network also has the potential for large scale parallel evaluation. This is important because about one-third of the processing time in the scene analyses was spent doing geometric reasoning.

The IMAGINE I system showed the importance of having a model invocation process (Fisher, 1989a) to identify quickly candidate models from the model database. The work undertaken as this part of the project resulted in: (1) extensions for including inhibiting relationships, which produced considerably improved invocation behaviour, (2) extensions for using binary feature evidence (i.e. spatial relationships between two features, such as relative distance, orientation or size), and (3) implementing the model invocation process in an explicit value-passing network. This work is still continuing, and is awaiting more complete experimentation before having a proper report.

In addition, Paechter (1987) observed that many database objects required similar properties, such as requiring that principal curvatures must be zero. From this, he introduced a hierarchy of low-level symbolic description types, such as 'planar', for the example above. This did not change the network competence, but dramatically simplified the definition of object properties. Another major class of improvements were for a family of evidence evaluation functions, for example when a property's exact value is unimportant provided it is positive. The evidence evaluation functions were changed to have gaussian form, which linked the properties more closely to their statistical characterization. A more uniform evidence integration function based on an harmonic mean was introduced, which then allowed subcomponent evidence to be uniformly integrated with property evidence.

To match models to surface patches, one has to overcome occlusion and fragmentation, organise these features into groups, describe properties of the objects, select models, pair model features to the data features, estimate object positions and reason about missing features. To do these, the IMAGINE II system [26] was designed. Based on this, a framework was built for undertaking these actions, and developed sufficiently to demonstrate one complete recognition before the end of the grant period. The data surfaces were correctly paired to the model surfaces, and the substructure hierarchy developed correctly. Object position was estimated accurately enough to be barely distinguishable from the perfectly correct position. The successfully recognized object was an oil bottle using laser range data[3]. This recognition, by itself, was not significant, but was a promising first step, in that it was of a non-polyhedral object.

REFERENCES

Attneave, F. (1954) Some Information aspects of visual perception. *Psychological Review* **61** 183-193.

---

[3] Editors' Note. The *Needles* stereo algorithm (see [20]) would now be able to provide similar dense range data from visual images but it was not available at the ime Fisher's work required it.

Aylett, J. C., Fisher, R. B., and Fothergill, A. P., (1988) Predictive computer vision for robotic assembly. *Journal of Intelligent and Robotic Systems* **1** 185-201.

Baumgart, B.G. (1972) Winged edge polyhedral representation, STAN-CS-320, AIM-179, Stanford AI Lab.

Binford, T.O. (1982) Survey of model-based image analysis systems. *International Journal of Robotics Research* **1** 18-64.

Bolles, R.C., Howard, P. and Hannah, M.J. (1983) Three dimensional part orientation system. Proc. *International Joint Conference on AI*, 1116-1120.

Brooks, R.A. (1981) Symbolic reasoning among 3-D models and 2-D images. *Artificial Intelligence* **17** 285-348.

Brown, C. M. (1982) PADL-2: A technical summary. *IEEE Computer Graphics* **2** 69-85.

Cameron, S. A. (1984) *Model solids in motion.* PhD Thesis, Department of Artificial Intelligence, University of Edinburgh.

Fisher, R. B. (1987a) SMS: A suggestive modeling system for object recognition. *Image and Vision Computing* **5** 98-104.

Fisher, R. B. (1987b) Model invocation for three dimensional scene understanding. *Proc. Int. Joint Conf. AI*, 805-807.

Fisher, R. B. (1987c) Modeling second-order volumetric features. *Proc. 3rd Alvey Vision Conference*, 79-86, Cambridge.

Fisher, R. B. (1988) Solving geometric constraints in a parallel network. *Image and Vision Computing* **6** 1988.

Fisher, R. B. (1989a) *From surfaces to objects: computer vision and three dimensional scene analysis.* Chichester: John Wiley & Sons.

Fisher, R. B. (1989b) Experiments with a network-based geometric reasoning engine. Proc. *International Joint Conference on AI*, 1632-1628.

Fisher, R. B. and Orr, M. J. (in press) Geometric reasoning in a parallel network. *International Journal of Robotics Research.*

Hrechanyck, L.M. and Ballard, D.H. (1982) A connectionist model of form perception. *IEEE*, 44-52.

Koenderink, J.J. and Van Doorn, A.J. (1979) The internal representation of solid shape with respect to vision. *Biological Cybernetics* **32** 211-216.

Marr, D. and H.K. Nishihara (1978) Representation and recognition of the spatial organisation of three dimensional shapes. *Proc. of the Royal Society of London, B.* **200**, 269-294.

Orr, M. J. L. and Fisher, R. B. (1987) Geometric reasoning for computer vision. *Image and Vision Computing* **5** 233-238.

Paechter, B. (1987) *A new look at model invocation with special regard to supertype hierarchies,* MSc Dissertation, Department of Artificial Intelligence, University of Edinburgh.

Perrett, D.I. and Harries, M.H. (1988) Characteristic views and the visual inspection of simple faceted and smooth objects: tetrahedra and potatoes. *Perception* **17** 703-720.

Rieger, J.H. (1987) On the classification of views of piecewise smooth objects. *Image and Vision Computing* **5** 91-97.

Rieger, J.H. (1990) The geometry of view space of opaque objects bounded by smooth surfaces. *Artificial Intelligence* (in press).

Requicha, A.A.A.G. (1980) Representations for rigid solids: theory, methods and systems. *Computing Surveys* **12** 437-464.

Requicha, A.A.A.G. and Voelcker, H.B. (1982) Solid modelling: a historical survey. *IEEE Computer Graphics* **2** 9-26.

[21] Advances in 3D Model Identification from Stereo Data

John Knapman

IBM UK Scientific Centre
Winchester, SO23 9DR, UK

Abstract

Volumetric (CAD) models of objects are converted to a wire frame representation which is compiled into a data base and represented in vectors and matrices that characterise both local geometrical relationships and the structure of the models. This characterisation is independent of position and orientation and supports variable size. Using a stereo vision system, instances of these objects are then identified from pairs of images containing single objects or more than one object.

Introduction

The term "data base" is taken to imply a repository of a number, potentially a large number, of models that are to be selected and matched to the 3D data obtained from a scene. Sometimes, selecting models in this way is called "invocation" and it appears in principle to be more difficult than matching a single, given model to the data.

Results have been obtained distinguishing among twelve objects in a data base using synthetic images employing the vision system developed at the AIVRU, University of Sheffield (Mayhew et al, 1986). This delivers 3D geometrical descriptions of the edges in a scene from a stereo pair of images. These are classified as straight, circular, planar or otherwise.

Some images have been of isolated objects, with results reported elsewhere (Knapman, 1987). Other images have contained more than one object with limited occlusion.

The work of Grimson and Lozano-Pérez (1984) emphasises the need to find powerful constraints that are nevertheless cheap to implement in order to reduce the magnitude of the combinatorial problem inherent in matching even one model to the data in a scene. One cannot afford the expense of generating and testing many hypotheses for the transformation between model co-ordinates and real world co-ordinates. Such a transformation in 3D involves three degrees of rotational freedom and three of translation. In addition, it may involve a scale factor. Recently, Grimson (1987) considers the further possibility of a stretching transformation. As Grimson (1986, p662) remarks, the use of constraints to reduce the number of hypotheses to be generated and tested is the key to efficiency.

The present work addresses ways in which objects can be recognised efficiently from a data base of models rather than just a single model. Consequently, there is even more need to discover powerful constraints that can be applied cheaply to avoid generating and testing too many hypotheses. The outcome of the model identification method described in this paper is a *short list* of model hypotheses that can then then be tested by established means, e.g. by the matcher of Pollard et al (1987). Often, however, the method leads to a short list containing only one hypothesis (modulo a symmetry or two).

Nature of the Sensing Device

Whereas Grimson and Lozano-Pérez aim to be independent of the sensing modality (sonar, tactile, visual) we are particularly interested in using the data from the binocular stereoscopic vision system (Mayhew et al, 1986). This delivers 3D vector descriptions of straight lines and (less reliably) circular arcs in a scene. So far, it has not been possible to deliver surface descriptions. The constraints used by Grimson and Lozano-Pérez assume the availability of surface normals and are not therefore ideally suited. They also rely solely on sparse, unconnected points, whereas the stereo system delivers descriptions of connected edge segments. Although the system often breaks edges and junctions, it very seldom connects them erroneously, adopting a conservative principle of least commitment. Consequently, there is no point in throwing away these edge descriptions.

Therefore, we describe pair-wise relationships between edges in the data rather than between points, whereas Grimson and Lozano-Pérez, followed by Murray

(1986), consider pair-wise relationships between points and their surface normals in a surrounding neighbourhood.

The advantages of using pair-wise relationships are retained, namely that they provide a description that is independent of an object's position and orientation and can also be made independent of size. At the same time, an edge of some length can provide more geometrical information, and hence more discriminating power, than a neighbourhood of a point.

Stereo System Design

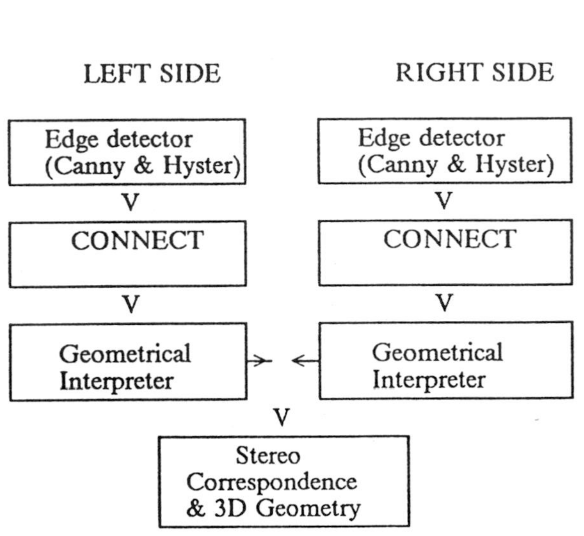

Figure 1. Alternative design of stereo vision system

Some of the experiments have been conducted using the Sheffield system and others with a somewhat different design, as illustrated in Figure 1. The primary motivation for trying this alternative design was to improve the quality of descriptions of circular arcs for use in the later matching process. Instead of fitting point by point as PMF (Pollard et al, 1985) does the method is to fit straight lines and ellipses to the monocular data and then solve the stereo correspondence problem between them, using the same constraints (notably disparity gradient) that PMF uses.

The results so far have been inconclusive. In some instances this method has yielded circular arcs with normals accurate to within 1° or 2° but in other cases has failed to classify them at all. Sometimes, the Sheffield system yields errors in normals as high as 28°, with commensurate errors in estimates of radius. Such errors render the arcs almost useless for recognition. However, better results have recently been reported with TINA (Frisby and Mayhew, 1987) and it is hoped that those improvements will be repeatable at this site.

Building Models

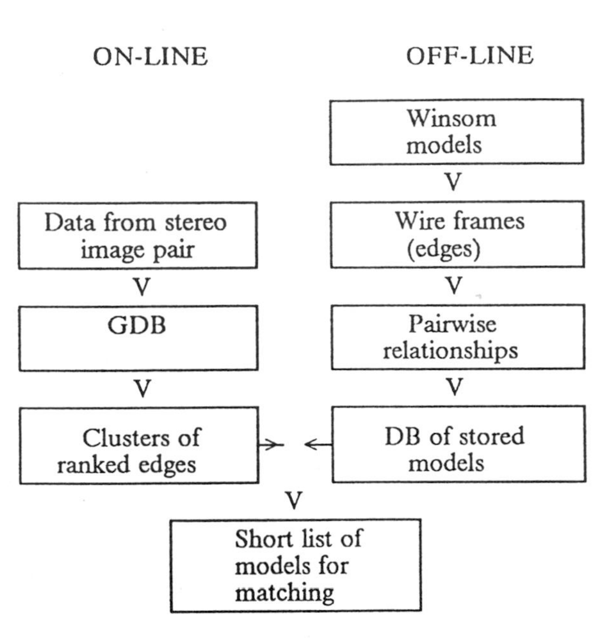

Figure 2. Summary of data flow

The IBM Winchester Solid Modeller - Winsom (Quarendon, 1984) - accepts volumetric descriptions of objects in terms of primitive solids. An extension of Winsom known as FASTDRAW (Halbert and Todd, 1987) produces a list of edge segments which are then classified (Herbert, 1987) as straight or circular. FASTDRAW was designed for a fast display of a model in outline for interactive use in defining models but it lends itself well to this different use.

The wire frames thus produced are then analysed to yield the pair-wise relationships between edges. These are stored in the data base in the form of *identification matrices* and *offset vectors* (see below). All this is done off-line as a kind of compilation.

On-line, the list of edges given by the vision system is examined. Earlier tests were conducted on scenes containing isolated objects. There, the edges were ranked by saliency, which in practice meant longest first. Later tests on scenes containing more than one object employed a simple clustering technique in which close edges (separation in 3-space less than an arbitrary threshold) were put together and ranked closest first.

Identifying Models

The recognition method can be thought of as providing an engine that implements a mapping from a set of features in the scene to a set of models in the data base.

D: $\{f | f \text{ in scene}\} \rightarrow \{m | m \text{ in DB}\}$

The set $M = D(F)$ is the short list of models that could be represented by the set F of features.

Underlying the mapping D are several primitive functions on features and pairs of features that produce vectors over the features and pairs in the data base. These are described below in the section "Primitives". They rely on the presence of matrices of data derived from the models and stored conveniently.

Perhaps the most important of these primitives is APPLY-RELATIONSHIP. It makes use of the structure of all the models in the data base to eliminate interpretations between pairs that share a common feature if they are inconsistent. This structure is encoded in offset vectors.

Whereas the recognition problem is usually posed as a search through n^k possible nodes for k features from the scene and n features in the data base, many of those possible nodes represent structurally inconsistent hypotheses. Here the problem is formulated as a step by step evaluation of the subsets of F. Each evaluation performs work in proportion to the number of models in the data base, so that the work increases linearly with the number of models. The actual operations involved are very simple, are local within models and hence are well suited to implementation on parallel hardware.

Clustering

In general a scene will comprise several objects and some sort of background. There exists the problem of segmenting the scene into objects. Since the vision system segments it into edges we are faced with a clustering problem in deciding which edges comprise a particular object. This is the "wire frame completion" problem. A complete solution would use visual cues such as connectivity, evidence for occlusion, type of junctions and uniformity of surfaces, as well as consistency with models in the data base.

Here we are interested mainly in the latter. The vision system delivers geometrical but not topological information about edges. A crude clustering scheme has been implemented, however, in which pairs of edges are sorted closest first and clusters are composed of those features nearer than an arbitrary threshold. This worked well on the example of two pegs (Figure 10).

Once a set F of features has been obtained, we wish to know whether it, or some subset of it, matches a small number of models in the data base. In other words, we wish to find $G \in P(F)$ such that $D(G)$ is non-empty but small, where $P(F)$ is the power set of F, the set of subsets of F which includes F itself.

The efficiency with which $P(F)$ is searched now determines the efficiency of the object recognition process. The heuristics employed assume that a set F of features is likely to consist predominantly of edges from one object. The rules are:

1. Grow a subset G starting from the closest two edges in F until $D(G)$ has one member (a unique identification) or $D(G)$ is empty (set G does not represent a known object).
2. If $D(G)$ is empty and G is of size j, consider each subset of G that is of size $j-1$. Try to grow these without the discarded feature.

The most obvious thing that can go wrong is accidental identification of an incorrect model from a set of edges that actually lie on different objects. No matter how good the constraints built into the model identification mapping D, accidental identification will always remain a logical possibility because of the possibility of genuine coincidence in the scene. In such cases it will be necessary to rely on model verification.

In general terms, one can envisage a more sophisticated (intelligent?) process that could, for instance, reason about the possibilities of occlusion. The present system simply makes no assumptions about occlusion, allowing for the possibility that any edge may be partially occluded. Another improvement would be to re-process the scene through the stereo vision system to remove ambiguities once the first object is identified. It might also be possible to use contextual knowledge to further constrain the mapping D, although the very existence of the data base constitutes a strong form of knowledge already.

Primitives

The data base contains an ordered set of models, each containing features, each of which participates in relationships. Each relationship has a *source* and a *target*. Consider all the relationships $R_1, R_2, \ldots, R_q$ in the data base grouped by source feature within model. These can be thought of as defining a *vector base* over which *property vectors* and *score vectors* are defined. For some property (e.g. the angle between two lines) a property vector $\underline{p} = (p_1, p_2, \ldots, p_q)$ would have $p_m = 45°$ if relationship R_m in the data base has this value for this property.

Given a pair of features f_1, f_2 in the scene, we would like to know to which relationships in the data base it could correspond. If the angle between f_1 and f_2 is in the range (θ, ϕ) then the *Boolean vector* $\vec{b} = (b_1, b_2, \ldots, b_q)$ is such that

$$b_m = 1 \text{ if } \theta \leq p_m \leq \phi$$
$$= 0 \text{ otherwise}$$

A Boolean vector is a special case of a score vector. The values in a score vector can also be numerical ranges (size factors). Union and intersection can be performed on them.

We define functions $E_{property}$ from pairs of features in the scene onto score vectors for every property that a relationship can have. The score vector of a pair is obtained as the union of these individual vectors.

$$E(f_1,f_2) = E_A(f_1,f_2) \cup E_B(f_1,f_2) \cup \ldots$$

Note that, although the functions $E_{property}$ are defined in terms of property vectors, they are implemented more efficiently using *identification matrices* (see below).

Structural Primitives

The two structural primitives are CONTRACT-BASE and APPLY-RELATIONSHIP. CONTRACT-BASE (abbreviated CB) changes the base of a score vector from relationships to features, or from features to models. The score s_m of relationship R_m is transferred to its source feature. Since a feature will have several relationships, a union is performed. Similarly, a union is performed contracting to a base of models.

APPLY-RELATIONSHIP (abbreviated AR) sets the score s_m of relationship R_m to be the same as that of its target feature.

The implementation of these two primitives relies on *offset vectors* that are prepared when the data base is loaded. They indicate the appropriate feature for each relationship R_m in the data base. Further efficiencies could be gained by exploiting the regularities in these offsets using bit masks and shift operations.

These two primitives allow the propagation of constraints from one relationship to another in a manner that is consistent with the structure of the models. Conceptually, this is done for all models at once. Suppose that a pair of scene features f_1, f_2 have a score vector $\vec{s} = E(f_2,f_1)$ (source f_2, target f_1). Then f_2 has a score vector $\vec{s}'_2 = CB(\vec{s})$. Now introduce a third scene feature f_3 giving score vectors $E(f_3,f_1)$ and $E(f_3,f_2)$. None of these three vectors takes account of the structural constraints implied by the other two. However, we can produce a score vector $\vec{s}'_3$ for f_3 that consolidates all the constraints as follows.

$$\vec{s}'_3 = CB(E(f_3,f_2) \cap AR(\vec{s}'_2)) \cap CB(E(f_3,f_1))$$

This score vector is now available to propagate to feature f_4. The general expression is

$$\vec{s}'_j = CB(E(f_j,f_{j-1}) \cap AR(\vec{s}'_{j-1})) \cap \bigcap_{i=1}^{j-2} CB(E(f_j,f_i))$$

Geometrical Constraints

These are much as described elsewhere (Knapman, 1987), relying on the angle between two lines and the two distances

CL	orthogonal distance at closest separation of extended lines
CE	average distance from each centroid perpendicular to the other lines

The length of a line is now regarded as a property of its relationships. This enables us to use the ratios of the lengths to CL and CE as properties of the relationship that are independent of size. The use of ratios minimises the need for size factor vectors, which are now only required for ensuring consistency between relationships that share a common feature.

The ratios utilised are

$$CL/(CL+CE),\ L1/CL,\ L2/CL,\ L1/CE,\ L2/CE$$

where $L1$, $L2$ are the line lengths. (Similar arrangements have been implemented for circular arcs and relationships between arcs and lines.)

Tolerance Vectors

Before using data produced by the vision system from a scene, it is advisable to allow certain tolerances. Crudely, one may apply tolerances of $\pm 5°$ to all angles and ± 5 pixels to all distances computed as properties of pair-wise relationships, with additional allowance for lines that are nearly parallel. This is wasteful because it fails to take account of the high accuracy with which displacements in the image plane can be measured compared with displacements in depth. Consequently, discriminating power is thrown away. On the other hand, a scheme of tolerances must not be too sophisticated because efficiency must be maintained.

The tolerance in each vector is here described by a cuboid around it, defined by a pair of vectors representing opposite corners in a viewer centred co-ordinate frame. The vector representing the end point of a straight line, for example, has a cuboid with x- and y-sides of length 0.2 pixels and a z length corresponding to 5.2 pixels if the line length p in the image plane is 50 pixels. These express tolerances of ± 0.1, ± 0.1 and ± 2.6 respectively. (They are proportional to $1/\sqrt{p}$, reflecting the way that the accuracy of measurement depends on the number of points in both the left and right images.)

Such a vector pair is termed a *tolerance vector*. Operations, including dot and cross products, are defined on tolerance vectors by finding the maxima and minima of the individual components of these products. When using the dot product, a pair of numbers results. Care must be taken over the sign ambiguity when finding a range of angles by way of the inverse cosines of such a pair. This is done by checking for a sign change in the cross product.

Identification Matrices

In order to minimise arithmetic operations, a scheme of bit maps is introduced. It depends for its success on the use of size independent values of properties of pair-wise relationships wherever possible.

On a pair of straight lines, for instance, use of the tolerance vectors leads to a range of values of *CL* and *CE*. Hence ranges are found for the ratios and the angle between the lines. Lengths are regarded only as a lower bound on the true length because of possible occlusion or broken lines.

Once a range of values has been found for a property of a relationship between two edge features, *identification matrices* are used to produce a Boolean vector as illustrated below.

	R_1	R_2	R_3	R_4	R_5	R_6	R_7	R_8	...	R_n
90°	1	0	0	0	0	1	1	0	...	0
89°	1	1	0	0	0	1	1	0	...	0
.	.	.	.	.	.	.	.	.	.	.
.	.	.	.	.	.	.	.	.	.	.
1°	1	1	0	1	1	1	1	1	...	1
0°	1	1	1	1	1	1	1	1	...	1

In the identification matrix there is one Boolean vector (row) for each angular value between 0° and 90°. Every relationship (R_1, ..., R_n) in every model in the data base is represented by a column. Relationship R_2 has an angle of 89° so it has a 1 in the vector for 89° and in all those beneath it. In row θ°, the 1s indicate those relationships with angle greater than or equal to θ.

Our models are rigid and so the complement of this Boolean matrix is used to indicate those relationships with angle less than θ. More generally, two identification matrices could be used to support models with ranges of allowable values. This is a possible approach to describing hinged or articulated objects.

At present, when an angular range (θ, ϕ) is found from the scene by way of the vision system and the tolerances, we take the intersection of two vectors, one the complement of that found in the matrix, to obtain a Boolean vector showing those relationships R_i in the data base with angles ψ such that $\theta \leq \psi \leq \phi$. These are the relationships that could correspond to the relationship found in the scene.

A more sophisticated arrangement of identification matrices is used for the ratios that may range over thousands of significant values. The method uses overlapping ranges so that a potential set of 65536 vectors is reduced to an optimum set of 64. 17 operations on bit strings are then needed to obtain a Boolean vector representing a range of data values.

Results

The seven test objects illustrated in Figures 3 to 9 were distinguished against a data base containing models of all of them after considering the number of edge features from the scene indicated in the table. This test used the sizes of the objects. Each scene was of an isolated object.

Object	**Number of scene features used**
Widget	3
Plug	3
Wedge	2
Cube	3
Ice cream	2
Frame	6
Chair	2

In another test, the scene in Figure 10 consisting of two "pegs" was successfully divided into two clusters, both of which were identified correctly against a data base of 12 models. When the size was used, 3 features from each cluster were sufficient for a unique identification. When size was not used, 6 features from one cluster were needed and 7 from the other for unique identification.

Acknowledgements

I have had valuable discussions relevant to this topic with John Mayhew, John Frisby, Stephen Pollard, Eric Grimson, Daniel Huttenlocher, Bernard Buxton, Andrew Blake, Bob Fisher, Mark Orr, John Woodwark, Rod Cuff, Steve Rake, Alex Lebek and Tom Troscianko. I am grateful to Simon Herbert, Rod Cuff and John Holland for assistance and co-operation.

References

1. **Frisby, J P and Mayhew, J E W** 'TINA: A Stereo Computer Vision System' A I Vision Research Unit, University of Sheffield, UK (January 1987)

2. **Grimson, W E L and Lozano-Pérez T** 'Model based recognition from sparse range or tactile data' *International Journal of Robotics Research* 3(3) pp 3-35 (1984)

3. **Grimson, W E L** 'The Combinatorics of Local Constraints in Model-Based Recognition and Localization from Sparse Data' *JACM* 33(4) pp 658-86 (1986)

4. **Grimson, W E L** 'Recognition of Object Families using Parameterized Models' *Proc 1st International Conference on Computer Vision* pp 93-101, London, UK (June 1987)

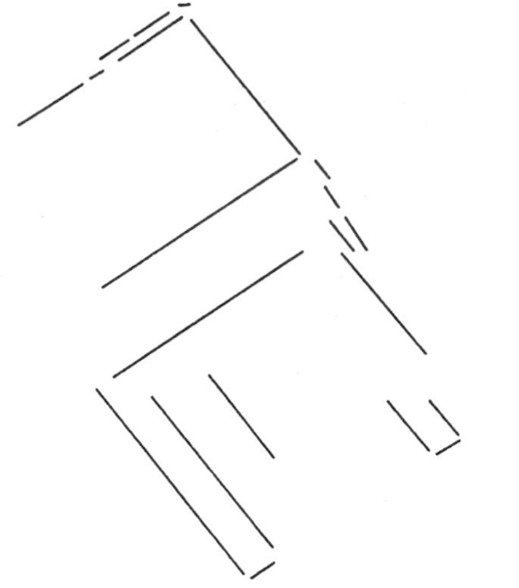

Figure 3. The chair

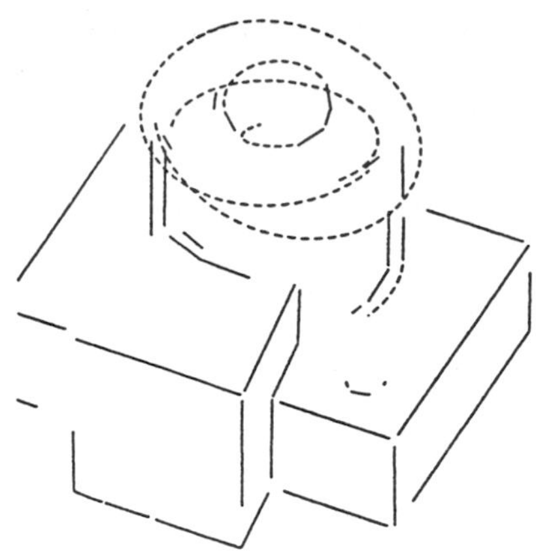

Figure 5. The widget

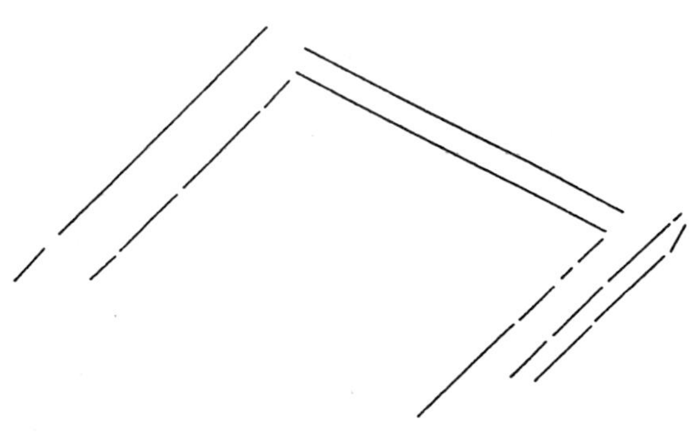

Figure 4. The frame

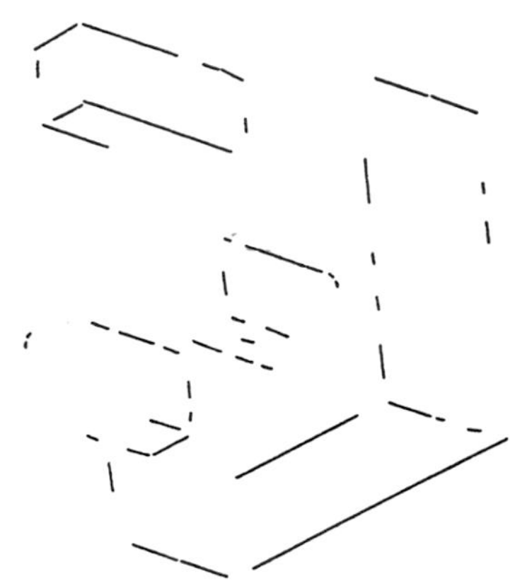

Figure 6. The plug

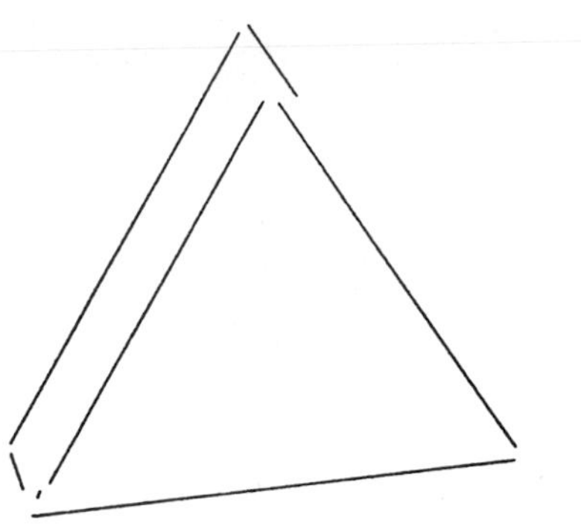

Figure 7. The wedge

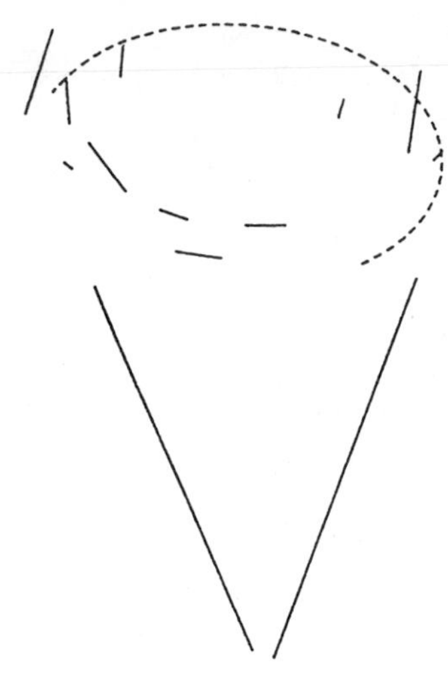

Figure 9. The ice cream cone

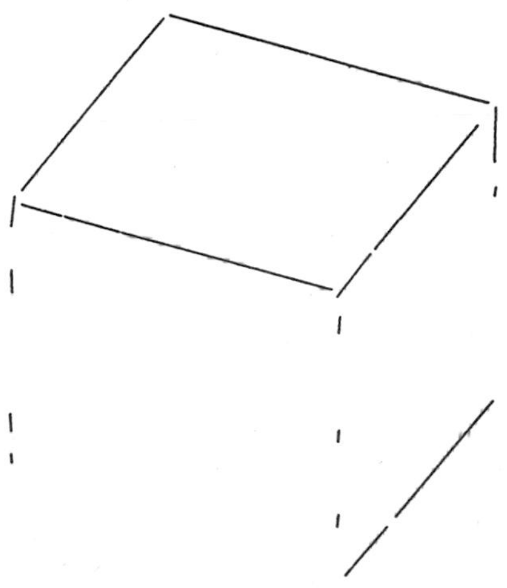

Figure 8. The cube

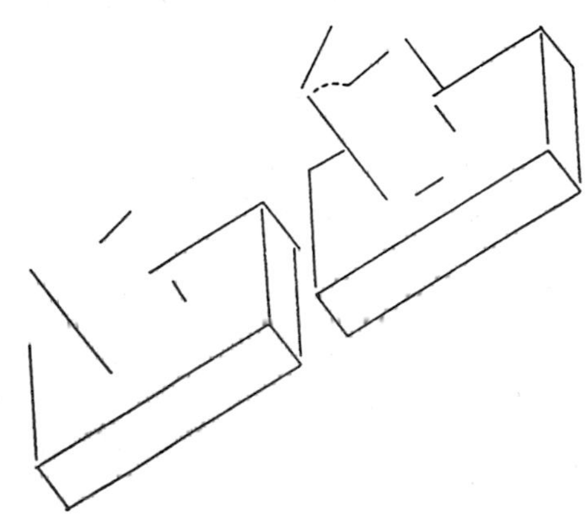

Figure 10. Two pegs

5. **Halbert, A and Todd, S** 'FASTDRAW' IBM U K Scientific Centre, St Clement St, Winchester, UK (forthcoming 1987)

6. **Herbert, S** 'Description of FASTDRAW post processor prototype' unpublished memo, IBM U K Scientific Centre, St Clement St, Winchester, UK (May 1987)

7. **Knapman, J M** '3D Model Identification from Stereo Data' *Proc 1st International Conference on Computer Vision* pp 547-51, London, UK (June 1987)

8. **Mayhew, J E W et al** 'GDB Release 1.0 User Documentation' A I Vision Research Unit ref no 014, University of Sheffield, UK (1986)

9. **Murray, D W** 'Model-based recognition using 3d shape alone' GEC Research Ltd., Wembley, UK (1986)

10. **Pollard, J, Mayhew, J E W and Frisby, J P** 'PMF: A stereo correspondence algorithm using a disparity gradient limit' *Perception*, 14, pp 449-70 (1985)

11. **Pollard, S B, Porrill, J, Mayhew, J E W and Frisby, J P** 'Matching geometrical descriptions in three space' A I Vision Research Unit ref no 022, University of Sheffield, UK (1986)

12. **Quarendon, P** 'Winsom User's Guide' IBM U K Scientific Centre report no 123, St Clement St, Winchester, UK (August 1984)

[22] Dupin's Cyclide and the Cyclide Patch

John Knapman

IBM UK Scientific Centre
Winchester, SO23 9DR, UK

Reprinted, with permission of Butterworth Scientific Ltd, from *Image and Vision Computing*, 1987, **5**, 167-173.

Abstract

To retrieve models from a data base for recognizing objects in stereo, a new formulation of patches of Dupin's Cyclide provides a succinct representation of surface shape.

The parameters can be extracted from the Weingarten Map and its derivatives at a point where a contour meets an extremal boundary.

Introduction

This work is part of a project to design and build a data base of object descriptions[1] for use together with a stereo vision system such as that proposed by Blake and Mayhew[2] in order to recognize objects in a scene.

There is here a requirement for a succinct representation of surface shape in order to keep the data base search reasonably simple and to ensure that shapes that are intuitively similar have similar search arguments.

Considerable effort has gone into exploring various representations for surface shape for the purposes of object recognition and also for geometric reasoning. Ikeuchi[3] advocates use of the extended Gaussian image. Pentland[4] has produced some impressive graphics based on super-quadrics enhanced by the use of fractals. Other representations include Bézier (bi-cubic) patches, B-splines, planar patches, quadrics, Coons patches and generalized cones.

The requirements are that a representation be economical, expressive, recoverable from real image data and stable under different conditions. Surface patches all suffer from lack of economy when the need arises to describe irregular surfaces precisely. Any formulation of surface patches can be made to fit to an actual surface shape by sufficiently fine sub-division but some require less sub-division than others at the expense of needing more parameters. Planar patches are at one extreme, requiring few parameters but fine sub-division. Cyclide patches - as formulated here - are near the middle of the range, having five numerical parameters plus patch size. Moreover, one of these parameters - the ratio of the principle curvatures at a point of symmetry - seems to capture something of the essence of shape to a remarkable degree.

Recoverability from real image data is perhaps the most stringent requirement for a representation. The extended Gaussian image requires knowledge of the surface normal at every point on the surface, something that even the human visual system is incapable of[5]. A super-quadric under a general translation and rotation requires 15 points to be known on a surface (see ref. 4, footnote 11, p.21). This may well be too many.

Koenderink and van Doorn[6] make a case for representing a surface shape qualitatively in terms of viewpoint catatrophes that appear as the observer moves about the object. For the problem of representing surface shape from a single stereo pair in order to recognize an object, the idea of qualitative representation can be thought of as deciding whether the surface is synclastic, anticlastic or developable (i.e. the Gaussian curvature is positive, negative, or zero, respectively) and distinguishing concave from convex (both synclastic) and recognising cylinders, cones and planes (all developable).

Such a representation would see a torus as composed of a convex outer patch with an anticlastic inner patch. However, it would not distinguish a rugby ball from a soccer ball. It is therefore recoverable and economical but not expressive. Problems may also arise in classifying surfaces that are on the borderline between two types (e.g. almost flat).

For these reasons the cyclide representation is preferred. This uses numerical parameters but can be related very simply to the qualitative description.

The Cyclide

Differential geometry teaches us that the shape of a surface in three dimensions is characterized by its lines of curvature, which form an orthogonal mesh upon it. (The tangents to a line of curvature are principal directions.) Hence at any point there are two orthogonal lines of curvature, one being the line of greatest curvature and the other being the line of least curvature. Working on applications to Computer Aided Design, Martin[7] and Nutbourne examined the class of patches having plane circular arcs as their lines of curvature.

Describing surfaces in terms of such patches is in some ways analogous to describing lines in terms of straight and circular segments as done by Pridmore et al[8].

The general class of surfaces having (planar) circles as their lines of curvature seems useful for object recognition because it provides a reasonable descriptive power but is based on simple geometric primitives. This class was first discovered by Dupin[9] in 1822 - whence the name Dupin's cyclide - and was studied by James Clerk Maxwell[10] (for its applications to optics), Cayley[11] and Darboux[12] in the last century.

The Dupin's cyclide is a surface of the fourth order having as special cases the torus, the cylinder, the cone and the sphere. Another interesting cyclide shape is the *spindle* which I call the *right spindle* when its axis is a straight line. It is the closest approximation to an ellipsoid of revolution when the lines of curvature are constrained to be circular arcs. It resembles a rugby ball or an American foot ball.

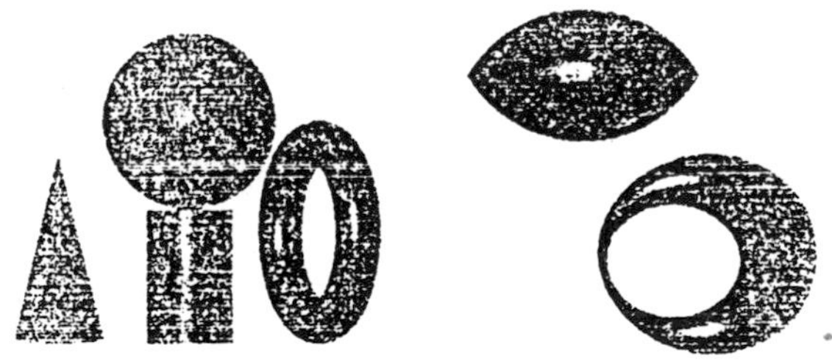

Figure 1. Special cases of the cyclide. Also the right spindle and ring cyclide

It is notable that these are the shapes proposed by Fisher[13] for modelling objects for purposes of recognition. There are obvious advantages in having a common parametrization to them, as furnished by the cyclide formulation. A more general case is the ring cyclide, sometimes called a "squashed torus". Essentially, a ring cyclide is to a torus as a cone is to a cylinder.

Cayley's Construction

Dupin defined the cyclide as the locus of a variable sphere touching three fixed spheres, but Cayley[11] gives a much simpler construction based on centres of symmetry of two circles.

Figure 2 shows the centres of symmetry S and T of two circles outside one another. It can be shown that S and T are at respective distances E_1 and E_2 from the centre of the smaller circle, where

$$E_1 = \frac{R_2 E}{R_1 + R_2} \text{ and } E_2 = \frac{R_2 E}{R_1 - R_2}$$

E being the distance between the centres. Similarly their respective distances from the centre H of the larger circle are

$$E'_1 = \frac{R_1 E}{R_1 + R_2} \text{ and } E'_2 = \frac{R_1 E}{R_1 - R_2}$$

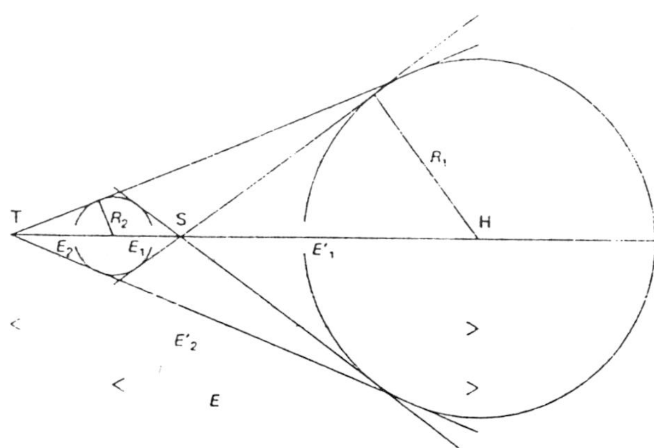

Figure 2. Centres of symmetry at S and T

These formulae apply also when one circle is inside another or when they are touching. Hence we can interpret Cayley's construction paraphrased as follows and illustrated in Figure 3.

> *Consider two circles in a plane. From either one of their centres of symmetry (S or T), draw a line cutting the circles at points A, B on the first circle and P, Q on the second. Now the tangent at A is parallel to the tangent at one of the two points P or Q. Let P be that point. On the line AQ construct a circle in the perpendicular plane having AQ as diameter. Do the same on BP. As the line is rotated about S or T, the locus of these two circles is a cyclide.*
>
> *A different cyclide results if the other centre of symmetry is taken.*

With the help of this construction, it is easy to visualize several cases of the cyclide. Consider the two circles in Figure 3. The centres of symmetry are marked.

Using the centre of symmetry S at distance E'_1 from the larger circle, the surface constructed is a ring cyclide like the one shown in Figure 1. If the circles become concentric the ring cyclide becomes a torus.

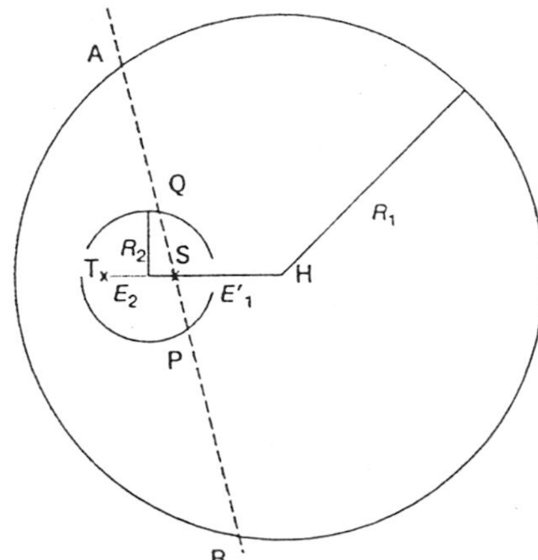

Figure 3. Example of Cayley's construction (ring cyclide)

As the radii of the circles tend to infinity while they remain concentric, the torus tends to a cylinder. If they are not concentric but their radii tend to infinity, the ring cyclide tends to a cone.

If the centre of symmetry at T instead of S is used, a spindle cyclide is constructed. The spindle itself is the central part, so that the small circle is its cross-section with its ends pointing upwards and downwards above and below the paper, as it were.

The locus of centres of the circles standing on AQ and PB is either an ellipse (see Figure 4) or a hyperbola. It can be shown[14] that the eccentricity of this conic is equal, in the respective cases, to

$$\varepsilon = \frac{E}{R_1 \pm R_2}$$

I call this quantity the *eccentricity* of the cyclide. It can also be shown[14] that the eccentricity in the limiting case of the cone is equal to the sine of the half angle, or slope, of the cone.

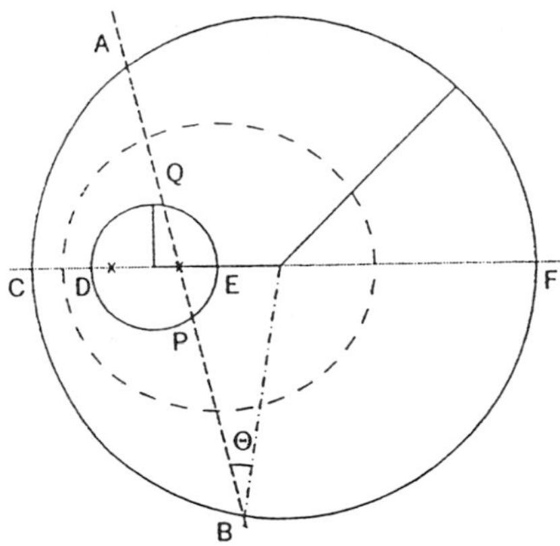

Figure 4. Locus of centres of circular lines of curvature. Also points of symmetry

If we continue the line of centres until it intersects the two circles, we find four points CDEF. These I call the *points of symmetry* of the cyclide.

The Cyclide Patch

Martin[7] and Nutbourne parametrize a cyclide patch in terms of the lines of curvature at a point. These can be continued to generate a complete cyclide if desired.

One of the difficulties in describing shape is that in order to give the complete differential geometry of a surface one needs the principal curvatures at every point. In machine vision, such information is not usually available. Sometimes it is difficult to extract even for one point. If it can be found at a point, it is useful to have some geometrical conventions on how the curvature might then be extrapolated over the surface.

The assumption that the surface has circles as its lines of curvature provides such conventions. Nutbourne and Martin show that once the two lines of curvature are given, the shape of the patch is constrained to within one further parameter. Their interpretation of this parameter is not suitable to our purpose and so we appeal to the underlying geometry of the cyclide for a more suitable formulation of this parameter. The eccentricity seems to be appropriate in this role.

Given a surface normal frame aligned with the principal directions of curvature at a point, a line of curvature is specified with three parameters.

1. Curvature κ of the line (reciprocal of radius)
2. Angle ϕ between the curve normal and the surface normal (so that the principal curvature of the surface in this direction is $\kappa \cos \phi$)
3. The arc length s

We adapt the notation of Forsyth[15,14] and name the two radii of principal curvature at a point on a cyclide R_θ, R_ψ and the two angles between the normals Θ, Ψ. Angle Θ is illustrated in Figure 4 and Ψ is analogous in a perpendicular plane. There are two position parameters θ, ψ related to the angles Θ, Ψ by

$$\tan\Psi = \frac{1}{\eta}\tan\psi \quad \text{and} \quad \tan\Theta = \frac{\varepsilon}{\eta}\sin\theta$$

where $\eta^2 = 1 - \varepsilon^2$. Following the usual parametrization of an ellipse, θ is the angle about the centre of the ellipse in Figure 4 on page 3. It is characteristic of the cyclide that Θ and R_θ are independent of ψ and that Ψ and R_ψ are independent of θ.

I parametrize the cyclide in terms of the ratio ρ of the principal curvatures at a point of symmetry, one of the principal curvatures there and the eccentricity ε. The ratio is defined as $\rho = \kappa_1/\kappa_2$ where κ_1 and κ_2 are the principal curvatures with $\kappa_1 < \kappa_2$ and therefore $\rho \leq 1$. It has the same sign as the Gaussian curvature with $\rho = 0$ indicating a developable surface (e.g. a cylinder or cone) while $\rho = 1$ indicates a spherical surface.

The second parameter is taken to be $\sigma = \kappa_2$, also at a point of symmetry. Then $\sigma = 1/r$ for a sphere or cylinder of radius r.

Taking the point of symmetry to be where $\theta = \pi$ and $\psi = \pi$ we can write the radii of curvature at an arbitrary point as[14]

$$R_\theta = \frac{1}{\sigma\rho(1-\varepsilon)}\left[\rho - \varepsilon - \varepsilon(1-\rho)\cos\theta\right] \qquad (1\theta)$$

and

$$R_\psi = \frac{1}{\sigma\rho(1-\varepsilon)}\left[\rho - \varepsilon - (1-\rho)\sec\psi\right] \qquad (1\psi)$$

Thus if the curvatures, angles and eccentricity can be found at some point in a scene, the parameters ρ, σ can readily be found. In particular, if we know the scale independent ratio $\mathrm{P} = R_\theta/R_\psi$ we can find ρ independently of σ. In fact, from equation (1),

$$\rho = \frac{\mathrm{P}(\varepsilon + \sec\psi) - \varepsilon(1+\cos\theta)}{\mathrm{P}(1+\sec\psi) - (1+\varepsilon\cos\theta)}$$

The next sections explain how to find at some points the curvatures, the angles Θ, Ψ and the eccentricity from stereo data so that the values of ρ and σ can be determined as described in this section.

Curvatures from a Profile and a Contour

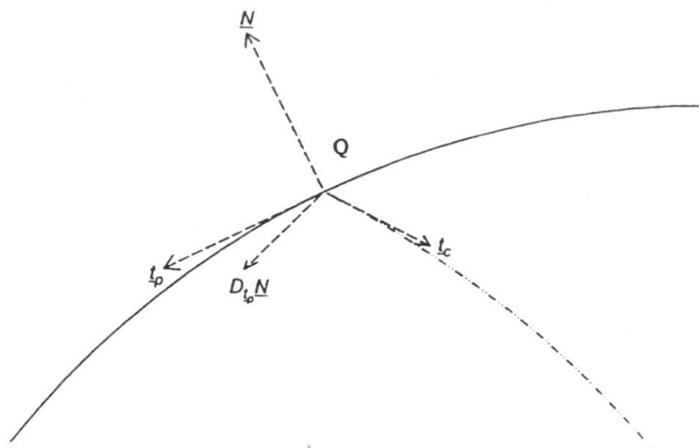

Figure 5. The Weingarten Map

A profile is the three dimensional curve at an extremal boundary, the line at which the surface normal is perpendicular to the line of sight. A contour is a line on the surface; it may be an intersection with another surface.

Proceeding purely from the local differential geometry of a point on a regular[16] surface in real Euclidean 3-space, it is possible to determine the principal curvatures and principal directions at a point where the profile meets a contour. This is because the surface normal (the *Gauss Map*) is known along a profile and can therefore be differentiated along it, yielding a vector that is tangent to the surface and therefore has two independent components. This is not generally true of contours.

The derivative of the Gauss Map is the *Weingarten Map* [17] (Figure 5) written $D_{\underline{t}_p}\underline{N}$. This means the derivative of the surface normal $\underline{N}$ in the direction of the tangent vector $\underline{t}_p$ along the profile. $D_{\underline{t}_p}\underline{N}$ is a tangent vector that differs from $\underline{t}_p$ unless $\underline{t}_p$ happens to be a principal direction. The Weingarten Map maps tangent vectors into tangent vectors. The eigenvectors of the Weingarten Map are the principal directions and its eigenvalues are the principal curvatures.

At a profile, the surface normal can be determined from a monocular image or a stereo pair, since it must be othogonal to the tangent of the curve and to the line of sight. In fact if $\underline{l}$ is the line of sight then $\underline{N}$ is given by the vector product.

$$\underline{N} = \frac{\underline{t}_p \times \underline{l}}{|\underline{t}_p \times \underline{l}|}$$

Note that the same analysis applies to a line of shadow on a surface if the position of the light source is known. We would simply replace $\underline{l}$ by a vector representing a ray of light.

The vision system[8] delivers a usable geometric description of a profile from a stereo pair, although strictly speaking the correspondences made are inexact. Since the surface normal is available along the profile, it is possible to calculate its derivative from a stereo pair as well. Differentiating the surface normal in the direction of $\underline{t}_p$ yields a vector

$$D_{\underline{t}_p}\underline{N} = -\underline{t}_1\kappa_1 \cos\gamma - \underline{t}_2\kappa_2 \sin\gamma \qquad (2)$$

where $\underline{t}_1$ and $\underline{t}_2$ are principal directions, κ_1 and κ_2 are the principal curvatures and γ is the angle between $\underline{t}_p$ and $\underline{t}_1$ [16]. Hence, writing $\underline{t}_p = \underline{t}_1 \cos\gamma + \underline{t}_2 \sin\gamma$, the (normal) curvature of the surface along the profile is

$$\kappa_p = -\underline{t}_p.D_{\underline{t}_p}\underline{N} = \kappa_1 \cos^2\gamma + \kappa_2 \sin^2\gamma$$

which is Euler's relation. By setting $H = (\kappa_1 + \kappa_2)/2$ and $S = (\kappa_1 - \kappa_2)/2$ it can more conveniently be written

$$\kappa_p = H + S\cos 2\gamma \qquad (3)$$

The vector $D_{\underline{t}_p}\underline{N}$ also has an orthogonal component which we will call τ.

$$\tau = -\underline{t}_o.D_{\underline{t}_p}\underline{N} = \kappa_1 \cos\gamma \sin\gamma - \kappa_2 \sin\gamma \cos\gamma$$

where $\underline{t}_o = \underline{t}_1 \sin\gamma - \underline{t}_2 \cos\gamma$. Therefore

$$\tau = S\sin 2\gamma \qquad (4)$$

We have two equations, (3) and (4), in the three unknowns H, S and γ. Summing the squares to eliminate γ we obtain

$$(\kappa_p - H)^2 + \tau^2 = S^2 \qquad (5)$$

If a contour - such as a surface intersection - meets the profile at a point Q, we can discover all three quantities at such a point. Let the tangent to the curve at this point be $\underline{t}_c$.

If α is the angle between $\underline{t}_c$ and the principal direction ($\cos\alpha = \underline{t}_c.\underline{t}_1$), the surface (normal) curvature in the direction of $\underline{t}_c$ is given by Euler's relation

$$\kappa_c = \kappa_1 \cos^2\alpha + \kappa_2 \sin^2\alpha \qquad (6)$$

Here $\alpha = \gamma + \beta$ where β is the known angle between the profile and the intersection ($\cos\beta = \underline{t}_c.\underline{t}_p$) and γ is as in equations (3) and (4).

The curvature of the contour at Q is given by Meusnier's theorem as

$$\kappa = \frac{\kappa_c}{\cos\phi} \qquad (7)$$

where $\cos\phi = \underline{n}.\underline{N}$ with $\underline{n}$ being the normal to the contour curve. The curvature κ_c is thus readily available by a linear equation (7). Then, rewriting equation (6) to be consistent with equations (3), (4) and (5),

$$\begin{aligned}\kappa_c &= H + S\cos(2\gamma + 2\beta)\\ &= H + S(\cos 2\beta \cos 2\gamma - \sin 2\beta \sin 2\gamma)\end{aligned} \qquad (8)$$

Therefore, after substituting $\cos 2\gamma$ and $\sin 2\gamma$ from equations (3) and (4),

$$\kappa_c = H + (\kappa_p - H)\cos 2\beta - \tau \sin 2\beta$$

This is a linear equation in H. Equation (5) then gives a linear expression for S^2 and equation (4) determines γ.

A Surface Frame

We now have the principal curvatures at Q and a surface frame $[\underline{t}_1, \underline{t}_2, \underline{N}]$ there since

$$\underline{t}_1 = \underline{t}_p \cos\gamma + \underline{t}_o \sin\gamma \text{ and } \underline{t}_2 = \underline{t}_p \sin\gamma - \underline{t}_o \cos\gamma$$

Rate of Change of Curvature

Progress has been made[18] in estimating not only the curvature but also the rate of change of curvature from a stereo pair of images. It is therefore realistic to contemplate using these quantities to determine the cyclide patch parameters Θ and Ψ. To interpret the derivatives in this way assumes that the surface is a cyclide patch, whereas the derivation of the curvatures in the previous section makes no such assumption.

Differentiating all three quantities κ_p, τ and κ_c yields three equations in two unknowns, leaving some redundancy that might be used to estimate how close the patch is to being part of a cyclide.

Let v be the displacement in the direction of the tangent $\underline{t}_c$ to the contour at Q. We wish to find an expression for $\frac{d\kappa}{dv}$, the rate of change of curvature of the line, since this quantity should be obtainable from stereo images by discovering curvatures along the curve near Q.

Write $C = \cos\phi = \underline{n}.\underline{N}$. Then, differentiating equation (7),

$$\frac{d\kappa}{dv}\cos\phi = \frac{d\kappa_c}{dv} - \frac{dC}{dv}\kappa \qquad (9)$$

Here

$$\frac{d\kappa_c}{dv} = 3(\kappa_1 - \kappa_2)\cos\alpha \sin\alpha \begin{bmatrix}\kappa_1 \cos\alpha \tan\Psi \\ -\kappa_2 \sin\alpha \tan\Theta\end{bmatrix} \qquad (10)$$

and

$$\frac{dC}{dv} = \underline{N}.D_{\underline{t}_c}\underline{n} + \underline{n}.D_{\underline{t}_c}\underline{N} \qquad (11)$$

where

$$D_{\underline{t}_c}\underline{N} = -\underline{t}_1\kappa_1 \cos\alpha - \underline{t}_2\kappa_2 \sin\alpha$$

similarly to equation (2) and the derivative of $\underline{n}$ must be obtained from the stereo image data.

The derivation of equation (10) is given elsewhere[14], as are those of equations (12) and (13) below, which are obtained by differentiating equation (2).

$$- \underline{t}_p . D_{\underline{t}_p}(D_{\underline{t}_p}\underline{N})$$

$$= 3(\kappa_1 - \kappa_2) \cos \gamma \sin \gamma \begin{bmatrix} \kappa_1 \cos \gamma \tan \Psi \\ - \kappa_2 \sin \gamma \tan \Theta \end{bmatrix} \quad (12)$$

and

$$- \underline{t}_o . D_{\underline{t}_p}(D_{\underline{t}_p}\underline{N})$$

$$= (\kappa_1 - \kappa_2) \begin{bmatrix} \kappa_1 \cos \gamma (1 - 3 \sin^2 \gamma) \tan \Psi \\ - \kappa_2 \sin \gamma (1 - 3 \cos^2 \gamma) \tan \Theta \end{bmatrix} \quad (13)$$

These are readily solved for $\tan \Theta$ and $\tan \Psi$.

We note that equation (12) represents the rate of change, in the direction $\underline{t}_p$, of the surface (normal) curvature in the direction $\underline{t}_p$. On the other hand, equation (13) represents the rate of change, in the direction $\underline{t}_o$, of the surface (normal) curvature in the direction $\underline{t}_p$.

The second derivative of $\underline{N}$ also has a component normal to the surface. This yields no new information but might be useful as a check on the accuracy of the differentiation. In fact,

$$- \underline{N} . D_{\underline{t}_p}(D_{\underline{t}_p}\underline{N}) = \kappa_1^2 \cos^2 \gamma + \kappa_2^2 \sin^2 \gamma \quad (14)$$

Note that this relationship is not unique to cyclides but follows directly from twice differentiating the equation $\underline{N}.\underline{N} = 1$ and substituting equation (2).

Eccentricity

This is a higher order quantity that can be obtained geometrically from considering two points P and Q at both of which a profile meets an intersection. In the most notable special case, the cone, geometrical methods are obviously applicable, as the eccentricity is the sine of the half angle (see "Cayley's Construction").

More generally, a local method is more satisfactory, not least because it affords, in principle, an exact determination at the point in question. This involves a further differentiation along a profile or an intersection and a somewhat lengthy calculation, so there must be some reservations about the accuracy of numerical methods from stereo images for this purpose.

The details appear in a fuller paper[14] where it is shown that differentiating equation (12) (or equation (10) along a contour) results in an equation of the form

$$P = Q \begin{bmatrix} \kappa_1 \cos \gamma \dfrac{d}{du} (\tan \Psi) \\ - \kappa_2 \sin \gamma \dfrac{d}{du} (\tan \Theta) \end{bmatrix} \quad (15)$$

This leads to a quadratic in ε^2 as follows.

$$\begin{bmatrix} (1 - \varepsilon^2) P \\ - Q \kappa_1 \kappa_2 \cos \gamma \sin \gamma \begin{pmatrix} \sec^2 \Psi + \tan^2 \Theta \\ - \varepsilon^2 (\sec^2 \Theta - \tan^2 \Psi) \end{pmatrix} \end{bmatrix}^2 \quad (16)$$

$$= 4(\varepsilon^2 \sec^2 \Theta - \tan^2 \Theta)(\sec^2 \Psi - \varepsilon^2 \tan^2 \Psi)$$

The underlying cyclide may be derived by the methods of "The Cyclide Patch".

A Test

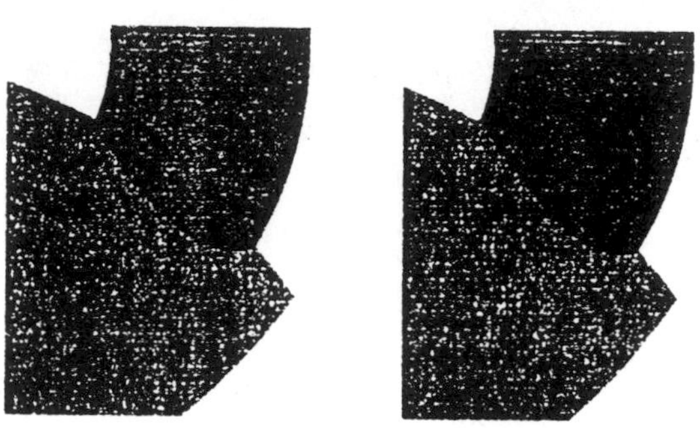

Figure 6. Right and left eye views of an intersection between a torus and a spindle

To verify the above principles, a test was conducted using the stereo vision system produced at the University of Sheffield[8] on stereo images prepared using Winsom[19], the IBM Winchester Solid Modeller. The test data is shown in Figure 6 where the left image is on the right and vice versa so that some readers will be able to obtain a stereoscopic impression by crossing the eyes. The scene is the intersection of a torus with a spindle.

Although internally the Sheffield system calculates curvature and rate of change of curvature at each point of every edge, this information was not used directly in this test but only indirectly, in that the vision system itself uses it to classify edges as straight, circular, planar or space curves. These classifications and the associated geometrical descriptions were used here to infer the parameters at the point at which the contour meets the profile.

The radius of the profile was found by the vision system to be 289 (in pixel units). Thus $\kappa_p = 1/289$ and $\tau = 0$. Note that the system is not able to distinguish profiles from other edges and this labelling was done manually. The radius of the circular approximation to the intersection curve was 53. The angle ϕ between the normal $\underline{n}$ to this curve and the surface normal $\underline{N}$ was 34°. The angle β between the contour and the profile was 97°. Substituting these values into equations (7) and (8) gives a value for H of 0.009648. Then from equation (5) we obtain S and thus κ_1 and κ_2.

The ratio κ_1/κ_2 was 0.22 as against the true ratio of the small and large radii of the torus which was 0.25. This discrepancy can be explained by the circular approximation made to the curve of intersection and by the vagaries of the stereo process itself, sensitive as it is to pixellation errors and the like, particularly when converting from disparity to depth. It is also true that the

Sheffield system takes no special account of the error in depth estimation at the profile caused by the fact that correspondence is made between slightly differing points on the surface in the two images, since the right eye sees a bit more of the surface, so to speak, than the left eye.

Equation (4) implies that $\gamma = 0$. Equations (12) and (13) both vanish, implying that both Θ and Ψ are zero. Also, in equation (16), $P = 0$ and $Q = 0$ implying that $\varepsilon = 0$.

Describing Surfaces

Once the geometry of a surface at some points is determined, a description of the surface as a whole is needed. Such a description has two purposes: recognition and geometric reasoning. As stated in the introduction, recognition in a data base of stored models is the primary focus of this work.

For this purpose, a stable description of the overall shape between edges is needed. If information is only available from one point, the surface may be assumed to be an extrapolation from there. Recognition, however, needs to proceed from a consistent point, not from the point that happens to be known. Appeal to the underlying geometry suggests the use of a point of symmetry of the cyclide. To be exact, we take a point at which the parameters Θ, Ψ and hence θ, ψ take the value π as stated in "The Cyclide Patch".

The two principal curvatures at that point then become the primary candidates to be arguments in searching a data base of object descriptions. The eccentricity can also be a search argument when available.

The ratio of the principal curvatures is probably more useful for recognition than the principal curvatures themselves. The ratio is all that is required to characterize the appearance of the profile.

Its utility is most apparent where only a plane intersection with an unknown surface is available with no other information about the surface. In such circumstances, it is possible to interpret the curve as an approximation to the Dupin indicatrix at a point P in the middle if the curve is close to a conic section. With suitable choice of co-ordinate direction, the equation of this curve is

$$\kappa_1 x^2 + \kappa_2 y^2 = 2\delta$$

where δ is a small (unknown) perpendicular displacement between the tangent plane at P and the plane of intersection, which are assumed parallel in this approximation. Hence the ratio ρ can be estimated even though κ_1 and κ_2 cannot.

If ρ is interpreted as the first parameter of a patch, the second parameter is most naturally taken (also at a point of symmetry) to be $\sigma = \kappa_2$. Thus a flat surface is indicated by $\sigma = 0$. In this case ρ is indeterminate.

The Gaussian curvature $K = \kappa_1\kappa_2$ does not seem to be useful in machine vision, a point noted also by Brady et al[20]. The mean curvature $H = (\kappa_1 + \kappa_2)/2$ does not appear suitable either, mainly because of its ambiguity when κ_1 and κ_2 have opposite signs.

More Information

When several points are known, a method for approximating a larger patch to fit a number of smaller patches is needed. The method chosen depends partly on how much is known. It may be that the principal curvatures at many points are available as would be the case using the "weak plate" method of surface interpolation described by Blake and Zisserman[21].

If, however, the differential geometry at just a few points is known, a possible approach would be to try to fit a large patch as close as possible to the smaller ones. A geometrical method would be to consider every patch's centre of symmetry and find the mean of their position, orientation and parameter values ρ and σ if some threshold is not breached. Some account would have to be taken of the reliability of the measurements of the patch parameters, based on the reliability of the data itself.

Further study of these possibilities is needed.

Conclusions

In stereo vision using normal lighting it is often impracticable to obtain a complete description of a surface in a scene. Rather, information about its curvature at some points can be gleaned from various sources, such as shading, specularities, extremal boundaries, and intersections.

Patches of surfaces from Dupin's cyclides have a parametrization that permits representation of surface shape with varying specificity. Given the principal curvatures at a point, the remaining three parameters of a patch, Θ , Ψ and ε, determine how the lines of curvature can be extended as circular arcs into the neighbourbood of the point.

The eccentricity ε relies on a higher order derivative than the other quantities and, in general, is likely to be available less often than the other parameters. The default assumption $\varepsilon = 0$ can conveniently be made when the data is unavailable, meaning that the surface patch is interpreted as part of a surface of revolution.

Once the parameters at certain points have been determined, they provide a basis for extrapolating the surface shape nearby. For purposes of geometric reasoning, methods for fitting and blending Cyclide Patches developed by de Pont[22] can be used.

For recognition, an overall shape description is needed, and this is perhaps best stated in terms of the scale independent ratio ρ of principal curvatures and the factor σ. These need to be given at a consistent point irrespective of viewpoint and a point of symmetry of the cyclide appears a particularly suitable place, the analysis then being at its simplest.

Among the various possible sources of information about shape, we have examined the surface normal and its derivatives along a profile (extremal boundary) and shown that, where a contour meets the profile, all five parameters can be determined locally. This has been tested on a pair of synthetic stereo images. Note that the use of the Weingarten Map along a profile to determine the local differential geometry is independent of the use of a cyclide representation. The assumption only affects the interpretation of the derivatives of this map.

Since the cyclide patch parameters are based on fundamental and well known quantities in differential geometry, other sources of estimation such as shading and specularity will also yield these parameters. Blake[23], for instance, derives equations for determining (under certain conditions) the Hessian of the height function of a surface in the neighbourhood of a point by using specular stereo. The principal curvatures and directions are readily obtainable from this Hessian[16].

Acknowledgements

I have had valuable discussions relevant to this topic with Tony Nutbourne, John Mayhew, Andrew Blake, John Porrill, Bob Fisher, John Woodwark and Alan Halbert. I am grateful to Steve Rake and Mike Gray for comments on an earlier version of this paper and to Simon Gee for checking the calculations.

References

1 **Knapman, J M** 'Vision Data Base: Requirements and Initial High Level Design' IBM UK Scientific Centre, Winchester, UK (April 1986)

2 **Blake, A and Mayhew, J E W** 'Alvey 2½D sketch project: Proposed structure for a development system' Department of Computer Science, University of Edinburgh, UK and A I Vision Research Unit, University of Sheffield, UK (November 1985)

3 **Ikeuchi, K** 'Recognition of 3-d objects using the extended Gaussian image' *Proc 7th IJCAI* Vancouver, B.C., Canada (1981) p 595

4 **Pentland, A P** 'Perceptual organization and the representation of natural form' Artificial Intelligence Center, SRI International, Menlo Park, CA, USA (1985)

5 **Langdon, P** Personal communication, A I Vision Research Unit, University of Sheffield, UK (1986)

6 **Koenderinck J J and van Doorn, A J** 'How the ambulant observer can construct a model of the environment from the geometrical structure of the visual inflow' in *Kybernetik* ed by Hausske, G and Butenandt, E, Oldenburg, Munich, W. Germany (1977)

7 **Martin, R R** 'Principle patches for computational geometry' Ph.D. thesis, Department of Engineering, University of Cambridge, UK (1982)

8 **Pridmore, T P, Bowen, J B and Mayhew, J E W** 'Geometrical description of the CONNECT Graph #2. The Geometrical Descriptor Base: A specification' A I Vision Research Unit ref no 012, University of Sheffield, UK

9 **Dupin, C.** 'Applications de géometrie et de méchanique' Bachelier, Paris, France (1822)

10 **Maxwell, J C** 1868 'On the cyclide' *Quarterly Journal of Pure and Applied Mathematics* vol IX (1868) p 111

11 **Cayley, A** 1873 'On the cyclide' *Quarterly Journal of Pure and Applied Mathematics* vol XII (1873) p 148

12 **Darboux, G** *La théorie générale des surfaces* Gautier - Villars, France (1887)

13 **Fisher, R** 'A proposal for a suggestive modeling system for object recognition' Working Paper, Department of Artificial Intelligence, University of Edinburgh, UK (November 1985)

14 **Knapman, J M** 'Dupin's Cyclide and the Cyclide Patch' UKSC Report number 156, IBM UK Scientific Centre, Winchester, UK (1986)

15 **Forsyth, A R** *Lectures on differential geometry of curves and surfaces*, Cambridge University Press, UK (1912)

16 **do Carmo, M P** *Differential Geometry of Curves and Surfaces* Prentice-Hall, Englewood Cliffs, NJ, USA (1976) pp 52,145,164

17 **Hicks, N J** *Notes on differential geometry*, van Nostrand, Princeton, NJ, USA (1965)

18 **Pridmore, T** Personal communication, A I Vision Research Unit, University of Sheffield, UK (1986)

19 **Quarendon, P** 'Winsom User's Guide' IBM U K Scientific Centre report no 123, St Clement St, Winchester, UK (August, 1984)

20 **Brady, M, Ponce, J, Yuille, A and Asada, H** Describing Surfaces' A I Memo 822, Massachusetts Institute of Technology, Artificial Intelligence Laboratory, Cambridge, Mass., USA (1985)

21 **Blake, A and Zisserman, A** 'Weak continuity constraints in computer vision' Internal Report CSR-197-86, Department of Computer Science, University of Edinburgh, UK (1986)

22 **de Pont, J J** 'Essays on the cyclide patch Ph.D. thesis, Department of Engineering, University of Cambridge, UK (1984)

23 **Blake, A** 'Specular Stereo' *Proc 9th IJCAI* Los Angeles, CA, USA (1985) p 973

[23] Interval-Based Geometric Reasoning in a Parallel Network

Mark J L Orr and Robert B Fisher

Department of Artificial Intelligence
University of Edinburgh, Edinburgh EH1 2QL, UK

Reprinted, with permission of Butterworth Scientific Ltd, from parts of *Image and Vision Computing*, 1987, **5**, 100-106 and *Image and Vision Computing*, 1988, **6**, 233-238

1. Introduction

Reasoning about geometry is a key process in visual perception. Not only is the discovery of geometric facts often the goal of a perceptual act (*where is the chair?*) but such facts can be used to aid the attainment of other goals such as identification (*this is a chair because it has four legs and a seat in all the right places*). A geometric reasoner inside a vision system is a kind of *quantity knowledge base* in the terms of (Davis 1987), receiving constraints from the vision system along with requests to draw inferences from them (*where in space is ...?, where in the image is ...?, can this be a ...?*).

The design of a geometric reasoner for computer vision can be split into three stages (Orr and Fisher 1987). The first stage consists in identifying the tasks to be delegated to the reasoner by the vision system. The second is the design of abstract data types and their associated operations which can carry out these tasks. The third and final stage is the design and testing of an implementation of the abstract types.

This paper reports our work using this method of design. In section 2 we discuss mainly tasks and abstract data types while also making reference to previous attempts at implementing geometric reasoning. The next section introduces a new parallel method of doing SUP/INF arithmetic which is the basis of our current implementation. Section 4 reveals how the reasoner was tailored to deal with the particular set of constraint types (which we catalogue) coming from our own vision system, or any similar, which uses 3D models and 3D data.

2. Tasks and Data Types

We divide geometric reasoning into three aspects: tasks, data types and implementation. The first aspect deals with the various tasks which seem appropriate for a vision system to delegate to a geometric reasoning package. The second involves the ideal data types and operations required in order to carry out these tasks and the third concerns the machinery of implementation.

Before proceeding we should mention that we make certain assumptions about the nature of the model and image entities used by the parent vision system. We assume that object models are built up from primitive geometric features (such as points, curves, surfaces and volumes) placed in a coordinate frame belonging to the model. We further assume that models are structured hierarchically, that is, complex models are built out of simpler ones by specifying the placing of the subcomponents in a frame pertaining to the aggregate. The key point about images is that they should contain entities which can correspond with the entities in the models at all levels: features (to correspond with model features), clusters of features (with simple models) and clusters of clusters of features (with complex models). How image segmentation into clusters is achieved or how model to image entity matches are hypothesised does not concern us here. We are also unconcerned whether the data is 2D or 3D: although the latter contains more information, the principles of geometric reasoning are the same for both.

Tasks

The nature of the geometric reasoning component within a vision system is characterised by the tasks which it is expected to carry out. Exactly which tasks come under the heading of geometric reasoning is debatable, but some stand out as obvious candidates. Included in these are establishing position estimates and image prediction.

Every identified feature in an image can be used to form position constraints, first because it is visible, and second by its measurable properties (location, shape, dimensions and so on). Take for example the identification of a point in the image with a point belonging to some object model. This hypothesis constrains the translation of the object in relation to the line of sight to the visible point, and some orientations of the object are excluded as they would cause the point to be obscured behind the object.

Having established a set of constraints on the position of a model from its individual features, the next step is to combine them into a single position estimate. The detection of inconsistent constraints is an important task here to eliminate false hypotheses (formed, for example, due to erroneous feature identifications). If a consistent estimate can be found it may contain degrees of freedom (especially if there is any rotational symmetry), or there may be more than one estimate (mirror symmetry).

In a similar way, position estimates for subcomponents have to be aggregated into an estimate for the parent object, but with one important difference. Since the subcomponent estimates refer to the placement of the subcomponents and not (as in the case of features) to the placement of the parent, the subcomponent estimates must first be transformed, using their known positions relative to the parent, into estimates for the parent object.

Having established a position estimate for an object the next step is to predict the appearance and location of its features. This allows a critical comparison between the predicted and observed features, and affords a basis for reasoning about occlusion effects. Additionally, image prediction can be used to search for features not already found in the image and to subsequently refine the position estimate of the object on the basis of any new information obtained. As an example, suppose an estimate of the position of a bicycle is obtained from the positions of two coplanar wheels at the correct distance apart, and then used to predict the location and appearance of the saddle and handle bars. Using this prediction, the image is then searched for these subcomponents with the following questions in mind: If found, are they where they should be and can they be used to refine the position already obtained from the wheels? If not found, can their absence be explained?

Two points need mentioning here which complicate matters. Firstly, predicted features are not necessarily pixel type entities. Although observed features are derived from pixel based information, they are normally described in terms of symbolic entities such as points, lines, surfaces and so on. Image prediction must be capable of handling both pixel and symbolic descriptions. Secondly, real images are formed from objects which have exact positions in the world, but prediction involves objects whose positions are only estimated and must reflect this by being able to form uncertain descriptions.

We now come to the second level of description of our geometric reasoner - the abstract data types and operations required in order to carry out the tasks outlined above.

Positions

The first and most obvious requirement is a data type for representing positions. Positions are traditionally represented by six independent quantities, three translational and three rotational. Unfortunately, this representation is not adequate for our purposes, for two reasons. Firstly, because we want to model objects which have flexible attachments, we need to be able to represent positions with degrees of freedom, and secondly, because a certain amount of uncertainty is present in image measurements we also wish to represent positions which are uncertain.

In what follows we will be giving some simple data type specifications (Guttag, Horowitz and Musser 1978) using the operators FRAME and PLACED (capital letters will be used for all operators). Both operate on members of the set Position and return members of the set Model. The latter includes the special 'models' World and Camera so that we can have world centered and viewer centered coordinate systems as well as relative positions between models. The functionality of FRAME and PLACED are written:

FRAME: Position $\rightarrow$ Model

PLACED: Position $\rightarrow$ Model

In other words, FRAME tells us which object the given position is with respect to and PLACED tells us what object is at the specified position.

Both FRAME and PLACED are termed *observer* functions because they reveal a single aspect of a multifaceted object. Other observer functions would reveal information about particular position parameters and would map to pairs of real numbers (to denote a permitted range) or perhaps to the mean and standard deviation of a Guassian probability distribution. In the next subsection we will introduce some *constructor* functions which generate instances of the Position data type from other types or from other positions.

Estimating Positions from Features

Each pairing of a model to a data feature produces constraints on the position of the model to which the feature belongs. We have then an operation, LOCATE, whose inputs are the model and image features:

LOCATE: Image_feature, Model_feature $\rightarrow$
  Position $\cup$ {undefined}
for all
  $f_i \in$ Image_Feature &
  $f_m \in$ Model_Feature:

  let p = LOCATE(f_i, f_m)
  if p $\neq$ undefined

    FRAME(p) = Camera &
    PLACED(p) = m

(f_m belongs to model m).

As well as the functionality of the LOCATE operator we have stated a rule which must always apply, *viz.* that LOCATE always places the model to which the feature belongs relative to the camera frame (because the geometric features of the image are in the Camera frame), unless an illegal pairing has been attempted, an image surface with a model edge for instance, when the result is undefined. The latter possibility shows why the range of the LOCATE function has to include the undefined object.

Merging Positions

In general models consists of more than just a single feature. A surface model, for instance, might consist of several curve features to represent its boundary and two vectors for its principle axes of curvature. If some or all of these features have been identified and produced constraints on the position of the surface then there must be some way of verifying consistency and merging the separate estimates into one.

Consequently, we need an operation MERGE which operates on a set of positions and returns a position. If #(Position) is the power set of Position (the set of all possible subsets of Position) then:

MERGE: #(Position) → Position ∪
{undefined, inconsistent}
for all m_1, m_2 ∈ Model, S ∈ #(Position):

if q ∈ S → FRAME(q) = m_1 &
PLACED(q) = m_2
then
let p = MERGE(S)
if p ≠ inconsistent

FRAME(p) = m_1 &
PLACED(p) = m_2

else MERGE(S) = undefined

The result is only defined when all the input positions have the same coordinate frame and refer to the same object. Another special device - the inconsistent object - is used to signal that the positions in S are contradictory, that is, when the intersection in 6D parameter space of the volumes corresponding to the elements of S is empty.

Transforming Position Constraints

Often we know the position of two objects relative to one another, perhaps because they are parts of the same model assembly or because there is *a priori* knowledge (e.g. the position of the camera in the world). Suppose we know the position of object A relative to object B, and consider two different problems. First, if we know the position of A in the frame of some other object C, what is the position of B in this frame? Second, if instead we know the position of C in A's frame, what is the position of C in B's frame? These problems require the operations TRANSFORM and INVERSE which obey the following rules in relation to the operators FRAME and PLACED.

TRANSFORM: Position, Position →
Position ∪ {undefined}

INVERSE: Position → Position
for all p, q ∈ Position:

let t = TRANSFORM(p, q)
if PLACED(p) = FRAME(q) then

FRAME(t) = FRAME(p)
PLACED(t) = PLACED(q)

else t = undefined
for all p ∈ Position:

let q = INVERSE(p)

FRAME(q) = PLACED(p) &
PLACED(q) = FRAME(p)

Now if we represent by X/Y a position whose FRAME is X and whose PLACED object is Y, our two problems can be written as:

First problem: know A/B and C/A, want C/B:

C/B = TRANSFORM(C/A, A/B)

Second problem: know A/B and A/C, want B/C:

B/C = TRANSFORM(INVERSE(A/B), A/C)

Image Prediction

Subsumed under the heading image prediction are a number of operations, ranging from the simple to the complex, and differing by what is being predicted. Simple predictions include feature properties (the projected length of an edge for example) and visibility (whether something can be seen). The most complicated prediction would be the whole image, pixel by pixel.

The operation to be performed in any given prediction task depends not only on the task but also on the nature of the object whose image is to be predicted. To predict whether a plane surface is front-facing merely requires the calculation of surface normal projected along the line of sight. For non-planar surfaces something more complicated has to be done. We abstract all such predictions into the operation PREDICT:

PREDICT: Model_feature, Position ->
Pred_feature

where Pred_feature is a separate data type from Image_feature because it must incorporate uncertainty due to positions which are only estimated.

Finally, we illustrate the use of the operators we have introduced. Suppose the vision system and the geometric reasoner together have hypothesised and located an object based on some subset of its constituent surfaces. The position of any of its surfaces can be obtained by TRANSFORMing the known (from the model) position of the surface relative to the object by the estimated position of the object relative to the camera. Suppose that one of the object's surfaces which has not yet been found, but whose position has been estimated, is PREDICTed to be visible. The vision system then conducts a search for this image feature. If it cannot be found then some explanation for its absence (e.g. occlusion) is required if the object hypothesis is to stand up. If it is present in the image, the LOCATE operator can estimate its position which can then be TRANSFORMed into a new estimate for the object position. The hypothesis can then fail if this estimate does not MERGE successfully with the original.

Review

Part of the motivation for an abstract specification of geometric reasoning is to make explicit the important implementation decisions. On the one hand, there may not be easy solutions to some of the problems posed in the specification. On the other, it might be possible to relax the requirements of the specification so as to permit a particular implementation solution but still retain an acceptable level of competence. Each practical system is made interesting by its own particular set of compromises between what is desired and what can be achieved. We next review some existing geometric reasoners, and discuss them in the light of the previous sections.

Our own vision system IMAGINE (see "The design of the IMAGINE II scene analysis program" in this volume) uses 3D image data and 3D models. Its current geometric reasoning engine is described below in sections 3 and 4. The old version used intervals for the six position parameters to represent uncertainty. MERGEs were done by intersecting the intervals. TRANSFORMs were achieved by partitioning the intervals, taking means, transforming each possible combination of six means by matrix multiplication and then finding the smallest rectangular box enclosing the transformed points in six dimensional parameter space. Problems were encountered with the use of slant and tilt for rotations because when zero was in the range of slant values the tilt became unbounded (we now use quaternions for representing rotations). Some of the problems with the old method were caused by the LOCATE operation which did not handle data errors well, could only operate on surface patches and required the location of the patch central point so that difficulties arose when a patch was partially occluded.

ACRONYM (Brooks 1981) is a vision system which uses 2D data and 3D model primitives. Positions are represented by variables, one for each of the six degrees of freedom. Constraints on positions are formed by relating expressions in the variables to uncertain quantities measured from the image. A constraint manipulation system (CMS) processed multiple constraints symbolically leading to bounds on the individual position parameters. The operations MERGE, TRANSFORM and PREDICT (sections 3.3, 3.4 and 3.5) were achieved by, respectively, unioning restriction sets, simplifying symbolic compositions of positions and bounding expressions in variables. Underpinning the geometric reasoner is SUP/INF or interval arithmetic which the current IMAGINE reasoner also uses although it is implemented differently and has certain advantages over ACRONYM (see section 3).

RAPT (Popplestone, Ambler and Bellos 1980) is an off-line programming language for planning robot assembly tasks. Embedded in RAPT is a geometric reasoner which takes assertions about the relative positions of bodies from the programming language and infers their Cartesian positions. In the programming language, relations are stated rather like a human might state them, e.g. *face 1 of body A is against face 2 of body B*. Internally, however, a relation is represented by a symbolic composition of translations and rotations which may involve variables to represent the unconstrained degrees of freedom. A graph is formed whose nodes are the bodies in the assembly task and whose arcs are the relations between the bodies. If at least two independent paths can be found between two nodes then there is an equation which relates two or more independent expressions for the body's position and some or all of the variables (degrees of freedom) can be eliminated. The difficulties with RAPT relations for our purposes are the absence of any mechanism for incorporating uncertainty and the restriction to relations which lead to algebraic equalities and not to inequalities.

In (Faugeras and Herbert 1983) models and images have features but are unstructured. The features (model and image) are planar surface patches characterised by surface normal and distance from the origin. The problem is to find the transformation that best maps the model features into the image features. It is interpreted as a least squares problem and elegantly solved by reducing it into the problem of finding the eigenvalues of a symmetric 3 by 3 matrix. Their work can be viewed as an implementation of the MERGE operator for a particular class of feature.

An alternative way of treating uncertain positions, reported by (Durrant-Whyte 1987) has come out of work in stochastic geometry (Harding and Kendall 1974) Durrant-Whyte tackles the problem of applying (exact) coordinate transformations to uncertain positions. Uncertainty is represented by a probability distribution in parameter space, and its functional form is chosen to be Gaussian because the transformation of a Gaussian distribution is also a Gaussian (though only to an approximation). Thus, all that is needed to specify an uncertain position are the mean parameter values and a variance-covariance matrix. The latter may be transformed by multiplication with the matrix representing the (exact) relation between the two coordinate frames. The method is not a full implementation of the TRANSFORM function since the transforming position must be exact.

3. A Network Implementation

Of the various implementation alternatives discussed above algebraic inequalities of the type used in the CMS of ACRONYM (Brooks 1981) have several desirable properties. They provide a uniform mechanism for a variety of relationships including *a priori* relationships (e.g. the position of the camera), and model variations (variable dimensions or flexible attachments). Such constraints involve known (observable) and unknown quantities and estimates are sought for the unknowns. To find such estimates the CMS symbolically combined and simplified multiple constraints until the expressions they bound reduced to single quantifiers. This had drawbacks of a high cost for symbolic processing and an inability to properly handle non-linear constraints. Below we describe a new implementation of this method which confronts these problems.

The basic constraint solving method we use is Bledsoe's SUP-INF algorithm (Bledsoe 1975), later refined by Shostak (Shostak 1977) and Brooks (Brooks 1981). Constraints are expressed in the form:

$$x_i \le f_i$$

or

$$x_i \ge g_i$$

where the x_i are members of a set $\{x_1, x_2, ... x_n\}$ of variables and f_i and g_i are values or expressions involving some or all of the x_i. A solution of the constraints would be a substitution of real values for the variables that maintained the truth of each inequality. The goal of the algorithm, for a given set of constraints, is:

(1) to decide whether the set of possible solutions is empty,

(2) to find bounds on the value that a given expression (involving some or all of the x_i) can attain over the solution set.

The algorithm is based on the recursive application of the functions SUP and INF on the expression to be bound and its sub-expressions. SUP returns an upper bound (supremum) and INF a lower bound (infimum). In Brooks' (Brooks 1981) program the simplification of constraints and the application of SUP and INF was handled by symbolic manipulation at run time. We present a new implementation of the SUP-INF method that transfers the cost of symbolic manipulation from run-time to compile-time, improves the performance of the algorithm for non-linear constraints and has a natural parallel structure.

Structure of the network

The implementation has the structure of a network with nodes and connections. There are two types of nodes: value nodes and operation nodes. The value nodes acquire numerical SUP and INF bounds on their associated algebraic variable or expression. The bounds are computed from connections with other value nodes or with operation nodes that receive inputs from other value or operation nodes. Each time new bounds are computed the change propagates over the network causing other nodes to acquire new bounds. The changes become smaller as the bounds get closer and the network converges asymptotically to a stable state when the desired bounds on variables or expressions of interest can be extracted from the associated value nodes.

Operation nodes implement a simple unary or binary function and take their inputs from value nodes and other operation nodes. The operators implemented are: {"+", "-", "*", "/", "sup_of_max", "sup_of_min", "inf_of_max", "inf_of_min", "extract_sup", "extract_inf", "constant", "cos", "sin", "sqrt", "<", "≤", ">", "≥", "and", "or", "select", and "enable"}.

Network Creation

A network is constructed by linking together several network fragments or modules. Each module represents a particular instance of a common constraint type and there may be more than one module of the same type in the network. The structure of modules is defined by an off-line compilation process. Consequently, an on-line program that uses the network, such as a geometric reasoner, only has to connect instances of the appropriate modules to solve the problem at hand.

A module is compiled from a list of algebraic inequalities such as:

$$x \le y + z$$

The inequalities are written by a human programmer after due consideration of the 'problem' that the module 'solves'. An example from geometric reasoning is finding the rotation that maps one pair of direction vectors to another. The relations between all the variables occurring in the problem are expressed as inequalities. If an equality is encountered then it is split into two inequalities:

$x = \text{expr}$ becomes:

$x \le \text{expr}$ & $x \ge \text{expr}$

If a product is encountered, then it is split into four inequalities involving the signed reciprocal ('srecip') function:

$x * y \le z$ becomes:

$$x \le z * \text{srecip}(y)$$

$$y \le z * \text{srecip}(x)$$

$$x \ge -z * \text{srecip}(-y)$$

$$y \ge -z * \text{srecip}(-x)$$

This function has the definition:

srecip(x) = if x > 0 then 1/x
else 'undefined'

and consequently has the effect of turning off and on constraints according to the sign of its argument. Explicit conditionals are also possible such as:

if (z == 0) then $x \le y$

so that the constraint $x \le y$ is only turned on if z is zero (meaning $\text{INF}(z) \le 0 \le \text{SUP}(z)$).

Recursive constraints are allowed such as:

$$x^2 \ge 1 - y^2$$

which becomes:

$$x \ge (1 - y^2) * \text{srecip}(x)$$

$$x \le (y^2 - 1) * \text{srecip}(-x)$$

but are treated differently by bound simplification (see below).

A parallel network based case construction is needed because some operations produce different output according to conditions on their input. Two special operation types were used to implement the case structure. One is the 'enable' operation, a function of a test argument and a result argument whose output is the result only if the test is true. The other is the 'select' operation that returns the first of its arguments to become defined. Using these, the 'enable' operation turns on and off results according to their applicability (as determined by the test argument), and the 'select' operation passes through the "true" value. The logical value of the test argument is generated by using a numerical comparison operator (e.g. "<") or a logical operator (e.g. "and").

Ordinarily, an operator will not be evaluated until all arguments have values. This causes problems when using the operators that may not evaluate, such as the 'srecip' function. A problem also occurs at initial startup, because not all operators have all arguments ready, which may block the evaluation of other nodes, which may in turn block the evaluation of the operator, resulting in deadlock. The problem occurs often because the bounds on value nodes are "max" and "min" operators of (typically) many arguments.

To solve this problem, the "max" and "min" operators are evaluated differently according to whether the SUP or INF is desired. The "sup_of_max" ("inf_of_min") operator does not evaluate until all arguments are ready, because increasing the upper (decreasing the lower) bound may be necessary as other arguments become ready, and the SUP (INF) bound is only allowed to decrease (increase). However, the "inf_of_max" ("sup_of_min") operator can evaluate when one argument is ready, because later arguments either have no effect or improve the bound.

Symbolic Manipulation

Before compiling the network, the list of inequalities is checked for correct syntax, simplified and processed by the functions SUP and INF. In general this is a hard problem but the constraint manipulation system (CMS) of Brooks' program ACRONYM (Brooks 1981) at least provides some competence. We have extended this CMS to cope with square roots, powers of variables, the unsigned reciprocal function, conditionals, the undefined value and 'minus'!

Simplification is only applied to non-recursive constraints where the variable on the left hand side of the inequality does not appear anywhere in the right hand side. Recursive constraints are difficult to handle and if simplified would generally just lead to the trivial:

$$-\infty \leq x \leq +\infty$$

The CMS could be used directly (as in ACRONYM) by the on-line program. Measurements made by the program would add new constraints providing more scope for simplification and eventually to bounds on variables and expressions that are not measured directly. However, symbolic reasoning is computationally expensive and not suited to wide scale parallelism.

A more compelling reason for using a network is that it can iterate to better bounds over non-linear constraints than the single pass method of the CMS. Consider the following example.

$$x \leq 1 + 1/y$$

$$y \geq 1 + 1/x$$

$$0.1 \leq x \leq 10$$

$$0.1 \leq y \leq 10$$

The CMS (somewhat simplified) finds:

$$SUP(x) = 1 + 1/INF(y)$$

$$= 1 + 1/(1 + 1/SUP(x))$$

When it gets to the embedded SUP(x) it uses the numerical bound 10 to produce:

$$SUP(x) = 1 + 1/(1 + 1/10)$$

$$= 1.91$$

However the network computation iterates to the (analytically) best bound:

$$SUP(x) = 1.62$$

$$= (1 + \sqrt{5})/2$$

Network Compilation

Value nodes are created for all variables occurring in the constraint list. These are connected by various operator nodes that extract values from value nodes or other operators. The connections are determined by the expressions found in the constraints. The following is a list of the actions taken by the compiler when it encounters the specified expression type:

constant:
An operation node (with no inputs) is created that supplies the given constant.

variable:
An operation node is created that extracts the SUP (or INF) of the associated value node.

plus: An operation node is created that adds the results of the recursively compiled sub-expressions.

max (or min):
SUP(max(list)) is compiled to be max(SUP(list)) (analogously for INF and 'min'). Thus subfragments for each sub-expression in the list are created and linked to a series of connected binary 'max' (or 'min') nodes. Network evaluation is different for max (or min) nodes created from SUP or INF in their use of defaults when not all argu-

ments are evaluated (which may arise from timing delays or alternative expressions being undefined). The INF max function returns a value if at least one argument is evaluated; the SUP max function only returns a value when all arguments are evaluated.

times:

SUP(A*B) is expanded to:

max(INF(A) * INF(B),
INF(A) * SUP(B),
SUP(A) * INF(B),
SUP(A) * SUP(B))

and then compiled. The same for INF(A*B) except 'max' is replaced by 'min'.

recip(E) (where E is an expression):

A test-case node is required for the reciprocal function. Test-case nodes select their output according to a test defined at compile-time and carried out at run-time. If SUP is the desired bound, the test-case construction is:

if INF(E)>0 or SUP(E)<0

then 1/INF(E)

else plus_infinity

If INF is the desired bound then:

if INF(E)>0 or SUP(E)<0

then 1/SUP(E)

else minus_infinity

srecip(E) (where E is an expression):

This is the signed reciprocal function where:

srecip(x) = if x > 0 then 1/x
else 'undefined'

If SUP is the desired bound, a test-case node is created selecting:

if INF(E)>0

then 1/INF(E)

else 'undefined'

If INF is the desired bound then the test-case construction is:

if INF(E) > 0

then 1/SUP(E)

else 'undefined'

v^n (where v is a variable and n is odd):

A sequence of 'times' operation nodes are created and linked to the SUP (or INF) of the variable. The output of each 'times' operation becomes the input to the next.

v^n (where v is a variable and n is even):

If SUP is the desired bound then sequences of 'times' nodes are created and linked to both the INF and SUP of the variable and a final 'max' node linked to the output of each sequence. If INF is the desired bound then a 'test-case' node is created selecting:

if SUP(v) < 0

then $[SUP(v)]^n$

else if INF(v) > 0

then $[INF(v)]^n$

else 0

square_root(E) (where E is an expression):

The positive square root is assumed. If SUP is the desired bound then:

if SUP(E) ≥ 0

then sqrt(SUP(E))

else 'undefined'

If INF is the desired bound:

if INF(E) ≥ 0

then sqrt(INF(E))

else 'undefined'

As the same expressions may be used more than once in different constraints in the same module, the recursive compiler uses a previous compilation for a expression if one exists, thus avoiding duplication. Another simplification is the reduction of multiple constraints to a single 'min' or 'max' function:

$v \leq E_1$, $v \leq E_2$, ... becomes:

$v \leq \min(E_1, E_2, ...)$

A similar simplification is performed for lower bounds using the 'max' function.

To illustrate the creation of a network module, suppose we are interested in the 'problem':

$A \leq B - C$

which entails the further constraints:

$B \geq A + C$

$C \leq B - A$

This list of constraints would be the input to the CMS, that would have little to simplify but would recursively apply the SUP and INF functions symbolically to find:

SUP(A) = SUP(B) - INF(C)

INF(B) = INF(A) + INF(C)

SUP(C) = SUP(B) - INF(A)

The compiler then produces the network shown in figure 1. This is a trivial example that even fails to compute both bounds on the parameters involved. In practice (see section 3) modules are larger and more complicated.

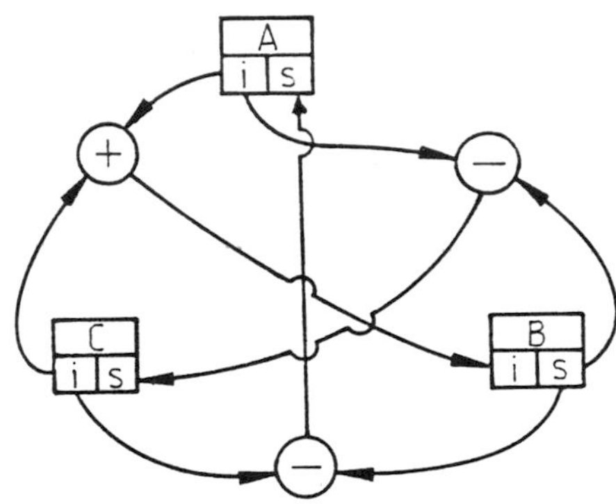

Figure 1: the network for $A \leq B - C$.

Modularisation

The run-time program constructs and evaluates its own networks according to the problems it is presented with. We assume that problems can be broken down into several parts each of which can be managed by an instance of some previously compiled module. Suppose we have the following two constraints:

$x \leq y - z$

$y \leq z - w$

A network for this problem would be constructed out of two instances of the module defined above for the constraint type:

$A \leq B - C$

and connected as shown in figure 2. The modules can be thought of as black boxes with connections to the outside world. For the first constraint the connections A->x, B->y and C->z are made, while for the second constraint A->y, B->z and C->w.

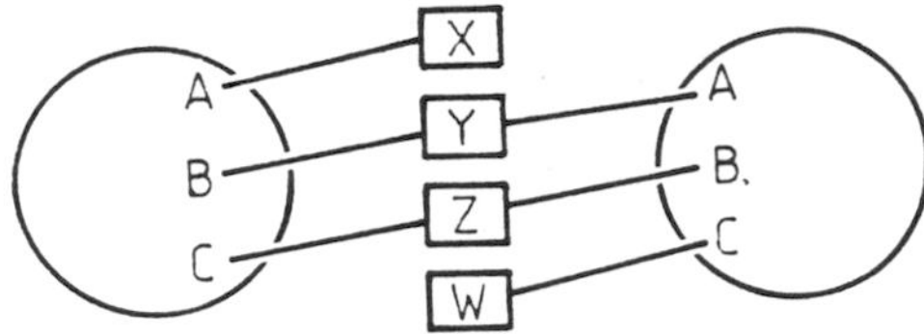

Figure 2: two connected modules.

Network Evaluation

The values at each node are computed using the values at the connecting nodes. The SUP (INF) computation chooses the minimum (maximum) of each of its current bounds and its current value. Including the current value in the calculation ensures that bounds can only get tighter. Thus if:

$SUP(A) \leq a_1$, $SUP(A) \leq a_2$, ...

then:

$SUP(A_{t+1}) = \min(SUP(A_t), a_1, a_2, ...)$

is the updating function for the supremum of A from time t to time t+1.

The following defines the evaluation functions for the different operation types:

constant:
returns a constant value

extract_sup (extract_inf):
returns the SUP (INF) of the referenced value

plus:
returns a result if both arguments are initialised:
if $+\infty + +\infty$, then return $+\infty$
if $-\infty + -\infty$, then return $-\infty$
if $+\infty + -\infty$, then indeterminate
if $-\infty + +\infty$, then indeterminate
if only one argument is infinite then return it
otherwise return the sum of arguments

minus:
returns a result if both arguments are initialised:
if $+\infty - +\infty$, then indeterminate
if $-\infty - -\infty$, then indeterminate
if $+\infty - -\infty$, then return $+\infty$
if $-\infty - +\infty$, then $-\infty$
if only the first argument is infinite then return it
if only the second argument is infinite then return its negative
otherwise return the difference of arguments

times:

returns a result if both arguments are initialised:
if one argument is $+\infty$ and the other is > 0, then return $+\infty$
if one argument is $+\infty$ and the other is $= 0$, then return 0
if one argument is $+\infty$ and the other is < 0, then return $-\infty$
if one argument is $-\infty$ and the other is > 0, then return $-\infty$
if one argument is $-\infty$ and the other is $= 0$, then return 0
if one argument is $-\infty$ and the other is < 0, then return $+\infty$
otherwise return product of arguments

recip:

returns a result if the argument is initialised:
if argument is $\pm\infty$, then return 0
if $0 <$ argument $< +\varepsilon$, then return $+\infty$
if $-\varepsilon <$ argument < 0, then return $-\infty$ otherwise return 1/argument

sup_of_max:

returns the largest of the arguments if both initialised

sup_of_min:

returns the largest of any initialised arguments

inf_of_max:

returns the smallest of any initialised arguments

inf_of_min:

returns the smallest of the arguments if both initialised

sqrt:

returns a result if the argument is initialised and greater than or equal to0:
if argument is $+\infty$, then return $+\infty$
otherwise return $\sqrt{(\text{argument})}$

cos (sin):

returns a result if the argument is initialised:
if argument is $\pm\infty$, then indeterminate
otherwise return cos(argument) (sin(argument))

greater:

returns a result if both arguments are initialised:
if first argument is $-\infty$, then return false
if second argument is $-\infty$, then return true
if first argument is $+\infty$, then return true
if second argument is $+\infty$, then return false
if first argument > second argument, then return true
otherwise return false
(similarly for *greatereq, less, lesseq*)

and:

returns a result if both arguments are initialised:
if both arguments are true, then return true
otherwise return false

or:

returns a result if at least one argument is initialised:
if the first argument is not initialised, then return the second
if the second argument is not initialised, then return the first
if either argument is true, then return true
otherwise return false

enable:

returns the value argument if both arguments are initialised and the test argument is true

select:

returns the value of any initialised argument (arbitrary if more than one).

The networks of modules are designed to be evaluated in parallel. The whole network could be evaluated synchronously or asynchronously in a MIMD processor with non-local connectivity. Ideally, each node would be stored in a separate processor, continually polling its inputs and updating its output if appropriate.

So far we only simulate the network serially. To increase efficiency each node contains a list of its dependent nodes and when its value changes its dependents are put on a 'pending evaluation' list. When the change at a node drops below a preset threshold its dependent nodes no longer require re-evaluation. When the pending evaluation list is empty the network has reached a stable state and processing can stop. Alternatively, the network stops when inconsistency is detected when a pair of bounds cross over (the SUP of some value node becomes lower than its INF).

It is easy to show that the networks must converge asymtotically, that is, not oscillate. At any time when a new bound becomes available for some variable V, if it is a larger upper bound than the current SUP or a smaller lower bound than the current INF then it has no effect, as it makes no sense to increase the range of potential values for V. As the bounds can at most be equal (inconsistency is declared if they cross), each bound has a limit so must converge. In practice, when the change in a value is below a threshold, no change is recorded, thus forcing finite termination. Further details can be found in (Fisher 1987b).

Implementing the Geometric Reasoning Functions

The TRANSFORM function is implemented as a network module. Looked at as a black box, it has three sets of ports to the outside world representing three positions (18 parameters in total): the position being transformed, the transforming position and the resulting position. When operating in the context of an evaluating network, if any two of the sets of ports receive bounds from outside, the module will reflect the new situation by setting new bounds on the third set of ports. The INVERSE function can be implemented using TRANSFORM and the 'bi-directional' nature of network modules. Recall the second of the two problems relating to TRANSFORM and INVERSE which were discussed in section 2:

Second problem: we know A/B and A/C and want B/C:

B/C = TRANSFORM(INVERSE(A/B), A/C)

(X/Y = the position of Y relative to X)

By rearranging we can eliminate the INVERSE function:

A/C = TRANSFORM(A/B, B/C)

Now if we set up a TRANSFORM module for this problem, because of bi-directionality, it does not matter which of the three positions are constrained the other(s) will be forced into agreement by evaluation. In particular, we can always generate constraints on B/C given constraints on A/B and A/C.

In general we cannot always achieve the elimination of INVERSE, for example if:

We know A/B and B/C and want C/A, then:

C/A = INVERSE(TRANSFORM(A/B, B/C))

and rearranging will not remove the INVERSE operator. In this case we must use the identity position (I) and solve the problem with two linked TRANSFORM modules implementing the relation:

I = TRANSFORM(
TRANSFORM(A/B, B/C), C/A)

The MERGE function is carried out at the nodes linking the ports from different modules. Each port is 'saying something' about the bounds on some variable and if two or more ports are linked then they either agree (the bounds intersect and the intersection improves the estimate) or disagree. In the latter case, an inconsistency has been detected - precisely what the MERGE function was designed to do.

The functionalities of LOCATE and PREDICT, unlike the other operations, depend on the types of models and image entities used by the vision system. We therefore postpone discussion of these operators until the next section when we discuss a particular vision system.

Example

We illustrate the foregoing with an example of estimating an object's 3D orientation. Assume the following (exact) model direction vectors

$\underline{m}_1$ = (-0.51, 0.83, 0.22)
$\underline{m}_2$ = (0.68,-0.23, 0.69)

are rotated rigidly by rotation Q to give the vectors Q($\underline{m}_1$) and Q($\underline{m}_2$). Then, assume we observe two (exact) data vectors

$\underline{d}_1$ = (-0.40, 0.91, 0.04)
$\underline{d}_2$ = (-0.52,-0.67, 0.51)

Because these vectors are exact, it can be shown analytically that the rotation (represented as a quaternion) which maps $\underline{m}_1$ and $\underline{m}_2$ into $\underline{d}_1$ and $\underline{d}_2$ is:

Q = (0.73, 0.25,-0.62,-0.14)

Now suppose (more realistically) that we observe *uncertain* data vectors

$\underline{d}_1$ =

Low	(-0.450, 0.892,-0.005)
High	(-0.359, 0.932, 0.095)

$\underline{d}_2$ =

Low	(-0.566,-0.711, 0.476)
High	(-0.481,-0.637, 0.561)

These are the above exact vectors with ε = 0.05 radians isotropic error added. Evaluating a network which consists of a single module for transforming a pair of vectors (see section 4) the following bounds are achieved on the rotation:

Q =

Low	(0.674, 0.177,-0.761,-0.209)
High	(0.784, 0.342,-0.497,-0.087)

The result required 46 network update cycles with an average of 85 operation node evaluations per cycle. In a true parallel implementation (we can only simulate) the node evaluations in each cycle can be done in parallel. As ε increases the bounds on Q diverge, while as ε tends to zero the bounds converge and the solution approaches the analytic result.

If we had had three pairs of vectors instead of just two, there would be three different ways of pairing them and therefore the network for this constraint would consist of three modules. This is illustrated schematically in figure 3 where the modules are the boxes labelled "(2,0)" (the name is due to the module transforming two directions and no locations - see section 4) and the circles are the linking external variables with "Q" representing the rotation parameters.

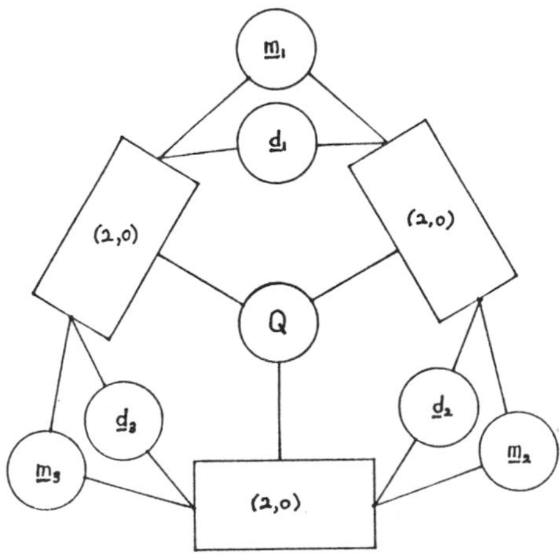

Figure 3: the network structure for three pairs of vectors.

In general for *n* matched pairs of vectors there are *(n-1)n/2* different pairings and the complexity of the corresponding network is of order n^2. Tests have revealed the existence of at least one heuristic which can be used to reduce the complexity, which is to discard the pairings of matched vectors which have the high uncertainty.

Related Work

The use of algebraic inequalities to represent geometric constraints derives from Brooks' ACRONYM (Brooks 1981), as does the symbolic constraint manipulation methods. The network computation is similar to the many relaxation or constraint satisfaction algorithms that are suitable for parallel processing. However, it differs from the relaxation algorithms in that it is not a probabilistic labelling computation and from constraint satisfaction in that there is reduction of an infinite continuous range of values rather than selection from a finite set of discrete values. While the network relies on connections between units, the computation is not in the distributed connectionist form where the results are expressed as states of the network. Instead, the results are the values current at selected processors.

The work presented here differs significantly from two other network based geometric reasoning systems. Hinton and Lang (1985) learned and deduced positions of 2D patterns using a distributed connectionist network, whose intermediate nodes represented object position and gated connections between iconic image and model representations. Ballard and Tanaka (1985) demonstrated a 3D reasoning network whose nodes represent instances of parameter values and whose connections represent consistency according to model-determined algebraic relationships. In both cases, patterns of network activity result, with the dominant pattern accepted as the answer (unlike here, where the result is explicit). Both systems also simultaneously select a model, which is treated separately in our analysis.

Davis (Davis 1987) has classified the types of constraint propagation systems. The system described here is an interval label constraint machine applied over full algebraic constraints (with some transcendental operations). It is used for geometric reasoning without dependence on "sin" and "cos" because rotations are represented by quaternions. His complexity analysis indicates execution times may be doubly exponential and termination may not even occur (unless forced by truncating small changes, as is done here).

Here, the complexity does not appear to be a problem, with execution time of the order of network size, presumably due to the truncation of small changes. Davis also raises the problem of disjoint parameter intervals. We believe the geometry understanding embedded in the vision program will detect most cases of this in advance (e.g. will know about n-fold symmetry) and create separate hypotheses with only single intervals.

4. 3D Models and 3D Images

In the previous section it has been shown how, with the aid of a special module for transforming positions, SUP/INF networks can be constructed which implement the geometric reasoning operators TRANSFORM, INVERSE and MERGE and the data type Position. It remains to be shown how the remaining operators, LOCATE and PREDICT, can be implemented. These operators depend on the type of models and image data used by the vision system. Our own system has 3D models (Fisher 1986 and "SMS: a suggestive modeling system for object recognition" in this volume) and 3D images and the implementation of these operators for this and similar systems is the subject of this section. For 2D images, in ACRONYM for example (Brooks 1981), the operators must account for projection from the camera frame onto the image plane as well as transformations from the model frames to the camera frame.

General Constraints

Since we are dealing with 3D geometric entities the general position constraint from a match between a model feature and an image feature involves *m* matched directions and *n* matched points. However, since any two points are equivalent to a single point and one direction, an (m, n>1) constraint can always be reduced to (m+n-1, 1) by pairing up points. Further, since two directions are sufficient to constrain rotation, an (m>2, n) constraint can be split into m(m-1)/2 separate (2, n) constraints (or less if we use heuristics). Consequently, we lose no generality if we only have network modules for the constraints (1, 0), (0, 1), (1, 1), (2, 0) and (2, 1). Three matched vectors and three matched points, for example, would be dealt with by ten (2, 1) modules linked together. There is a lot of redundancy in such a constraint but in the presence of noise the redundancy helps.

An important point to note is that two linked modules representing constraints (m_1, n_1) and (m_2, n_2) are not, in general, equivalent to one module representing the constraint (m_1+m_2, n_1+n_2). The equivalence only exists when the separate constraints are individually sufficient to fully constrain the unknown quantity. For example, for PREDICT, two (1, 0) constraints are equivalent to one (2, 0) constraint because a rotated vector is completely determined by the rotation and the vector to be rotated. However, for LOCATE, a single pair of matched vectors is not sufficient to fully constrain the rotation and so the equivalence no longer holds. Curiously, a (2, 1) module *is* equivalent to linked (2, 0) and (0, 1) modules, even though neither fully constrains position. This works because rotation is fully constrained by the (2, 0) module from which it can be 'exported' to the (0, 1) module where it combines with the pair of matched points to fully constrain translation. More details can be found in (Orr 1987a).

Thus, to summarise, we can cope with any (m, n) position constraint with some combination of four types of module: (1, 0), (0, 1), (1, 1), (2, 0). For geometric reasoning we need these four modules plus the module implementing the TRANSFORM and INVERSE operators as discussed in section 3. The number of operation nodes in each of these modules is listed in table 1.

For illustration the mathematics underlying one of the modules, the (0, 1) module (transformation of a location), is given in an appendix. Other less crucial modules may also be defined, such as those dealing with isotropic errors (location spheres, direction cones) (Fisher 1987a).

Table 1	
Module	Nodes
(1, 0)	1704
(0, 1)	1080
(1, 1)	3016
(2, 0)	3155
TRANSFORM	2088

Table 2		
Feature	Constraint	Symmetry
points	(1, 0)	none
curves		
lines	(0, 2)	2-fold
circular arc	(2, 1)	2-fold
ellipses	(2, 1)	4-fold
surface patches		
plane	(1, 0)	none
cylinder	(1, 0)	2-fold
cone	(1, 1)	none
torus	(1, 1)	none
volumes		
stick	(1, 1)	2-fold
bent stick	(1, 2)	2-fold
plate	(1, 1)	2-fold
bent plate	(1, 1)	none
blob	(3, 1)	8-fold

Particular Constraints

Our implementation of the operators LOCATE and PREDICT uses a catalogue of constraints from all legal pairings between model and image features. For each pairing the catalogue lists:

1) what vectors to extract from the model,
2) what vectors to extract from the image,
3) what modules to use, how they link to the vectors and how they link with each other.

In PREDICTing, the position of the model (in the Camera frame) is known while some of the data vectors are not. The opposite is true for the LOCATE operator - the vectors are known and an estimate is sought for the position. The same network solves both problems because it is inherently 'bi-directional'.

Table 2 lists legal pairings of features in our modeling system with image features, their constraint types and possible rotation ambiguities. Note that the boundaries of a surface patch are not part of the patch feature but separate features themselves.

Ambiguities are caused by n-fold symmetric features and are handled by the vision system (rather than the geometric reasoner) by the creation of n-fold multiple hypotheses. Each hypothesis receives a position estimate, the wrong ones are eventually eliminated by the lack of other hypotheses with which they can MERGE. More details are in (Orr 1987b) which includes some discussion of isotropic data errors and methods of overcoming partial occlusion.

5. Conclusions

The methodology we have investigated is summarised here. We start with sets of algebraic constraints associated with particular geometric relationships. (For reasoning with 3D models and 3D images there seem to be at least five of these: the four vector combination transformations of section 4 and the position transformation of section 3.) Image observables are represented by variables at this stage. These constraints are then processed by a CMS to produce symbolic bounds on each variable. The bounds are compiled into a network module where the structure of the module reflects the structure of the expressions for the bounds. All the foregoing is an off-line process and need not be repeated unless new relationships or constraints are added. The on-line program solves geometric problems with networks created by connecting compiled modules together according to the structure of each problem. When observable variables get bound to measured values the other variables (position or model parameters) are forced into consistency by evaluating the networks.

ACRONYM's CMS was optimal when producing numerical bounds on single variables over sets of linear constraints. Since we reproduce the symbolic reasoning in the network, only substituting data values later, the network must have the same performance over linear constraint sets. Over non-linear constraints, as we have here, we cannot expect optimality, but our extensions to the CMS and iterative evaluation in the network improve the performance.

The SUP/INF method is only a partial decision procedure in the sense that although consistent data will always lead to a consistent network, inconsistent data can occasionally also lead to a consistent network. We are currently engaged in evaluating the importance of this limitation and preliminary results suggest if the data errors are low (less than about 10%) or if there is enough data to over constrain the problem then the likelyhood of reaching a consistent network state with an inconsistent set of data is small (about 10% or less). Probably these 10% of incorrect evaluations involve data which is 'nearly consistent', although we have yet to demonstrate this.

We intend to apply the network formulation to the problem of camera calibration by compiling a module to do simultaneous equation solving. The coefficients in the equations will depend on the uncertain components of matched points in space and in the image and the variables will be the camera parameters. The key question will be the extent to which errors in the reference points are magnified in the camera parameters.

Further work is required to analyse the constraints from feature matches in which a parameterised range of model vectors corresponds to a measured image vector. This often occurs when a feature is partially obscured (e.g. a circular arc whose endpoints are not visible). Such constraints are only important for heavily obscured objects where there are few alternative constraints.

References

Ballard, D. and Tanaka, H., 1985, "Transformational Form Perception in 3D: Constraints, Algorithms and Implementation", Proc. 9th Int. Joint Conf. on Artif. Intel., p964.

Brooks, R.A., 1981, "Symbolic reasoning among 3-D models and 2-D images", Artificial Intelligence, **17**, p285.

Davis, E., 1987, "Constraint Propagation with Interval Labels", Artificial Intelligence, **32**, p281.

Durrant-Whyte, H.F., 1987, "Uncertain geometry in robotics", Proceedings of the IEEE Conference on Robotics and Automation, vol.2, p851.

Faugeras, O.D. and Hebert, H., 1983, "A 3-D recognition and positioning algorithm using geometrical matching between primitive surfaces", IJCAI Proceedings, p996.

Fisher, R.B, 1986, "SMS - a suggestive modeling system for object recognition", Image and Vision Computing, **5**, p98.

Fisher, R.B, 1987a, "Solving algebraic constraints in a parallel network, as applied to geometric reasoning", Working paper No. 205, Department of Artificial Intelligence, Edinburgh University.

Fisher, R.B, 1987b, "Details of a network engine for algebraic and geometric reasoning", Working paper (forthcoming), Department of Artificial Intelligence, Edinburgh University.

Guttag, J.V., Horowitz, E. and Musser, D.R., 1978, "The design of data type specifications", in "Current trends in programming methodology", IV, (Ed. Yeh, R.), Prentice-Hall.

Harding, E.F. and Kendall, D.G., 1974, "Stochastic Geometry", Wiley.

Hinton, G. and Lang, K., 1985, "Shape recognition and illusory conjunctions", Proc. 9th Int. Joint Conf. on Artif. Intel., p252.

Orr, M.J.L., 1987a, "Coordinate transforms using quaternions", Working Paper No. 204, Department of Artificial Intelligence, University of Edinburgh.

Orr, M.J.L., 1987b, "Geometric constraints in 3D computer vision", Working Paper No. 203, Department of Artificial Intelligence, University of Edinburgh.

Orr, M.J.L. and Fisher, R.B., 1987, "Geometric Reasoning for Computer Vision", Image and Vision Computing, **5**, p233.

Popplestone, R.J., Ambler, A.P. and Bellos, I.M., 1980, "An interpreter for a language describing assemblies", Artificial Intelligence, **14**, p79.

Appendix

Here, for illustration, we write out the mathematics underlying one of the geometric reasoning modules and briefly describe the modifications necessary to enable its compilation into a module. The module is for transforming a single location vector by a position P. We use quaternions (in bold letters) and vectors (underlined). If **q** is a quaternion then q_0 is its scalar part and $\underline{q}$ its vector part. "*" and "'" stand for the quaternion operations of, respectively, multiplication and conjugation (where the sign of the vector part is reversed). Let:

$$P = (\mathbf{r}, \mathbf{t})$$

where:

r is a unit quaternion (the rotation)

t is a pure vector ($t_0 = 0$) (the translation)
and let:

u be the untransformed vector ($u_0 = 0$)

v be the transformed vector ($v_0 = 0$)
then:

$$\mathbf{v} = \mathbf{r} * \mathbf{u} * \mathbf{r}' + \mathbf{t} \quad \text{(A1)}$$

It follows from equation A1 that:

$$\mathbf{t} = \mathbf{v} - \mathbf{r} * \mathbf{u} * \mathbf{r}' \quad \text{(A2)}$$

$$\mathbf{u} = \mathbf{r}' * (\mathbf{v} - \mathbf{t}) * \mathbf{r} \quad \text{(A3)}$$

$$(\mathbf{v} - \mathbf{t}) * \mathbf{r} = \mathbf{r} * \mathbf{u}$$

From this last equation we deduce that:

$$\underline{r}.\underline{u} = \underline{r}.(\underline{v} - \underline{t}) \quad \text{(A4)}$$

$$q_0(\underline{v} - \underline{t} - \underline{u}) = \underline{q} \times (\underline{v} - \underline{t} + \underline{u}) \quad \text{(A5)}$$

Equations A1-5 constitute the underlying mathematics for the module. To prepare this as input to the network compiler the following must be done:

1) write each vector (quaternion) equation as three (four) separate scalar equations,

2) for product expressions on the left hand side take one subexpression to the right hand side operated on by *srecip* or *recip*,

3) replace each scalar equation by two equivalent inequalities (≤ and ≥),

For example, equation A5 is a vector equation, the first component of which is:

$$q_0(v_1 - t_1 - u_1) = q_2(u_3 + v_3 - t_3) - q_3(u_2 + v_2 - t_2)$$

Since the sign of $(v_1 - t_1 - u_1)$ is not known *a priori* we use the *srecip* function and write:

$$q_0 = (q_2(u_3 + v_3 - t_3) - q_3(u_2 + v_2 - t_2)) *$$
$$\text{srecip}(v_1 - t_1 - u_1)$$

$$q_0 = (q_3(u_2 + v_2 - t_2) - q_2(u_3 + v_3 - t_3)) *$$
$$\text{srecip}(t_1 + u_1 - v_1)$$

Finally, these two equations are replaced by four inequalities.

[24] SMS: A Suggestive Modeling System for Object Recognition

Robert B Fisher

Department of Artificial Intelligence
University of Edinburgh, Edinburgh EH1 2QL, UK

Reprinted, with permission of Butterworth Scientific Ltd, from *Image and Vision Computing,* 1987, **5**, 98-104.

1. Introduction

SMS [4,6] is an object representation system motivated by the requirements of recognition instead of depiction. It is designed for model invocation, reference frame estimation and matching (roughly as in IMAGINE [5], only with many extensions). It represents strongly visible features and relationships of non-polyhedral man-made objects, integrating curve, surface and volumetric structural descriptions in a subcomponent hierarchy.

The central principles of the modeling philosophy are:

- The models are suggestive rather than literal. By suggestive, we mean that: (1) surface shapes and volumes may be only approximate, (2) only salient features will be modeled, omitting minor or hard-to-segment features and (3) the model may not be completely closed or connected (e.g. representative surface patches may be used instead of complete surfaces). Literal models are suitable for image generation; suggestive models represent salient features without excessive metrical detail. Suggestiveness is needed for generic model representation, otherwise rough matchability is not possible.
- The modeled features should be observable data features. This facilitates matching without having to compute the visible appearance of a feature (Marr's accessibility criterion [12]).
- Both data and model features are assumed to be segmented similarly for matching correspondence and are symbolically described for efficiency.
- Marr's uniqueness criteria is to be slightly relaxed so there may not be a canonical description. Alternative object representations are allowed to cope with both incomplete descriptions and scale-based description change.
- Marr's scope, stability and sensitivity criteria [12] still apply.

It is presumed that most of the information in the model will be explicit, instead of being computed when necessary. This cannot always be the case because: (1) descriptions of incompletely constrained objects (e.g. variable size or flexibly connected) cannot be fully predictable and (2) the many less significant features create a combinatorial explosion in *a priori* description prediction, whereas their visibility is directly deducible given a roughly oriented model.

2. Requirements on SMS

Object representations are required for the following purposes:

- object feature and relationship descriptions are needed to constrain model-to-data matches and 3D location,
- visible object features and their configurations are needed for model invocation,
- predicted feature relationships are also needed to understand feature visibility from a given viewpoint.

The most important representation is the geometric model. From this, one can predict features and relationships as seen from any particular viewpoint, as well as verify observed relationships.

For matching, the geometric model should:

- represent strong edges,
- make surface information explicit, because surfaces are the primary visible features,
- make volumetric information explicit, because volumes represent the spatial distribution of the object, and because volumetric relationships can be deduced from the data when matchable surface information is not,
- be able to represent solid and laminar objects,
- have three dimensional, transformable representations for understanding appearance from arbitrary viewpoints,
- have geometric part-whole relationships, and
- allow partially constrained size and placement relationships.

Competent vision systems with large model bases need some form of model invocation. There are many approaches to this problem, but here it is based on accumulating evidence for objects, mediated by the associations between objects [5].

Direct evidence is computed by comparing the degree to which observed data properties meet modeled (unary or binary) property constraints, which must therefore be part of the model. Unary constraints specify the value ranges that are acceptable for different attributes of individual features. Binary constraints specify the 3D spatial configuration of the features. (Examples are the expected area of a surface and the angles at which two surfaces meet.) This information is made explicit for efficient invocation and matching.

The plausibility of related objects provides indirect evidence for the object, through the subcomponent, supercomponent, subtype (specialization) and supertype (generalization) relationships. Component relationships are implicit in the subcomponent hierarchy of the geometric model and the generic relationships must be given separately.

Invocation also requires subcomponent visibility groups, to indicate which possibly related objects contribute evidence for a given object. Each group specifies the major object features seen together from a given range of viewpoints. Only the prominent features and configurations are represented and only for significant viewpoint ranges.

3. Relationship to Previous Modeling Systems

The SMS models are most closely related to those used in ACRONYM [2] and IMAGINE [5]. The hierarchical reference frame and volumetric method used in SMS follows ACRONYM, though the primitive solids used are not generalized cylinders. IMAGINE used surfaces as its primitives in a subcomponent hierarchy to make explicit the shape of individual objects.

The volumetric primitives of Shapiro et. al. [15] were chosen to represent the essential character and relationships of solids.

Several recent 3D vision systems are based primarily on surface patch representations. Faugeras and Hebert [3] used an empirically derived fragmentary planar patch decomposition of an irregular object's surface, (patches were characterized by nominal position and surface orientation). Grimson and Lozano-Perez [8] used a similar representation. The models also included additional information, such as angles between normals and distances between points to improve recognition efficiency.

Bolles et al [1] used a vertex, edge, surface and volume representation, linked in a winged-edge-like representation. Features were also represented in classification (size,type) trees, to promote quick indexing of candidate models from observed data.

Many modeling systems use wire frames, and while no complete wire frame is used here, strong object edges are represented.

The variable and constraint method of ACRONYM has been followed with some modifications. The specialization method is similar to that of Marr and Nishihara [13], where specializations have different structural models and are linked by subcomponent and generic indices to associated models.

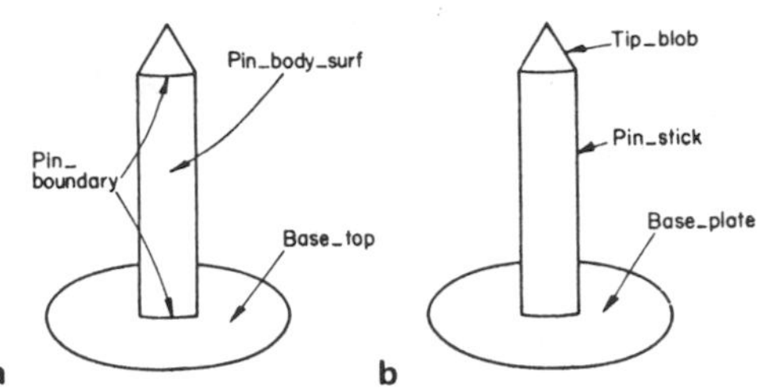

Figure 1: Drawing Pin Model

The viewer-centered representation is based on the subcomponent group of IMAGINE, the view potential of Koenderink and van Doorn [10] and the aspect graph information proposed for the YASA representation [7]. Here, descriptions of structures are represented according to their visibility and apparent configuration from given viewpoints.

The terms for local relations between solids follow Shapiro et al [15]. The axis relations are similar to those given by Marr [12] and express the relative size and placement of axes.

4. A Brief Summary of SMS

This section illustrates the contents of an SMS model (figure 1) through use of a drawing pin model.

SMS's data primitives are viewpoint independent object features organized in an object-centered geometric reference frame. The primitives are chosen for their visible salience:

space curves - represented by curvature and extent. Closed ellipses are represented explicitly, and other space curves are assumed to be segmented into straight lines and circular arcs. (Curves with torsion are not modeled, but this would be an easy extension.)

surfaces - segmented by roughly constant principal curvatures, and represented using surface patches from a torus (because its two surface curvatures correspond with the two observable principal curvatures). Degenerate and other cases such as planes, cylinders and cones are also represented. Patch boundaries are nominal and are defined using space curves.

volumes - represent extended spatial distributions, and have primarily 1, 2 or 3 directions of extension. The three first-order primitives are the STICK, PLATE and BLOB, which roughly characterize mass distribution without precise surface shape description. The extensions are parameterized, so slightly distorted volumes are allowed. Recently, second order volumetric primitives have been added to improve model sensitivity (see section 4.1).

These primitives and their parameters are used because they correspond closely with descriptions derived from 2 1/2 D sketch data. The different feature types are treated as alternatives, because of data unpredictability. Hence, a model will contain a mixture of each of the three types, and the intention is that evidence of any type would be sufficient.

Examples of feature definitions in the pin model are:

space curve - the curve of the orientation discontinuity where the pin shaft meets the base.

```
(ELLIPSE pin_boundary
        MAJOR_RADIUS        0.1
        MINOR_RADIUS        0.1
)
```

surface patch - the spherical patch of the top surface of the pin base. The negative minor radius declares the surface to be concave. The definition defines a complete torus, which needs to be trimmed by patch boundaries to form the object surface. The boundary list shows several curves that lie approximately on the surface, including the pin_boundary defined above. These boundaries delimit a spherical cap with a hole in it; the included point designates which region of the segmented torus is the patch. Translations and rotations are described below. The scale factor allows local rescaling of features.

```
(TORUS base_top
   MAJOR_RADIUS 0.0
   MINOR_RADIUS -1.0
   BOUNDARY_LIST    (

      ((PLACED_FEATURE base_boundary
         AT TRANSLATION (0,0,0.84)
           ROTATION VECTOR
             (0,0,-1) (0,0,-1)
         SCALE 1.0
      ))

      ((PLACED_FEATURE pin_boundary
         AT TRANSLATION (0,0,0.995)
           ROTATION VECTOR
             (0,0,-1) (0,0,-1)
         SCALE 1.0
      )))

   (INCLUDED_POINT (0.2,0,0.98))
)
```

volume - a bent PLATE is the volumetric approximation to the pin head, having two directions of extension. The thickness of the plate is small relative to the radius

```
(PLATE base_plate
   RADIUS          0.58
   THICKNESS       0.1
   BEND            0.85
)
```

Assemblies are formed from previously defined subassemblies and surfaces, where the features are placed using reference-frame transformations. The assemblies also record volumetric relationships between the solids, such as whether a STICK connects to a PLATE in the center or the edge, and relative relationships between volume axes, such as size, orientation and placement.

Reference frame rotations are specified in three forms, according to whether:

(1) the rotation is completely constrained (but may be a variable quantity, as in a robot joint angle),

(2) the rotation is symmetric about an axis, or

(3) the rotation is completely unconstrained, as with a spherically symmetric feature.

Translations are specified by a transforming vector (possibly variable, too).

Two types of assembly are defined. The first is a PRIMARY_ASSEMBLY, whose role is to group alternate representations (e.g. curves, surfaces or volumes) for primitive unstructured objects, because alternative evidence may be available for the recognition of primitive features. Any evidence should be allowed, without making the existence of the structure in larger structures contingent on the type of data evidence.

The PRIMARY_ASSEMBLY for the cylindrical pin is given below. Here, the curve, surface and volume alternatives are placed in the reference frame for the whole assembly. The ASM_ALT sections separate the equivalent alternative evidence groups. The PLACED_FEATURE blocks place an instance of the named feature in the object's local coordinate frame. The AT block gives the reference frame transformation from the feature's local frame to that of the object, with the required TRANSLATION and ROTATION.

```
(PRIMARY_ASSEMBLY pin_body

   (VARS (NONE))

   ((ASM_ALT /* curves */

      ((PLACED_FEATURE pin_boundary
         AT TRANSLATION (0,0,0)
           ROTATION VECTOR
             (0,0,-1) (-1,0,0)
         SCALE 1.0)

      (PLACED_FEATURE pin_boundary
         AT TRANSLATION (length,0,0)
           ROTATION VECTOR
             (0,0,-1) (1,0,0)
         SCALE 1.0)))

   (ASM_ALT /* surfaces */
      ((PLACED_FEATURE pin_body_surf
         AT TRANSLATION (0,0,0)
           ROTATION VECTOR
             (1,0,0) (1,0,0)
         SCALE 1.0)))
```

```
(ASM_ALT /* volumes */
  ((PLACED_FEATURE pin_stick
     AT TRANSLATION ((length/2),0,0)
       ROTATION VECTOR
         (1,0,0) (1,0,0)
     SCALE 1.0))))

( /* structure properties */ NONE)
)
```

The second type of assembly is the STRUCTURED_ASSEMBLY, whose role is to group subcomponents into an object, using the reference frame transformation mechanism. An example of this is shown here, where the pin_head and pin_body PRIMARY_ASSEMBLYs are joined to form the pin assembly. The assembly also has new properties specified. The first constraint states that the head and body surfaces are adjacent. Full path names are used because the referenced features are not always defined at the current level of assembly. The connection constraints describe the relationship that the volumetric primitives have (following [15]). Here, the END of the pin_body, a STICK, is attached to the CENTER of the pin_head, a BLOB.

```
(STRUCTURED_ASSEMBLY pin

   (VARS (length (DEFAULT_VALUE 1.0)))

   (/* substructures */
    (PLACED_FEATURE pin_body
      AT TRANSLATION (0,0,0)
        ROTATION VECTOR
           (1,0,0) (1,0,0)
      SCALE 1.0)

    (PLACED_FEATURE pin_head
      AT TRANSLATION (length+0.2,0,0)
        ROTATION VECTOR
           (1,0,0) (-1,0,0)
      SCALE 1.0))

   ( /* properties */
      (CONNECTED
           pin_head->pin_head_surf
            pin_body->pin_body_surf)
      (CONN_CONST pin_body
           END_CENTER pin_head))
)
```

Variables represent incompletely determined aspects of the models, such as shape, size or relative position and are bound in local contexts. Use of variables follows structured programming techniques and define the contexts within which variables are bound (dynamic binding). The defining context is the smallest hierarchical superobject context binding the variable. A robot finger joint angle can then be defined in the context of the finger only, so has a distinct value for each finger instance. If a hand scale variable is then defined in the context of the hand, but referenced in each finger subcontext, it has a distinct value in each hand instance and the same value in each finger subinstance.

Constraints on expressions containing variables are allowed, as in ACRONYM. The following limits the value of the "length" variable in the "pin" context:

```
(CONSTRAINT ((length > 0.5)) ASSEMBLY pin)
(CONSTRAINT ((length < 2.0)) ASSEMBLY pin)
```

There is a hierarchy of descriptions representing both substructure abstraction and identity refinement. This mechanism unifies two processes: (1) generic representations, and (2) scale dependent descriptions. The first case occurs when new constraints or features are added to refine an object's identity, much as when refining the definition of a wide-bodied aircraft to define a 747 as in ACRONYM [2]. The second case occurs when the same identity is described, but at several conceptual scale dependent representations. Marr and Nishihara [13] gave an example of this in their expansion of the "human" cylinder to "head, body and limbs" cylinders.

SMS uses one mechanism for both of these processes. Related models are linked using ELABORATION/SIMPLIFICATION statements. Subcomponents common to the linked objects may reference the same subcomponent definition, or may reference refined subcomponents. Additional property constraints as well as new models can distinguish refined models from their predecessors.

Associated with the geometric model are viewpoint dependent relationships among visible features. This information records visibly significant features, such as observability and surface ordering, for the principal distinct viewpoints associated with the object. While this information could be derived from the geometric model, the justification for including the information explicitly in the model is twofold: (1) on-line derivation is computationally expensive and (2) the theory of visual salience is not yet well developed.

The two key types of information represented are:

(1) an explicit classification of the visibility of prominent features in topologically different viewpoints, and

(2) new viewer-dependent features that only exist because the object is observed from a viewpoint, such as tangential occluding boundaries, obscuring surface relationships and tee junctions.

We now show part of the viewpoint dependent feature group for the whole drawing pin model. Only the visibility group associated with the viewpoint seen in figure 1 is given. The definition lists the two subcomponents visible from this viewpoint (the pin and base) and records that no features are tangential (i.e. possibly visible or not according to minor changes in viewpoint). The next group records the constraints between new viewpoint dependent features. The first two define TEE junctions, and list the boundary curves involved by their full path names, because the correct list of transformations from object to subobject is needed. The next two list boundaries that are occluding from this viewpoint, along with the background surfaces. The last item lists which model features (at this level) are partially obscured (the base). Finally, the model records the position constraints that define this particular viewpoint. The constraints say that the dot product between the vector from the viewer (i.e. (0,0,-1)) and the vector (1,0,0) transformed by the object position must lie between -0.9 and 0.

```
(VDFG drawing_pin
  (
    ...

   (VIS_GROUP (pin base) /* above side */

    TAN_GROUP (NONE)

    NEW_FEAT_CONSTRAINTS (
      (VPD_TEE
        FRONTCURVE pin->pin_body->
           pin_body_surf->body_tan_bnd1
        BACKCURVE
           base->base_circumference)
      (VPD_TEE
        FRONTCURVE pin->pin_body->
           pin_body_surf->body_tan_bnd2
        BACKCURVE
           base->base_circumference)
      (VPD_OCCLBND pin->pin_body->
           pin_body_surf->body_tan_bnd1
        BACKGROUND (base->base_top))
      (VPD_OCCLBND pin->pin_body->
           pin_body_surf->body_tan_bnd2
        BACKGROUND (base->base_top))
      (VPD_POFEAT base)
  )

    POSITION_CONSTRAINTS
     (((VIEWER DOTPR MAP((1,0,0))
           < 0))
      ((VIEWER DOTPR MAP((1,0,0))
           > -0.9)))
  )

      ...

  )
)
```

Several images of the drawing pin model are shown. Figure 2 shows the surface and space curve components of the model and figure 3 shows the volumetric model. While this is only a simple object, the different representations still give a reasonable characterization.

For the viewpoint dependent feature groups, a nominal object orientation from the supplied position constraints is deduced for each visibility group, which can then be drawn. Figure 4 shows the four significant visibility groups for the drawing pin.

The pin model demonstrates the main model features. Figures 5 and 6 show more complicated models used as part of our Alvey project. Figures 7, 8 and 9 show other models created using SMS: a PUMA robot model (surfaces and curves shown), an oilcan

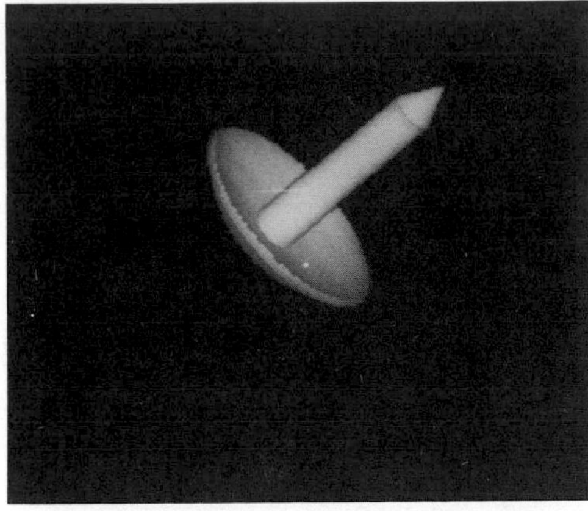

Figure 2: Surfaces and Space Curves of the Drawing Pin

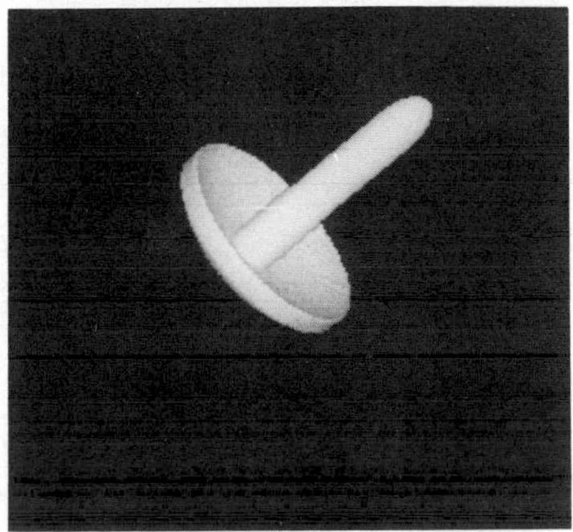

Figure 3: Volumes of the Drawing Pin

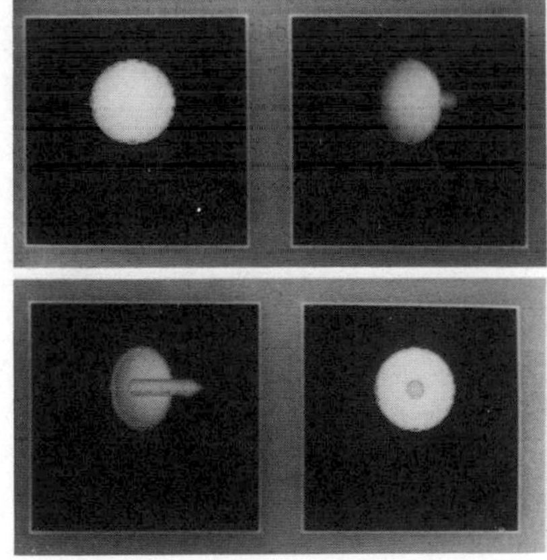

Figure 4: Visible Feature Groups for the Four Significant Viewpoints of Pin

(volumes and curves shown) and a parameterized ashtray (surfaces and curves shown).

4.1 Second Order Volumetric Primitives

Model creation using SMS's volumetric primitives revealed that these models often lacked the highly salient visual details representable using the surface and space curve primitives, although the first-order mass distribution of the features was well characterized. SMS links

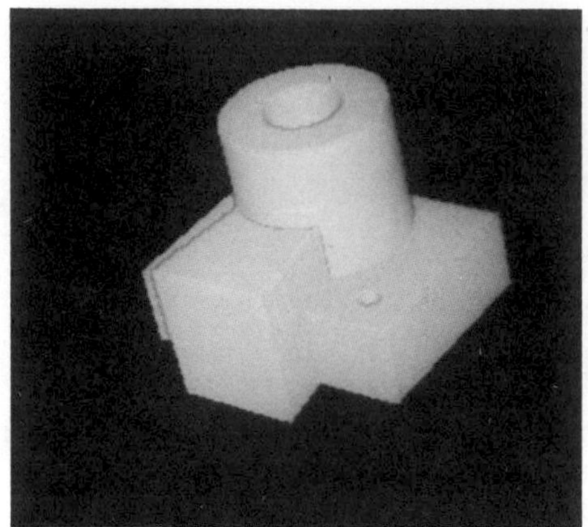

Figure 5: Surfaces and Space Curves of Widget

Figure 6: Volumes of the Widget

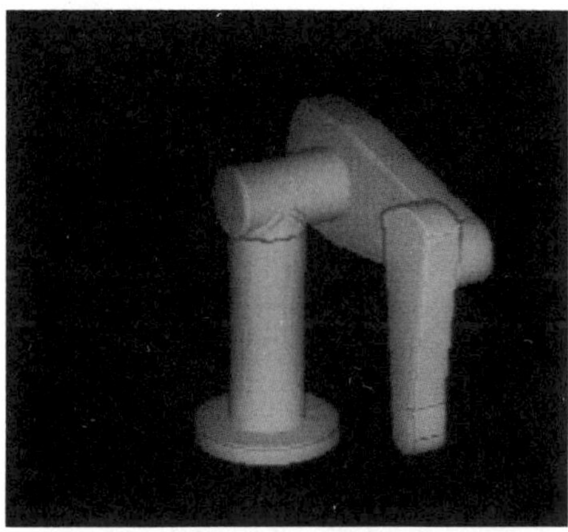

Figure 7: Surfaces and Space Curves of Robot

models by ELABORATION and SIMPLIFICATION, where linked models may have radically different structures (as in replacing a hand with 5 separate fingers by a BLOB), but exactly what the model differences are has not been clear. Hence, the motivation for the second-order primitives is to introduce new capabilities needed for having alternative conceptual scale object representations.

The major deficiencies were not having primitives for small intruding (or negative) features, like holes, and small extruding (or positive) features, such as bumps. This section introduces eight second-order volumetric primitives [6] (four small positive extruding and four negative intruding) that add detail to models, as might be required in a recognition scheme that used conceptual scale, and provides a taxonomy for them. These features increase the 'sensitivity' of the modeling scheme [12].

The extensions to SMS given here are related to the set-theoretic or constructive solid geometry [14] approach. However, here, the intent is to represent only volumetric features that can be directly and easily identified from 2 1/2D data. The primitives are also related to the shape features identified by Jared [9] and Kyprianou [11] (protrusions or depressions, which were further refined to slots, holes and pockets). Here, their role is related to part function and manufacturing method.

4.1.1 Positive Second-Order Volumetric Features

These are small extrusions modifying a major volumetric feature that do not merit a first-order feature description. They can be classified according to their having one, two or three primary directions of extension and are shown schematically in figure 10.

The first one dimensional positive feature is the **SPIKE**, which is a feature that sticks out from a volume and possibly bends (figure 10a). It is defined primarily by its length and bend curvature.

The second one dimensional positive feature is the **RIDGE**, which is a feature that lies on the surface of a volume (figure 10b). It is again defined primarily by its length and bend curvature.

The two dimensional positive feature is the **FIN**, which represents something like a **RIDGE**, but extends substantially out of the object (figure 10c). It is defined primarily by its length, height and bend curvature.

The three dimensional positive feature is the **BUMP**, representing a small hemi-ellipsoidal extrusion from a volume (figure 10d). It is defined by its three radii of curvature, given as height, major_radius and minor_radius.

4.1.2 Negative Second-Order Volumetric Features

These are small intrusions modifying a major volumetric feature. They differ from the positive features in that they cannot be approximated by SMS's current volumetric primitives. They sculpt out portions of volumetric primitives, rather than add minor extensions.

The negative second-order volumetric features can be classified according to their having one, two or three primary directions of extension and have an exact correspondence with the positive second-order features. The features are the **HOLE**, **GROOVE**, **SLOT** and **DENT**, which correspond to the SPIKE, RIDGE, FIN and BUMP, as shown in figure 11.

4.1.3 Examples

Figure 12 shows examples of an object containing SPIKE, RIDGE, FIN and BUMP features. Figure 13 shows examples of an object containing HOLE, GROOVE, SLOT and DENT features. Since the first-

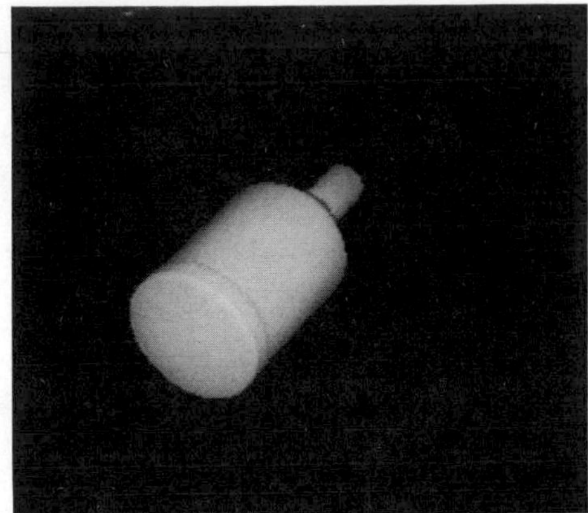

Figure 8: Volumes and Curves of Oilcan

Figure 9: Surfaces and Space Curves of Ashtray

order feature in both cases is only a STICK (e.g. the largish cylindrical shape), the second-order features clearly add important distinguishing detail. Figure 14 show the volumetric model of the widget with the second order features.

Figure 12: Example Using Positive Features

5. Discussion

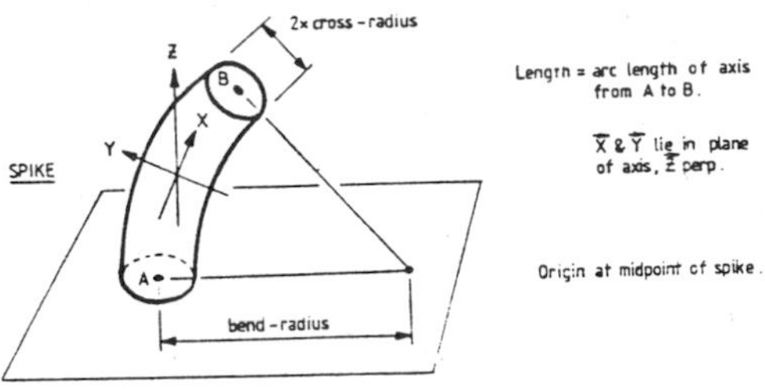

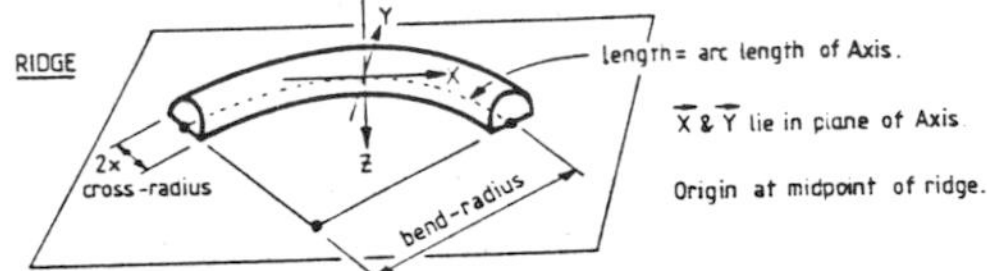

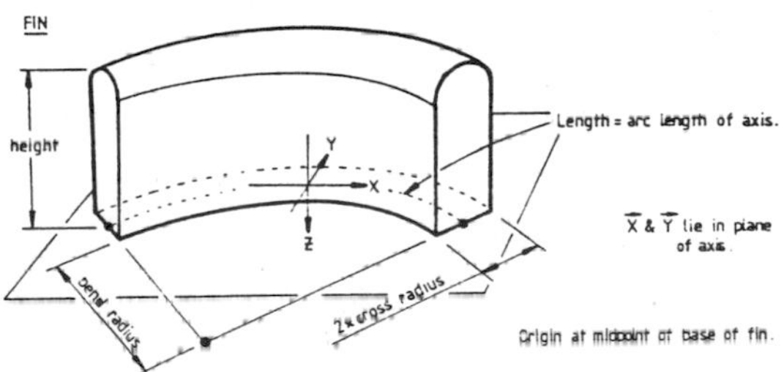

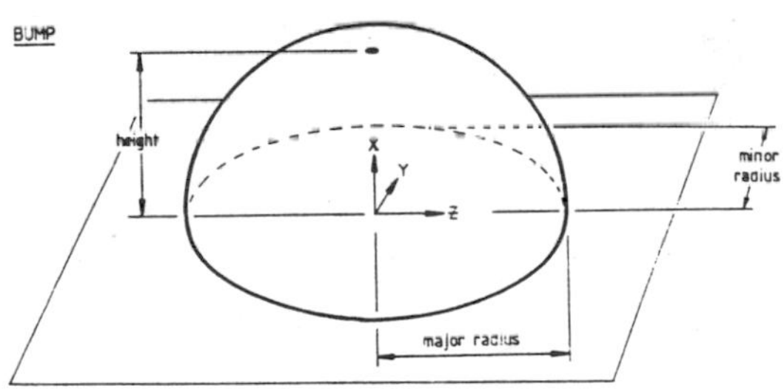

Figure 10: Second-Order Positive Features

The SMS representation is designed for use in the IMAGINE II object recognition system. This system expects 2 1/2D sketch features as inputs (such as fragmentary 3D edges and surface patches). Model invocation occurs as described in section 2, in a network created from the SMS model and the image structure. High plausibility nodes are selected for model directed matching. These nodes provide direct linking of model to data features, including several subcomponent pairings (which are then used for initial position estimation). Additionally, invocation specifies a rough object orientation, which indexes a viewpoint dependent feature group.

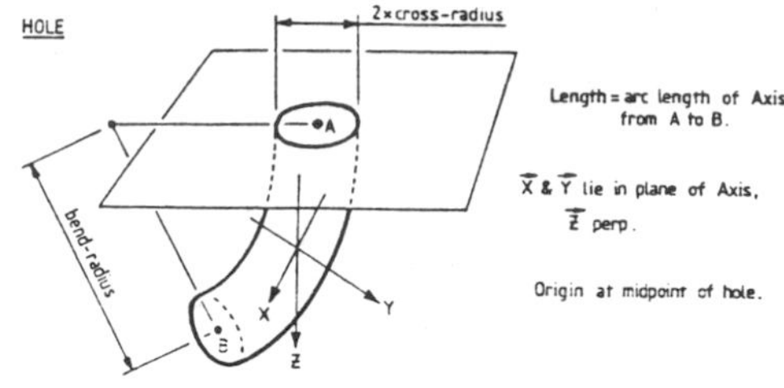

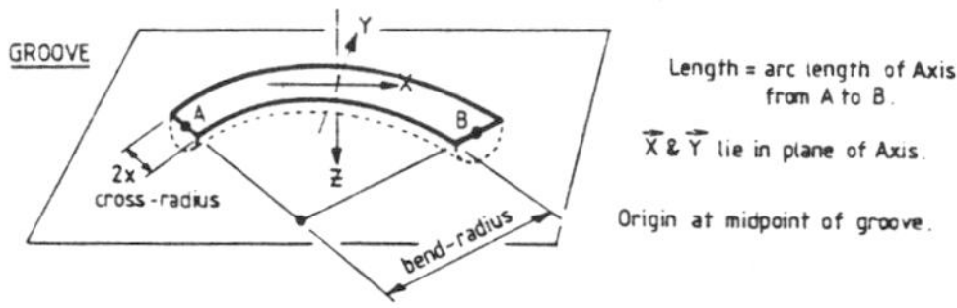

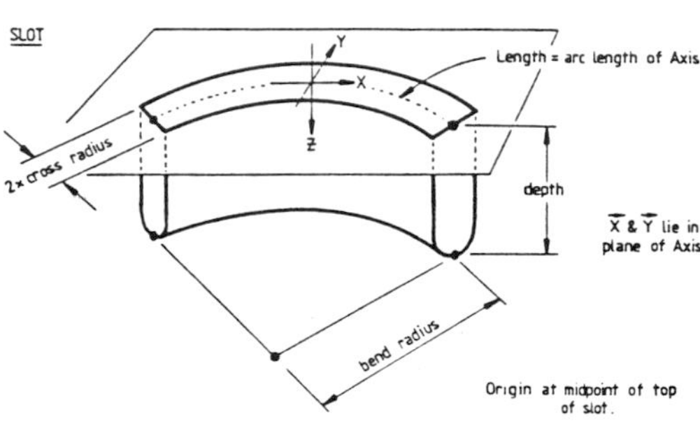

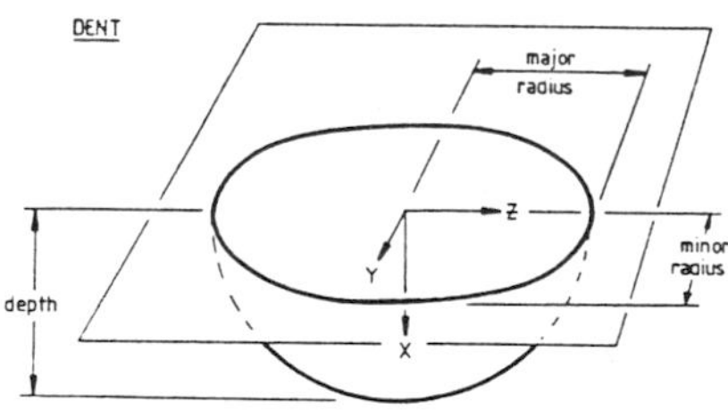

Figure 11: Second-Order Negative Features

Using this information, high performance object recognition can be quickly achieved:

- reference frames can be established from model-data feature pairings
- all visible features can be searched for, using predicted image positions and 3D constraints (from the oriented model and visibility lists),
- multiple feature fragments can be associated with oriented model features,
- back-facing and self-obscured features can be ignored,
- features obscured by unrelated objects can be verified as not visible by comparing the predicted 3D scene location with observed closer surfaces and
- viewpoint dependent features can be used as additional corroborating evidence.

The second-order features introduce the problem of whether a feature should be represented as a first or a second-order volumetric feature. For example, a nose on a face seems like a second-order BUMP relative to the whole face, but an arm on a torso is probably instead a first-order STICK extension. We hypothesize that the first-order features will be useful for broad class identifications and rough location, and the second-order features will refine subclass identifications and locations (much as in ACRONYM [2]).

There are some object representation problems that SMS does not attempt to solve:

(1) there are no primitives for surfaces whose shapes vary continuously, other than the cone - hence these can only be modeled piecewise.

(2) natural object shapes exhibit controlled irregularity, which is not represented.

(3) no metafeatures are included - such as a row of dots.

Typical objects have many (e.g. 50+) characteristic views, when viewed as a whole, potentially requiring an enormous model. To overcome this, we exploit the hierarchical structure decomposition of the objects: the viewpoints for the structured object will be classified according to the visibility of the subcomponents, rather than according to the features of the subcomponents. Further, only the significant views are represented, with minor variations remaining unmodeled.

SMS does not presume that all of an object's modeled aspects will be directly specified by the model creator. Rather, it advocates what a recognition-oriented object model should contain, irrespective of how the model is created. From the geometric model, some of the other information may be automatically derived. These include the properties of various features, such as surface curvature, angular relationships between pairs of surfaces or curve length. Some open problems are how to generate the generic and scale relationships represented by the elaboration mechanism, how to partition the features into a subcomponent hierarchy, and how to deduce unconstrained, partially constrained or variable relationships from a few observed instances of the objects.

6. Summary

SMS is an object representation system motivated by the requirements of object recognition instead of object depiction. Strongly visible features and relationships were represented as distinct symbolic primitives, which allow direct symbolic matching. It still has a structural flavor, however, and can produce reasonable pictures of objects.

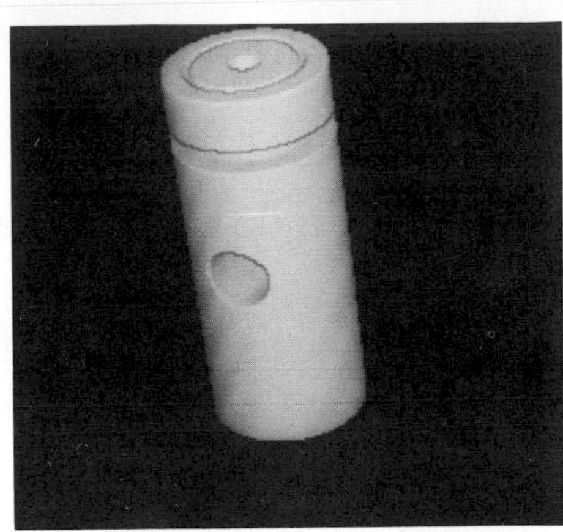

Figure 13: Example Using Negative Features

Figure 14: Second Order Widget Features

The key novelty of this representation is its integrated use of multiple alternative representations - allowing curve, surface or volumetric entities at the primitive level and refined alternative models at all levels. The advantage of these is that recognition is then achievable using a variety of evidence or recognition pathways. The alternative model mechanism combines both generic and descriptive refinement mechanisms.

It uses symbolic primitives that suggestively characterize the object and its shape, using properties that are easily extractable from image data. The result is that the object is described not literally, but instead by the character of features useful for its recognition.

The primitives are chosen for representation of solid and laminar objects with smooth surfaces (and is not restricted to the polyhedral world). This allows surface and volumetric shapes to be represented instead of simply orientation discontinuities and vertices, or infinitesimal surface patches.

Viewer-centered properties based on feature visibility and occlusion relationships are provided. They link directly with the object-centered descriptions, allowing access to viewpoint independent models from observed features.

Acknowledgements

Funding for the research described herein was under Alvey grant GR/D/1740.3. The ideas in this paper benefited greatly from discussions with A. P. Fothergill, J. Aylett, J. Frisby, M. Gray, J. Knapman, J. Mayhew and M. Orr. J. Aylett, M. Orr and F. Seytter helped considerably with the software and modeling.

References

[1] Bolles, R.C., Horaud, P., Hannah, M.J., "3DPO: A Three-Dimensional Part Orientation System", Proc. 8th Int. Joint. Conf. on Artificial Intelligence, pp 1116-1120, 1983.

[2] Brooks, R. A., "Symbolic reasoning among 3-D models and 2-D images", Artif. Intel., **17**, pp285-348, 1981.

[3] Faugeras, O.D., Hebert, M., "A 3-D Recognition and Positioning Algorithm Using Geometrical Matching Between Primitive Surfaces", Proc. 8th Int. Joint. Conf. on Artificial Intelligence, pp 996-1002, 1983.

[4] Fisher, R. B., "SMS: A Suggestive Modeling System for Object Recognition", University of Edinburgh, Dept. of A.I. Working Paper 185, 1985.

[5] Fisher, R. B., "From Surfaces to Objects: Recognizing Objects Using Surface Information and Object Models", PhD Thesis, University of Edinburgh, 1986.

[6] Fisher, R. B., "Modeling Second-Order Volumetric Features" Proc. 3rd Alvey Vision Conference, Cambridge, pp79-86, 1987.

[7] Gray, M. "Recognition Planning From Solid Models", Proc. 1986 Alvey Computer Vision and Image Interpretation Meeting, Bristol, 1986.

[8] Grimson, W.E.L., and Lozano-Perez, T., "Model-Based Recognition and Localization from Sparse Range or Tactile Data", Int. J. of Robotic Research, Vol. 3, No. 3, pp 3-35, 1984.

[9] Jared, G. E. M., "Shape Features in Geometrical Modeling", Unpublished report(?), Dept. of Engineering, Univ. of Cambridge.

[10] Koenderink, J. J., van Doorn, A. J., "The Shape of Smooth Objects and the Way Contours End", Perception, Vol 11, pp 129-137.

[11] Kyprianou, L. K., "Shape Classification in Computer-Aided Design", PhD thesis, Univ. of Cambridge Computer Lab, 1980.

[12] Marr, D., "Vision", pubs: W.H. Freeman and Co., 1982.

[13] Marr, D., Nishihara, H. K., "Representation and Recognition of the Spatial Organization of Three Dimensional Shapes", Proc. Royal Soc. London, B200, pp269-294, 1978.

[14] Requicha, A. A. G., Voelcker, H. B., "Constructive Solid Geometry", Univ. of Rochester, Production

Automation Project, memo TM-25, 1977.

[15] Shapiro, L,, Moriarty, J., Mulgaonkar, P., Haralick, R., "Sticks, Plates, And Blobs: A Three-Dimensional Object Representation For Scene Analysis", AAAI-80, Aug 1980.

[25] WPFM: The Workspace Prediction and Fast Matching System

Jonathan C Aylett and Robert B Fisher

Department of Artificial Intelligence
University of Edinburgh, Edinburgh EH1 2QL, UK

A Pat Fothergill

Department of Computer Science
University of Aberdeen, Aberdeen, UK

Reprinted, with permission of *Journal of Intelligent and Robotic Systems*, 1988, **1**, 185-201.

1. Introduction

An important area for the application of machine vision is to industrial assembly tasks, where the effective automation of such tasks is often dependent on the use of robots with sensing capabilities. The micro-world environment of a typical industrial assembly robot, although complex may also be highly constrained, with considerable information available *a priori* about objects and their disposition within a robot workcell. In order to maximise the efficiency with which a computer vision system can operate within this domain *a priori* information can be utilised to avoid extensive visual processing for constant scene features, or for objects in the scene for which there are accurate estimates of current position. The use of this information can then allow a reduction of the high computational cost of vision processing. This quantitative geometric information can be derived from a CAD based model of the robot workstation and from the known location of the camera system used to view the scene.

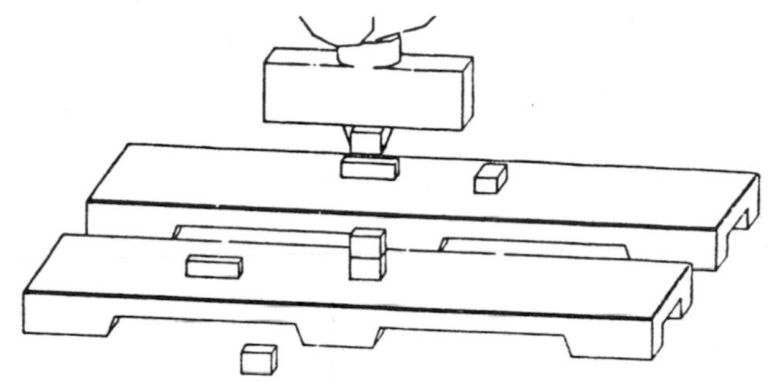

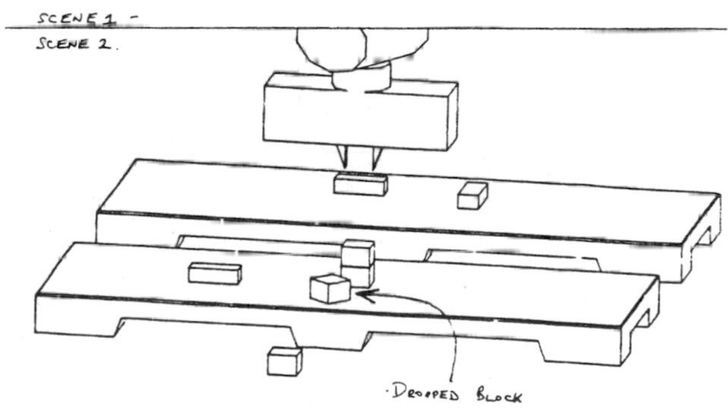

Figure 1 - A Typical Scenario

2. Workspace Prediction and Fast Matching

The *WPFM System* was developed to use *a priori* knowledge about a given scene so that some stereo data extracted from the scene could be quickly matched to model features, and then subtracted out of the scene data, leaving unknown data to be dealt with by a more comprehensive (and computationally expensive) vision matcher [9]. A schematic illustration of the type of target scenario is shown in Figure(1), where the only difference between the two modeled scenes is that in one case the robot gripper has "dropped it's block".

The *WPFM System* is composed of two major components, the off-line *workspace prediction system (WP System)* and the on-line *fast a priori matching system (FAPM System)*. The off-line prediction system was developed from the Robmod [7 & 8] solid modelling system and can produce a *workspace prediction graph (WP Graph)* for any modeled scene. The on-line fast matching phase consists of an edge based matching system, where stereo edge data derived from a real scene by a stereo vision system [5, 14], can be matched to model edge features in an appropriate *WP Graph*.

Although the *WP System* (and Robmod) is limited to a polyhedral representation of objects, curved edges can be modeled by approximating a curve with a series of linear tessellation edges. This then enables the matching of *curved* edge features extracted by the stereo process. The scene subtraction process implemented by the *WPFM System* is a "*symbolic subtraction*" of edge features, rather than an "*image subtraction*" of pixels, as an image subtraction process would generate image artifacts and other errors.

3. The Workspace Prediction Graph

Unlike boundary based modelling systems, CSG systems build objects by combining primitive solid shapes together, using boolean set operations. By including information about the way an object is constructed from these primitive solid shapes into a boundary representation, we construct a data structure containing the geometrical and topological information about an object, as well as a relational aspect which comprises a description of the *visually salient parts* that go to make up an object. This extends the concept of a boundary representation to include information specifically useful to vision processing [2] and is a development from the classical winged edge type structures used by Weiler [19] and others [4, 6, 10, 16 17, & 20]. Our variant has a hierarchical structure which composes distinct objects into *separate assemblies,* then decomposes them into *CSG primatives* (convex or concave), into *surfaces,* and then *edge boundaries* of the surfaces. The geometry is associated with edge, vertex and surface descriptions. A *Workspace Prediction Graph* can be produced by the modelling system analysing a CSG model of a scene from a particular viewpoint and adding the following visibility information to the boundary representation :

1. Total number of visible, part visible and non-visible edges.
2. Total number of visible, virtual and non-visible vertices.
3. Viewing parameters - viewing angles, viewed point and frame size.
4. Edges sorted by visibility type - visible, part-visible and non-visible. Some edges may be tagged as extremal, for "curved" primatives.
5. Vertices sorted by visibility type - visible and non-visible.
6. Virtual vertices. These are produced at T junctions where model edges are partially occluded.

Generally, the edges of the facets used to model curved surfaces by polyhedral approximation are treated as non-visible edges, as these are features which are not seen in real objects. However *extremal* edges are represented, as they correspond to a visible facet edge bounding the first non-visible facet. Although the *FAPM System* only requires the use of the edge and vertex features in the *WP Graph,* we produce a more complete representation [2] which could be adapted to be used with a more general purpose vision system, or in an enhanced *FAPM System.*

4. GDB Data

The details of the operation of the *GDB System* and the data structures produced by it can be found elsewhere [14]. The fast matching system requires the 3D geometrical descriptions of linear data segments and circular arcs contained within GDB data to perform the matching process.

5. Problems of Matching

Although we use *a priori* information about an expected scene, there will not be a perfect correspondence between the features extracted from the scene by the *GDB System* and the features produced by the *WP System* because of extra, missing or different features occurring in the *WP Graph* and the *GDB data.* These imperfections can be caused by :

Imperfections in the WP Graph

1. Simplification of the shapes of the objects when modelled in order to be able to represent them in the modelling system.
2. The WP graph may include features which are too small to recovered by the vision system.
3. Incorrect locations of a some model features, caused by objects with locations different to those predicted.
4. Missing model features, because the system will not attempt to predict features arising from objects with unknown locations.

Imperfections in GDB data

1. Features may not be appear in the data because lighting conditions can make them invisible.
2. Extra features can also be produced by the GDB system, caused by reflectance changes, shadows (shadow edges), specularities or texture.
3. Features may be occluded in the image that were predicted to be visible.
4. A single feature may be fragmented by an unpredicted partial occlusion.
5. Data can be fragmented by imperfections in an image, such as noise.
6. Tangential occluding boundaries on curved surfaces are difficult to resolve accurately by a stereo process and may be placed inaccurately, particularly in depth.
7. Linear edge features parallel to the plane of the stereo camera system are difficult to resolve stereoscopically and may also be placed inaccurately.
8. Curved edge features may be inaccurately segmented into several linear data segments.

6. Fast A Priori Matching

The *FAPM System* matches data input from a *GDB File* and model input from a *WP Graph.* Matching proceeds by pairing data to model edges using geometrical algorithms. The objective is to find all data segments that match the model, and to determine how well the data matches the model features. Tolerance values are required for this matching process and the choice of values for these parameters depends on the quality of the data. The tolerance parameters are :

1. The *maximum divergence angle* between linear model and linear data segments.
2. The *maximum tessellation divergence angle* between model tessellation and linear data segments within which the model curve (approximated by a linear tessellation) and data segment are considered to be parallel.
3. The *maximum perpendicular divergence angle* between the axis of a circular arc in the data and a "curved" model segment.
4. The minimum proportion of the data segment to model segment *overlap margin.* This defines the length of data segment allowed to fall outside a model edge.
5. The maximum *separation distance* between a linear model edge and a linear data segment at the point of closest approach.

After setting the calibration and tolerance parameters, model edges can be matched against data segments as follows :

1. For each data segment, determine if it lies within a *model circumsphere,* and if not, mark as unmatched.
2. For each model edge, scan all data segments and attempt a match. Mark paired data segments and model segments as matched, and for each model edge, record a total accumulated length of data segments matched.

Stage 1 of the process acts as a coarse filter, and thereby improves performance. The circumsphere surrounds the modelled object, and is generated by Robmod as part of the WP Graph. For speed, the test used is a *quick point test* on each data segment. Data segments have both endpoints tested to determine if one or both lie within the circumsphere. This is a conservative test as it does not remove all features located too far from the model, because the circumsphere does not "fit tightly" (it is not a convex hull), and approximate calculations are used to minimise the amount of computation required. However, the test can remove a considerable number of data segments quickly from the matching process and it becomes significant as the number of distinct objects in a scene increases.

Stage 2 is the main matching process. Each model edge is matched against all the remaining data segments. For linear model edges, there is allowed only a unique pairing of data segments to model edges, such that if one data segment is matched to a linear model edge, that data segment cannot be matched to another model feature. The data segments are paired to the first matching model edge, and a "*best fit*" test for any competing model edges is not applied, as this situation should only occur with very loose matching tolerances or with a data/model mismatch. Hence for m model edges and d data segments, this matching process is of the order of $(m*d)/2$ complexity, although this is reduced by the use of the circumsphere test or increased as the number of "curved" model edges increases (as these do not have a unique pairing relationship to data segments). The computational complexity of the matching process is kept within these bounds, as it is not necessary to estimate a reference frame transformation to register model to data [12 & 18], or to select which model to match to data by a process of model invocation [9], as this information is determined *a priori.*

6.1. Matching Linear Features

The matching process for each linear model edge is subdivided into four tests, and data is rejected at the first test in the sequence that fails. Linear edge segments in the model are represented by ($\mathbf{v_m},\mathbf{m_1},\mathbf{m_2}, M_l$) and in the data by ($\mathbf{v_d},\mathbf{d_1},\mathbf{d_2}, D_l$), where the four components are the unit direction vector $\mathbf{v_m} = \mathbf{m_2} - \mathbf{m_1}$, the two endpoints and the length. The tests are as follows :

1. *Quick point test.* Tests if either point on the data segment has an approximate separation distance from a point on the the model edge greater than the length of the model edge. The test will succeed if all the following conditions are true :

   $$|m_{1i} - d_{1i}| < M_l$$

   $$|m_{1i} - d_{2i}| < M_l$$

   $$|m_{2i} - d_{1i}| < M_l$$

   $$|m_{2i} - d_{2i}| < M_l$$

   where $i \in [1,2,3]$, the vector components.
2. *Angular deviation test.* Tests if the angle of separation of the direction vectors of the data segments and model edges is within the specified tolerance angle. For a maximum deviation angle D_a the test will succeed iff

   $$|\mathbf{v_m}.\mathbf{v_d}| > \cos(D_a)$$

3. *Sub-segment test.* Tests if the projection of a data segment onto a model edge falls within that model edge. A tolerance parameter requires the data to overlap the model edge by a fractional proportion of the model edge length, and for a linear data segment both endpoints must fall within this interval. The overlap parameters are given by :

$$O_1 = (\mathbf{d_1} - \mathbf{m_2}).\mathbf{v_m}$$

and $$O_2 = (\mathbf{d_2} - \mathbf{m_2}).\mathbf{v_m}$$

And the test will succeed iff

$$-F_oM_l \le O_1 \le M_l + F_oM_l$$

and $$-F_oM_l \le O_2 \le M_l + F_oM_l$$

Where F_o is the overlap proportion tolerance parameter.

4. *Minimum distance test.* Tests to determine if the closest point between the the data segment and the model edge is within the specified separation distance limit. This test will succeed iff

$$|(O_1 \mathbf{v_m}) + \mathbf{m_2} - \mathbf{d_1} | < S_d$$

and $$|(O_2 \mathbf{v_m}) + \mathbf{m_2} - \mathbf{d_2} | < S_d$$

where S_d is the minimum separation tolerance parameter, and O_1 and O_2 are as defined above.

The algorithms used in tests (2-4) above were derived from algorithms originally developed by Watson [18] for use in a wire frame based vision matching system, and are similar to those used in other combinatorial matching systems [11 & 12]. A linear data segment that passes all of the above tests will be paired to the linear model edge and the uniqueness criterion will be enforced.

6.2. Matching Data and Model Tessellations

There are two further cases of matching, both of which involve the matching of a "*curved*" model edge to data. As curved model edges are represented in the WP Graph by a tessellation of the curve into a number of smaller linear edges, it is these *tessellation edges* that are matched to the data. The two cases differ in that curved features may be segmented by the GDB as *linear* or *circular arc* data segments. Hence in the first case, the GDB tessellates curved data into a number of linear data segments, whilst in the second case circular features are segmented into one or more circular arcs. To match model tessellations to data tessellations, we use a similar (but not identical) method as used above for the linear case. This matching process is :

1. *Quick point test,* similar to test(1) above, except that only one pair of conditions is required to be true. Hence the test will succeed if :

$$|m_{1i} - d_{1i}| < M_l$$

and $$|m_{1i} - d_{2i}| < M_l$$

or $$|m_{2i} - d_{1i}| < M_l$$

and $$|m_{2i} - d_{2i}| < M_l$$

2. *Angle test* as test(2) above, although the maximum deviation angle is normally set to a larger value than used for the linear case, to allow for possible extra divergence between model and data segments which can occur if the tessellation of the data and the tessellation of the model are out of step.

3. *Sub-segment test* as in test(3) above, except to allow for the possible "*stepping*" problem between tessellations, we use initially a zero overlap and require only one endpoint to overlap. If both overlap, the process is as before, otherwise we then run a subsidiary test to determine how much of the *data segment* overlaps the model edge. This subsidiary test is passed if a sufficient proportion of the data segment overlaps the model edge, (an overlap of 30% was used). In some cases, the data segment can be larger than the model edge. This is usually caused by the GDB segmenting a curve into one rather than several linear segments which will then correspond to several tessellation edges in the model. For this case, the algorithms are as described above, except that the relationship between a model edge and a data segment is reversed as several model edge segments will be paired to one data segment.

4. *Minimum distance test* as in test(4) above, unless the overlap is only partial, in which case one minimum distance is tested corresponding to the one valid overlap.

Due to the "*stepping*" problem described above, the uniqueness criteria cannot be applied in this matching process. To minimise the possibility of incorrect pairings between model and data occurring, the linear model edges are matched to the data before the tessellated model edges. The lower accuracy of this matching process is partially offset by the stronger pairing relationship implied by a match between a curved model edge and a curved data segment.

6.3. Matching Curved Features - Data Arcs

A circular arc in the GDB is represented by (R_l, $\mathbf{c_c}$, $\mathbf{d_1}$, $\mathbf{d_2}$) where R_l is the radius of the arc, $\mathbf{c_c}$ the centre point and $\mathbf{d_1}$ & $\mathbf{d_2}$ the two endpoints of the arc. To match a model tessellation edge to a circular arc, the test sequence is as follows :

1. *Quick point test* as in test(1) above, except that the point distance is the radius and the data point used is the centre of the circular arc.

2. *Angular deviation test.* The normal to the plane in which the data arc lies is compared to the direction vector of the model edge. It matches if these are perpendicular to each other to within the maximum

deviation angle.

The unit direction vectors for the two radii are given by :

$$\mathbf{r_1} = (\mathbf{d_1} - \mathbf{c_c}) / R_l$$

$$\mathbf{r_2} = (\mathbf{d_2} - \mathbf{c_c}) / R_l$$

and the unit normal vector $\mathbf{n_d}$ to the plane of the arc is given by :

$$\mathbf{n_d} = \mathbf{r_1} \times \mathbf{r_2} / ||\mathbf{r_1} \times \mathbf{r_2}||$$

For a maximum deviation angle D_a the test will succeed iff

$$|\mathbf{v_m} . \mathbf{n_d}| < \sin(D_a)$$

3. *Minimum distance test.* Determines if the end points of the model edge fall within the radius distance from the centre of the data arc segment, within the separation distance limit. For a separation distance limit S_d the test will succeed iff

$$|(||(\mathbf{c_c} - \mathbf{m_1})|| - R_l)| < S_d$$

and $|(||(\mathbf{c_c} - \mathbf{m_2})|| - R_l)| < S_d$

4. *Circular arc sub-segment test.* This determines if the model edge overlaps the data arc, by intersecting the two angle ranges of the two model edge endpoints with the angle range of the data arc. The test passes if the required proportion of the angle range of the model tessellation edge is found to overlap the data arc, (the required overlap was set to 30%). The overlap between the data and model angle ranges is given by :

$$O_a = | [0, A_a] \cap [A_{m1}, A_{m2}] |$$

and the test will succeed iff

$$|O_a / (A_{m1} - A_{m2})| > 0.3$$

(See [3] for further details of this algorithm).

In some cases, the data arc may be smaller than the model tessellation edge, usually due to data fragmentation. For this case, the test is the same, except that 30% of the *data arc* is required to overlap the model edge for the test to succeed.

Although the algorithms used for matching circular data arcs differ from the previous case of matching tessellation to tessellation, the uniqueness constraint still does not apply in the matching process, as again one data segment may be required to be matched to several model tessellation edges. However, the problem of a lower resolution in the matching process is reduced as the "*stepping*" problem encountered with tessellation to tessellation matching does not arise.

7. Results of Matching

At the end of the matching process an updated GDB file is output, with indicators of which data segments have been matched, as well as graphics indicating which model edges and data segments have been matched, (see Figures(2c-2i)). A matching "*goodness*" summary is also produced to indicate how close a match was obtained between model and data and this can then be used to determine whether a match is acceptable, and which data segments can be safely ignored in further vision processing.

8. Experimental Results

The workspace prediction and fast matching system has been implemented in C and run on our SUN computers, although not yet in conjunction with the overall vision system, which is the eventual objective. We have run the system on several test cases, the results of one of which is given below. The test data used for this was from a set of stereo images provided by AIVRU Sheffield and had an image resolution of 256 by 256 pixels. The imaged scene contained a single known test object in a cluttered environment and we attempted to match only this test object at a predicted position. The test object was a moderately complex engineering type object generally known as the "*widget*". The dimensions of the rectangular base of this test object were (20, 50, 70)mm.

Figure 2a

One of the stereo image pairs of this scene is shown in Figure(2a) and the 3D GDB data extracted from this in Figure(2b).

Although, the matcher requires *a priori* the known location of objects, this was not available for this data and had to be estimated, so it is therefore not exact. The tolerance values used in the matching process were :

Figure 2b

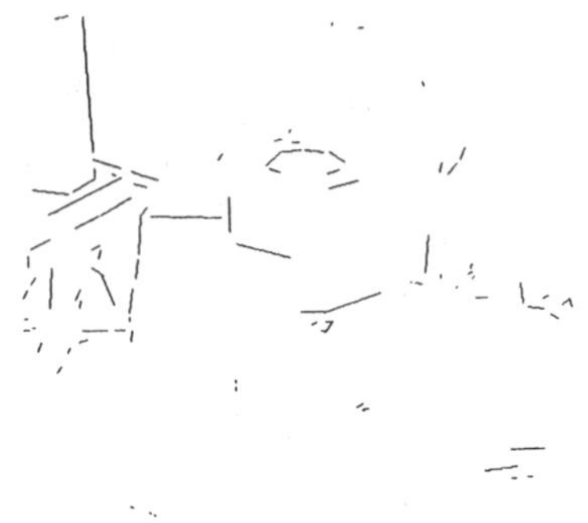

Figure 2e

Maximum divergence angle: 0.25 Radians.

Maximum tessellation divergence angle: 0.30 Radians.

Perpendicular divergence angle (circular arcs): 0.20 Radians.

Minimum Overlap Proportion: 90%.

Maximum separation distance limit: 18mm

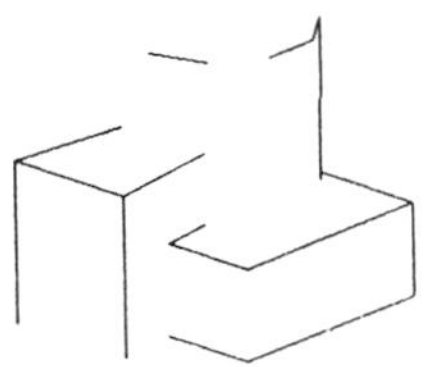

Figure 2f

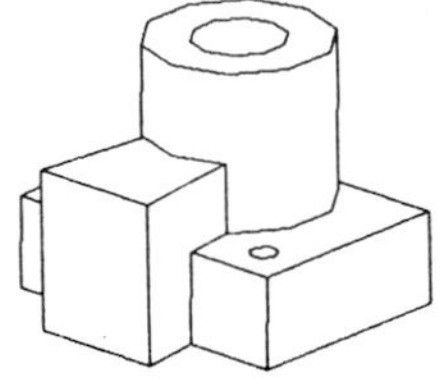

Figure 2c

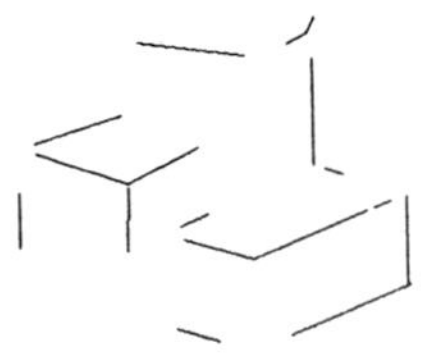

Figure 2g

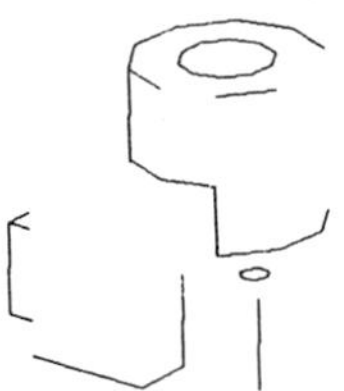

Figure 2d

Figure 2h

The matching sequence between model and data is illustrated in figures(2c-2i), with the *WP Graph* to be matched (2c), the unmatched model edges (2d), the unmatched data segments (2e), the matched model edges (2f) and the matched data segments (2g). Lastly, the data and model are shown overlaid (2h), and the data segments outside the model circumsphere are shown (2i). This matching process ran in 0.75 seconds on a SUN-3

Figure 2i

computer producing the following matching summary :

59 MODEL EDGES PREDICTED VISIBLE

19 MATCHED MODEL EDGES

32% OF PREDICTED MODEL EDGES MATCHED

830mm OF MODEL EDGES PREDICTED VISIBLE

464mm OF MODEL EDGES MATCHED

320mm OF DATA SEGMENTS MATCHED

69% OF MATCHED MODEL EDGE LENGTH MATCHED TO DATA

39% OF PREDICTED EDGE LENGTH MATCHED TO DATA

Of the model edges predicted to be visible 32% were matched to data, and 69% of the total length of these matched edges was accounted for by the total matched data length. The total matched data length also accounted for 39% of the total length of the model edges predicted to be visible. We can see that the circumsphere test was useful in eliminating much of the data from the matching process and enabling a faster run time (Figure(2i)).

Model matching failed in several cases because of problems with the GDB data. No data was produced by the GDB System for a large part of the top of the cylindrical projection of the widget as stereo processing failed to recover this (although edge detection did extract it). There was a similar problem for the left front corner of the base and for the vertical edge on the right front corner. The equivalent model features were therefore not matched. Data loss was also caused by the occlusion of parts of the widget by other objects and this contributes to the low figure for the proportion of model edges predicted visible and matched (32%). In practice a model of the entire scene would be constructed. This would then reduce the number of model edges and the total edge length predicted visible for the widget, increasing the figures for the proportions matched. This low figure is also explained by the failure to match some curved features. As each model curve is tessellated into several linear edges a large number of these can fail to be matched if only a few curved features are not matched. The curved features were not matched as they were either too small to be resolved by the GDB, or were segmented into tessellations which were inaccurate rather than into circular arcs. Matching with circular arcs has been successfully tested [3], and this would have avoided the problems associated with the tessellated data. Despite these problems, the matching system performed well, with nearly all (visible) linear data segments being matched.

9. Conclusion

The purpose of the *WPFM System* we have described is to identify areas of local discrepancy between the *GDB data* and *WP graph* as quickly as possible so that attention may be centred on them by a full vision system. Thus unmatched data may indicate a local area of discrepancy, which combined with information on any expected model features not matched, could indicate to the full vision system that objects have moved, or are missing. However, some unmatched data will be due to noise and other distortions in the data. The matching goodness summary, combined with the use of the full topological and geometric information in the *WP Graph*, could be used by the full vision system to disambiguate this noise and distortion from real differences in expected scenes.

The system has been implemented and run on synthetic data generated by the *Winsom* solid modelling system [15] and on real test data [3], which it can process rapidly to produce a reasonable result. Matching performance with real data will be improved as the resolution of the GDB system is increased by the use of improved calibration techniques and better camera systems. Better data is already provided by the latest version of the GDB System, and this will be used in future testing.

Acknowledgements

Funding for this work was under Alvey grant GR/D/1740.3. Vision test data was provided by T P Pridmore and S B Pollard of AIVRU Sheffield, who also provided help and advice with the GDB System.

References

[1] AIVRU (1986). GDB Release (1.0) User Documentation. AIVRU report 014, University of Sheffield.

[2] Aylett. J.C. (1987). A Boundary Representation for Machine Vision, Working Paper, University Of Edinburgh. (In preparation).

[3] Aylett. J.C. (1987). WPFM: The Workspace Prediction and Fast Matching System, Working Paper, University Of Edinburgh.

[4] Baer, A. et al. (1979). Geometric Modelling: A Survey. Computer Aided Design, Volume 11 Number 5.

[5] Blake, A. and Mayhew, J.E.W. (1985). Alvey 2-1/2D sketch project: Proposed structure for a development sys-

tem. AIVRU report, University of Sheffield.

[6] Boyse, J. W. (1982). GMSolid: Interactive Modeling for Design and Analysis of Solids. IEEE Computer Graphics and Automation, Mar. 1982, pp. 27-40.

[7] Cameron, S.A. (1984). Modelling Solids in Motion, PhD Thesis, University Of Edinburgh.

[8] Cameron, S.A., Aylett, J.C. (1986). Robmod User Guide, DAI Software Paper, University Of Edinburgh.

[9] Fisher, R.B. (1986). From Surfaces to Objects, PhD Thesis, University of Edinburgh.

[10] Gray, M. (1985). Proposal for Representing 3-D Objects. IBM UK Scientific Centre.

[11] Grimson, W. E. L. and Lozano-Perez T. Model-Based Recognition and Localisation from Sparse Range or Tactile Data. The International Journal of Robotics Research, Vol. 3, No. 3, Fall 1984.

[12] Pollard, S. B. et al. (1986). Matching Geometrical Descriptions in Three Space. AIVRU Working Paper 22, University of Sheffield.

[13] Popplestone, R.J., Ambler, A.P. and Bellos, I.M.. An Interpreter for a Language Describing Assemblies. Artificial Intelligence, Vol. 14, pp. 79, 1980.

[14] Pridmore, T.P., Bowen, J.B., Mayhew, J.E.W. (1986). Geometrical description of the connect graph (version 2). The geometrical base description : a specification. AIVRU report 012, University of Sheffield.

[15] Quarendon, P. (1984). WINSOM User's Guide (UKSC 123). IBM UK Scientific Centre.

[16] Requicha A. A. G. (1980). Representations for Rigid Solids: Theory, Methods and Systems. Computing Surveys, Volume 12, No 4.

[17] Requicha A. A. G. and Voelcker, H. B. (1982). Solid Modeling: A Historical Summary and Contemporary Assessment. Computing Surveys, Volume 12, No 4.

[18] Watson, R. (1985). An Edge-Based 3D Geometrical Model Matching System. MSc Dissertation, Department of Artificial Intelligence, University of Edinburgh.

[19] Weiler, K. (1985). Edge Based Data Structures for Solid Modeling in Curved Surface Environments. IEEE Computer Graphics and Automation, Jan. 1985, pp. 21-40.

[20] Wilson, P. R. et al (1985). Interfaces for Data Transfer Between Solid Modeling Systems. IEEE Computer Graphics and Automation, Jan. 1985, pp. 41-51.

[26] The Design of the IMAGINE II Scene Analysis Program

Robert B Fisher

Department of Artificial Intelligence
University of Edinburgh, Edinburgh EH1 2QL, UK

Reprinted, with permission of John Wiley and Sons Ltd, from *From Surfaces to Objects: Computer Vision and Three Dimensional Scene Analysis* 1989.

1. Introduction

The IMAGINE I [1] system was designed for scene analysis in a laboratory or factory domain. The scenes will contain multiple overlapping man-made, but non-polyhedral, objects. Its inputs were segmented surface patches with associated range and surface orientation measurements, and surface-based hierarchically structured object models. Experience with this program has led us to the complete redesign embodied in the IMAGINE II system.

While the re-implementation is complete for only a few of the modules now, the design of the system is complete. This brief paper summarizes the key features of the design, to help place some of the other papers in this book and their motivations into context.

1.1 Critical Review of IMAGINE I

IMAGINE I [1] was designed for scene analysis starting from a labeled, segmented 2 1/2D sketch. That is, it used a surface-based description of the scene, where the surfaces were segmented into regions of nearly constant curvature class, and the boundaries between the regions were labeled with the discontinuity type (i.e. whether a depth, orientation or curvature discontinuity).

From this, individual surface patches were joined or extended across occlusion boundaries, to deduce as much of the original surface shape as possible.

Next, surface patches were grouped to form surface-clusters [2], which were an indentity-independent volumetric scene representation. The purpose of the representation, in the context of 3D scene analysis, was to create contexts within which to accumulate or find evidence for model invocation and hypothesis completion. That is, when working with a given model, only evidence from within the context would be used.

Three-dimensional properties of the surfaces and surface clusters were then estimated (e.g. surface curvatures and areas) using the 3D information present in the data.

Model invocation [5] then occurred. To allow:

- complete access to the whole model base,
- efficient, non-directed computation over all models,
- integration of structural and generic as well as property evidence, and
- graceful degradation as property values become unreliable or missing

the model invocation process was formulated as an evidence accumulation computation evaluated in a network suitable for wide-scale parallelism.

The object models were based on quadratic surface patches linked together to form laminar or solid assemblies, which could then be used to hierarchically construct larger assemblies. Variables could be included in the reference frame transformations.

Model matching was initiated by the invocation process and occurred between models and data features found in the surface or surface cluster contexts. The matching process used the geometrical models to deduce a reference frame for the object, and from this deduced which features of the object were likely to be invisible, partially obscured or fully visible. Then, it searched the image data for evidence justifying all the unlocated visible features (or evidence for their absence, such as being obscured by other objects).

The key example scene analysed was that of a PUMA robot with its gripper obscured by a trashcan. The program successfully deduced the identity of all subcomponents, was largely correct in its visibility analysis and made reasonable estimates of all components (including deducing the joint angles between the links of the robot).

Some of the weaknesses of IMAGINE I are identified here, and provide the impetus for the IMAGINE II design:

- Only reasonably complete surface patches could be used (i.e. no patch fragmentation).
- Data could have some numerical errors, but completely erroneous data (e.g. boundary mis-labeling) would thwart successful scene analysis.
- Object models used only surface patches and these could not extend around the model. Holes and

non-surface evidence were not modeled.

- Data contexts were based only on surface information and did not exploit or account for curve and volumetric data.
- Model invocation did not correctly account for generic relationships and did not exploit spatial configuration evidence.
- Model matching was primarily bottom-up and required complete surface patches.
- The geometric reasoning was based largely on transforming and intersecting parameter ranges represented as 6D parameter rectangular solids, resulting in weak parameter estimation.

2. Overview of the IMAGINE II Design

Figure 1 shows a block diagram of the main modules of the IMAGINE II system. As in IMAGINE I, this program assumes the data comes from segmented 2 1/2D sketch-like data, only here curve and volumetric scene features may be part of the input. Also, the data is allowed to be fragmented and possibly incomplete. The input data structure is a REV graph (Region, Edge, Vertex). In the context of Alvey consortium II, the REV is instantiated using data from the Sheffield GDB system (elsewhere in this book). Alternatively, the data might come from segmented laser ranging data.

The system output is, as before, a list of object hypotheses with position and parameter estimates and a set of image evidence and justifications supporting the object hypothesis.

The rest of this section summarizes the design and some of the ideas behind the modules and data structures shown in figure 1.

2.1 Building the VSCP Structure

The first new representation is the VSCP structure (Volume, Surface, Curve, Point), which is constructed from the REV by knowledge-based structure completion processes. The goal of this process is to group curve and surface features from the REV to overcome fragmentation and occlusion effects and to remove non-structural artifacts (e.g. reflectance edges). It is possible that the original raw data might be interrogated to help verify deductions, but this is not planned for at present.

An example of an occlusion rule is:

- If two valid "TEE" junctions lying on the boundary of the same surface can be extended (using the local boundary shape) until they intersect, and the curve extensions lie behind closer surfaces, then hypothesize that the original shape of the partially obscured surface is that of the extended surface.

An example of a fragmentation rule is:

- If two surface patches are "adjacent", have similar shape, depth and orientation and there are not intervening space curves (e.g. from patch edges or closer surfaces), then merge the two patches.

Here "adjacent" is a heuristic concept because the surface characterization is assumed to be neither complete nor dense (i.e. there may be missing surfaces and there might be substantial gaps between adjacent patches).

2.2 Building the Contexts Structure

Invocation and matching will still occur in data contexts, only now contexts are provided for curve and volume hypotheses as well as surface and surface clusters. The point of these structures is three-fold:

(1) They improve matching efficiency by grouping related data and thereby isolating irrelevant data.

(2) They create a structure that can accumulate plausibility for model invocation.

(3) They represent the 3D scene structure in an identity-independent manner and support vision-related processes such as autonomous vehicle navigation or robot grasping.

Points (1) and (2) are most relevant here.

The context structures are hierarchical in that contexts can be grouped to form larger contexts. Contexts are designed to support recognition of curves, surfaces, volumes and larger assemblies of features, so one context type exists for each. For example, the information contained in an surface context might link to both curve fragments and surface patches, because either might help define a complete surface.

Examples of context-forming rules are:

- If a set of adjacent surface patches are completely isolated by depth discontinuity boundaries and there are no such boundaries internal to the group, then these surfaces form a context for recognizing an assembly.
- If a set of space curves roughly surrounds a region of 2D image space and the curves are not radically different in depth, then hypothesize a surface context lies within the curves.

2.3 Structure Description

Model invocation and hypothesis completion require property estimates for image features. Because we are using 2 1/2D sketch data, 3D properties can be directly measured. These properties may be associated with isolates features, such as:

curve fragment properties: length, curvature, ...

surface fragment properties: area, curvature, elongation, ...

or they may be associated with pairs or groups of features, such as:

curve fragment pairs: relative orientation, relative size, ...

surface fragment pairs: relative orientation, relative size, ...

While this project mainly considers structural properties, this module could also attach non-structural properties, such as colour, gloss, texture or surface markings.

2.4 Model Invocation

Model invocation occurs roughly as in IMAGINE I (section 1.1). A network implements the computation in

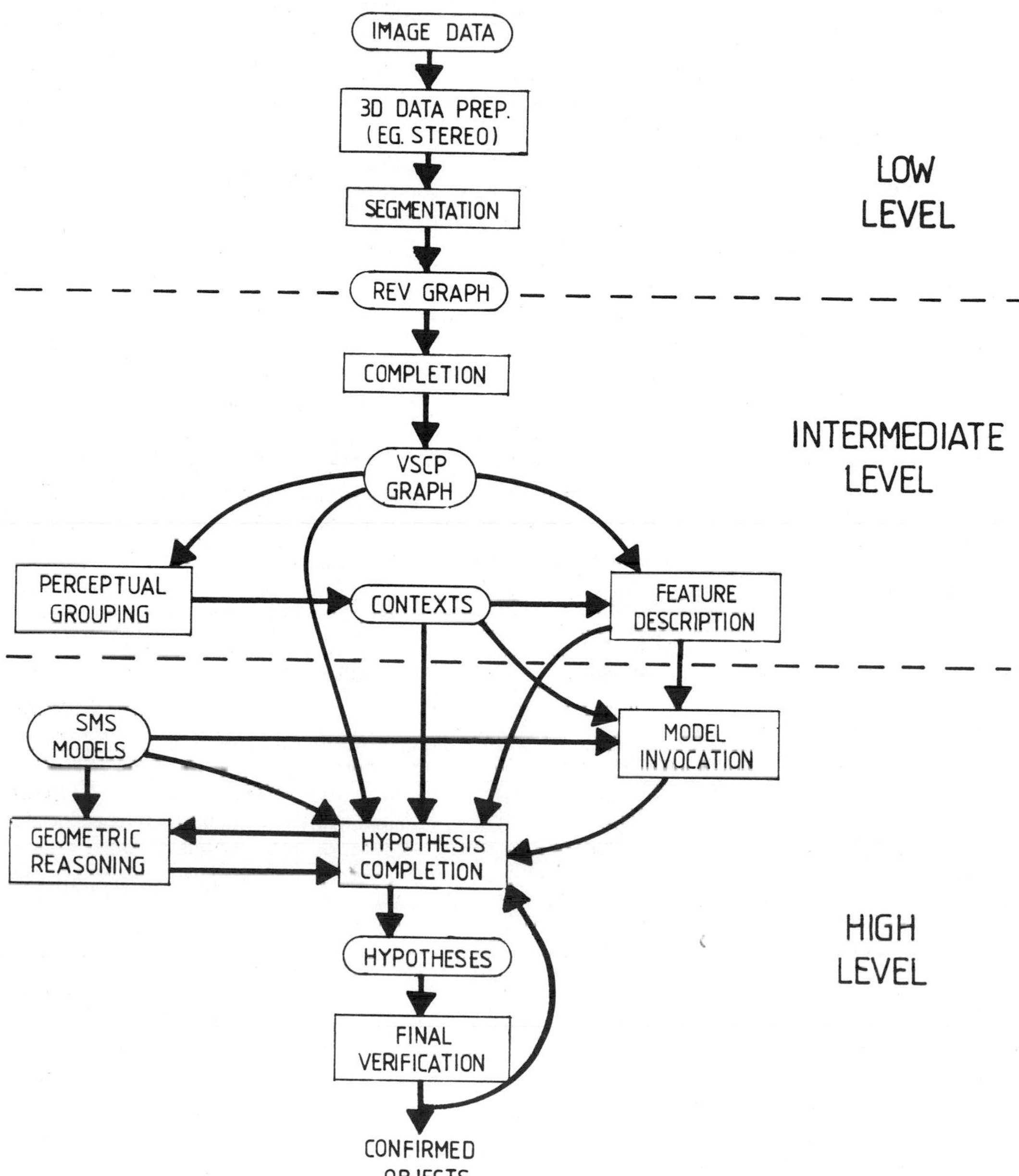

Figure 1 - Structure of the IMAGINE II System

a manner suitable for parallel evaluation. Nodes represent the pairing between individual model and data features, and are connected to other nodes according to the type of relation. Relations include: structural (e.g. "subcomponent of"), generic (e.g. "visual specialization of"), class (e.g. "non-visual specialization of"), inhibiting and general association. Invocation occurs as a result of a plausibility computation, where plausibilities arise from direct evidence (e.g. from a measure of the fit between data and model properties) and indirect evidence imported from the related nodes.

Improvements over IMAGINE I include those of Paechter [8] relating to generics, symbolic properties, property evaluation and uniform integration of direct evidence types. Other extensions include: property evidence from spatial configurations and data feature re-use inhibitions.

2.5 Object Models

The object models used are the SMS models [4,6], as described in a companion paper in this book ("SMS: A Suggestive Modeling System for Object Recognition").

The SMS models are primarily structural with model primitives designed to match with either curve, surface or volumetric data as alternatives. The models are hierarchical, building larger models from previously defined substructures. Substructure placement is by local reference frame transformation.

All model dimensions and reference frame transformations may involve variables and expressions, and algebraic constraints can bound the range of the variables.

A generic hierarchy can be constructed to embody both scale-based and abstraction simplifications.

An important part of the models are the viewpoint-dependent feature groups, which record the fundamentally distinct viewpoints of the object. They also identify model features visible from the viewpoint and identify new viewpoint dependent features (such as occlusion relationships or extremal boundaries).

2.6 Hypothesis Completion

Initial selection of the model may come bottom-up from invocation or top-down as part of another hypothesis being completed. Hypothesis completion then attempts to find evidence concerning all model features.

Feature visibility information comes from selection of a viewpoint-dependent feature group from the SMS model (section 2.5) as selected according to the estimated orientation of the model (from geometric reasoning - section 2.7). This will inform on the visibility of most model features (i.e. whether tangential, backfacing, self-obscured, etc.).

Completion is largely a hierarchical synthesis process that groups recognized subcomponents to form larger hypotheses. The most primitive features are designed to be recognized using either curve, surface or volumetric data, depending on what is available. At all stages, geometric consistency is required, which also results in more precise position estimates and estimates for embedded variables (such as a variable rotation angle about an axis).

Completion is a heuristic process whereby various approaches are tried to find evidence for a feature. For example, some heuristics for surface finding are:

(1) Use a reasonable image patch if it is in the predicted position, with the predicted orientation and has the correct shape and size.

(2) Use a smaller image patch if it is in the predicted position, with the predicted orientation and has the correct shape and no patch of the correct size is found (i.e. expect fragmented patches).

(3) Ignore the surface if it is small and far away.

Application of the heuristics is controlled through routines that know what approaches are available for finding features (and when to try them). Process management uses a task agenda (section 2.8).

2.7 Geometric Reasoning

The geometric reasoning [3,7] is described in detail in a companion paper in this book ("Geometric Reasoning for Computer Vision").

The geometric relationships between model features, model and data pairings and *a priori* scene knowledge are fundamentally represented using algebraic equalities and inequalities.

Algebraic expressions are expensive and difficult to manipulate, so to acquire estimates of object positions, for example, the set of inequalities is transformed into networks expressing the computational relationships between the variables contained in the constraints. These networks have the side-benefits of:

- improving on the first-order bounding methods through iteration and
- having a naturally parallel structure

Analysis of the types of geometric relationships occurring in scene analysis showed that most relationships could be expressed using only a small (5-6) set of standard relationships (e.g. a transformed model point maps to a data point). The standard relationships could then be used to construct standard network modules, which can then be allocated and connected as needed when solving larger problems.

By analyzing the possible pairings of SMS model features to 2 1/2D sketch features, a catalogue of network modules has been developed, to be compiled once, then allocated and connected appropriately for any given model-to-data pairing. This promotes convenient geometric testing and parameter estimation during hypothesis completion.

2.8 Agenda Management

To facilitate experimentation with different control regimes, the hypothesis completion processes are activated from a priority-ordered agenda. An agenda item embodies a request for applying a specified hypothesis completion process on a given datum or hypothesis. The activated process may then enter other requests into the agenda. We use the agenda to implement a mixed control regime involving both top-down and bottom-up hypothesis completion.

2.9 Hypothesis Verification

Because data can be fragmented or erroneous, object hypotheses may be incomplete. Further, spurious hypotheses may be created from coincidental alignments between scene features. Hypothesis completion with geometric reasoning will eliminate some spurious hypotheses, but some instances of global inconsistency may remain, such as when three unconnected planes at right angles may match a cube.

This module is not designed yet, but is intended to consider 2 problems:

(1) global consistency of evidence (e.g. connectedness and proper depth ordering of all components)

(2) heuristic criteria for when to accept incomplete models.

3 Conclusions

The system design given here is intended to cope with fragmented and somewhat incorrect data deriving from scenes containing self and externally obscured complex, non-polyhedral manmade objects including possible degrees of freedom (e.g. robot joints). The test scenes we are planning to use involve both stereo data (from the Alvey "widget" and PUMA robot scenes) and laser ranging scenes (the "oilcan", "lightbulb", "renault part" scenes, ...). While some components of this design are still in the exploratory stage, others are sufficiently developed that parallel implementations can be investigated, leading to eventual re-implementation for realtime efficiency.

This book is being written before all modules have been implemented, integrated and tested; however, it is hoped that the character of the planned IMAGINE II system is clear.

References

[1] Fisher, R. B., "From Surfaces to Objects: Recognizing Objects Using Surface Information and Object Models", PhD Thesis, University of Edinburgh, 1986.

[2] Fisher, R. B., "Identity Independent Object Segmentation in 2 1/2D Sketch Data", Proc. 1986 European Conference on Artificial Intelligence, pp148-153, July 1986.

[3] Orr, M. J. L., Fisher, R. B. "Geometric Reasoning for Computer Vision", Image and Vision Computing, Vol 5, No 3, pp233-238, August 1987.

[4] Fisher, R. B., "SMS: A Suggestive Modeling System for Object Recognition", Image and Vision Computing, Vol 5, No 2, May 1987. Also University of Edinburgh, Dept. of A.I. Working Paper 185, 1985.

[5] Fisher, R. B., "Model Invocation for Three Dimensional Scene Understanding", Proc. 10th Int. Joint Conf. on Artificial Intelligence, pp805-807, 1987.

[6] Fisher, R. B., "Modeling Second-Order Volumetric Features", Proc. 3rd Alvey Vision Conference, pp79-86, Cambridge, 1987.

[7] Fisher, R. B., Orr, M. J. L., "Solving Geometric Constraints in a Parallel Network", Proc. 3rd Alvey Vision Conference, pp87-95, Cambridge, 1987.

[8] Paechter, B., "A New Look At Model Invocation With Special Regard To Supertype Hierarchies", MSc Dissertation, University of Edinburgh, 1987.

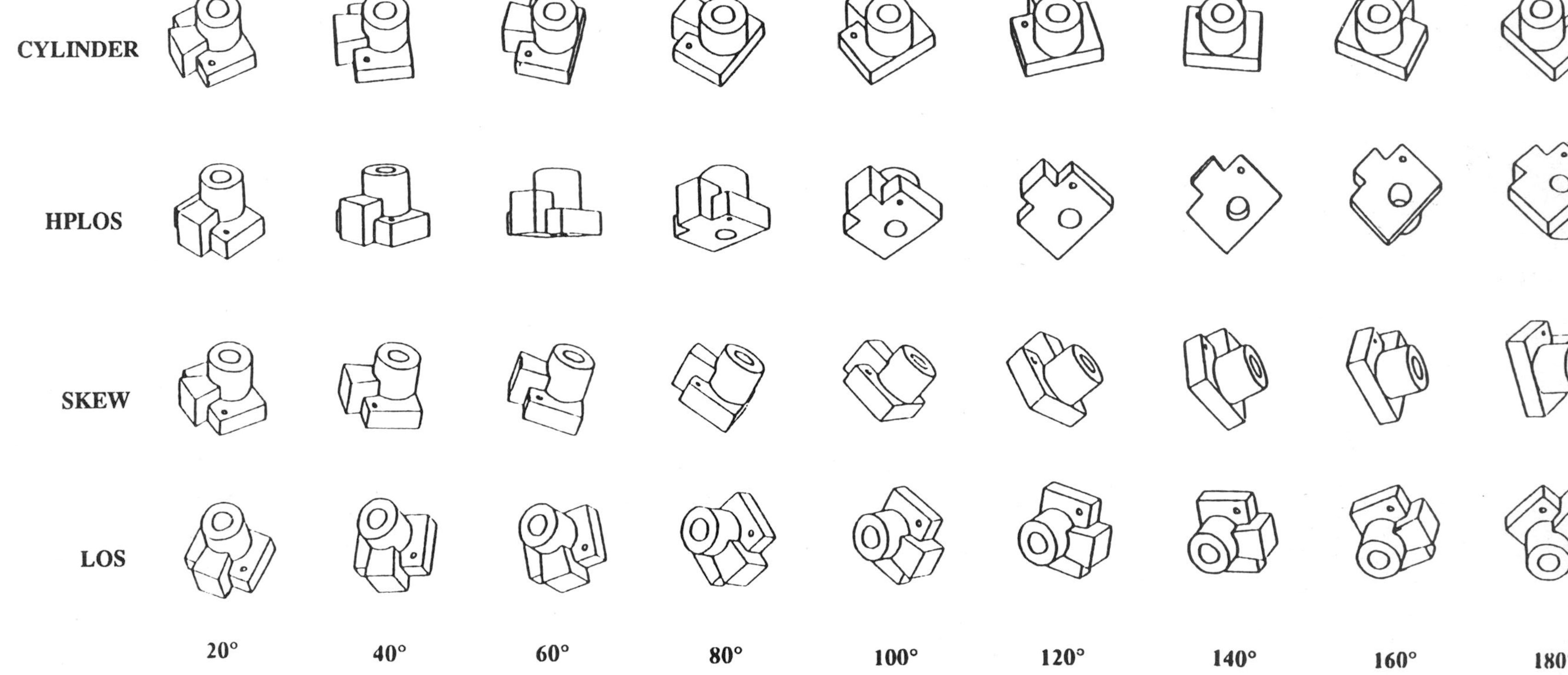

Figure 1. The complete set of rotated views used in the experimrnt arranged by axis and increment of rotation around the axis. Each rotated view was paired with the reference view (bottom).

[27] In Search of 'Characteristic View' 3D Object Representations in Human Vision Using Ratings of Perceived Differences Between Views

Patrick M Langdon, John E W Mayhew and John P Frisby

AI Vision Research Unit,
University of Sheffield, Sheffield S10 2TN

Nineteen subjects were required to rate the perceived difference between a reference view of a 3D object and another view of the object. The latter views were created using four different axes of rotation from the reference view. Ratings of perceived difference increased with increasing angle of view point rotation. The main results, however, were that the amount of perceived difference created by a given angle of view point rotation depended greatly on the axis of rotation and that discontinuities were present in the functions relating perceived difference ratings to view point rotation angle. The latter discontinuities were matched by steps in a simple measure of feature visibility. The implications of these results for 'characteristic view' theories of object recognition are discussed. It is noted that the results are inconsistent with models incorporating shortest-path mental rotation.

1 INTRODUCTION

One possible object representation for view-based recognition is a small set of 'characteristic views' each of which contains information about critical features of the object visible from the same general direction (e.g. Minsky, 1975; Koenderink, 1987; Koenderink & van Doorn, 1979; Chakravarty and Freeman, 1982). Mayhew's YASA representation (described in the introduction to this section of this book) also exploits the characteristic view idea. YASA incorporates a hierarchical organisation of clusters of 3D features such as edges, vertices, and surface regions, stable over a range of view points, to map an object's view potential for recognition.

If human object recognition uses features in this general way then it might be expected that views of an object which possess a high degree of feature commonality would be perceived as more similar than those which do not. Moreover, the function relating perceived difference to view point rotation might be expected to reveal 'steps' reflecting any qualitative changes in visible feature commonality as view point angle varies. That is, perceived difference should increase slowly (if at all) with quantitative feature distortions resulting from small changes in view point but decline sharply as the boundary between characteristic views is traversed and substantial qualitative feature changes occur[1].

Hence, the present study investigated whether visibility of face, edge and vertex features predicts perceived differences between views. The stimuli were line drawings of views of the industrial widget used by various sites within the consortium as a test object (figure 1). The views were created by rotating the view point used for a reference view around four different axes. The study had two parts: (a) measurement of differences in feature visibilities between the reference view and other views; and (b) a psychophysical experiment in which subjects were required to rate their perceived differences between the reference view and the other views.

[1] The term qualitative is used here to refer to presence/absence of a feature in a view. The term quantitative is used for changes in the appearance of a feature with changes in view point.

2 METHOD

2.1 Stimuli

The stimuli were high contrast black and white slides of line drawings of pictures of an object (figure 1) generated by the IBM solid body modeller WINSOM, programmed with the appropriate 3 x 3 rotation matrices. Each slide presented two perspective views of the object, each subtending 3° of the subject's visual angle. There were 43 slides, 36 of which portrayed a reference view paired with a rotated view of the object and 7 which showed a pair of identical reference views. The reference view portrayed the object rotated 45° about the y-axis and -55° about the x-axis (i.e. rotated towards the view point). This view was paired with one of 36 rotated views, the latter taking a random left or right position over conditions.

There were four rotation axes (figure 2). For each axis the object was rotated from the starting orientation of the reference view in 20° steps from 20° to 180° and a view created for each step. For the *CYLINDER* axis condition the object was rotated around an axis of the object which corresponded to the axis of its cylindrical component. This created 9 views, each of which was paired with the reference view to form a slide. In the *HPLOS* (Horizontal Perpendicular to the Line Of Sight) condition the object was rotated around an axis perpendicular to the line of sight and lying in the horizontal plane (parallel to the picture x-axis). In the *LOS* (Line Of Sight) axis condition the object was rotated around the observer's line of sight through the object. Finally, in the *SKEW* axis condition, intended to be an axis which bore no relation to the object or principal axes of the observer's reference frame, the object was rotated around the axis in the direction of the unit axis x = 0.512, y = 0.384, z = - 0.768 (figures 1 and 2).

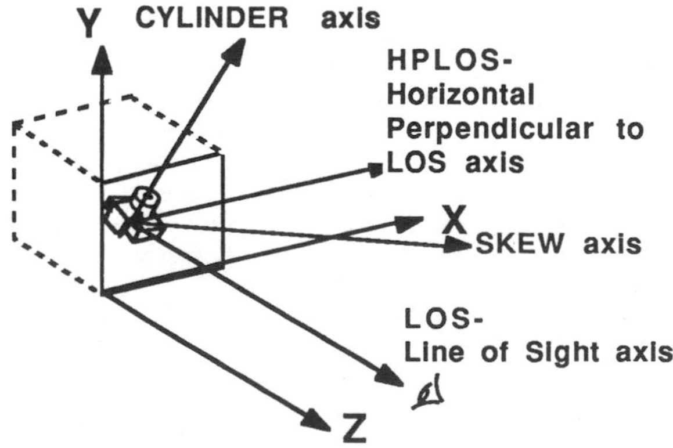

Figure 2. The four rotation axes used for the generation of the rotated views.

As view point is changed there occasionally occur views which are 'singular' or 'degenerate', in the sense that they offer a radically unrepresentative appearance available only from a single or very restricted range of view points (Koenderink 1987; Chakravarty, 1982). An extreme example is a face-on view of a block where only one face is visible. Views of this type were avoided as far as possible but the simple form of view sampling adopted did not preclude them altogether: see, for example, the 140° views for the *CYLINDER* and *HPLOS* axes.

2.2 Measures of Feature Differences Between Views

A count of the number of common and distinctive features between stimulus pairs was made by hand for three feature classes: faces, edges and vertices. Each feature was numbered and a feature was counted as common when the same feature was visible in two views. A 3D vertex was counted as visible even when its appearance was different (e.g. a 3D vertex projecting into a 2D arrow junction which changes to a 2D Y-junction with view point rotation).

It was possible for views to possess the same set of common features but differ in that one view contained additional distinctive features. Hence, the following definition of feature difference was used:

(Features in reference view) - (Common - Distinctive)

For present purposes, a 'combined' feature difference measure was obtained based on all three feature types measured: faces, edges, and vertices. Separate analyses for each feature type, however, have provided a similar overall picture (Langdon, 1989).

2.3 Experimental Design and Procedure

Nineteen volunteer subjects with normal or corrected to normal vision took part. They saw the stimuli at eye-level back-projected on to a ground glass screen which they viewed from a distance of about 150 cm while seated.

The experimental session began with subjects being invited to examine a small hand-held model of the test object for 2 minutes. They were then shown an identical pair of reference views and told these corresponded to zero difference on the perceived difference scale which they would be taught to use. Then followed a set of ten example views, taken from view points different from those used in the experimental stimulus sets. Subjects examined these for one minute to gain familiarity with the range of the scale. This scale was defined to them in formal instructions in the following way: 0 was described as as "*a pair of identical views*" and 100 as "*the most different views imaginable*", and judgements were to be made on the basis of "*the visual appearance of the object's shape*". For the experiment proper subjects were instructed to call out their ratings as quickly as possible. Response latencies were measured from the onset of stimulus to verbal response, the latter recorded with a throat microphone. The latency data are reported in Langdon (1989).

Each subject performed 86 trials, the same 42 slides being presented in two blocks. The first and every sixth slide presented an identical pair of reference views to remind subjects of the meaning of zero difference on the perceived difference scale (see below). The order of presentation of all remaining slides was randomised for each subject.

3 RESULTS

3.1 Feature Difference Measures

Figure 3a shows how the combined feature difference measure varied with rotation angle around each axis. Data from the LOS axis are not shown because for that axis feature visibility remained constant over all view points. Inevitably, feature difference increased with rotation angle for all axes but two aspects of the graphs are worthy of special note, as follows:

(a) The feature difference scores from the different rotation axes tend to form separate sub-populations. That is, the data points are not scattered homogeneously around a single regression line. Those from the *HPLOS* and *CYLINDER* axes are fairly well intermingled but the *SKEW* axis points fall distinctly below them.

(b) There are some indications of step changes in feature visibility. For example, in the *HPLOS* case there is a clear step between 40° and 60°, and another between 120° and 140°. For the *SKEW* axis, there is step between 60° and 80° and a suggestion of another between 100° and 140°. The *CYLINDER* axis presents much more of a straight line, except for the suggestion of a step between 20° and 40°.

3.2 Perceived Difference Ratings

The means of each subject's two ratings for each stimulus were analysed using a two-factor ANOVA, with group means and standard errors plotted in figure 3b. The ±1 standard error bars around these means reveal remarkably good concordance between subject's ratings, suggesting that they interpreted the task similarly.

As was to be expected, perceived difference increased with increased view point rotation for all axes ($F_{5,92}$ = 135.5, $p<0.001$). The important points of detail to note from figure 3b are as follows:

(a) There were considerable disparities in overall mean perceived difference ratings for the different axes ($F_{2,30}$ = 81.6, $p<0.001$). Paired comparisons between means revealed that the *CYLINDER* axis ratings were lower than all the others, and that the *HPLOS* axis ratings were higher than those for the *LOS* and *SKEW* axes (all at $p<0.01$, Newman-Keuls).

(b) The interaction between axis and rotation angle is highly significant ($F_{9,164}$ = 5.9, $p<0.001$). In the *HPLOS* case, a sharp decrease in slope is noticeable at 60°; the curve flattens off at that point although there is some suggestion of another discontinuity between 120° and 140°. For the *SKEW* axis, there is a shallow step between 60° and 80°, and some suggestion of an even shallower one between 120° and 140°. The *CYLINDER* axis data fall more or less on a straight line except for a 'bump' at the 140° point which may be a reflection of the rather degenerate character of the 140° view.

4 DISCUSSSION

The fact that both perceived difference ratings and feature differences scores rise with view point rotation is not at all surprising and does not in itself provide interesting evidence that our simple feature visibility measure predicts perceived difference/similarity. For an examination of this issue, various details of the data need to be considered.

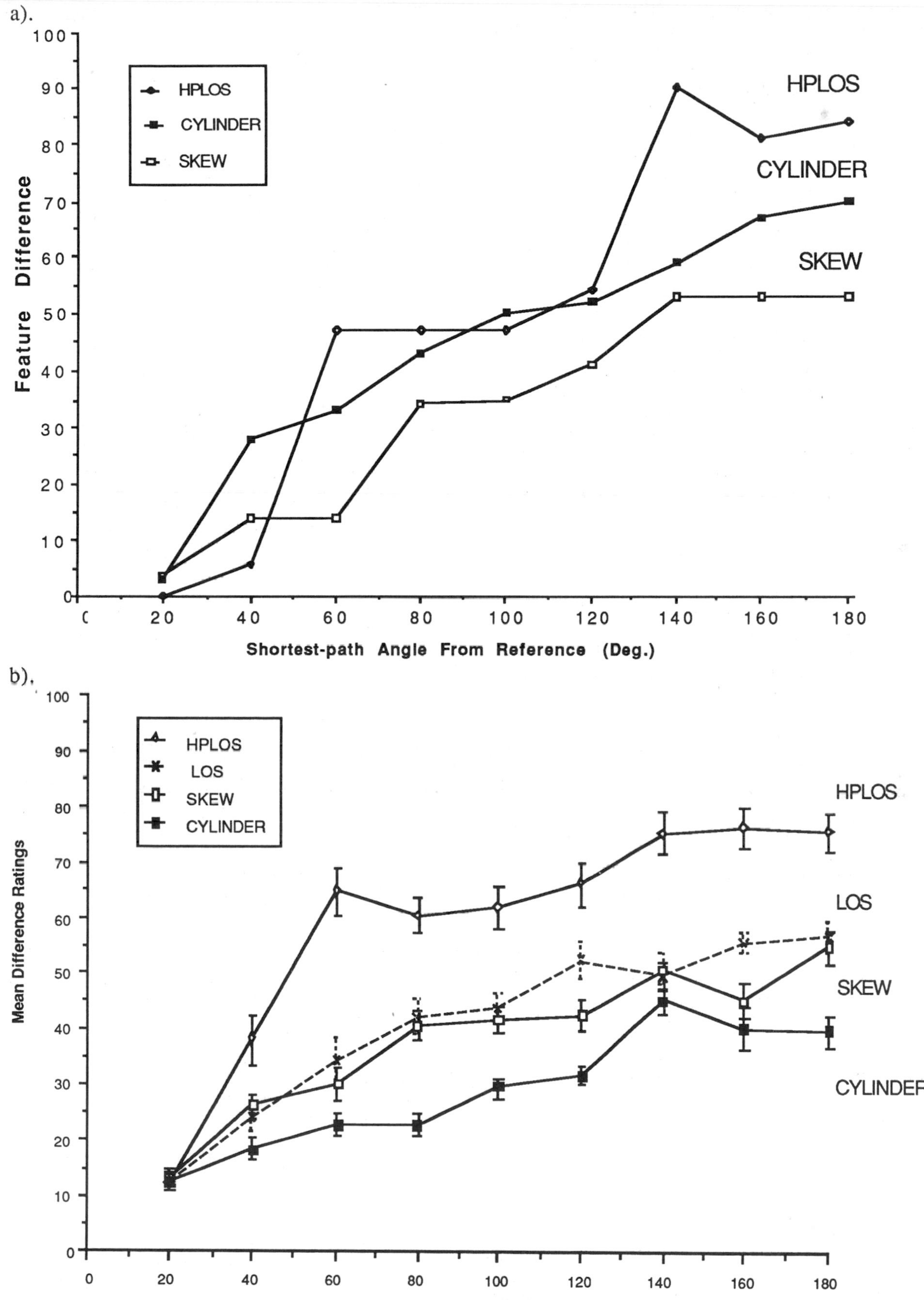

Figure 3 Relationships of rotation angle from reference with (a) Combined face, edge and vertex feature difference (top), and (b) Perceived difference (bottom).

(a) Both the ratings and the feature difference data for the various axes tended to form separate sub-populations, with the *HPLOS* axis having the greatest effect in each case. However, whereas *SKEW* axis rotations had least effect on feature difference scores, that position was clearly taken by the *CYLINDER* axis for the perceived difference ratings. This qualitative dissimilarity suggests that our simple feature difference score is a rather poor predictor of perceived difference ratings, but it can be argued that mean overall ratings could be influenced in part by other factors. For example, the *CYLINDER* axis conditions stayed closest throughout the rotation angle range to the 'three-quarters canonical perspective' view customarily preferred for 3D objects (Palmer, Rosch and Chase, 1981). This might have led subjects to judge them overall as 'less different'. Hence, perhaps more weight should be given to the changes within each axis rotation condition than to overall mean differences between them.

(b) In general, there is a suprisingly good match between steps in the two cases. The clearest correlation occurs for *HPLOS* at 40-60°. Another reasonably strong linkage occurs at 60-80° for the *SKEW* axis. Matches are rather less pronounced for the steps in the *HPLOS* and *SKEW* feature difference curves at around 140° but there is suggestive evidence of parallel steps in the perceived diffrence curves, at any rate for *HPLOS*. Also, the failure to find any steps in either case for the *CYLINDER* axis over the range 40-180° is in keeping with the general conclusion we draw, namely that the psychophysical data do show some interesting and encouraging signs of transitions which are broadly in keeping with the characteristic view idea. (Note: we have already suggested that the 'bump', not step, located at 140° on the *CYLINDER* perceived difference curve could be caused by subjects' responding to the degeneracy of that view.)

(c) Since no feature differences at all result from increasing rotation angles around the LOS axis, feature visibility completely fails to account both for the monotonic increase in perceived difference obtained for this axis and its mid-way position in the overall perceived difference ordering of conditions (figure 3b). It might be argued, however, that perceived difference ratings for this axis were a special case for which subjects used their ratings to reflect sensitivity to stimulus orientation rather than feature differences.

We conclude that our simple model of feature visibility provides a remarkably good account of some aspects of the perceived difference judgments, namely the locations of step discontinuities. However, it is also clear that not all the details of the judgement data can be predicted by simple feature visibility - but perhaps that would anyway be too much to expect given the intrinsically ill-defined and general character of the 'perceived difference' rating scale which subjects were asked to use.

To sum up, we regard the results as providing some limited support for characteristic view theories founded on simple lists of visible features.

5 MENTAL ROTATION

Driven by the observation that subjects seemed sensitive to rotation of the image in the LOS condition even though feature visibility there remained constant, we have also attempted to interpret the data within the context of the literature on mental rotation. However, both analogue and propositional mental rotation theories (e.g. Shepard and Metzler, 1971; Just and Carpenter, 1976) would predict that perceived difference should vary with rotation angle in the same way for all rotation axes. This is because all rotated views were generated using shortest-path rotations around their respective axes, and hence could be brought into congruence using the same-sized shortest-path rotations; and shortest-path rotation is assumed in those mental rotation models. Yet it is clear that marked disparities in perceived difference ratings were obtained for the four axes. Langdon (1989) shows how these ratings can be well-described by a 'spin-precession' mental rotation model (Parsons, 1987). Langdon suggests that the perceived difference ratings could reflect two simultaneous mental rotations: one (precession) brings a major axis of the object, here the CYLINDER axis, into alignment, while the other comprises a rotation around that axis (spin).

Acknowledgements
Patrick Langdon was supported by a SERC IT-linked studentship. We are grateful to IBM UK Ltd for the use of the WINSOM body modeller.

REFERENCES

Chakravarty, I. and Freeman, H. (1982) Characteristic views as a basis for three-dimensional object recognition. *SPIE, Robot Vision* **336** 37- 45.

Just, M.A. and Carpenter, P.A. (1976). Eye fixations and cognitive processes.*Cognitive Psychology* **8** 441-480.

Koenderink, J.J., & Van Doorn, A.J. (1979). Internal representation of solid shape with respect to vision. *Biological Cybernetics* **32** 211- 216.

Koenderink, J.J. (1987). An internal representation for solid shape based on the topological properties of the apparent contour. In Whitman R. and Ullman, S. (Eds.) *Image Understanding*. Ablex Publ. Pp. 85-86.

Langdon, P.M. (1989). *Perceived similarity judgments between multiple views of 3D objects and 'Characteristic View' theories of recognition.* PhD thesis, University of Sheffield.

Minsky, M. (1975). A framework for representing knowledge. In Winston, P.H. (Ed.). *The psychology of computer vision.* New York: McGraw-Hill.

Palmer, S. Rosch, E and Chase P. (1981) Canonical perspective and the perception of objects. In Long, J. and Baddeley, A.D. (Eds.) *Attention and Performance* ***IX***. Hillsdale, N.J.: Larence Erlbaum Associates Inc. Pp. 135-151.

Parsons, L.M. (1987) Visual discrimination of abstract mirror-reflected three-dimensional objects at many orientations. *Perception & Psychophysics* **42** 49-59.

Shepard, R.N. and Metzler, J. (1971). Mental rotation of three dimensional objects. *Science* **171** 701- 703.

[28] Matching Geometrical Descriptions in Three-Space

Stephen B Pollard, John Porrill, John E W Mayhew and John P Frisby

AI Vision Research Unit
University of Sheffield, Sheffield S10 2TN, UK

Reprinted, with permission of Butterworth Scientific Ltd, from *Image and Vision Computing*, 1987, **5**, 73-78.

Abstract

A matching strategy for combining two or more three space descriptions, obtained here from edge based binocular stereo, of a scene is discussed. The scheme combines features of a number of recent model matching algorithms with heuristics aimed to reduce the space of potential rigid transformations that relate scene descriptions.

1. Introduction

The topic addressed by this paper is the matching of stereo-based 3D edge descriptions obtained from two or more different views of a scene. We describe a matching algorithm with wide potential application in the temporal aggregation of scene descriptions for scene model evolution and autonomous vehicle guidance.

The algorithm is for example of use as a precursor to the combination of data about the 3D geometry of a given edge into an improved estimate (Porrill et al[1]). It is also useful for obtaining an accurate estimate of the location of the viewpoint with respect to the scene. Moreover, the algorithm is shown to be useful as a primitive model matcher in which a visual description of a known model can be matched to an instance of the modelled object in a cluttered scene.

The algorithm can also be used for a purely visual method of creating an object model description. Given descriptions of the object-to-be-modelled from multiple viewpoints, the algorithm can combine these into a single description which can then serve as a model of the object-to-be-recognised in subsequent views of cluttered scenes containing the object. For this and other model matching applications it will clearly be desirable to incorporate into the model description some organisation of its view potential[2–4] including the flagging of non-rigid relationships (eg hinges). However, whilst we have obtained some success in this regard it remains a topic beyond the scope of the current paper.

The reasonable assumption that the geometry of the scene remains constant between views provides a powerful matching constraint. It allows our goal to be defined as identifying the best set of matches that is consistent with a single rigid transformation. The rigidity constraint can either be explicit, requiring each primitive to undergo the same global transformation, or implicit, requiring that local geometrical relationships between primitives be preserved. Tree searching strategies based upon each have been exploited by Faugeras *et al*[5, 6] and Grimson *et al*[7–9] respectively. Constraints based upon local geometrical relationships have the computational advantage that such relationships can be precompiled for each scene and stored in look up tables, with the result that simple pairwise comparisons are all that is necessary to exploit rigidity. Under the alternative strategy, each potential global transformation requires both computation and then application to each descriptive primitive in one scene to locate matching descriptive primitives in the other.

The matching strategy described here differs from that of Grimson et al in that tree search is replaced by a hypothesis and test strategy based upon a number of focus features[10, 11]. Exhaustive tree searching strategies are only computationally efficient where all the data in one scene is known to be present in the other[12, 13], otherwise, despite the powerful constraint provided by rigidity they tend to be combinatorially explosive. Here, unfortunately, due to the difference in viewpoint, the vagaries of the image formation process, and the imaging process itself the mapping between two geometrical descriptions of the same scene is generally many-to-many. Hence major computational problems will arise with simple tree search. Concentrating initial attention to the matches of a relatively small number of heuristically determined focus features allows, at the expense of some generality, the search space to be reduced considerablely.

2. Geometrical Description

The task of matching three space descriptions of well carpentered scenes is discussed. For brevity and simplicity we shall restrict our attention to scenes, or regions of scenes, that are amenable to characterisation by their straight surface discontinuities. However extensions to include both circular and space curve descriptions in the matching process are currently under investigation. All such descriptions are obtained here from edge based binocular stereo triangulation[14–16]. Matched edge points are aggregated into extended edge structures[3] and described by a process of recursive segmentation and description as either straight, circular, planar or space curves[17–19]. The grouping of edge descriptions in this way provides an initial, though impoverished, viewer centred scene description called the Geometric Descriptive Base[20] (GDB).

In the GDB straight lines are represented (in an overdetermined fashion) by the triple $(\mathbf{v},\mathbf{p}_1,\mathbf{p}_2)$, that is, their two end points $\mathbf{p}_1$ and $\mathbf{p}_2$ and the direction vector between them $\mathbf{v}$. The centroid of a line (its midpoint $(\mathbf{p}_1+\mathbf{p}_2)/2$) shall be denoted $\mathbf{c}$. Where the actual physical occupancy of a line is not important it is sometimes helpful to represent them by the vector pair $(\mathbf{v},\mathbf{c})$.

3. The Matching Problem

In general it is not possible to place a restriction on the allowable transformations that take primitives from one scene description into another unless an a priori estimate of the difference in their viewpoint is available. Of course in the domain of autonomous navigation and scene evolution it is likely that just such an estimate exists. If for instance the temporal delay that separates scene descriptions obtained by an autonomous vehicle is sufficiently small (ie the frame rate is sufficiently high) the transformation that takes one view point into another will be of a limited magnitude. Alternatively if a less intensive rate of low level image processing is to be preferred an estimate of the trajectory could be used to approximate the geometry that relates successive viewpoints. The design of our matching algorithm is general in this regard. An estimate of the global transformation is not required to achieve successful matching; if however such information is readily available it can be exploited to reduce the set of potential matches and thus also the computational requirements.

Given the somewhat impoverished nature of our descriptive basis and the potential for unfortunate, and unforeseen, occlusion relationships to arise, it seems prudent not to restrict potential matches on the basis of the descriptive properties of the line primitives (eg length, contrast etc). Hence in principle, each primitive extracted from one scene is able to match with each of the primitives in the other. Furthermore we do not feel, at the present time, able reliably to obtain higher level features and topological relationships (eg vertices or connected edge segments describing a polyhedral face) and focus initial matching about these. Frequently relationships of this kind will not be preserved between views. It has not even assumed that the locations of the end points of lines remains constant as continuous lines in one image may appear broken in the other. Lines are however expected to overlap significantly.

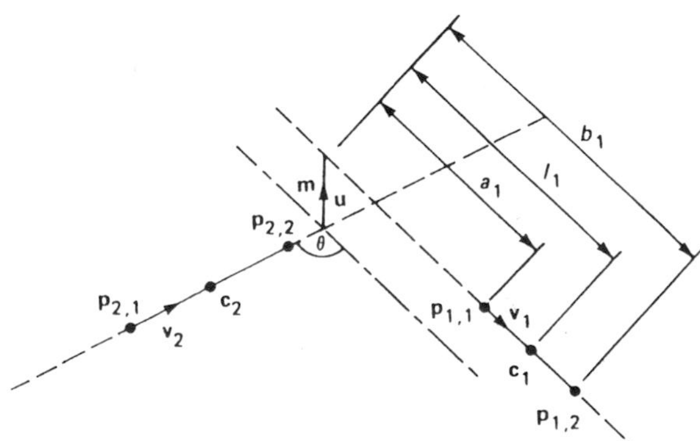

Figure 1. Geometrical relationships are illustrated for a pair of lines. These are: their orientation difference θ, the distance m between their extensions, and the distances a_1 and b_1 from the ends of the physical line to the point of minimum separation.

3.1. Exploiting Rigidity

Matches for two non-parallel line segments are sufficient to constrain all six degrees of freedom that constitute a putative transformation between scene descriptions[6]. Once a transformation is hypothesised, rigidity provides a powerful constraint upon other consistent matches (subject to tolerance errors; the details of which are not discussed here for reasons of brevity). As discussed above rigidity can be exploited more cheaply (though less strongly) if expressed in terms of the consistency in a number of pairwise relationships. Here we adopt just three, they are (illustrated also in figure 1):

(i) orientation differences, given by $\theta = \cos^{-1}(\mathbf{v}_1.\mathbf{v}_2)$.

(ii) minimum separations between (extended) lines. The unit vector in the direction of closest approach (normal to each line) is given by $\mathbf{u} = (\mathbf{v}_1 \times \mathbf{v}_2)/|\mathbf{v}_1 \times \mathbf{v}_2|$ and component of the vector difference between the lines in that direction by $m = (\mathbf{c}_2 - \mathbf{c}_1).\mathbf{u}$. However if the lines are close to parallel it is more sensible to simply measure the perpendicular distance between the lines $m = |(\mathbf{c}_2 - \mathbf{c}_1) - ((\mathbf{c}_2 - \mathbf{c}_1).\mathbf{v}_1)\mathbf{v}_1|$.

(iii) distance to the beginning and end of each physical line with respect to the point of minimum separation and in the direction of the line. This relationship is only applicable for non-parallel lines. The vector between the points of closest approach is given by $\mathbf{m} = ((\mathbf{c}_2 - \mathbf{c}_1).\mathbf{u})\mathbf{u}$. Adding $\mathbf{m}$ to $\mathbf{c}_2$ gives $\mathbf{c}'_2$, where lines $(\mathbf{v}_1, \mathbf{c}_1)$ and $(\mathbf{v}_2, \mathbf{c}'_2)$ are coplanar and meet at the point of closest approach on $(\mathbf{v}_1, \mathbf{c}_1)$. The signed distance to that point from $\mathbf{c}_1$ in the direction $\mathbf{v}_1$ is given by $l_1 = ((\mathbf{v}_2 \times \mathbf{v}_1).(\mathbf{v}_2 \times (\mathbf{c}'_2 - \mathbf{c}_1)))/|\mathbf{v}_2 \times \mathbf{v}_1|^2$. Hence the distance from $\mathbf{p}_{1_1}$ and $\mathbf{p}_{1_2}$ to that point are given by $a_1 = l_1 + (\mathbf{c}_1 - \mathbf{p}_{1_1}).\mathbf{v}_1$ and $b_1 = l_1 + (\mathbf{c}_1 - \mathbf{p}_{1_2}).\mathbf{v}_1$ respectively. Similarly for distances to the point of closest separation on the other line $a_2 = l_2 + (\mathbf{c}_2 - \mathbf{p}_{2_1}).\mathbf{v}_2$ and $b_2 = l_2 + (\mathbf{c}_2 - \mathbf{p}_{2_2}).\mathbf{v}_2$.

Potential matches for each pair of descriptive elements from one scene description can be checked for geometrical consistency in the other. Rigidity implies that each of the pairwise relationships will be preserved between scene descriptions, hence any measured discrepancies must lie within a range predicted by the magnitude of allowable errors. Furthermore a pair of consistent non-parallel matches provides a powerful constraint upon the remaining matches. Hence they can be thought to represent, implicitly and weakly, a global transformation. The representation is weak because it is possible, on occasion, for matches that are not consistent with a single global transformation to satisfy the pairwise relationships. In practice such problems are not major. Furthermore if the basis of the implicit transforms is raised from a pair to a triple, quadruple or even a quintuple of matches, such inconsistencies are far less likely (additionally the margin of allowable error on each new match will be reduced).

3.2. Look Up Tables

The pairwise geometrical relationships, upon which local constraints are based, have the advantage that they can be precomputed for each pair of lines independently for each scene description and stored as look up tables [as with [7–9, 12]]. Each relational property is stored as a range of values consistent with the allowable error. It is these ranges that must overlap for a pair of matches to be considered geometrically consistent. Errors in centroid location and orientation are considered separately and combined in a conservative fashion that simply adds their contributions resulting in the largest feasible range of pairwise geometrical relationships.

Given a pair of lines with allowable errors $|\varepsilon_1| < \alpha_1$ and $|\varepsilon_2| < \alpha_2$ on the location of their centroid and solid angles ϕ_1 and ϕ_2 on their direction vector the following ranges can be derived:

(i) on orientation differences: the interval $[\max(\theta-\phi_1-\phi_2,0),\min(\theta+\phi_1+\phi_2,\pi)]$.

(ii) on minimum separations between (extended) lines: the interval

$$m \pm (\alpha_1+\alpha_2+|l_1|\tan\phi_1+|l_2|\tan\phi_2)$$

(iii) on the distances to the beginning and end of each physical line with respect to the point of minimum separation: the approximate intervals

$$a_1 \pm (\alpha_1+\alpha_2+|l_2|\tan\phi_2/\sin\theta)$$

$$b_1 \pm (\alpha_1+\alpha_2+|l_2|\tan\phi_2/\sin\theta)$$

$$a_2 \pm (\alpha_1+\alpha_2+|l_1|\tan\phi_1/\sin\theta)$$

$$b_2 \pm (\alpha_1+\alpha_2+|l_1|\tan\phi_1/\sin\theta)$$

3.3. Feature Focus

Our current approach to matching is to apply heuristics similar to those of feature focus[10, 11] in order to avoid unbounded search. The strategy is to concentrate initial attention upon a number of salient features. Only matches associated with these features are subsequently entitled to *grow* hypothetical transformations. Currently processing terminates only after all focus features have been considered. As an alternative it could be possible to complete computation once a *sufficiently good* match has been located. However, at the present time, a suitable definition of *sufficiently good* is not available. The feature focus strategy adopted here differs from those considered previously as familiarity with the scene it is not assumed. As a result focus features and matching strategies are not an integral component of our scene description: they must be generated at run time.

Focus features are identified in a single scene description. Currently they are chosen simply on the basis of their length, a property associated with salience. Some effort is expended to ensure that all regions of the scene are represented by chosen features, ie a feature is identified as a focus if there are not more than a certain number of longer features within a predetermined radius of it.

Our matching strategy proceeds as follows

(1) a focus features is selected (in turn);

(2) the S closest features to it with length greater than L are identified;

(3) potential matches for the focus feature are considered, unlike matching in general, these are selected conservatively on the basis of length (which must lie within 30% of each other);

(4) consistent matches for each of the neighbouring primitives are located;

(5) this set of matches (including that of the focus feature) is searched for maximally consistent cliques of cardinality at least C, each of these can be thought of as a potential implicit transformation;

(6) each clique is extended by adding new matches for all other lines in the scene if they are consistent with each of the matches in the clique;

(7) mutually consistency can be ensured by some further (cheap) tree search;

(8) extended cliques are ranked on the basis of the sum of the length of their matched lines, the contribution from each match being the lesser of the lengths of its constituent lines;

Note that any/all of the focus features are potentially able to discover the implicit transformation (clique of correct matches) that takes one viewpoint into the other. Hence only allowing focus features to match conservatively does not greatly hinder the matching strategy. Furthermore some unnecessary computation can be avoided if consistent cliques arrived at via different focus features are identified and combined prior to their extension in step (6).

Insisting that at least one focus feature obtains a match places a bound upon depth of search to which current assignments are allowed to be all null. In a similar fashion, restricting the set of focus feature matches reduces the breadth of search. Furthermore requiring that mutually consistent matches be found for C of the S near neighbouring primitives further controls the search. Consider each matched focus feature to be the origin of an independent search tree; paths below the depth S are bounded unless at least C matches occur above them. In practice it is this constraint that provides the greatest prune, as very few incorrect transformations satisfy this requirement.

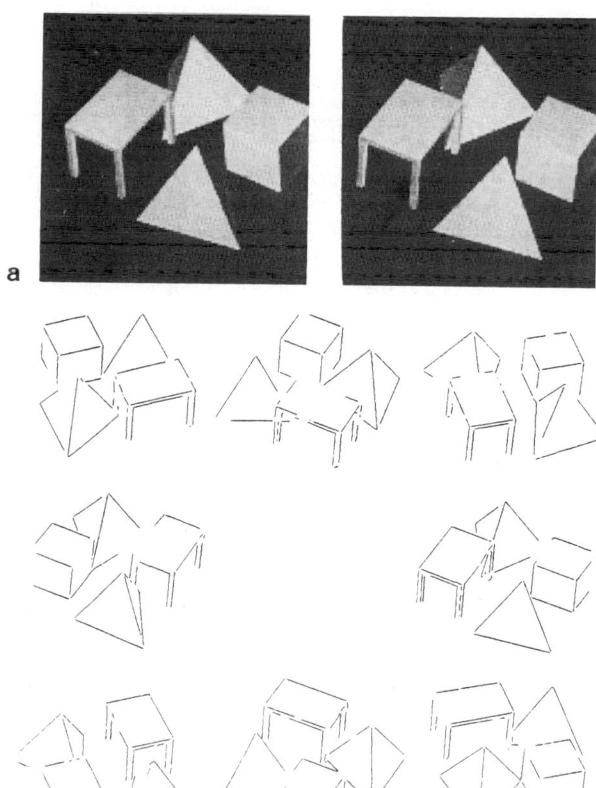

Figure 2. Part (a) is a stereogram of one view of a synthesised scene (arranged for cross eyed fusion). Part (b) shows GDB descriptions of this scene from eight equally spaced viewpoints.

The power of our focusing heuristics are dependent upon the choice of S and C; if C is too small many putative transformations will be explored at great expense, hence C must be large enough to impose considerable constraint upon potential transformations. Conversely, whilst S must be sufficiently large that C amongst them will locate consistent matches, if S becomes too large the time spent searching increases dramatically. In practice, as will be illustrated below, very few consistent sets of matches, beyond the correct one, are found if $C = 4$ and $S = 7$.

The set of S primitives are chosen to neighbour the focus feature in question for two reasons. First, the constraints provided by pairwise consistency are strongest over modest physical separations as the allowable error ranges are smaller. And second, in the absence of a more sophisticated scheme, neighbouring primitives are thought *more likely* to occupy similer view potentials and hence appear simultaneously in scene descriptions obtained from different views.

The number of focus features used for matching is increased with n (in the experiments below approximately $0.2 \times n$). Similarly the number of potential matches, the number of potential transformations, and the cost of extending each transformation all increase with n. However as S and C remain constant the the expense of exploring each focus match will on average also remain constant. Hence whilst computational expense is high (increasing with some multiple of n^4) combinatorial explosion is avoided. Furthermore if an appropriate computer architecture were available it may be possible to do some proportion of this work in parallel (for example the consideration of each match of each focus feature).

A similar matching strategy has been proposed recently by Ayache *et al*[21], except that they consider transformations for all consistent matches of pairs of privileged lines (equivalent to chosing C to be 2), of which there may be a great many. Furthermore each pair of such matches is used by them to compute an explicit transformation, rather than the implicit representation we prefer.

4. Matching Experiments

Performance of the matching algorithm is illustrated quantitatively for artificial stereo data provided by the IBM Winsom[22] body modeller and qualitatively for natural stereo data. The former is used to obviate the accurate stereo calibration problem which is a current research topic in the laboratory.

Consider first the synthesised scene depicted in the stereogram in figure 2a. GDB descriptions of this scene, obtained from eight equally spaced viewpoints (45 degrees apart) are shown in 2b. Each description consists of approximately 40 above-threshold GDB line primitives. These are to be matched between viewpoints to construct a more complete model of the scene. The results of the matching process between the first two views is illustrated in figure 3. The ten focus features chosen in view 1 obtained a total of 174 potential matches in view 2. Setting S to 7 and C to 4 only 13 independent implicit transformations result. After extension the best consistent transformation included 18 matched lines. The best rigid rotation and translation (in that order) that takes view 1 to view 2 is computed by the least squares method discussed by Faugeras *et al*[6] in which rotations are represented as quaternions (though for simplicity the optimal rotation is recovered before translation). In figure 3a view 1 is transformed into view 2 (the error in the computed rotation is 0.48 degrees) and matching lines are shown bold, many of the the unmatched lines are not visible in both

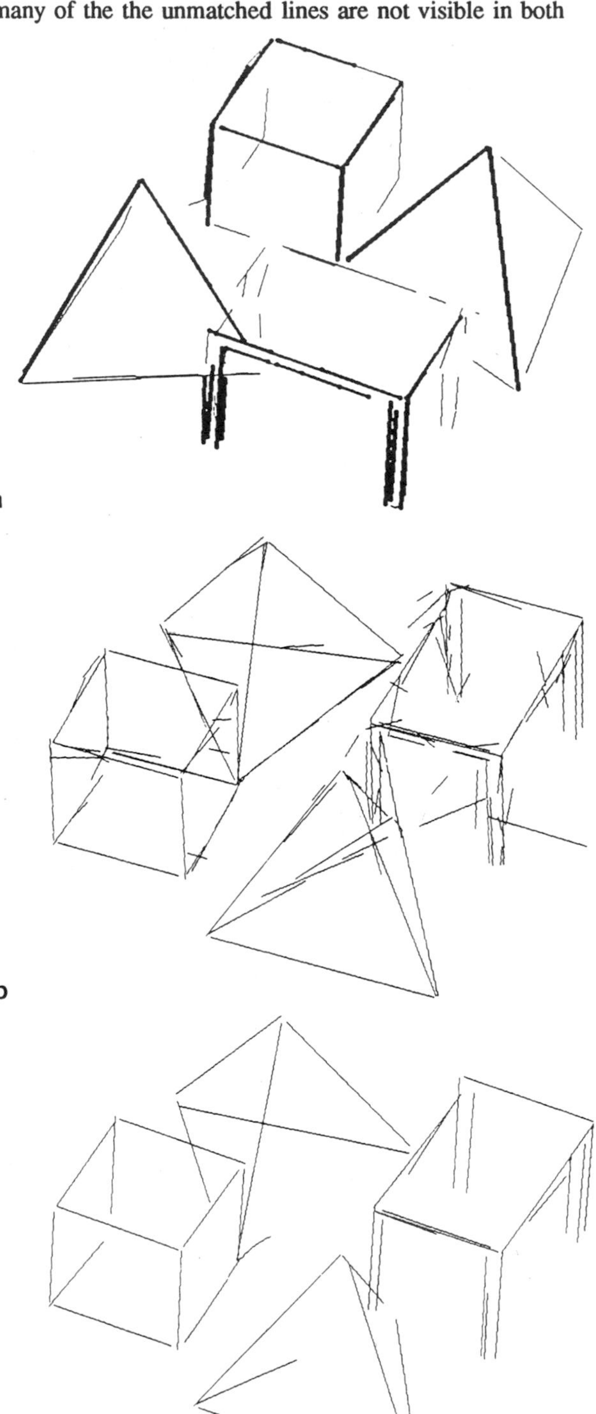

Figure 3. The results of matching the first two views in figure 2 are shown in (a); matched lines are shown bold. All views when combined by the matcher result in (b). Those lines that have been matched (and hence appear in more than one view) are shown in (c).

views. If the model is matched and updated with respect to each view in the sequence (chosing focus features only from the features that were matched in the previous cycle) the scene description in figure 3b results. This description contains a large quantity of noisy data that appeared in one or other view. A cleaner model can be obtained by filtering out primitives that have never been matched (see figure 3c).

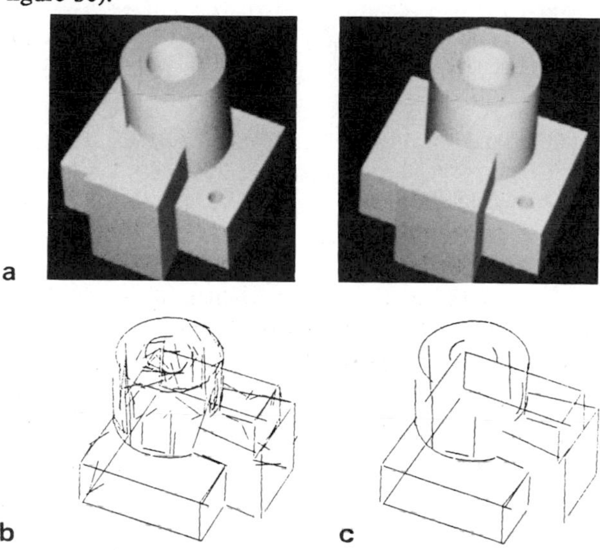

Figure 4. A single view of a synthesised test object is shown in (a). Noisy and clean models are shown in (b) and (c) respectively.

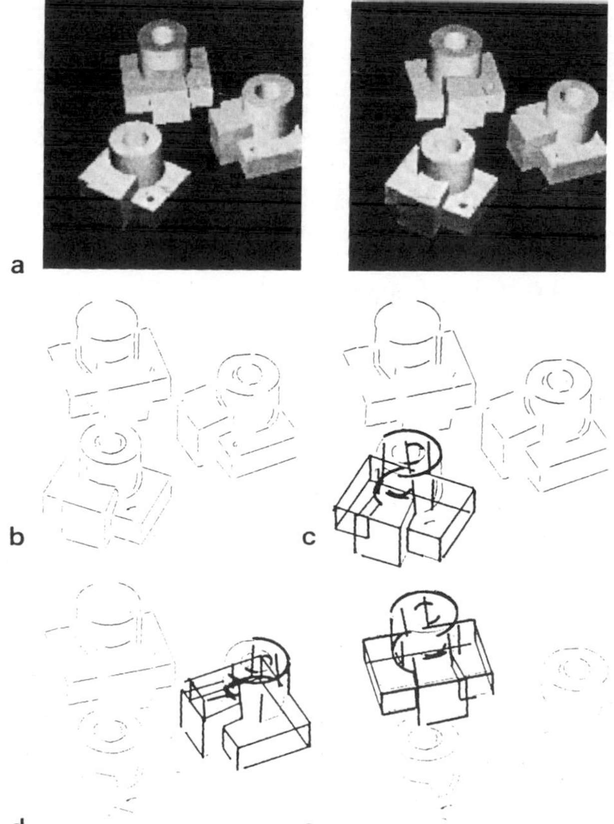

Figure 5. A synthesised bin picking scenario is depicted in (a), with corresponding GDB description in (b). Model instances are identified in (c), (d) and (e).

A similar sequence of processing has been performed for the artificial test object shown in figure 4a. Noisy and clean models obtained for it are shown in figure 4b and 4c respectively. Notice that few of the occluding contours that arise from the cylinder are ever matched. The matcher does not match the circular section of object, the unsophisticated update procedure simply passes through circles that were observed in the last known view. Matching was not hindered by the presence of circular data.

Once obtained this simplistic model (consisting of 41 line sections) can be matched in a bin picking scenario. Figures 5 and 6 illustrate this process for artificial and natural disparity data. The latter suffers camera calibration error; the resolution of our current calibration technique is suitable for epipolar stereo matching but not for accurate disparity interpretation. Figures 5a and 6a show scenes of a number of test objects, and figures 5b and 6b GDB data extracted from these. The best match of our model is superimposed, and shown bold, over each in 5c and 6c. Whilst the match for artificial data is near perfect, some geometrical distortion is visible in the real data. Removing matched portions of the GBD data allows the second (figures 5d and 6d) and third (figures 5e and 6e) best matches to be located. Unfortunately the third match of the real data results in mismatch.

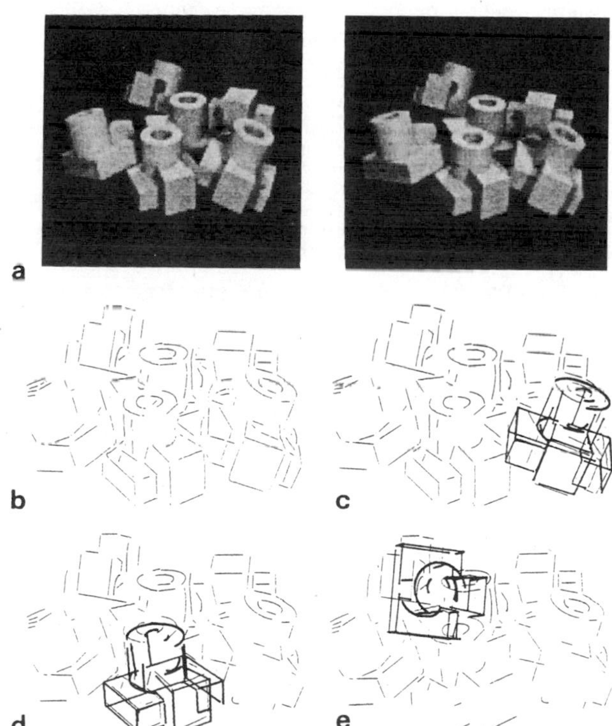

Figure 6. A real bin picking scenario is depicted in (a), with corresponding GDB description in (b) (current camera calibration is unreliable). Model instances are identified in (c) and (d). Mismatch results in (e).

5. Concluding Comments

A matching strategy for combining two or more three space descriptions of a scene has been discussed. It combines features of a number of algorithms that have appeared recently in the literature on three dimensional model matching. Its has two principal (almost novel) features. First, a number of pairwise relationships are seen as implicitly specifying the rigid transformation that relates the scenes. And secondly, search has been controlled by requiring that local cliques of mutually consistent matches must be located in the vicinity of at least one of a number of focus features, with the result that very few hypothetical transformations require attention.

A number of extensions to this strategy are currently under investigation. These fall into two categories: (i) those concerned with description and model building, eg the primitive base, occluding contours, partial rigidity, and view potential (all discussed briefly above); (ii) and those concerning the matching process itself. Currently the pairwise relation table is computed exhaustively, relationships between every primitive are stored. It should be possible to exploit rigidity using only a subset of the pairwise relations. Furthermore the scheme could be expanded to include unforeseen non-rigidity (when acquiring a model of a scene with moving objects in it).

Acknowledgements

We would like to thank Tony Pridmore and Ian Elsley for useful comments and advice and Chris Brown for his valuable technical assistance. This research was supported by SERC project grant no. GR/D/16796-IKBS/099 awarded under the Alvey programme. Stephen Pollard is an SERC IT Research Fellow.

References

1 Porrill J, SB Pollard and JEW Mayhew (1986) The optimal combination of multiple sensors including stereo vision, Alvey Computer Vision and Image Interpretation Meeting, Bristol, and submitted to Image and Vision Computing.

2 Chakravarty,I. and Freeman,H (1982) Characteristic Views as a Basis for Three-dimensional Object Recognition, SPIE Vol.336 Robot Vision.

3 Koenderink JJ (1985) The Internal Representation of Solid Shape Based on the Topological Properties of the Apparent Contour, Image Understanding.

4 Mayhew JEW (1986) Review of the YASA Project : May 1986, AIVRU Memo 014, University of Sheffield.

5 Faugeras OD, M Hebert, J Ponce and E Pauchon (1984) Object representation, identification, and positioning from range data, Proc. 1st Int. Symp. on Robotics Res, M Brady and R Paul (eds), MIT Press, 425-446.

6 Faugeras OD and M Hebert (1985) The representation, recognition and positioning of 3D shapes from range data, submitted to Int. J. Robotics Res.

7 Grimson WEL and T Lozano-Perez (1984) Model based recognition from sparse range or tactile data, Int. J. Robotics Res. 3(3): 3-35.

8 Grimson WEL and T Lozano-Perez (1985) Recognition and localisation of overlapping parts from sparse data in two and three dimensions, Proc IEEE Int. Conf. on Robotics and Automation, Silver Spring: IEEE Computer Society Press, 61-66.

9 Grimson WEL and T Lozano-Perez (1985) Search and sensing strategies for recognition and localization of two and three dimensional objects, Proc. Third Int. Symp. on Robotics Res.

10 Bolles RC and RA Cain (1982) Recognizing and locating partially visible objects, the local feature focus method, Int. J. of Robotics Res. 1(3): 57-82.

11 Bolles RC, P Horaud and MJ Hannah (1983) 3DPO: A three dimensional part orientation system, Proc. IJCAI 8, Karlshrue, West Germany, 116-120.

12 Gaston PC and T Lozano-Perez (1984) Tactile recognition and localization using object models: the case of the polyhedra on a plane, IEEE Trans. on Pattern Analysis and Machine Intelligence, Vol PAMI-6, No. 3, 257-266.

13 Grimson WEL (1984) The combinatorics of local constraints in model-based recognition and localization from sparse data, MIT AI Lab. Memo 763.

14 Pollard SB, JEW Mayhew and JP Frisby (1985) PMF: A stereo correspondence algorithm using a disparity gradient limit, Perception 14, 449-470.

15 Pollard SB, J Porrill, JEW Mayhew and JP Frisby (1985) Disparity gradient, Lipschitz continuity and computing binocular correspondences, Proc. Third Int. Symp. on Robotics Res.

16 Pollard SB (1985) Identifying correspondences in Binocular stereo, unpublished Phd thesis, Dept of Psychology, University of Sheffield.

17 Porrill J, TP Pridmore, JEW Mayhew and JP Frisby (1986) Fitting planes, lines and circles to stereo disparity data, AIVRU memo 017.

18 Pridmore TP, JEW Mayhew and JP Frisby (1985) Production rules for grouping edge-based disparity data, AIVRU memo 015, University of Sheffield.

19 Pridmore TP, J Porrill and JEW Mayhew (1986) Segmentation and description of binocularly viewed contours, Alvey Computer Vision and Image Interpretation Meeting, Bristol, and submitted to Image and Vision Computing.

20 Pridmore TP, JB Bowen and JEW Mayhew (1985) Geometrical description of the CONNECT graph #2, the geometrical descriptive base: a specification, AIVRU Memo, 012.

21 Ayache N, OD Faugeras, B Faverjon and G Toscani (1985) Matching depth maps obtained by passive stereo, Proc. Third Workshop on Computer Vision: Representation and Control, 197-204.

22 Quarendon P (1984) WINSOM user's guide, IBM Doc. No. UKSC 123.

[29] TINA: A 3D Vision System for Pick and Place

John Porrill, Stephen B Pollard, Tony P Pridmore, Jonathan B Bowen,
John E W Mayhew and John P Frisby

AI Vision Research Unit
University of Sheffield, Sheffield S10 2TN, UK

Reprinted, with permission of Butterworth Scientific Ltd, from *Image and Vision Computing*, 1988, **6**, 91-99.

Abstract

This paper provides an overview of the Sheffield AIVRU 3D vision system for robotics. The system currently supports model based object recognition and location; its potential for robotics applications is demonstrated by its guidance of a UMI robot arm in a pick and place task. The system comprises:

1) The recovery of a sparse depth map using edge based passive stereo triangulation.
2) The grouping, description and segmentation of edge segments to recover a 3D description of the scene geometry in terms of straight lines and circular arcs.
3) The statistical combination of 3D descriptions for the purpose of object model creation from multiple stereo views, and the propagation of constraints for within view refinement.
4) The matching of 3D wireframe models to 3D scene descriptions, to recover an initial estimate of their position and orientation.

The system is currently being developed to allow robot navigation by utilising visual feedback. The idea is to exploit the temporal coherence that exist in a sequence of images in order to provide quickening strategies.

1. Introduction.

The following is a brief description of the system. Edge based binocular stereo is used to recover a depth map of the scene from which a geometrical description comprising straight lines and circular arcs is computed. Scene to scene matching and statistical combination allows multiple stereo views to be combined into more complete scene descriptions with obvious application to autonomous navigation and path planning. Here we show how a number of views of an object can be integrated to form a useful visual model, which may subsequently be used to identify the object in a cluttered scene. The resulting position and attitude information is used to guide the robot arm.

Figure 1 illustrate our system at work. A pair of Panasonic WV-CD50 CCD cameras are mounted on an adjustable stereo rig. Here they are positioned with optical centers approximately 15cm apart with asymmetric convergent gaze of approximately 16 degrees verged upon a robot workspace some 50cm distant. The 28mm Olympus lens (with effective focal length of approximately 18.5mm) subtends a visual angle of about 27 degrees. The system is able to identify and accurately locate a modelled object in the cluttered scene. This information is used to compute a grasp plan for the known object (which is precompiled with respect to one corner of the object which acts as its coordinate frame). The UMI robot which is at a predetermined position with respect to the viewer centered coordinates of the visual system is able to pick up the object.

The system is a continuing research project: the scene description is currently being augmented with surface geometry and topological information. We are also exploring the use of predictive feed forward to quicken the stereo algorithm. The remainder of the paper will describe the modules comprising the system in more detail.

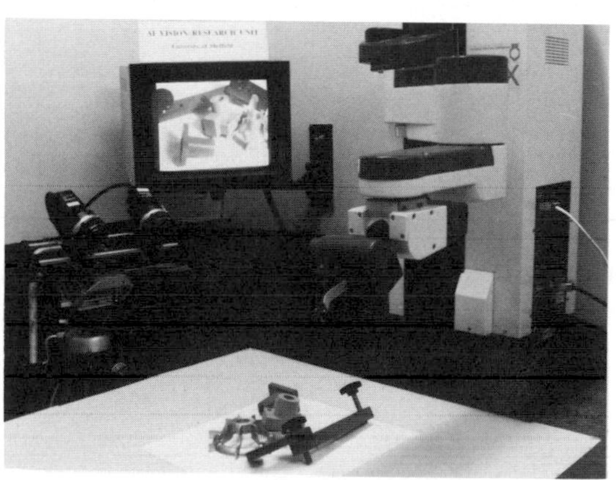

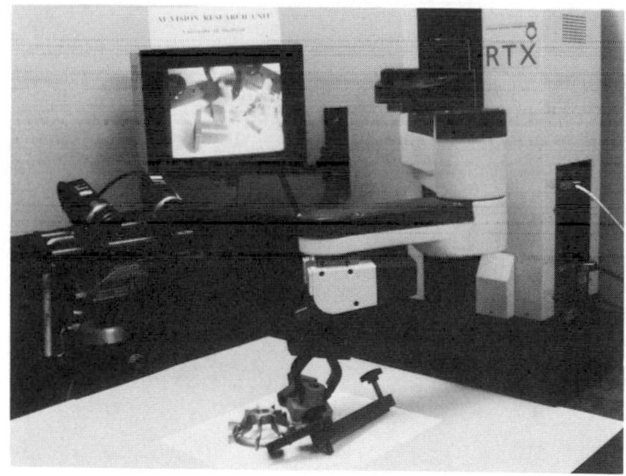

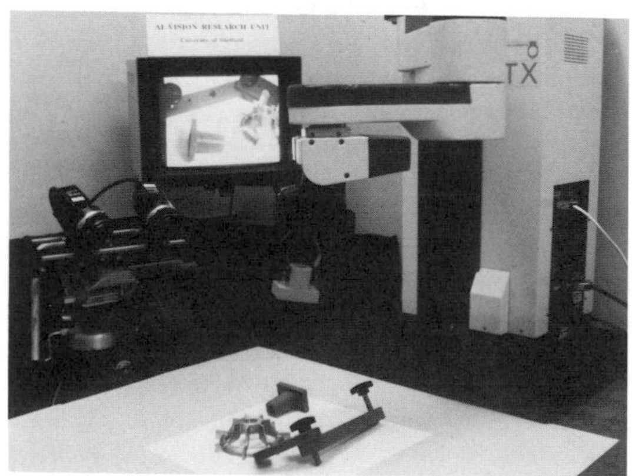

Figure 1. A visually guided robot arm.

a

b

Figure 2. **a, b,** *Stereo images*

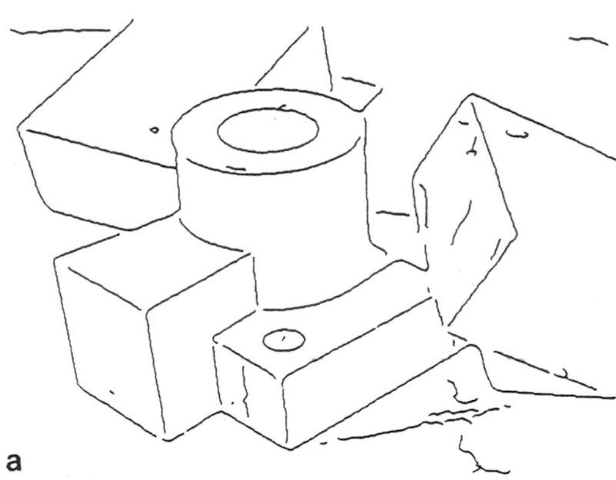
a

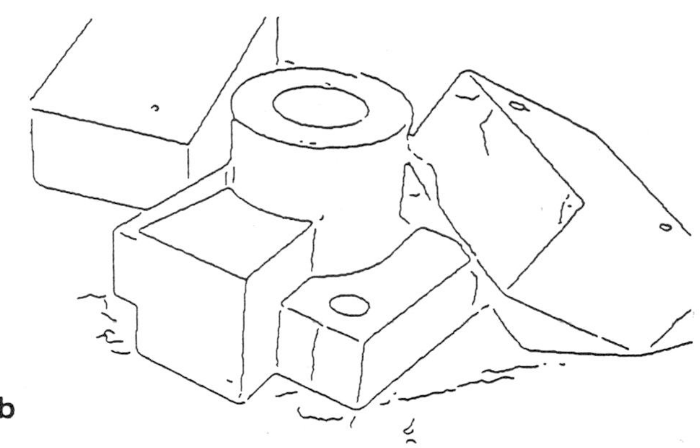
b

Figure 3. **a, b,** *Edge maps*

2. PMF: The recovery of a depth map.

The basis is a fairly complete implementation the Canny edge operator[1] applied to two images obtained from the CCD cameras (Figure 2). The images are 256x256 with 8 bit grey level resolution. In the camera calibration stage, a planar tile containing 16 squares equally spaced in a square grid was accurately placed in the workspace at a position specified with respect to the robot coordinate system such that the orientation of the grid corresponded to the x and y axes. The position of the corners on the calibration stimulus were measured to within 15 microns using a Steko 1818 stereo comparator. Tsai's calibration method was used to calibrate each camera separately. We have found errors of the same order as Tsai reported which are sufficiently small for the purposes of stereo matching. The camera attitudes are used to transform the edge data into parallel camera geometry to facilitate the stereo matching process. To recover the world to camera transform the calibration images are themselves used as input to the system, ie are stereoscopically fused and the geometrical description of the edges and vertices of the squares statistically combined. The best fitting plane, the directions of the orientations of the lines of the grid corresponding to the x and y axes, and the point of their intersection gives the direction cosines and position of the origin of the robot coordinate system in the camera coordinate system. The use of the geometrical descriptions recovered from stereo as feedback to iterate over the estimates of the camera parameters is a project for the future.

Currently a single scale Canny operator with $\sigma = 1$ pixel is used (Figure 3). The non maxima suppression which employs quadratic interpolation gives a resolution of 0.1 of a pixel (though dependent to some extent upon the structure of the image). After thresholding with hysteresis (currently non adaptive), the edge segments are rectified (Figure 4) so as to present parallel camera geometry to the stereo matching process. This also changes the location of the centre of the image appropriately, allows for the aspect ratio of the CCD array (fixing the vertical and stretching the horizontal) and adjusts the focal lengths to be consistent between views.

Camera calibration returns good estimates of the optical centre, focal length and orientation of each camera. This *original* geometry is illustrated in Figure 4 behind the interocular axis O_lO_r. The point at which the principal axis of the camera intersects the image plane is denoted P_l and P_r for the left and right hand cameras respectively. Not that (i) the principal axes need not meet in space (though it is advantageous if they almost do), and (ii) the focal lengths are not necessarily equal. It is desirable to construct an equivalent parallel camera geometry. For convenience this is based upon the left camera; the principal axis of the imaginary left camera $\overrightarrow{O_lQ_l}$ is chosen to be of focal length F, perpendicular to $\overrightarrow{O_lO_r}$, and to be coplanar with $O_rO_lP_l$ (as is the x axis of the image plane). An identical imaginary camera geometry is constructed for the right camera (ie $\overrightarrow{O_lQ_l}$ and $\overrightarrow{O_rQ_r}$ are parallel). Note that $\overrightarrow{O_rQ_r}$ need not be coplanar with $O_lO_rP_r$. For pictorial simplicity the new coordinate frames are shown in front of the interocular axis. Points on the original image planes can now be projected through the optical centres of each camera onto the new and imaginary image planes. With the result that corresponding image points will appear on corresponding *virtual* rasters. For the sake of economy and to avoid aliasing problems this transformation is applied to edge points rather than image pixels themselves.

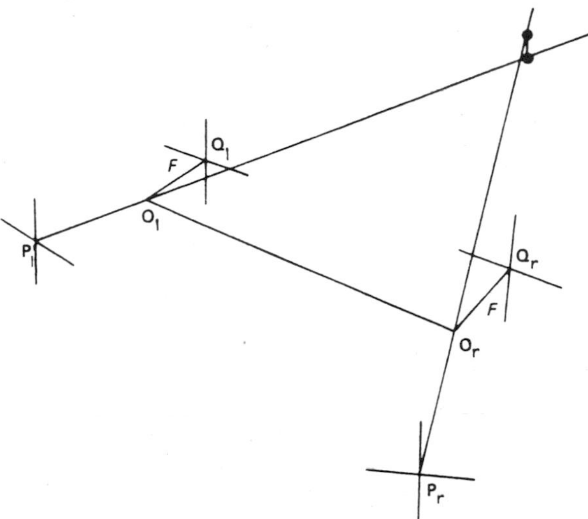

Figure 4. Parallel Camera Geometry.

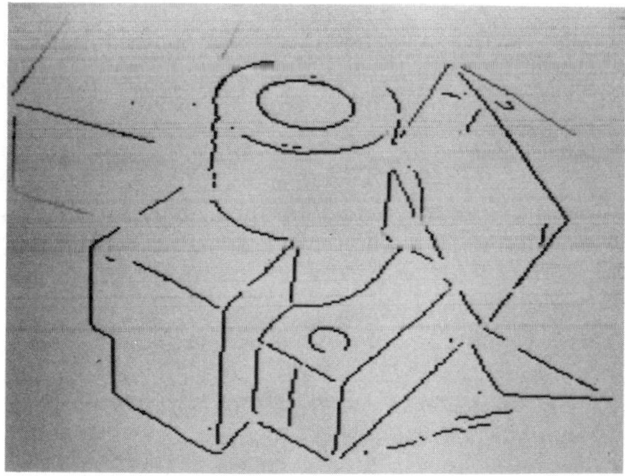

Figure 5. The depth map, displayed with respect to the left image, with disparities coded by intensity (near-dark far-light). The total range of disparities in the scene was approximately 35 pixels from a search window of 200 pixels. PMF is a neighbourhood support algorithm and in this case the neighbourhood was 10 pixels radius. The limiting disparity gradient employed in PMF was 0.5. The iteration strategy used a conservative heuristic for the identification of correct matches, and their scores were frozen. This effectively removes them from succeeding iterations and reduces the computational cost of the algorithm as it converges to the solution. 5 iterations were sufficient.

The two edge maps are and stereoscopically combined to form a depth map (Figure 5). The PMF[2, 3] stereo algorithm uses the disparity gradient constraint to solve the stereo correspondence problem. The parallel camera geometry allows potential matches to be restricted to corresponding rasters. Initial matches are further restricted to edge segments of the same contrast polarity and of roughly similar orientations (determined by the choice of a disparity gradient limit). Matches for a neighbouring point may support a candidate match provided the disparity gradient between the two does not exceed a particular threshold. Essentially, the strategy is for each point to choose from among its candidate matches the one best supported by its neighbours.

The disparity gradient limit provides a parameter for controlling the disambiguating power of the algorithm. The theoretical maximum disparity gradient is 2.0 (along the epipolars), but at such a value the disambiguating power of the constraint is negligible. False matches frequently receive as much support as their correct counterparts. However, as the limit is reduced the effectiveness of the algorithm increases and below 1.0 (a value proposed as the psychophysical maximum disparity gradient by Burt and Julesz[4]), we typically find that more than 90% of the matches are assigned correctly on a single pass of the algorithm. The reduction of the threshold to a value below the theoretical limit has little overhead in reduction of the complexity of the surfaces that can be fused until it is reduced close to the other end of the scale (a disparity gradient of 0.0 corresponds to fronto-parallel surfaces). In fact we find that a threshold disparity gradient of 0.5 is very powerful constraint for which less than 7% of surfaces (assuming uniform distribution over the Gaussian sphere: following Arnold and Binford[5]) project with a maximum disparity gradient greater than 0.5 when the viewing distance is four times the interocular distance. With greater viewing distances, the proportion is even lower.

It has been shown[6,7] that enforcing a disparity gradient ensures Lipschitz continuity on the disparity map. Such continuity is more general than and subsumes the more usual use of continuity assumptions in stereo.

The method used to calibrate the stereo cameras was based on that described by Tsai[8] (using a single plane calibration target) which recovers the six extrinsic parameters (3 translation and 3 rotation) and the focal length of each camera. This method has the advantage that all except the latter are measured in a fashion that is independent of any radial lens distortion that may be present. The image origin, and aspect ratios of each camera had been recovered previously. The calibration target which was a tile of accurately measured black squares on a white background was positioned at a known location in the XY plane of the robot work space. After both cameras have been calibrated their relative geometry is calculated.

Whilst camera calibration provides the transformation from the viewer/camera to the world/robot coordinate spaces we have found it more accurate to recover the position of the world coordinate frame directly. Stereo matching of the calibration stimulus allows its position in space to be determined. A geometrical description of the position and orientation of the calibration target is obtained by statistically combining the stereo geometry of the edge descriptions and vertices[9].

3. GDB: The recovery of the geometric descriptive base.

In this section we briefly report the methods for segmenting and describing the edge based depth map to recover the 3D geometry of the scene in terms of straight lines and circular arcs. A complete description of the process can be found in Pridmore *et al*[10] and Porrill *et al*[11].

The core process is an algorithm (GDF) which recursively attempts to describe, then smooth and segment, linked edge segments recovered from the stereo depth map. GDF is handed a list of edge elements by CONNECT[12]. Orthogonal regression is used to classify the input string as a straight line, plane or space curve. If the edge list is not a statistically satisfactory straight line but does form an acceptable plane curve, the algorithm attempts to fit a circle. If this fails, the curve is smoothed and segmented at the extrema of curvature and curvature difference. The algorithm is then applied recursively to the segmented parts of the curve.

Some subtlety is required when computing geometrical descriptions of stereo acquired data. This arises in part from the transformation between the geometry in disparity coordinates and the camera/world coordinates. The former is in a basis defined by the X coordinates in the left and right images and the common vertical Y coordinate, the latter, for practical considerations (eg there is no corresponding average or cyclopean image), is with respect to the left imaging device, the optical centre of the camera being at (0,0,0) and the centre of the image is at (0,0,f) where f is the focal length of the camera. While the transformation between disparity space and the world is projective, and hence preserves lines and planes, circles in the world have a less simple description in disparity space. The strategy employed to deal with circles is basically as follows: given a string of edge segments in disparity space, our program will only attempt to fit a circle if it has already passed the test for planarity, and the string is then replaced by its projection into this plane. Three well chosen points are projected into the world/camera coordinate frame and a circle hypothesised, which then predicts an ellipse lying in the plane in disparity space. The mean square errors of the points from this ellipse combined with those from the plane provide a measure of the goodness of fit. In practice, rather than change coordinates to work in the plane of the ellipse, we work entirely in the left eye's image, but change the metric so that it measures distances as they would be in the plane of the ellipse.

Typically, stereo depth data are not complete; some sections of continuous edge segments in the left image may not be matched in the right due to image noise or partial occlusion. Furthermore disparity values tend to be erroneous for extended horizontal or near horizontal segments of curves. It is well known that the stereo data associated with horizontal edge segments is very unreliable, though of course the image plane information is no less usable than for the other orientations. Our solution to these problems is to use 3D descriptions to predict 2D data. Residual components derived from reliable 3D data and the image projection of unreliable or unmatched (2D) edges are then statistically combined and tested for acceptance. Where an edge segment from the left image is entirely unmatched in the right then a 2D description is obtained (and flagged as such). By these methods we obtain more complete 2D and 3D geometrical description of the scene from the left eyes view than if we used only the stereo data. Figure 6 illustrates the GDB description.

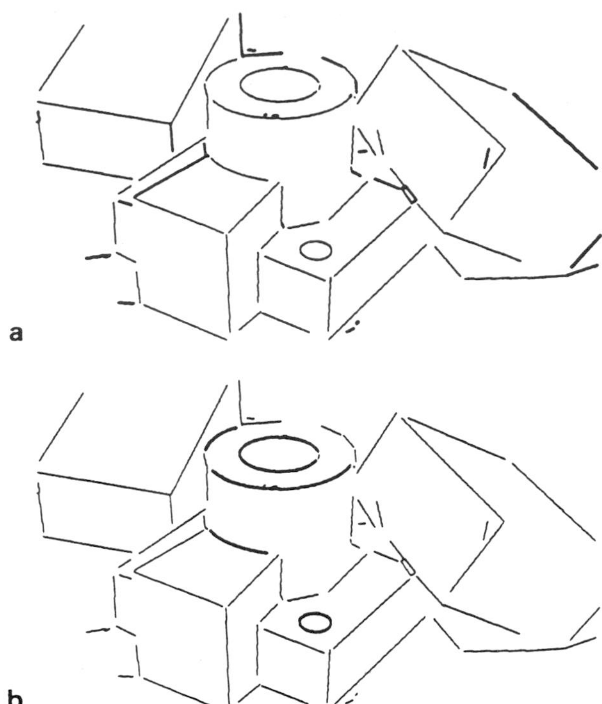

Figure 6. Geometrical descriptions. In (a) both 2 and 3 dimensional descriptions, with respect to the left hand image, are shown. Primitives of the GDB that are flagged as 2D, as a result of the fact that no depth data has been recovered for them by the stereo algorithm (perhaps as a result occlusion), are displayed bold. It is important to note that these exist only as descriptions in the image plane and not as descriptions in the world. In (b) again both 2 and 3 dimensional data are shown, but on this occasion circular sections (in three dimensions and not only in the image plane) of the GDB are the ones that have been highlighted by displaying them bold. Before segmentation each edge list is smoothed either by diffusion or by the approximately equivalent Gaussian (σ=2.5).

Evaluation of the geometrical accuracy of the descriptions returned by the GDF has employed both natural and CAD graphics generated images. The latter were subject to quantisation error and noise due to the illumination model but had near perfect camera geometry; they were thus used to provide the control condition, enabling us to decouple the errors due to the camera calibration stage of the process. A full description of the experiments are to be found in[13], suffice it to say that we find that typical errors for the orientation of lines is less than a degree, and for the normals of circular arcs subtending more than a radian, the errors are less than 3 degrees in the CAD generated images and only about twice that for images acquired from natural scene. The positional accuracy of features and curvature segmentation points has also been evaluated, errors are typically of the order of a few millimetres which maybe argues well for the adequacy of Tsai's camera calibration method more than anything else.

4. SMM: The Scene and Model Matcher.

The matching algorithm[14], which can be used for scene to scene and model to scene matching, exploits ideas from several sources: the use of a pairwise geometrical relationships table as the object model from Grimson and Lozano-Perez[15–17], the least squares computation of transformations by exploiting the quaternion representation for rotations from Faugeraus *et al*[18,19], and the use of focus features from Bolles *et al*[21]. We like to think that the whole is greater than the sum of its parts!

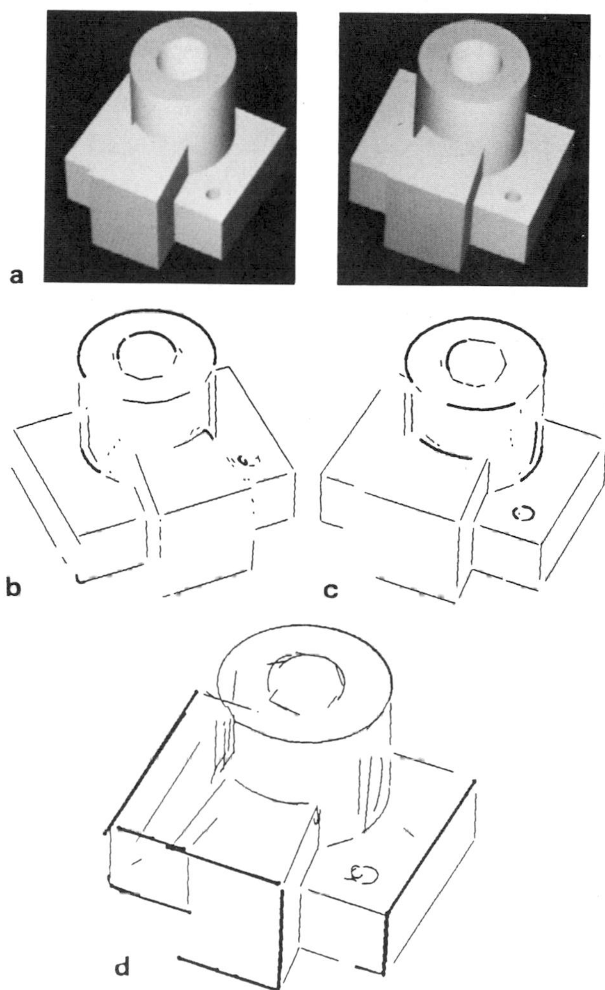

Figure 7. Matching scene descriptions: (a) shows a stereo view of the object/scene (obtained from the IBM WINSOM CSG body modeler); (b) and (c) GDB data extracted for two views of this object. Each description consists of approximately 50 above-threshold GDB line primitives. The 10 focus features chosen in view (b) obtained a total of 98 potential matches in view (c). Setting S to 7 and C to 4 only 78 independent implicit transformations result. After extension the best consistent transformation included 9 matched. The least square transformation (rotation followed by translation) that takes view (b) to view (c) is computed by the method discussed by Faugeras et al [18] in which rotations are represented as quaternions. In figure (d) view (b) is transformed into view (c) (the error in the computed rotation is 0.7 degrees) and matching lines are shown bold, the vast majority of the unmatched lines are not visible in both views (often as a result of noise).

The matching strategy proceeds as follows:

1) a focus feature is chosen from the model;
2) the S closest salient features are identified (currently salient means lines with length greater than L);
3) potential matches for the focus feature are selected;
4) consistent matches, in terms of a number of pairwise geometrical relationships, for each of the neighbouring features are located;
5) the set of matches (including the set of focus features) is searched for maximally consistent cliques of cardinality at least C, each of these can be thought of as an implicit transformation.
6) synonymous cliques (that represent the same implicit transformation) are merged and then each clique is extended by adding new matches for all other lines in the scene if they are consistent with each of the matches in the clique. Rare inconsistency amongst an extended clique is dealt with by a final economical tree search.
7) extended cliques are ranked on the basis of the number and length of their members.
8) the transformation implicitly defined by the clique is recovered using the method described by Faugeras *et al*[18].

The use of the parameters S (the neighbours of the focus feature), and C (the minimum subset of S) are powerful search pruning heuristics that are obviously model dependent. Work is currently in hand to extend the matcher with a richer semantics of features and their pairwise geometrical relationships, and also to exploit negative or incompatible information in order to reduce the likelihood of false positive matches.

The pairwise geometrical relationships made explicit in the matching algorithm can be used to provide a useful indexing scheme. Each primitive has associated with it a 1 dimensional hash table quantised by θ (their angular difference), each element of which includes a list, sorted by their absolute minimum separation, of pointers to look up table entries that lie within the associated θ, bucket (this can be searched rapidly using a binary search). This scheme allows relationships found in one scene description to be compared rapidly with relationships present in the other.

An example of the performance of the matching algorithm is given in Figure 7.

5. TIED: the integration of edge descriptions.

The geometrical information recovered from the stereo system described above is uncertain and error prone, however the errors are highly anisotropic, being much greater in depth than in the image plane. This anisotropy can be exploited if information from different but approximately known positions is available, as the statistical combination of the data from the two viewpoints provides improved location in depth. From a single stereo view the uncertainity can only be improved by exploiting geometrical constraints. A method for the optimal combination of geometry from multiple sensors based on the work of Faugeras *et al*[21] and Durrant-Whyte[22] has been developed[23], clique found by the matcher contained 13 matched lines. Figure 10 (c) depicts the scene viewed by the camera rig in figure 1.

The information provided by matching gives the RHS of the inverse kinematics equation which must be solved if our manipulator is to grasp the object (Figure 11).

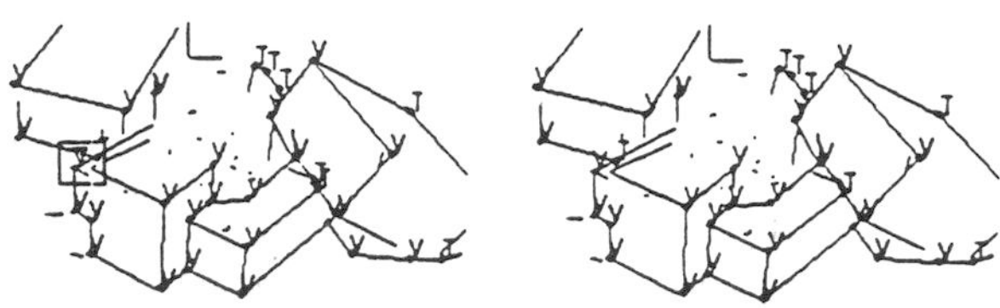

Figure 12. Wireframe completion.

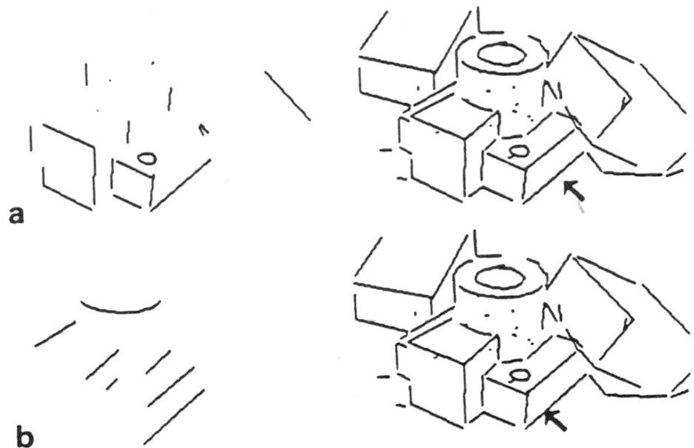

Figure 13. Pairwise relations: (a) all the lines perpendicular to the arrowed line have been generated; (b) all the lines parallel to the arrowed line have been generated.

6. REV: The regions, edges, vertices graph.

The system may be regarded as generating a sequence of representations each spatially registered with respect to a coordinate system based on the left eye: image, edge map, depth map and geometrical description. In the initial stages of processing a pass oriented approach may be appropriate but we consider that it is desirable to provide easy and convenient access between the representations at a higher level of processing. The REVgraph is an environment, built in Franz Lisp, in which the lower level representations are all indexed in the same co-ordinate system. On top of this a number of tools have been and are being written for use in the development of higher level processes which we envisage overlaying the geometrical frame with surface and topological information. Such processes will employ both qualitative and quantitative geometrical reasoning heuristics. In order to aid debugging by keeping a history of reasoning, and increase search efficiency by avoiding backtracking, the REVgraph contains a consistency maintenance system (CMS), to which any processes may be easily interfaced. The CMS is our implementation of most of the good ideas in Doyle[24] and DeKleer[25] augmented with some our own. The importance of truth maintenance in building geometrical models of objects was originally highlighted by Hermann[26]. Details of the REVgraph and CMS implementation may be found in Bowen[27].

Figure 12 illustrates a prototype wireframe completion algorithm. It links straight edges together to form T-junctions or vertices as appropriate. Inconsistencies between such labelings are identified and handled by the CMS. In this case the ambiguity is slight only 6 possible solutions (contexts) result, two of which are shown above (with vertices labeled V and T-junctions labeled T). The context on the right was adjudged by the program to be the most complete, while the one on the left contains a rather dubious T-junction where there should be a vertex (marked on the far left of the modeled object). The search space was bounded by some simple heuristics, using evaluations over the various CMS contexts, which is why a few lines are left incomplete where insufficient depth information is available. Note that incorrect decisions are possible (eg. the edge along the right hand side of the base of the cylinder which forms a vertex with the block on its right).

Figure 13 showe some useful pairwise relationships that are made explicit within the REVgraph environment. The formation of a pairwise relations table is a utility in the REVgraph. It generates pairs of lines and the geometric relations between them according to certain user requests.

7. Conclusions

We demonstrate the ability of our system to support visual guided pick and place in a visually cluttered but, in terms of trajectory planning, benign manipulator workspace. It is not appropriate at this time to ask how long the visual processing stages of the demonstration take, suffice it to say that they deliver geometrical information of sufficient quality, not only for the task in hand but to serve as a starting point for the development of other visual and geometrical reasoning competences.

Acknowledgements

We gratefully acknowledge Dr Chris Brown for his valuable technical assistance. This research was supported by SERC project grant no. GR/D/1679.6-IKBS/025 awarded under the Alvey programme.

References

1 Canny J.F. (1983), Finding edges and lines in images, MIT AI memo, 720, 1983.

2 Pollard S.B., J.E.W. Mayhew and J.P. Frisby (1985), PMF: a stereo correspondence algorithm using a disparity gradient limit, *Perception,* 14, 449-470.

3 Pollard S.B., J. Porrill, J.E.W. Mayhew and J.P. Frisby (1985), Disparity gradient, Lipschitz continuity and computing binocular correspondences, *Proc. Third Int. Symp. on Robotics Res.* 19-26.

4 Burt P. and B. Julesz (1980), Modifications of the classical notion of panum's fusional area, *Perception* 9, 671-682.

5 Arnold R. D. and T. O. Binford (1980) Geometric constraints in stereo vision, *Soc. Photo-Optical Instr. Engineers,* 238, 281-292.

6 Trivedi H.P. and S.A. Lloyd (1985), The role of disparity gradient in stereo vision, Comp. Sys. Memo 165, GEC Hirst Research Centre, Wembley, England.

7 Porrill J. (1985) Notes on: the role of the disparity gradient in stereo vision, AIVRU Lab Memo 009, University of Sheffield.

8 Tsai R.Y. (1986), An efficient and accurate camera calibration technique for 3D machine vision, *Proc IEEE CVPR 86,* 364-374.

9 Pollard S.B. and J. Porill (1986), Using camera calibration techniques to obtain a viewer centred coordinate frame, AIVRU Lab Memo 026, University of Sheffield.

10 Pridmore T.P., J. Porrill and J.E.W. Mayhew (1986), Segmentation and description of binocularly viewed contours, *Alvey Computer Vision and Image Interpretation Meeting,* University of Bristol, and *Image and Vision Computing* 5 No 2 132-138.

11 Porrill J., T. P. Pridmore, J. E. W. Mayhew and Frisby, J. P. (1986a) Fitting planes, lines and circles to stereo disparity data, AIVRU memo 017

12 Pridmore T.P., J.E.W. Mayhew and J.P. Frisby (1985), Production rules for grouping edge-based disparity Data, *Alvey Vision Conference,* University of Sussex, and AIVRU memo 015, University of Sheffield.

13 Pridmore T.P. (1987), The Interpretation of edge based binocular disparity information, Phd Thesis, University of Sheffield.

14 Pollard S.B., J.Porrill, J.E.W. Mayhew and J.P. Frisby (1986), matching geometrical descriptions in 3-space, *Alvey Computer Vision and Image Interpretation Meeting,* Bristol, AIVRU Memo 022 and *Image and Vision Computing* 5 No 2 73-78.

15 Grimson W.E.L. and T. Lozano-Perez (1984), Model based recognition from sparse range or tactile data, *Int. J. Robotics Res.* 3(3): 3-35.

16 Grimson W.E.L. and T. Lozano-Perez (1985), Recognition and localisation of overlapping parts from sparse data in two and three dimensions, *Proc IEEE Int. Conf. on Robotics and Automation,* Silver Spring: IEEE Computer Society Press, 61-66.

17 Grimson W.E.L. and T. Lozano-Perez (1985), Search and sensing strategies for recognition and localization of two and three dimensional objects, *Proc. Third Int. Symp. on Robotics Res.*

18 Faugeras O.D., M. Hebert, J. Ponce and E. Pauchon (1984), Object representation, identification, and positioning from range data, *Proc. 1st Int. Symp. on Robotics Res,* J.M. Brady and R. Paul (eds), MIT Press, 425-446.

19 Faugeras O.D. and M. Hebert (1985), The representation, recognition and positioning of 3D shapes from range data, *Int. J. Robotics Res*

20 Bolles R.C., P. Horaud and M.J. Hannah (1983), 3DPO: A three dimensional part orientation system, *Proc. IJCAI 8,* Karlshrue, West Germany, 116-120.

21 Faugeras O.D., N. Ayache and B. Faverjon (1986), Building visual maps by combining noisy stereo measurements, *IEEE Robotics conference,* San Francisco.

22 Durrant-Whyte H.F. (1985), Consistent integration and propagation of disparate sensor observations, *Thesis, University of Pennsylvania.*

23 Porrill J., S.B. Pollard and J.E.W Mayhew (1986b), The optimal combination of multiple sensors including stereo vision, *Alvey Computer Vision and Image Interpretation Meeting,* Bristol, AIVRU Memo 25 and *Image and Vision Computing* 5 No 2 174-180.

24 Doyle J. (1979), A truth maintenance system, *Artificial Intelligence* 12, 231-272.

25 DeKleer J. (1984), Choices without backtracking, *Proc, National Conference on Artificial Intelligence,*

26 Herman M. (1985), Representation and incremental construction of a three-dimensional scene model, CMU-CS-85-103, Dept. of Computer Science, Carnegie-Mellon University.

27 Bowen J.B. and J.E.W. Mayhew (1986), Consistency maintenance in the REV graph environment, *Alvey Computer Vision and Image Interpretation Meeting,* University of Bristol, AIVRU Memo 20, and *Image and Vision Computing* (in press).

makes it possible, under favourable circumstances, to compute T and U and the structure of the scene from the two images alone.

There are, however, certain pairs of images that admit of two or more interpretations, in the sense that all the pairs (Q,Q') satisfy two distinct equations of type (1), namely

(3) $p_1'Q' = U_1(p_1Q-T_1)$ and

(4) $p_2'Q' = U_2(p_2Q-T_2)$.

In (3) and (4) the subscripts 1 and 2 refer, of course, to the two interpretations; in each interpretation p is a function of Q and p' is a function of Q':

(5) $p_1 = p_1(Q)$, $p_1' = p_1'(Q')$,
$p_2 = p_2(Q)$, $p_2' = p_2'(Q')$.

An ambiguous pair of images therefore satisfies the identity

(6) $Q' = U_1(p_1Q-T_1)/p_1' = U_2(p_2Q-T_2)/p_2'$.

The second equality in (6) implies that, for every image point Q, $U_1(p_1Q-T_1)$ is a linear combination of U_2Q and U_2T_2; and it entitles us to infer that

(7) $[U_1(p_1Q-T_1), U_2Q, U_2T_2] = 0$.

Multiply the second term in (7) by p_1, and abbreviating the vector p_1Q as R, we arrive at the equation

(8) $[U_1(R-T_1), U_2R, U_2T_2] = 0$.

The triple product on the left hand side is clearly a second-order polynomial in (X, Y, Z), the components of R, and so (8) is the equation of a quadric passing through the points O and O', where R = 0 and R = T_1 respectively. But not every quadric passing through 0 and 0' can be represented in the form (8), since for given T_1 and U_1 this form has only 5 degrees of freedom (2 for the unit vector T_2 and 3 for the rotation matrix U_2). We deduce that although twofold ambiguity is quite likely to arise (and usually does - T S Huang, personal communication) if not more than 5 texture elements can be identified in both photographs, with 6 or more elements the two images will generally permit only one interpretation even when all the elements lie on a quadric passing through both 0 and 0'.

Equation (7) may be written as an explicit equation for $p_1(Q)$:

(9) $p_1(Q) = [U_1T_1, U_2Q, U_2T_2]/[U_1Q, U_2Q, U_2T_2]$.

Interchanging the subscripts 1 and 2 we deduce that on the other interpretation the equation for p(Q) is

(10) $p_2(Q) = [U_2T_2, U_1Q, U_1T_1]/[U_2Q, U_1Q, U_1T_1]$.

3 MULTIPLE AMBIGUITY

In his discussion of optic flow fields Maybank established (Maybank 1985) that 3 is the maximum number of distinct alternative interpretations of such a field, each being associated with distinct values of the camera's angular velocity and direction of motion. We shall show that the same is true of a pair of finitely separated projections.

If there are two interpretations of a pair of images, $p_1(Q)$ must satisfy (9); if there are 3, it must also satisfy

(11) $p_1(Q) = [U_1T_1, U_3Q, U_3T_3]/[U_1Q, U_3Q, U_3T_3]$.

It is the necessary equivalence of (9) and (11) that forms the basis of the following discussion.

The numerators of (9) and (11) are first order polynomials in the components of Q, and the denominators are polynomials of the second order. The most straightforward case is that in which each numerator divides its denominator algebraically, so that both (9) and (11) reduce to

(12) $p_1(Q) = 1/(N.Q)$.

This is the equation of a plane, the vector N being the inverse normal to the plane. The potential ambiguity of a pair of views of a plane has been fully discussed elsewhere (Longuet-Higgins 1984b), so we shall confine ourselves from now on to the case in which $p_1(Q)$ is not a plane, and the numerators in (9) and (11) do not divide their denominators. It follows at once that the numerators and the denominators in (9) and (11) are directly proportional - that there exists a constant c such that

(13) $[U_1Q, U_2Q, U_2T_2] = c[U_1Q, U_3Q, U_3T_3]$ and

(14) $[U_1T_1, U_2Q, U_2T_2] = c[U_1T_1, U_3Q, U_3T_3]$.

Though it is by no means obvious, the insertion of arbitrary values of U_1, U_2 and U_3 into (13), and subsequent comparison of the polynomial coefficients, determines the magnitude of c and the directions of T_2 and T_3. (The signs of the translation vectors cannot be determined until later, when the values of the distances p(Q) and p'(Q') are being computed; for each of the three interpretations of the sign of T must be such as to make all these distances positive, and if this is not possible the interpretation fails.) T_1 is then determined (again with unknown sign) by inserting the values of the other parameters into (14).

The detailed justification of these assertions will be given elsewhere; here we give the results of just one such computation, illustrating the fact that the three interpretations of a triply ambiguous pair of images may be uncomfortably close together.

First, the Q vectors of 5 points in the first image:

0.396	-0.172	0.902
0.180	0.438	0.881
0.171	0.371	0.913
-0.118	0.061	0.991
-0.272	0.164	0.948

Next, the Q' vectors of the corresponding points in the other image:

0.322	-0.200	0.925
0.172	0.411	0.895
0.162	0.342	0.926
-0.062	-0.011	0.998
-0.204	0.100	0.974

Finally, the vector T, the matrix U and the p values of the 5 points, in the 3 distinct interpretations:

Interpretation 1

-0.239	0.541	-0.807

0.999	0.019	-0.035
-0.015	0.996	0.092
0.036	-0.091	0.995

2.637	6.782	6.227	2.779	3.477

Interpretation 2

-0.846	0.435	0.310

0.995	0.056	-0.083
-0.056	0.998	0.001
0.082	0.004	0.997

62.751	21.478	19.194	6.095	5.405

Interpretation 3

-0.830	0.401	0.387

0.995	0.048	-0.088
-0.048	0.999	-0.002
0.087	0.006	0.996

52.076	18.157	16.592	5.813	5.066

4 GEOMETRICAL CONSIDERATIONS

In this section we briefly review what is known about triply ambiguous flow fields, and show that the surfaces from which they arise are of the same type as those that give rise to triply ambiguous image pairs. We conclude that the number of distinct interpretations of two views of a textured surface cannot exceed 3.

In his 1985 paper Maybank showed that ambiguous flow fields can only arise from planes or quadric surfaces of a special form, namely

(15) M: $[v', v, R] = (W'.R)(v'.R) - (W'.v')R^2$,

where (v, Ω) and (v', Ω') are alternative values of the camera's linear and angular velocity,

(16) $W' = \Omega' - \Omega$ and

(17) $R = pQ = (X, Y, Z)$.

The quadric M has several interesting properties: (a) it passes through the viewpoint $R = 0$; (b) its tangent at the viewpoint is the common plane of v and v' (since when R is small the triple product $[v', v, R]$ is very small); (c) it contains the line $R = \lambda v'$ (such a value of R causing both sides of (15) to vanish); and (d) its quadratic part has a specially simple diagonal form. If the X and Z axes are taken as the internal and external bisectors of the angle 2ϕ between W' and v', the right hand side of (15) becomes

(18) $k[s^2X^2 + (s^2-c^2)Y^2 - c^2Z^2]$

where k is the product of the lengths of W' and v', $c = \cos\phi$ and $s = \sin\phi$. Since the line $R = \lambda v'$ lies entirely in M, M must be a ruled quadric, the most general such surface being a hyperboloid of one sheet. A hyperbolic paraboloid is also a possibility (if $c^2=s^2$), but in either case the middle coefficient in (18) is the sum of the other two.

We shall refer to the directions of W' and v' as the principal directions of the quadric M. A triply ambiguous flow field arises if in addition to (v, Ω) and (v', Ω') there exists a third pair of velocities (v'', Ω'') such that W'' $(= \Omega''-\Omega)$ is parallel to v' and W" is parallel to v". Then the principal directions of M can, as it were, exchange roles, the one that was parallel to W' now being regarded as parallel to v", and the one that was parallel to v' being seen as parallel to W". It is, essentially, this duality that limits the number of interpretations; given the "correct" interpretation (v,Ω) of two views of M, the two other interpretations, (v', Ω') and (v'', Ω''), exhaust the possible ways of associating a linear velocity and an angular velocity difference with the principal directions of M.

At first sight equation (8), describing the type of surface that gives rise to ambiguous pairs of views, looks rather different from equation (18), for the optic flow case. But as we shall see in a moment, there is a close relation between the surfaces they represent.

We begin by writing (8) in the form

(19) L: $[U(R-T_1),R,T] = 0$,
where $U = (U_2)^{-1}U_1$ and $T= T_2$.

Like Maybank's quadric M, the surface L is a ruled quadric containing the viewpoints $R = O$ and $R =T_1$ and the straight line $R = \lambda T$. We now show that the second-order terms of L are identical in form with those of M.

Writing $R = (X, Y, Z)$, and using lower-case letters to denote the 3 components of T and the 9 components of U, we begin by expanding the second-order part of (19) in the form

$$(20)\quad \begin{aligned}[UR, R, T] &= X^2(u_{31}t_2 - u_{21}t_3) \\ &+ Y^2(....) + Z^2(....) \\ &+ YZ(u_{22}t_1 - u_{12}t_2 + u_{13}t_3 - u_{33}t_1) \\ &+ ZX(....) + XY(....)\end{aligned}$$

where the dots indicate that the subscripts 1, 2 and 3 have been cyclically permuted. In order to proceed we need a parametric representation of the elements of U. A convenient one for the present purpose is in terms of 3+1 real numbers p, q, r and s whose squares add up to 1:

(21) $u_{11}=p^2-q^2-r^2+s^2$, $u_{12}=2(pq - rs)$, $u_{13}=2(rp + qs)$,
$u_{21}=2(pq + rs)$, $u_{22}=-p^2+q^2-r^2+s^2$, $u_{23}=2(qr-ps)$,
$u_{31}=2(rp -qs)$, $u_{32}=2(qr+ps)$,
$u_{33}=-p^2-q^2+r^2+s^2$.

(In point of fact $s = \cos(\psi/2)$, where ψ is the rotation angle of U and (p, q, r) are the direction cosines of the rotation axis, multiplied by $\sin(\psi/2)$.) Substituting from (21) we obtain the coefficient of X^2 in (17) as

(22) $2(pr - qs)t_2 - 2(pq + rs)t_3$

and that of YZ as

(23) $2(q^2-r^2)t_1 - 2(pq - rs)t_2 + 2(pr - qs)t_3$,

with analogous expressions for the other coefficients.

Defining three new vectors

(24) $u = (p, q, r)$, $v = u \times T$, $w = sT - v$,

we obtain, after some algebra,

(25) $[UR, R, T] = 2[(u.R)(w.R) - (u.w)R^2]$.

The right hand side of (25) is identical in form with that of (15), showing that L as defined by (19) is indeed a Maybank quadric.

To recapitulate: we showed in section 2 that in order to present an ambiguous pair of views from camera positions related by the relative orientation (T_1,U_1), a surface must be of the form (8) or equivalently (19). The second-order terms in its equation are of the same form as those of the Maybank quadric (15); the principal directions - those of u and w - are functions of U_1 and of the translation T_2 and the rotation U_2 associated with the alternative interpretation.

In the triply ambiguous case the same functions of U_1, T_3 and U_3 must also yield the principal directions of <u>the same</u> quadric; this is only possible if u' is parallel to w and w' is parallel to u, and leaves no room for any further distinct interpretation. Three is therefore the maximum number of distinct interpretations of two views of a visually textured surface.

5 DISCUSSION

What we have shown is that the existence of two alternative interpretations of a pair of views of a visually textured surface implies that the surface is either a plane or a quadric of the form (8). Given any "true" relative orientation (T_1, U_1) and any "spurious" one (T_2, U_2), one can construct a quadric of type (8) such that its two images will sustain either of the associated interpretations. This quadric passes through both viewpoints and contains the line $R = \lambda T_2$; it is, in fact, a surface of the type first considered by Maybank in connection with the interpretation of optic flow fields. The spurious interpretation will not necessarily satisfy the visibility conditions - that p(Q) and p'(Q') are both positive for all the image points. But the more nearly equal are the two relative orientations, the greater the likelihood that the alternative interpretation will survive the visibility test.

Three is the maximum number of distinct interpretations of a pair of views of a surface patch. Triply ambiguous view pairs may be constructed by assigning arbitrary values to the three associated rotation matrices; the corresponding translation vectors are then uniquely determined, as well as the three alternative surfaces on which the visible points may be deemed to lie.

Apart from their purely mathematical interest, these results have both a reassuring and a disturbing aspect for the designers of computer vision systems. Reassuring, in that they demonstrate the existence of an upper limit to the number of interpretations that two images will sustain if a sufficient number of visible texture elements (5 or more, in general) appears in both images; disturbing, in that they remind us of the untrustworthiness of vision algorithms based on the implicit assumption that there must be a single "best" interpretation of any given set of visual data.

Perhaps the most useful fact to emerge from the present analysis is that the most hazardous scenes for computational analysis are those in which all the visible texture elements lie in one smooth surface. The simplest scenes are often the most perceptually confusing!

ACKNOWLEDGEMENTS

I am indebted to C G Harris, S D Isard and S J Maybank for useful comments on an earlier version of this paper, and to the Royal Society and SERC for research support, and to Grace Crookes for much appreciated help in preparation of the camera ready copy.

REFERENCES

Hadani, I., Ishai, G. and Gur, M. (1980) Visual Stability and space perception in monocular vision: a mathematical model. *J. Opt. Soc. Amer.*, **70**, 60-65.

Hay, J.C. (1966) Optical motions and space perception: an extension of Gibson's analysis. *Psychological Review*, **73**, 550-565.

Koenderink, J.J. and van Doorn, A.J. (1976) Local structure of movement parallax of the plane. *J. Opt. Soc. Amer.*, **66**, 717-723.

Lee, D.N. (1974) Visual information during locomotion. *Perception: Essays in honour of James J. Gibson* (eds. R. B. MacLeod and H.L. Pick), 250-267, Cornell Univ. Press, Ithaca N.Y.

Longuet-Higgins, H.C. and Prazdny, K. (1980) The interpretation of a moving retinal image. *Proc. Roy. Soc. Lond. B 208*, 385-397.

Longuet-Higgins, H.C. (1981) A computer algorithm for reconstructing a scene from two projections. *Nature*, **293**, 133-135.

Longuet-Higgins, H.C. (1984a) The reconstruction of a scene from two projections: configurations that defeat the 8-point algorithm. *IEEE: Proceedings of the first conference on artificial intelligence applications*, 395-397.

Longuet-Higgins, H.C. (1984b) The visual ambiguity of a moving plane. *Proc. Roy. Soc. Lond. B 223*, 165-175.

Longuet-Higgins, H.C. (1986) The reconstruction of a plane surface from two perspective projections. *Proc. Roy. Soc. Lond B 227*, 399-410.

Maybank, S.J. (1985) The angular velocity associated with the optical flow field arising from motion through a rigid environment. *Proc. Roy. Soc. Lond. A 401*, 317-326.

Nakayama, I. and Loomis, J.M. (1974) Optical velocity patterns, velocity sensitive neurons and space perception. *Perception*, **3**, 63-80.

Subbarao, M. (1986) Interpretation of image motion fields: rigid curved surfaces in motion. *Research report CAR-TR-199*, Centre for Automation Research, Univ. of Maryland.

Tsai, R.Y. and Huang, T.S. (1981a) Estimating three-dimensional motion paramaters of a rigid planar patch. *Technical report R-922*, Coordinated Science Laboratory, Univ. of Illinois, Urbana.

Tsai, R.Y. and Huang, T.S. (1981b) Uniqueness and estimation of three-dimensional motion parameters of rigid objects with curved surfaces. *Technical report R-921*, Coordinated Science Laboratory, Univ. of Illinois, Urbana.

Yen, B.L. and Huang, T.S. (1983) Determining 3D motion and structure of a rigid body using the spherical projection. *Computer Vision Graphics and Image Processing*. **21**, 21-32.

INDEX OF CONTRIBUTORS

Artificial Intelligence

Patrick Henry Winston and J. Michael Brady, founding editors
J. Michael Brady, Daniel G. Bobrow, and Randall Davis, current editors

Artificial Intelligence: An MIT Perspective, Volume I: Expert Problem Solving, Natural Language Understanding, Intelligent Computer Coaches, Representation and Learning, edited by Patrick Henry Winston and Richard Henry Brown, 1979

Artificial Intelligence: An MIT Perspective, Volume II: Understanding Vision, Manipulation, Computer Design, Symbol Manipulation, edited by Patrick Henry Winston and Richard Henry Brown, 1979

NETL: A System for Representing and Using Real-World Knowledge, Scott Fahlman, 1979

The Interpretation of Visual Motion, by Shimon Ullman, 1979

A Theory of Syntactic Recognition for Natural Language, Mitchell P. Marcus, 1980

Turtle Geometry: The Computer as a Medium for Exploring Mathematics, Harold Abelson and Andrea di Sessa, 1981

From Images to Surfaces: A Computational Study of the Human Visual System, William Eric Leifur Grimson, 1981

Robot Manipulators: Mathematics, Programming, and Control, Richard P. Paul, 1981

Computational Models of Discourse, edited by Michael Brady and Robert C. Berwick, 1982

Robot Motion: Planning and Control, edited by Michael Brady, John M. Hollerbach, Timothy Johnson, Tomás Lozano-Pérez, and Matthew T. Mason, 1982

In-Depth Understanding : A Computer Model of Integrated Processing for Narrative Comprehension, Michael G. Dyer, 1983

Robotic Research: The First International Symposium, edited by Hideo Hanafusa and Hirochika Inoue, 1985

Robot Hands and the Mechanics of Manipulation, Matthew T. Mason and J. Kenneth Salisbury, Jr., 1985

The Acquisition of Syntactic Knowledge, Robert C. Berwick, 1985

The Connection Machine, W. Daniel Hillis, 1985

Legged Robots that Balance, Marc H. Raibert, 1986

Robotics Research: The Third International Symposium, edited by O.D. Faugeras and Georges Giralt, 1986

Machine Interpretation of Line Drawings, Kokichi Sugihara, 1986

ACTORS: A Model of Concurrent Computation in Distributed Systems, Gul A. Agha, 1986

Knowledge-Based Tutoring: The GUIDON Program, William Clancey, 1987

AI in the 1980s and Beyond: An MIT Survey, edited by W. Eric L. Grimson and Ramesh S. Patil, 1987

Visual Reconstruction, Andrew Blake and Andrew Zisserman, 1987

Reasoning about Change: Time and Causation from the Standpoint of Artificial Intelligence, Yoav Shoham, 1988

Model-Based Control of a Robot Manipulator, Chae H. An, Christopher G. Atkeson, and John M. Hollerbach, 1988

A Robot Ping-Pong Player: Experiment in Real-Time Intelligent Control, Russell L. Andersson, 1988

Robotics Research: The Fourth International Symposium, edited by Robert C. Bolles and Bernard Roth, 1988

The Paralation Model: Architecture-Independent Parallel Programming, Gary Sabot, 1988

Concurrent System for Knowledge Processing: An Actor Perspective, edited by Carl Hewitt and Gul Agha, 1989

Automated Deduction in Nonclassical Logics: Efficient Matrix Proof Methods for Modal and Intuitionistic Logics, Lincoln Wallen, 1989

Shape from Shading, edited by Berthold K.P. Horn and Michael J. Brooks, 1989

Ontic: A Knowledge Representation System for Mathematics, David A. McAllester, 1989

Solid Shape, Jan J. Koenderink, 1990

Expert Systems: Human Issues, edited by Dianne Berry and Anna Hart, 1990

Artificial Intelligence: Concepts and Applications, edited by A. R. Mirzai, 1990

Robotics Research: The Fifth International Symposium, edited by Hirofumi Miura and Suguru Arimoto, 1990

Theories of Comparative Analysis, Daniel S. Weld, 1990

Artificial Intelligence at MIT: Expanding Frontiers, edited by Patrick Henry Winston and Sarah Alexandra Shellard, 1990

Vector Models for Data-Parallel Computing, Guy E. Blelloch, 1990

Experiments in the Machine Interpretation of Visual Motion, David W. Murray and Bernard F. Buxton, 1990

Object Recognition by Computer: The Role of Geometric Constraints, W. Eric L. Grimson, 1990

3D Model Recognition from Stereoscopic Cues, edited by John E.W. Mayhew and John P. Frisby, 1991

The MIT Press, with Peter Denning as general consulting editor, publishes computer science books in the following series:

ACM Doctoral Dissertation Award and Distinguished Dissertation Series

Artificial Intelligence
Patrick Winston, Founding editor
Michael Brady, Daniel Bobrow, and Randall Davis, editors

Charles Babbage Institute Reprint Series for the History of Computing
Martin Campbell-Kelly, editor

Computer Systems
Herb Schwetman, editor

Explorations with Logo
E. Paul Goldenberg, editor

Foundations of Computing
Michael Garey and Albert Meyer, editors

History of Computing
I. Bernard Cohen and William Aspray, editors

Information Systems
Michael Lesk, editor

Logic Programming
Ehud Shapiro, editor; Fernando Pereira, Koichi Furukawa, Jean-Louis Lassez, and David H. D. Warren, Associate editors

The MIT Press Electrical Engineering and Computer Science Series

Research Monographs in Parallel and Distributed Processing
Christopher Jesshope and David Klappholz, editors

Scientific and Engineering Computation
Janusz Kowalik, editor

Technical Communication
Ed Barrett, editor